GIVE ME LIBERTY!

AN AMERICAN HISTORY

★

Fifth Edition

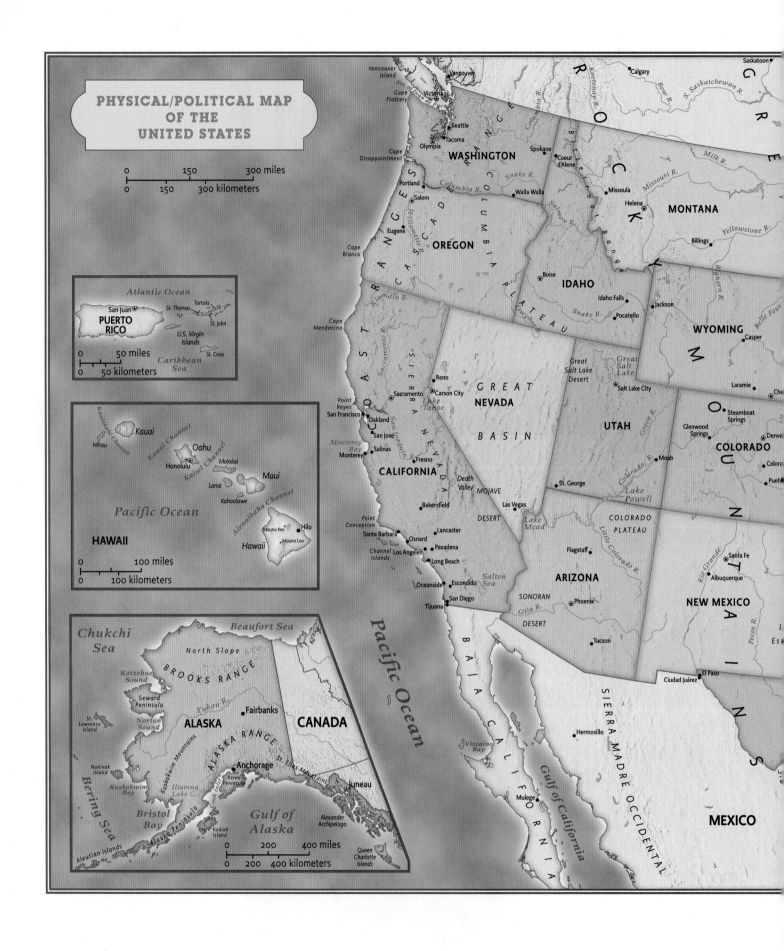

PHYSICAL/POLITICAL MAP OF THE UNITED STATES

0   150   300 miles
0   150   300 kilometers

Atlantic Ocean

San Juan ⊛
PUERTO RICO   St. Thomas Tortola
St. John
U.S. Virgin Islands
St. Croix
Caribbean Sea

0   50 miles
0   50 kilometers

Kauai
Nihau
Kauai Channel
Oahu
Molokai
Honolulu ⊛
Lanai   *Maui*
Kaiwi Channel
Kahoolawe
Alenuihaha Channel
Pacific Ocean

HAWAII
Mauna Kea
Hilo
Hawaii   Mauna Loa

0   100 miles
0   100 kilometers

Chukchi Sea
Beaufort Sea
North Slope
Kotzebue Sound   **BROOKS RANGE**
Seward Peninsula
Yukon R.
St. Lawrence Island
Norton Sound
Fairbanks
ALASKA   **CANADA**
Nunivak Island
Kuskokwim Mountains
Kuskokwim Bay
Iliamna Lake   ALASKA RANGE
St. Elias Mountains
Anchorage
Cook Inlet   Kenai Peninsula
Juneau
Bering Sea
Bristol Bay
Alaska Peninsula   **Gulf of Alaska**
Alexander Archipelago
Aleutian Islands   Kodiak Island
Queen Charlotte Islands

0   200   400 miles
0   200   400 kilometers

Vancouver Island
Cape Flattery
Vancouver
Victoria
Cape Disappointment
Seattle
Tacoma
Olympia
WASHINGTON
Spokane
Coeur d'Alene
Portland
Salem
Walla Walla
Missoula
Helena
MONTANA
Billings
Eugene
OREGON
Boise
IDAHO
Idaho Falls
Jackson
Pocatello
WYOMING
Casper
ROCKY
Kootenay R.
Columbia R.
Calgary
Saskatoon
Milk R.
Missouri R.
Yellowstone R.
S. Saskatchewan R.
Bow R.
Bighorn R.
Belle Four
Cape Blanco
Cape Mendocino
Klamath R.
Snake R.
COLUMBIA
PLATEAU
Salmon R.
Owyhee R.
Snake R.
CASCADE RANGE
Reno
Sacramento
Carson City
Lake Tahoe
GREAT
NEVADA
BASIN
Great Salt Lake Desert
Great Salt Lake
Salt Lake City
UTAH
Laramie
COLORADO
Steamboat Springs
Glenwood Springs
Denver
Point Reyes
San Francisco
Oakland
San Jose
Sacramento R.
San Joaquin R.
SIERRA NEVADA
Monterey Bay
Monterey
Salinas
Fresno
CALIFORNIA
Death Valley
MOJAVE
DESERT
Las Vegas
Lake Mead
St. George
Moab
Green R.
Colorado R.
Lake Powell
COLORADO PLATEAU
Colo
Pueblo
Bakersfield
Lancaster
Point Conception
Santa Barbara
Oxnard
Pasadena
Los Angeles
Long Beach
Channel Islands
Salton Sea
Flagstaff
Little Colorado R.
Santa Fe
Albuquerque
Rio Grande
NEW MEXICO
Oceanside
Escondido
San Diego
Tijuana
ARIZONA
SONORAN
DESERT
Gila R.
Phoenix
Tucson
El Paso
Ciudad Juárez
Pecos R.
Es
BAJA
CALIFORNIA
Vizcaíno Bay
Gulf of California
Mulege
Hermosillo
SIERRA MADRE OCCIDENTAL
MEXICO
MOUNTAINS
Pacific Ocean
GRE

GIVE ME LIBERTY!

AN AMERICAN HISTORY

★

Fifth Edition

Volume 1: To 1877

ERIC FONER

W · W · NORTON & COMPANY
NEW YORK · LONDON

For my mother, Liza Foner (1909–2005), an accomplished artist who lived through most of the twentieth century and into the twenty-first

W. W. Norton & Company has been independent since its founding in 1923, when William Warder Norton and Mary D. Herter Norton first published lectures delivered at the People's Institute, the adult education division of New York City's Cooper Union. The firm soon expanded its program beyond the Institute, publishing books by celebrated academics from America and abroad. By midcentury, the two major pillars of Norton's publishing program—trade books and college texts—were firmly established. In the 1950s, the Norton family transferred control of the company to its employees, and today—with a staff of four hundred and a comparable number of trade, college, and professional titles published each year—W. W. Norton & Company stands as the largest and oldest publishing house owned wholly by its employees.

Editor: Steve Forman
Associate Editor: Scott Sugarman
Project Editor: Jennifer Barnhardt
Editorial Assistants: Travis Carr, Kelly Rafey
Managing Editor, College: Marian Johnson
Managing Editor, College Digital Media: Kim Yi
Production Manager: Sean Mintus
Media Editor: Laura Wilk
Media Project Editor: Rachel Mayer
Media Associate Editor: Michelle Smith
Media Assistant Editor: Chris Hillyer
Marketing Manager, History: Sarah England Bartley
Associate Design Director: Hope Miller Goodell
Designer: Chin-Yee Lai
Photo Editor: Stephanie Romeo
Permissions Manager: Megan Schindel
Permissions Specialist: Bethany Salminen
Composition: Jouve
Illustrations: Mapping Specialists, Ltd.
Manufacturing: Transcontinental

Permission to use copyrighted material is included on page A-83.

The Library of Congress has cataloged the Full Edition as follows:

Names: Foner, Eric, 1943- author.
Title: Give me liberty!: an American history / Eric Foner.
Description: Fifth edition. | New York: W. W. Norton & Company, 2016 |
 Includes bibliographical references and index.
Identifiers: LCCN 2016018497 | ISBN 9780393283167 (hardcover)
Subjects: LCSH: United States—History. | United States—Politics and
 government. | Democracy—United States—History. | Liberty—History.
Classification: LCC E178 .F66 2016 | DDC 973—dc23 LC record available at
 https://lccn.loc.gov/2016018497

ISBN this edition: 978-0-393-28312-9

W. W. Norton & Company, Inc., 500 Fifth Avenue, New York, NY 10110-0017
wwnorton.com
W. W. Norton & Company Ltd., 15 Carlisle Street, London W1D 3BS

1 2 3 4 5 6 7 8 9 0

ABOUT THE AUTHOR

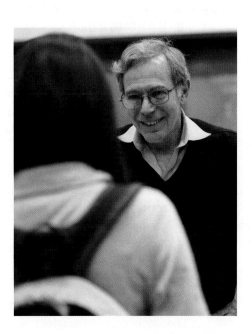

ERIC FONER is DeWitt Clinton Professor of History at Columbia University, where he earned his B.A. and Ph.D. In his teaching and scholarship, he focuses on the Civil War and Reconstruction, slavery, and nineteenth-century America. Professor Foner's publications include *Free Soil, Free Labor, Free Men: The Ideology of the Republican Party before the Civil War*; *Tom Paine and Revolutionary America*; *Nothing but Freedom: Emancipation and Its Legacy*; *Reconstruction: America's Unfinished Revolution, 1863–1877*; *The Story of American Freedom*; and *Forever Free: The Story of Emancipation and Reconstruction*. His history of Reconstruction won the *Los Angeles Times* Book Award for History, the Bancroft Prize, and the Parkman Prize. He has served as president of the Organization of American Historians and the American Historical Association. In 2006 he received the Presidential Award for Outstanding Teaching from Columbia University. His most recent books are *The Fiery Trial: Abraham Lincoln and American Slavery,* winner of the Bancroft and Lincoln Prizes and the Pulitzer Prize for History, and *Gateway to Freedom: The Hidden History of the Underground Railroad*, winner of the New York Historical Society Book Prize.

CONTENTS

Eng^d by H.B.Hall.Jr N.Y

MARGARET FUl

PREFACE

Give Me Liberty! An American History is a survey of American history from the earliest days of European exploration and conquest of the New World to the first decades of the twenty-first century. It offers students a clear, concise narrative whose central theme is the changing contours of American freedom.

I am extremely gratified by the response to the first four editions of Give Me Liberty!, which have been used in survey courses at many hundreds of two- and four-year colleges and universities throughout the country. The comments I have received from instructors and students encourage me to think that Give Me Liberty! has worked well in their classrooms. Their comments have also included many valuable suggestions for revisions, which I greatly appreciate. These have ranged from corrections of typographical and factual errors to thoughts about subjects that needed more extensive treatment. In making revisions for this Fifth Edition, I have tried to take these suggestions into account. I have also incorporated the findings and insights of new scholarship that has appeared since the original edition was written.

The most significant changes in this Fifth Edition reflect my desire to integrate the history of the American West and especially the regions known as borderlands more fully into the narrative. In recent years these aspects of American history have been thriving areas of research and scholarship. Of course earlier editions of Give Me Liberty! have discussed these subjects, but in this edition their treatment has been deepened and expanded. I have also added notable works in these areas to many chapter bibliographies and lists of websites.

The definition of the West has changed enormously in the course of American history. In the colonial period, the area beyond the Appalachians—present-day Kentucky, Tennessee, and western Pennsylvania and New York—constituted the West. In the first half of the nineteenth century, the term referred to Ohio, Michigan, Alabama, and Mississippi. After the Civil War, the West came to mean the area beyond the Mississippi River. Today, it is sometimes used to refer mainly to the Pacific coast. But whatever its geographic locale, the West has been as much an idea as a place—an area beyond the frontier of settlement that promised newcomers new kinds of freedom, sometimes at the expense of the freedom of others, such as native inhabitants and migrant laborers. In this edition we follow Americans as they constructed their Wests, and debated the kinds of freedom they would enjoy there.

Borderlands is a more complex idea that has influenced much recent historical scholarship. Borders are lines dividing one country, region, or state from another. Crossing them often means becoming subject to different laws and customs, and enjoying different degrees of freedom. Borderlands are regions that exist on both sides of borders. They are fluid areas where people of different cultural and social backgrounds converge. At various points in American history, shifting borders have opened new opportunities and closed off others in the borderlands. Families living for decades or centuries in a region have suddenly found themselves divided by a newly created border but still living in a borderland that transcends the new division. This happened to Mexicans in modern-day California, Arizona, and New Mexico, for example, in 1848, when the treaty ending the Mexican-American War transferred the land that would become those states from Mexico to the United States.

Borderlands exist within the United States as well as at the boundaries with other countries. For example, in the period before the Civil War, the region straddling the Ohio River contained cultural commonalities that in some ways overrode the division there between free and slave states. The borderlands idea also challenges simple accounts of national development in which empires and colonies pave the way for territorial expansion and a future transcontinental nation. It enables us, for example, to move beyond the categories of conquest and subjugation in understanding how Native Americans and Europeans interacted over the early centuries of contact. This approach also provides a way of understanding how the people of Mexico and the United States interact today in the borderland region of the American Southwest, where many families have members on both sides of the boundary between the two countries.

Small changes relating to these themes may be found throughout the book. The major additions seeking to illuminate the history of the West and of borderlands are as follows:

Chapter 1 now introduces the idea of borderlands with a discussion of the areas where European empires and Indian groups interacted and where authority was fluid and fragile. Chapter 4 contains expanded treatment of the part of the Spanish empire now comprising the borderlands United States (Arizona, California, New Mexico, Texas, and Florida) and how Spain endeavored, with limited success, to consolidate its authority in these regions. In Chapter 6, a new subsection, "The American Revolution as a Borderlands Conflict," examines the impact on both Americans and Canadians of the creation, because of American independence, of a new national boundary separating what once had been two parts of the British empire. Chapter 8 continues this theme with a discussion of the borderlands aspects of the War of 1812. Chapter 9 discusses how a common culture came into being along the Ohio River in the early nineteenth century despite the existence of slavery on one side and free labor on the other. Chapter 13 expands the treatment of Texan independence from Mexico by discussing its impact on both Anglo and Mexican residents of this borderland region. Chapter 14 contains a new examination of the Civil War in the American West.

In Chapter 16, I have expanded the section on the industrial west with new discussions of logging and mining, and added a new subsection on the dissemination of a mythical image of the Wild West in the late nineteenth century. Chapter 17 contains an expanded discussion of Chinese immigrants in the West and the battle over exclusion and citizenship, a debate that centered on what kind of population should be allowed to inhabit the West and enjoy the opportunities the region offered. Chapter 18 examines Progressivism, countering conventional narratives that emphasize the origins of Progressive political reforms in eastern cities by relating how many, from woman suffrage to the initiative, referendum, and recall, emerged in Oregon, California, and other western states. Chapter 20 expands the treatment of western agriculture in the 1920s by highlighting the acceleration of agricultural mechanization in the region and the agricultural depression that preceded the general economic collapse of 1929 and after. In Chapter 22 we see the new employment opportunities for Mexican-American women in the war production factories that opened in the West. In Chapter 26, there is a new subsection on conservatism in the West and the Sagebrush Rebellion of the 1970s and 1980s. Chapter 27 returns to the borderlands theme by discussing the consequences of the creation, in the 1990s, of a free trade zone connecting the two sides of the Mexican-American border. And Chapters 27 and 28 now include expanded discussions of the southwestern borderland as a site of an acrimonious battle over immigration—legal and undocumented—involving the federal and state governments, private vigilantes, and continuing waves of people trying to cross into the United States. The contested borderland now extends many miles into the United States north of the boundary between the two nations, and southward well into Mexico and even Central America.

I have also added a number of new selections to Voices of Freedom, the paired excerpts from primary documents in each chapter. Some of the new documents reflect the stronger emphasis on the West and borderlands; others seek to sharpen the juxtaposition of divergent concepts of freedom at particular moments in American history. And this edition contains many new images—paintings, broadsides, photographs, and others—related to these themes.

Americans have always had a divided attitude toward history. On the one hand, they tend to be remarkably future-oriented, dismissing events of even the recent past as "ancient history" and sometimes seeing history as a burden to be overcome, a prison from which to escape. On the other hand, like many other peoples, Americans have always looked to history for a sense of personal or group identity and of national cohesiveness. This is why so many Americans devote time and energy to tracing their family trees and why they visit historical museums and National Park Service historical sites in ever-increasing numbers. My hope is that this book will convince readers with all degrees of interest that history does matter to them.

The novelist and essayist James Baldwin once observed that history "does not refer merely, or even principally, to the past. On the contrary, the great force of history comes from the fact that we carry it within us, . . . [that] history is literally present in all that we do." As Baldwin recognized, the force of history is evident in our own world. Especially in a political democracy like the United States, whose government is designed to rest on the consent of informed citizens, knowledge of the past is essential—not only for those of us whose profession is the teaching and writing of history, but for everyone. History, to be sure, does not offer simple lessons or immediate answers to current questions. Knowing the history of immigration to the United States, and all of the tensions, turmoil, and aspirations associated with it, for example, does not tell us what current immigration policy ought to be. But without that knowledge, we have no way of understanding which approaches have worked and which have not—essential information for the formulation of future public policy.

History, it has been said, is what the present chooses to remember about the past. Rather than a fixed collection of facts, or a group of interpretations that cannot be challenged, our understanding of history is constantly changing. There is nothing unusual in the fact that each generation rewrites history to meet its own needs, or that scholars disagree among themselves on basic questions like the causes of the Civil War or the reasons for the Great Depression. Precisely because each generation asks different questions of the past, each generation formulates different answers. The past thirty years have witnessed a remarkable expansion of the scope of historical study. The experiences of groups neglected by earlier scholars, including women, African-Americans, working people, and others, have received unprecedented attention from historians. New subfields—social history, cultural history, and family history among them—have taken their place alongside traditional political and diplomatic history.

Give Me Liberty! draws on this voluminous historical literature to present an up-to-date and inclusive account of the American past, paying due attention to the experience of diverse groups of Americans while in no way neglecting the events and processes Americans have experienced in common. It devotes serious attention to political, social, cultural, and economic history, and to their interconnections. The narrative brings together major events and prominent leaders with the many groups of ordinary people who make up American society. *Give Me Liberty!* has a rich cast of characters, from Thomas Jefferson to campaigners for woman suffrage, from Franklin D. Roosevelt to former slaves seeking to breathe meaning into emancipation during and after the Civil War.

Aimed at an audience of undergraduate students with little or no detailed knowledge of American history, *Give Me Liberty!* guides readers through the complexities of the subject without overwhelming them with excessive detail. The unifying theme of freedom that runs through the text gives shape to the narrative and integrates the numerous strands that make up the American experience. This approach builds on that of my earlier book, *The Story of American Freedom* (1998), although *Give Me Liberty!* places events and personalities in the foreground and is more geared to the structure of the introductory survey course.

Freedom, and the battles to define its meaning, have long been central to my own scholarship and undergraduate teaching, which focuses on the nineteenth century and especially the era of the Civil War and Reconstruction (1850–1877). This was a time when the future of slavery tore the nation apart and emancipation produced a national debate over what rights the former slaves, and all Americans, should enjoy as free citizens. I have found that attention to clashing definitions of freedom and the struggles of different groups to achieve freedom as they understood it offers a way of making sense of the bitter battles and vast transformations of that pivotal era. I believe that the same is true for American history as a whole.

No idea is more fundamental to Americans' sense of themselves as individuals and as a nation than freedom. The central term in our political language, freedom—or liberty, with which it is almost always used interchangeably—is deeply embedded in the record of our history and the language of everyday life. The Declaration of Independence lists liberty among mankind's inalienable rights; the Constitution announces its purpose as securing liberty's blessings. The United States fought the Civil War to bring about a new birth of freedom, World War II for the Four Freedoms, and the Cold War to defend the Free World. Americans' love of liberty has been represented by liberty poles, liberty caps, and statues of liberty, and acted out by burning stamps and burning draft cards, by running away from slavery, and by demonstrating for the right to vote. "Every man in the street, white, black, red, or yellow," wrote the educator and statesman Ralph Bunche in 1940, "knows that this is 'the land of the free' . . . 'the cradle of liberty.'"

The very universality of the idea of freedom, however, can be misleading. Freedom is not a fixed, timeless category with a single unchanging definition. Indeed, the history of the United States is, in part, a story of debates, disagreements, and struggles over freedom. Crises like the American Revolution, the Civil War, and the Cold War have permanently transformed the idea of freedom. So too have demands by various groups of Americans to enjoy greater freedom. The meaning of freedom has been constructed not only in congressional debates and political treatises, but on plantations and picket lines, in parlors and even bedrooms.

Over the course of our history, American freedom has been both a reality and a mythic ideal—a living truth for millions of Americans, a cruel mockery for others. For some, freedom has been what some scholars call a "habit of the heart," an ideal so taken for granted that it is lived out but rarely analyzed. For others, freedom is not a birthright but a distant goal that has inspired great sacrifice.

Give Me Liberty! draws attention to three dimensions of freedom that have been critical in American history: (1) the *meanings* of freedom; (2) the *social conditions* that make freedom possible; and (3) the *boundaries* of freedom that determine who is entitled to enjoy freedom and who is not. All have changed over time.

In the era of the American Revolution, for example, freedom was primarily a set of rights enjoyed in public activity—the right of a community to be governed by laws to which its representatives had consented and of individuals to engage in religious worship without governmental interference. In the nineteenth century, freedom came to be closely identified with each person's opportunity to develop to the fullest his or her innate talents. In the twentieth, the "ability to choose," in both public and private life, became perhaps the dominant understanding of freedom. This development was encouraged by the explosive growth of the consumer marketplace (a development that receives considerable attention in *Give Me Liberty!*), which offered Americans an unprecedented array of goods with which to satisfy their needs and desires. During the 1960s, a crucial chapter in the history of American freedom, the idea of personal freedom was extended into virtually every realm, from attire and "lifestyle" to

INVICTA.

relations between the sexes. Thus, over time, more and more areas of life have been drawn into Americans' debates about the meaning of freedom.

A second important dimension of freedom focuses on the social conditions necessary to allow freedom to flourish. What kinds of economic institutions and relationships best encourage individual freedom? In the colonial era and for more than a century after independence, the answer centered on economic autonomy, enshrined in the glorification of the independent small producer—the farmer, skilled craftsman, or shopkeeper—who did not have to depend on another person for his livelihood. As the industrial economy matured, new conceptions of economic freedom came to the fore: "liberty of contract" in the Gilded Age, "industrial freedom" (a say in corporate decision-making) in the Progressive era, economic security during the New Deal, and, more recently, the ability to enjoy mass consumption within a market economy.

The boundaries of freedom, the third dimension of this theme, have inspired some of the most intense struggles in American history. Although founded on the premise that liberty is an entitlement of all humanity, the United States for much of its history deprived many of its own people of freedom. Non-whites have rarely enjoyed the same access to freedom as white Americans. The belief in equal opportunity as the birthright of all Americans has coexisted with persistent efforts to limit freedom by race, gender, and class and in other ways.

Less obvious, perhaps, is the fact that one person's freedom has frequently been linked to another's servitude. In the colonial era and nineteenth century, expanding freedom for many Americans rested on the lack of freedom—slavery, indentured servitude, the subordinate position of women—for others. By the same token, it has been through battles at the boundaries—the efforts of racial minorities, women, and others to secure greater freedom—that the meaning and experience of freedom have been deepened and the concept extended into new realms.

Time and again in American history, freedom has been transformed by the demands of excluded groups for inclusion. The idea of freedom as a universal birthright owes much both to abolitionists who sought to extend the blessings of liberty to blacks and to immigrant groups who insisted on full recognition as American citizens. The principle of equal protection of the law without regard to race, which became a central element of American freedom, arose from the antislavery struggle and the Civil War and was reinvigorated by the civil rights revolution of the 1960s, which called itself the "freedom movement." The battle for the right of free speech by labor radicals and birth-control advocates in the first part of the twentieth century helped to make civil liberties an essential element of freedom for all Americans.

Although concentrating on events within the United States, *Give Me Liberty!* also situates American history in the context of developments in other parts of the world. Many of the forces that shaped American history, including the international migration of peoples, the development of slavery, the spread of democracy, and the expansion of capitalism, were worldwide processes not confined to the United States. Today, American ideas, culture, and economic and military power exert unprecedented influence throughout the world. But beginning with the earliest days of settlement, when European empires competed to colonize North America and enrich themselves from its trade, American history cannot be understood in isolation from its global setting.

Freedom is the oldest of clichés and the most modern of aspirations. At various times in our history, it has served as the rallying cry of the powerless and as a justification of the status quo. Freedom helps to bind our culture together and exposes the contradictions between what America claims to be and what it sometimes has been. American history is not a narrative of continual progress toward greater and greater freedom. As the abolitionist Thomas Wentworth Higginson noted after the Civil War, "revolutions may go backward." Though freedom can be achieved, it may also be taken away. This happened, for example, when the equal rights granted to former slaves immediately after the Civil War were essentially nullified during the era of segregation. As was said in the eighteenth century, the price of freedom is eternal vigilance.

In the early twenty-first century, freedom continues to play a central role in American political and social life and thought. It is invoked by individuals and groups of all kinds, from critics of economic globalization to those who seek to secure American freedom at home and export it abroad. I hope that *Give Me Liberty!* will offer beginning students a clear account of the course of American history, and of its central theme, freedom, which today remains as varied, contentious, and ever-changing as America itself.

ACKNOWLEDGMENTS

All works of history are, to a considerable extent, collaborative books, in that every writer builds on the research and writing of previous scholars. This is especially true of a textbook that covers the entire American experience, over more than five centuries. My greatest debt is to the innumerable historians on whose work I have drawn in preparing this volume. The Suggested Reading list at the end of each chapter offers only a brief introduction to the vast body of historical scholarship that has influenced and informed this book. More specifically, however, I wish to thank the following scholars, who generously read portions of this work and offered valuable comments, criticisms, and suggestions:

Joel Benson, Northwest Missouri State University
Lori Bramson, Clark College
Tonia Compton, Columbia College
Adam Costanzo, Texas A&M University
Carl Creasman Jr., Valencia College
Blake Ellis, Lone Star College–CyFair
Carla Falkner, Northeast Mississippi Community College
Van Forsyth, Clark College
Aram Goudsouzian, University of Memphis
Michael Harkins, Harper College
Sandra Harvey, Lone Star College–CyFair
Robert Hines, Palo Alto College
Traci Hodgson, Chemeketa Community College
Tamora Hoskisson, Salt Lake Community College
William Jackson, Salt Lake Community College
Alfred H. Jones, State College of Florida
David Kiracofe, Tidewater Community College

Brad Lookingbill, Columbia College
Jennifer Macias, Salt Lake Community College
Thomas Massey, Cape Fear Community College
Derek Maxfield, Genesee Community College
Marianne McKnight, Salt Lake Community College
Jonson Miller, Drexel University
Ted Moore, Salt Lake Community College
Robert Pierce, Foothills College
Ernst Pinjing, Minot State University
Harvey N. Plaunt, El Paso Community College
Steve Porter, University of Cincinnati
John Putman, San Diego State University
R. Lynn Rainard, Tidewater Community College
Nicole Ribianszky, Georgia Gwinnett College
Nancy Marie Robertson, Indiana University—Purdue University Indianapolis
John Shaw, Portland Community College
Danielle Swiontek, Santa Barbara Community College
Richard Trimble, Ocean County College
Alan Vangroll, Central Texas College
Eddie Weller, San Jacinto College
Andrew Wiese, San Diego State University
Matthew Zembo, Hudson Valley Community College

I am particularly grateful to my colleagues in the Columbia University Department of History: Pablo Piccato, for his advice on Latin American history; Evan Haefeli and Ellen Baker, who read and made many suggestions for improvements in their areas of expertise (colonial America and the history of the West, respectively); and Sarah Phillips, who offered advice on treating the history of the environment.

I am also deeply indebted to the graduate students at Columbia University's Department of History who helped with this project. For this edition, Michael "Mookie" Kidackel offered invaluable assistance in gathering material related to borderlands and Western history. For previous editions, Theresa Ventura assisted in locating material for new sections placing American history in a global context, April Holm did the same for new coverage of the history of American religion and debates over religious freedom, James Delbourgo conducted research for the chapters on the colonial era, and Beverly Gage did the same for the twentieth century. In addition, Daniel Freund provided all-around research assistance. Victoria Cain did a superb job of locating images. I also want to thank my colleagues Elizabeth Blackmar and Alan Brinkley for offering advice and encouragement throughout the writing of this book. I am also grateful to students who, while using the textbook, pointed out to me errors or omissions that I have corrected in this edition: Jordan Farr, Chris Jendry, Rafi Metz, Samuel Phillips-Cooper, Richard Sereyko, and David Whittle.

Many thanks to Joshua Brown, director of the American Social History Project, whose website, History Matters, lists innumerable online resources for the study of American history. Thanks also to the instructors who helped build our robust digital resource and ancillary package. The new InQuizitive for History was developed by Tonia M. Compton (Columbia College), Matt Zembo (Hudson Valley Community College), Jodie Steeley (Merced Community College District), Bill Polasky (Stillman Valley High School), and Ken Adler (Spring Valley High School). Our new History Skills Tutorials were created by Geri Hastings. The Coursepack was thoroughly updated by Beth Hunter (University of Alabama at Birmingham). Allison Faber (Texas A&M University) and Ben Williams (Texas A&M University) revised the Lecture PowerPoint slides. And our Test Bank and Instructor's Manual was revised to include new questions authored by Robert O'Brien (Lone Star College–CyFair and Tamora M. Hoskisson (Salt Lake Community College).

At W. W. Norton & Company, Steve Forman was an ideal editor—patient, encouraging, and always ready to offer sage advice. I would also like to thank Steve's editorial assistants, Travis Carr and Kelly Rafey, and associate editor, Scott Sugarman, for their indispensable and always cheerful help on all aspects of the project; Ellen Lohman and Bob Byrne for their careful copyediting and proofreading work; Stephanie Romeo and Fay Torresyap for their resourceful attention to the illustrations program; Hope Miller Goodell and Chin-Yee Lai for their refinements of the book design; Leah Clark, Tiani Kennedy, and Debra Morton-Hoyt for splendid work on the covers for the Fifth Edition; Jennifer Barnhardt for keeping the many threads of the project aligned and then tying them together; Sean Mintus for his efficiency and care in book production; Laura Wilk for orchestrating the rich media package that accompanies the textbook; Jessica Brannon-Wranowsky for the terrific new web quizzes and outlines; Sarah England Bartley, Steve Dunn, and Mike Wright for their alert reads of the U.S. survey market and their hard work in helping establish *Give Me Liberty!* within it; and Drake McFeely, Roby Harrington, and Julia Reidhead for maintaining Norton as an independent, employee-owned publisher dedicated to excellence in its work.

Many students may have heard stories of how publishing companies alter the language and content of textbooks in an attempt to maximize sales and avoid alienating any potential reader. In this case, I can honestly say that W. W. Norton allowed me a free hand in writing the book and, apart from the usual editorial corrections, did not try to influence its content at all. For this I thank them, while I accept full responsibility for the interpretations presented and for any errors the book may contain. Since no book of this length can be entirely free of mistakes, I welcome readers to send me corrections at ef17@columbia.edu.

My greatest debt, as always, is to my family—my wife, Lynn Garafola, for her good-natured support while I was preoccupied by a project that consumed more than its fair share of my time and energy, and my daughter, Daria, who while a ninth and tenth grader read every chapter as it was written and offered invaluable suggestions about improving the book's clarity, logic, and grammar.

Eric Foner
New York City
July 2016

W. W. Norton offers a robust digital package to support teaching and learning with *Give Me Liberty!* These resources are designed to make students more effective textbook readers, while at the same time developing their critical thinking and history skills.

RESOURCES FOR STUDENTS

All resources are available through digital.wwnorton.com/givemeliberty5v1 with the access card at the front of this text.

NORTON INQUIZITIVE FOR HISTORY

Norton InQuizitive for history is an adaptive quizzing tool that improves students' understanding of the themes and objectives from each chapter, while honing their critical-analysis skills with primary source, image, and map analysis questions. Students receive personalized quiz questions with detailed, guiding feedback on the topics in which they need the most help, while the engaging, gamelike elements motivate them as they learn.

HISTORY SKILLS TUTORIALS

The History Skills Tutorials feature three modules—Images, Documents, and Maps—to support students' development of the key skills needed for the history course. These tutorials feature videos of Eric Foner modeling the analysis process, followed by interactive questions that will challenge students to apply what they have learned.

STUDENT SITE

The free and easy-to-use Student Site offers additional resources for students to use outside of class. Resources include interactive iMaps from each chapter, author videos, and a comprehensive Online Reader with a collection of historical longer works, primary sources, novellas, and biographies.

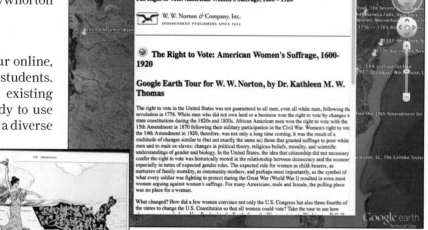

EBOOK

Free and included with new copies of the text, the **Norton Ebook Reader** provides an enhanced reading experience that works on all computers and mobile devices. Features include intuitive highlighting, note-taking, and bookmarking as well as pop-up definitions and enlargeable maps and art. Direct links to InQuizitive also appear in each chapter. Instructors can focus student reading by sharing notes with their classes, including embedded images and video. Reports on student and class-wide access and time on task allow instructors to monitor student reading and engagement.

RESOURCES FOR INSTRUCTORS

All resources are available through www.wwnorton.com/instructors.

NORTON COURSEPACKS

Easily add high-quality digital media to your online, hybrid, or lecture course—all at no cost to students. Norton's Coursepacks work within your existing Learning Management System and are ready to use and easy to customize. The coursepack offers a diverse collection of assignable and assessable resources: **Primary Source Exercises, Guided Reading Exercises, Review Quizzes, U.S. History Tours powered by Google Earth, Flashcards, Map Exercises**, and all of the resources from the **Student Site.**

NORTON AMERICAN HISTORY DIGITAL ARCHIVE

The Digital Archive offers roughly 2,000 additional primary source images, audio, and video files spanning American history that can be used in assignments and lecture presentations.

TEST BANK

The Test Bank is authored by Robert O'Brien, Lone Star College–CyFair, and Tamora M. Hoskisson, Salt Lake Community College, and contains more than 4,000 multiple-choice, true/false, short-answer, and essay questions.

INSTRUCTOR'S MANUAL

The Instructor's Manual contains detailed Chapter Summaries, Chapter Outlines, Suggested Discussion Questions, and Supplemental Web, Visual, and Print Resources.

LECTURE AND ART POWERPOINT SLIDES

The Lecture PowerPoint sets authored by Allison Faber, Texas A&M University, and Ben Williams, Texas A&M University, combine chapter review, art, and maps.

GIVE ME LIBERTY!

AN AMERICAN HISTORY

Fifth Edition

PART 1

AMERICAN COLONIES TO 1763

The colonial period of American history was a time of enormous change, as the people of four continents—North America, South America, Europe, and Africa—were suddenly and unexpectedly thrown into contact with one another. The period also initiated a new era in the history of freedom. It was not, however, a desire for freedom that drove early European explorations of North and South America. Contact between Europe and the Americas began as a by-product of the quest for a sea route for trade with Asia. But it quickly became a contest for power between rival empires, who moved to conquer, colonize, and exploit the resources of the New World.

At the time of European contact, the Western Hemisphere was home to tens of millions of people. Within the present borders of the United States there existed Indian societies based on agriculture, hunting, or fishing, with their own languages, religious practices, and forms of government. All experienced wrenching changes after Europeans arrived, including incorporation into the world market and epidemics of disease that devastated many native groups.

The colonies that eventually came to form the United States originated in very different ways. Virginia, the first permanent colony to be established, was created by a private company that sought to earn profits through exploration for gold and the development of transatlantic trade. Individual proprietors—well-connected Englishmen given large grants of land by the king—established Maryland and Pennsylvania. New York, which had been founded by the Dutch, came into British hands as the result of a war. Religious groups seeking escape from persecution in England and hoping to establish communities rooted in their understanding of the principles of the Bible founded colonies in New England.

In the seventeenth century, all the British colonies experienced wrenching social conflicts as groups within them battled for control. Relations with Indians remained tense and sometimes violent. Religious and political divisions in England, which experienced a civil war in the 1640s and the ouster of the king in 1688, reverberated in the colonies. So did wars between European powers, which spilled over into North America. Nonetheless, after difficult beginnings, Britain's mainland colonies experienced years of remarkable growth in population and economic activity. By the eighteenth century, the non-Indian population of Britain's North American colonies had far outstripped that of the colonies of France and Spain.

In every colony in British America, well-to-do landowners and merchants dominated economic and political life. Nonetheless, emigration to the colonies offered numerous settlers opportunities they had not enjoyed at home, including access to land, the freedom to worship as they pleased, and the right to vote. Every British colony had an elected assembly that shared power with a governor, who was usually appointed from London. Even this limited degree of self-government contrasted sharply with the lack of representative institutions in the Spanish and French empires. All these circumstances drew thousands of English emigrants to North America in the seventeenth century, and thousands more from Ireland, Scotland, and the European continent in the eighteenth century.

Yet the conditions that allowed colonists to enjoy such freedoms were made possible by lack of freedom for millions of others. For the native inhabitants of the Western Hemisphere, European colonization brought the spread of devastating epidemics and either dispossession from the land or forced labor for the colonizers. Millions of Africans were uprooted from their homes and transported to the New World to labor on the plantations of Brazil, the Caribbean, and England's North American colonies. Even among European immigrants, the majority arrived not as completely free individuals but as indentured servants who owed a prearranged number of years of labor to those who paid their passage.

In colonial America, many modern ideas of freedom did not exist, or existed in very different forms than today. Equality before the law was unknown—women, non-whites, and propertyless men enjoyed far fewer rights than landowning white male citizens. Economic freedom, today widely identified with participation in an unregulated market, meant independence—owning land or a shop and not relying on another person for a livelihood. Most colonies had official churches, and many colonists who sought religious liberty for themselves refused to extend it to others. Speaking or writing critically of public authorities could land a person in jail.

Nonetheless, ideas about freedom played a major role in justifying European colonization. The Spanish and French claimed to be liberating Native Americans by bringing them advanced civilization and Roman Catholicism. England insisted that true freedom for Indians meant adopting English ways, including Protestantism. Moreover, the expansion of England's empire occurred at a time when freedom came to be seen as the defining characteristic of the English nation. Slavery existed in every New World colony. In many, it became the basis of economic life. Yet most Britons, including colonists, prided themselves on enjoying "British liberty," a common set of rights that included protection from the arbitrary exercise of governmental power.

Thus, freedom and lack of freedom expanded together in the colonies of British North America that would eventually form the United States.

CHAPTER 1

A
NEW WORLD

★

"The discovery of America," the British writer Adam Smith announced in his celebrated work *The Wealth of Nations* (1776), was one of "the two greatest and most important events recorded in the history of mankind." Historians no longer use the word "discovery" to describe the European exploration, conquest, and colonization of a hemisphere already home to millions of people. But there can be no doubt that when Christopher Columbus made landfall in the West Indian islands in 1492, he set in motion some of the most pivotal developments in human history. Immense changes soon followed in both the Old and New Worlds; the consequences of these changes are still with us today.

The peoples of the American continents and Europe, previously unaware of each other's existence, were thrown into continuous interaction. Crops new to each hemisphere crossed the Atlantic, reshaping diets and transforming the natural environment. Because of their long isolation, the inhabitants of North and South America had developed no immunity to the germs that also accompanied the colonizers. As a result, they suffered a series of devastating epidemics, the greatest population catastrophe in human history. Within a decade of Columbus's voyage, a fourth continent—Africa—found itself drawn into the new Atlantic system of trade and population movement. In Africa, Europeans found a supply of unfree labor that enabled them to exploit the fertile lands of the Western Hemisphere. Indeed, of approximately 10 million men, women, and children who crossed from the Old World to the New between 1492 and 1820, the vast majority, about 7.7 million, were African slaves.

From the vantage point of 1776, the year the United States declared itself an independent nation, it seemed to Adam Smith that the "discovery" of America had produced both great "benefits" and great "misfortunes." To the nations of western Europe, the development of American colonies brought an era of "splendor and glory." The emergence of the Atlantic as the world's major avenue for trade and population movement, Smith noted, enabled millions of Europeans to increase the "enjoyments" of life. To the "natives" of the Americas, however, Smith went on, the years since 1492 had been ones of "dreadful misfortunes" and "every sort of injustice." And for millions of Africans, the settlement of America meant a descent into the abyss of slavery.

Long before Columbus sailed, Europeans had dreamed of a land of abundance, riches, and ease beyond the western horizon. Once the "discovery" of this New World had taken place, they invented an America of the imagination, projecting onto it their hopes for a better life. Here, many believed, would arise unparalleled opportunities for riches, or at least liberation from poverty. Europeans envisioned America as a religious refuge, a society of equals, a source of power and glory. They searched the New World for golden cities and fountains of eternal youth. Some sought to establish ideal communities based on the lives of the early Christian saints or other blueprints for social justice.

Some of these dreams of riches and opportunity would indeed be fulfilled. To many European settlers, America offered a far greater chance to own land and worship as they pleased than existed in Europe, with its rigid, unequal

FOCUS QUESTIONS

What were the major patterns of Native American life in North America before Europeans arrived? *–p. 6*

How did Indian and European ideas of freedom differ on the eve of contact? *–p. 15*

What impelled European explorers to look west across the Atlantic? *–p. 18*

What happened when the peoples of the Americas came in contact with Europeans? *–p. 21*

What were the chief features of the Spanish empire in America? *–p. 24*

What were the chief features of the French and Dutch empires in North America? *–p. 35*

Painted around 1725, *Genealogy of the Inca Rulers and Their Spanish Successors from Manco Capac, the First Inca King, to Ferdinand VI of Spain*, depicts Spanish conquistadors and rulers as direct successors of Inca kings. The unknown artist aimed both to assimilate the pre-conquest history of the Americas into Spanish history and to legitimate Spain's colonial rule over the former Inca empire.

social order and official churches. Yet the conditions that enabled millions of settlers to take control of their own destinies were made possible by the debasement of millions of others. The New World became the site of many forms of unfree labor, including indentured servitude, forced labor, and one of the most brutal and unjust systems ever devised by man, plantation slavery. The conquest and settlement of the Western Hemisphere opened new chapters in the long histories of both freedom and slavery.

There was a vast human diversity among the peoples thrown into contact with one another in the New World. Exploration and settlement took place in an era of almost constant warfare among European nations, each racked by internal religious, political, and regional conflicts. Native Americans and Africans consisted of numerous groups with their own languages and cultures. They were as likely to fight one another as to unite against the European newcomers. All these peoples were changed by their integration into the new Atlantic economy. The complex interactions of Europeans, American Indians, and Africans would shape American history during the colonial era.

THE FIRST AMERICANS

The Settling of the Americas

The residents of the Americas were no more a single group than Europeans or Africans. They spoke hundreds of different languages and lived in numerous kinds of societies. Most, however, were descended from bands of hunters and fishers who had crossed the Bering Strait via a land bridge at various times between 15,000 and 60,000 years ago—the exact dates are hotly debated by archaeologists. Others may have arrived by sea from Asia or Pacific islands. Around 14,000 years ago, when glaciers began to melt at the end of the last Ice Age, the land link became submerged under water, separating the Western Hemisphere from Asia.

History in North and South America did not begin with the coming of Europeans. The New World was new to Europeans but an ancient homeland to those who already lived there. The hemisphere had witnessed many changes during its human history. First, the early inhabitants and their descendants spread across the two continents, reaching the tip of South America perhaps 11,000 years ago. As the climate warmed, they faced a food crisis as the immense animals they hunted, including woolly mammoths and giant bison, became extinct. Around 9,000 years ago, at the same time that agriculture was being developed in the Near East, it also emerged in modern-day Mexico and the Andes, and then spread to other parts of the Americas, making settled civilizations possible. Throughout the hemisphere, maize (corn), squash, and beans formed the basis of agriculture. The absence of livestock in the Western Hemisphere, however, limited farming by preventing the plowing of fields and the application of natural fertilizer.

THE FIRST AMERICANS

A map illustrating the probable routes by which the first Americans settled the Western Hemisphere at various times between 15,000 and 60,000 years ago.

Indian Societies of the Americas

North and South America were hardly an empty wilderness when Europeans arrived. The hemisphere contained cities, roads, irrigation systems, extensive trade networks, and large structures such as pyramid-temples, whose beauty still inspires wonder. With a population close to 250,000, **Tenochtitlán**, the capital of the **Aztec** empire in what is now Mexico, was one of the world's largest cities. Its great temple, splendid royal palace, and a central market comparable to that of European capitals made the city seem "like an enchanted vision," according to one of the first Europeans to encounter it. Farther south lay the Inca kingdom, centered in modern-day Peru. Its population of perhaps 12 million was linked by a complex system of roads and bridges that extended 2,000 miles along the Andes mountain chain.

When Europeans arrived, a wide variety of native peoples lived within the present borders of the United States. Indian civilizations in North America had not developed the scale, grandeur, or centralized organization of the Aztec and Inca societies to their south. North American Indians lacked the technologies Europeans had mastered, such as metal tools and machines, gunpowder, and the scientific knowledge necessary for long-distance navigation. No society north of Mexico had achieved literacy (although some made maps on bark and animal hides). They also lacked wheeled vehicles, since they had no domestic animals like horses or oxen to pull them. Their "backwardness" became a central justification for European conquest. But, over time, Indian societies had perfected

Roads, irrigation systems, and trade networks

This world map, produced in 1507 by the German mapmaker Martin Waldseemüller, was the first to depict the full Western Hemisphere and the first to include the name "America" (on the lower part of South America) for part of the New World. It also seems to indicate the Pacific Ocean, but no European encountered that ocean until the Spanish explorer Balboa in 1513.

techniques of farming, hunting, and fishing, developed structures of political power and religious belief, and engaged in far-reaching networks of trade and communication.

Map of the Aztec capital Tenochtitlán and the Gulf of Mexico, probably produced by a Spanish conquistador and published in 1524 in an edition of the letters of Hernán Cortés. The map shows the city's complex system of canals, bridges, and dams, with the Great Temple at the center. Gardens and a zoo are also visible.

Mound Builders of the Mississippi River Valley

Remarkable physical remains still exist from some of the early civilizations in North America. Around 3,500 years ago, before Egyptians built the pyramids, Native Americans constructed a large community centered on a series of giant semicircular mounds on a bluff overlooking the Mississippi River in present-day Louisiana. Known today as Poverty Point, it was a commercial and governmental center whose residents established trade routes throughout the Mississippi and Ohio River valleys. Archaeologists have found there copper from present-day Minnesota and Canada, and flint mined in Indiana.

More than a thousand years before Columbus sailed, Indians of the Ohio River valley, called "mound builders" by eighteenth-century settlers who encountered the large earthen burial mounds they created, had traded across half the continent. After their decline, another culture flourished in the Mississippi River valley, centered on the city of Cahokia near present-day St. Louis, a fortified community with between 10,000 and 30,000 inhabitants in the year 1200. Its

Cahokia

A modern aerial photograph of the ruins of Pueblo Bonita, in Chaco Canyon in present-day New Mexico. The rectangular structures are the foundations of dwellings, and the circular ones are *kivas*, or places of religious worship.

Cliff dwellings in Cañon de Chelly, in the area of modern-day Arizona, built sometime between 300 and 1300 and photographed in 1873.

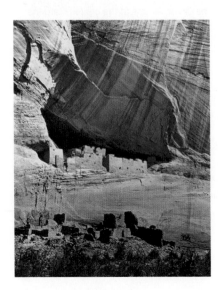

residents, too, built giant mounds, the largest of which stood 100 feet high and was topped by a temple. Little is known of Cahokia's political and economic structure. But it stood as the largest settled community in what is now the United States until surpassed in population by New York and Philadelphia around 1800.

Western Indians

In the arid northeastern area of present-day Arizona, the Hopi and Zuni and their ancestors engaged in settled village life for over 3,000 years. During the peak of the region's culture, between the years 900 and 1200, these peoples built great planned towns with large multiple-family dwellings in local canyons, constructed dams and canals to gather and distribute water, and conducted trade with groups as far away as central Mexico and the Mississippi River valley. The largest of their structures, Pueblo Bonita, in Chaco Canyon, New Mexico, stood five stories high and had more than 600 rooms. Not until the 1880s was a dwelling of comparable size constructed in the United States.

After the decline of these communities, probably because of drought, survivors moved to the south and east, where they established villages and perfected the techniques of desert farming, complete with irrigation systems to provide water for crops of corn, beans, and cotton. These were the people Spanish explorers called the Pueblo Indians (because they lived in small villages, or *pueblos*, when the Spanish first encountered them in the sixteenth century).

On the Pacific coast, another densely populated region, hundreds of distinct groups resided in independent villages and lived primarily by fishing, hunting sea mammals, and gathering wild plants and nuts. As many as 25 million salmon swam up the Columbia River each year, providing Indians with abundant food. On the Great Plains, with its herds of buffalo—descendants of the prehistoric giant bison—many Indians were hunters (who tracked animals on foot before the arrival of horses with the Spanish), but others lived in agricultural communities.

Indians of Eastern North America

In eastern North America, hundreds of tribes inhabited towns and villages scattered from the Gulf of Mexico to present-day Canada. They lived on corn, squash, and beans, supplemented by fishing and hunting deer, turkeys, and other animals. Indian trade routes crisscrossed the eastern part of the continent. Tribes frequently warred with one another to obtain goods, seize captives, or take revenge for the killing of relatives. They conducted diplomacy and made peace. Little in the way of centralized authority existed until, in the fifteenth century, various leagues or confederations emerged in an effort to bring order to local regions. In the Southeast, the

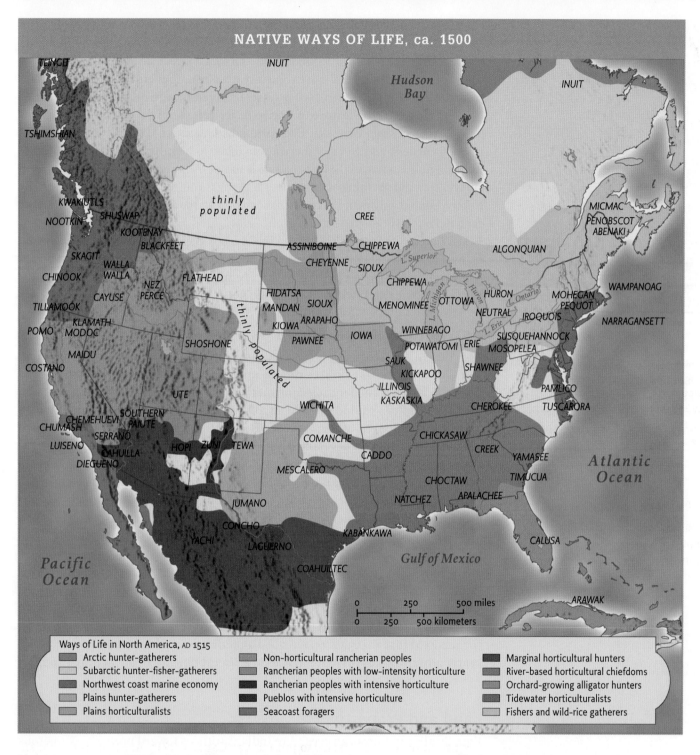

NATIVE WAYS OF LIFE, ca. 1500

Ways of Life in North America, AD 1515

- Arctic hunter-gatherers
- Subarctic hunter-fisher-gatherers
- Northwest coast marine economy
- Plains hunter-gatherers
- Plains horticulturalists
- Non-horticultural rancherian peoples
- Rancherian peoples with low-intensity horticulture
- Rancherian peoples with intensive horticulture
- Pueblos with intensive horticulture
- Seacoast foragers
- Marginal horticultural hunters
- River-based horticultural chiefdoms
- Orchard-growing alligator hunters
- Tidewater horticulturalists
- Fishers and wild-rice gatherers

The native population of North America at the time of first contact with Europeans consisted of numerous tribes with their own languages, religious beliefs, and economic and social structures. This map suggests the numerous ways of life existing at the time.

The Village of Secoton, by John White, an English artist who spent a year on the Outer Banks of North Carolina in 1585–1586 as part of an expedition sponsored by Sir Walter Raleigh. A central street links houses surrounded by fields of corn. In the lower part, dancing Indians take part in a religious ceremony.

Rituals

Choctaw, Cherokee, and Chickasaw each united dozens of towns in loose alliances. In present-day New York and Pennsylvania, five Iroquois peoples—the Mohawk, Oneida, Cayuga, Seneca, and Onondaga—formed a **Great League of Peace**, bringing a period of stability to the area. Each year a Great Council, with representatives from the five groupings, met to coordinate behavior toward outsiders.

The most striking feature of Native American society at the time Europeans arrived was its sheer diversity. Each group had its own political system and set of religious beliefs, and North America was home to literally hundreds of mutually unintelligible languages. Indians had no sense of "America" as a continent or hemisphere. They did not think of themselves as a single unified people, an idea invented by Europeans and only many years later adopted by Indians themselves. Indian identity centered on the immediate social group—a tribe, village, chiefdom, or confederacy. When Europeans first arrived, many Indians saw them as simply one group among many. Their first thought was how to use the newcomers to enhance their standing in relation to other native peoples, rather than to unite against them. The sharp dichotomy between Indians and "white" persons did not emerge until later in the colonial era.

Native American Religion

Nonetheless, the diverse Indian societies of North America did share certain common characteristics. Their lives were steeped in religious ceremonies often directly related to farming and hunting. Spiritual power, they believed, suffused the world, and sacred spirits could be found in all kinds of living and inanimate things—animals, plants, trees, water, and wind—an idea known as "animism." Through religious ceremonies, they aimed to harness the aid of powerful supernatural forces to serve the interests of man. In some tribes, hunters performed rituals to placate the spirits of animals they had killed. Other religious ceremonies sought to engage the spiritual power of nature to secure abundant crops or fend off evil spirits. Indian villages also held elaborate religious rites, participation in which helped to define the boundaries of community membership. In all Indian societies, those who seemed to possess special abilities to invoke supernatural powers—shamans, medicine men, and other religious leaders—held positions of respect and authority.

Indian religion did not pose a sharp distinction between the natural and the supernatural, or secular and religious activities. In some respects, however, Indian religion was not that different from popular spiritual beliefs in Europe. Most Indians held that a single Creator stood atop the spiritual hierarchy. Nonetheless, nearly all Europeans arriving in the New World quickly concluded that Indians were in dire need of being converted to a true, Christian faith.

Land and Property

Equally alien in European eyes were Indian attitudes toward property. Numerous land systems existed among Native Americans. Generally, however, village leaders assigned plots of land to individual families to use for a season or more, and tribes claimed specific areas for hunting. Unclaimed land remained free for anyone to use. Families "owned" the right to use land, but they did not own the land itself. Indians saw land, the basis of economic life for both hunting and farming societies, as a common resource, not an economic commodity. In the nineteenth century, the

Indian leader Black Hawk would explain why, in his view, land could not be bought and sold: "The Great Spirit gave it to his children to live upon, and cultivate as far as necessary for their subsistence; and so long as they occupy and cultivate it, they have a right to the soil." Few if any Indian societies were familiar with the idea of a fenced-off piece of land belonging forever to a single individual or family. There was no market in real estate before the coming of Europeans.

Land as a common resource

Nor were Indians devoted to the accumulation of wealth and material goods. Especially east of the Mississippi River, where villages moved every few years when soil or game became depleted, acquiring numerous possessions made little sense. However, status certainly mattered in Indian societies. Tribal leaders tended to come from a small number of families, and chiefs lived more splendidly than average members of society. But their reputation often rested on their willingness to share goods with others rather than hoarding them for themselves.

A few Indian societies had rigid social distinctions. Among the Natchez, descendants of the mound-building Mississippian culture, a chief, or "Great Sun," occupied the top of the social order, with nobles, or "lesser suns," below him, and below them, the common people. In general, however, wealth mattered far less in Indian society than in European society at the time. Generosity was among the most valued social qualities, and gift giving was essential to Indian society. Trade, for example, meant more than a commercial transaction—it was accompanied by elaborate ceremonies of gift exchange. Although Indians had no experience of the wealth enjoyed at the top of European society, under normal circumstances no one in Indian societies went hungry or experienced the extreme inequalities of Europe. "There are no beggars among them," reported the English colonial leader Roger Williams of New England's Indians.

Gift giving

A Catawba map illustrates the differences between Indian and European conceptions of landed property. The map depicts not possession of a specific territory, but trade and diplomatic connections between various native groups and with the colony of Virginia, represented by the rectangle on the lower right. The map, inscribed on deerskin, was originally presented by Indian chiefs to Governor Francis Nicholson of South Carolina in 1721. This copy, the only version that survives, was made by the governor for the authorities in London. It added English labels that conveyed what the Indians had related orally with the gift.

Gender Relations

The system of gender relations in most Indian societies also differed markedly from that of Europe. Membership in a family defined women's lives, but they openly engaged in premarital sexual relations and could even choose to divorce their husbands. Most, although not all, Indian societies were matrilineal—that is, centered on clans or kinship groups in which children became members of the mother's family, not the father's. Tribal leaders were almost always men, but women played an important role in certain religious ceremonies, and female elders often helped to select male village leaders and took part in tribal meetings. Under English law, a married man controlled the family's property and a wife had no independent legal identity. In contrast, Indian women owned dwellings and tools, and a husband generally moved to live with the family of his wife. In Indian societies, men contributed to the community's well-being and demonstrated their masculinity by success in hunting or, in the Pacific Northwest, by catching fish with nets and harpoons. Because men were frequently away on the hunt, women took responsibility not only for household duties but for most agricultural work as well. Among the Pueblo of the Southwest, however, where there was less hunting than in the East, men were the primary cultivators.

Matrilineal societies

European Views of the Indians

Europeans tended to view Indians in extreme terms. They were regarded either as "noble savages," gentle, friendly, and superior in some ways to Europeans, or as uncivilized barbarians. Giovanni da Verrazano, a Florentine navigator who sailed up and down the eastern coast of North America in 1524, described Indians he encountered as "beautiful of stature and build." (For their part, many Indians, whose diet was probably more nutritious than that of most Europeans, initially found the newcomers weak and ugly.)

Indians fishing, in a 1585 drawing by John White. The canoe is filled with fish, while two men harpoon others in the background. Among the wildlife illustrated are hammerhead sharks and catfish.

Over time, however, negative images of Indians came to overshadow positive ones. Early European descriptions of North American Indians as barbaric centered on three areas—religion, land use, and gender relations. Whatever their country of origin, European newcomers concluded that Indians lacked genuine religion, or in fact worshiped the devil. Their shamans and herb healers were called "witch doctors," their numerous ceremonies and rituals at best a form of superstition, their belief in a world alive with spiritual power a worship of "false gods." Christianity presented no obstacle to the commercial use of the land, and indeed in some ways encouraged it, since true religion was thought to promote the progress of civilization. Whereas the Indians saw nature as a world of spirits and souls, the Europeans viewed it as a collection of potential commodities, a source of economic opportunity.

Europeans invoked the Indians' distinctive pattern of land use and ideas about property to answer the awkward question raised by a British minister at an early stage of England's colonization: "By what right or warrant can we enter into the land of these Savages, take away their rightful inheritance from them, and plant ourselves in their places?" While the Spanish claimed title to land in America by right of conquest and papal authority, the English, French, and Dutch came to rely on the idea that Indians had not actually "used" the land and thus had no claim to it. Despite the Indians' highly developed agriculture and well-established towns, Europeans frequently described them as nomads without settled communities. The land was thus deemed to be a vacant wilderness ready to be claimed by newcomers who would cultivate and improve it. European settlers believed that mixing one's labor with the earth, which Indians supposedly had failed to do, gave one title to the soil.

In the Indians' gender division of labor and matrilineal family structures, Europeans saw weak men and mistreated women. Hunting and fishing, the primary occupations of Indian men, were considered leisure activities in much of Europe, not "real" work. Because Indian women worked in the fields, Europeans often described them as lacking freedom. They were "not much better than slaves," in the words of one English commentator. Europeans considered Indian men "unmanly"—too weak to exercise authority within their families and restrain their wives' open sexuality, and so lazy that they forced their wives to do most of the productive labor. Throughout North America, Europeans promoted the ideas that women should confine themselves to household work and that men ought to exercise greater authority within their families. Europeans insisted that by subduing the Indians, they were actually bringing them freedom—the freedom of true religion, private property, and the liberation of both men and women from uncivilized and unchristian gender roles.

A seventeenth-century engraving by a French Jesuit priest illustrates many Europeans' view of Indian religion. A demon hovers over an Iroquois longhouse, suggesting that Indians worship the devil.

European view of Indian gender roles

INDIAN FREEDOM, EUROPEAN FREEDOM

Indian Freedom

And what of liberty as the native inhabitants of the New World understood it? Many Europeans saw Indians as embodying freedom. The Iroquois, wrote one colonial official, held "such absolute notions of liberty that they allow of no kind of superiority of one over another, and banish all servitude from their territories." But

Indian women planting crops while men break the sod. An engraving by Theodor de Bry, based on a painting by Jacques Le Moyne de Morgues. Morgues was part of an expedition of French Huguenots to Florida in 1564; he escaped when the Spanish destroyed the outpost in the following year.

most colonizers quickly concluded that the notion of "freedom" was alien to Indian societies. Early English and French dictionaries of Indian languages contained no entry for "freedom" or *liberté*. Nor, wrote one early trader, did Indians have "words to express despotic power, arbitrary kings, oppressed or obedient subjects."

Indeed, Europeans considered Indians barbaric in part because they did not appear to live under established governments or fixed laws, and had no respect for authority. "They are born, live, and die in a liberty without restraint," wrote one religious missionary. In a sense, they were *too* free, lacking the order and discipline that Europeans considered the hallmarks of civilization. When Giovanni da Verrazano described the Indians as living in "absolute freedom," he did not intend this as a compliment.

The familiar modern understanding of freedom as personal independence, often based on ownership of private property, had little meaning in most Indian societies. But Indians certainly had their own ideas of freedom. While the buying and selling of slaves was unknown, small-scale slavery existed in some Indian societies. So too did the idea of personal liberty as the opposite of being held as a slave. Indians would bitterly resent the efforts of some Europeans to reduce them to slavery.

Although individuals were expected to think for themselves and did not always have to go along with collective decision making, Indian men and women judged one another according to their ability to live up to widely understood ideas of appropriate behavior. Far more important than individual autonomy were kinship ties, the ability to follow one's spiritual values, and the well-being and security of one's community. In Indian culture, group autonomy and self-determination, and the mutual obligations that came with a sense of belonging and connectedness, took precedence over individual freedom. Ironically, the coming of Europeans, armed with their own language of liberty, would make freedom a preoccupation of American Indians, as part and parcel of the very process by which they were reduced to dependence on the colonizers.

Christian Liberty

On the eve of colonization, Europeans held numerous ideas of freedom. Some were as old as the city-states of ancient Greece, others arose during the political struggles of the early modern era. Some laid the foundations for modern conceptions of freedom, others are quite unfamiliar today. Freedom was not a single idea but a collection of distinct rights and privileges, many enjoyed by only a small portion of the population.

Freedom as a spiritual condition

One conception common throughout Europe was that freedom was less a political or social status than a moral or spiritual condition. Freedom meant abandoning the life of sin to embrace the teachings of Christ. "Where the Spirit of the Lord is," declares the New Testament, "there is liberty." In this definition, servitude and freedom were mutually reinforcing, not contradictory states, since those who accepted the teachings of Christ simultaneously became "free from sin" and "servants to God."

"Christian liberty" had no connection to later ideas of religious toleration, a notion that scarcely existed anywhere on the eve of colonization. Every nation in

Europe had an established church that decreed what forms of religious worship and belief were acceptable. Dissenters faced persecution by the state as well as condemnation by church authorities. Religious uniformity was thought to be essential to public order; the modern idea that a person's religious beliefs and practices are a matter of private choice, not legal obligation, was almost unknown. The religious wars that racked Europe in the sixteenth and seventeenth centuries centered on which religion would predominate in a kingdom or region, not the right of individuals to choose which church in which to worship.

Freedom and Authority

In its secular form, the equating of liberty with obedience to a higher authority suggested that freedom meant obedience to law. Aristotle had described the law as liberty's "salvation," not its enemy. The identification of freedom with the rule of law did not, however, mean that all subjects of the crown enjoyed the same degree of freedom. Early modern European societies were extremely hierarchical, with marked gradations of social status ranging from the king and hereditary aristocracy down to the urban and rural poor. Inequality was built into virtually every social relationship. The king claimed to rule by the authority of God. Persons of high rank demanded deference from those below them.

Within families, men exercised authority over their wives and children. According to the widespread legal doctrine known as "coverture," when a woman married she surrendered her legal identity, which became "covered" by that of her husband. She could not own property or sign contracts in her own name, control her wages if she worked, write a separate will, or, except in the rarest of circumstances, go to court seeking a divorce. The husband conducted business and testified in court for the entire family. He had the exclusive right to his wife's "company," including domestic labor and sexual relations.

Everywhere in Europe, family life depended on male dominance and female submission. Indeed, political writers of the sixteenth century explicitly compared the king's authority over his subjects with the husband's over his family. Both were ordained by God. To justify this argument, they referred to a passage in the New Testament: "As the man is the head of the woman, so is Christ the head of the Church." Neither kind of authority could be challenged without threatening the fabric of social order.

Liberty and Liberties

In this hierarchical society, liberty came from knowing one's social place and fulfilling the duties appropriate to one's rank. Most men lacked the freedom that came with economic independence. Property qualifications and other restrictions limited the electorate to a minuscule part of the adult male population. The law required strict obedience of employees, and breaches of labor contracts carried criminal penalties.

European ideas of freedom still bore the imprint of the Middle Ages, when "liberties" meant formal, specific privileges such as self-government, exemption from taxation, or the right to practice a particular trade, granted to individuals or groups by contract, royal decree, or purchase. One legal dictionary defined a liberty

The title page of *The Great Voyage to the Country of the Hurons*, published in Paris in 1632 by Gabriel Sagard, one of the first missionaries to New France, includes images of Native Americans and Catholic friars. Father Sagard also produced a dictionary of the Huron language.

Hierarchy in society

as "a privilege . . . by which men may enjoy some benefit beyond the ordinary subject." Only those who enjoyed the "freedom of the city," for example, could engage in certain economic activities. Numerous modern civil liberties did not exist. The law decreed acceptable forms of religious worship. The government regularly suppressed publications it did not like, and criticism of authority could lead to imprisonment. Personal independence was reserved for a small part of the population, and this was one reason why authorities found "masterless men"—those without regular jobs or otherwise outside the control of their social superiors—so threatening. Nonetheless, every European country that colonized the New World claimed to be spreading freedom—for its own population and for Native Americans.

THE EXPANSION OF EUROPE

It is fitting that the second epochal event that Adam Smith linked to Columbus's voyage of 1492 was the discovery by Portuguese navigators of a sea route from Europe to Asia around the southern tip of Africa. The European conquest of America began as an offshoot of the quest for a sea route to India, China, and the islands of the East Indies, the source of the silk, tea, spices, porcelain, and other luxury goods on which international trade in the early modern era centered. For centuries, this commerce had been conducted across land, from China and South Asia to the Middle East and the Mediterranean region. Profit and piety—the desire to eliminate Islamic middlemen and win control of the lucrative trade for Christian western Europe—combined to inspire the quest for a direct route to Asia.

Chinese and Portuguese Navigation

At the beginning of the fifteenth century, one might have predicted that China would establish the world's first global empire. Between 1405 and 1433, Admiral Zheng He led seven large naval expeditions in the Indian Ocean. The first convoy consisted of 62 ships that were larger than those of any European nation, along with 225 support vessels and more than 25,000 men. On his sixth voyage, Zheng explored the coast of East Africa. China was already the world's most important trading economy, with trade routes dotting the Indian Ocean. Zheng's purpose was not discovery, but to impress other peoples with China's might. Had his ships continued westward, they could easily have reached North and South America. But as a wealthy land-based empire, China did not feel the need for overseas expansion, and after 1433 the government ended support for long-distance maritime expeditions. It fell to Portugal, situated on the western corner of the Iberian Peninsula, far removed from the overland route to Asia, to take advantage of new techniques of sailing and navigation to begin exploring the Atlantic.

The development of the **caravel**, a ship capable of long-distance travel, and of the compass and quadrant, devices that enabled sailors to determine their location and direction with greater accuracy than in the past, made it possible to sail down the coast of Africa and return to Portugal. Portuguese seafarers initially hoped to locate the source of gold that for centuries had been transported in caravans

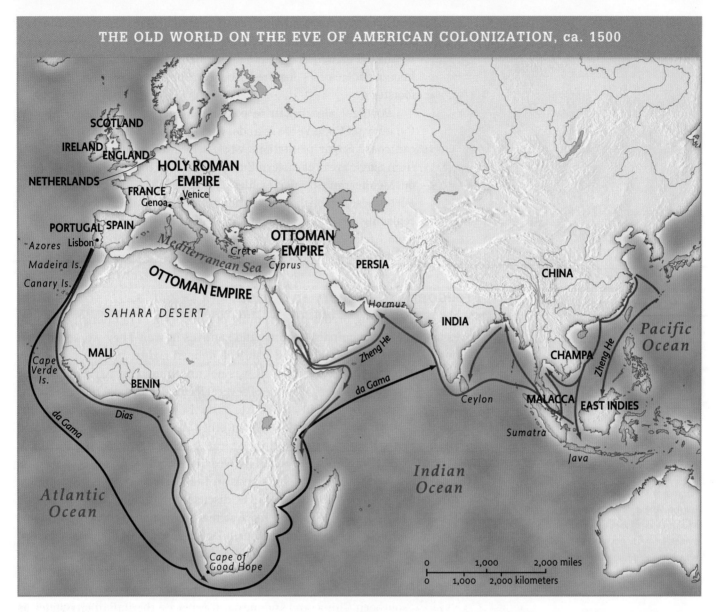

THE OLD WORLD ON THE EVE OF AMERICAN COLONIZATION, ca. 1500

across the Sahara Desert to North Africa and Europe. This commerce, which passed through the African kingdom of Mali on the southern edge of the Sahara, provided Europe with most of its gold. Around 1400, it rivaled trade with the East in economic importance. And like trade with Asia, it was controlled by Muslim merchants.

In the fifteenth century, the world known to Europeans was limited to Europe, parts of Africa, and Asia. Explorers from Portugal sought to find a sea route to the East in order to circumvent the Italian city-states and Middle Eastern rulers who controlled the overland trade.

Portugal and West Africa

Until 1434, no European sailor had seen the coast of Africa below the Sahara, or the forest kingdoms south of Mali that contained the actual gold fields. But in that year, a Portuguese ship brought a sprig of rosemary from West Africa, proof that one could sail beyond the desert and return. Little by little, Portuguese ships moved farther down the coast. In 1485, they reached Benin, an imposing city whose crafts-men produced bronze sculptures that still inspire admiration for their artistic

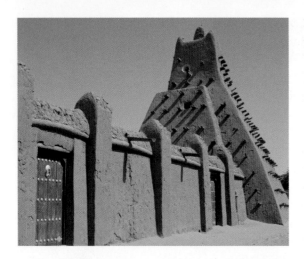

Sankore University in Timbuktu, in present-day Mali, was one of the great Islamic centers of learning in fourteenth-century Africa.

A detail from the *Cantino World Map* depicting the western coast of Africa at the beginning of the Atlantic slave trade. Created by an anonymous Portuguese mapmaker in 1502, the map included Europe, Africa, and a small part of the Western Hemisphere, described as "the islands lately discovered in the parts of India." It was smuggled out of Portugal by Alberto Cantino, a diplomat representing an Italian city-state.

beauty and superb casting techniques. The Portuguese established fortified trading posts on the western coast of Africa. The profits reaped by these Portuguese "factories"—so named because merchants were known as "factors"—inspired other European powers to follow in their footsteps.

Portugal also began to colonize Madeira, the Azores, and the Canary and Cape Verde Islands, which lie in the Atlantic off the African coast. Sugar plantations worked by Muslim captives and slaves from Slavic areas of eastern Europe had flourished in the Middle Ages on Mediterranean islands like Cyprus, Malta, and Crete. Now, the Portuguese established plantations on the Atlantic islands, eventually replacing the native populations with thousands of slaves shipped from Africa—an ominous precedent for the New World. Soon, the center of sugar production would shift again, to the Western Hemisphere.

Freedom and Slavery in Africa

Slavery in Africa long predated the coming of Europeans. Traditionally, African slaves tended to be criminals, debtors, and captives in war. They worked within the households of their owners and had well-defined rights, such as possessing property and marrying free persons. It was not uncommon for African slaves to acquire their freedom. Slavery was one of several forms of labor, not the basis of the economy as it would become in large parts of the New World. The coming of the Portuguese, soon followed by traders from other European nations, accelerated the buying and selling of slaves within Africa. At least 100,000 African slaves were transported to Spain and Portugal between 1450 and 1500. In 1502, the first African slaves were transported to islands in the Caribbean. The transatlantic slave trade, and its impact on Africa, will be discussed in Chapter 4.

Having reached West Africa, Portuguese mariners pushed their explorations ever southward along the coast. Bartholomeu Dias reached the Cape of Good Hope at the continent's southern tip in 1487. In 1498, Vasco da Gama sailed around it to India, demonstrating the feasibility of a sea route to the East. With a population of under 1 million, Portugal established a vast trading empire, with bases in India, southern China, and Indonesia. It replaced the Italian city-states as the major European commercial partner of the East. But six years before da Gama's voyage, Christopher Columbus had, he believed, discovered a new route to China and India by sailing west.

The Voyages of Columbus

A seasoned mariner and fearless explorer from Genoa, a major port in northern Italy, Columbus had for years sailed the Mediterranean and North Atlantic, studying ocean currents and wind patterns. Like nearly all navigators of the time, Columbus knew the earth was round. But he drastically underestimated its size. He believed that by sailing westward he could relatively quickly cross the Atlantic and reach Asia. No one in Europe knew that two giant continents lay 3,000 miles to the west. The Vikings, to be sure, had sailed from Greenland to Newfoundland around the year 1000 and established a settlement, Vinland, at a site now known as L'Anse aux Meadows. But this outpost was abandoned after a few years and had been forgotten, except in Norse legends.

For Columbus, as for other figures of the time, religious and commercial motives reinforced one another. A devout Catholic, he drew on the Bible for his estimate of the size of the globe. Along with developing trade with the East, he hoped to convert Asians to Christianity and enlist them in a crusade to redeem Jerusalem from Muslim control. Columbus sought financial support throughout Europe for the planned voyage. Most of Columbus's contemporaries, however, knew that he considerably underestimated the earth's size, which helps to explain why he had trouble gaining backers for his expedition. Eventually, King Ferdinand and Queen Isabella of Spain agreed to become sponsors. Their marriage in 1469 had united the warring kingdoms of Aragon and Castile. In 1492, they completed the *reconquista*—the "reconquest" of Spain from the Moors, African Muslims who had occupied part of the Iberian Peninsula for centuries. To ensure its religious unification, Ferdinand and Isabella ordered all Muslims and Jews to convert to Catholicism or leave the country. Along with the crown, much of Columbus's financing came from bankers and merchants of Spain and the Italian city-states, who desperately desired to circumvent the Muslim stranglehold on eastern trade. Columbus set sail with royal letters of introduction to Asian rulers, authorizing him to negotiate trade agreements.

Columbus's sponsors

CONTACT

Columbus in the New World

On October 12, 1492, after only thirty-three days of sailing from the Canary Islands, where he had stopped to resupply his three ships, Columbus and his expedition arrived at the Bahamas. His exact landing site remains in dispute, but it was probably San Salvador, a tiny spot of land known today as Watling Island. Soon afterward, he encountered the far larger islands of Hispaniola (today the site of Haiti and the Dominican Republic) and Cuba. When one of his ships ran aground, he abandoned it and left thirty-eight men behind on Hispaniola. But he found room to bring ten inhabitants of the island back to Spain for conversion to Christianity.

In the following year, 1493, European colonization of the New World began. Columbus returned with seventeen ships and more than 1,000 men to explore the area and establish a Spanish outpost. Columbus's settlement on the island of Hispaniola, which he named La Isabella, failed, but in 1502 another Spanish explorer, Nicolás de Ovando, arrived with 2,500 men and established a permanent base, the first center of the Spanish empire in America. Before he died in 1506, Columbus made two more voyages to the New World, in 1498 and 1502. He went to his grave believing that he had discovered a westward route to Asia. The explorations of another Italian, Amerigo Vespucci, along the coast of South America between 1499 and 1502 made plain that a continent entirely unknown to Europeans had been encountered. The New World would come to bear not Columbus's name but one

Columbus's Landfall, an engraving from *La lettera dell'isole* (Letter from the Islands). This 1493 pamphlet reproduced, in the form of a poem, Columbus's first letter describing his voyage of the previous year. Under the watchful eye of King Ferdinand of Spain, Columbus and his men land on a Caribbean island, while local Indians flee.

VOYAGES OF DISCOVERY

EUROPE

Vinland
Cabot (1497)

NEWFOUNDLAND

NORTH AMERICA

Cortés (1519)

Columbus (1492)

Columbus (1493)

Columbus (1502)

AFRICA

Balboa (1513)

Atlantic Ocean

Columbus (1498)

Magellan (1519-1522)

Vespucci (1501-1502)

Cabral (1500)

Pacific Ocean

SOUTH AMERICA

Magellan (1519-1522)

| 0 | 1,000 | 2,000 miles |

| 0 | 1,000 | 2,000 kilometers |

Christopher Columbus's first Atlantic crossing, in 1492, was soon followed by voyages of discovery by English, Portuguese, Spanish, and Italian explorers.

based on Vespucci's—America. Vespucci also realized that the native inhabitants were distinct peoples, not residents of the East Indies as Columbus had believed, although the name "Indians," applied to them by Columbus, has endured to this day.

Vespucci

Exploration and Conquest

The speed with which European exploration proceeded in the aftermath of Columbus's first voyage is remarkable. The technique of printing with movable type, invented in the 1430s by the German craftsman Johannes Gutenberg, had made possible the rapid spread of information in Europe, at least among the educated minority. News of Columbus's achievement traveled quickly. One writer hailed him as "a hero such as the ancients made gods of." Others were inspired to follow in his wake. John Cabot, a Genoese merchant who had settled in England, reached Newfoundland in 1497. Soon, scores of fishing boats from France, Spain, and England were active in the region. Pedro Cabral claimed Brazil for Portugal in 1500.

But the Spanish took the lead in exploration and conquest. Inspired by a search for wealth, national glory, and the desire to spread Catholicism, Spanish *conquistadores*, often accompanied by religious missionaries and carrying flags emblazoned with the sign of the cross, radiated outward from Hispaniola. In 1513, Vasco Núñez de Balboa trekked across the isthmus of Panama and became the first European to gaze upon the Pacific Ocean. Between 1519 and 1522, Ferdinand Magellan led the first expedition to sail around the world, encountering Pacific islands and peoples previously unknown to Europe. Magellan was killed in the Philippines, but his fleet completed the journey, correcting once and for all Columbus's erroneous assessment of the earth's size.

The first explorer to encounter a major American civilization was Hernán Cortés, who in 1519 arrived at Tenochtitlán, the nerve center of the Aztec empire, whose wealth and power rested on domination of numerous subordinate peoples nearby. The Aztecs were violent warriors who engaged in the ritual sacrifice of captives and others, sometimes thousands at a time. This practice thoroughly alienated their neighbors and reinforced the Spanish view of America's native inhabitants as barbarians, even though in Europe at this time thousands of men and women were burned at the stake as witches or religious heretics, and criminals were executed in public spectacles that attracted throngs of onlookers.

With only a few hundred European men, the daring Cortés conquered the Aztec city, relying on superior military technology such as iron weapons and gunpowder, as well as shrewdness in enlisting the aid of some of the Aztecs' subject peoples, who supplied him with thousands of warriors. His most powerful ally, however, was disease—a smallpox epidemic that devastated Aztec society. A few years later, Francisco Pizarro conquered the great Inca kingdom centered in modern-day Peru. Pizarro's tactics were typical of the conquistadores. He captured the Incan king,

Engravings, from the *Florentine Codex*, of the forces of Cortés marching on Tenochtitlán and assaulting the city with cannon fire. The difference in military technology between the Spanish and Aztecs is evident. Indians who allied with Cortés had helped him build vessels and carry them in pieces over mountains to the city. The codex (a volume formed by stitching together manuscript pages) was prepared under the supervision of a Spanish missionary in sixteenth-century Mexico.

TABLE 1.1 Estimated Regional Populations: The Americas, ca. 1500	
North America	3,800,000
Mexico	17,200,000
Central America	5,625,000
Hispaniola	1,000,000
The Caribbean	3,000,000
The Andes	15,700,000
South America	8,620,000
Total	54,945,000

A drawing from around 1700 shows an Indian suffering from smallpox. The Columbian Exchange—the flow of goods and people across the Atlantic—included animals, plants, technology, and diseases.

demanded and received a ransom, and then killed the king anyway. Soon, treasure fleets carrying cargoes of gold and silver from the mines of Mexico and Peru were traversing the Atlantic to enrich the Spanish crown.

The Demographic Disaster

The transatlantic flow of goods and people, sometimes called the **Columbian Exchange**, altered millions of years of evolution. Plants, animals, and cultures that had evolved independently on separate continents were now thrown together. Products introduced to Europe from the Americas included corn, tomatoes, potatoes, peanuts, tobacco, and cotton, while people from the Old World brought wheat, rice, sugarcane, horses, cattle, pigs, and sheep to the New. But Europeans also carried germs previously unknown in the Americas.

No one knows exactly how many people lived in the Americas at the time of Columbus's voyages—current estimates range between 50 and 90 million. By comparison, the European population in 1492 (including Russia) was around 90 million, the African population was around 40 million, and about 210 million lived in China and modern-day India. Most inhabitants of the New World lived in Central and South America. In 1492, the Indian population within what are now the borders of the United States was between 2 and 5 million.

Whatever their numbers, the Indian populations suffered a catastrophic decline because of contact with Europeans and their wars, enslavement, and especially diseases like smallpox, influenza, and measles. Never having encountered these diseases, Indians had not developed antibodies to fight them. The result was devastating. Many West Indian islands were all but depopulated. On Hispaniola, the native population, estimated at between 300,000 and 1 million in 1492, had nearly disappeared fifty years later. The population of Mexico would fall by more than 90 percent in the sixteenth century, from perhaps 20 million to less than 2 million. As for the area that now forms the United States, its Native American population fell continuously. It reached its lowest point around 1900, at only 250,000.

Overall, the death of perhaps 80 million people—close to one-fifth of humankind—in the first century and a half after contact with Europeans represents the greatest loss of life in human history. It was disease as much as military prowess and more-advanced technology that enabled Europeans to conquer the Americas.

THE SPANISH EMPIRE

By the middle of the sixteenth century, Spain had established an immense empire that reached from Europe to the Americas and Asia. The Atlantic and Pacific oceans, once barriers separating different parts of the world, now became highways for the exchange of goods and the movement of people. Spanish galleons carried gold and silver from Mexico and Peru eastward to Spain and westward to Manila in the Philippines and on to China.

The Spanish empire included the most populous parts of the New World and the regions richest in natural resources. Stretching from the Andes Mountains of

South America through present-day Mexico and the Caribbean and eventually into Florida and the southwestern United States, Spain's empire exceeded in size the Roman empire of the ancient world. Its center in North America was Mexico City, a magnificent capital built on the ruins of the Aztec city of Tenochtitlán that boasted churches, hospitals, monasteries, government buildings, and the New World's first university. Unlike the English and French New World empires, Spanish America was essentially an urban civilization, an "empire of towns." For centuries, its great cities, notably Mexico City, Quito, and Lima, far outshone any urban centers in North America and most of those in Europe.

Governing Spanish America

Spain's system of colonial government rivaled that of ancient Rome. Alarmed by the destructiveness of the conquistadores, the Spanish crown replaced them with a more stable system of government headed by lawyers and bureaucrats. At least in theory, the government of Spanish America reflected the absolutism of the newly unified nation at home. Authority originated with the king and flowed downward through the Council of the Indies—the main body in Spain for colonial administration—and then to viceroys in Mexico and Peru and other local officials in America. The Catholic Church also played a significant role in the administration of Spanish colonies, frequently exerting its authority on matters of faith, morals, and treatment of the Indians.

Successive kings kept elected assemblies out of Spain's New World empire. Royal officials were generally appointees from Spain, rather than *criollos*, or **creoles**, as persons born in the colonies of European ancestry were called. The imperial state was a real and continuous presence in Spanish America. But as its power declined in Europe beginning in the seventeenth century, the local elite came to enjoy more and more effective authority over colonial affairs. Given the vastness of the empire, local municipal councils, universities, merchant organizations, and craft guilds enjoyed considerable independence.

Colonists in Spanish America

Despite the decline in the native population, Spanish America remained populous enough that, with the exception of the West Indies and a few cities, large-scale importations of African slaves were unnecessary. Instead, the Spanish forced tens of thousands of Indians to work in gold and silver mines, which supplied the empire's wealth, and on large-scale farms, or **haciendas**, controlled by Spanish landlords. In Spanish America, unlike other New World empires, Indians performed most of the labor, and although the Spanish introduced livestock, wheat, and sugar, the main agricultural crops were the same ones grown before colonization—corn, beans, and squash.

"The maxim of the conqueror must be to settle," said one Spanish official. The government barred non-Spaniards from emigrating to its American domains, as well as non-Christian

TABLE 1.2 Estimated Regional Populations: The World, ca. 1500	
India	110,000,000
China	103,000,000
Other Asia	55,400,000
Western Europe	57,200,000
The Americas	54,000,000
Russia and Eastern Europe	34,000,000
Sub-Saharan Africa	38,300,000
Japan	15,400,000
World Total	467,300,000

An image from the *Tlaxcala Codex*, which chronicles events in a region of central Mexico in the sixteenth century. Aztec warriors dressed in eagle and jaguar costumes dance before Spanish officials and priests.

Young Woman with a Harpsichord, a colorful painting from Mexico in the early 1700s, depicts an upper-class woman. Her dress, jewelry, fan, the cross around her neck, and the musical instrument all emphasize that while she lives in the colonies, she embodies the latest in European fashion and culture.

Spaniards, including Jews and Moors. But the opportunity for social advancement drew numerous colonists from Spain—225,000 in the sixteenth century and a total of 750,000 in the three centuries of Spain's colonial rule. Eventually, a significant number came in families, but at first the large majority were young, single men, many of them laborers, craftsmen, and soldiers. Many also came as government officials, priests, professionals, and minor aristocrats, all ready to direct the manual work of Indians, since living without having to labor was a sign of noble status. The most successful of these colonists enjoyed lives of luxury similar to those of the upper classes at home.

Colonists and Indians

Although persons of European birth, called *peninsulares*, stood atop the social hierarchy, they never constituted more than a tiny proportion of the population of Spanish America. Unlike in the later British empire, Indian inhabitants always outnumbered European colonists and their descendants in Spanish America, and large areas remained effectively under Indian control for many years. Like the later French empire and unlike the English, Spanish authorities granted Indians certain rights within colonial society and looked forward to their eventual assimilation.

The Spanish crown ordered wives of colonists to join them in America and demanded that single men marry. But with the population of Spanish women remaining low, the intermixing of the colonial and Indian peoples soon began. As early as 1514, the Spanish government formally approved of such marriages, partly as a way of bringing Christianity to the native population. By 1600, **mestizos** (persons of mixed origin) made up a large part of the urban population of Spanish America. In the century that followed, *mestizos* repopulated the Valley of Mexico, where disease had decimated the original inhabitants. Over time, Spanish America evolved into a hybrid culture, part Spanish, part Indian, and in some areas part African, but with a single official faith, language, and governmental system. In

Four Racial Groups, taken from a series of paintings by the eighteenth-century Mexican artist Andrés de Islas, illustrates the racial mixing that took place in the Spanish empire and some of the new vocabulary invented to describe it. *First:* The offspring of a Spaniard and Indian is a *mestizo*. *Second:* A Spaniard and a *mestiza* produce a *castizo*. *Third:* The child of an Indian and a *mestiza* is a *coyote*. *Fourth:* And the child of an Indian man and African woman is a *chino*.

An illustration from the *Huexotzinco Codex* (1531) depicts Mexicans providing products and services as taxes to the Spanish conquerors. The banner of the Virgin Mary and baby Jesus reflects the early spread of Christianity. The people of Huexotzinco, a town near Mexico City, had aided Hernán Cortés in his conquest of the Aztec empire. The codex was part of a successful lawsuit, endorsed by Cortés, in which the Indians challenged excessive taxation by colonial officials.

1531, a poor Indian, Juan Diego, reported seeing a vision of the Virgin Mary, looking very much like a dark-skinned Indian, near a Mexican village. Miracles began to be reported, and a shrine was built in her honor. The Virgin of Guadalupe would come to be revered by millions as a symbol of the mixing of Indian and Spanish cultures, and later of the modern nation of Mexico.

The Virgin of Guadalupe

Justifications for Conquest

What allowed one nation, the seventeenth-century Dutch legal thinker Hugo Grotius wondered, to claim possession of lands that "belonged to someone else"? This question rarely occurred to most of the Europeans who crossed the Atlantic in the wake of Columbus's voyage, or to rulers in the Old World. They had immense confidence in the superiority of their own cultures to those they encountered in America. They expected these societies to abandon their own beliefs and traditions and embrace those of the newcomers. Failure to do so reinforced the conviction that these people were uncivilized "heathens" (non-Christians).

Europeans brought with them not only a long history of using violence to subdue their internal and external foes but also missionary zeal to spread the benefits of their own civilization to others, while reaping the rewards of empire. Spain was no exception. The establishment of its empire in America took place in the wake of Spain's own territorial unification, the rise of a powerful royal government, and the enforcement of religious orthodoxy by the expulsion of Muslims and Jews in 1492. To further legitimize Spain's claim to rule the New World, a year after Columbus's first voyage Pope Alexander VI divided the non-Christian world between Spain and Portugal. The line was subsequently adjusted to give Portugal control of Brazil, with the remainder of the Western Hemisphere falling under Spanish authority.

Religious motivation

The Virgin of Guadalupe, a symbol of Mexican culture, in an image from 1770. She is portrayed as the protector of the Indians.

Converting Indians

Spreading the Faith

Not surprisingly, the pope justified this pronouncement by requiring Spain and Portugal to spread Catholicism among the native inhabitants of the Americas. The missionary element of colonization, already familiar because of the long holy war against Islam within Spain itself, was powerfully reinforced in the sixteenth century, when the Protestant Reformation divided the Catholic Church. In 1517, Martin Luther, a German priest, posted his ***Ninety-Five Theses***, which accused the church of worldliness and corruption. Luther wanted to cleanse the church of abuses such as the sale of indulgences (official dispensations forgiving sins). He insisted that all believers should read the Bible for themselves, rather than relying on priests to interpret it for them. His call for reform led to the rise of new Protestant churches independent of Rome and plunged Europe into more than a century of religious and political strife.

Spain, the most powerful bastion of orthodox Catholicism, redoubled its efforts to convert the Indians to the "true faith." National glory and religious mission went hand in hand. Convinced of the superiority of Catholicism to all other religions, Spain insisted that the primary goal of colonization was to save the Indians from heathenism and prevent them from falling under the sway of Protestantism. The aim was neither to exterminate nor to remove the Indians, but to transform them into obedient, Christian subjects of the crown. Indeed, lacking the later concept of "race" as an unchanging, inborn set of qualities and abilities, many Spanish writers insisted that Indians could in time be "brought up" to the level of European civilization. Of course, this meant not only the destruction of existing Indian political structures but also a transformation of their economic and spiritual lives. Religious orders established missions throughout the empire, and over time millions of Indians were converted to Catholicism.

On the other hand, Spanish rule, especially in its initial period, witnessed a disastrous fall in Indian population, not only because of epidemics but also because of the brutal conditions of labor to which Indians were subjected. The

A benign view of Spanish colonization. This engraving from a 1621 book depicts Spanish missionaries bringing Christianity to New World natives while priests do construction work. A fortified colonial town is visible in the background.

conquistadores and subsequent governors, who required conquered peoples to acknowledge the Catholic Church and provide gold and silver, saw no contradiction between serving God and enriching themselves. Others, however, did.

Las Casas's Complaint

As early as 1537, Pope Paul III, who hoped to see Indians become devout subjects of Catholic monarchs, outlawed their enslavement (an edict never extended to apply to Africans). His decree declared Indians to be "truly men," who must not be "treated as dumb beasts." Fifteen years later, the Dominican priest **Bartolomé de Las Casas** published an account of the decimation of the Indian population with the compelling title *A Very Brief Account of the Destruction of the Indies*. Las Casas's father had sailed on Columbus's second voyage, and he himself had participated in the conquest of Cuba. But in 1514 Las Casas freed his own Indian slaves and began to preach against the injustices of Spanish rule.

Las Casas's writings denounced Spain for causing the death of millions of innocent people. He narrated in shocking detail the "strange cruelties" carried out by "the Christians," including the burning alive of men, women, and children and the imposition of forced labor. The Indians, he wrote, had been "totally deprived of their freedom and were put in the harshest, fiercest, most terrible servitude and captivity." Long before the idea was common, Las Casas insisted that Indians were rational beings, not barbarians, and that Spain had no grounds on which to deprive them of their lands and liberty. "The entire human race is one," he proclaimed, and while he continued to believe that Spain had a right to rule in America, largely on religious grounds, he called for Indians to enjoy "all guarantees of liberty and justice" from the moment they became subjects of Spain. "Nothing is certainly more precious in human affairs, nothing more esteemed," he wrote, "than freedom." Yet Las Casas also suggested that importing slaves from Africa would help to protect the Indians from exploitation.

> *Spain's "strange cruelties"*

Reforming the Empire

Like other Spaniards, Las Casas believed that the main justification for empire was converting the Indians to Christianity. Spanish cruelty, he feared, undermined this effort. Largely because of Las Casas's efforts, Spain in 1542 promulgated the New Laws, commanding that Indians no longer be enslaved. In 1550, Spain abolished the *encomienda* system, under which the first settlers had been granted authority over conquered Indian lands with the right to extract forced labor from the native inhabitants. In its place, the government established the ***repartimiento* system**, whereby residents of Indian villages remained legally free and entitled to wages, but were still required to perform a fixed amount of labor each year. The Indians were not slaves—they had access to land, were paid wages, and could not be bought and sold. But since the requirement that they

Spanish conquistadores murdering Indians at Cuzco, in Peru. The Dutch-born engraver Theodor de Bry and his sons illustrated ten volumes about New World exploration published between 1590 and 1618. A Protestant, de Bry created vivid images that helped to spread the Black Legend of Spain as a uniquely cruel colonizer.

A view of San Carlos Borromeo de Carmelo, or Mission Carmel, in 1786, two years after the death of Father Junipero Serra, depicts Native Americans lined up to welcome a French scientific expedition. Sketched by a French explorer, this is the earliest known image of California.

Indian labor

work for the Spanish remained the essence of the system, it still allowed for many abuses by Spanish landlords and by priests who required Indians to toil on mission lands as part of the conversion process. Indeed, a long struggle ensued among settlers, missionaries, and colonial authorities for control of Indian labor. Each party proclaimed itself a humane overlord and denounced the others for exploiting the native population.

By the end of the sixteenth century, work in the Spanish empire consisted largely of forced wage labor by native inhabitants and slave labor by Africans on the West Indian islands and a few parts of the mainland. Like all empires, Spain's always remained highly exploitative. Over time, the initial brutal treatment of Indians improved somewhat. The Spanish established their domination not just through violence and disease but by bringing education, medical care, and European goods, and because many Indians embraced Christianity. But Las Casas's writings, translated almost immediately into several European languages, contributed to the spread of the **Black Legend**—the image of Spain as a uniquely brutal and exploitative colonizer. This would provide a potent justification for other European powers to challenge Spain's predominance in the New World. Influenced by Las Casas, the eighteenth-century French historian Guillaume Thomas Raynal would write of Columbus's arrival in the New World, "Tell me, reader, whether these were civilized people landing among savages, or savages among civilized people?"

Exploring North America

New colonies

While the Spanish empire centered on Mexico, Peru, and the West Indies, the hope of finding a new kingdom of gold soon led Spanish explorers into new territory. In 1508, Spain established the first permanent colony in what is now the United States.

EARLY SPANISH CONQUESTS AND EXPLORATIONS
IN THE NEW WORLD

Cabrillo

Pueblo
Revolt,
1680

Oñate
Acoma
Santa
Fe

de Soto

Roanoke

*Atlantic
Ocean*

Cabeza de Vaca

Coronado

Fort Caroline
St. Augustine

Ponce de León

*Gulf of
Mexico*

Cortés

Hispaniola

Mexico City

Caribbean Sea

*Pacific
Ocean*

Pizarro

PERU

— Cabrillo
— Oñate
-·- Coronado
— de Soto
— Cabeza de Vaca
--- Ponce de León
— Cortés
— Pizarro
▢ Extent of Incan peoples
▢ Extent of Aztec peoples

0   500   1,000 miles
0   500   1,000 kilometers

By around 1600, New Spain had become a vast empire stretching from the modern-day American Southwest through Mexico and Central America and into the former Inca kingdom in South America. This map shows early Spanish exploration, especially in the present-day United States.

That first colony was not, as many people believe, at Jamestown, Virginia, or St. Augustine, Florida, but on the island of Puerto Rico, now a U.S. "commonwealth." Unlike many other European settlements that followed it, Puerto Rico had gold; Juan Ponce de León, who led the colony, sent a considerable amount to Spain, while keeping some for himself. In 1513, Ponce embarked for Florida, in search of wealth, slaves, and a fountain of eternal youth, only to be repelled by local Indians. In 1528, another expedition seeking plunder in Florida embarked from Spain, but after a series of storms only a handful of men reached the Gulf Coast. For seven years they traversed the Southwest until a few survivors arrived in Mexico in 1536. One, Álvar Núñez Cabeza de Vaca, wrote an account of his adventures, including tales told by native inhabitants (possibly to persuade the newcomers to move on) of the seven golden cities of Cibola, somewhere over the horizon.

Exploring the West

In the late 1530s and 1540s, Juan Rodriguez Cabrillo explored the Pacific coast as far north as present-day Oregon, and expeditions led by Hernando de Soto, Cabeza de Vaca, Francisco Vásquez de Coronado, and others marched through the Gulf region and the Southwest, fruitlessly searching for another Mexico or Peru. Coronado explored much of the interior of the continent, reaching as far north as the Great Plains, and became the first European to encounter the immense herds of buffalo that roamed the West. These expeditions, really mobile communities with hundreds of adventurers, priests, potential settlers, slaves, and livestock, spread disease and devastation among Indian communities. De Soto's was particularly brutal. His men tortured, raped, and enslaved countless Indians and transmitted deadly diseases. When Europeans in the seventeenth century returned to colonize the area traversed by de Soto's party, little remained of the societies he had encountered. Where large towns had existed, explorers found only herds of grazing bison.

Spanish Florida

Nonetheless, these explorations established Spain's claim to a large part of what is now the American South and Southwest. The first region to be colonized within the present-day United States was Florida. Spain hoped to establish a military base there to combat pirates who threatened the treasure fleet that each year sailed from Havana for Europe loaded with gold and silver from Mexico and Peru. Spain also wanted to forestall French incursions in the area. In 1565, Philip II of Spain authorized the nobleman Pedro Menéndez de Avilés to lead a colonizing expedition to Florida. Menéndez destroyed a small outpost at Fort Caroline, which a group of Huguenots (French Protestants) had established in 1562 near present-day Jacksonville. Menéndez and his men massacred the 500 colonists and went on to establish Spanish forts on St. Simons Island, Georgia, and at St. Augustine, Florida. The latter remains the oldest site in the continental United States continuously inhabited by European settlers and their descendants.

Military base

Forts and missions

Spanish expeditions soon established forts from present-day Miami into South Carolina, and Spanish religious missionaries set up outposts in Florida and on the Sea Islands, hoping to convert the local Indians to Christianity. In 1566, 500 Spanish colonists landed near modern-day Port Royal, South Carolina, and established the settlement of Santa Elena. It survived until 1587, when the government in Spain ordered it abandoned and the inhabitants resettled (over their vocal protests) at St. Augustine, to protect them from English naval raids. Most of the forts fell into disuse, and many of the missions were destroyed by local Guale Indians in an uprising that began in 1597. The Indians explained their revolt by noting that the missionaries had sought to eliminate "our dances, banquets, feasts, celebrations, and wars. . . . They persecute our old people by calling them witches." The missions were soon rebuilt, only to be devastated again a century later, this time by English and Indian forces from South Carolina. In general, Florida failed to attract settlers, remaining an isolated military settlement, in effect a fortified outpost of Cuba. As late as 1763, Spanish Florida had only 4,000 inhabitants of European descent.

Spain in the Southwest

Spain took even longer to begin the colonization of the American Southwest. Although Coronado and others made incursions into the area in the sixteenth century, their explorations were widely considered failures, since they had discovered neither gold nor advanced civilizations whose populations could be put to work for the Spanish empire. Spain then neglected the area for another half-century. It was not until 1598 that Juan de Oñate led a group of 400 soldiers, colonists, and missionaries north from Mexico to establish a permanent settlement. While searching for fabled deposits of precious metals, Oñate's nephew and fourteen soldiers were killed by inhabitants of Acoma, the "sky city" located on a high bluff in present-day New Mexico.

> *Oñate and Acoma*

Oñate decided to teach the local Indians a lesson. After a two-day siege, his forces scaled the seemingly impregnable heights and destroyed Acoma, killing more than 800 of its 1,500 or so inhabitants, including 300 women. Of the 600 Indians captured, the women and children were consigned to servitude in Spanish families, while adult men were punished by the cutting off of one foot. Not until the 1640s was Acoma, which had been inhabited since the thirteenth century, rebuilt. Oñate's message was plain—any Indians who resisted Spanish authority would be crushed. But his method of rule, coupled with his failure to locate gold, alarmed authorities in Mexico City. In 1606, Oñate was ordered home and punished for his treatment of New Mexico's Indians. In 1610, Spain established the capital of New Mexico at Santa Fe, the first permanent European settlement in the Southwest.

Acoma, the "sky city," as it appeared in 1904.

The Pueblo Revolt

In 1680, New Mexico's small and vulnerable colonist population numbered fewer than 3,000. Most were *mestizos* (persons of mixed Spanish and Indian origin), since few European settlers came to the region. Relations between the Pueblo Indians and colonial authorities had deteriorated throughout the seventeenth century, as governors, settlers, and missionaries sought to exploit the labor of an Indian population that declined from about 60,000 in 1600 to some 17,000 eighty years later. Franciscan friars worked relentlessly to convert Indians to Catholicism, often using intimidation and violence. Their spiritual dedication and personal courage impressed many Indians, however, as did the European goods and technologies they introduced. Some natives welcomed them as a counterbalance to the depredations of soldiers and settlers and accepted baptism, even as they continued to practice their old religion, adding Jesus, Mary, and the Catholic saints to their already rich spiritual pantheon. But as the Inquisition—the persecution of non-Catholics—became more and more intense in Spain, so did the friars' efforts to stamp out traditional religious ceremonies in New Mexico. By burning Indian idols, masks, and other sacred objects, the missionaries alienated far more Indians than they converted. A prolonged drought that began around 1660 and the authorities' inability to protect the villages and missions from attacks by marauding Navajo and Apache Indians added to local discontent.

The Pueblo peoples had long been divided among themselves. The Spanish assumed that the Indians could never unite against the colonizers. In August 1680, they were proven wrong.

Little is known about the life of Popé, who became the main organizer of an uprising that aimed to drive the Spanish from the colony and restore the Indians' traditional autonomy. A religious leader born around 1630 in San Juan Pueblo, Popé first appears in the historical record in 1675, when he was one of forty-seven Pueblo Indians arrested for "sorcery"—that is, practicing their traditional religion. Four of the prisoners were hanged, and the rest, including Popé, were brought to Santa Fe to be publicly whipped. After this humiliation, Popé returned home and began holding secret meetings in Pueblo communities.

Under Popé's leadership, New Mexico's Indians joined in a coordinated uprising. Ironically, because the Pueblos spoke six different languages, Spanish became the revolt's "lingua franca" (a common means of communication among persons of different linguistic backgrounds). Some 2,000 warriors destroyed isolated farms and missions, killing 400 colonists, including 21 Franciscan missionaries. They then surrounded Santa Fe. The Spanish resisted fiercely but eventually had no choice but to abandon the town. Most of the Spanish survivors, accompanied by several hundred Christian Indians, made their way south out of New Mexico. Within a few weeks, a century of colonization in the area had been destroyed. From their own point of view, the Pueblo Indians had triumphantly reestablished the freedom lost through Spanish conquest.

The **Pueblo Revolt** was the most complete victory for Native Americans over Europeans and the only wholesale expulsion of settlers in the history of North America. According to a royal attorney who interviewed the Spanish survivors in Mexico City, the revolt arose from the "many oppressions" the Indians had suffered. The victorious Pueblos turned with a vengeance on all symbols of European culture, uprooting fruit trees, destroying cattle, burning churches and images of Christ and the Virgin Mary, and wading into rivers to wash away their Catholic baptisms. They rebuilt their places of worship, called "kivas," and resumed sacred dances the friars had banned. "The God of the Spaniards," they shouted, "is dead."

Cooperation among the Pueblo peoples, however, soon evaporated. By the end of the 1680s, warfare had broken out among several villages, even as Apache and Navajo raids continued. Popé died around 1690. In 1692, the Spanish launched an invasion that reconquered New Mexico. Some communities welcomed them back

St. Anthony and the Infant Jesus, painted on a tanned buffalo hide by a Franciscan priest in New Mexico in the early eighteenth century. This was not long after the Spanish reconquered the area, from which they had been driven by the Pueblo Revolt.

as a source of military protection. But Spain had learned a lesson. In the eighteenth century, colonial authorities adopted a more tolerant attitude toward traditional religious practices and made fewer demands on Indian labor.

THE FRENCH AND DUTCH EMPIRES

If the Black Legend inspired a sense of superiority among Spain's European rivals, the precious metals that poured from the New World into the Spanish treasury aroused the desire to try to match Spain's success. The establishment of Spain's American empire transformed the balance of power in the world economy. The Atlantic replaced the overland route to Asia as the major axis of global trade. During the seventeenth century, the French, Dutch, and English established colonies in North America. England's mainland colonies, to be discussed in the next chapter, consisted of agricultural settlements with growing populations whose hunger for land produced incessant conflict with native peoples. New France and New Netherland were primarily commercial ventures that never attracted large numbers of colonists. More dependent on Indians as trading partners and military allies, these French and Dutch settlements allowed Native Americans greater freedom than the English.

Shifts in global trade

French Colonization

The first of Spain's major European rivals to embark on New World explorations was France. The French initially aimed to find gold and to locate a Northwest Passage—a sea route connecting the Atlantic to the Pacific. But early French explorers were soon disappointed, and North America came to seem little more than a barrier to be crossed, not a promising site for settlement or exploitation. For most of the sixteenth century, only explorers, fishermen, pirates preying on Spanish shipping farther south, and, as time went on, fur traders visited the eastern coast of North America. French efforts to establish settlements in Newfoundland and Nova Scotia failed, beset by native resistance and inadequate planning and financing. Not until the seventeenth century would France, as well as England and the Netherlands, establish permanent settlements in North America.

Northwest Passage

The explorer Samuel de Champlain, sponsored by a French fur-trading company, founded Quebec in 1608. In 1673, the Jesuit priest Jacques Marquette and the fur trader Louis Joliet located the Mississippi River, and by 1681 René-Robert Cavelier, Sieur de La Salle, had descended to the Gulf of Mexico, claiming the entire Mississippi River valley for France. New France eventually formed a giant arc along the St. Lawrence, Mississippi, and Ohio rivers.

Until 1663, when the population of European origin was fewer than 3,000, French Canada was ruled by the Company of New France through a governor-general appointed in Paris. There was no representative assembly. In that year, the French government established a new company. It granted land along the St. Lawrence River to well-connected nobles and army officers who would transport colonists to take their place in a feudal society. But most of the **indentured servants**

The Company of New France

VOICES OF FREEDOM

From BARTOLOMÉ DE LAS CASAS, HISTORY OF THE INDIES (1528)

Las Casas was the Dominican priest who condemned the treatment of Indians in the Spanish empire. His widely disseminated *History of the Indies* helped to establish the Black Legend of Spanish cruelty.

———————————

The Indians [of Hispaniola] were totally deprived of their freedom and were put in the harshest, fiercest, most horrible servitude and captivity which no one who has not seen it can understand. Even beasts enjoy more freedom when they are allowed to graze in the fields. But our Spaniards gave no such opportunity to Indians and truly considered them perpetual slaves, since the Indians had not the free will to dispose of their persons but instead were disposed of according to Spanish greed and cruelty, not as men in captivity but as beasts tied to a rope to prevent free movement. When they were allowed to go home, they often found it deserted and had no other recourse than to go out into the woods to find food and to die. When they fell ill, which was very frequently because they are a delicate people unaccustomed to such work, the Spaniards did not believe them and pitilessly called them lazy dogs and kicked and beat them; and when illness was apparent they sent them home as useless. . . . They would go then, falling into the first stream and dying there in desperation; others would hold on longer but very few ever made it home. I sometimes came upon dead bodies on my way, and upon others who were gasping and moaning in their death agony, repeating "Hungry, hungry." And this was the freedom, the good treatment and the Christianity the Indians received.

About eight years passed under [Spanish rule] and this disorder had time to grow; no one gave it a thought and the multitude of people who originally lived on the island . . . was consumed at such a rate that in these eight years 90 per cent had perished. From here this sweeping plague went to San Juan, Jamaica, Cuba and the continent, spreading destruction over the whole hemisphere.

From "DECLARATION OF JOSEPHE"
(DECEMBER 19, 1681)

Josephe was a Spanish-speaking Indian questioned by a royal attorney in Mexico City investigating the Pueblo Revolt. The revolt of the Indian population, in 1680, temporarily drove Spanish settlers from present-day New Mexico.

―――――――――――――

Asked what causes or motives the said Indian rebels had for renouncing the law of God and obedience to his Majesty, and for committing so many of crimes, [he answered] the causes they have were alleged ill treatment and injuries received from [Spanish authorities], because they beat them, took away what they had, and made them work without pay. Thus he replies.

Asked if he has learned if it has come to his notice during the time that he has been here the reason why the apostates burned the images, churches, and things pertaining to divine worship, making a mockery and a trophy of them, killing the priests and doing the other things they did, he said that he knows and had heard it generally stated that while they were besieging the villa the rebellious traitors burned the church and shouted in loud voices, "Now the God of the Spaniards, who was their father, is dead, and Santa Maria, who was their mother, and the saints, who were pieces of rotten wood," saying that only their own god lived. Thus they ordered all the temples and images, crosses and rosaries burned, and their function being over, they all went to bathe in the rivers, saying that they thereby washed away the water of baptism. For their churches, they placed on the four sides and in the center of the plaza some small circular enclosures of stone where they went to offer flour, feathers, and the seed of maguey [a local plant], maize, and tobacco, and performed other superstitious rites, giving the children to understand that they must all do this in the future. The captains and the chiefs ordered that the names of Jesus and Mary should nowhere be uttered. . . . He has seen many houses of idolatry which they have built, dancing the dance of the cachina [part of a traditional Indian religious ceremony], which this declarant has also danced. Thus he replies to the question.

QUESTIONS

1. *Why does Las Casas, after describing the ill treatment of Indians, write, "And this was the freedom, the good treatment and the Christianity the Indians received"?*

2. *What role did religion play in the Pueblo Revolt?*

3. *What ideas of freedom are apparent in the two documents?*

returned home after their contracts expired. More than 80 percent of the migrants were men. Apart from nuns, fewer than 1,800 women (compared with more than 12,000 men) emigrated to French Canada in the seventeenth century. And during the entire colonial period, only about 250 complete families did so.

Settlement in New France

By 1700, the number of white inhabitants of New France had risen to only 19,000. With a far larger population than England, France sent many fewer emigrants to the Western Hemisphere. The government at home feared that significant emigration would undermine France's role as a European great power and might compromise its effort to establish trade and good relations with the Indians. Unfavorable reports about America circulated widely in France. Canada was widely depicted as an icebox, a land of savage Indians, a dumping ground for criminals. Most French who left their homes during these years preferred to settle in the Netherlands, Spain, or the West Indies. The revocation in 1685 of the Edict of Nantes, which had extended religious toleration to French Protestants, led well over 100,000 Huguenots to flee their country. But they were not welcome in New France, which the crown desired to remain an outpost of Catholicism.

New France and the Indians

Alliances with Indians

The viability of New France, with its small white population and emphasis on the fur trade rather than agricultural settlement, depended on friendly relations with local Indians. The French prided themselves on adopting a more humane policy than their imperial rivals. "Only our nation," declared one French writer, "knows the secret of winning the Indians' affection." Lacking the need for Indian labor of the Spanish and the voracious appetite for land of the English colonies, and relying on Indians to supply furs to trading posts, the French worked out a complex series of military, commercial, and diplomatic connections, the most enduring alliances between Indians and settlers in colonial North America. Samuel de Champlain,

This engraving, which appears in Samuel de Champlain's 1613 account of his voyages, is the only likeness of the explorer from his own time. Champlain, wearing European armor and brandishing an arquebus (an advanced weapon of the period), stands at the center of this pitched battle between his Indian allies and the hostile Iroquois.

the intrepid explorer who dominated the early history of New France, insisted on religious toleration for all Christians and denied that Native Americans were intellectually or culturally inferior to Europeans—two positions that were unusual for his time. Although he occasionally engaged in wars with local Indians, he dreamed of creating a colony based on mutual respect between diverse peoples. The Jesuits, a missionary religious order, did seek, with some success, to convert Indians to Catholicism. But unlike Spanish missionaries in early New Mexico, they allowed Christian Indians to retain a high degree of independence and much of their traditional social structure, and they did not seek to suppress all traditional religious practices.

Jesuits

Like other colonists throughout North America, however, the French brought striking changes in Indian life. Contact with Europeans was inevitably followed by the spread of disease. Participation in the fur trade drew natives into the burgeoning Atlantic economy, introducing new goods and transforming hunting from a search for food into a quest for marketable commodities. Indians were soon swept into the rivalries among European empires, and Europeans into conflicts among Indians. As early as 1615, the Huron of present-day southern Ontario and upper New York State forged a trading alliance with the French, and many converted to Catholicism. In the 1640s, however, after being severely weakened by a smallpox epidemic, the tribe was virtually destroyed in a series of attacks by Iroquois armed by the Dutch.

As in the Spanish empire, New France witnessed considerable cultural exchange and intermixing between colonial and native populations. On the "middle ground" of the upper Great Lakes region in French America, Indians and whites encountered each other for many years on a basis of relative equality. And *métis*, or children of marriages between Indian women and French traders and officials, became guides, traders, and interpreters. Like the Spanish, the French seemed willing to accept Indians as part of colonial society. They encouraged Indians to adopt the European division of labor between men and women, and to speak French. Indians who converted to Catholicism were promised full citizenship. In fact, however, it was far rarer for natives to adopt French ways than for French settlers to become attracted to the "free" life of the Indians.

The middle ground

The Dutch Empire

In 1609, Henry Hudson, an Englishman employed by the Dutch East India Company, sailed into New York Harbor searching for a Northwest Passage to Asia. Hudson and his crew became the first Europeans to sail up the river that now bears his name. Hudson did not find a route to Asia, but he did encounter abundant fur-bearing animals and Native Americans more than willing to trade furs for European goods. He claimed the area for the Netherlands, and his voyage planted the seeds for what would eventually become a great metropolis, New York City. By 1614, Dutch traders had established an outpost at Fort Orange, near present-day Albany. Ten years later, the Dutch West India Company, which had been awarded a monopoly of Dutch trade with America, settled colonists on Manhattan Island.

Henry Hudson

These ventures formed one small part in the rise of the Dutch overseas empire. In the early seventeenth century, the Netherlands dominated international

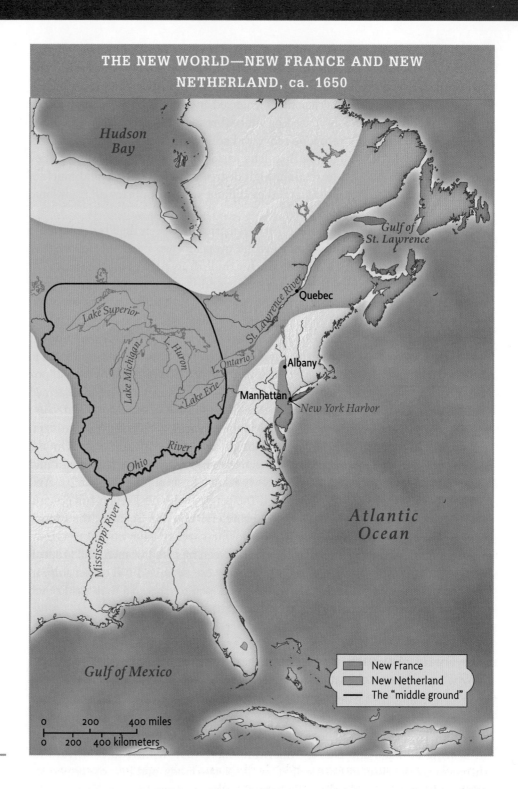

THE NEW WORLD—NEW FRANCE AND NEW NETHERLAND, ca. 1650

Hudson Bay

Gulf of St. Lawrence

Lake Superior

L. Huron

Lake Michigan

St. Lawrence River

Quebec

L. Ontario

Lake Erie

Albany

Manhattan

New York Harbor

Ohio River

Atlantic Ocean

Mississippi River

Gulf of Mexico

New France
New Netherland
The "middle ground"

0   200   400 miles
0   200   400 kilometers

New France and New Netherland.

Dutch trade

commerce, and Amsterdam was Europe's foremost shipping and banking center. The small nation had entered a golden age of rapidly accumulating wealth and stunning achievements in painting, philosophy, and the sciences. The Dutch invented the joint stock company, a way of pooling financial resources and sharing the risk of maritime voyages, which proved central to the development of modern capitalism. With a population of only 2 million, the Netherlands established a far-flung empire that reached from Indonesia to South Africa and the Caribbean and temporarily wrested control of Brazil from Portugal.

Dutch Freedom

The Dutch prided themselves on their devotion to liberty. Indeed, in the early seventeenth century they enjoyed two freedoms not recognized elsewhere in Europe—freedom of the press and of private religious practice. Even though there was an established church, the Dutch Reformed, individuals could hold whatever religious beliefs they wished. Amsterdam had become a haven for persecuted Protestants from all over Europe, including French Huguenots, German Calvinists, and those, like the Pilgrims, who desired to separate from the Church of England. Jews, especially those fleeing from Spain, also found refuge there. Other emigrants came to the Netherlands in the hope of sharing in the country's prosperity. During the seventeenth century, the nation attracted about half a million migrants from elsewhere in Europe. Many of these newcomers helped to populate the Dutch overseas empire.

Religious freedom

Freedom in New Netherland

Despite the Dutch reputation for cherishing freedom, New Netherland was hardly governed democratically. New Amsterdam, the main population center, was essentially a fortified military outpost controlled by appointees of the West India Company. Although the governor called on prominent citizens for advice from time to time, neither an elected assembly nor a town council, the basic unit of government at home, was established.

In other ways, however, the colonists enjoyed more liberty, especially in religious matters, than their counterparts elsewhere in North America. Even their slaves possessed rights. The Dutch dominated the Atlantic slave trade in the early seventeenth century, and they introduced slaves into New Netherland as a matter of course. By 1650, the colony's 500 slaves outnumbered those in the Chesapeake. Some enjoyed "half-freedom"—they were required to pay an annual fee to the company and work for it when called upon, but they were given land to support their families. Settlers employed slaves on family farms or for household or craft labor, not on large plantations as in the West Indies.

Women in the Dutch settlement enjoyed far more independence than in other colonies. According to Dutch law, married women retained their separate legal identity. They could go to court, borrow money, and own property. Men were used to sharing property with their wives. Their wills generally left their possessions to their widows and daughters as well as sons. Margaret Hardenbroeck, the widow of a New Amsterdam merchant, expanded her husband's business and became one of the town's richest residents after his death in 1661.

Women's rights

The Dutch and Religious Toleration

New Netherland attracted a remarkably diverse population. As early as the 1630s, at least eighteen languages were said to be spoken in New Amsterdam, whose

NIEUW AMSTERDAM
of 't Eylant Manhattans.

A view of New Amsterdam from 1651 illustrates the tiny size of the outpost.

Limits of religious toleration

Governor Stuyvesant

residents included not only Dutch settlers but also Africans, Belgians, English, French, Germans, Irish, and Scandinavians. Of course, these settlers adhered to a wide variety of religions.

The Dutch long prided themselves on being uniquely tolerant in religious matters compared to other European nations and their empires. It would be wrong, however, to attribute modern ideas of religious freedom to either the Dutch government and company at home or the rulers of New Netherland. Both Holland and New Netherland had an official religion, the Dutch Reformed Church, one of the Protestant national churches to emerge from the Reformation. The Dutch commitment to freedom of conscience extended to religious devotion exercised in private, not public worship in nonestablished churches. It did not reflect a willing acceptance of religious diversity.

The West India Company's officials in the colony, particularly Governor Petrus Stuyvesant, were expected to be staunch defenders of the Dutch Reformed Church. When Jews, Quakers, Lutherans, and others demanded the right to practice their religion openly, Stuyvesant adamantly refused, seeing such diversity as a threat to a godly, prosperous order. Under Stuyvesant, the colony was more restrictive in its religious policies than the Dutch government at home. Twenty-three Jews arrived in New Amsterdam in 1654 from Brazil and the Caribbean. Referring to them as "members of a deceitful race," Stuyvesant ordered the newcomers to leave. But the company overruled him, noting that Jews at home had invested "a large amount of capital" in its shares.

As a result of Stuyvesant's policies, challenges arose to the limits on religious toleration. One, known as the Flushing Remonstrance, was a 1657 petition by a group of English settlers protesting the governor's order barring Quakers from living in the town of Flushing, on Long Island. Although later seen as a landmark of religious liberty, the Remonstrance had little impact at the time. Stuyvesant ordered several signers arrested for defying his authority.

Nonetheless, it is true that the Dutch dealt with religious pluralism in ways quite different from the practices common in other New World empires. Religious dissent was tolerated—often grudgingly, as in the case of Catholics—as long as it did not involve open and public worship. No one in New Netherland was forced to attend the official church, nor was anyone executed for holding the wrong religious beliefs (as would happen in Puritan New England around the time of the Flushing Remonstrance).

Settling New Netherland

In an attempt to attract settlers to North America, the Dutch West India Company promised colonists not only the right to practice their religion freely (in private) but also cheap livestock and free land after six years of labor. Eventually, it even surrendered its monopoly of the fur trade, opening this profitable commerce to all comers. Many settlers, Stuyvesant complained, had been lured by "an imaginary liberty" and did not display much respect for the company's authority.

In 1629, the company adopted a plan of "Freedoms and Exemptions," offering large estates to *patroons*—shareholders who agreed to transport tenants for agricultural labor. The patroon was required to purchase a title to the land from Indians, but otherwise his "freedoms" were like those of a medieval lord, including the right to 10 percent of his tenants' annual income and complete authority over law enforcement within his domain. Only one patroonship became a going concern, that of Kiliaen van Rensselaer, who acquired some 700,000 acres in the Hudson Valley. His family's autocratic rule over the tenants, as well as its efforts to extend its domain to include lands settled by New Englanders who claimed that they owned their farms, would inspire sporadic uprisings into the mid-nineteenth century.

During the seventeenth century, the Netherlands sent 1 million people overseas (many of them recent immigrants who were not in fact Dutch) to populate and govern their far-flung colonies. Very few, however, made North America their destination. By the mid-1660s, the European population of New Netherland numbered only 9,000. New Netherland remained a tiny backwater in the Dutch empire. So did an even smaller outpost near present-day Wilmington, Delaware, established in 1638 by a group of Dutch merchants. To circumvent the West India Company's trade monopoly, they claimed to be operating under the Swedish flag and called their settlement New Sweden. Only 300 settlers were living there when New Netherland seized the colony in 1655.

> Patroons

The seal of New Netherland, adopted by the Dutch West India Company in 1630, suggests the centrality of the fur trade to the colony's prospects. Surrounding the beaver is wampum, a string of beads used by Indians in religious rituals and as currency.

New Netherland and the Indians

The Dutch came to North America to trade, not to conquer. They were less interested in settling the land than in exacting profits from it. Mindful of the Black Legend of Spanish cruelty, the Dutch determined to treat the native inhabitants more humanely. Having won their own independence from Spain after the longest and bloodiest war of sixteenth-century Europe, many Dutch identified with American Indians as fellow victims of Spanish oppression.

From the beginning, Dutch authorities recognized Indian sovereignty over the land and forbade settlement in any area until it had been purchased. But they also required tribes to make payments to colonial authorities. Near the coast, where most newcomers settled, New Netherland was hardly free of conflict with the Indians. The expansionist ambitions of Governor William Kieft, who in the 1640s

AMERICAE SIVE NOVI ORBIS, NOVA DESCRIPTIO.

A map of the Western Hemisphere, published in 1592 in Antwerp, then ruled by Spain and now part of Belgium. It shows North America divided between New France and New Spain before the coming of the English.

began seizing fertile farmland from the nearby Algonquian Indians, sparked a three-year war that resulted in the death of 1,000 Indians and more than 200 colonists. With the powerful Iroquois Confederacy of the upper Hudson Valley, however, the Dutch established friendly commercial and diplomatic relations.

Borderlands and Empire in Early America

A **borderland**, according to one historian, is "a meeting place of peoples where geographical and cultural borders are not clearly defined." Numerous such places came into existence during the era of European conquest and settlement, including the "middle ground" of the upper Great Lakes in New France. Boundaries between empires, and between colonists and native peoples, shifted constantly, overlapping claims to authority abounded, and hybrid cultures developed. As Europeans consolidated their control in some areas, the power of native peoples weakened. But at the edges of empire, power was always unstable, and overlapping cultural interactions at the local level defied any single pattern. European conquest was not a simple story of expanding domination over either empty space or powerless peoples, but of a continual struggle to establish authority. The Spanish, French, and Dutch empires fought each other for dominance in various parts of the continent, and Indians often wielded both economic and political power, pitting European empires against each other. Despite laws restricting commerce between empires, traders challenged boundaries, traversing lands claimed by both Europeans and Indians. People of European and Indian descent married and exchanged cultural attributes.

Thus, before the planting of English colonies in North America, other European nations had established various kinds of settlements in the New World. Despite their differences, the Spanish, French, and Dutch empires shared certain features. All brought Christianity, new forms of technology and learning, new legal systems and family relations, and new forms of economic enterprise and wealth creation. They also brought savage warfare and widespread disease. These empires were aware of one another's existence. They studied and borrowed from one another, each lauding itself as superior to the others.

> *Shared features of the Spanish, French, and Dutch empires*

From the outset, dreams of freedom—for Indians, for settlers, for the entire world through the spread of Christianity—inspired and justified colonization. It would be no different when, at the beginning of the seventeenth century, England entered the struggle for empire in North America.

SUGGESTED READING

BOOKS

- Bender, Thomas. *A Nation among Nations: America's Place in World History* (2006). Attempts to place American history in an international context; the opening chapters offer a global portrait of the age of exploration and conquest.

- Calloway, Colin G. *One Vast Winter Count: The American West before Lewis and Clark* (2003). A comprehensive portrait of Indian life in one key region of North America.

- Crosby, Alfred J. *The Columbian Exchange: Biological and Cultural Consequences of 1492* (1972). Examines the flow of goods and diseases across the Atlantic and their consequences.

- Elliott, J. H. *Empires of the Atlantic World: Britain and Spain in America 1492–1830* (2006). A fascinating comparison of the development of two New World empires.

- Fernández-Armesto, Felipe. *Pathfinders: A Global History of Exploration* (2006). A history of explorations throughout the centuries, including those of the fifteenth and sixteenth centuries.

- Fischer, David H. *Champlain's Dream* (2008). A lively account of Samuel de Champlain's effort to build a French colony in North America based on toleration and mutual respect between settlers and Native Americans.

- Gutiérrez, Ramón A. *When Jesus Came, the Corn Mothers Went Away: Marriage, Sexuality, and Power in New Mexico, 1500–1846* (1991). Discusses the changes in Indian life in New Mexico as a result of Spanish colonization.

- Haefeli, Evan. *New Netherland and the Dutch Origins of American Religious Liberty* (2012). Explores the complex conditions of religious life in New Netherland.

- Knaut, Andrew L. *The Pueblo Revolt of 1680: Conquest and Resistance in Seventeenth-Century New Mexico* (1997). A recent account of the largest revolt of native peoples.

- Mann, Charles C. *1491: New Revelations of the Americas before Columbus* (2005). A comprehensive portrait of life in the Western Hemisphere before the arrival of Europeans.

- Parry, J. H. *The Age of Reconnaissance* (1981). A global history of the era of European exploration and colonization.

- Richter, Daniel K. *Facing East from Indian Country* (2001). Examines the era of exploration and settlement as viewed through the experience of Native Americans.

- ———. *The Ordeal of the Longhouse: The Peoples of the Iroquois League in the Era of European Colonization* (1992). Describes life among one of the most important Indian groups before and after the arrival of Europeans.

- Witgen, Michael. *An Infinity of Nations: How the Native New World Shaped Early North America* (2012). An imaginative account of how native peoples and Europeans interacted in the Great Lakes region.

WEBSITES

- American Indians and the Natural World: http://carnegiemnh.org/online/indians/index.html

- Archive of Early American Images: www.brown.edu/academics/libraries/john-carter-brown/jcb-online/image-collections/archive-early-american-images

- Cahokia Mounds: http://cahokiamounds.org

- Exploring the Early Americas: www.loc.gov/exhibits/earlyamericas/

- France in America: http://international.loc.gov/intldl/fiahtml

- Jamestown, Quebec, Santa Fe: Three North American Beginnings: http://americanhistory.si.edu/jamestown-quebec-santafe/en/introduction

CHAPTER REVIEW AND ONLINE RESOURCES

REVIEW QUESTIONS

1. Describe why the "discovery" of America was one of the "most important events recorded in the history of mankind," according to Adam Smith.

2. Describe the different global economies that Europeans participated in or created during the European age of expansion.

3. One of the most striking features of Indian societies at the time of the encounter with Europeans was their diversity. Support this statement with several examples.

4. Compare and contrast European values and ways of life with those of the Indians. Consider addressing religion, views about ownership of land, gender relations, and notions of freedom.

5. What were the main factors fueling the European age of expansion?

6. Compare the different economic and political systems of Spain, Portugal, the Netherlands, and France in the age of expansion.

7. Compare the political, economic, and religious motivations behind the French and Dutch empires with those of New Spain.

8. Describe how the idea of the "Black Legend" affected subsequent policies and practices of Spain as well as those of the Netherlands and France.

9. How would European settlers explain their superiority to Native Americans and justify both the conquest of Native lands and terminating their freedom?

KEY TERMS

Tenochtitlán (p. 8)

Aztec (p. 8)

Great League of Peace (p. 12)

caravel (p. 18)

reconquista (p. 21)

conquistadores (p. 23)

Columbian Exchange (p. 24)

creoles (p. 25)

hacienda (p. 25)

mestizos (p. 26)

Ninety-Five Theses (p. 28)

Bartolomé de Las Casas (p. 29)

repartimiento system (p. 29)

Black Legend (p. 30)

Pueblo Revolt (p. 34)

indentured servants (p. 35)

métis (p. 39)

borderland (p. 44)

Go to INQUIZITIVE

To see what you know—and learn what you've missed—with personalized feedback along the way.

Visit the *Give Me Liberty!* Student Site for primary source documents and images, interactive maps, author videos featuring Eric Foner, and more.

CHAPTER 2

BEGINNINGS OF ENGLISH AMERICA

★

1607-1660

Port St Louis

toise
100   600   2000

On April 26, 1607, three small ships carrying colonists from England sailed out of the morning mist at what is now called Cape Henry into the mouth of Chesapeake Bay. After exploring the area for a little over two weeks, they chose a site sixty miles inland on the James River for their settlement, hoping to protect themselves from marauding Spanish warships. Here they established Jamestown (named for the king of England) as the capital of the colony of Virginia (named for his predecessor, Elizabeth I, the "virgin queen"). But despite these bows to royal authority, the voyage was sponsored not by the English government, which in 1607 was hard-pressed for funds, but by the **Virginia Company,** a private business organization whose shareholders included merchants, aristocrats, and members of Parliament, and to which the queen had given her blessing before her death in 1603.

When the three ships returned home, 104 settlers remained in Virginia. All were men, for the Virginia Company had more interest in searching for gold and in other ways of exploiting the area's natural resources than in establishing a functioning society. Nevertheless, Jamestown became the first permanent English settlement in the area that is now the United States. The settlers were the first of tens of thousands of Europeans who crossed the Atlantic during the seventeenth century to live and work in North America. They led the way for new empires that mobilized labor and economic resources, reshaped societies throughout the Atlantic world, and shifted the balance of power at home from Spain and Portugal to the nations of northwestern Europe.

The founding of Jamestown took place at a time of heightened European involvement in North America. Interest in colonization was spurred by national and religious rivalries and the growth of a merchant class eager to invest in overseas expansion and to seize for itself a greater share of world trade. As noted in Chapter 1, it was quickly followed by the founding of Quebec by France in 1608, and Henry Hudson's exploration in 1609 of the river that today bears his name, leading to the founding of the Dutch colony of New Netherland. In 1610, the Spanish established Santa Fe as the capital of New Mexico. More than a century after the voyages of Columbus, the European penetration of North America had finally begun in earnest. It occurred from many directions at once—from east to west at the Atlantic coast, north to south along the St. Lawrence and Mississippi rivers, and south to north in what is now the American Southwest.

English North America in the seventeenth century was a place where entrepreneurs sought to make fortunes, religious minorities hoped to worship without governmental interference and to create societies based on biblical teachings, and aristocrats dreamed of re-creating a vanished world of feudalism. Those who drew up blueprints for settlement expected to reproduce the social structure with which they were familiar, with all its hierarchy and inequality. The lower orders would occupy the same less-than-fully-free status as in England, subject to laws regulating their labor and depriving them of a role in politics. But for ordinary men and women, emigration offered an escape from lives of deprivation and inequality. "No man," wrote John Smith, an early leader of Jamestown, "will go from [England] to

FOCUS QUESTIONS

What were the main contours of English colonization in the seventeenth century? *–p. 50*

What obstacles did the English settlers in the Chesapeake overcome? *–p. 54*

How did Virginia and Maryland develop in their early years? *–p. 58*

What made the English settlement of New England distinctive? *–p. 64*

What were the main sources of discord in early New England? *–p. 70*

How did the English Civil War affect the colonies in America? *–p. 79*

Samuel de Champlain's 1605 sketch of Plymouth Harbor, made when he was exploring the coast of modern-day New England in search of a site for a French settlement, shows the area dotted with wigwams and fields of corn, squash, and beans. By the time the Pilgrims arrived in 1620, epidemics had destroyed this thriving Indian community.

have less freedom" in America. The charter of the Virginia Company, granted by James I in 1606, promised that colonists would enjoy "all liberties" of those residing in "our realm of England." The settlers of English America came to enjoy greater rights than colonists of other empires, including the power to choose members of elected assemblies, protections of the common law such as the right to trial by jury, and access to land, the key to economic independence. In some colonies, though by no means all, colonists enjoyed considerably more religious freedom than existed in Europe.

Many degrees of freedom coexisted in seventeenth-century North America, from the slave, stripped completely of liberty, to the independent landowner, who enjoyed a full range of rights. During a lifetime, a person might well occupy more than one place on this spectrum. The settlers' success, however, rested on depriving Native Americans of their land and, in some colonies, on importing large numbers of African slaves as laborers. Freedom and lack of freedom expanded together in seventeenth-century America.

ENGLAND AND THE NEW WORLD

Unifying the English Nation

Although John Cabot, sailing from England in 1497, had been the first European since the Vikings to encounter the North American continent, English exploration and colonization would wait for many years. As the case of Spain suggests, early empire building was, in large part, an extension of the consolidation of national power in Europe. But during the sixteenth century, England was a second-rate power racked by internal disunity. Henry VII, who assumed the throne in 1485, had to unify the kingdom after a long period of civil war. His son and successor, Henry VIII, launched the Reformation in England. When the pope refused to annul his marriage to Catherine of Aragon, Henry severed the nation from the Catholic Church. In its place he established the Church of England, or **Anglican Church**, with himself at the head. Decades of religious strife followed. Under Henry's son Edward VI, who became king at the age of ten in 1547, the regents who governed the country persecuted Catholics. When Edward died in 1553, his half sister Mary became queen. Mary temporarily restored Catholicism as the state religion and executed a number of Protestants. Her rule was so unpopular that reconciliation with Rome became impossible. Mary's successor, Elizabeth I (reigned 1558–1603), restored the Anglican ascendancy and executed more than 100 Catholic priests.

England and Ireland

England's long struggle to conquer and pacify Ireland, which lasted well into the seventeenth century, absorbed money and energy that might have been directed toward the New World. In subduing Ireland, whose Catholic population was deemed a threat to the stability of Protestant rule in England, the government employed a variety of approaches, including military conquest, the slaughter of civilians, the seizure of land and introduction of English economic practices, and the dispatch of large numbers of settlers. Rather than seeking to absorb the Irish into English society, the English excluded the native population from a territory of settlement known as the Pale, where the colonists created their own social order.

Just as the "reconquest" of Spain from the Moors established patterns that would be repeated in Spanish New World colonization, the methods used in Ireland anticipated policies England would undertake in America. Some sixteenth-century English writers directly compared the allegedly barbaric "wild Irish" with American Indians. Like the Indians, the Irish supposedly confused liberty and license. They refused to respect English authority and resisted conversion to English Protestantism. The early English colonies in North America and the West Indies were known as "plantations" (that is, communities "planted" from abroad among an alien population); the same term was originally used to describe Protestant settlements in Ireland.

England and North America

Not until the reign of Elizabeth I did the English turn their attention to North America, although sailors and adventurers still showed more interest in raiding Spanish cities and treasure fleets in the Caribbean than establishing settlements. The government granted charters (grants of exclusive rights and privileges) to Sir Humphrey Gilbert and Sir Walter Raleigh, authorizing them to establish colonies in North America at their own expense.

With little or no support from the crown, both ventures failed. Gilbert, who had earned a reputation for brutality in the Irish wars by murdering civilians and burning their crops, established a short-lived settlement on Newfoundland in 1582. Three years later, Raleigh dispatched a fleet of five ships with some 100 colonists (many of them his personal servants) to set up a base on Roanoke Island, off the North Carolina coast, partly to facilitate continuing raids on Spanish shipping. But the colonists, mostly young men under military leadership, abandoned the venture in 1586 and returned to England. A second group of 100 settlers, composed of families who hoped to establish a permanent colony, was dispatched that year. Their fate remains a mystery. When a ship bearing supplies arrived in 1590, the sailors found the **Roanoke colony** abandoned, with the inhabitants evidently having moved to live among the Indians. The word "Croatoan," the Indian name for a nearby island or tribe, had been carved on a tree. Raleigh, by now nearly bankrupt, lost his enthusiasm for colonization. To establish a successful colony, it seemed clear, would require more planning and economic resources than any individual could provide.

Spreading Protestantism

As in the case of Spain, national glory, profit, and religious mission merged in early English thinking about the New World. The Reformation heightened the English government's sense of Catholic Spain as its mortal enemy (a belief reinforced in 1588

Mary I, the queen who tried to restore Catholicism in England, as painted in 1554 by Antonis Mor, a Dutch artist who made numerous portraits of European royalty. He depicts her as a women of firm determination. During her brief reign (1553–1558), nearly three hundred Protestants were burned at the stake.

The Armada Portrait of Queen Elizabeth I, by the artist George Gower, commemorates the defeat of the Spanish Armada in 1588 and appears to link it with English colonization of the New World. England's victorious navy is visible through the window, while the queen's hand rests on a globe, with her fingers pointing to the coast of North America.

An engraving by Theodor de Bry depicts colonists hunting and fishing in Virginia. Promotional images such as this emphasized the abundance of the New World and suggested that colonists could live familiar lives there.

Empire and freedom

when a Spanish naval armada unsuccessfully attempted to invade the British Isles). Just as Spain justified its empire in part by claiming to convert Indians to Catholicism, England expressed its imperial ambitions in terms of an obligation to liberate the New World from the tyranny of the pope. The very first justification James I offered for the English settlement of Virginia was "propagating of the Christian religion [by which he meant Protestantism] to such people as yet live in darkness and miserable ignorance of the true knowledge and worship of God." By the late sixteenth century, anti-Catholicism had become deeply ingrained in English popular culture. English translations of Bartolomé de Las Casas's writings appeared during Elizabeth's reign. One, using a common Protestant term for the Catholic Church, bore the title, "Popery Truly Displayed."

Although atrocities were hardly confined to any one nation—as England's own conduct in Ireland demonstrated—the idea that the empire of Catholic Spain was uniquely murderous and tyrannical enabled the English to describe their own imperial ambitions in the language of freedom. In *A Discourse Concerning Western Planting*, written in 1584 at the request of Sir Walter Raleigh, the Protestant minister and scholar Richard Hakluyt listed twenty-three reasons why Queen Elizabeth I should support the establishment of colonies. Among them was the idea that English settlements would strike a blow against Spain's empire and therefore form part of a divine mission to rescue the New World and its inhabitants from the influence of Catholicism and tyranny. "Tied as slaves" under Spanish rule, he wrote, the Indians of the New World were "crying out to us . . . to come and help." They would welcome English settlers and "revolt clean from the Spaniard," crying "with one voice, Liberta, Liberta, as desirous of liberty and freedom." England would repeat much of Spain's behavior in the New World. But the English always believed that they were unique. In their case, empire and freedom would go hand in hand.

But bringing freedom to Indians was hardly the only argument Hakluyt marshaled as England prepared to step onto the world stage. National power and glory were never far from the minds of the era's propagandists of empire. Through colonization, Hakluyt and other writers argued, England, a relatively minor power in Europe at the end of the sixteenth century, could come to rival the wealth and standing of great nations like Spain and France.

The Social Crisis

Equally important, America could be a refuge for England's "surplus" population, benefiting mother country and emigrants alike. The late sixteenth century was a time of social crisis in England, with economic growth unable to keep pace with the needs of a population that grew from 3 million in 1550 to about 4 million in 1600. For many years, English peasants had enjoyed a secure hold on their plots of land. But in the sixteenth and seventeenth centuries, landlords sought profits by raising sheep for the expanding trade in wool and introducing more modern farming practices such as crop rotation. They evicted small farmers and fenced in "commons" previously open to all.

While many landlords, farmers, and town merchants benefited from the **enclosure movement**, as this process was called, thousands of persons were uprooted from the land. Many flooded into England's cities, where wages fell dramatically. Others, denounced by authorities as rogues, vagabonds, and vagrants, wandered the roads in search of work. Their situation grew worse as prices throughout Europe rose, buoyed by the influx of gold and silver from the mines of Latin America into Spain. A pioneering study of English society conducted at the end of the seventeenth century estimated that half the population lived at or below the poverty line. The cost of poor relief fell mainly on local communities. "All our towns," wrote the Puritan leader John Winthrop in 1629, shortly before leaving England for Massachusetts, "complain of the burden of poor people and strive by all means to rid any such as they have." England, he added somberly, "grows weary of her inhabitants."

> **Responses to poverty**

The government struggled to deal with this social crisis. Under Henry VIII, those without jobs could be whipped, branded, forced into the army, or hanged. During Elizabeth's reign, a law authorized justices of the peace to regulate hours and wages and put the unemployed to work. "Vagrants" were required to accept any job offered to them and could be punished if they sought to change employment. Another solution was to encourage the unruly poor to leave for the New World. Richard Hakluyt wrote of the advantages of settling in America "such needy people of our country who now trouble the commonwealth and . . . commit outrageous offenses." As colonists, they could become productive citizens, contributing to the nation's wealth.

Masterless Men

As early as 1516, when Thomas More published *Utopia*, a novel set on an imaginary island in the Western Hemisphere, the image of America as a place where settlers could escape from the economic inequalities of Europe had been circulating in England. This ideal coincided with the goals of ordinary Englishmen. Although authorities saw wandering or unemployed "masterless men" as a danger to society and tried to force them to accept jobs, popular attitudes viewed economic dependence as itself a form of servitude. Working for wages was widely associated with servility and loss of liberty. Only those who controlled their own labor could be regarded as truly free. Indeed, popular tales and ballads romanticized the very vagabonds, highwaymen, and even beggars denounced by the propertied and powerful, since despite their poverty they at least enjoyed freedom from wage work.

William Hogarth's well-known engraving *Gin Lane* (1751) offers a satiric glimpse of lower-class life in London. Hogarth was particularly concerned about the abuse of alcohol. A drunken woman allows her baby to fall from her arms while, on the left, a man and his wife pawn their coats, tools, and cooking utensils for money for liquor.

The image of the New World as a unique place of opportunity, where the English laboring classes could regain economic independence by acquiring land and where even criminals would enjoy a second chance, was deeply rooted from the earliest days of settlement. John Smith had scarcely landed in Virginia in 1607 when he wrote that in America "every man may be the master and owner of his own labor and land." In 1623, the royal letter approving the recruitment of emigrants to New England promised that any settler could easily become "lord of 200 acres of land"—an amount far beyond the reach of most Englishmen. The main lure for emigrants from England to the New World was not so much riches in gold and silver as the promise of independence that followed from owning land. Economic freedom and the possibility of passing it on to one's children attracted the largest number of English colonists.

THE COMING OF THE ENGLISH

English Emigrants

Dangers of emmigration

Seventeenth-century North America was an unstable and dangerous environment. Diseases decimated Indian and settler populations alike. Colonies were racked by religious, political, and economic tensions and drawn into imperial wars and conflict with Indians. They remained dependent on the mother country for protection and economic assistance. Without sustained immigration, most settlements would have collapsed. With a population of between 4 million and 5 million, about half that of Spain and a quarter of that of France, England produced a far larger number of men, women, and children willing to brave the dangers of emigration to the New World. In large part, this was because economic conditions in England were so bad.

Between 1607 and 1700, more than half a million people left England. North America was not the destination of the majority of these emigrants. Approximately 180,000 settled in Ireland, and about the same number migrated to the West Indies, where the introduction of sugar cultivation promised riches for those who could obtain land. Nonetheless, the population of England's mainland colonies quickly outstripped that of their rivals. The Chesapeake area, where the tobacco-producing colonies of Virginia and Maryland developed a constant demand for cheap labor, received about 120,000 settlers, most of whom landed before 1660. New England attracted 21,000 emigrants, nearly all of them arriving before 1640. In the second part of the seventeenth century, the Middle Colonies (New York, New Jersey, and Pennsylvania) attracted about 23,000 settlers. Although the arrivals to New England and the Middle Colonies included many families, the majority of newcomers were young, single men from the bottom rungs of English society, who had little to lose by emigrating. Many had already moved from place to place in England. Colonial settlement was in many ways an extension of the migration at home of an increasingly mobile English population.

Indentured Servants

Settlers who could pay for their own passage—government officials, clergymen, merchants, artisans, landowning farmers, and members of the lesser nobility—arrived in America as free persons. Most quickly acquired land. In the seventeenth century, however, nearly two-thirds of English settlers came as indentured servants, who voluntarily surrendered their freedom for a specified time (usually five to seven years) in exchange for passage to America.

Like slaves, servants could be bought and sold, could not marry without the permission of their owner, were subject to physical punishment, and saw their obligation to labor enforced by the courts. To ensure uninterrupted work by female servants, the law lengthened the term of their indenture if they became pregnant. "Many Negroes are better used," complained Elizabeth Sprigs, an indentured

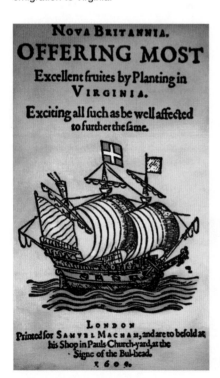

A pamphlet published in 1609 promoting emigration to Virginia.

NOVA BRITANNIA.
OFFERING MOST
Excellent fruites by Planting in VIRGINIA.
Exciting all such as be well affected to further the same.

LONDON
Printed for SAMVEL MACHAM, and are to be sold at his Shop in Pauls Church-yard, at the Signe of the Bul-head.
1609.

servant in Maryland who described being forced to work "day and night . . . then tied up and whipped." But, unlike slaves, servants could look forward to a release from bondage. Assuming they survived their period of labor, servants would receive a payment known as "freedom dues" and become free members of society.

For most of the seventeenth century, however, indentured servitude was not a guaranteed route to economic autonomy. Given the high death rate, many servants did not live to the end of their terms. Freedom dues were sometimes so meager that they did not enable recipients to acquire land. Many servants found the reality of life in the New World less appealing than they had anticipated. Employers constantly complained of servants running away, not working diligently, or being unruly, all manifestations of what one commentator called their "fondness for freedom."

Land and Liberty

Access to land played many roles in seventeenth-century America. Land, English settlers believed, was the basis of liberty. Owning land gave men control over their own labor and, in most colonies, the right to vote. The promise of immediate access to land lured free settlers, and freedom dues that included land persuaded potential immigrants to sign contracts as indentured servants. Land in America also became a way for the king to reward relatives and allies. Each colony was launched with a huge grant of land from the crown, either to a company or to a private individual known as a proprietor. Some grants, if taken literally, stretched from the Atlantic Ocean to the Pacific.

Land was a source of wealth and power for colonial officials and their favorites, who acquired enormous estates. Without labor, however, land would have little value. Since emigrants did not come to America intending to work the land of others (except temporarily in the case of indentured servants), the very abundance of "free" land eventually led many property owners to turn to slaves as a workforce.

Englishmen and Indians

Land in North America, of course, was already occupied. And the arrival of English settlers presented the native inhabitants of eastern North America with the greatest crisis in their history. Unlike the Spanish, English colonists did not call themselves "conquerors" (*conquistadores*). They wanted land, not dominion over the existing population. The Chesapeake and New England attracted more settlers than New Mexico, Florida, and New France combined, thus placing far greater pressure on Indian landholdings and provoking more frequent wars. The English were chiefly interested in displacing the Indians and settling on their land, not intermarrying with them, organizing their labor, or making them subjects of the crown. The

An indenture (a contract for labor for a period of years) signed by James Mahoney, who emigrated from Ireland to North America in 1723.

The English and Indian land

Another drawing by the artist John White shows an Indian village surrounded by a stockade.

marriage between John Rolfe and Pocahontas, the daughter of Virginia's leading chief, discussed below, is well known but almost unique. No such mixed marriage took place in seventeenth-century Massachusetts and only two more occurred in Virginia before the legislature outlawed the practice in 1691. The English exchanged goods with the native population, and Indians often traveled through colonial settlements. Fur traders on the frontiers of settlement sometimes married Indian women, partly as a way of gaining access to native societies and the kin networks essential to economic relationships. Most English settlers, however, remained obstinately separate from their Indian neighbors.

Purchasing land

Despite their insistence that Indians had no real claim to the land since they did not cultivate or improve it, most colonial authorities in practice recognized Indians' title based on occupancy. They acquired land by purchase, often in treaties forced upon Indians after they had suffered military defeat. Colonial courts recorded numerous sales of Indian land to governments or individual settlers. To keep the peace, some colonial governments tried to prevent the private seizure or purchase of Indian lands, or they declared certain areas off-limits to settlers. But these measures were rarely enforced and ultimately proved ineffective. New settlers and freed servants sought land for themselves, and those who established families in America needed land for their children.

Recurrent warfare between colonists and Indians

The seventeenth century was marked by recurrent warfare between colonists and Indians. These conflicts generated a strong feeling of superiority among the colonists and left them intent on maintaining the real and imagined boundaries separating the two peoples. In the initial stages of settlement, English colonists often established towns on sites Indians had cleared, planted Indian crops, and adopted Indian technology such as snowshoes and canoes, which were valuable for travel in the American wilderness. But over time the English displaced the original inhabitants more thoroughly than any other European empire.

The Transformation of Indian Life

The coming of English settlers profoundly affected Indian societies. Like the other colonial empires, the English used native people as guides, trading partners, and allies in wars and for other purposes. Many eastern Indians initially welcomed the newcomers, or at least their goods, which they appreciated for their practical advantages. Items like woven cloth, metal kettles, iron axes, fishhooks, hoes, and guns were quickly integrated into Indian life. Indians also displayed a great desire for goods like colorful glass beads and copper ornaments that could be incorporated into their religious ceremonies.

European goods

As Indians became integrated into the Atlantic economy, subtle changes took place in Indian life. European metal goods changed their farming, hunting, and cooking practices. Men devoted more time to hunting beaver for fur trading. Older skills deteriorated as the use of European products expanded, and alcohol became increasingly common and disruptive. Indians learned to bargain effectively and to supply items that Europeans desired. Later observers would describe this trade as one in which Indians exchanged valuable commodities like furs and animal skins for worthless European trinkets. In fact, both Europeans and Indians gave up goods they had in abundance in exchange for items in short supply in their own society. But as the colonists achieved military superiority over the Indians, the profits of trade mostly flowed to colonial and European merchants. Growing connections with Europeans stimulated warfare among Indian tribes, and the overhunting of beaver and deer forced some groups to encroach on territory claimed by others. And newcomers from Europe brought epidemics that decimated Indian populations.

The only known contemporary portrait of a New England Indian, this 1681 painting by an unknown artist was long thought to represent Ninigret II, a leader of the Narragansetts of Rhode Island. It has been more recently identified as Robin Cassacinamon, an influential Pequot leader and friend of John Winthrop II, a governor of colonial Connecticut, who originally owned the painting. Apart from the wampum beads around his neck, everything the Indian wears is of English manufacture.

Changes in the Land

Traders, religious missionaries, and colonial authorities all sought to reshape Indian society and culture. But as settlers spread over the land, they threatened Indians' ways of life more completely than any company of soldiers or group of bureaucrats. As settlers fenced in more and more land and introduced new crops and livestock, the natural environment changed in ways that undermined traditional Indian agriculture and hunting. Pigs and cattle roamed freely, trampling Indian cornfields and gardens. The need for wood to build and heat homes and export to England depleted forests on which Indians relied for hunting. The rapid expansion of the fur trade diminished the population of beaver and other animals. "Since you are here strangers, and come into our country," one group of Indians told early settlers in the Chesapeake, "you should rather conform yourselves to the customs of our country, than impose yours on us." But it was the Indians whose lives were most powerfully altered by the changes set in motion in 1607 when English colonists landed at Jamestown.

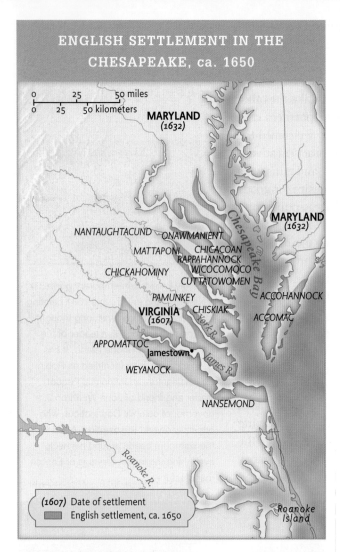

ENGLISH SETTLEMENT IN THE CHESAPEAKE, ca. 1650

MARYLAND (1632)

NANTAUGHTACUND
ONAWMANIENT
MATTAPONI
CHICACOAN
RAPPAHANNOCK
CHICKAHOMINY
WICOCOMOCO
CUTTATOWOMEN
PAMUNKEY
ACCOHANNOCK
VIRGINIA (1607)
CHISKIAK
ACCOMAC
APPOMATTOC
Jamestown
WEYANOCK
NANSEMOND

Chesapeake Bay
York R.
James R.
Roanoke R.
Roanoke Island

MARYLAND (1632)

(1607) Date of settlement
English settlement, ca. 1650

By 1650, English settlement in the Chesapeake had spread well beyond the initial colony at Jamestown, as tobacco planters sought fertile land near navigable waterways.

SETTLING THE CHESAPEAKE

The Jamestown Colony

The early history of Jamestown was, to say the least, not promising. The colony's leadership changed repeatedly, its inhabitants suffered an extraordinarily high death rate, and, with the company seeking a quick profit, supplies from England proved inadequate. The hopes of locating riches such as the Spanish had found in Mexico were quickly dashed. "Silver and gold they have none," one Spanish observer commented, their local resources were "not much to be regarded," and they had "no commerce with any nation." The first settlers were "a quarrelsome band of gentlemen and servants." They included few farmers and laborers and numerous sons of English gentry and high-status craftsmen (jewelers, stonecutters, and the like), who preferred to prospect for gold rather than farm. They "would rather starve than work," declared **John Smith**, one of the colony's first leaders.

Jamestown lay beside a swamp containing malaria-carrying mosquitoes, and the garbage settlers dumped into the local river bred germs that caused dysentery and typhoid fever. Disease and lack of food took a heavy toll. By the end of the first year, the original population of 104 had fallen by half. New arrivals (including the first two women, who landed in 1608) brought the numbers up to 400 in 1609, but by 1610, after a winter long remembered as the "starving time," only 65 settlers remained alive. At one point, the survivors abandoned Jamestown and sailed for England, only to be intercepted and persuaded to return to Virginia by ships carrying a new governor, 250 colonists, and supplies. By 1616, about 80 percent of the immigrants who had arrived in the first decade were dead.

Only rigorous military discipline held the colony together. John Smith was a forceful man whose career before coming to America included a period fighting the Turks in Hungary, where he was captured and for a time enslaved. He imposed a regime of forced labor on company lands. "He that will not work, shall not eat," Smith declared. Smith's autocratic mode of governing alienated many of the colonists. After being injured in an accidental gunpowder explosion in 1609, he was forced to return to England. But his immediate successors continued his iron rule.

From Company to Society

The Virginia Company slowly realized that for the colony to survive it would have to abandon the search for gold, grow its own food, and find a marketable commodity. It would also have to attract more settlers. With this end in view, it announced new policies in 1618 that powerfully shaped Virginia's development as a functioning society rather than an outpost of London-based investors. Instead of retaining all the land for itself, the company introduced the **headright system**, awarding fifty acres of land to any colonist who paid for his own or another's passage. Thus, anyone who brought in a sizable number of servants would immediately acquire a large estate. In place of the governor's militaristic regime, a "charter of grants and liberties" was issued, including the establishment of a **House of Burgesses**. When it convened in 1619, this became the first elected assembly in colonial America.

The House of Burgesses was hardly a model of democracy—only freemen could vote, and the company and its appointed governor retained the right to nullify any measure the body adopted. But its creation established a political precedent that all English colonies would eventually follow. Also in 1619, the first twenty blacks arrived in Virginia on a Dutch vessel. The full significance of these two events would not be apparent until years later. But they laid the foundation for a society that would one day be dominated economically and politically by slaveowning planters.

Powhatan and Pocahontas

When the English arrived at Jamestown, they landed in an area inhabited by some 15,000 to 25,000 Indians living in numerous small agricultural villages. Most acknowledged the rule of Wahunsonacock, a shrewd and forceful leader who had recently consolidated his authority over the region and collected tribute from some thirty subordinate tribes. Called Powhatan by the settlers after the Indian word for both his tribe and his title of paramount chief, he quickly realized the advantages of trade with the newcomers. For its part, mindful of Las Casas's condemnation of Spanish behavior, the Virginia Company instructed its colonists to treat local Indians kindly and to try to convert them to Christianity. Realizing that the colonists depended on the Indians for food, John Smith tried to stop settlers from seizing produce from nearby villages, lest the Indians cut off all trade.

In the first two years of Jamestown's existence, relations with Indians were mostly peaceful and based on a fairly equal give-and-take. At one point, Smith was captured by the Indians and threatened with execution by Powhatan, only to be rescued by Pocahontas, reputedly the favorite among his many children by dozens of wives. The incident has come down in legend (most recently a popular animated film) as an example of a rebellious, love-struck teenager defying her father. In fact, it was probably part of an elaborate ceremony designed by Powhatan to demonstrate his power over the colonists and incorporate them into his realm. Pocahontas subsequently became an intermediary between the two peoples, bringing food and messages to Jamestown.

John Smith's return to England raised tensions between the two groups, and a period of sporadic conflict began in 1610, with the English massacring villagers indiscriminately and destroying Indian crops. Pocahontas herself was captured and held as a hostage by the settlers in 1613. While confined to Jamestown, she converted to Christianity. As part of the restoration of peace in 1614, she married

A portrait of John Smith, the leader of the early Virginia colony, engraved on a 1624 map of New England.

The only portrait of Pocahontas during her lifetime was engraved by Simon van de Passe in England in 1616. After converting to Christianity, Pocahontas took the name Rebecca.

POWHATAN *Appamattuck*

Held this state & fashion when Capt. Smith ✠ was delivered to him prissner 1607

Powhatan, the most prominent Indian leader in the original area of English settlement in Virginia. This image, showing Powhatan and his court, was engraved on John Smith's map of Virginia and included in Smith's *General History of Virginia*, published in 1624.

the English colonist John Rolfe. Two years later, she accompanied her husband to England, where she caused a sensation in the court of James I as a symbol of Anglo-Indian harmony and missionary success. But she succumbed to disease in 1617. Her father died the following year.

The Uprising of 1622

Once it became clear that the English were interested in establishing a permanent and constantly expanding colony, not a trading post, conflict with local Indians was inevitable. The peace that began in 1614 ended abruptly in 1622 when Powhatan's brother and successor, Opechancanough, led a brilliantly planned surprise attack that in a single day wiped out one-quarter of Virginia's settler population of 1,200. The surviving 900 colonists organized themselves into military bands, which then massacred scores of Indians and devastated their villages. A spokesman for the Virginia Company explained the reason behind the Indian assault: "The daily fear that . . . in time we by our growing continually upon them would dispossess them of this country." But by going to war, declared Governor Francis Wyatt, the Indians had forfeited any claim to the land. Virginia's policy, he continued, must now be nothing less than the "expulsion of the savages to gain the free range of the country."

Indians remained a significant presence in Virginia, and trade continued throughout the century. But the unsuccessful **Uprising of 1622** fundamentally shifted the balance of power in the colony. The settlers' supremacy was reinforced in 1644 when a last desperate rebellion led by Opechancanough, now said to be 100 years old, was crushed after causing the deaths of some 500 colonists. Virginia forced a treaty on the surviving coastal Indians, who now numbered fewer than 2,000, that acknowledged their subordination to the government at Jamestown and required them to move to tribal reservations to the west and not enter areas of European settlement without permission. This policy of separation followed the precedent already established in Ireland. Settlers spreading inland into the Virginia countryside continued to seize Indian lands.

The destruction caused by the uprising of 1622 was the last in a series of blows suffered by the Virginia Company. Two years later, it surrendered its charter and Virginia became the first royal colony, its governor now appointed by the crown. Virginia had failed to accomplish any of its goals for either the company or the settlers. Investors had not turned a profit, and although the company had sent 6,000 settlers to Virginia, its white population numbered only 1,200 when the king assumed control. Preoccupied with affairs at home, the government in London for years paid little attention to Virginia. Henceforth, the local elite, not a faraway company, controlled the colony's development. And that elite was growing rapidly in wealth and power thanks to the cultivation of a crop introduced from the West Indies by John Rolfe—tobacco.

A Tobacco Colony

King James I considered tobacco "harmful to the brain and dangerous to the lungs" and issued a spirited warning against its use. But increasing numbers of Europeans enjoyed smoking and believed the tobacco plant had medicinal benefits. As a commodity with an ever-expanding mass market in Europe, tobacco became Virginia's substitute for gold. It enriched an emerging class of tobacco planters, as well as members of the colonial government who assigned good land to themselves. The crown profited from customs duties (taxes on tobacco that entered or left the kingdom). By 1624, more than 200,000 pounds were being grown, producing startling profits for landowners. Forty years later, the crop totaled 15 million pounds, and it doubled again by the 1680s. The spread of tobacco farming produced a dispersed society with few towns and little social unity. It inspired a get-rich-quick attitude and a frenzied scramble for land and labor. By the middle of the seventeenth century, a new influx of immigrants with ample financial resources—sons of merchants and English gentlemen—had taken advantage of the headright system and governmental connections to acquire large estates along navigable rivers. They established themselves as the colony's social and political elite.

Theodor de Bry's engraving of the 1622 Indian uprising in Virginia depicts the Indians massacring defenseless colonists (who are shown unarmed although many in fact owned guns).

The expansion of tobacco cultivation also led to an increased demand for field labor, met for most of the seventeenth century by young, male indentured servants. Despite harsh conditions of work in the tobacco fields, a persistently high death rate, and laws mandating punishments from whipping to an extension of service for those who ran away or were unruly, the abundance of land continued to attract migrants. Of the 120,000 English immigrants who entered the Chesapeake region during the seventeenth century, three-quarters came as servants. Virginia's white society increasingly came to resemble that of England, with a wealthy landed gentry at the top; a group of small farmers, mostly former indentured servants who had managed to acquire land, in the middle; and an army of poor laborers—servants and landless former indentured servants—at the bottom. By 1700, the region's white population had grown to nearly 90,000.

An advertisement for tobacco includes images of slaves handling barrels and tobacco plants.

Women and the Family

Virginia, however, lacked one essential element of English society—stable family life. The colony avidly promoted the immigration of women, including several dozen "tobacco brides" who arrived in 1620 and 1621 for arranged marriages. But given the demand for male servants to work in the tobacco fields, men in the Chesapeake outnumbered women for most of the seventeenth century by four or five to one. The vast majority of women who emigrated to

Englishmen smoking tobacco. European demand for tobacco enriched Virginia planters, British merchants, and the English government, and spurred an ever-increasing demand for field labor.

the region came as indentured servants. Since they usually had to complete their terms of service before marrying, they did not begin to form families until their mid-twenties. The high death rate, unequal ratio between the sexes, and late age of marriage for those who found partners retarded population growth and produced a society with large numbers of single men, widows, and orphans. Although patriarchal ideals remained intact in Virginia, in practice the traditional authority of husbands and fathers was weakened. Because of their own low life expectancy, fathers found it difficult to supervise the careers and marriages of their children.

Slow population growth

In the colonies as in England, a married woman possessed certain rights before the law, including a claim to **dower rights** of one-third of her husband's property in the event that he died before she did. When the widow died, however, the property passed to the husband's male heirs. (English law was far less generous than in Spain, where a woman could hold independently any property inherited from her parents, and a man and wife owned jointly all the wealth accumulated during a marriage.)

Social conditions in the colonies, however, opened the door to roles women rarely assumed in England. Widows and the few women who never married took advantage of their legal status as *feme sole* (a "woman alone," who enjoyed an independent legal identity denied to married women) to make contracts and conduct business. Margaret Brent, who emigrated to the Chesapeake in 1638, acquired land, managed her own plantation, and acted as a lawyer in court. Some widows were chosen to administer their husbands' estates or were willed their husbands' property outright, rather than receiving only the one-third "dower rights." But because most women came to Virginia as indentured servants, they could look forward only to a life of hard labor in the tobacco fields and early death. Servants were frequently subjected to sexual abuse by their masters. Those who married often found themselves in poverty when their husbands died.

Women's lives

The Maryland Experiment

Although it began under very different sponsorship and remained much smaller than Virginia during the seventeenth century, the second Chesapeake colony, Maryland, followed a similar course of development. As in Virginia, tobacco came to dominate the economy and tobacco planters the society. But in other ways, Maryland's history was strikingly different.

Maryland was established in 1632 as a proprietary colony, that is, a grant of land and governmental authority to a single individual. This was Cecilius Calvert, the son of a recently deceased favorite of King Charles I. The charter made Calvert proprietor of the colony and granted him "full, free, and absolute power," including control of trade and the right to initiate all legislation, with an elected assembly confined to approving or disapproving his proposals. Calvert imagined Maryland as a feudal domain. Land would be laid out in manors with the owners paying "quitrents" to the proprietor. Calvert disliked representative institutions and believed ordinary people should not meddle in governmental affairs. On the other hand, the charter also guaranteed to colonists "all privileges, franchises, and liberties" of Englishmen. While these were not spelled out, they undoubtedly included the idea of a government limited by the law. Here was a recipe for conflict, and Maryland had more than its share during the seventeenth century.

Proprietary colony

Religion in Maryland

Further aggravating instability in the colony was the fact that Calvert, a Catholic, envisioned Maryland as a refuge for his persecuted coreligionists, especially the

Processing tobacco was as labor-intensive as caring for the plant in the fields. Here scantily clad slaves and female indentured servants work with the crop after it has been harvested.

younger sons of Catholic gentry who had few economic or political prospects in England. In Maryland, he hoped, Protestants and Catholics could live in a harmony unknown in Europe. The first group of 130 colonists included a number of Catholic gentlemen and two priests. Most appointed officials were also Catholic, including relatives of the proprietor, as were those to whom he awarded the choicest land grants. But Protestants always formed a majority of the settlers. Most, as in Virginia, came as indentured servants, but others took advantage of Maryland's generous headright system to acquire land by transporting workers to the colony.

As in Virginia, the death rate remained very high. In one county, half the marriages during the seventeenth century lasted fewer than eight years before one partner died. Almost 70 percent of male settlers in Maryland died before reaching the age of fifty, and half the children born in the colony did not live to adulthood. But at least initially, Maryland seems to have offered servants greater opportunity for landownership than Virginia. Unlike in the older colony, freedom dues in Maryland included fifty acres of land. As tobacco planters engrossed the best land later in the century, however, the prospects for landless men diminished.

THE NEW ENGLAND WAY

The Rise of Puritanism

As Virginia and Maryland evolved toward societies dominated by a small aristocracy ruling over numerous bound laborers, a very different social order emerged in seventeenth-century New England. The early history of that region is intimately connected to the religious movement known as "Puritanism," which arose in England late in the sixteenth century. The term was initially coined by opponents to ridicule those not satisfied with the progress of the Protestant Reformation in England, who called themselves not Puritans but "godly" or "true Protestants." Puritanism came to define a set of religious principles and a view of how society should be organized. **Puritans** differed among themselves on many issues. But all shared the conviction that the Church of England retained too many elements of Catholicism in its religious rituals and doctrines. Puritans saw elaborate church ceremonies, the rule that priests could not marry, and ornate church decorations as vestiges of "popery." Many rejected the Catholic structure of religious authority descending from a pope or king to archbishops, bishops, and priests. Only independent local congregations, they believed, should choose clergymen and determine modes of worship. These Puritans were called "Congregationalists." All Puritans shared many of the beliefs of the Church of England and the society as a whole, including a hatred of Catholicism and a pride in England's greatness as a champion of liberty. But they believed that neither the church nor the nation was living up to its ideals.

Puritans considered religious belief a complex and demanding matter and urged believers to seek the truth by reading the Bible and listening to sermons by educated ministers, rather than devoting themselves to sacra-

The first book printed in the English mainland colonies, *The Whole Book of Psalmes Faithfully Translated into English Metre* was published in Cambridge, Massachusetts, in 1640. Worshipers used it to sing psalms (religious songs from the Bible, sung in Massachusetts unaccompanied by music, which Puritan churches banned).

ments administered by priests and to what Puritans considered formulaic prayers. The sermon was the central rite of Puritan practice. In the course of a lifetime, according to one estimate, the average Puritan listened to some 7,000 sermons. In their religious beliefs, Puritans followed the ideas of the French-born Swiss theologian John Calvin. The world, Calvin taught, was divided between the elect and the damned. All persons sought salvation, but whether one was among the elect destined to be saved had already been determined by God. His will, ultimately, was unknowable, and nothing one did on earth—including prayers, good works, and offerings—would make any difference. But while there were no guarantees of salvation, worldly success—leading a good life, prospering economically—might well be indications of God's grace. Idleness and immoral behavior were sure signs of damnation.

Moral Liberty

Puritanism, however, was not simply a set of ideas but a state of mind, a zealousness in pursuing the true faith that alienated many who held differing religious views. A minority of Puritans (such as those who settled in Plymouth Colony) became separatists, abandoning the Church of England entirely to form their own independent churches. Most, however, hoped to purify the church from within. But in the 1620s and 1630s, as Charles I seemed to be moving toward a restoration of Catholic ceremonies and the Church of England dismissed Puritan ministers and censored their writings, many Puritans decided to emigrate. They departed England not so much because of persecution, but because they feared that "Popish" practices had grown to such "an intolerable height," as one minister complained, that "the consciences of God's saints . . . could no longer bear them." By the same token, Puritans blamed many of England's social problems on the wandering poor, whom they considered indolent and ungodly. When Puritans emigrated to New England, they hoped to escape what they believed to be the religious and worldly corruptions of English society. They would establish a "city set upon a hill," a Bible Commonwealth whose influence would flow back across the Atlantic and rescue England from godlessness and social decay.

Like so many other emigrants to America, Puritans came in search of liberty, especially the right to worship and govern themselves in what they deemed a truly Christian manner. Freedom for Puritans was primarily a spiritual affair. It implied the opportunity and the responsibility to obey God's will through self-government and self-denial. It certainly did not mean unrestrained action, improper religious practices, or sinful behavior, of which, Puritans thought, there were far too many examples in England. In a 1645 speech to the Massachusetts legislature explaining the Puritan conception of freedom, **John Winthrop**, the colony's governor, distinguished sharply between two kinds of liberty. "Natural" liberty, or acting without restraint, suggested "a liberty to do evil." This was the false idea of freedom supposedly adopted by the Irish, Indians, and bad Christians generally. Genuine "moral" liberty—the Christian liberty described in Chapter 1—meant "a liberty to that only which is good." It was quite compatible with severe restraints on speech, religion, and personal behavior. True freedom, Winthrop insisted, depended on "subjection to authority," both religious and secular; otherwise, anarchy was sure to follow. To Puritans, liberty meant that

A portrait of John Winthrop, first governor of the Massachusetts Bay Colony, painted in the 1640s.

"City set upon a hill"

"Moral" liberty

the elect had a right to establish churches and govern society, not that others could challenge their beliefs or authority.

The Pilgrims at Plymouth

The first Puritans to emigrate to America were a group of separatists known as the **Pilgrims**. They had already fled to the Netherlands in 1608, believing that Satan had begun "to sow errors, heresies and discords" in England. A decade later, fearing that their children were being corrupted by being drawn into the surrounding culture, they decided to emigrate to Virginia. The expedition was financed by a group of English investors who hoped to establish a base for profitable trade. In September 1620, the *Mayflower*, carrying 150 settlers and crew (among them many non-Puritans), embarked from England. Blown off course, they landed not in Virginia but hundreds of miles to the north, on Cape Cod. Here the 102 who survived the journey established the colony of Plymouth. Before landing, the Pilgrim leaders drew up the **Mayflower Compact**, in which the adult men going ashore agreed to obey "just and equal laws" enacted by representatives of their own choosing. This was the first written frame of government in what is now the United States.

A century earlier, when Giovanni da Verrazano explored the Atlantic coast of North America, he encountered thickly settled villages and saw the smoke of innumerable Indian bonfires. By the time the Pilgrims landed, hundreds of European fishing vessels had operated off New England, landing to trade with Indians and bringing, as elsewhere, epidemics. The Pilgrims arrived in an area whose native population had recently been decimated by smallpox. They established Plymouth on the site of an abandoned Indian village whose fields had been cleared before the epidemic and were ready for cultivation. Nonetheless, the settlers arrived six weeks before winter without food or farm animals. Half died during the first winter. The colonists only survived through the help of local Indians, notably Squanto, who with twenty other Indians had been kidnapped and brought to Spain in 1614 by the English explorer Thomas Hunt, who planned to sell them as slaves. Rescued by a local priest, Squanto somehow made his way to London, where he learned English. He returned to Massachusetts in 1619 only to find that his people, the Patuxet, had succumbed to disease. He served as interpreter for the Pilgrims, taught them where to fish and how to plant corn, and helped in the forging of an alliance with Massasoit, a local chief. In the autumn of 1621, the Pilgrims invited their Indian allies to a harvest feast celebrating their survival, the first Thanksgiving in North America. (Feasts of Thanksgiving were a feature of Puritan religious practice, not something conducted in this one instance.)

The Pilgrims hoped to establish a society based on the lives of the early Christian saints. Their government rested on the principle of consent, and voting was not restricted to church members. All land was held in common until 1627, when it was divided among the settlers. Plymouth survived as an independent colony until 1691, but it was soon overshadowed by Massachusetts Bay to its north.

The Mayflower

In this engraving, Theodor de Bry depicts an encounter between an English explorer and the Wampanoag Indians on Cape Cod or Martha's Vineyard in 1602. The region's Indians had much experience with Europeans before the Pilgrims settled there.

The Great Migration

Chartered in 1629, the Massachusetts Bay Company was founded by a group of London merchants who hoped to further the Puritan cause and turn a profit through trade with the Indians. The first five ships sailed from England in 1629, and by 1642 some 21,000 Puritans had emigrated to Massachusetts. Long remembered as the **Great Migration**, this flow of population represented less than one-third of English emigration in the 1630s. Far more English settlers arrived in Ireland, the Chesapeake, and the Caribbean. After 1640, migration to New England virtually ceased, and in some years more colonists left the region than arrived. Nonetheless, the Great Migration established the basis for a stable and thriving society.

In many ways, the settling of New England was unique. Although servants represented about one-quarter of the Great Migration, most settlers arrived in Massachusetts in families. They came for many reasons, including the desire to escape religious persecution, anxiety about the future of England, and the prospect of economic betterment. Compared with colonists in Virginia and Maryland, they were older and more prosperous, and the number of men and women more equally balanced. Because of the even sex ratio and New England's healthier climate, the population grew rapidly, doubling every twenty-seven years. Although the region received only a small fraction of the century's migration, by 1700 New England's white population of 91,000 outnumbered that of both the Chesapeake and the West Indies. Nearly all were descendants of those who crossed the Atlantic during the Great Migration.

Seal of the Massachusetts Bay Colony. The Indian's scanty attire suggests a lack of civilization. His statement "Come Over and Help Us," based on an incident in the Bible, illustrates the English conviction that they were liberating the native population, rather than exploiting them as other empires had.

The Puritan Family

While the imbalance between male and female migrants made it difficult for patriarchal family patterns fully to take root in the Chesapeake until the end of the seventeenth century, they emerged very quickly in New England. Whatever their differences with other Englishmen on religious matters, Puritans shared with the larger society a belief in male authority within the household as well as an adherence to the common-law tradition that severely limited married women's legal and economic rights. Puritans in America carefully emulated the family structure of England, insisting that the obedience of women, children, and servants to men's will was the foundation of social stability. The father's authority was all the more vital because in a farming society without large numbers of slaves or servants, control over the labor of one's family was essential to a man's economic success.

Male authority

To be sure, Puritans deemed women to be the spiritual equals of men, and women were allowed to become full church members. Although all ministers were men, the Puritan belief in the ability of believers to interpret the Bible opened the door for some women to claim positions of religious leadership. The ideal Puritan marriage was based on reciprocal affection and companionship, and divorce was legal. Yet within the household, the husband's authority was virtually absolute. Indeed, a man's position as head of his family was thought to replicate God's authority in spiritual matters and the authority of the government in the secular realm. Magistrates sometimes intervened to protect wives from physical abuse,

The Savage Family, a 1779 painting by the New England artist Edward Savage, depicts several generations of a typically numerous Puritan family.

The New England town

The Massachusetts Bay Charter

but they also enforced the power of fathers over their children and husbands over their wives. Moderate physical "correction" was considered appropriate for women who violated their husbands' sense of proper behavior.

Their responsibilities as wives and mothers defined women's lives. In his 1645 speech on liberty, John Winthrop noted that a woman achieved genuine freedom by fulfilling her prescribed social role and embracing "subjection to her husband's authority." The family was the foundation of strong communities, and unmarried adults seemed a danger to the social fabric. An early law of Plymouth declared that "no single person be suffered to live of himself." The typical New England woman married at twenty-two, a younger age than her English counterpart, and gave birth seven times. Because New England was a far healthier environment than the Chesapeake, more children survived infancy. Thus, much of a woman's adult life was devoted to bearing and rearing children.

Government and Society in Massachusetts

In a sermon aboard the *Arabella*, on which he sailed for Massachusetts in 1630, John Winthrop spoke of the settlers binding themselves together "in the bond of brotherly affection" in order to promote the glory of God and their own "common good." Puritans feared excessive individualism and lack of social unity. Unlike the dispersed plantation-centered society of the Chesapeake, the leaders of Massachusetts organized the colony in self-governing towns. Groups of settlers received a land grant from the colony's government and then subdivided it, with residents awarded house lots in a central area and land on the outskirts for farming. Much land remained in commons, either for collective use or to be divided among later settlers or the sons of the town's founders. Each town had its own Congregational Church. Each, according to a law of 1647, was required to establish a school, since the ability to read the Bible was central to Puritan belief. To train an educated ministry, Harvard College was established in 1636 (nearly a century after the Royal University of Mexico, founded in 1551), and two years later the first printing press in English America was established in Cambridge.

The government of Massachusetts reflected the Puritans' religious and social vision. Wishing to rule the colony without outside interference and to prevent non-Puritans from influencing decision making, the shareholders of the Massachusetts Bay Company emigrated to America, taking the charter with them and transforming a commercial document into a form of government. At first, the eight shareholders chose the men who ruled the colony. In 1634, a group of deputies elected by freemen (landowning church members) was added to form a single ruling body, the General Court. Ten years later, company officers and elected deputies were divided into two legislative houses. Unlike Virginia, whose governors were appointed first by a faraway company and after 1624 by the crown, or Maryland, where authority rested with a single proprietor, the freemen of Massachusetts elected their governor.

The principle of consent was central to Puritanism. Church government was decentralized—each congregation, as one minister put it, had "complete liberty to stand alone." Churches were formed by voluntary agreement among members, who elected the minister. No important church decision was made without the agreement of the male members. Towns governed themselves, and local officials, delegates to the General Court, and the colonial governor were all elected. Puritans, however, were hardly believers in equality. Church membership, a status that carried great prestige and power, was a restrictive category. Anyone could worship at a church, or, as the Puritans preferred to call it, meeting house, but to be a full member required demonstrating that one had experienced divine grace and could be considered a "visible saint," usually by testifying about a conversion experience. Although male property holders generally chose local officials, voting in colony-wide elections was limited to men who had been accepted as full church members. As time went on, this meant that a smaller and smaller percentage of the population controlled the government. Puritan democracy was for those within the circle of church membership; those outside the boundary occupied a secondary place in the Bible Commonwealth.

An embroidered banner depicting the main building at Harvard, the first college established in the English colonies. It was probably made by a Massachusetts woman for a husband or son who attended Harvard.

Church and State in Puritan Massachusetts

Seventeenth-century New England was a hierarchical society in which socially prominent families were assigned the best land and the most desirable seats in church. "Some must be rich and some poor, some high and eminent in power and dignity; others mean and in subjection," declared John Winthrop. This was part of God's plan, reinforced by man-made law and custom. The General Court forbade ordinary men and women from wearing "the garb of gentlemen." Ordinary settlers were addressed as "goodman" and "goodwife," while the better sort were called "gentleman" and "lady" or "master" and "mistress." When the General Court in 1641 issued a Body of Liberties outlining the rights and responsibilities of Massachusetts colonists, it adopted the traditional understanding of liberties as privileges that derived from one's place in the social order. Inequality was considered an expression of God's will, and while some liberties applied to all inhabitants, there were separate lists of rights for freemen, women, children, and servants. The Body of Liberties also allowed for slavery. The first African slave appears in the records of Massachusetts Bay in 1640.

The Body of Liberties

Massachusetts forbade ministers from holding office so as not to interfere with their spiritual responsibilities. But church and state were closely interconnected.

The law required each town to establish a church and to levy a tax to support the minister. There were no separate church courts, but the state enforced religious devotion. The Body of Liberties affirmed the rights of free speech and assembly and equal protection of the law for all within the colony, but the laws of Massachusetts prescribed the death penalty for, among other things, worshiping "any god, but the lord god," practicing witchcraft, or committing blasphemy.

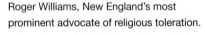

Church and state

Like many others in the seventeenth century, Puritans believed that religious uniformity was essential to social order. They did not believe in religious toleration—there was one truth, and their faith embodied it. Religious liberty meant the liberty to practice this truth. The purpose of the Puritan experiment was to complete the Reformation and, they hoped, spread it back to England. Religious dissent might fatally undermine these goals. But the principle of autonomy for local congregations soon clashed with the desire for religious uniformity.

NEW ENGLANDERS DIVIDED

The Puritans exalted individual judgment—hence their insistence on reading the Bible. The very first item printed in English America was a broadside, *The Oath of a Freeman* (1638), explaining the rights and duties of the citizens of Massachusetts and emphasizing that men should vote according to their "own conscience ... without respect of persons, or favor of any men." Yet modern ideas of individualism, privacy, and personal freedom would have struck Puritans as quite strange. They considered too much emphasis on the "self" dangerous to social harmony and community stability. In the closely knit towns of New England, residents carefully monitored one another's behavior and chastised or expelled those who violated communal norms. In the Puritan view, as one colonist put it, the main freedom possessed by dissenters was the "liberty to keep away from us." Towns banished individuals for such offenses as criticizing the church or government, complaining about the colony in letters home to England, or, in the case of one individual, Abigail Gifford, for being "a very burdensome woman." Tolerance of difference was not high on the list of Puritan values.

Roger Williams, New England's most prominent advocate of religious toleration.

Roger Williams

Differences of opinion about how to organize a Bible Commonwealth, however, emerged almost from the founding of Massachusetts. With its emphasis on individual interpretation of the Bible, Puritanism contained the seeds of its own fragmentation. The first sustained criticism of the existing order came from the young minister Roger Williams, who arrived in Massachusetts in 1631 and soon began to insist that its congregations withdraw from the Church of England and that church and state be separated. "Soul liberty," Williams believed, required that individuals be allowed to follow their consciences wherever they led. To most Puritans, the social fabric was held together by certain religious truths, which could not be questioned. To Williams, any law-abiding citizen should be allowed to practice whatever form of religion he chose. For the government to "molest any person, Jew or Gentile, for either professing doctrine or practicing worship" violated the principle that genuine religious faith is voluntary.

Williams and religious liberty

Williams aimed to strengthen religion, not weaken it. The embrace of government, he insisted, corrupted the purity of Christian faith and drew believers into endless religious wars like those that wracked Europe. To leaders like John Winthrop, the outspoken minister's attack on the religious-political establishment of Massachusetts was bad enough, but Williams compounded the offense by rejecting the conviction that Puritans were an elect people on a divine mission to spread the true faith. Williams denied that God had singled out any group as special favorites.

Rhode Island and Connecticut

Banished from Massachusetts in 1636, Williams and his followers moved south, where they established the colony of Rhode Island, which eventually received a charter from London. In a world in which the right of individuals to participate in religious activities without governmental interference barely existed, Rhode Island became a beacon of religious freedom. It had no established church, no religious qualifications for voting until the eighteenth century, and no requirement that citizens attend church. It became a haven for **Dissenters** (Protestants who belonged to denominations other than the established church) and Jews persecuted in other colonies. Rhode Island's frame of government was also more democratic. The assembly was elected twice a year, the governor annually, and town meetings were held more frequently than elsewhere in New England.

Religious freedom in Rhode Island

Religious disagreements in Massachusetts generated other colonies as well. In 1636, the minister Thomas Hooker established a settlement at Hartford. Its system of government, embodied in the Fundamental Orders of 1639, was modeled on that of Massachusetts—with the significant exception that men did not have to be church members to vote. Quite different was the colony of New Haven, founded in 1638 by emigrants who wanted an even closer connection between church and state. In 1662, Hartford and New Haven received a royal charter that united them as the colony of Connecticut.

The Trial of Anne Hutchinson

More threatening to the Puritan establishment, both because of her gender and because she attracted a large and influential following, was Anne Hutchinson. A midwife and the daughter of a clergyman, Hutchinson, wrote John Winthrop, was "a woman of a ready wit and bold spirit." She arrived in Massachusetts with her husband in 1634 to join their minister, John Cotton, who had been expelled from his pulpit in England by church authorities. Hutchinson began holding meetings in her home, where she led discussions of religious issues among men and women, including a number of prominent merchants and public officials. In Hutchinson's view, salvation was God's direct gift to the elect and could not be earned by good works, devotional practices, or other human effort. Most Puritans shared this belief. What set Hutchinson apart was her charge that nearly all the ministers in Massachusetts were guilty of faulty preaching for distinguishing "saints" from the damned on the basis of activities such as church attendance and moral behavior rather than an inner state of grace.

Hutchinson's criticisms of Puritan leaders

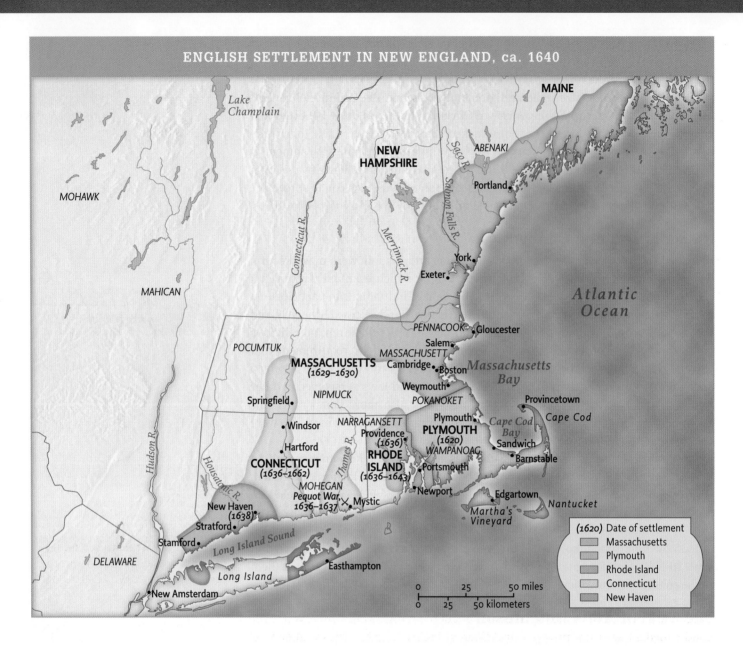

ENGLISH SETTLEMENT IN NEW ENGLAND, ca. 1640

Lake Champlain

MAINE

MOHAWK

NEW HAMPSHIRE

ABENAKI

Saco R.

Portland

Salmon Falls R.

Connecticut R.

Merrimack R.

Atlantic Ocean

MAHICAN

York

Exeter

POCUMTUK

PENNACOOK Gloucester

Salem

MASSACHUSETT

MASSACHUSETTS (1629–1630)

Cambridge Boston

Massachusetts Bay

Weymouth

Springfield

NIPMUCK

POKANOKET

Provincetown

Cape Cod

Plymouth *Cape Cod Bay*

Windsor

NARRAGANSETT

Providence (1636)

PLYMOUTH (1620)

WAMPANOAC

Sandwich

Hudson R.

Hartford

Thames R.

RHODE ISLAND (1636–1643)

Barnstable

Housatonic R.

CONNECTICUT (1636–1662)

Portsmouth

MOHEGAN Pequot War 1636–1637 ✕ Mystic

Newport

Edgartown

Nantucket

New Haven (1638)

Martha's Vineyard

Stratford

Stamford

Long Island Sound

DELAWARE

Easthampton

Long Island

New Amsterdam

| (1620) Date of settlement |
| Massachusetts |
| Plymouth |
| Rhode Island |
| Connecticut |
| New Haven |

0   25   50 miles

0   25   50 kilometers

By the mid-seventeenth century, English settlement in New England had spread well inland and up and down the Atlantic coast.

Hutchinson's trial

In Massachusetts, where most Puritans found the idea of religious pluralism deeply troubling and church and state reinforced each other, both ministers and magistrates were intent on suppressing any views that challenged their own leadership. Their critics denounced Cotton and Hutchinson for Antinomianism (a term for putting one's own judgment or faith above both human law and the teachings of the church). In 1637, she was placed on trial before a civil court for sedition (expressing opinions dangerous to authority). Her position as a "public woman" made her defiance seem even more outrageous. Her meetings, said Governor Winthrop, were neither "comely in the sight of God nor fitting to your sex." A combative and articulate woman, Hutchinson ably debated interpretation of the Bible with her university-educated accusers. She more than held her own during her trial. But when she spoke of divine revelations, of God speaking to her directly rather than through ministers or the Bible, she violated

Puritan doctrine and sealed her own fate. Such a claim, the colony's leaders felt, posed a threat to the very existence of organized churches—and, indeed, to all authority. Hutchinson and a number of her followers were banished. Her family made its way to Rhode Island and then to Westchester, north of what is now New York City, where Hutchinson and most of her relatives perished during an Indian war.

Anne Hutchinson lived in New England for only eight years, but she left her mark on the region's religious culture. As in the case of Roger Williams, her career showed how the Puritan belief in each individual's ability to interpret the Bible could easily lead to criticism of the religious and political establishment. It would take many years before religious toleration—which violated the Puritans' understanding of "moral liberty" and social harmony—came to Massachusetts.

> *Significance of Anne Hutchinson*

Puritans and Indians

Along with disruptive religious controversies, New England, like other colonies, had to deal with the difficult problem of relations with Indians. The native population of New England numbered perhaps 100,000 when the Puritans arrived. But because of recent epidemics, the migrants encountered fewer Indians near the coast than in other parts of eastern North America. In areas of European settlement, colonists quickly outnumbered the native population. Some settlers, notably Roger Williams, sought to treat the Indians with justice. Williams learned complex Indian languages, and he insisted that the king had no right to grant land already belonging to someone else. No town, said Williams, should be established before its site had been purchased. While John Winthrop believed uncultivated land could legitimately be taken by the colonists, he also recognized the benefits of buying land rather than simply seizing it. But he insisted that such purchases (usually completed after towns had already been settled) must carry with them Indian agreement to submit to English authority and pay tribute to the colonists.

> *Treating Indians with justice*

To New England's leaders, the Indians represented both savagery and temptation. In Puritan eyes, they resembled Catholics, with their false gods and deceptive rituals. They enjoyed freedom, but of the wrong kind—what Winthrop condemned as undisciplined "natural liberty" rather than the "moral liberty" of the civilized Christian. Always concerned that sinful persons might prefer a life of ease to hard work, Puritans feared that Indian society might prove attractive to colonists who lacked the proper moral fiber. In 1642, the Connecticut General Court set a penalty of three years at hard labor for any colonist who abandoned "godly society" to live with the Indians. To counteract the attraction of Indian life, the leaders of New England also encouraged the publication of **captivity narratives** by those captured by Indians. The most popular was *The Sovereignty and Goodness of God* by Mary Rowlandson, who had emigrated with her parents as a child in 1639 and was seized along with a group of other settlers and held for three months until ransomed during an Indian war in the 1670s. Rowlandson acknowledged that she had been well treated and suffered "not the least abuse or unchastity," but her book's overriding theme was her determination to return to Christian society.

The title page of a translation of the Bible into the Massachusett Indian language, published by John Eliot in 1663.

VOICES OF FREEDOM

From "THE TRIAL OF ANNE HUTCHINSON" (1637)

A midwife and the daughter of a clergyman, Anne Hutchinson began holding religious meetings in her home in Massachusetts in 1634. She attracted followers who believed that most ministers were not adhering strictly enough to Puritan theology. In 1637 she was placed on trial for sedition. In her defense, she claimed to be inspired by a direct revelation from God, a violation of Puritan beliefs. The examination of Hutchinson by Governor John Winthrop and Deputy Governor Thomas Dudley is a classic example of the clash between established power and individual conscience.

GOV. JOHN WINTHROP: Mrs. Hutchinson, you are called here as one of those that have troubled the peace of the commonwealth and the churches here; you are known to be a woman that hath had a great share in the promoting and divulging of those opinions that are the cause of this trouble, . . . and you have maintained a meeting and an assembly in your house that hath been condemned by the general assembly as a thing not tolerable nor comely in the sight of God nor fitting for your sex . . . .

MRS. ANNE HUTCHINSON: What have I said or done?

GOV. JOHN WINTHROP: [Y]ou did harbor and countenance those that are parties in this faction. . . .

MRS. ANNE HUTCHINSON: That's matter of conscience, Sir.

GOV. JOHN WINTHROP: Your conscience you must keep, or it must be kept for you.

* * *

GOV. JOHN WINTHROP: Your course is not to be suffered for. Besides we find such a course as this to be greatly prejudicial to the state. . . . And besides that it will not well stand with the commonwealth that families should be neglected for so many neighbors and dames and so much time spent. We see no rule of God for this. We see not that any should have authority to set up any other exercises besides what authority hath already set up . . . .

MRS. ANNE HUTCHINSON: I bless the Lord, he hath let me see which was the clear ministry and which the wrong. . . . Now if you do condemn me for speaking what in my conscience I know to be truth I must commit myself unto the Lord.

MR. NOWEL (ASSISTANT TO THE COURT): How do you know that was the spirit?

MRS. ANNE HUTCHINSON: How did Abraham know that it was God that bid him offer his son, being a breach of the sixth commandment?

DEP. GOV. THOMAS DUDLEY: By an immediate voice.

MRS. ANNE HUTCHINSON: So to me by an immediate revelation.

DEP. GOV. THOMAS DUDLEY: How! an immediate revelation.

* * *

GOV. JOHN WINTHROP: Mrs. Hutchinson, the sentence of the court you hear is that you are banished from out of our jurisdiction as being a woman not fit for our society, and are to be imprisoned till the court shall send you away.

From JOHN WINTHROP,
SPEECH TO THE MASSACHUSETTS GENERAL COURT
(JULY 3, 1645)

John Winthrop, governor of the Massachusetts Bay Colony, describes two very different definitions of liberty in this speech.

The great questions that have troubled the country, are about the authority of the magistrates and the liberty of the people. . . . Concerning liberty, I observe a great mistake in the country about that. There is a twofold liberty, natural (I mean as our nature is now corrupt) and civil or federal. The first is common to man with beasts and other creatures. By this, man, as he stands in relation to man simply, hath liberty to do what he lists; it is a liberty to do evil as well as to [do] good. This liberty is incompatible and inconsistent with authority, and cannot endure the least restraint of the most just authority. The exercise and maintaining of this liberty makes men grow more evil, and in time to be worse than brute beasts. . . . This is that great enemy of truth and peace, that wild beast, which all the ordinances of God are bent against, to restrain and subdue it.

The other kind of liberty I call civil or federal, it may also be termed moral. . . . This liberty is the proper end and object of authority, and cannot subsist without it; and it is a liberty to that only which is good, just, and honest. . . . This liberty is maintained and exercised in a way of subjection to authority; it is of the same kind of liberty wherewith Christ hath made us free. The woman's own choice makes . . . a man her husband; yet being so chosen, he is her lord, and she is to be subject to him, yet in a way of liberty, not of bondage; and a true wife accounts her subjection her honor and freedom, and would not think her condition safe and free, but in her subjection to her husband's authority. Such is the liberty of the church under the authority of Christ.

QUESTIONS

1. *To what extent does Hutchinson's being a woman play a part in the accusations against her?*

2. *Why does Winthrop consider "natural" liberty dangerous?*

3. *How do Hutchinson and Winthrop differ in their understanding of religious liberty?*

An engraving from John Underhill's *News from America*, published in London in 1638, shows the destruction of the Pequot village on the Mystic River in 1637. The colonial forces, firing guns, are aided by Indian allies with bows and arrows.

Massacre at Mystic

Puritans announced that they intended to bring Christian faith to the Indians, but they did nothing in the first two decades of settlement to accomplish this. They generally saw Indians as an obstacle to be pushed aside.

The Pequot War

Indians in New England lacked a paramount chief like Powhatan in Virginia. Coastal Indian tribes, their numbers severely reduced by disease, initially sought to forge alliances with the newcomers to enhance their own position against inland rivals. But as the white population expanded and new towns proliferated, conflict with the region's Indians became unavoidable. The turning point came in 1637 when a fur trader was killed by Pequots—a powerful tribe who controlled southern New England's fur trade and exacted tribute from other Indians. A force of Connecticut and Massachusetts soldiers, augmented by Narragansett allies, surrounded the main Pequot fortified village at Mystic and set it ablaze, killing those who tried to escape. Over 500 men, women, and children lost their lives in the massacre. By the end of the **Pequot War** a few months later, most of the Pequots had been exterminated or sold into Caribbean slavery. The treaty that restored peace decreed that their name be wiped from the historical record.

The destruction of one of the region's most powerful Indian groups not only opened the Connecticut River valley to rapid white settlement but also persuaded other Indians that the newcomers possessed a power that could not be resisted. The colonists' ferocity shocked their Indian allies, who considered European military practices barbaric. A few Puritans agreed. "It was a fearful sight to see them frying in the fire," the Pilgrim leader William Bradford wrote of the raid on Mystic. But to most Puritans, including Bradford, the defeat of a "barbarous nation" by "the sword of the Lord" offered further proof that they were on a sacred mission and that Indians were unworthy of sharing New England with the visible saints of the church.

The New England Economy

The leaders of the New England colonies prided themselves on the idea that religion was the primary motivation for emigration. "We all came into these parts of America," proclaimed an official document of the 1640s, "with one and the same end and aim, namely, to advance the kingdom of our Lord Jesus Christ and to enjoy the liberties of the Gospel in purity with peace." But economic motives were hardly unimportant. One promotional pamphlet of the 1620s spoke of New England as a place "where religion and profit jump together."

Most Puritans came to America from East Anglia, an internationally renowned cloth-producing region. One of the most economically advanced areas of England, East Anglia in the 1620s and 1630s was suffering from a series of poor harvests and the dislocations caused by a decline in the cloth trade. A majority of the emigrants from this area were weavers, tailors, or farmers. But while they were leaving a depressed region, they were relatively well-off. Most came from the middle ranks of society and paid for their family's passage rather than indenturing themselves to labor. They sought in New England not only religious liberty but also economic advancement—if not riches, then at least a "competency," the economic independence that came with secure landownership or craft status. When one preacher proclaimed that the "main end" of settlement was to honor God, a man in the congregation cried out, "Sir, you are mistaken . . . our main end was to catch fish." But to Puritans no contradiction existed between piety and profit so long as one did not forget the needs of the larger community. Success in one's calling might be taken as a sign of divine grace.

"Competency"

Lacking a marketable staple like sugar or tobacco, New Englanders turned to fishing and timber for exports. But the economy centered on family farms producing food for their own use and a small marketable surplus. Although the Body of Liberties of 1641, as noted above, made provision for slavery in the Bible Commonwealth, there were very few slaves in seventeenth-century New England. Nor were indentured servants as central to the economy as in the Chesapeake. Most households relied on the labor of their own members, including women in the home and children in the fields. Sons remained unmarried into their mid-twenties, when they could expect to receive land from their fathers, from local authorities, or by moving to a new town. Indeed, while religious divisions spawned new settlements, the desire for land among younger families and newcomers was the major motive for New England's expansion. In Sudbury, Massachusetts, for example, one resident proposed in 1651 that every adult man be awarded an equal parcel of land. When a town meeting rejected the idea, a group of young men received a grant from the General Court to establish their own town farther west.

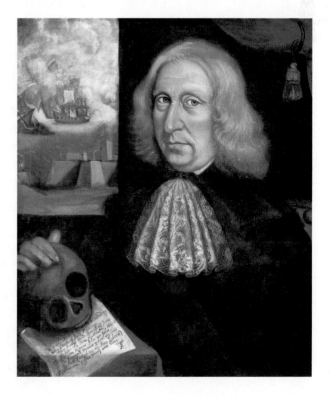

A self-portrait from around 1680, painted by Thomas Smith. A sailor who came to New England from Bermuda around 1650, Smith acquired considerable wealth, as evidenced by his fashionable clothing. The background depicts a naval battle involving Dutch and English ships (possibly a reference to their joint attack on a North African port in 1670). In the foreground is a poem with Smith's initials. This is the earliest-known American self-portrait.

The Merchant Elite

Per capita wealth in New England lagged far behind that of the Chesapeake, but it was much more equally distributed. A majority of New England families achieved the goal of owning their own land, the foundation for a comfortable independence. Nonetheless, as in the Chesapeake, economic development produced a measure of social inequality. On completing their terms, indentured servants rarely achieved full church membership or received grants of land. Most became disenfranchised wage earners.

New England gradually assumed a growing role within the British empire based on trade. As early as the 1640s, New England merchants shipped and marketed the staples of other colonies to markets in Europe and Africa. They engaged in a particularly profitable trade with the West Indies, whose growing slave plantations they supplied with fish, timber, and agricultural produce gathered at home. Especially in Boston, a powerful class of merchants arose who challenged some key

Mrs. Elizabeth Freake and Baby Mary. Painted by an anonymous artist in the 1670s, this portrait depicts the wife and daughter of John Freake, a prominent Boston merchant and lawyer. To illustrate the family's wealth, Mrs. Freake wears a triple strand of pearls, a garnet bracelet, and a gold ring, and her child wears a yellow silk dress.

"Jeremiads"

Puritan policies, including the subordination of economic activity to the common good. As early as the 1630s, when the General Court established limits on prices and wages—measures common in England—and gave a small group of merchants a monopoly on imports from Europe, others protested. Indeed, merchants were among the most prominent backers of Anne Hutchinson's challenge to colonial authority. Some left Boston to establish a new town at Portsmouth, in the region eventually chartered as the royal colony of New Hampshire. Others remained to fight, with increasing success, for the right to conduct business as they pleased. By the 1640s, Massachusetts had repealed many of its early economic regulations.

Although the Puritans never abandoned the idea that economic activity should serve the general welfare, Boston merchants soon came to exercise a decisive influence in public affairs. The government of Massachusetts Bay Colony actively promoted economic development by building roads and bridges, offering bounties to economic enterprises, and abandoning laws limiting prices. Eventually, the Puritan experiment would evolve into a merchant-dominated colonial government.

The Half-Way Covenant

In the mid-seventeenth century, some Puritan leaders began to worry about their society's growing commercialization and declining piety, or "declension." By 1650, less than half the population of Boston had been admitted to full church membership. Massachusetts churches were forced to deal with a growing problem—the religious status of the third generation. Children of the elect could be baptized, but many never became full church members because they were unable to demonstrate the necessary religious commitment or testify to a conversion experience. What was the status of their children? New Englanders faced a difficult choice. They could uphold rigorous standards of church admission, which would limit the size and social influence of the Congregational Church. Or they could make admission easier, which would keep the church connected to a larger part of the population but would raise fears about a loss of religious purity.

The **Half-Way Covenant** of 1662 tried to address this problem by allowing for the baptism and a kind of subordinate, or "half-way," membership for grandchildren of those who emigrated during the Great Migration. In a significant compromise of early Puritan beliefs, ancestry, not religious conversion, became the pathway to inclusion among the elect. But church membership continued to stagnate.

By the 1660s and 1670s, ministers were regularly castigating the people for selfishness, manifestations of pride, violations of the Sabbath, and a "great backsliding" from the colony's original purposes. These warnings, called "jeremiads" after the ancient Hebrew prophet Jeremiah, interpreted crop failures and disease as signs of divine disapproval and warned of further punishment to come if New Englanders did not mend their ways. Yet hard work and commercial success in one's chosen calling had always been central Puritan values. In this sense, the commercialization of New England was as much a fulfillment of the Puritan mission in America as a betrayal.

RELIGION, POLITICS, AND FREEDOM

The Rights of Englishmen

Even as English emigrants began the settlement of colonies in North America, England itself became enmeshed in political and religious conflict, in which ideas of liberty played a central role. The struggle over **English liberty** in the first half of the seventeenth century expanded the definition of freedom at home and spilled over into early English North America.

By 1600, the traditional definition of "liberties" as a set of privileges confined to one or another social group still persisted, but alongside it had arisen the idea that certain "rights of Englishmen" applied to all within the kingdom. This tradition rested on the Magna Carta (or Great Charter) of 1215. An agreement between King John and a group of barons—local lords whose private armies frequently fought against each other and the crown—the Magna Carta attempted to put an end to a chronic state of civil unrest. It listed a series of "liberties" granted by the king to "all the free men of our realm." This was a restricted group at the time, since a large part of the English population still lived as serfs—peasants working land owned by feudal lords and legally bound to provide labor and other services. The liberties mentioned in the Magna Carta included protection against arbitrary imprisonment and the seizure of one's property without due process of law.

The principal beneficiaries of the Magna Carta were the barons, who obtained the right to oversee the king's conduct and even revolt if he violated their privileges. But over time, the document came to be seen as embodying the idea of "English freedom"—that the king was subject to the rule of law, and that all persons should

> *The Magna Carta*

The Court of Common Pleas. Trial by jury was a central element in the definition of "English liberty." This watercolor appeared in a three-volume series, *The Microcosm of London* (1808–1810).

enjoy security of person and property. These rights were embodied in the common law, whose provisions, such as habeas corpus (a protection against being imprisoned without a legal charge), the right to face one's accuser, and trial by jury came to apply to all free subjects of the English crown. And as serfdom slowly disappeared, the number of Englishmen considered "freeborn," and therefore entitled to these rights, expanded enormously.

The English Civil War

English freedom

At the beginning of the seventeenth century, when English emigrants began arriving in the New World, "freedom" still played only a minor role in England's political debates. But the political upheavals of that century elevated the notion of "English freedom" to a central place. The struggle for political supremacy between Parliament and the Stuart monarchs James I and Charles I culminated in the English Civil War of the 1640s and early 1650s. This long-running battle arose from religious disputes about how fully the Church of England should distance its doctrines and forms of worship from Catholicism. Conflict also developed over the respective powers of the king and Parliament, a debate that produced numerous invocations of the idea of the "freeborn Englishman" and led to a great expansion of the concept of English freedom.

Parliament vs. monarchy

The leaders of the House of Commons (the elective body that, along with the hereditary aristocrats of the House of Lords, made up the English Parliament) accused the Stuart kings of endangering liberty by imposing taxes without parliamentary consent, imprisoning political foes, and leading the nation back toward Catholicism. Civil war broke out in 1642, resulting in a victory for the forces of Parliament. In 1649, Charles I was beheaded, the monarchy abolished, and England declared "a Commonwealth and Free State"—a nation governed by the will of the people. Oliver Cromwell, the head of the victorious Parliamentary army, ruled for almost a decade after the execution of the king. In 1660, the monarchy was restored and Charles II assumed the throne. But by then, the breakdown of authority had stimulated intense discussions of liberty, authority, and what it meant to be a "freeborn Englishman."

England's Debate over Freedom

The Levellers

The idea of freedom suddenly took on new and expanded meanings between 1640 and 1660. The writer John Milton, who in 1649 called London "the mansion-house of liberty," called for freedom of speech and of the press. New religious sects sprang up, demanding the end of public financing and special privileges for the Anglican Church and religious toleration for all Protestants. The Levellers, history's first democratic political movement, proposed a written constitution, the Agreement of the People, which began by proclaiming "at how high a rate we value our just freedom." At a time when "democracy" was still widely seen as the equivalent of anarchy and disorder, the document proposed to abolish the monarchy and House of Lords and to greatly expand the right to vote. "The poorest he that lives in England hath a life to live as the greatest he," declared the Leveller Thomas Rainsborough, and therefore "any man that is born in England . . . ought to have his voice in election." Rainsborough even condemned slavery.

The Levellers offered a glimpse of the modern definition of freedom as a universal entitlement in a society based on equal rights, not a function of social class.

Another new group, the Diggers, went even further, hoping to give freedom an economic underpinning through the common ownership of land. Previous discussion of freedom, declared Gerard Winstanley, the Diggers' leader, had been misguided: "You are like men in a mist, seeking for freedom and know not what it is." True freedom applied equally "to the poor as well as the rich"; all were entitled to "a comfortable livelihood in this their own land." Even before the restoration of the monarchy, the Levellers, Diggers, and other radical movements spawned by the English Civil War had been crushed or driven underground. But some of the ideas of liberty that flourished during the 1640s and 1650s would be carried to America by English emigrants.

English Liberty

These struggles elevated the notion of "English liberty" to a central place in Anglo-American political culture. It became a major building block in the assertive sense of nationhood then being consolidated in England. The medieval idea of liberties as a collection of limited entitlements enjoyed by specific groups did not suddenly disappear. But it was increasingly overshadowed by a more general definition of freedom grounded in the common rights of all individuals within the English realm. All Englishmen were governed by a king, but "he rules over free men," according to the law, unlike the autocratic monarchs of France, Spain, Russia, and other countries.

The belief in freedom as the common heritage of all Englishmen and the conception of the British empire as the world's guardian of liberty helped to legitimize English colonization in the Western Hemisphere and to cast its imperial wars against Catholic France and Spain as struggles between freedom and tyranny.

The Civil War and English America

These struggles, accompanied by vigorous discussions of the rights of freeborn Englishmen, inevitably reverberated in England's colonies, dividing them from one another and internally. Most New Englanders sided with Parliament in the Civil War of the 1640s. Some returned to England to join the Parliamentary army or take up pulpits to help create a godly commonwealth at home. But Puritan leaders were increasingly uncomfortable as the idea of religious toleration for Protestants gained favor in England. It was the revolutionary Parliament that in 1644 granted Roger Williams his charter for the Rhode Island colony he had founded after being banished from Massachusetts.

Meanwhile, a number of followers of Anne Hutchinson became Quakers, one of the sects that sprang up in England during the Civil War. Quakers held that the spirit of God dwelled within every individual, not just the elect, and that this "inner light," rather than the Bible or teachings of the clergy, offered the surest guidance in spiritual matters. When Quakers appeared in Massachusetts, colonial officials had them whipped, fined, and banished. In 1659 and 1660, four Quakers who returned from exile were hanged, including Mary Dyer, a former disciple of Hutchinson.

The frontispiece of *Leviathan*, by Thomas Hobbes. Written during the English Civil War and published in 1651, two years after the execution of King Charles I, *Leviathan* argues that the only effective form of government is an absolute monarchy. Hobbes designed this image himself to illustrate his thesis. The king wields the sword of justice in one hand and the staff of an archbishop in the other—he combines the powers of church and state. His person is composed of his people; he is literally a body politic. Beneath him is a peaceful, orderly country, and beneath that, images of threats to public order, both secular and religious, against which the king must guard.

The execution of Charles I in 1649, a central event of the English Civil War.

The treatment of Quakers gave Massachusetts a reputation in England as a hotbed of religious persecution. When Charles II, after the restoration of the monarchy in 1660, reaffirmed the Massachusetts charter, he ordered the colony to recognize the "liberty of conscience" of all Protestants. But while hangings ceased, efforts to suppress the Quakers continued, as did attacks on Baptists, whose disdain for a learned ministry also seemed to threaten Puritan beliefs.

The Crisis in Maryland

Unlike the New England colonies, Virginia sided with Charles I. Its leaders even proclaimed Charles II king after his father's execution in 1649, although Oliver Cromwell's government in London soon brought the rebellious colony under control. In Maryland, the combination of the religious and political battles of the Civil War, homegrown conflict between Catholic and Protestant settlers, and anti-proprietary feeling produced a violent civil war within the colony, later recalled as the "plundering time." Indeed, Maryland in the 1640s verged on total anarchy, with a pro-Parliament force assaulting those loyal to Charles I. The emerging Protestant planter class longed to seize power from the Catholic elite created by Cecelius Calvert. The assembly's Protestant majority rejected laws proposed by the proprietor and claimed the same power to legislate and levy taxes enjoyed by the House of Commons in England.

To stabilize the colony and attract more settlers, Calvert appointed a Protestant governor and offered refuge to Protestant Dissenters being persecuted in Virginia, where Anglicanism was the established religion and laws restricted the religious and political rights of others. In 1649, Maryland adopted an **Act Concerning Religion (or Maryland Toleration Act)**, which institutionalized the principle of toleration that had prevailed from the colony's beginning. All Christians were guaranteed the "free exercise" of religion. The act did not establish religious liberty in a modern sense, since it punished those who denied the divinity of Jesus Christ

Meeting of the General Council of the Army at Putney, scene of the debate in 1647 over liberty and democracy between Levellers and more conservative army officers.

or the doctrine of the Holy Trinity. Indeed, a Jewish physician was soon arrested under its provisions. Nonetheless, the law was a milestone in the history of religious freedom in colonial America.

Turmoil, however, continued. During the 1650s, the Commonwealth government in London placed Maryland under the control of a Protestant council, which repealed the Toleration Act and forbade Catholics from openly practicing their religion. In 1657, however, Calvert's authority was restored and with it Maryland's experiment in religious freedom.

Cromwell and the Empire

Oliver Cromwell, who ruled England from 1649 until his death in 1658, undertook an aggressive policy of colonial expansion, the promotion of Protestantism, and commercial empowerment in the British Isles and the Western Hemisphere. His army forcibly extended English control over Ireland, massacring civilians, banning the public practice of Catholicism, and seizing land owned by Catholics. In the Caribbean, England seized Jamaica, a valuable sugar island, from Spain. In 1651, as will be related in Chapter 3, Parliament passed the first Navigation Act, which sought to challenge the Dutch hold on international commerce by confining colonial trade to English ships and ports.

Thus, by the middle of the seventeenth century, several English colonies existed along the Atlantic coast of North America. Established as part of an ad hoc process rather than arising under any coherent national plan, they differed enormously in economic, political, and social structure. The seeds had been planted, in the Chesapeake, for the development of plantation societies based on unfree labor, and in New England, for settlements centered on small towns and family farms. Throughout the colonies, many residents enjoyed freedoms they had not possessed at home, especially access to land and the right to worship as they desired. Others found themselves confined to unfree labor for many years or an entire lifetime.

The next century would be a time of crisis and consolidation as the population expanded, social conflicts intensified, and Britain moved to exert greater control over its flourishing North American colonies.

A portrait of Oliver Cromwell, who ruled England after the execution of Charles I, by the artist Sir Peter Lely.

England's colonial expansion

SUGGESTED READING

BOOKS

- Anderson, Virginia. *Creatures of Empire: How Domestic Animals Transformed Early America* (2006). Shows how livestock brought by English settlers helped to transform the colonial landscape and provoked conflict with Native Americans.

- Banner, Stuart. *How the Indians Lost Their Land: Law and Power on the Frontier* (2005). Argues that most Indian land came into settlers' hands by legal processes rather than conquest.

- Bonomi, Patricia. *Under the Cope of Heaven: Religion, Society, and Politics in Colonial America* (1986). Traces the interrelationship of religion and politics and the rise of religious diversity in the colonies.

- Brown, Kathleen. *Good Wives, Nasty Wenches, and Anxious Patriarchs: Gender, Race, and Power in Colonial Virginia* (1996). A pioneering study of gender relations and their impact on Virginia society.

- Cronon, William. *Changes in the Land: Colonists and the Ecology of New England* (1983). A pathbreaking examination of how English colonization affected the natural environment in New England.

- Gleach, Frederic W. *Powhatan's World and Colonial Virginia: A Conflict of Cultures* (1997). A study of Indian culture and the impact of European colonization upon it.

- Hill, Christopher. *The Century of Revolution* (1961). A survey stressing the causes and consequences of the English Civil War.

- Horn, James. *Adapting to a New World: English Society in the Seventeenth-Century Chesapeake* (1994). A detailed examination of the lives of early settlers in England and later in Virginia.

- Morgan, Edmund S. *The Puritan Family* (1944). An early examination of family life and gender relations in colonial America.

- Noll, Mark. *The Old Religion in a New World: The History of North American Christianity* (2001). Relates how the transplantation of European religions to America changed religious institutions and practices.

- Pestana, Carla G. *The English Atlantic in an Age of Revolution, 1640–1661* (2001). Analyzes how the English Civil War reverberated in the American colonies.

- Philbrick, Nathaniel. *Mayflower* (2006). An account of one of the most celebrated voyages of the colonial era, and the early history of the Plymouth colony.

- Price, David A. *Love and Hate in Jamestown: John Smith, Pocahontas, and the Start of a New Nation* (2003). Presents the legend and reality of John Smith, Pocahontas, and early Virginia.

- Taylor, Alan. *American Colonies* (2001). A comprehensive survey of the history of North American colonies from their beginnings to 1763.

- Winship, Michael. *Making Heretics: Militant Protestantism and Free Grace in Massachusetts, 1636–1641* (2002). The most recent account of Anne Hutchinson and the Antinomian controversy.

WEBSITES

- The Plymouth Colony Archive Project: www.histarch.illinois.edu/plymouth

- Virtual Jamestown: www.virtualjamestown.org

CHAPTER REVIEW AND ONLINE RESOURCES

REVIEW QUESTIONS

1. Compare and contrast settlement patterns, treatment of Indians, and religion of the Spanish and English in the Americas.

2. For English settlers, land was the basis of independence and liberty. Explain the reasoning behind that concept and how it differed from the Indians' conception of land.

3. Describe the factors promoting and limiting religious freedom in the New England and Chesapeake colonies.

4. Describe who chose to emigrate to North America from England in the seventeenth century and explain their reasons.

5. In what ways did the economy, government, and household structure differ in New England and the Chesapeake colonies?

6. The English believed that, unlike the Spanish, their motives for colonization were pure, and that the growth of empire and freedom would always go hand in hand. How did the expansion of the British empire affect the freedoms of Native Americans, the Irish, and even many English citizens?

7. Considering politics, social tensions, and debates over the meaning of liberty, how do the events and aftermath of the English Civil War demonstrate that the English colonies in North America were part of a larger Atlantic community?

8. How did the tobacco economy draw the Chesapeake colonies into the greater Atlantic world?

KEY TERMS

Virginia Company (p. 49)
Anglican Church (p. 50)
Roanoke colony (p. 51)
enclosure movement (p. 52)
John Smith (p. 58)
headright system (p. 59)
House of Burgesses (p. 59)
Uprising of 1622 (p. 60)
dower rights (p. 62)
Puritans (p. 64)
John Winthrop (p. 65)
Pilgrims (p. 66)
Mayflower Compact (p. 66)
Great Migration (p. 67)
Dissenters (p. 71)
captivity narratives (p. 73)
Pequot War (p. 76)
Half-Way Covenant (p. 78)
English liberty (p. 79)
Act Concerning Religion (or Maryland Toleration Act) (p. 82)

Go to 🐰 INQUIZITIVE

To see what you know—and learn what you've missed—with personalized feedback along the way.

Visit the *Give Me Liberty!* **Student Site** for primary source documents and images, interactive maps, author videos featuring Eric Foner, and more.

CHAPTER 3

CREATING

ANGLO-AMERICA

★

1660-1750

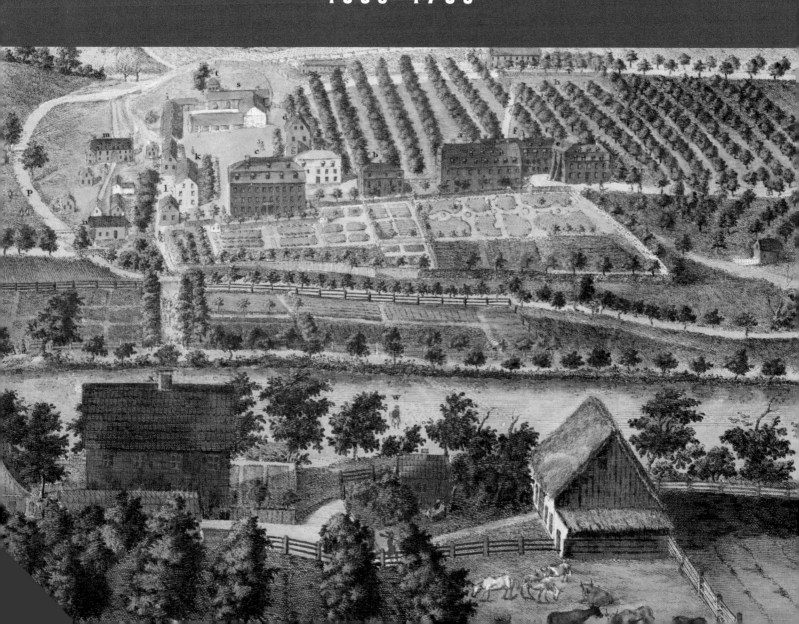

In the last quarter of the seventeenth century, a series of crises rocked the European colonies of North America. Social and political tensions boiled over in sometimes ruthless conflicts between rich and poor, free and slave, settler and Indian, and members of different religious groups. At the same time, struggles within and between European empires echoed in the colonies. Aggrieved groups seized upon the language of freedom to advance their goals. Although each conflict had its own local causes, taken together they added up to a general crisis of colonial society in the area that would become the United States.

The bloodiest and most bitter conflict occurred in southern New England, where in 1675 an Indian alliance launched attacks on farms and settlements that were encroaching on Indian lands. It was the most dramatic and violent warfare in the region in the entire seventeenth century.

New Englanders described the Wampanoag leader **Metacom** (known to the colonists as King Philip) as the uprising's mastermind, although in fact most tribes fought under their own leaders. By this time, the white population considerably outnumbered the Indians. But the fate of the New England colonies hung in the balance for several months. By 1676, Indian forces had attacked nearly half of New England's ninety towns. Twelve in Massachusetts were destroyed. As refugees fled eastward, the line of settlement was pushed back almost to the Atlantic coast. Some 1,000 settlers, out of a population of 52,000, and 3,000 of New England's 20,000 Indians perished in the fighting.

In mid-1676, the tide of battle turned and a ferocious counterattack broke the Indians' power once and for all. Although the uprising united numerous tribes, others remained loyal to the colonists. The role of the Iroquois in providing essential military aid to the colonists helped to solidify their developing alliance with the government of New York. Together, colonial and Indian forces inflicted devastating punishment on the rebels. Metacom was captured and executed, Indian villages were destroyed, and captives, including men, women, and children, were killed or sold into slavery in the West Indies. Most of the survivors fled to Canada or New York. Even the "praying Indians"—about 2,000 Indians who had converted to Christianity and lived in autonomous communities under Puritan supervision—suffered. Removed from their towns to Deer Island in Boston Harbor, supposedly for their own protection, many perished from disease and lack of food. Both sides committed atrocities in this merciless conflict, but in its aftermath the image of Indians as bloodthirsty savages became firmly entrenched in the New England mind.

In the long run, **King Philip's War** produced a broadening of freedom for white New Englanders by expanding their access to land. But this freedom rested on the final dispossession of the region's Indians.

FOCUS QUESTIONS

How did the English empire in America expand in the mid-seventeenth century? –p. 88

How was slavery established in the Western Atlantic world? –p. 94

What major social and political crises rocked the colonies in the late seventeenth century? –p. 101

What were the directions of social and economic change in the eighteenth-century colonies? –p. 106

How did patterns of class and gender roles change in eighteenth-century America? –p. 117

A View of Bethlehem, One of the Brethren's Principal Settlements in Pennsylvania, a lithograph produced in London in 1757, depicts a prosperous Moravian community, one of numerous settlements established by religious groups who emigrated from Europe to Britain's American colonies. In the left foreground, with a roof made of tiles from a local workshop, is the Crown Inn, which stood for over a century until razed to make way for a railroad. To its right is a large barn, with animals grazing nearby.

GLOBAL COMPETITION AND THE EXPANSION OF ENGLAND'S EMPIRE

The Mercantilist System

As the New World became a battleground in European nations' endless contests for wealth and power, England moved to seize control of Atlantic trade, solidify its hold on North America's eastern coast, and exert greater control over its empire. By the middle of the seventeenth century, it was apparent that the colonies could be an important source of wealth for the mother country. According to the prevailing theory known as **mercantilism**, the government should regulate economic activity so as to promote national power. It should encourage manufacturing and commerce by special bounties, monopolies, and other measures. Above all, trade should be controlled so that more gold and silver flowed into the country than left it. That is, exports of goods, which generated revenue from abroad, should exceed imports, which required paying foreigners for their products. In the mercantilist outlook, the role of colonies was to serve the interests of the mother country by producing marketable raw materials and importing manufactured goods from home. "Foreign trade," declared an influential work written in 1664 by a London merchant, formed the basis of "England's treasure." Commerce, not territorial plunder, was the foundation of empire.

Under Oliver Cromwell, Parliament passed in 1651 the first **Navigation Act**, which aimed to wrest control of world trade from the Dutch, whose merchants profited from free trade with all parts of the world and all existing empires. Additional measures followed in 1660 and 1663. England's new economic policy, mercantilism, rested on the idea that England should monopolize the profits arising from the English empire.

According to the Navigation laws, certain "enumerated" goods—essentially, the most valuable colonial products, such as tobacco and sugar—had to be transported in English ships and sold initially in English ports, although they could then be re-exported to foreign markets. Similarly, most European goods imported into the colonies had to be shipped through England, where customs duties were paid. This enabled English merchants, manufacturers, shipbuilders, and sailors to reap the benefits of colonial trade, and the government to enjoy added income from taxes. As members of the empire, American colonies would profit as well, since their ships were considered English. Indeed, the Navigation Acts stimulated the rise of New England's shipbuilding industry.

The Conquest of New Netherland

The restoration of the English monarchy when Charles II assumed the throne in 1660 sparked a new period of colonial expansion. The government chartered new trading ventures, notably the Royal African Company, which was given a monopoly of the slave trade. Within a generation, the number of English colonies in North America doubled. First to come under English control was New Netherland, seized in 1664 during an Anglo-Dutch war that also saw England gain control of Dutch trading posts in Africa. Charles II awarded the colony to his younger brother

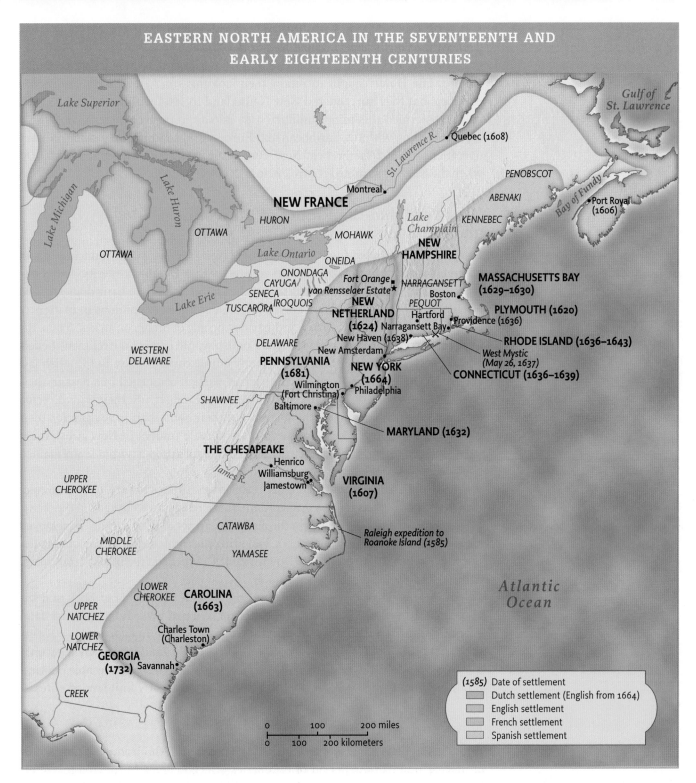

EASTERN NORTH AMERICA IN THE SEVENTEENTH AND EARLY EIGHTEENTH CENTURIES

Gulf of St. Lawrence

Lake Superior

Quebec (1608)

PENOBSCOT

Montreal

Lake Michigan

Lake Huron

NEW FRANCE

HURON

OTTAWA

ABENAKI

Bay of Fundy

Port Royal (1606)

KENNEBEC

Lake Champlain

NEW HAMPSHIRE

MOHAWK

OTTAWA

Lake Ontario

ONEIDA

ONONDAGA

CAYUGA

SENECA

IROQUOIS

TUSCARORA

Lake Erie

Fort Orange
van Rensselaer Estate ★

NARRAGANSETT

MASSACHUSETTS BAY (1629–1630)

Boston

NEW NETHERLAND (1624)

PEQUOT

PLYMOUTH (1620)

Hartford

Providence (1636)

Narragansett Bay

New Haven (1638)

RHODE ISLAND (1636–1643)

West Mystic (May 26, 1637)

CONNECTICUT (1636–1639)

New Amsterdam

WESTERN DELAWARE

DELAWARE

PENNSYLVANIA (1681)

NEW YORK (1664)

Wilmington (Fort Christina)

Philadelphia

SHAWNEE

Baltimore

MARYLAND (1632)

THE CHESAPEAKE

Henrico

James R.

Williamsburg

Jamestown

VIRGINIA (1607)

UPPER CHEROKEE

CATAWBA

Raleigh expedition to Roanoke Island (1585)

MIDDLE CHEROKEE

YAMASEE

Atlantic Ocean

LOWER CHEROKEE

CAROLINA (1663)

UPPER NATCHEZ

LOWER NATCHEZ

Charles Town (Charleston)

GEORGIA (1732) Savannah

CREEK

(1585)	Date of settlement
	Dutch settlement (English from 1664)
	English settlement
	French settlement
	Spanish settlement

0   100   200 miles
0 100 200 kilometers

By the early eighteenth century, numerous English colonies populated eastern North America, while the French had established their own presence to the north and west.

James, the duke of York, with "full and absolute power" to govern as he pleased. (Hence the colony's name became New York.)

New Netherland had always remained peripheral to the far-flung Dutch empire. The Dutch fought to retain their holdings in Africa, Asia, and South America, but they surrendered New Netherland in 1664 without a fight. English rule transformed this minor military base into an important imperial outpost, a seaport trading with the Caribbean and Europe, and a launching pad for military operations against the French. New York's European population, around 9,000 when the English assumed control, rose to 20,000 by 1685.

English rule in New York

New York and the Rights of Englishmen and Englishwomen

English rule expanded the freedom of some New Yorkers, while reducing that of others. Many English observers had concluded that Dutch prosperity—what one writer called "the prodigious increase of the Netherlanders in their domestic and foreign trade"—stemmed from "their toleration of different opinions in matters of religion," which attracted "many industrious people of other countries." Thus, the terms of surrender guaranteed that the English would respect the religious beliefs and property holdings of the colony's many ethnic communities. But English law ended the Dutch tradition by which married women conducted business in their own name. As colonists of Dutch origin adapted to English rule, their wills directed more attention to advancing the fortunes of their sons than providing for their wives and daughters. There had been many female traders in New Amsterdam (often widows who had inherited a deceased husband's property), but few remained by the end of the seventeenth century.

English rule and women

The English also introduced more restrictive attitudes toward blacks. In colonial New York City, as in New Amsterdam, those residents who enjoyed the status of "freeman," obtained by birth in the city or by an act of local authorities, enjoyed special privileges compared to others, including the right to work in various trades. But the English, in a reversal of Dutch practice, expelled free blacks from many skilled jobs.

English rule and blacks

Others benefited enormously from English rule. The duke of York and his appointed governors continued the Dutch practice of awarding immense land grants to favorites, including 160,000 acres to Robert Livingston and 90,000 to Frederick Philipse. By 1700, nearly 2 million acres of land were owned by only five New York families who intermarried regularly, exerted considerable political influence, and formed one of colonial America's most tightly knit landed elites.

New York and the Indians

Initially, English rule also strengthened the position of the Iroquois Confederacy of upstate New York. After a complex series of negotiations in the mid-1670s, Sir Edmund Andros, who had been appointed governor of New York after fighting the French in the Caribbean, formed an alliance known as the **Covenant Chain**, in which the imperial ambitions of the English and Indians reinforced one another. The Five (later Six) Iroquois Nations assisted Andros in clearing parts of New York of rival tribes and helped the British in attacks on the French and their Indian

The Covenant Chain

An engraving representing the Grand Council of the Iroquois Nations of the area of present-day upstate New York. From a book about American Indians published in Paris by a Jesuit missionary, who depicts the Indians in the attire of ancient Romans. Note the prevalence of wampum belts in the image, in the foreground and in the hand and at the feet of the central figure. Wampum was used to certify treaties and other transactions.

allies. Andros, for his part, recognized the Iroquois claim to authority over Indian communities in the vast area stretching to the Ohio River. But beginning in the 1680s, Indians around the Great Lakes and Ohio Valley regrouped and with French aid attacked the Iroquois, pushing them to the east. By the end of the century, the Iroquois Nations adopted a policy of careful neutrality, seeking to play the European empires off one another while continuing to profit from the fur trade.

The Iroquois Nations

The Charter of Liberties

Many colonists, meanwhile, began to complain that they were being denied the "liberties of Englishmen," especially the right to consent to taxation. There had been no representative assembly under the Dutch, and the governors appointed by the duke of York at first ruled without one. Discontent was especially strong on Long Island, which had been largely settled by New Englanders used to self-government.

In 1683, the duke agreed to call an elected assembly, whose first act was to draft a Charter of Liberties and Privileges. The charter required that elections be held every three years among male property owners and the freemen of New York City; it also reaffirmed traditional English rights such as trial by jury and security of property, as well as religious toleration for all Protestants. In part, the charter reflected an effort by newer English colonists to assert dominance over older Dutch settlers by establishing the principle that the "liberties" to which New Yorkers were entitled were those enjoyed by Englishmen at home.

English rights

The Founding of Carolina

For more than three decades after the establishment of Maryland in 1632, no new English settlement was planted in North America. Then, in 1663, Charles II awarded to eight proprietors the right to establish a colony to the north of Florida, as a barrier to Spanish expansion. Not until 1670 did the first settlers arrive to found Carolina. In its early years, Carolina was the "colony of a colony." It began as an offshoot of the tiny island of Barbados. In the mid-seventeenth century, Barbados was the Caribbean's richest plantation economy, but a shortage of available land led wealthy planters to seek opportunities in Carolina for their sons. The early settlers of Carolina sought Indian allies by offering guns for deer hides and captives, a policy that unleashed widespread raiding among Indians for slaves to sell. The colonists also encouraged native allies to attack Indians in Spanish Florida; in one series of wars between 1704 and 1706 the Creek, Savannah, and Yamasee enslaved almost 10,000 Florida Indians, most of them shipped to other mainland colonies and the West Indies. Indeed, between 1670 and 1720, the number of Indian slaves exported from Charleston was larger than the number of African slaves imported. In 1715, the Yamasee and Creek, alarmed by the enormous debts they had incurred in trade with the settlers and by slave traders' raids into their territory, rebelled. The **Yamasee uprising** was crushed, and most of the remaining Indians were enslaved or driven out of the colony into Spanish Florida, from where they occasionally launched raids against English settlements.

Indian slavery

The Fundamental Constitutions of Carolina, issued by the proprietors in 1669, proposed to establish a feudal society with a hereditary nobility (with strange titles like landgraves and caciques), serfs, and slaves. Needing to attract settlers quickly, however, the proprietors also provided for an elected assembly and religious toleration—by now recognized as essential to enticing migrants to North America. They also instituted a generous headright system, offering 150 acres for each member of an arriving family (in the case of indentured servants, of course, the land went to the employer) and 100 acres to male servants who completed their terms.

The Fundamental Constitutions of Carolina

None of the baronies envisioned in the Fundamental Constitutions were actually established. Slavery, not feudalism, made Carolina an extremely hierarchical society. The proprietors instituted a rigorous legal code that promised slaveowners "absolute power and authority" over their human property and included imported slaves in the headright system. This allowed any persons who settled in Carolina and brought with them slaves, including planters from Barbados who resettled in the colony, instantly to acquire large new landholdings. In its early days, however, the economy centered on cattle raising and trade with local Indians, not agriculture. Carolina grew slowly until planters discovered the staple—rice—that would make them the wealthiest elite in English North America and their colony an epicenter of mainland slavery.

The Holy Experiment

The last English colony to be established in the seventeenth century was Pennsylvania. The proprietor, William Penn, envisioned it as a place where those facing religious persecution in Europe could enjoy spiritual freedom, and colonists and Indians would coexist in harmony. Penn's late father had been a supporter and creditor of Charles II. To cancel his debt to the Penn family and bolster the English presence in North America, the king in 1681 granted Penn a vast tract of land south and west of New York, as well as the old Swedish-Dutch colony that became Delaware.

A portrait of William Penn, founder of Pennsylvania, by the British artist Francis Place.

A devout member of the **Society of Friends, or Quakers**, Penn was particularly concerned with establishing a refuge for his coreligionists, who faced increasing persecution in England. He had already assisted a group of English Quakers in purchasing half of what became the colony of New Jersey from Lord John Berkeley, who had received a land grant from the duke of York. Penn was largely responsible for the frame of government announced in 1677, the West Jersey Concessions, one of the most liberal of the era. Based on Quaker ideals, it created an elected assembly with a broad suffrage and established religious liberty. Penn hoped that West Jersey would become a society of small farmers, not large landowners.

Quaker Liberty

Like the Puritans, Penn considered his colony a "holy experiment," but of a different kind—"a free colony for all mankind that should go hither." He hoped that Pennsylvania could be governed according to Quaker principles, among them the equality of all persons (including women, blacks, and Indians) before God and the primacy of the individual conscience. To Quakers, liberty was a universal entitlement, not the possession of any single people—a position that would eventually make them the first group of whites to repudiate slavery. Penn also treated Indians with a consideration almost unique in the colonial experience, arranging to purchase land before reselling it to colonists and offering refuge to tribes driven out of other colonies by warfare. Sometimes, he even purchased the same land twice, when more than one Indian tribe claimed it. Since Quakers were pacifists who came to America unarmed and did not even organize a militia until the 1740s, peace with the native population was essential. Penn's Chain of Friendship appealed to the local Indians, promising protection from rival tribes who claimed domination over them.

Religious freedom was Penn's most fundamental principle. He condemned attempts to enforce "religious Uniformity" for depriving thousands of "free inhabitants" of England of the right to worship as they desired. His Charter of Liberty, approved by the assembly in 1682, offered "Christian liberty" to all who affirmed a belief in God and did not use their freedom to promote "licentiousness." There was no established church in Pennsylvania, and attendance at religious services was entirely voluntary, although Jews were barred from office by a required oath affirming belief in the divinity of Jesus Christ. At the same time, the Quakers upheld a strict code of personal morality. Penn's Frame of Government prohibited swearing, drunkenness, and adultery, as well as popular entertainments of the era such as "revels, bull-baiting, and cock-fighting." Private religious belief may not have been enforced by the government, but moral public behavior certainly was. Not religious uniformity but a virtuous citizenry would be the foundation of Penn's social order.

An early-eighteenth-century engraving depicts William Penn welcoming a German immigrant on the dock in Philadelphia. Penn sought to make migrants from all over Europe feel at home in Pennsylvania.

Penn and religious liberty

Land in Pennsylvania

Given the power to determine the colony's form of government, Penn established an appointed council to originate legislation and an assembly elected by male taxpayers and "freemen" (owners of 100 acres of land for free immigrants and 50 acres for former indentured servants). These rules made a majority of the male population eligible to vote. Penn owned all the colony's land and sold it to settlers at low prices rather than granting it outright. Like other proprietors, he expected to turn a profit, and like most of them, he never really did. But if Penn did not prosper, Pennsylvania did. A majority of the early settlers were Quakers from the British Isles. But Pennsylvania's religious toleration, healthy climate, and inexpensive land, along with Penn's aggressive efforts to publicize the colony's advantages, soon attracted immigrants from all over western Europe.

Ironically, the freedoms Pennsylvania offered to European immigrants contributed to the deterioration of freedom for others. The colony's successful efforts to attract settlers would eventually come into conflict with Penn's benevolent Indian policy. And the opening of Pennsylvania led to an immediate decline in the number of indentured servants choosing to sail for Virginia and Maryland, a development that did much to shift those colonies toward reliance on slave labor.

A Quaker Meeting, a painting by an unidentified British artist, dating from the late eighteenth or early nineteenth century. It illustrates the prominent place of women in Quaker gatherings.

ORIGINS OF AMERICAN SLAVERY

The turn to slavery

No European nation, including England, embarked on the colonization of the New World with the intention of relying on African slaves for the bulk of its labor force. But the incessant demand for workers spurred by the spread of tobacco cultivation eventually led Chesapeake planters to turn to the transatlantic trade in slaves. Compared with indentured servants, slaves offered planters many advantages. As Africans, they could not claim the protections of English common law. Slaves' terms of service never expired, and they therefore did not become a population of unruly landless men. Their children were slaves, and their skin color made it more difficult for them to escape into the surrounding society. African men, moreover, unlike their Native American counterparts, were accustomed to intensive agricultural labor, and they had encountered many diseases known in Europe and developed resistance to them, so were less likely to succumb to epidemics.

Englishmen and Africans

English views of alien peoples

The English had long viewed alien peoples with disdain, including the Irish, Native Americans, and Africans. They described these strangers in remarkably similar language as savage, pagan, and uncivilized, often comparing them to animals. "Race"—the idea that humanity is divided into well-defined groups associated with skin color—is a modern concept that had not fully developed in the seventeenth century. Nor had "racism"—an ideology based on the belief that some

Race and racism

races are inherently superior to others and entitled to rule over them. The main lines of division within humanity were thought to be civilization versus barbarism or Christianity versus heathenism, not color or race.

Nonetheless, anti-black stereotypes flourished in seventeenth-century England. Africans were seen as so alien—in color, religion, and social practices—that they were "enslavable" in a way that poor Englishmen were not. Most English also deemed Indians to be uncivilized. But the Indian population declined so rapidly, and it was so easy for Indians, familiar with the countryside, to run away, that Indian slavery never became viable. Some Indians were sold into slavery in the Caribbean. But it is difficult to enslave a people on their native soil. Slaves are almost always outsiders, transported from elsewhere to their place of labor.

Slavery in History

Slavery has existed for nearly the entire span of human history. It was central to the societies of ancient Greece and Rome. Slavery survived for centuries in northern Europe after the collapse of the Roman Empire. Germans, Vikings, and Anglo-Saxons all held slaves. Slavery persisted even longer in the Mediterranean world, where a slave trade in Slavic peoples survived into the fifteenth century. (The English word "slavery" derives from "Slav.") Pirates from the Barbary Coast of North Africa regularly seized Christians from ships and enslaved them. In West Africa, as noted in Chapter 1, slavery and a slave trade predated the coming of Europeans, and small-scale slavery existed among Native Americans. But slavery in nearly all these instances differed greatly from the institution that developed in the New World.

In the Americas, slavery was based on the **plantation**, an agricultural enterprise that brought together large numbers of workers under the control of a single owner. This imbalance magnified the possibility of slave resistance and made it necessary

Plantation slavery

In *Free Women of Color with Their Children and Servants in a Landscape*, Agostino Brunias, an Italian artist who was sent to the West Indies by the British government in the 1760s to paint the local population, portrays an outing of fashionable free women with their children and slaves, some dressed in livery. Although the scene depicted is in the Caribbean, the work resembles numerous paintings of the leisure activities of the well-to-do in Britain. The painting reflects the three-race system that developed in the British Caribbean— the free women are light-skinned but not white. The woman at the center looks directly at the viewer, emphasizing her aristocratic bearing.

Cutting Sugar Cane, an engraving from *Ten Views in Antigua*, published in 1823. Male and female slaves harvest and load the sugar crop while an overseer on horseback addresses a slave. During the eighteenth century, sugar was the chief crop produced by Western Hemisphere slaves.

to police the system rigidly. It encouraged the creation of a sharp boundary between slavery and freedom. Labor on slave plantations was far more demanding than in the household slavery common in Africa, and the death rate among slaves much higher. In the New World, slavery would come to be associated with race, a concept that drew a permanent line between whites and blacks. Unlike in Africa, slaves in the Americas who became free always carried with them in their skin color the mark of bondage—a visible sign of being considered unworthy of incorporation as equals into free society.

Slavery in the West Indies

A sense of Africans as alien and inferior made their enslavement by the English possible. But prejudice by itself did not create North American slavery. For this institution to take root, planters and government authorities had to be convinced that importing African slaves was the best way to solve their persistent shortage of labor. During the seventeenth century, the shipping of slaves from Africa to the New World became a major international business. But only a relative handful were brought to England's mainland colonies. By the time plantation slavery became a major feature of life in English North America, it was already well entrenched elsewhere in the Western Hemisphere. By 1600, huge sugar plantations worked by slaves from Africa had made their appearance in Brazil, a colony of Portugal. In the seventeenth century, England, Holland, Denmark, and France joined Spain as owners of West Indian islands. English emigrants to the West Indies outnumbered those to North America in the first part of the seventeenth century. In 1650, the English population of the West Indies exceeded that in all of North America. Generally, the first settlers established mixed economies with small farms worked by white indentured servants. But as sugar planters engrossed the best land, they forced white

Slaves and the shortage of labor

Sugar plantations

farmers off island after island. White indentured servants proved as discontented as elsewhere. In 1629, when a Spanish expedition attacked the British island of Nevis, servants in the local militia joined them shouting, "Liberty, joyful liberty!"

With the Indian population having been wiped out by disease, and with the white indentured servants unwilling to do the back-breaking, monotonous work of sugar cultivation, the massive importation of slaves from Africa began. In 1645, for example, Barbados, a tiny island owned by England, was home to around 11,000 white farmers and indentured servants and 5,000 slaves. As sugar cultivation intensified, planters turned increasingly to slave labor. By 1660, the island's population had grown to 40,000, half European and half African. Ten years later, the slave population had risen to 82,000, concentrated on some 750 sugar plantations. Meanwhile, the white population stagnated. By the end of the seventeenth century, huge sugar plantations manned by hundreds of slaves dominated the West Indian economy, and on most of the islands the African population far outnumbered that of European origin.

Barbados

Sugar was the first crop to be mass-marketed to consumers in Europe. Before its emergence, international trade consisted largely of precious metals like gold and silver, and luxury goods aimed at an elite market, like the spices and silks imported from Asia. Sugar was by far the most important product of the British, French, and Portuguese empires, and New World sugar plantations produced immense profits for planters, merchants, and imperial governments. Saint Domingue, today's Haiti, was the jewel of the French empire. In 1660, Barbados generated more trade than all the other English colonies combined.

Sugar

Compared to its rapid introduction in Brazil and the West Indies, slavery developed slowly in North America. Slaves cost more than indentured servants, and the high death rate among tobacco workers made it economically unappealing to pay for a lifetime of labor. For decades, servants from England formed the backbone of the Chesapeake labor force, and the number of Africans remained small. As late as 1680, there were only 4,500 blacks in the Chesapeake, a little more than 5 percent of the region's population. The most important social distinction in

Slow development in North America

A lithograph by the German artist Johann Moritz Rugendas, who visited Brazil in the early 1820s, depicts the operation of a sugar mill. Slaves feed the cane into rollers, which grind it to crush out the juice.

In this scene depicted on an English handkerchief, male and female slaves work in the tobacco fields alongside a white indentured servant (*right*).

the seventeenth-century Chesapeake was not between black and white but between the white plantation owners who dominated politics and society and everybody else—small farmers, indentured servants, and slaves.

Slavery and the Law

English and Spanish empires compared on slavery

Centuries before the voyages of Columbus, Spain had enacted *Las Siete Partidas*, a series of laws granting slaves certain rights relating to marriage, the holding of property, and access to freedom. These laws were transferred to Spain's American empire. They were often violated, but nonetheless gave slaves opportunities to claim rights under the law. Moreover, the Catholic Church often encouraged masters to free individual slaves. The law of slavery in English North America would become far more repressive than in the Spanish empire, especially on the all-important question of whether avenues existed by which slaves could obtain freedom.

Chesapeake blacks

For much of the seventeenth century, however, the legal status of Chesapeake blacks remained ambiguous and the line between slavery and freedom more permeable than it would later become. The first Africans, twenty in all, arrived in Virginia in 1619. British pirates sailing under the Dutch flag had seized them from a Portuguese ship carrying slaves from Angola, on the southwestern coast of Africa, to modern-day Mexico. Small numbers followed in subsequent years. Although the first black arrivals were almost certainly treated as slaves, it appears that at least some managed to become free after serving a term of years. To be sure, racial distinctions were enacted into law from the outset. As early as the 1620s, the law barred blacks from serving in the Virginia militia. The government punished sexual relations outside of marriage between Africans and Europeans more severely than the same acts involving two white persons. In 1643, a poll tax (a tax levied on individuals) was imposed on African but not white women. In both Virginia and Maryland, however, free blacks could sue and testify in court, and some even managed to acquire land and purchase white servants or African slaves. It is not known exactly how Anthony Johnson, who apparently arrived in Virginia as a slave during the 1620s, obtained his freedom. But by the 1640s, he was the owner of slaves and of several hundred acres of land on Virginia's eastern shore. Blacks and whites labored side by side in the tobacco fields, sometimes ran away together, and established intimate relationships.

The Rise of Chesapeake Slavery

Evidence of blacks being held as slaves for life appears in the historical record of the 1640s. In registers of property, for example, white servants are listed by the number of years of labor, while blacks, with higher valuations, have no terms of service associated with their names. Not until the 1660s, however, did the laws of Virginia and Maryland refer explicitly to slavery. As tobacco planting spread and the demand for labor increased, the condition of black and white servants diverged sharply. Authorities sought to improve the status of white servants, hoping to counteract the widespread impression in England that Virginia was a death trap. At the same time, access to freedom for blacks receded.

The development of slavery

A Virginia law of 1662 provided that in the case of a child one of whose parents was free and one slave, the status of the offspring followed that of the mother. (This provision not only reversed the European practice of defining a child's status through the father but also made the sexual abuse of slave women profitable for slaveholders, since any children that resulted remained the owner's property.) In 1667, the Virginia House of Burgesses decreed that religious conversion did not release a slave from bondage. Thus, Christians could own other Christians as slaves. Moreover, authorities sought to prevent the growth of the free black population by defining all offspring of interracial relationships as illegitimate, severely punishing white women who begat children with black men, and prohibiting the freeing of any slave unless he or she was transported out of the colony. By 1680, even though the black population was still small, notions of racial difference were well entrenched in the law. In England's American empire, wrote one contemporary, "these two words, Negro and Slave [have] by custom grown homogenous and convertible." In British North America, unlike the Spanish empire, no distinctive mulatto, or mixed-race, class existed; the law treated everyone with African ancestry as black.

Black slavery

Bacon's Rebellion: Land and Labor in Virginia

Virginia's shift from white indentured servants to African slaves as the main plantation labor force was accelerated by one of the most dramatic confrontations of this era, **Bacon's Rebellion** of 1676. Governor William Berkeley had for thirty years run a corrupt regime in alliance with an inner circle of the colony's wealthiest tobacco planters. He rewarded his followers with land grants and lucrative offices. At first, Virginia's tobacco boom had benefited not only planters but also smaller farmers, some of them former servants who managed to acquire farms. But as tobacco farming spread inland, planters connected with the governor engrossed the best lands, leaving freed servants (a growing population, since Virginia's death rate was finally falling) with no options but to work as tenants or to move to the frontier. At the same time, heavy taxes on tobacco and falling prices because of overproduction reduced the prospects of small farmers. By the 1670s, poverty among whites had reached levels reminiscent of England. In addition, the right to vote, previously enjoyed by all adult men, was confined to landowners in 1670. Governor Berkeley maintained peaceful relations with Virginia's remaining native population. His refusal to allow white settlement in areas reserved for Indians angered many land-hungry colonists.

Social tensions in Virginia

Sir William Berkeley, governor of colonial Virginia, 1641–1652 and 1660–1677, in a portrait by Sir Peter Lely. Berkeley's authoritarian rule helped to spark Bacon's Rebellion.

Effects of Bacon's Rebellion

In 1676, long-simmering social tensions coupled with widespread resentment against the injustices of the Berkeley regime erupted in Bacon's Rebellion. The spark was a minor confrontation between Indians and colonists on Virginia's western frontier. Settlers now demanded that the governor authorize the extermination or removal of the colony's Indians, to open more land for whites. Fearing all-out warfare and continuing to profit from the trade with Indians in deerskins, Berkeley refused. An uprising followed that soon careened out of control. Beginning with a series of Indian massacres, it quickly grew into a full-fledged rebellion against Berkeley and his system of rule.

To some extent, Bacon's Rebellion was a conflict within the Virginia elite. The leader, Nathaniel Bacon, a wealthy and ambitious planter who had arrived in Virginia in 1673, disdained Berkeley's coterie as men of "mean education and employments." His backers included men of wealth outside the governor's circle of cronies. But Bacon's call for the removal of all Indians from the colony, a reduction of taxes at a time of economic recession, and an end to rule by "grandees" rapidly gained support from small farmers, landless men, indentured servants, and even some Africans. The bulk of his army consisted of discontented men who had recently been servants.

The End of the Rebellion, and Its Consequences

Bacon promised freedom (including access to Indian lands) to all who joined his ranks. His supporters invoked the tradition of "English liberties" and spoke of the poor being "robbed" and "cheated" by their social superiors. In 1676, Bacon gathered an armed force for an unauthorized and indiscriminate campaign against those he called the governor's "protected and darling Indians." He refused Berkeley's order to disband and marched on Jamestown, burning it to the ground. The governor fled, and Bacon became the ruler of Virginia. His forces plundered the estates of Berkeley's supporters. Only the arrival of a squadron of warships from England restored order. Bacon's Rebellion was over. Twenty-three of his supporters were hanged (Bacon himself had taken ill and died shortly after Berkeley's departure).

The specter of a civil war among whites greatly frightened Virginia's ruling elite, who took dramatic steps to consolidate their power and improve their image. They restored property qualifications for voting, which Bacon had rescinded. At the same time, planters developed a new political style in which they cultivated the support of poorer neighbors. Meanwhile, the authorities reduced taxes and adopted a more aggressive Indian policy, opening western areas to small farmers, many of whom prospered from a rise in tobacco prices after 1680. To avert the further rise of a rebellious population of landless former indentured servants, Virginia's authorities accelerated the shift to slaves (who would never become free) on the tobacco plantations. As Virginia reduced the number of indentured servants, it redefined their freedom dues to include fifty acres of land.

A Slave Society

Between 1680 and 1700, slave labor began to supplant indentured servitude on Chesapeake plantations. Bacon's Rebellion was only one among several factors that contributed to this development. As the death rate finally began to fall, it became more economical to purchase a laborer for life. Improving conditions in England reduced the number of transatlantic migrants, and the opening of Pennsylvania, where land was readily available, attracted those who still chose to leave for America. Finally, the ending of a monopoly on the English slave trade previously enjoyed by the Royal Africa Company opened the door to other traders and reduced the price of imported African slaves.

The spread of slavery

By 1700, blacks constituted more than 10 percent of Virginia's population. Fifty years later, they made up nearly half. Recognizing the growing importance of slavery, the House of Burgesses in 1705 enacted a new slave code, bringing together the scattered legislation of the previous century and adding new provisions that embedded the principle of white supremacy in the law. Slaves were property, completely subject to the will of their masters and, more generally, of the white community. They could be bought and sold, leased, fought over in court, and passed on to one's descendants. Henceforth, blacks and whites were tried in separate courts. No black, free or slave, could own arms, strike a white man, or employ a white servant. Any white person could apprehend any black to demand a certificate of freedom or a pass from the owner giving permission to be off the plantation. Virginia had changed from a "society with slaves," in which slavery was one system of labor among others, to a "slave society," where slavery stood at the center of the economic process.

Slave code of 1705

Notions of Freedom

Throughout history, slaves have run away and in other ways resisted bondage. They did the same in the colonial Chesapeake. Colonial newspapers were filled with advertisements for runaway slaves. These notices described the appearance and skills of the fugitive and included such comments as "ran away without any cause" or "he has great notions of freedom." Some of the blacks brought to the region during the seventeenth century were the offspring of encounters between European traders and Africans on the western coast of Africa or the Caribbean. Familiar with European culture and fluent in English, they turned to the colonial legal system in their quest for freedom. Throughout the seventeenth century, blacks appeared in court claiming their liberty, at first on the basis of conversion to Christianity or having a white father. This was one reason Virginia in the 1660s closed these pathways to freedom. But although legal avenues to liberty receded, the desire for freedom did not. After the suppression of a slave conspiracy in 1709, Alexander Spotswood, the governor of Virginia, warned planters to be vigilant. The desire for freedom, he reminded them, can "call together all those who long to shake off the fetters of slavery."

Runaway slaves

COLONIES IN CRISIS

King Philip's War of 1675–1676 and Bacon's Rebellion the following year coincided with disturbances in other colonies. In Maryland, where the proprietor, Lord Baltimore, in 1670 had suddenly restricted the right to vote to owners of fifty acres of land or a certain amount of personal property, a Protestant uprising unsuccessfully sought to oust his government and restore the suffrage for all freemen. In several

Uprisings

A scene from King Philip's War, included on a 1675 map of New England.

colonies, increasing settlement on the frontier led to resistance by alarmed Indians. A rebellion by Westo Indians was suppressed in Carolina in 1680. The Pueblo Revolt of the same year (discussed in Chapter 1) indicated that the crisis of colonial authority was not confined to the British empire.

The Glorious Revolution

Parliamentary supremacy

Turmoil in England also reverberated in the colonies. In 1688, the long struggle for domination of English government between Parliament and the crown reached its culmination in the **Glorious Revolution**, which established parliamentary supremacy once and for all and secured the Protestant succession to the throne. Under Charles II, Parliament had asserted its authority in the formation of national policy. It expanded its control of finance, influenced foreign affairs, and excluded from political and religious power Catholics and Dissenters (Protestants who belonged to a denomination other than the official Anglican Church).

When Charles died in 1685, he was succeeded by his brother James II (formerly the duke of York), a practicing Catholic and a believer that kings ruled by divine right. In 1687, James decreed religious toleration for both Protestant Dissenters and Catholics. The following year, the birth of James's son raised the prospect of a Catholic succession, alarming those who equated "popery" with tyranny. A group of English aristocrats invited the Dutch nobleman William of Orange, the husband of James's Protestant daughter Mary, to assume the throne in the name of English liberties. William arrived in England in November 1688 with an army of 21,000 men, two-thirds of them Dutch. As the landed elite and leaders of the Anglican Church rallied to William's cause, James II fled and the revolution was complete.

Liberty as the birthright of all Englishmen

Unlike the broad social upheaval that marked the English Civil War of the 1640s, the Glorious Revolution was in effect a coup engineered by a small group of aristocrats in alliance with an ambitious Dutch prince. They had no intention of challenging the institution of the monarchy. But the overthrow of James II entrenched more firmly than ever the notion that liberty was the birthright of all Englishmen and that the king was subject to the rule of law. To justify the ouster of James II, Parliament in 1689 enacted an **English Bill of Rights**, which listed parliamentary powers such as control over taxation as well as rights of individuals, including trial by jury. These were the "ancient" and "undoubted . . . rights and liberties" of all Englishmen. In the following year, the Toleration Act allowed Protestant Dissenters (but not Catholics) to worship freely, although only Anglicans could hold public office.

As always, British politics were mirrored in the American colonies. After the Glorious Revolution, Protestant domination was secured in most of the colonies, with the established churches of England (Anglican) and Scotland (Presbyterian) growing the fastest, while Catholics and Dissenters suffered various forms of discrimination. Despite the new regime's language of liberty, however, religious freedom was far more advanced in some American colonies, such as Rhode Island, Pennsylvania, and Carolina, than in England. Nonetheless, throughout English America the Glorious Revolution powerfully reinforced among the colonists the sense of sharing a proud legacy of freedom and Protestantism with the mother country.

King William III, a portrait by an unknown artist, painted around 1697. William, who came to power in England as a result of the Glorious Revolution, wears an ermine cape.

The Glorious Revolution in America

The Glorious Revolution exposed fault lines in colonial society and offered local elites an opportunity to regain authority that had recently been challenged. Until the mid-1670s, the North American colonies had essentially governed themselves, with little interference from England. Governor Berkeley ran Virginia as he saw fit; proprietors in New York, Maryland, and Carolina governed in any fashion they could persuade colonists to accept; and New England colonies elected their own officials and openly flouted trade regulations. In 1675, England established the **Lords of Trade** to oversee colonial affairs. Three years later, the Lords questioned the Massachusetts government about its compliance with the Navigation Acts. They received the surprising reply that since the colony had no representatives in Parliament, the acts did not apply to it unless the Massachusetts General Court approved.

In the 1680s, England moved to reduce colonial autonomy. Shortly before his death, Charles II revoked the Massachusetts charter, citing wholesale violations of the Navigation Acts. Hoping to raise more money from America in order to reduce his dependence on Parliament, James II between 1686 and 1689 combined Connecticut, Plymouth, Massachusetts, New Hampshire, Rhode Island, New York, and East and West Jersey into a single super-colony, the **Dominion of New England**. It was ruled by the former New York governor Sir Edmund Andros, who did not have to answer to an elected assembly. These events reinforced the impression that James II was an enemy of freedom. In New England, Andros's actions alienated nearly everyone not dependent on his administration for favors. He appointed local officials in place of elected ones, imposed taxes without the approval of elected representatives, declared earlier land grants void unless approved by him, and enforced religious toleration for all Protestants. His rule threatened both English liberties and the church-state relationship at the heart of the Puritan order.

> *English authority and colonial autonomy*

The Maryland Uprising

In 1689, news of the overthrow of James II triggered rebellions in several American colonies. In April, the Boston militia seized and jailed Edmund Andros and other officials, whereupon the New England colonies reestablished the governments

> *Rebellions in American colonies*

abolished when the Dominion of New England was created. In May, a rebel militia headed by Captain Jacob Leisler established a Committee of Safety and took control of New York. Two months later, Maryland's Protestant Association overthrew the government of the colony's Catholic proprietor, Lord Baltimore.

All of these new regimes claimed to have acted in the name of English liberties and looked to London for approval. But the degrees of success of these coups varied markedly. Most triumphant were the Maryland rebels. Concluding that Lord Baltimore had mismanaged the colony, William revoked his charter (although the proprietor retained his land and rents) and established a new, Protestant-dominated government. Catholics retained the right to practice their religion but were barred from voting and holding office. In 1715, after the Baltimore family had converted to Anglicanism, proprietary power was restored. But the events of 1689 transformed the ruling group in Maryland and put an end to the colony's unique history of religious toleration.

Leisler's Rebellion

Turmoil in New York

The outcome in New York was far different. The German-born Leisler, one of the wealthiest merchants in the city, was a fervent Calvinist who feared that James II intended to reduce England and its empire to "popery and slavery." Although it was not his intention, Leisler's regime divided the colony along ethnic and economic lines. Members of the Dutch majority seized the opportunity to reclaim local power after more than two decades of English rule, while bands of rebels ransacked the homes of wealthy New Yorkers. Prominent English colonists, joined by some wealthy Dutch merchants and fur traders, protested to London that Leisler was a tyrant. William refused to recognize Leisler's authority and dispatched a new governor, backed by troops. Many of Leisler's followers were imprisoned, and he himself was condemned to be executed. The grisly manner of his death—Leisler was hanged and then had his head cut off and body cut into four parts—reflected the depths of hatred the rebellion had inspired. For generations, the rivalry between Leisler and anti-Leisler parties polarized New York politics.

Changes in New England

Political change in Massachusetts

After deposing Edmund Andros, the New England colonies lobbied hard in London for the restoration of their original charters. Most were successful, but Massachusetts was not. In 1691, the crown issued a new charter that absorbed Plymouth into Massachusetts and transformed the political structure of the Bible Commonwealth. Town government remained intact, but henceforth property ownership, not church membership, would be the requirement to vote in elections for the General Court. The governor was now appointed in London rather than elected. Thus, Massachusetts became a royal colony, the majority of whose voters were no longer Puritan "saints." Moreover, it was required to abide by the **English Toleration Act** of 1690—that is, to allow all Protestants to worship freely. The demise of the "New England way" greatly benefited non-Puritan merchants and large landowners, who came to dominate the new government.

These events produced an atmosphere of considerable tension in Massachusetts, exacerbated by raids by French troops and their Indian allies on the northern New England frontier. The advent of religious toleration heightened anxieties

An engraving from Ralph Gardiner's *England's Grievance Discovered*, published in 1655, depicts women hanged as witches in England. The letters identify local officials: A is the hangman, B the town crier, C the sheriff, and D a magistrate.

among the Puritan clergy, who considered other Protestant denominations a form of heresy. "I would not have a hand in setting up their Devil worship," one minister declared of the Quakers. Indeed, not a few Puritans thought they saw the hand of Satan in the events of 1690 and 1691.

The Prosecution of Witches

Belief in magic, astrology, and witchcraft was widespread in seventeenth-century Europe and America, existing alongside the religion of the clergy and churches. Many Puritans believed in supernatural interventions in the affairs of the world. They interpreted as expressions of God's will such events as lightning that struck one house but spared another, and epidemics that reduced the population of their Indian enemies. Evil forces could also affect daily life. Witches were individuals, usually women, who were accused of having entered into a pact with the devil to obtain supernatural powers, which they used to harm others or to interfere with natural processes. When a child was stillborn or crops failed, many believed that witchcraft was at work.

Belief in witchcraft

In Europe and the colonies, witchcraft was punishable by execution. It is estimated that between the years 1400 and 1800, more than 50,000 people were executed in Europe after being convicted of witchcraft. Witches were, from time to time, hanged in seventeenth-century New England. Most were women beyond childbearing age who were outspoken, economically independent, or estranged from their husbands, or who in other ways violated traditional gender norms. The witch's alleged power challenged both God's will and the standing of men as heads of family and rulers of society.

Executions

The Salem Witch Trials

Until 1692, the prosecution of witches had been local and sporadic. But in the heightened anxiety of that year, a series of trials and executions took place in the town of Salem, Massachusetts that made its name to this day a byword for fanaticism and persecution. The crisis began late in 1691 when several young girls began to suffer fits and nightmares, attributed by their elders to witchcraft. Soon, three "witches" had been named, including Tituba, an Indian from the Caribbean who was a slave in the home of one of the girls. Since the only way to avoid prosecution was to confess and name others, accusations of witchcraft began to snowball. By the middle of 1692, hundreds of residents of Salem had come forward to accuse their neighbors. Some, it appears, used the occasion to settle old scores within the Salem community. Local authorities took legal action against nearly 150 persons, the large majority of them women. Many confessed to save their lives, but fourteen women and five men were hanged, protesting their innocence to the end. One man was pressed to death (crushed under a weight of stones) for refusing to enter a plea.

Accusations in Salem

In the **Salem witch trials**, accusations of witchcraft spread far beyond the usual profile of middle-aged women to include persons of all ages (one was a child of four) and those with no previous history of assertiveness or marital discord. As accusations and executions multiplied, it became clear that something was seriously wrong with the colony's system of justice. Toward the end of 1692, the governor of Massachusetts dissolved the Salem court and ordered the remaining prisoners released. At the same time, the prominent clergyman Increase Mather published an influential treatise, *Cases of Conscience Concerning Evil Spirits*, warning that juries should not take seriously either the testimony of those who claimed to be possessed or the confessions and accusations of persons facing execution. The events in Salem discredited the tradition of prosecuting witches and accelerated a commitment among prominent colonists to finding scientific explanations for natural events like comets and illnesses, rather than attributing them to magic. In future years, only two accused witches would be brought to trial in Massachusetts, and both were found not guilty.

The Salem court

THE GROWTH OF COLONIAL AMERICA

The Salem witch trials took place precisely two centuries after Columbus's initial voyage. The Western Hemisphere was dramatically different from the world he had encountered. Powerful states had been destroyed and the native population decimated by disease and in some areas deprived of its land. In North America, three new and very different empires had arisen, competing for wealth and power. The urban-based Spanish empire, with a small settler elite and growing mestizo population directing a large Indian labor force, still relied for wealth primarily on the gold and silver mines of Mexico and South America. The French empire centered on Saint Domingue, Martinique, and Guadeloupe, plantation islands of the West Indies. On the mainland, it consisted of a thinly settled string of farms and trading posts in the St. Lawrence Valley. In North America north of the Rio Grande, the English colonies had far outstripped their rivals in population and trade.

Three empires

As stability returned after the crises of the late seventeenth century, English North America experienced an era of remarkable growth. Between 1700 and 1770, crude backwoods settlements became bustling provincial capitals. Even as epidemics continued in Indian country, the hazards of disease among colonists diminished, agricultural settlement pressed westward, and hundreds of thousands of newcomers arrived from the Old World. Thanks to a high birthrate and

Population increase

TABLE 3.1 Origins and Status of Migrants to British North American Colonies, 1700–1775

	TOTAL	SLAVES	INDENTURED SERVANTS	CONVICTS	FREE
Africa	278,400	278,400	—	—	—
Ireland	108,600	—	39,000	17,500	52,100
Germany	84,500	—	30,000	—	54,500
England/Wales	73,100	—	27,200	32,500	13,400
Scotland	35,300	—	7,400	2,200	25,700
Other	5,900	—	—	—	5,900
Total	585,800	278,400	103,600	52,200	151,600

continuing immigration, the population of England's mainland colonies, 265,000 in 1700, grew nearly tenfold, to over 2.3 million seventy years later. (It is worth noting, however, that because of the decline suffered by the Indians, the North American population was considerably lower in 1770 than it had been in 1492.)

A Diverse Population

Probably the most striking characteristic of colonial American society in the eighteenth century was its sheer diversity. In 1700, the colonies were essentially English outposts. Relatively few Africans had yet been brought to the mainland, and the overwhelming majority of the white population—close to 90 percent—was of English origin. In the eighteenth century, African and non-English European arrivals skyrocketed, while the number emigrating from England declined.

African and non-English European arrivals surge

As economic conditions in England improved, the government began to rethink the policy of encouraging emigration. No longer concerned with an excess population of vagabonds and "masterless men," authorities began to worry that large-scale emigration was draining labor from the mother country. About 40 percent of European immigrants to the colonies during the eighteenth century continued to arrive as bound laborers who had temporarily sacrificed their freedom to make the voyage to the New World. But as the colonial economy prospered, poor indentured migrants were increasingly joined by professionals and skilled craftsmen—teachers, ministers, weavers, carpenters—whom England could ill afford to lose. This brought to an end official efforts to promote English emigration.

Attracting Settlers

Yet while worrying about losing desirable members of its population, the government in London remained convinced that colonial development enhanced the nation's power and wealth. To bolster the Chesapeake labor force, nearly 50,000 convicts (a group not desired in Britain) were sent to work in the tobacco fields.

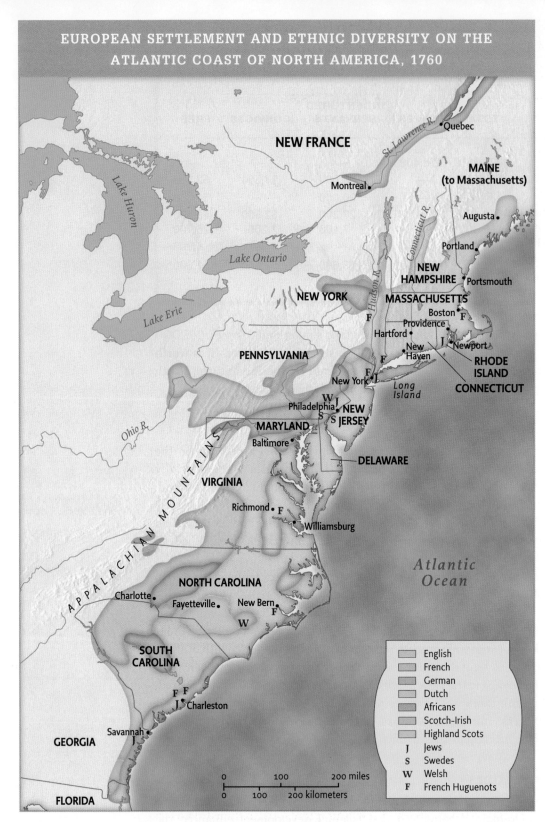

EUROPEAN SETTLEMENT AND ETHNIC DIVERSITY ON THE ATLANTIC COAST OF NORTH AMERICA, 1760

NEW FRANCE

Quebec

St. Lawrence R.

Montreal

MAINE
(to Massachusetts)

Lake Huron

Augusta

Lake Ontario

Portland

Connecticut R.

NEW
HAMPSHIRE

Portsmouth

Lake Erie

NEW YORK

MASSACHUSETTS

Hudson R.

Boston F

Providence

Hartford

New
Haven

J Newport

PENNSYLVANIA

New York

RHODE
ISLAND

CONNECTICUT

Long
Island

Philadelphia

W J

NEW

Ohio R.

S S JERSEY

MARYLAND

Baltimore

DELAWARE

VIRGINIA

APPALACHIAN MOUNTAINS

Richmond F

Williamsburg

Atlantic
Ocean

NORTH CAROLINA

Charlotte

Fayetteville

New Bern

F

W

SOUTH
CAROLINA

F F

J Charleston

Savannah

GEORGIA

J

FLORIDA

0   100   200 miles
0   100   200 kilometers

	English
	French
	German
	Dutch
	Africans
	Scotch-Irish
	Highland Scots
J	Jews
S	Swedes
W	Welsh
F	French Huguenots

Among the most striking features of eighteenth-century colonial society was the racial and ethnic diversity of the population (except in New England). This resulted from increased immigration from the non-English parts of the British Isles and from mainland Europe, as well as the rapid expansion of the slave trade from Africa.

Officials also actively encouraged Protestant immigration from the non-English (and less prosperous) parts of the British Isles and from the European continent, promising newcomers easy access to land and the right to worship freely. A law of 1740 even offered European immigrants British citizenship after seven years of residence, something that in the mother country could be obtained only by a special act of Parliament. The widely publicized image of America as an asylum for those "whom bigots chase from foreign lands," in the words of a 1735 poem, was in many ways a by-product of Britain's efforts to attract settlers from non-English areas to its colonies.

Scottish and Scotch-Irish immigrants

Among eighteenth-century migrants from the British Isles, the 80,000 English newcomers (a majority of them convicted criminals) were considerably outnumbered by 145,000 from Scotland and Ulster, the northern part of Ireland, where many Scots had settled as part of England's effort to subdue the island. Scottish and Scotch-Irish immigrants had a profound impact on colonial society. Mostly Presbyterians, they added significantly to religious diversity in North America. Their numbers included not only poor farmers seeking land but also numerous merchants, teachers, and professionals (indeed, a large majority of the physicians in eighteenth-century America were of Scottish origin).

The German Migration

Germans, 110,000 in all, formed the largest group of newcomers from the European continent. Most came from the valley of the Rhine River, which stretches through present-day Germany into Switzerland. In the eighteenth century, Germany was divided into numerous small states, each with a ruling prince who determined the official religion. Those who found themselves worshiping the "wrong" religion—Lutherans in Catholic areas, Catholics in Lutheran areas, and everywhere, followers of small Protestant sects such as Mennonites, Moravians, and Dunkers—faced persecution. Many decided to emigrate. Other migrants were motivated by persistent agricultural crises and the difficulty of acquiring land. Indeed, the emigration to America represented only a small part of a massive reshuffling of the German population within Europe. Millions of Germans left their homes during the eighteenth century, most of them migrating eastward to Austria-Hungary and the Russian empire, which made land available to newcomers.

Germans the largest group of newcomers from Europe

Wherever they moved, Germans tended to travel in entire families. English and Dutch merchants created a well-organized system whereby **redemptioners** (as indentured families were called) received passage in exchange for a promise to work off their debt in America. Most settled in frontier areas—rural New York, western Pennsylvania, and the southern backcountry—where they formed tightly knit farming communities in which German for many years remained the dominant language. Their arrival greatly enhanced the ethnic and religious diversity of Britain's colonies.

German settlements

Religious Diversity

Eighteenth-century British America was not a "melting pot" of cultures. Ethnic groups tended to live and worship in relatively homogeneous communities. But outside of New England, which received few immigrants and retained its overwhelmingly English ethnic character, American society had a far more diverse population than Britain. Nowhere was this more evident than in the practice

American society more diverse than Britain

In 1685, Louis XIV of France revoked the Edict of Nantes of 1598, which had granted basic civil rights to Protestants in the predominantly Catholic nation. This lithograph, *The Escape of the Reformed Refugees from France*, depicts Protestant families, known as Huguenots, fleeing France. Many made their way to British North America and Dutch South Africa, where they could enjoy religious freedom.

"Liberty of conscience"

of religion. In 1700, nearly all the churches in the colonies were either Congregational (in New England) or Anglican. In the eighteenth century, the Anglican presence expanded considerably. New churches were built and new ministers arrived from England. But the number of Dissenting congregations also multiplied.

Apart from New Jersey (formed from East and West Jersey in 1702), Rhode Island, and Pennsylvania, the colonies did not adhere to a modern separation of church and state. Nearly every colony levied taxes to pay the salaries of ministers of an established church, and most barred Catholics and Jews from voting and holding public office. But increasingly, de facto toleration among Protestant denominations flourished, fueled by the establishment of new churches by immigrants, as well as new Baptist, Methodist, and other congregations created as a result of the Great Awakening, a religious revival that will be discussed in Chapter 4. By the mid-eighteenth century, Dissenting Protestants in most colonies had gained the right to worship as they pleased and own their churches, although many places still barred them from holding public office and taxed them to support the official church. Although few in number (perhaps 2,000 at their peak in eighteenth-century America), Jews also contributed to the religious diversity. German Jews, in particular, were attracted by the chance to escape the rigid religious restrictions of German-speaking parts of Europe; many immigrated to London and some, from there, to cities like Charleston and Philadelphia. A visitor to Pennsylvania in 1750 described the colony's religious diversity: "We find there Lutherans, Reformed, Catholics, Quakers, Menonists or Anabaptists, Herrnhuters or Moravian Brethren, Pietists, Seventh Day Baptists, Dunkers, Presbyterians, . . . Jews, Mohammedans, Pagans."

"Liberty of conscience," wrote a German newcomer in 1739, was the "chief virtue" of British North America, "and on this score I do not repent my immigration." Equally

Baptists were among the numerous religious denominations in the eighteenth-century colonies. In this engraving, from a history of American Baptists published in 1770, a minister baptizes a new member in the Schuylkill River in Pennsylvania, while members of the congregation look on.

important to eighteenth-century immigrants, however, were other elements of freedom, especially the availability of land, the lack of a military draft, and the absence of restraints on economic opportunity common in Europe. Skilled workers were in great demand. "They earn what they want," one emigrant wrote to his brother in Switzerland in 1733. Letters home by immigrants spoke of low taxes, the right to enter trades and professions without paying exorbitant fees, and freedom of movement. "In this country," one wrote, "there are abundant liberties in just about all matters."

Indian Life in Transition

The tide of newcomers, who equated liberty with secure possession of land, threatened to engulf the surviving Indian populations. By the eighteenth century, Indian communities were well integrated into the British imperial system. Indian warriors did much of the fighting in the century's imperial wars. Their cultures were now quite different from what they had been at the time of first contact. Indian societies that had existed for centuries had disappeared, the victims of disease and warfare. New tribes, like the Catawba of South Carolina and the Creek Confederacy, which united dozens of Indian towns in South Carolina and Georgia, had been created from their remnants. Few Indians chose to live among whites rather than in their own communities. But they had become well accustomed to using European products like knives, hatchets, needles, kettles, and firearms. Alcohol introduced by traders created social chaos in many Indian communities. One Cherokee told the governor of South Carolina in 1753, "The clothes we wear, we cannot make ourselves, they are made to us. We use their ammunition with which we kill deer. . . . Every necessary thing we must have from the white people."

Indians and European empire

While traders saw in Indian villages potential profits and British officials saw allies against France and Spain, farmers and planters viewed Indians as little more than an obstruction to their desire for land. They expected Indians to give way to white settlers. The native population of the Virginia and South Carolina frontier had already been displaced when large numbers of settlers arrived. In Pennsylvania, however, the flood of German and Scotch-Irish settlers into the backcountry upset the relatively peaceful Indian-white relations constructed by William Penn. At a 1721 conference, a group of colonial and Indian leaders reaffirmed Penn's Chain of Friendship. But conflicts over land soon multiplied. The infamous **Walking Purchase** of 1737 brought the fraudulent dealing so common in other colonies to Pennsylvania. The Lenni Lanape Indians agreed to an arrangement to cede a tract of land bounded by the distance a man could walk in thirty-six hours. To their amazement, Governor James Logan hired a team of swift runners, who marked out an area far in excess of what the Indians had anticipated.

Settlers and Indian land

Walking Purchase of 1737

By 1760, when Pennsylvania's population, a mere 20,000 in 1700, had grown to 220,000, Indian-colonist relations, initially the most harmonious in British North America, had become poisoned by suspicion and hostility. One group of Susquehanna Indians declared "that the white people had abused them and taken their lands from them, and therefore they had no reason to think that they were now concerned for their happiness." They longed for the days when "old William Penn" treated them with fairness and respect.

VOICES OF FREEDOM

From LETTER BY A SWISS-GERMAN IMMIGRANT TO PENNSYLVANIA (AUGUST 23, 1769)

Germans were among the most numerous immigrants to the eighteenth-century colonies. Many wrote letters to family members at home, relating their experiences and impressions.

———————————

Dearest Father, Brother, and Sister and Brother-in-law,

I have told you quite fully about the trip, and I will tell you what will not surprise you—that we have a free country. Of the sundry craftsmen, one may do whatever one wants. Nor does the land require payment of tithes [taxes to support a local landlord, typical in Europe]. . . . The land is very big from Canada to the east of us to Carolina in the south and to the Spanish border in the west. . . . One can settle wherever one wants without asking anyone when he buys or leases something. . . .

I have always enough to do and we have no shortage of food. Bread is plentiful. If I work for two days I earn more bread than in eight days [at home]. . . . Also I can buy many things so reasonably [for example] a pair of shoes for [roughly] seven Pennsylvania shillings. . . . I think that with God's help I will obtain land. I am not pushing for it until I am in a better position.

I would like for my brother to come . . . and it will then be even nicer in the country. . . . I assume that the land has been described to you sufficiently by various people and it is not surprising that the immigrant agents [demand payment]. For the journey is long and it costs much to stay away for one year. . . .

Johannes Hänner

From MEMORIAL AGAINST NON-ENGLISH IMMIGRATION (DECEMBER 1727)

Only a minority of emigrants from Europe to British North America in the eighteenth century came from the British Isles. Some English settlers, such as the authors of this petition from Pennsylvania to the authorities in London, found the growing diversity of the colonial population quite disturbing.

———————————

How careful every European state, that has Colonies in America, has been of preserving the advantage arising from them wholly to their own Nation and People, is obvious to all who will consider the policy & conduct of the Spanish, French & others in relation to theirs. . . .

About the year 1710 a Company of religious People called Menists [Mennonites] from the Palatinate of the Rhine, transported themselves into the Province of Pennsylvania from Holland in British shipping, and purchased Lands at low rates towards the River Susquehanna. The Terms & Reception they met with proved so encouraging, that they invited diverse of their relations and friends to follow them. In the succeeding years . . . several thousands were settled in that Province. . . . We are now assured by the same people that five or six thousand more are to follow them this next ensuing year. . . .

All these men young & old who arrived since the first, come generally very well armed. Many of them are Papists, & most of them appear inured to War & other hardships. They retire commonly back into the woods amongst or behind the remoter inhabitants, sometimes purchase land, but often sit down on any piece they find vacant that they judge convenient for them without asking questions. . . . Few of them apply now to be Naturalized, [and as] they . . . generally . . . adhere to their own customs. The part of the country they principally settle in is that towards the French of Canada, whose interest, it may be apprehended, . . . (since several of them speak their language) [they] would as willingly favor as the English. . . . It is hoped therefore that nothing need be added to shew the present necessity of putting a stop to that augmentation of their strength. . . . A general provision against all Foreigners may be necessary.

QUESTIONS

1. *What does Johannes Hänner have in mind when he calls America a "free country"?*

2. *What do the petitioners find objectionable about non-English migrants to Pennsylvania?*

3. *How do these documents reflect different views of who should be entitled to the benefits of freedom in the American colonies?*

William Penn's Treaty with the Indians. Penn's grandson, Thomas, the proprietor of Pennsylvania, commissioned this romanticized painting from the artist Benjamin West in 1771, by which time harmony between Indians and colonists had long since turned to hostility. In the nineteenth century, many reproductions of this image circulated, reminding Americans that Indians had once been central figures in their history.

Regional Diversity

By the mid-eighteenth century, the different regions of the British colonies had developed distinct economic and social orders. Small farms tilled by family labor and geared primarily to production for local consumption predominated in New England and the new settlements of the **backcountry** (the area stretching from central Pennsylvania southward through the Shenandoah Valley of Virginia and into upland North and South Carolina). The backcountry was the most rapidly growing region in North America. In 1730, the only white residents in what was then called "Indian country" were the occasional hunter and trader. By the eve of the American Revolution, the region contained one-quarter of Virginia's population and half of South Carolina's. Most were farm families raising grain and livestock, but slave-owning planters, seeking fertile soil for tobacco farming, also entered the area.

> **The backcountry**

In the older portions of the Middle Colonies of New York, New Jersey, and Pennsylvania, farmers were more oriented to commerce than on the frontier, growing grain both for their own use and for sale abroad and supplementing the work of family members by employing wage laborers, tenants, and in some instances slaves. Because large landlords had engrossed so much desirable land, New York's growth lagged behind that of neighboring colonies. "What man will be such a fool as to become a base tenant," wondered Richard Coote, New York's governor at the beginning of the eighteenth century, "when by crossing the Hudson river that man can for a song purchase a good freehold?" With its fertile soil, favorable climate, initially peaceful Indian relations, generous governmental land distribution policy, and rivers that facilitated long-distance trading, Pennsylvania came to be known as "the best poor man's country." Ordinary colonists there enjoyed a standard of living unimaginable in Europe.

> **"The best poor man's country"**

The Consumer Revolution

During the eighteenth century, Great Britain eclipsed the Dutch as the leading producer and trader of inexpensive consumer goods, including colonial products like coffee and tea, and such manufactured goods as linen, metalware, pins, ribbons, glassware, ceramics, and clothing. Trade integrated the British empire. As the American colonies were drawn more and more fully into the system of Atlantic commerce, they shared in the era's consumer revolution. In port cities and small inland towns, shops proliferated and American newspapers were filled with advertisements for British goods. British merchants supplied American traders with loans to enable them to import these products, and traveling peddlers carried them into remote frontier areas.

Consumerism in a modern sense—the mass production, advertising, and sale of consumer goods—did not exist in colonial America. Nonetheless, eighteenth-century estate inventories—records of people's possessions at the time of death—revealed the wide dispersal in American homes of English and even Asian products. In the seventeenth century, most colonists had lived in a pioneer world of homespun clothing and homemade goods. Now, even modest farmers and artisans owned books, ceramic plates, metal cutlery, and items made of imported silk and cotton. Tea, once a luxury enjoyed only by the wealthy, became virtually a necessity of life. "People that are least able to go to the expense," one New Yorker noted, "must have their tea though their families want bread."

This 1772 broadside offers a rare view of the interior of a Philadelphia shop and lists some of the many European and West Indian goods on sale, including rum, tea, spices, and gunpowder—a sign of the ongoing consumer revolution linked to international trade.

Colonial Cities

Britain's mainland colonies were overwhelmingly agricultural. Nine-tenths of the population resided in rural areas and made their livelihood from farming. Colonial cities like Boston, New York, Philadelphia, and Charleston were quite small by the standards of Europe or Spanish America. In 1700, when the population of Mexico City stood at 100,000, Boston had 6,000 residents and New York 4,500. As late as 1750, eight cities in Spanish America exceeded in size any in English North America.

English American cities served mainly as gathering places for agricultural goods and for imported items to be distributed to the countryside. Nonetheless, the expansion of trade encouraged the rise of port cities, home to a growing population of colonial merchants and artisans (skilled craftsmen) as well as an increasing number of poor. In 1770, with some 30,000 inhabitants, Philadelphia was "the capital of the New World," at least its British component, and, after London and Liverpool, the empire's third busiest port. The financial, commercial, and cultural center of British America, its growth rested on economic integration with the rich agricultural region nearby. Philadelphia merchants organized the collection of farm goods, supplied rural storekeepers, and extended credit to consumers. They exported flour, bread, and meat to the West Indies and Europe.

Colonial Artisans

The city was also home to a large population of furniture makers, jewelers, and silversmiths serving wealthier citizens, and hundreds of lesser artisans like weavers, blacksmiths, coopers, and construction workers. The typical artisan owned his own tools and labored in a small workshop, often his home, assisted by family members and young journeymen and apprentices learning the trade. The artisan's skill, which set him apart from the common laborers below him in the social scale, was the key to his existence, and it gave him a far greater degree of economic freedom than those dependent on others for a livelihood. "He that hath a trade, hath an estate," wrote Benjamin Franklin, who had worked as a printer before achieving renown as a scientist and statesman.

Despite the influx of British goods, American craftsmen benefited from the expanding consumer market. Most journeymen enjoyed a reasonable chance of rising to the status of master and establishing a workshop of their own. Some achieved remarkable success. Born in New York City in 1723, Myer Myers, a Jewish silversmith of Dutch ancestry, became one of the city's most prominent artisans. Myers produced jewelry, candlesticks, coffeepots, tableware, and other gold and silver objects for the colony's elite, as well as religious ornaments for both synagogues and Protestant churches in New York and nearby colonies. He used some of his profits to acquire land in New Hampshire and Connecticut. Myers's career reflected the opportunities colonial cities offered to skilled men of diverse ethnic and religious backgrounds.

An Atlantic World

People, ideas, and goods flowed back and forth across the Atlantic, knitting together the empire and its diverse populations—British merchants and consumers, American colonists, African slaves, and surviving Indians—and creating webs of interdependence among the European empires. Sugar, tobacco, and other products of the Western Hemisphere were marketed as far away as eastern Europe. London bankers financed the slave trade between Africa and Portuguese Brazil. Spain spent its gold and silver importing goods from other countries. As trade expanded, the North American and West Indian colonies became the major overseas market for British manufactured goods. Although most colonial output was consumed at home, North Americans shipped farm products to Britain, the West Indies, and, with the exception of goods like tobacco "enumerated" under the Navigation Acts, outside the empire. Virtually the entire Chesapeake tobacco crop was marketed in Britain, with most of it then re-exported to Europe by British merchants. Most of the bread and flour exported from the colonies was destined for the West Indies. African slaves there grew sugar that could be distilled into rum, a product increasingly popular among both North American colonists and Indians, who obtained it by trading furs and deerskins that were then shipped to

This piece of china made in England in the 1690s and exported to New England depicts King William III and his wife Mary. It is an example of the growing colonial demand for English consumer goods.

American craftsmen and the expanding consumer market

Trade in the Atlantic world

Charles Town Harbor, a watercolor painted around 1740 by the artist Bishop Roberts, depicts the flourishing major port city of South Carolina. The ships all fly British flags, since the Navigation Acts prevented foreign vessels from carrying the colony's main export, rice. South Carolina was home to the wealthiest elite in Britain's mainland colonies, and ships carried imported luxury goods for them from Great Britain.

Europe. The mainland colonies carried on a flourishing trade in fish and grains with southern Europe. Ships built in New England made up one-third of the British empire's trading fleet.

Membership in the empire had many advantages for the colonists. Most Americans did not complain about British regulation of their trade because commerce enriched the colonies as well as the mother country and lax enforcement of the Navigation Acts allowed smuggling to flourish. In a dangerous world, moreover, the Royal Navy protected American shipping. And despite the many differences between life in England and its colonies, eighteenth-century English America drew closer and closer to, and in some ways became more and more similar to, the mother country across the Atlantic.

English America

SOCIAL CLASSES IN THE COLONIES

The Colonial Elite

Most free Americans benefited from economic growth, but as colonial society matured an elite emerged that, while neither as powerful nor as wealthy as the aristocracy of England, increasingly dominated politics and society. Indeed, the gap between rich and poor probably grew more rapidly in the eighteenth century

Growing gap between rich and poor

than in any other period of American history. In New England and the Middle Colonies, expanding trade made possible the emergence of a powerful upper class of merchants, often linked by family or commercial ties to great trading firms in London. There were no banks in colonial America. Credit and money were in short supply, and mercantile success depended on personal connections as much as business talent. By 1750, the colonies of the Chesapeake and Lower South were dominated by slave plantations producing **staple crops**, especially tobacco and rice, for the world market. Here great planters accumulated enormous wealth. The colonial elite also included the rulers of proprietary colonies like Pennsylvania and Maryland.

America had no titled aristocracy as in Britain. It had no system of legally established social ranks or family pedigrees stretching back to medieval times. Apart from the De Lanceys, Livingstons, and van Rensselaers of New York, the Penn family in Pennsylvania, and a few southern planters, it had no one whose land-holdings, in monetary value, rivaled those of the British aristocracy. But throughout British America, men of prominence controlled colonial government. In Virginia, the upper class was so tight-knit and intermarried so often that the colony was said to be governed by a "cousinocracy." Members of the gentry controlled the vestries, or local governing bodies, of the established Anglican Church, dominated the county courts (political as well as judicial institutions that levied taxes and enacted local ordinances), and were prominent in Virginia's legislature. In the 1750s, seven members of the same generation of the Lee family sat in the House of Burgesses.

Eighteenth-century Virginia was a far healthier environment than in the early days of settlement. Planters could expect to pass their wealth down to the next generation, providing estates for their sons and establishing family dynasties. Nearly every Virginian of note achieved prominence through family connections. The days when self-made men could rise into the Virginia gentry were long gone; by 1770, nearly all upper-class Virginians had inherited their wealth. Thomas Jefferson's grandfather was a justice of the peace (an important local official), militia captain, and sheriff, and his father a member of the House of Burgesses. George Washington's father, grandfather, and great-grandfather had been justices of the peace. The Virginia gentry used its control of provincial government to gain possession of large tracts of land as western areas opened for settlement. Grants of 20,000 to 40,000 acres were not uncommon. Robert "King" Carter, a speaker of the House of Burgesses, acquired 300,000 acres of land and 1,000 slaves by the time of his death in 1732.

Anglicization

For much of the eighteenth century, the American colonies had more regular trade and communications with Britain than

A 1732 portrait of Daniel, Peter, and Andrew Oliver, sons of a wealthy Boston merchant. The prominent display of their delicate hands tells the viewer that they have never had to do manual labor.

among themselves. Elites in different regions slowly developed a common lifestyle and sense of common interests. But rather than thinking of themselves as distinctively American, they became more and more English—a process historians call "Anglicization."

Wealthy Americans tried to model their lives on British etiquette and behavior. Somewhat resentful at living in provincial isolation—"at the end of the world," as one Virginia aristocrat put it—they sought to demonstrate their status and legitimacy by importing the latest London fashions and literature, sending their sons to Britain for education, and building homes equipped with fashionable furnishings modeled on the country estates and town houses of the English gentry. Their residences included large rooms for entertainment, display cases for imported luxury goods, and elaborate formal gardens. Some members of the colonial elite, like George Washington, even had coats of arms designed for their families, in imitation of English upper-class practice.

Desperate to follow an aristocratic lifestyle, many planters fell into debt. William Byrd III of Virginia lived so extravagantly that by 1770 he had accumulated a debt of £100,000, an amount almost unheard of in England or America. But so long as the world market for tobacco thrived, so did Virginia's gentry.

The South Carolina Aristocracy

The richest group of mainland colonists were South Carolina planters (although planters in Jamaica far outstripped them in wealth). Elite South Carolinians often traveled north to enjoy summer vacations in the cooler climate of Newport, Rhode Island, and they spent much of the remainder of their time in Charleston, the only real urban center south of Philadelphia and the richest city in British North America. Here aristocratic social life flourished, centered on theaters, literary societies, and social events. Like their Virginia counterparts, South Carolina grandees lived a lavish lifestyle amid imported furniture, fine wines, silk clothing, and other items from England. They surrounded themselves with house slaves dressed in specially designed uniforms. In 1774, the per capita wealth in the Charleston District was £2,300, more than four times that of tobacco areas in Virginia and eight times the figure for Philadelphia or Boston. But wealth in South Carolina was highly concentrated. The richest 10 percent of the colony owned half the wealth in 1770, the poorest quarter less than 2 percent.

Throughout the colonies, elites emulated what they saw as England's balanced, stable social order. Liberty, in their eyes, meant, in part, the power to rule—the right of those blessed with wealth and prominence to dominate over others. They viewed society as a hierarchical structure in which some men were endowed with greater talents than others and destined to rule. The social order, they believed, was held together by webs of influence that linked patrons and those dependent on them. Each place in the hierarchy carried with it different responsibilities, and one's status was revealed in dress, manners, and the splendor of one's home. "Superiority" and "dependence," as one colonial newspaper put it, were natural elements of any society. An image of refinement served to legitimize wealth and political power. Colonial elites prided themselves on developing aristocratic manners, cultivating the arts, and making productive use of leisure. Indeed, on both sides of the Atlantic,

A portrait of Elijah Boardman, a merchant in New Milford, Massachusetts. Boardman wears the attire of a gentleman and rests his arm on his counting desk. In the rear, bolts of cloth are visible. But Boardman chose to emphasize his learning, not his wealth, by posing with books, including two plays of Shakespeare, John Milton's *Paradise Lost*, and the *London Magazine*.

> *Charleston: America's richest city*

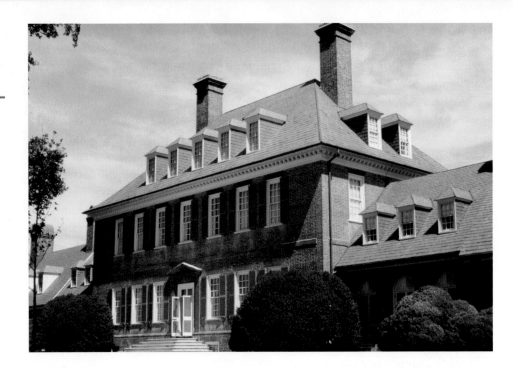

Built in the 1750s by Carter Burwell, grandson of the original Robert "King" Carter, Carter's Grove, near Williamsburg, Virginia, was a grand plantation mansion.

elites viewed work as something reserved for common folk and slaves. Freedom from labor was the mark of the gentleman.

Poverty in the Colonies

At the other end of the social scale, poverty emerged as a visible feature of eighteenth-century colonial life. Although not considered by most colonists part of their society, the growing number of slaves lived in impoverished conditions.

Poverty of free Americans

Among free Americans, poverty was hardly as widespread as in Britain, where in the early part of the century between one-quarter and one-half of the people regularly required public assistance. But as the colonial population expanded, access to land diminished rapidly, especially in long-settled areas. In New England, which received few immigrants, the high birthrate fueled population growth. With the supply of land limited, sons who could not hope to inherit farms were forced to move to other colonies or to try their hand at a trade in the region's towns. By mid-century, tenants and wage laborers were a growing presence on farms in the Middle Colonies.

In colonial cities, the number of propertyless wage earners subsisting at the poverty line steadily increased. In Boston, one-third of the population in 1771 owned no property at all. In rural Augusta County, carved out of Virginia's Shenandoah River valley in 1738, land was quickly engrossed by planters and speculators. By the 1760s, two-thirds of the county's white men owned no land and had little prospect of obtaining it unless they migrated farther west. Taking the colonies as a whole, half

The richest 10 percent

of the wealth at mid-century was concentrated in the hands of the richest 10 percent of the population.

Attitudes and policies toward poverty in colonial America mirrored British precedents. The better-off colonists generally viewed the poor as lazy, shiftless, and responsible for their own plight. Both rural communities and cities did accept responsibility for assisting their own. But to minimize the burden on taxpayers, poor persons were frequently set to labor in workhouses, where they produced goods that reimbursed authorities for part of their upkeep. Their children were sent to work as apprentices in local homes or workshops. And most communities adopted stringent measures to "warn out" unemployed and propertyless newcomers who might become dependent on local poor relief. This involved town authorities either expelling the unwanted poor from an area or formally declaring certain persons ineligible for assistance. In Essex County, Massachusetts, the number of poor persons warned out each year rose from 200 in the 1730s to 1,700 in the 1760s. Many were members of families headed by widowed or abandoned women.

The Middle Ranks

The large majority of free Americans lived between the extremes of wealth and poverty. Along with racial and ethnic diversity, what distinguished the mainland colonies from Europe was the wide distribution of land and the economic autonomy of most ordinary free families. The anonymous author of the book *American Husbandry*, published in 1775, reported that "little freeholders who live upon their own property" made up "the most considerable part" of the people, especially in the northern colonies and the nonplantation parts of the South. Altogether, perhaps two-thirds of the free male population were farmers who owned their own land. England, to be sure, had no class of laborers as exploited as American slaves, but three-fifths of its people owned no property at all.

By the eighteenth century, colonial farm families viewed landownership almost as a right, the social precondition of freedom. They strongly resented efforts, whether by Native Americans, great landlords, or colonial governments, to limit their access to land. A dislike of personal dependence and an understanding of freedom as not relying on others for a livelihood sank deep roots in British North

Landownership and freedom

The Residence of David Twining, a painting of a Pennsylvania farm as it appeared in the eighteenth century. Edward Hicks, who lived there as a youth, painted the scene from memory in the 1840s. Hicks depicts a prosperous farm, largely self-sufficient but also producing for the market, typical of colonial eastern Pennsylvania. One of the farm workers is a slave. Five-year-old Edward himself is pictured in the lower right-hand corner, listening to Mrs. Twining read the Bible.

America. These beliefs, after all, accorded with social reality—a wide distribution of property that made economic independence part of the lived experience of large numbers of white colonists.

Women and the Household Economy

In the household economy of eighteenth-century America, the family was the center of economic life. Most work revolved around the home, and all members—men, women, and children—contributed to the family's livelihood. The independence of the small farmer depended in considerable measure on the labor of dependent women and children. "He that hath an industrious family shall soon be rich," declared one colonial saying, and the high birthrate in part reflected the need for as many hands as possible on colonial farms. Most farmers concentrated first on growing food for their own consumption and acquiring enough land to pass it along to their sons. But the consumer revolution and expanding networks of Atlantic trade drew increasing numbers of farmers into production for the market as well.

Family as center of economic life

As the population grew and the death rate declined, family life stabilized and more marriages became lifetime commitments. Free women were expected to devote their lives to being good wives and mothers. Already enshrined in law and property relations, male domination took on greater and greater social reality. In several colonies, the law mandated primogeniture—meaning that estates must be passed intact to the oldest son. As colonial society became more structured, opportunities that had existed for women in the early period receded. In Connecticut, for example, the courts were informal and unorganized in the seventeenth century, and women often represented themselves. In the eighteenth century, it became necessary to hire a lawyer as one's spokesman in court. Women, barred from practicing

Receding opportunities for women

This portrait of the Cheney family by an unknown late-eighteenth-century artist illustrates the high birthrate in colonial America, and suggests how many years of a woman's life were spent bearing and raising children.

as attorneys, disappeared from judicial proceedings. Because of the desperate need for labor, men and women in the seventeenth century both did various kinds of work. In the eighteenth century, the division of labor along gender lines solidified. Women's work was clearly defined, including cooking, cleaning, sewing, making butter, and assisting with agricultural chores. The work of farmers' wives and daughters often spelled the difference between a family's self-sufficiency and poverty.

"Women's work is never done." This popular adage was literally true. Even as the consumer revolution reduced the demands on many women by making available store-bought goods previously produced at home, women's work seemed to increase. Lower infant mortality meant more time spent in child care and domestic chores. The demand for new goods increased the need for all family members to contribute to family income. For most women, work was incessant and exhausting. "I am dirty and distressed, almost wearied to death," wrote Mary Cooper, a Long Island woman, in her diary in 1769. "This day," she continued, "is forty years since I left my father's house and come here, and here have I seen little else but hard labor and sorrow."

Women's work

North America at Mid-Century

By the mid-eighteenth century, the area that would become the United States was home to a remarkable diversity of peoples and different kinds of social organization, from Pueblo villages of the Southwest to tobacco plantations of the Chesapeake, towns and small farms of New England, landholdings in the Hudson Valley that resembled feudal estates, and fur-trading outposts of the northern and western frontier. Elites tied to imperial centers of power dominated the political and economic life of nearly every colony. But large numbers of colonists enjoyed far greater opportunities for freedom—access to the vote, prospects of acquiring land, the right to worship as they pleased, and an escape from oppressive government—than existed in Europe. Free colonists probably enjoyed the highest per capita income in the world. The colonies' economic growth contributed to a high birthrate, long life expectancy, and expanding demand for consumer goods.

Opportunities for freedom

In the British colonies, writes one historian, lived "thousands of the freest individuals the Western world has ever known." Yet many others found themselves confined to the partial freedom of indentured servitude or to the complete absence of freedom in slavery. Both timeless longings for freedom and new and unprecedented forms of unfreedom had been essential to the North American colonies' remarkable development.

Freedom and unfreedom

SUGGESTED READING

BOOKS

- Bailyn, Bernard. *The Peopling of British North America* (1986). A brief survey of the movement of peoples across the Atlantic.

- Berlin, Ira. *Many Thousands Gone: The First Two Centuries of Slavery in North America* (1998). The most extensive study of the origins and development of colonial slavery.

- Bushman, Richard. *The Refinement of America: Persons, Houses, Cities* (1992). A study of how a more "refined" lifestyle emerged in the eighteenth-century colonies.

- Dayton, Cornelia H. *Women before the Bar: Gender, Law, and Society in Connecticut, 1639–1789* (1995). Examines the changing legal status of women in one American colony.

- Jordan, Winthrop D. *White over Black: American Attitudes toward the Negro, 1550–1812* (1968). A detailed look at how ideas about race developed over time in England and the American colonies.

- Kidd, Thomas S. *The Great Awakening* (2007). An account of the religious movement that swept the American colonies in the eighteenth century.

- Kulikoff, Allan. *Tobacco and Slaves: The Development of Southern Cultures in the Chesapeake, 1680–1800* (1986). Explores how the rise of slave-grown tobacco affected society in the Chesapeake.

- Lemon, James T. *The Best Poor Man's Country: A Geographical Study of Early Southeastern Pennsylvania* (1972). A study of agriculture and the environment in one of the most successful farming areas of colonial America.

- Mintz, Sidney. *Sweetness and Power: The Place of Sugar in Modern History* (1985). A global history of the significance of sugar in the making of the modern world.

- Morgan, Edmund S. *American Slavery, American Freedom: The Ordeal of Colonial Virginia* (1975). An influential study of the slow development of slavery in seventeenth-century Virginia.

- Norton, Mary Beth. *In the Devil's Snare: The Salem Witchcraft Crisis of 1692* (2002). A study of the witch trials that places them in the context of anxieties over Indian warfare on the Massachusetts frontier.

- Pestana, Carla G. Protestant Empire: *Religion and the Making of the British Atlantic World* (2009). Discusses the role of Protestantism in inspiring and justifying British overseas expansion.

- Saxton, Martha. *Being Good: Women's Moral Values in Early America* (2003). Examines social standards for women's behavior and how women tried to live up to them.

- Silver, Peter. *Our Savage Neighbors: How Indian War Transformed Early America* (2008). Argues that hostility to Indians provided a way of unifying the diverse population of European origin that made up colonial America.

WEBSITES

- The Atlantic Slave Trade and Slave Life in the Americas: http://hitchcock.itc.virginia.edu/Slavery/index.php

- Afro-Louisiana History and Genealogy: www.ibiblio.org /laslave/

CHAPTER REVIEW AND ONLINE RESOURCES

REVIEW QUESTIONS

1. Both the Puritans and William Penn viewed their colonies as "holy experiments." How did they differ?

2. The textbook states, "Prejudice by itself did not create American slavery." Examine the economic forces, events, and laws that shaped the experiences of enslaved people.

3. How did English leaders understand the place and role of the American colonies in England's empire?

4. How did King Philip's War, Bacon's Rebellion, and the Salem witch trials illustrate a widespread crisis in British North America in the late seventeenth century?

5. The social structure of the eighteenth-century colonies was growing more open for some but not for others. Consider the statement with respect to men and women, whites and blacks, and rich and poor.

6. By the end of the seventeenth century, commerce was the foundation of empire and the leading cause of competition between European empires. Explain how the North American colonies were directly linked to Atlantic commerce by laws and trade.

7. If you traveled from New England to the South, how would you describe the diversity you saw between the different colonies?

8. What impact did the family's being the center of economic life have on gender relations and the roles of women?

9. What experiences caused people in the colonies to be like people in England, and what experiences served to make them different?

KEY TERMS

Metacom (p. 87)

King Philip's War (p. 87)

mercantilism (p. 88)

Navigation Act (p. 88)

Covenant Chain (p. 90)

Yamasee uprising (p. 92)

Society of Friends (Quakers) (p. 93)

plantation (p. 95)

Bacon's Rebellion (p. 99)

Glorious Revolution (p. 102)

English Bill of Rights (p. 103)

Lords of Trade (p. 103)

Dominion of New England (p. 103)

English Toleration Act (p. 104)

Salem witch trials (p. 106)

redemptioners (p. 109)

Walking Purchase (p. 111)

backcountry (p. 114)

staple crops (p. 118)

Go to 🐰 INQUIZITIVE

To see what you know—and learn what you've missed—with personalized feedback along the way.

Visit the *Give Me Liberty!* **Student Site** for primary source documents and images, interactive maps, author videos featuring Eric Foner, and more.

CHAPTER 4

SLAVERY, FREEDOM, AND THE STRUGGLE FOR EMPIRE

★

TO 1763

Sometime in the mid-1750s, Olaudah Equiano, the eleven-year-old son of a West African village chief, was kidnapped by slave traders. He soon found himself on a ship headed for Barbados. After a short stay on that Caribbean island, Equiano was sold to a plantation owner in Virginia and then purchased by a British sea captain, who renamed him Gustavus Vassa. He accompanied his owner on numerous voyages on Atlantic trading vessels. While still a slave, he enrolled in a school in England where he learned to read and write, and then enlisted in the Royal Navy. He fought in Canada under General James Wolfe in 1758 during the Seven Years' War. In 1763, however, Equiano was sold once again and returned to the Caribbean. Three years later, he was able to purchase his freedom. Equiano went on to live through shipwrecks, took part in an English colonizing venture in Central America, and even participated in an expedition to the Arctic Circle.

Equiano eventually settled in London, and in 1789 he published *The Interesting Narrative of the Life of Olaudah Equiano, or Gustavus Vassa, the African*, which he described as a "history of neither a saint, a hero, nor a tyrant," but of a victim of slavery who through luck or fate ended up more fortunate than most of his people. He condemned the idea that Africans were inferior to Europeans and therefore deserved to be slaves. He urged the European reader to recall that "his ancestors were once, like the Africans, uncivilized" and asked, "Did nature make them inferior . . . and should they too have been made slaves?" Persons of all races, he insisted, were capable of intellectual improvement. The book became the era's most widely read account by a slave of his own experiences. Equiano died in 1797.

Recent scholars have suggested that Equiano may actually have been born in the New World rather than Africa. In either case, while his rich variety of experience was no doubt unusual, his life illuminates broad patterns of eighteenth-century American history. As noted in the previous chapter, this was a period of sustained development for British North America. Compared to England and Scotland—united to create Great Britain by the Act of Union of 1707—the colonies were growing much more rapidly. Some contemporaries spoke of British America as a "rising empire" that would one day eclipse the mother country in population and wealth.

It would be wrong, however, to see the first three-quarters of the eighteenth century simply as a prelude to American independence. As Equiano's life illustrates, the Atlantic was more a bridge than a barrier between the Old and New Worlds. Ideas, people, and goods flowed back and forth across the ocean. Even as the colonies' populations became more diverse, they were increasingly integrated into the British empire. Their laws and political institutions were extensions of those of Britain, their ideas about society and culture reflected British values, their economies were geared to serving the empire's needs. As European powers jockeyed for advantage in North America, colonists were drawn into an almost continuous series of wars with France and its Indian allies, which reinforced their sense of identification with and dependence on Great Britain.

Equiano's life also underscores the greatest irony or contradiction in the history of the eighteenth century—the simultaneous expansion of freedom and slavery. This was the era when the idea of the "freeborn Englishman" became

Benjamin Latrobe's watercolor, *An Overseer Doing His Duty*, was sketched near Fredericksburg, Virginia, in 1798. The title is meant to be ironic: the well-dressed overseer relaxes while two female slaves work in the fields.

powerfully entrenched in the outlook of both colonists and Britons. More than any other principle, liberty was seen as what made the British empire distinct. Yet the eighteenth century was also the height of the Atlantic slave trade, a commerce increasingly dominated by British merchants and ships. One of the most popular songs of the period included the refrain, "Britons never, never, never will be slaves." But during the eighteenth century, more than half the Africans shipped to the New World as slaves were carried on British vessels. Most were destined for the plantations of the West Indies and Brazil, but slaves also made up around 280,000 of the 585,000 persons who arrived in Britain's mainland colonies between 1700 and 1775. Although concentrated in the Chesapeake and areas farther south, slavery existed in every colony of British North America. And unlike Equiano, very few slaves were fortunate enough to gain their freedom.

SLAVERY AND EMPIRE

Of the estimated 10 million Africans transported to the New World between 1492 and 1820, more than half arrived between 1700 and 1800. The **Atlantic slave trade** would later be condemned by statesmen and general opinion as a crime against humanity. But in the eighteenth century, it was a regularized business in which European merchants, African traders, and American planters engaged in complex bargaining over human lives, all with the expectation of securing a profit. The slave trade was a vital part of world commerce. Every European empire in the New World utilized slave labor and battled for control of this lucrative trade. The *asiento*—an agreement whereby Spain subcontracted to a foreign power the right to provide slaves to Spanish America—was an important diplomatic prize. Britain's acquisition of the *asiento* from the Dutch in the Treaty of Utrecht of 1713 was a major step in its rise to commercial supremacy.

In the British empire of the eighteenth century, free laborers working for wages were atypical and slavery was the norm. Slave plantations contributed mightily to English economic development. The first mass consumer goods in international trade were produced by slaves—sugar, rice, coffee, and tobacco. The rising demand for these products fueled the rapid growth of the Atlantic slave trade.

Atlantic Trade

In the eighteenth century, the Caribbean remained the commercial focus of the British empire and the major producer of revenue for the crown. But slave-grown products from the mainland occupied a larger and larger part of Atlantic commerce. A series of triangular trading routes crisscrossed the Atlantic, carrying British manufactured goods to Africa and the colonies, colonial products to Europe, and slaves from Africa to the New World. Most colonial vessels, however, went back and forth between cities like New York, Charleston, and Savannah, and to ports in the Caribbean. Areas where slavery was only a minor institution also profited from slave labor. Merchants in New York, Massachusetts, and Rhode Island participated actively in the slave trade, shipping slaves from Africa to the Caribbean or southern

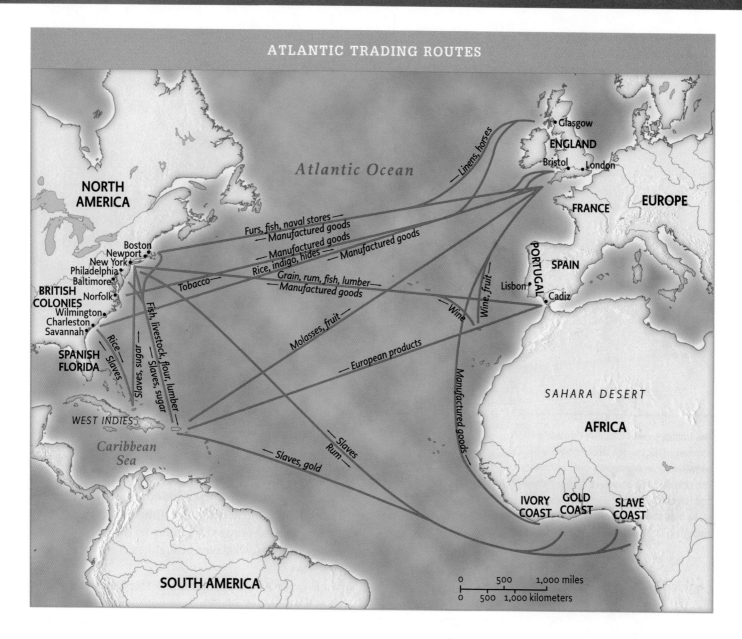

ATLANTIC TRADING ROUTES

A series of trading routes crisscrossed the Atlantic, bringing manufactured goods to Africa and Britain's American colonies, slaves to the New World, and colonial products to Europe.

colonies. The slave economies of the West Indies were the largest market for fish, grain, livestock, and lumber exported from New England and the Middle Colonies. Indeed, one historian writes, "The growth and prosperity of the emerging society of free colonial British America . . . were achieved as a result of slave labor." In Britain itself, the profits from slavery and the slave trade stimulated the rise of ports like Liverpool and Bristol and the growth of banking, shipbuilding, and insurance. They also helped to finance the early industrial revolution.

Overall, in the eighteenth century, Atlantic commerce consisted primarily of slaves, crops produced by slaves, and goods destined for slave societies. It should not be surprising that for large numbers of free colonists and Europeans, freedom meant in part the power and right to enslave others. And as slavery became more and more entrenched, so too, as the Quaker abolitionist John Woolman commented

A mid-eighteenth-century image of a woman going to church in Lima, Peru, accompanied by two slaves. Slavery existed throughout the Western Hemisphere.

in 1762, did "the idea of slavery being connected with the black color, and liberty with the white."

Africa and the Slave Trade

A few African societies, like Benin for a time, opted out of the Atlantic slave trade, hoping to avoid the disruptions it inevitably caused. But most African rulers took part, and they proved quite adept at playing the Europeans off against one another, collecting taxes from foreign merchants, and keeping the capture and sale of slaves under their own control. Few Europeans ventured inland from the coast. Traders remained in their "factories" and purchased slaves brought to them by African rulers and dealers.

The transatlantic slave trade made Africa a major market for European goods, especially textiles and guns. Both disrupted relationships within and among African societies. Cheap imported textiles undermined traditional craft production, while guns encouraged the further growth of slavery, since the only way to obtain European weapons was to supply slaves. By the eighteenth century, militarized states like Ashanti and Dahomey would arise in West Africa, with large armies using European firearms to prey on their neighbors in order to capture slaves. From a minor institution, slavery grew to become more and more central to West African society, a source of wealth for African merchants and of power for newly emerging African kingdoms. But the loss every year of tens of thousands of men and women in the prime of their lives to the slave trade weakened and distorted West Africa's society and economy.

The Middle Passage

For slaves, the voyage across the Atlantic—known as the **Middle Passage** because it was the second, or middle, leg in the triangular trading routes linking Europe, Africa,

The frontispiece of Olaudah Equiano's account of his life, the best-known narrative by an eighteenth-century slave. The portrait of Equiano in European dress and holding a Bible challenges stereotypes of blacks as "savages" incapable of becoming civilized.

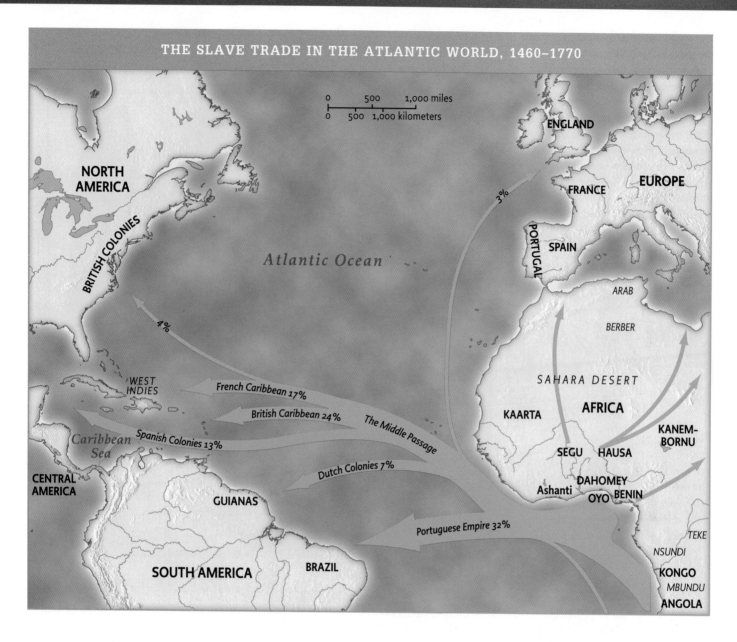

THE SLAVE TRADE IN THE ATLANTIC WORLD, 1460–1770

and America—was a harrowing experience. Since a slave could be sold in America for twenty to thirty times the price in Africa, men, women, and children were crammed aboard vessels as tightly as possible to maximize profits. "The height, sometimes, between decks," wrote one slave trader, "was only eighteen inches, so that the unfortunate human beings could not turn around, or even on their sides . . . and here they are usually chained to the decks by their necks and legs." Equiano, who later described "the shrieks of the women and the groans of the dying," survived the Middle Passage, but many Africans did not. Diseases like measles and smallpox spread rapidly, and about one slave in five perished before reaching the New World. Ship captains were known to throw the sick overboard in order to prevent the spread of epidemics. The crews on slave ships also suffered a high death rate.

The Atlantic slave trade expanded rapidly in the eighteenth century. The mainland colonies received only a tiny proportion of the Africans brought to the New World, most of whom were transported to Brazil and the West Indies.

This image, made by a sailor in 1769 for the ship's owner, a merchant in Nantes, France, depicts a slave-trading vessel, the *Marie-Séraphique*, anchored off the African coast, and the ship's interior. The cargo carried in barrels, generally guns, cloth, and metal goods, was to be traded for slaves. The third image from the left depicts the conditions under which slaves endured the Middle Passage across the Atlantic. The ship carried over 300 slaves. The broadside also included a calculation of the profit of the voyage.

Slave population

Only a small proportion (less than 5 percent) of slaves carried to the New World were destined for mainland North America. The vast majority landed in Brazil or the West Indies, where the high death rate on the sugar plantations led to a constant demand for new slave imports. As late as 1700, only about 20,000 Africans had been landed in Britain's colonies in North America. In the eighteenth century, however, their numbers increased steadily. Overall, the area that was to become the United States imported between 400,000 and 600,000 slaves. By 1770, due to the natural reproduction of the slave population, around one-fifth of the estimated 2.3 million persons (not including Indians) living in the English colonies of North America were Africans and their descendants.

Chesapeake Slavery

By the mid-eighteenth century, three distinct slave systems were well entrenched in Britain's mainland colonies: tobacco-based plantation slavery in the Chesapeake, rice-based plantation slavery in South Carolina and Georgia, and nonplantation slavery in New England and the Middle Colonies. The largest and oldest of these was the tobacco plantation system of the Chesapeake, where more than 270,000 slaves resided in 1770, nearly half of the region's population. On the eve of the Revolution, Virginia and Maryland were as closely tied to Britain as any other colonies and their economies were models of mercantilist policy (described in Chapter 3). They supplied the mother country with a valuable agricultural product, imported large amounts of British goods, and were closely linked in culture and political values to London. As we have seen, the period after 1680 witnessed a rapid shift from indentured servitude to slavery on the region's tobacco plantations. In the eighteenth century, the growing world demand for tobacco encouraged continued slave imports.

> *Ties to Britain*

As Virginia expanded westward, so did slavery. By the eve of the American Revolution, the center of gravity of slavery in the colony had shifted from the Tidewater (the region along the coast) to the Piedmont farther inland. Most Chesapeake slaves, male and female, worked in the fields, but thousands labored as teamsters, as boatmen, and in skilled crafts. Numerous slave women became cooks, seamstresses, dairy maids, and personal servants. The son of George Mason, one of Virginia's leading planters and statesmen, recorded that his father's slaves included "coopers, sawyers, blacksmiths, tanners, shoemakers, spinners, weavers, knitters, and even a distiller." Slavery was common on small farms as well as plantations; nearly half of Virginia's white families owned at least one slave in 1770.

> *Types of slave labor*

Slavery laid the foundation for the consolidation of the Chesapeake elite, a landed gentry that, in conjunction with merchants who handled the tobacco trade and lawyers who defended the interests of slaveholders, dominated the region's society and politics. Meanwhile, even as the consumer revolution improved the standard of living of lesser whites, their long-term economic prospects diminished. As slavery expanded, planters engrossed the best lands and wealth among the white population became more and more concentrated. Slavery transformed Chesapeake society into an elaborate hierarchy of degrees of freedom. At the top stood large planters, below them numerous lesser planters and landowning yeomen, and at the bottom a large population of convicts, indentured servants, tenant farmers (who made up half the white households in 1770), and, of course, the slaves.

Young Charles Calvert, a member of an aristocratic Maryland family, painted in 1761 by John Hesselius, who produced numerous portraits of prominent residents of the Chesapeake. The boy, obviously the son of wealthy parents, stands next to a young slave, a symbol of his family's wealth. Calvert holds drumsticks and the slave his drum, an allusion to a possible future military career.

Freedom and Slavery in the Chesapeake

With the consolidation of a slave society in the Chesapeake, planters filled the law books with measures enhancing the master's power over his human property and restricting blacks' access to freedom. Violence lay at the heart of the slave system. Even a planter like Landon Carter, who prided himself on his concern for the well-being of his slaves, noted casually in his diary, "They have been severely whipped day by day."

Race took on more and more importance as a line of social division. Whites increasingly considered free blacks dangerous and undesirable. Free blacks lost the right to employ white servants and to bear arms, were subjected to special taxes, and could be punished for striking a white person, regardless of the cause. In 1723, Virginia revoked the voting privileges of property-owning free blacks. When the Lords of Trade in London asked Virginia's governor to justify discriminating among "freemen, merely upon account of their complexion," he responded that "a distinction ought to be made between their offspring and the descendants of an Englishman, with whom they never were to be accounted equal." Because Virginia law required that freed slaves be sent out of the colony, free blacks remained only a tiny part of the population—less than 4 percent in 1750. "Free" and "white" had become virtually identical.

Indian Slavery in Early Carolina

Sale of Indian slaves

Farther south, a different slave system, based on rice production, emerged in South Carolina and Georgia. The Barbadians who initially settled South Carolina in the 1670s were quite familiar with African slavery, but their first victims were members of the area's native population. The local Creek Indians initially welcomed the settlers and began selling them slaves, generally war captives and their families, most of whom were sold to the West Indies. They even launched wars against neighboring tribes specifically for the purpose of capturing and selling slaves. As the plantation system expanded, however, the Creeks became more and more concerned, not only because it led to encroachments on their land but also because they feared enslavement themselves. They were aware that only a handful of slaves worked in nearby Spanish Florida. The Creeks, one leader remarked in 1738, preferred to deal with the Spanish, who "enslave no one as the English do."

The Rice Kingdom

As in early Virginia, frontier conditions allowed leeway to South Carolina's small population of African-born slaves, who farmed, tended livestock, and were initially allowed to serve in the militia to fight the Spanish and Indians. And as in Virginia, the introduction of a marketable staple crop, in this case rice, led directly to economic development, the large-scale importation of slaves, and a growing divide between white and black. South Carolina was the first mainland colony to achieve a black majority. By the 1730s (by which time North Carolina had become a separate colony), two-thirds of its population was black. In the 1740s, another staple, indigo (a crop used in producing blue dye), was developed. Like rice, indigo required large-scale cultivation and was grown by slaves.

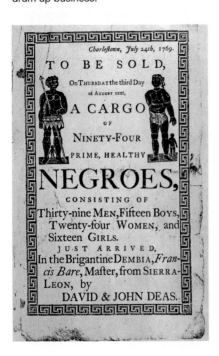

Slave Sale Broadside. This 1769 broadside advertises the sale of ninety-four slaves who had just arrived in Charleston from West Africa. Broadsides like this one were displayed prominently by slave traders to drum up business.

Charlestown, July 24th, 1769.
TO BE SOLD,
On Thursday the third Day of August next,
A CARGO OF NINETY-FOUR PRIME, HEALTHY
NEGROES,
CONSISTING OF
Thirty-nine Men, Fifteen Boys, Twenty-four Women, and Sixteen Girls.
JUST ARRIVED,
In the Brigantine Dembia, Francis Bare, Master, from Sierra-Leon, by
DAVID & JOHN DEAS.

Ironically, it was Africans, familiar with the crop at home, who taught English settlers how to cultivate rice, which then became the foundation of South Carolina slavery and of the wealthiest slaveowning class on the North American mainland. Since rice production requires considerable capital investment to drain swamps and create irrigation systems, it is economically advantageous for rice plantations to be as large as possible. Thus, South Carolina planters owned far more land and slaves than their counterparts in Virginia. Moreover, since mosquitoes bearing malaria (a disease to which Africans had developed partial immunity) flourished in the watery rice fields, planters tended to leave plantations under the control of overseers and the slaves themselves.

In the Chesapeake, field slaves worked in groups under constant supervision. Under the "task" system that developed in eighteenth-century South Carolina, individual slaves were assigned daily jobs, the completion of which allowed them time for leisure or to cultivate crops of their own. In 1762, one rice district had a population of only 76 white males among 1,000 slaves. Fearful of the ever-increasing black population majority, South Carolina's legislature took steps to encourage the immigration of "poor Protestants," offering each newcomer a cash bounty and occasionally levying taxes on slave imports, only to see such restrictions overturned in London. By 1770, the number of South Carolina slaves had reached 75,000, well over half the colony's population.

The Georgia Experiment

Rice cultivation also spread into Georgia in the mid-eighteenth century. The colony was founded in 1732 by a group of philanthropists led by James Oglethorpe, a wealthy reformer whose causes included improved conditions for imprisoned debtors and the abolition of slavery. Oglethorpe hoped to establish a haven where the "worthy poor" of England could enjoy economic opportunity. The government in London supported the creation of Georgia to protect South Carolina against the Spanish and their Indian allies in Florida.

Founding of Georgia

Initially, the proprietors banned the introduction of both liquor and slaves, leading to continual battles with settlers, who desired both. By the 1740s, Georgia offered the spectacle of colonists pleading for the "English liberty" of self-government so that they could enact laws introducing slavery. In 1751, the proprietors surrendered the colony to the crown. The colonists quickly won the right to an elected assembly, which met in Savannah, Georgia's main settlement. It repealed the ban on slavery (and liquor), as well as an early measure that had limited land holdings to 500 acres. Georgia became a miniature version of South Carolina. By 1770, as many as 15,000 slaves labored on its coastal rice plantations.

Slavery in the North

Compared to the plantation regions, slavery was far less central to the economies of New England and the Middle Colonies, where small farms predominated. Slaves made up only a small percentage of these colonies' populations, and it was unusual for even rich families to own more than one or two slaves. Nonetheless, slavery was not entirely marginal to northern colonial life. Slaves worked as farm hands, in artisan shops, as stevedores loading and unloading ships, and as personal servants. With slaves so small a part of the population that they seemed to pose no threat to the white majority, laws were less harsh than in the South. In New England, where in 1770 the 15,000 slaves represented less than 3 percent of the region's population, slave marriages were recognized in law, the severe physical punishment of slaves was prohibited, and slaves could bring suits in court, testify against whites, and own property and pass it on to their children—rights unknown in the South.

Slavery had been present in New York from the earliest days of Dutch settlement. With white immigration lagging behind that of Pennsylvania, the colony's Hudson Valley landlords, small farmers, and craftsmen continued to employ considerable amounts of slave labor in the eighteenth century. As New York City's role in the slave trade expanded, so did slavery in the city. In 1746, its 2,440 slaves

TABLE 4.1 Slave Population as Percentage of Total Population of Original Thirteen Colonies, 1770

COLONY	SLAVE POPULATION	PERCENTAGE
Virginia	187,600	42%
South Carolina	75,168	61
North Carolina	69,600	35
Maryland	63,818	32
New York	19,062	12
Georgia	15,000	45
New Jersey	8,220	7
Connecticut	5,698	3
Pennsylvania	5,561	2
Massachusetts	4,754	2
Rhode Island	3,761	6
Delaware	1,836	5
New Hampshire	654	1

A portrait of Ayuba Diallo, a Muslim merchant in Senegal who became a victim of the slave trade in 1731 and was transported to Maryland. He escaped in 1733 and with the help of wealthy patrons regained his freedom. Because of Diallo's unusual talents—he knew both English and Arabic and could relate the Koran from memory—he became a celebrity in England, which he visited in 1733. He sat for two portraits by the noted artist William Hoare. This is the earliest known painting of an African who experienced slavery in Britain's North American colonies. Diallo returned to his homeland in 1734.

Slave imports

amounted to one-fifth of New York City's total population. Some 30 percent of its laborers were slaves, a proportion second only to Charleston among American cities. Most were domestic workers, but slaves worked in all sectors of the economy. In 1770, about 27,000 slaves lived in New York and New Jersey, 10 percent of their total population. Slavery was also a significant presence in Philadelphia, although the institution stagnated after 1750 as artisans and merchants relied increasingly on wage laborers, whose numbers were augmented by population growth and the completion of the terms of indentured servants. In an urban economy that expanded and contracted according to the ups and downs of international trade, many employers concluded that relying on wage labor, which could be hired and fired at will, made more economic sense than a long-term investment in slaves.

SLAVE CULTURES AND SLAVE RESISTANCE

Becoming African-American

The nearly 300,000 Africans brought to the mainland colonies during the eighteenth century were not a single people. They came from different cultures, spoke different languages, and practiced many religions. Eventually, an African-American people would emerge from the diverse peoples transported to the British colonies in the Middle Passage. Slavery threw together individuals who would never otherwise have encountered one another and who had never considered their color or residence on a single continent a source of identity or unity. Their bond was not kinship, language, or even "race," but slavery itself. The process of creating a cohesive culture and community took many years, and it proceeded at different rates in different regions. But by the nineteenth century, slaves no longer identified themselves as Ibo, Ashanti, Yoruba, and so on, but as African-Americans. In music, art, folklore, language, and religion, their cultural expressions emerged as a synthesis of African traditions, European elements, and new conditions in America.

For most of the eighteenth century, the majority of American slaves were African by birth. Advertisements seeking information about runaways often described them by African origin ("young Gambia Negro," "new Banbara Negro fellow") and spoke of their bearing on their bodies "country marks"—visible signs of ethnic identity in Africa. Indeed, during the eighteenth century, black life in the colonies was "re-Africanized" as the earlier Creoles (slaves born in the New World) came to be outnumbered by large-scale importations from Africa. Compared with the earliest generation of slaves, the newcomers worked harder, died earlier, and had less access to freedom. Charles Hansford, a white Virginia blacksmith, noted in a 1753 poem that he had frequently heard slaves speak of their desire to "reenjoy" life in Africa:

> I oft with pleasure have observ'd how they
> Their sultry country's worth strive to display
> In broken language, how they praise their case
> And happiness when in their native place . . .
> How would they dangers court and pains endure
> If to their country they could get secure!

African Religion in Colonial America

No experience was more wrenching for African slaves in the colonies than the transition from traditional religions to Christianity. Islam had spread across North Africa and the region of the Sahara Desert. The slaves who ended up in British North America, however, came from the forest regions of West Africa, where traditional religions continued to be practiced. Although these religions varied as much as those on other continents, they shared some elements, especially belief in the presence of spiritual forces in nature and a close relationship between the sacred and secular worlds. West Africans, like Europeans, Equiano wrote, believed in a single "Creator of all things," who "governs events" on earth, but otherwise their religious beliefs seemed more similar to those of Native Americans than to Christianity. In West African religions, there was no hard and fast distinction between the secular and spiritual worlds. Nature was suffused with spirits and the dead could influence the living: the spirits of departed "friends or relations always attend them and guard them from the bad spirits of their foes."

West African religions

Although some slaves came to the colonies familiar with Christianity or Islam, the majority of North American slaves practiced traditional African religions (which many Europeans deemed superstition or even witchcraft) well into the eighteenth century. When they did adopt Protestant religious practices, many slaves melded them with traditional beliefs, adding the Christian God to their own pantheon of lesser spirits, whom they continued to worship. A similar process occurred in slave societies like Brazil and Cuba, where African spirits merged with Catholic saints.

Melding of Christianity with traditional beliefs

The Old Plantation, a late-eighteenth-century watercolor, depicts slaves dancing in a plantation's slave quarters, perhaps at a wedding. The musical instruments and pottery are African in origin while much of the clothing is of European manufacture, indicating the mixing of African and white cultures among the era's slaves. The artist has recently been identified as John Rose, owner of a rice plantation near Beaufort, South Carolina.

African-American Cultures

By the mid-eighteenth century, the three slave systems in British North America had produced distinct African-American cultures. In the Chesapeake, because of a more healthful climate, the slave population began to reproduce itself by 1740, creating a more balanced sex ratio than in the seventeenth century and making possible the creation of family-centered slave communities. Because of the small size of most plantations and the large number of white **yeoman farmers**, slaves here were continuously exposed to white culture. They soon learned English, and many were swept up in the religious revivals known as the Great Awakening, discussed later in this chapter.

In South Carolina and Georgia, two very different black societies emerged. On the rice plantations, slaves lived in extremely harsh conditions and had a low birthrate throughout the eighteenth century, making rice production dependent on continued slave imports from Africa. The slaves seldom came into contact with whites and enjoyed far more autonomy than elsewhere in the colonies. The larger structures of their lives were established by slavery, but they were able to create an African-based culture. They constructed African-style houses, chose African names for their children, and spoke Gullah, a language that mixed various African roots and was unintelligible to most whites. Despite a continuing slave trade in which young, single males predominated, slaves slowly created families and communities that bridged generations. The experience of slaves who labored in Charleston and Savannah as servants and skilled workers was quite different. These assimilated more quickly into Euro-American culture, and sexual liaisons between white owners and slave women produced the beginnings of a class of free mulattos.

In the northern colonies, where slaves represented a smaller part of the population, dispersed in small holdings among the white population, a distinctive African-American culture developed more slowly. Living in close proximity to whites, they enjoyed more mobility and access to the mainstream of life than their counterparts farther south. But they had fewer opportunities to create stable family life or a cohesive community.

Resistance to Slavery

The common threads that linked these regional African-American cultures were the experience of slavery and the desire for freedom. Throughout the eighteenth century, blacks risked their lives in efforts to resist enslavement. Colonial newspapers, especially in the southern colonies, were filled with advertisements for runaway slaves. Most fugitives were young African men who had arrived recently. In South Carolina and Georgia, they fled to Florida, to uninhabited coastal and river swamps, or to Charleston and Savannah, where they could pass for free. In the Chesapeake and Middle Colonies, fugitive slaves tended to be familiar with white culture and therefore, as one advertisement put it, could "pretend to be free."

What Edward Trelawny, the colonial governor of Jamaica, called "a dangerous spirit of liberty" was widespread among the New World's slaves. The eighteenth century's first slave uprising occurred in New York City in 1712, when a group of slaves set fire to houses on the outskirts of the city and killed the first nine whites

This portrait of William Duguid, a Boston textile merchant, was painted in 1773 by Prince Demah Barnes. It depicts Duguid wearing imported clothing with an elaborate floral pattern. What makes the painting unique, however, is that Barnes was a slave whose owner, a Massachusetts merchant, encouraged what he called Barnes's "natural genius" and took him on a brief visit to London for training. Still a slave, Barnes enlisted in the Massachusetts militia in 1777 after his Loyalist owners fled the state. He died of smallpox in 1778.

Running away

who arrived on the scene. Subsequently, eighteen conspirators were executed; some were tortured and burned alive in a public spectacle meant to intimidate the slave population. During the 1730s and 1740s, continuous warfare involving European empires and Indians opened the door to slave resistance. In 1731, a slave rebellion in Louisiana, where the French and Natchez Indians were at war, temporarily halted efforts to introduce the plantation system in that region. There were uprisings throughout the West Indies, including in the Virgin Islands, owned by Denmark, and on the French island of Guadeloupe. On Jamaica, a major British center of sugar production, communities of fugitive slaves known as "maroons" waged outright warfare against British authorities until a treaty of 1739 recognized their freedom, in exchange for which they agreed to return future escapees.

An advertisement seeking the return of four runaway slaves from New York City. Note the careful description of the fugitives' clothing and the diversity of the names, presumably given by their owners—two common English names, one of African origin and one alluding to ancient Rome. The reward offered is a substantial amount of money in the colonial era.

The Crisis of 1739–1741

On the mainland, slaves seized the opportunity for rebellion offered by the War of Jenkins' Ear, which pitted England against Spain. In September 1739, a group of South Carolina slaves, most of them recently arrived from Kongo where some, it appears, had been soldiers, seized a store containing numerous weapons at the town of Stono. Beating drums to attract followers, the armed band marched southward toward Florida, burning houses and barns, killing whites they encountered, and shouting "Liberty." (Florida's Spanish rulers offered "Liberty and Protection" to fugitives from the British colonies.) The group eventually swelled to some 100 slaves. After a pitched battle with the colony's militia, the rebels were dispersed. The rebellion took the lives of more than two dozen whites and as many as 200 slaves, including many who had no connection to the rebellion. Some slaves managed to reach Florida, where in 1740 they were armed by the Spanish to help repel an attack on St. Augustine by a force from Georgia. The **Stono Rebellion** led to a severe tightening of the South Carolina slave code and the temporary imposition of a prohibitive tax on imported slaves.

The Stono Rebellion

In 1741, a panic (which some observers compared to the fear of witches in Salem in the 1690s) swept New York City. After a series of fires broke out, rumors spread that slaves, with some white allies, planned to burn part of the city, seize weapons, and either turn New York over to Spain or murder the white population. More than 150 blacks and 20 whites were arrested, and 34 alleged conspirators, including 4 white persons, were executed. Historians still disagree as to how extensive the plot was or whether it existed at all. But dramatic events like revolts, along with the constant stream of runaways, disproved the idea, voiced by the governor of South Carolina, that slaves had "no notion of liberty." In eighteenth-century America, dreams of freedom knew no racial boundary.

Panic in New York

AN EMPIRE OF FREEDOM

British Patriotism

British power

Despite the centrality of slavery to its empire, eighteenth-century Great Britain prided itself on being the world's most advanced and freest nation. It was not only the era's greatest naval and commercial power but also the home of a complex governmental system with a powerful Parliament representing the interests of a self-confident landed aristocracy and merchant class. In London, the largest city in Europe with a population approaching 1 million by the end of the eighteenth century, Britain possessed a single political-cultural-economic capital. It enjoyed a common law, common language, and, with the exception of a small number of Jews, Catholics, and Africans, common devotion to Protestantism. For much of the eighteenth century, Britain found itself at war with France, which had replaced Spain as its major continental rival. This situation led to the development of a large military establishment, high taxes, and the creation of the Bank of England to help finance European and imperial conflicts. For both Britons and colonists, war helped to sharpen a sense of national identity against foreign foes.

British identity

British patriotic sentiment became more and more assertive as the eighteenth century progressed. Symbols of British identity proliferated: the songs "God Save the King" and "Rule, Britannia," and even the modern rules of cricket, the national sport. The rapidly expanding British economy formed another point of pride uniting Britons and colonists. Continental peoples, according to a popular saying, wore "wooden shoes"—that is, their standard of living was far below that of Britons. Especially in contrast to France, Britain saw itself as a realm of widespread prosperity, individual liberty, the rule of law, and the Protestant faith. Wealth, religion, and freedom went together. "There is no Popish nation," wrote the Massachusetts theologian Cotton Mather in 1710, "but what by embracing the Protestant Religion would . . . not only assert themselves into a glorious liberty, but also double their wealth immediately."

The British Constitution

British liberty

Central to this sense of British identity was the concept of liberty. The fierce political struggles of the English Civil War and the Glorious Revolution bequeathed to eighteenth-century Britons an abiding conviction that liberty was their unique possession. They believed power and liberty to be natural antagonists. To mediate between them, advocates of British freedom celebrated the rule of law, the right to live under legislation to which one's representatives had consented, restraints on the arbitrary exercise of political authority, and rights like trial by jury enshrined in the common law. On both sides of the Atlantic, every political cause, it seemed, wrapped itself in the language of liberty and claimed to be defending the "rights of Englishmen." Continental writers dissatisfied with the lack of liberty in their own countries looked to Britain as a model. The House of Commons, House of Lords, and king each checked the power of the others. This structure, wrote the French political philosopher Baron Montesquieu, made Britain "the one nation in the world whose constitution has political liberty for its purpose." In its "balanced constitution" and the principle that no man, even the king, is above the law, Britons claimed to have devised the best means of preventing political tyranny. Until the 1770s, most colonists believed themselves to be part of the freest political system mankind had ever known.

As the coexistence of slavery and liberty within the empire demonstrated, British freedom was anything but universal. It was closely identified with the Protestant religion and was invoked to contrast Britons with the "servile" subjects of Catholic countries. It viewed nearly every other nation on earth as "enslaved"—to popery, tyranny, or barbarism. One German military officer commented in 1743 on the British "contempt" of foreigners: "They [pride] themselves not only upon their being free themselves, but being the bulwarks of liberty all over Europe; and they vilify most of the Nations on the continent . . . for being slaves, as they call us." British liberty was fully compatible with wide gradations in personal rights. Yet in the minds of the free residents of Great Britain and its North American colonies, liberty was the bond of empire.

A 1770 engraving from the *Boston Gazette* by Paul Revere illustrates the association of British patriotism and liberty. Britannia sits with a liberty cap and her national shield, and releases a bird from a cage.

These ideas sank deep roots not only within the "political nation"—those who voted, held office, and engaged in structured political debate—but also far more broadly in British and colonial society. Laborers, sailors, and artisans spoke the language of British freedom as insistently as pamphleteers and parliamentarians. Although most white men in Britain and many in the colonies lacked the right to vote, they influenced public life in other ways, serving on juries, and taking to the streets to protest what they considered oppressive authority. Ordinary persons protested efforts by merchants to raise the cost of bread above the traditional "just price," and the Royal Navy's practice of "impressment"—kidnapping poor men on the streets for maritime service.

> *Protests against authority*

Republican Liberty

Liberty was central to two sets of political ideas that flourished in the Anglo-American world. One is termed by scholars **republicanism** (although few in eighteenth-century England used the word, which literally meant a government without a king and conjured up memories of the beheading of Charles I). Republicanism celebrated active participation in public life by economically independent citizens as the essence of liberty. Republicans assumed that only property-owning citizens possessed "virtue"—defined in the eighteenth century not simply as a personal moral quality but as the willingness to subordinate self-interest to the pursuit of the public good. "Only a virtuous people are capable of freedom," wrote Benjamin Franklin.

In eighteenth-century Britain, this body of thought about freedom was most closely associated with a group of critics of the established political order known as the "Country Party" because much of their support arose from the landed gentry. In Britain, Country Party publicists like John Trenchard and Thomas Gordon, authors of *Cato's Letters*, published in the 1720s, had little impact. But their writings were eagerly devoured in the American colonies, whose elites were attracted to Trenchard and Gordon's emphasis on the political role of the independent

> *The "Country Party"*

The Polling, by the renowned eighteenth-century British artist William Hogarth, satirizes the idea that British elections are decided by the reasoned deliberations of upstanding property owners. Inspired by a corrupt election of 1754, Hogarth depicts an election scene in which the maimed and dying are brought to the polls to cast ballots. At the center, lawyers argue over whether a man who has a hook for a hand can swear on the Bible.

landowner and their warnings against the constant tendency of political power to infringe upon liberty.

Liberal Freedom

The second set of eighteenth-century political ideas celebrating freedom came to be known as **liberalism** (although its meaning was quite different from what the word suggests today). Whereas republican liberty had a public and social quality, liberalism was essentially individual and private. The leading philosopher of liberty was John Locke, whose *Two Treatises of Government*, written around 1680, had limited influence in his own lifetime but became extremely well known in the next century. Government, he wrote, was formed by a mutual agreement among equals (the parties being male heads of households, not all persons). In this "social contract," men surrendered a part of their right to govern themselves in order to enjoy the benefits of the rule of law. They retained, however, their natural rights, whose existence predated the establishment of political authority. Protecting the security of life, liberty, and property required shielding a realm of private life and personal concerns—including family relations, religious preferences, and economic activity—from interference by the state. During the eighteenth century, Lockean ideas—individual rights, the consent of the governed, the right of rebellion against unjust or oppressive government—would become familiar on both sides of the Atlantic.

Like other Britons, Locke spoke of liberty as a universal right yet seemed to exclude many persons from its full benefits. While Locke was one of the first theorists to defend the property rights of women and even their access to divorce, and condemned slavery as a "vile and miserable estate of man," the free individual in liberal thought was essentially the propertied white man. Nonetheless,

Locke's Two Treatises of Government

by proclaiming that all individuals possess natural rights that no government may violate, Lockean liberalism opened the door to the poor, women, and even slaves to challenge limitations on their own freedom.

In the eighteenth century, these systems of thought overlapped and often reinforced each other. Both political outlooks could inspire a commitment to constitutional government and restraints on despotic power. Both emphasized the security of property as a foundation of freedom. Both traditions were transported to eighteenth-century America. Ideas about liberty imported from Britain to the colonies would eventually help to divide the empire.

THE PUBLIC SPHERE

Colonial politics for most of the eighteenth century was considerably less tempestuous than in the seventeenth, with its bitter struggles for power and frequent armed uprisings. Political stability in Britain coupled with the maturation of local elites in America made for more tranquil government. New York stood apart from this development. With its diverse population and bitter memories of Leisler's rebellion (see Chapter 3), New York continued to experience intense political strife among its many economic interests and ethnic groups. By the 1750s, semipermanent political parties competed vigorously for popular support in New York elections. But in most other colonies, although differences over policies of one kind or another were hardly absent, they rarely produced the civil disorder or political passions of the previous century.

The Right to Vote

In many respects, politics in eighteenth-century America had a more democratic quality than in Great Britain. Suffrage requirements varied from colony to colony, but as in Britain the linchpin of voting laws was the property qualification. Its purpose was to ensure that men who possessed an economic stake in society and the independence of judgment that supposedly went with it determined the policies of the government. The "foundation of liberty," the parliamentary leader Henry Ireton had declared during the English Civil War of the 1640s, "is that those who shall choose the lawmakers shall be men freed from dependence upon others." Slaves, servants, tenants, adult sons living in the homes of their parents, the poor, and women all lacked a "will of their own" and were therefore ineligible to vote. The wide distribution of property in the colonies, however, meant that a far higher percentage of the population enjoyed voting rights than in the Old World. It is estimated that between 50 and 80 percent of adult white men could vote in eighteenth-century colonial America, as opposed to fewer than 5 percent in Britain at the time.

Colonial politics, however, was hardly democratic in a modern sense. In a few instances—some towns in Massachusetts and on Long Island—propertied women, generally widows, cast ballots. But voting was almost everywhere considered a male prerogative. In some colonies, Jews, Catholics, and Protestant Dissenters like Baptists and Quakers could not vote. Propertied free blacks, who enjoyed the franchise in Virginia, South Carolina, and Georgia in the early days of settlement, lost

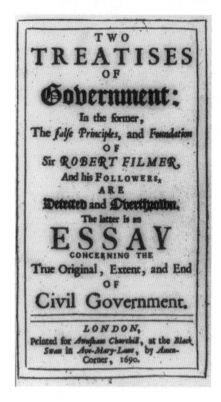

The title page of John Locke's *Two Treatises of Government*, which traced the origins of government to an original state of nature and insisted that political authorities must not abridge mankind's natural rights.

The British political philosopher John Locke, painted by Michael Dahl around 1696.

that right during the eighteenth century. In the northern colonies, while the law did not bar blacks from voting, local custom did. Native Americans were generally prohibited from voting.

Political Cultures

Despite the broad electorate among white men, "the people" existed only on election day. Between elections, members of colonial assemblies remained out of touch with their constituents. Strongly competitive elections were the norm only in the Middle Colonies. Elsewhere, many elections went uncontested, either because only one candidate presented himself or because the local culture stressed community harmony, as in many New England towns. Considerable power in colonial politics rested with those who held appointive, not elective, office. Governors and councils were appointed by the crown in the nine royal colonies and by the proprietors of Pennsylvania and Maryland. Only in Rhode Island and Connecticut were these offices elective. Moreover, laws passed by colonial assemblies could be vetoed by governors or in London. In New England, most town officers were elected, but local officials in other colonies were appointed by the governor or by powerful officials in London. The duke of Newcastle alone could appoint eighty-three colonial officials.

Property qualifications for officeholding were far higher than for voting. In South Carolina, for example, nearly every adult male could meet the voting qualification of fifty acres of land or payment of twenty shillings in taxes, but to sit in the assembly one had to own 500 acres of land and ten slaves or town property worth £1,000. As a result, throughout the eighteenth century nearly all of South Carolina's legislators were planters or wealthy merchants. Despite its boisterous and competitive politics, New York's diminutive assembly, with fewer than thirty members, was dominated by relatives and allies of the great landed families, especially the Livingstons and De Lanceys. Of seventy-two men who sat in the New York Assembly between 1750 and 1776, fifty-two were related to the families who owned the great Hudson River estates.

In some colonies, a majority of free men possessed the right to vote, but an ingrained tradition of "deference"—the assumption among ordinary people that wealth, education, and social prominence carried a right to public office—sharply limited effective choice in elections. Virginia politics, for example, combined political democracy for white men with the tradition that voters should choose among candidates from the gentry. Aspirants for public office actively sought to ingratiate themselves with ordinary voters, distributing food and liquor freely at the courthouse where balloting took place. In Thomas Jefferson's first campaign for the House of Burgesses in 1768, his expenses included hiring two men "for bringing up rum" to the polling place. Even in New England, with its larger number of elective positions, town leaders were generally the largest property holders and offices frequently passed from generation to generation in the same family.

Appointive office

This 1765 engraving depicting an election in Pennsylvania suggests the intensity of political debate in the Middle Colonies, as well as the social composition of the electorate. Those shown arguing outside the Old Court House in Philadelphia include physicians (with wigs and gold-topped canes), ministers, and lawyers. A line of men wait on the steps to vote.

Colonial Government

Preoccupied with events in Europe and imperial rivalries, successive British governments during the first half of the eighteenth century adopted a policy of **salutary neglect** toward the colonies, leaving them largely to govern themselves. With imperial authority so weak, the large landowners, merchants, and lawyers who dominated colonial assemblies increasingly claimed the right to control local politics.

Colonial assemblies

Convinced that they represented the will of the people, elected colonial assemblies used their control of finance to exert influence over appointed governors and councils. Although governors desired secure incomes for themselves and permanent revenue for their administrations (Robert Hunter of New York demanded a life salary), assemblies often authorized salaries only one year at a time and refused to levy taxes except in exchange for concessions on appointments, land policy, and other issues. Typically members of the British gentry who had suffered financial reversals and hoped to recoup their fortunes in America, governors learned that to rule effectively they would have to cooperate with the colonial elite.

The Rise of the Assemblies

In the seventeenth century, the governor was the focal point of political authority, and colonial assemblies were weak bodies that met infrequently. But in the eighteenth, as economic development enhanced the power of American elites, the assemblies they dominated became more and more assertive. Their leaders insisted that assemblies possessed the same rights and powers in local affairs as the House of Commons enjoyed in Britain. The most successful governors were those who accommodated the rising power of the assemblies and used their appointive powers and control of land grants to win allies among assembly members.

The most powerful assembly was Pennsylvania's, where a new charter, adopted in 1701, eliminated the governor's council, establishing the only unicameral (one-house) legislature in the colonies. Controlled until mid-century by an elite of Quaker merchants, the assembly wrested control of finance, appointments, and the militia from a series of governors representing the Penn family. Close behind in terms of power and legislative independence were the assemblies of New York, Virginia, South Carolina, and, especially, Massachusetts, which successfully resisted governors' demands for permanent salaries for appointed officials. Many of the conflicts between governors and elected assemblies stemmed from the colonies' economic growth. To deal with the scarcity of gold and silver coins, the only legal form of currency, some colonies printed paper money, although this was strongly opposed by the governors, authorities in London, and British merchants who did not wish to be paid in what they considered worthless paper. Numerous battles also took place over land policy (sometimes involving divergent attitudes toward the remaining Indian population) and the level of rents charged to farmers on land owned by the crown or proprietors.

Conflicts between governors and assemblies

In their negotiations and conflicts with royal governors, leaders of the assemblies drew on the writings of the English Country Party, whose emphasis on the constant tension between liberty and political power and the dangers of executive influence over the legislature made sense of their own experience. Of the European settlements in North America, only the British colonies possessed any considerable degree of popular participation in government. This fact reinforced the assemblies' claim to embody the rights of Englishmen and the principle of popular consent to government. They were defenders of "the people's liberty," in the words of one New York legislator.

Politics in Public

The public sphere

This language reverberated outside the relatively narrow world of elective and legislative politics. The "political nation" was dominated by the American gentry, whose members addressed each other in letters, speeches, newspaper articles, and pamphlets filled with Latin expressions and references to classical learning. But especially in colonial towns and cities, the eighteenth century witnessed a considerable expansion of the "public sphere"—the world of political organization and debate independent of the government, where an informed citizenry openly discussed questions that had previously been the preserve of officials.

In Boston, New York, and Philadelphia, clubs proliferated where literary, philosophical, scientific, and political issues were debated. Among the best known was the Junto, a "club for mutual improvement" founded by Benjamin Franklin in Philadelphia in 1727 for weekly discussion of political and economic questions. Beginning with only a dozen members, it eventually evolved into the much larger American Philosophical Society. Such groups were generally composed of men of property and commerce, but some drew ordinary citizens into discussions of public affairs. Colonial taverns and coffeehouses also became important sites not only for social conviviality but also for political debates. Philadelphia had a larger number of drinking establishments per capita than Paris. In Philadelphia, one clergyman commented, "the poorest laborer thinks himself entitled to deliver his sentiments in matters of religion or politics with as much freedom as the gentleman or scholar."

Benjamin Franklin's quest for self-improvement, or, as he put it in his autobiography, "moral perfection," is illustrated in this "Temperance diagram," which charts his behavior each day of the week with regard to thirteen virtues. They are listed on the left by their first letters: temperance, silence, order, resolution, frugality, industry, sincerity, justice, moderation, cleanliness, tranquility, chastity, and humility. Franklin did not always adhere to these virtues.

The Colonial Press

Neither the Spanish possessions of Florida and New Mexico nor New France possessed a printing press, although missionaries had established one in Mexico City in the 1530s. In British North America, however, the press expanded rapidly during the eighteenth century. So did the number of political broadsides and pamphlets published, especially at election time. Widespread literacy created an expanding market for printed materials. By the eve of the American Revolution, some three-quarters of the free adult male population in the colonies (and more than one-third of the women) could read and write, and a majority of American families owned at least one book. Philadelphia boasted no fewer than seventy-seven bookshops in the 1770s.

Circulating libraries appeared in many colonial cities and towns, making possible a wider dissemination of knowledge at a time when books were still expensive. The first, the Library Company of Philadelphia, was established by Benjamin Franklin in 1731. "So few were the readers at that time, and the majority of us so poor," Franklin recalled in his *Autobiography* (1791), that he could find only fifty persons, mostly "young tradesmen," anxious for self-improvement and willing to pay for the privilege of borrowing books. But reading, he added, soon "became fashionable." Libraries sprang up in other towns, and ordinary

Americans came to be "better instructed and more intelligent than people of the same rank" abroad.

The first continuously published colonial newspaper, the *Boston News-Letter*, appeared in 1704 (a predecessor, *Publick Occurrences, Both Foreign and Domestick*, established in Boston in 1690, had been suppressed by authorities after a single issue for criticizing military cooperation with the Iroquois). There were thirteen colonial newspapers by 1740 and twenty-five in 1765, mostly weeklies with small circulations—an average of 600 sales per issue. Probably the best-edited newspaper was the *Pennsylvania Gazette*, established in 1728 in Philadelphia and purchased the following year by Benjamin Franklin, who had earlier worked as an apprentice printer on his brother's Boston periodical, the *New England Courant*. At its peak, the *Gazette* attracted 2,000 subscribers. Newspapers initially devoted most of their space to advertisements, religious affairs, and reports on British society and government. But by the 1730s, political commentary was widespread in the American press.

Freedom of Expression and Its Limits

The public sphere thrived on the free exchange of ideas. But free expression was not generally considered one of the ancient rights of Englishmen. The phrase "freedom of speech" originated in Britain during the sixteenth century in Parliament's struggle to achieve the privilege of unrestrained debate. A right of legislators, not ordinary citizens, it referred to the ability of members of Parliament to express their views without fear of reprisal, on the grounds that only in this way could they effectively represent the people. Outside of Parliament, free speech had no legal protection. A subject could be beheaded for accusing the king of failing to hold "true" religious beliefs, and language from swearing to criticism of the government exposed a person to criminal penalties.

Freedom of speech

As for freedom of the press, governments on both sides of the Atlantic viewed this as extremely dangerous, partly because they considered ordinary citizens prone to be misled by inflammatory printed materials. During the English Civil War of the 1640s, the Levellers had called for the adoption of a written constitution, an Agreement of the People, containing guarantees of religious liberty and freedom of the press. But until 1695, when a British law requiring the licensing of printed works before publication lapsed, no newspaper, book, or pamphlet could legally be printed without a government license. The instructions of colonial governors included a warning about the "great inconveniences that may arise by the liberty of printing." After 1695, the government could not censor newspapers, books, and pamphlets before they appeared in print, although it continued to try to manage the press by direct payments to publishers and individual journalists. Authors and publishers could still be prosecuted for "seditious libel"—a crime that included defaming government officials—or punished for contempt.

Freedom of the press

Elected assemblies, not governors, most frequently discouraged freedom of the press in colonial America. Dozens of publishers were hauled before assemblies and forced to apologize for comments regarding one or another member. If they refused, they were jailed. James Franklin, Benjamin's older brother, spent a month in prison in 1722 after publishing a piece satirizing public authorities in Massachusetts. Colonial newspapers vigorously defended freedom of the press as a

The first page of the *New-York Weekly Journal*, edited by John Peter Zenger, one of four issues ordered to be burned by local authorities.

Benjamin Franklin

central component of liberty, insisting that the citizenry had a right to monitor the workings of government and subject public officials to criticism. Many newspapers reprinted passages from *Cato's Letters* in which Trenchard and Gordon strongly opposed prosecutions for libel. "Without freedom of thought," they declared, "there can be no such thing as wisdom, and no such thing as public liberty, without freedom of speech." But since government printing contracts were crucial for economic success, few newspapers attacked colonial governments unless financially supported by an opposition faction.

The Trial of Zenger

The most famous colonial court case involving freedom of the press demonstrated that popular sentiment opposed prosecutions for criticism of public officials. This was the 1735 trial of John Peter Zenger, a German-born printer who had emigrated to New York as a youth. Financed by wealthy opponents of Governor William Cosby, Zenger's newspaper, the *Weekly Journal*, lambasted the governor for corruption, influence peddling, and "tyranny." New York's council ordered four issues burned and had Zenger himself arrested and tried for seditious libel. The judge instructed the jurors to consider only whether Zenger had actually published the offending words, not whether they were accurate. But Zenger's attorney, Andrew Hamilton, urged the jury to judge not the publisher but the governor. If they decided that Zenger's charges were correct, they must acquit him, and, Hamilton proclaimed, "every man who prefers freedom to a life of slavery will bless you."

Zenger was found not guilty. The case sent a warning to prosecutors that libel cases might be very difficult to win, especially in the superheated atmosphere of New York partisan politics. To be sure, had Zenger lambasted the assembly rather than the governor, he would in all likelihood have been lodged in jail without even the benefit of a trial. The law of libel remained on the books. But the outcome helped to promote the idea that the publication of truth should always be permitted, and it demonstrated that the idea of free expression was becoming ingrained in the popular imagination.

The American Enlightenment

During the eighteenth century, many educated Americans began to be influenced by the outlook of the European **Enlightenment**. This philosophical movement, which originated among French thinkers and soon spread to Britain, sought to apply the scientific method of careful investigation based on research and experiment to political and social life. Enlightenment ideas crisscrossed the Atlantic along with goods and people. Enlightenment thinkers insisted that every human institution, authority, and tradition be judged before the bar of reason. The self-educated Benjamin Franklin's wide range of activities—establishing a newspaper, debating club, and library; publishing the widely circulated *Poor Richard's Almanack*; and conducting experiments to demonstrate that lightning is a form of electricity—exemplified the Enlightenment spirit and made him probably the best-known American in the eighteenth-century world.

One inspiration for the American Enlightenment was a reaction against the bloody religious wars that wracked Europe in the seventeenth century. Enlightenment thinkers hoped that "reason," not religious enthusiasm, could govern human life. The criticism of social and political institutions based on tradition and hereditary privilege rather than the dictates of reason could also be applied to established churches. John Locke himself had published *The Reasonableness of Christianity* in 1695, which insisted that religious belief should rest on scientific evidence. During the eighteenth century, many prominent Americans moved toward the position called Arminianism, which taught that reason alone was capable of establishing the essentials of religion. Others adopted **Deism**, a belief that God essentially withdrew after creating the world, leaving it to function according to scientific laws without divine intervention. Belief in miracles, in the revealed truth of the Bible, and in the innate sinfulness of mankind were viewed by Arminians, Deists, and others as outdated superstitions that should be abandoned in the modern age.

In the seventeenth century, the English scientist Isaac Newton had revealed the natural laws that governed the physical universe. Here, Deists believed, was the purest evidence of God's handiwork. Many Protestants of all denominations could accept Newton's findings while remaining devout churchgoers (as Newton himself had). But Deists concluded that the best form of religious devotion was to study the workings of nature, rather than to worship in organized churches or appeal to divine grace for salvation. By the late colonial era, a small but influential group of leading Americans, including Benjamin Franklin and Thomas Jefferson, could be classified as Deists.

THE GREAT AWAKENING

Like freedom of the press, religion was another realm where the actual experience of liberty outstripped its legal recognition. Religion remained central to eighteenth-century American life. Sermons, theological treatises, and copies of the Bible were by far the largest category of material produced by colonial printers. Religious disputes often generated more public attention than political issues. Yet many church leaders worried about lax religious observance as colonial economic growth led people to be more and more preoccupied with worldly affairs.

Religious Revivals

Many ministers were concerned that westward expansion, commercial development, the growth of Enlightenment rationalism, and lack of individual engagement in church services were undermining religious devotion. These fears helped to inspire the revivals that swept through the colonies beginning in the 1730s. Known as the **Great Awakening**, the revivals were less a coordinated movement than a series of local events united by a commitment to a "religion of the heart," a more emotional and personal Christianity than that offered by existing churches. The revivals redrew the religious landscape of the colonies.

The eighteenth century witnessed a revival of religious fundamentalism in many parts of the world, in part a response to the rationalism of the Enlightenment

A 1762 portrait of Benjamin Franklin, done in London by the English artist Mason Chamberlain while Franklin was in the city as agent for the Pennsylvania Assembly. Franklin is depicted as a scientist making notes on his experiments, rather than as a politician. In the background, an electrical storm rages—a reference to Franklin's pioneering experiments that demonstrated the electrical nature of lightning and led to his election as a member of the Royal Society, Britain's premier scientific organization. Franklin also invented the lightning rod. The storm in the painting is destroying buildings that have not installed Franklin's invention.

Threats to religious devotion

Jonathan Edwards, one of the most prominent preachers of the Great Awakening.

Emotional preaching

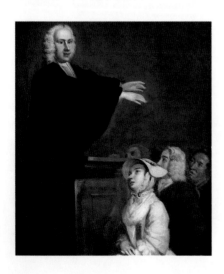

George Whitefield, the English evangelist who helped to spark the Great Awakening in the colonies. Painted around 1742 by John Wollaston, who had emigrated from England to the colonies, the work depicts Whitefield's powerful effect on male and female listeners. It also illustrates Whitefield's eye problem, which led critics to dub him "Dr. Squintum."

and a desire for greater religious purity. In the Middle East and Central Asia, where Islam was widespread, followers of a form of the religion known as Wahhabism called for a return to the practices of the religion's early days. In Eastern Europe, Hasidic Jews emphasized the importance of faith and religious joy as opposed to what they considered the overly academic study of Jewish learning and history in conventional Judaism. Methodism and other forms of enthusiastic religion were flourishing in Europe. Like other intellectual currents of the time, the Great Awakening was a transatlantic movement.

During the 1720s and 1730s, the New Jersey Dutch Reformed clergyman Theodore Frelinghuysen, his Presbyterian neighbors William and Gilbert Tennent, and the Massachusetts Congregationalist minister Jonathan Edwards pioneered an intensely emotional style of preaching. Edwards's famous sermon *Sinners in the Hands of an Angry God* portrayed sinful man as a "loathsome insect" suspended over a bottomless pit of eternal fire by a slender thread that might break at any moment. Edwards's preaching, declared a member of his congregation, inspired worshipers to cry out, "What shall I do to be saved—oh, I am going to hell!" Only a "new birth"—immediately acknowledging one's sins and pleading for divine grace—could save men from eternal damnation. "It is the new birth that makes [sinners] free," declared the Reverend Joshua Tufts.

The Preaching of Whitefield

More than any other individual, the English minister George Whitefield, who declared "the whole world his parish," sparked the Great Awakening. For two years after his arrival in America in 1739, Whitefield brought his highly emotional brand of preaching to colonies from Georgia to New England. God, Whitefield proclaimed, was merciful. Rather than being predestined for damnation, men and women could save themselves by repenting of their sins. Whitefield appealed to the passions of his listeners, powerfully sketching the boundless joy of salvation and the horrors of damnation. In every sermon, he asked his listeners to look into their own hearts and answer the question, "Are you saved?" If not, they must change their sinful ways and surrender their lives to Christ.

Tens of thousands of colonists flocked to Whitefield's sermons, which were widely reported in the American press, making him a celebrity and helping to establish the revivals as the first major intercolonial event in North American history. In Whitefield's footsteps, a host of traveling preachers or "evangelists" (meaning, literally, bearers of good news) held revivalist meetings, often to the alarm of established ministers.

Critics of the Great Awakening produced sermons, pamphlets, and newspaper articles condemning the revivalist preachers for lacking theological training, encouraging disrespect for "the established church and her ministers," and filling churches with "general disorder." Connecticut sought to stem the revivalist tide through laws punishing disruptive traveling preachers. By the time they subsided in the 1760s, the revivals had changed the religious configuration of the colonies and enlarged the boundaries of liberty. Whitefield had inspired the emergence of numerous Dissenting churches. Congregations split into factions headed by Old Lights (traditionalists) and New Lights (revivalists), and new churches proliferated—Baptist, Methodist, Presbyterian, and others. Many of these new churches began to criticize the colonial practice of levying taxes to support an established church; they defended religious freedom as one of the natural rights government must not restrict.

The Awakening's Impact

Although the revivals were primarily a spiritual matter, the Great Awakening reflected existing social tensions, threw into question many forms of authority, and inspired criticism of aspects of colonial society. They attracted primarily men and women of modest means—"rude, ignorant, void of manners, education or good breeding," one Anglican minister complained. Revivalist preachers frequently criticized commercial society, insisting that believers should make salvation, not profit, "the one business of their lives." In New England, they condemned merchants who ensnared the unwary in debt as greedy and unchristian. Preaching to the small farmers of the southern backcountry, Baptist and Methodist revivalists criticized the worldliness of wealthy planters and attacked as sinful activities such as gambling, horse racing, and lavish entertainments on the Sabbath.

A few preachers explicitly condemned slavery. And a few converts, such as Robert Carter III, the grandson of the wealthy planter Robert "King" Carter, emancipated their slaves after concluding that black and white were brothers in Christ. Most masters managed to reconcile Christianity and slaveholding. But especially in the Chesapeake, the revivals brought numerous slaves into the Christian fold, an important step in their acculturation as African-Americans. And a few blacks, touched by the word of God, took up preaching themselves. The revivals also spawned a group of female exhorters, who for a time shattered the male monopoly on preaching.

The revivals broadened the range of religious alternatives available to Americans, thereby leaving them more divided than before and at the same time more fully integrated into transatlantic religious developments. But the impact of the Great Awakening spread beyond purely spiritual matters. The newspaper and pamphlet wars it inspired greatly expanded the circulation of printed material in the colonies. The revivals encouraged many colonists to trust their own views rather than those of established elites. In listening to the sermons of self-educated preachers, forming Bible study groups, and engaging in intense religious discussions, ordinary colonists asserted the right to independent judgment. "The common people," proclaimed Baptist minister Isaac Backus, "claim as good a right to judge and act for themselves in matters of religion as civil rulers or the learned clergy." The revivalists' aim was spiritual salvation, not social or political revolution. But the independent frame of mind they encouraged would have significant political consequences.

A lithograph produced in Baltimore in 1791 by John Hagerty, a Methodist minister and publisher of religious works, illustrates a passage in the Bible ("on either side of the river was there the tree of life which bore twelve manner of fruits") and, more generally, the evangelical spirit of the Great Awakening. Beneath heavenly rays, the Tree of Life bears fruits of salvation for those seeking entry into the New Jerusalem. Sinners are noted with labels including "pride," "chambering & wantonness," "quack," "usury," and "extortion."

Right to independent judgment

IMPERIAL RIVALRIES

Spanish North America

The rapid growth of Britain's North American colonies took place at a time of increased jockeying for power among European empires, involving much of the area today included in the United States. But the colonies of England's rivals, although covering immense territories, remained thinly populated and far weaker

Missions played a crucial role in consolidating Spanish control over their vast American empire. In this watercolor from 1743 by a Jesuit priest, Indians at the Mission of San Javier in Paraguay are depicted paying elaborate homage to the King of Spain.

economically. The Spanish empire encompassed an area that stretched from the Pacific coast and New Mexico into the Great Plains and eastward through Texas and Florida. After 1763, it also included Louisiana, which Spain obtained from France. On paper a vast territorial empire, Spanish North America actually consisted of a few small and isolated urban clusters, most prominently St. Augustine in Florida, San Antonio in Texas, and Santa Fe and Albuquerque in New Mexico.

The Comanche and Apache

In the second half of the century, the Spanish government made a concerted effort to reinvigorate its empire north of the Rio Grande River. It sought to stabilize relations with Indians, especially the nomadic Comanche and Apache, who controlled much of the land claimed by Spain and whose raids on mines and ranches, settled Indian communities, and each other wreaked havoc. The Comanche, who had moved onto the southern Great Plains from the Rocky Mountains, violently displaced previous Native American residents of the area. They pushed the Apache, for example, into Texas and New Mexico, where they raided existing Pueblo villages, causing havoc among the Indians there and reducing Spain's power. Spain was also alarmed by the growing number of French merchants who made their way into the region from Louisiana.

Spanish reformers

During the reigns of Carlos II and Carlos III, Spanish reformers, like other Enlightenment figures, hoped that applying scientific methods to society would bring about progress, but at the same time they hoped to preserve the absolutist monarchy and Spain's American empire. They collected data about the area's native population and debated whether Indians were capable of being integrated into Spanish society or should remain subject peoples. Reformers condemned Spain's past treatment of Indians and called for more humane policies. They pointed out that despite the Black Legend of unique Spanish cruelty, Indians comprised well over half of the inhabitants of New Spain, but now amounted to less than 6 percent of the population of the mainland English colonies. But no coherent policy was adopted. In 1776, Spain put the region, previously governed from Mexico City, under a local military commander, who used a combination of coercion, gifts, and trade to woo unconquered Indians. These tactics to some extent strengthened

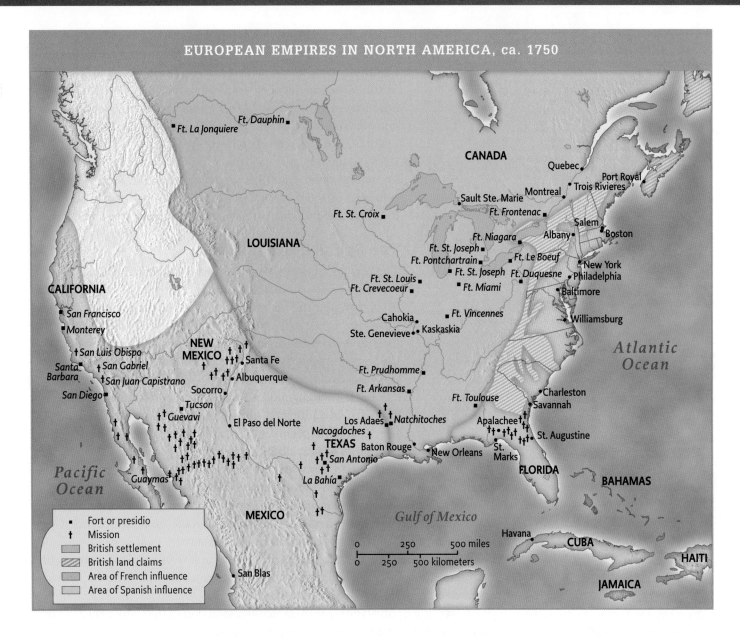

EUROPEAN EMPIRES IN NORTH AMERICA, ca. 1750

Legend:
- Fort or presidio
- † Mission
- British settlement
- British land claims
- Area of French influence
- Area of Spanish influence

Spain's hold on the northern part of its American empire, but did not succeed in eliminating Native power in the area.

Spain's problem stemmed in large part from the small size of the settler population. New Mexico in 1765 had only 20,000 inhabitants, with Pueblo Indians slightly outnumbering persons of European descent. About 15 percent of the Spanish were "crypto-Jews"—Jews who continued to practice their religion after converting to Catholicism, as required by Spanish law. Many had moved from Mexico City to escape the Inquisition there. Although ranching had expanded, the economy of New Mexico essentially rested on trading with and extracting labor from the surviving Indian population. Moreover, the manpower demands of wars in Europe made it impossible for the Spanish government to meet local military commanders' requests for more troops. The powerful Comanche and Apache continued to dominate large parts of northern New Spain.

Three great empires—the British, French, and Spanish—competed for influence in North America for much of the eighteenth century.

A rare map by a Comanche artist depicts the Battle of Sierra Blanca of July 30, 1787, between Comanche and Apache warriors in modern-day New Mexico. It was presented to the Spanish governor, who had recently formed an alliance with the Comanche. The battle was a resounding victory for the Comanche, who suffered only one dead and four wounded, while killing four Apache and capturing thirty-five. The letters on the map refer to an accompanying key, including A: the Comanche commander; B: Comanche warriors; D: Apache prisoners; and E: 16 captured horses—an indication of the importance of horses to southwestern Indians by this time.

Similar problems existed in Texas. Spain began the colonization of Texas at the beginning of the eighteenth century, partly as a buffer to prevent French commercial influence, then spreading in the Mississippi Valley, from intruding into New Mexico. The Spanish established complexes consisting of religious missions and *presidios* (military outposts) at Los Adaes, La Bahía, and San Antonio. But the region attracted few settlers. Texas had only 1,200 Spanish colonists in 1760. Florida stagnated as well, remaining an impoverished military outpost. Around 1770, its population consisted of about 2,000 Spanish, 1,000 black slaves, and a few hundred Indians, survivors of many decades of war and disease.

The Spanish in California

The clash of empires also took place on the Pacific Coast. In the mid-eighteenth century, empire builders in Moscow dreamed of challenging the Spanish for control of the region's fur trade, minerals, and ports. Russian traders established a series of forts in Alaska and then moved southward toward modern-day California. As late as 1812, Russians founded Fort Ross, only 100 miles north of San Francisco.

Even though only a small number of Russians actually appeared in California, the alarmed Spanish in 1769 launched the "Sacred Experiment" to take control of the coast north of San Diego to prevent its occupation by foreigners. In 1774, Juan Bautista de Anza, an explorer and military officer, led an expedition that discovered a usable overland route to California from northern Mexico. In 1776, he founded a new *presidio* and mission at San Francisco. But a Native American uprising in 1781 wrested control of the overland route from the Spanish. Given the distance and difficulties of communication, authorities in Mexico City decided to establish missions in California, run by the Franciscan religious order, rather than sending colonists. The friars would set up ranching and farming activities and convert Indians into loyal Spaniards.

A string of Spanish missions and *presidios* soon dotted the California coastline, from San Diego to Los Angeles, Santa Barbara, Monterey, San Francisco, and Sonoma. Born on the Spanish Mediterranean island of Mallorca, **Father Junípero Serra** became one of the most controversial figures in California's early history. He founded the first California mission, in San Diego, in 1769 and administered the mission network until his death in 1784. Serra was widely praised in Spain for converting thousands of Indians to Christianity, teaching them Spanish, and working to transform their hunting-and-gathering economies by introducing settled agriculture and skilled crafts. In 2015, he was elevated to sainthood by the Catholic Church. But forced labor and disease took a heavy toll among Indians who lived at the missions Serra directed. Many ran away, and the friars responded with whippings and imprisonment. "Naturally we want our liberty," one fugitive from the missions remarked.

Present-day California was a densely populated area, with a native population of perhaps 250,000 when Spanish settlement began. But as in other regions, the

An idealized view of mission life, painted by a Jesuit priest at Mission San José del Cabo, founded by Father Junípero Serra in modern-day Baja California, Mexico.

coming of soldiers and missionaries proved a disaster for the Indians. More than any other Spanish colony, California was a mission frontier. These outposts served simultaneously as religious institutions and centers of government and labor. Their aim was to transform the culture of the local population and eventually assimilate it into Spanish civilization. Father Serra and other missionaries hoped to convert the natives to Christianity and settled farming, although Serra accommodated native traditions such as dancing and traditional healing. The missions also relied on forced Indian labor to grow grain, work in orchards and vineyards, and tend cattle. The combination of new diseases, environmental changes caused by the introduction of Spanish crops and animals, and the resettlement of thousands of Indians in villages around the missions devastated Indian society. By 1821, when Mexico won its independence from Spain, California's native population had declined by more than one-third. But the area had not attracted Spanish settlers. In 1800, Los Angeles, with a population of 300, was the largest town. When Spanish rule came to an end in 1821, twenty missions were operating, with an average population of over 1,000 Indians, but *Californios* (California residents of Spanish descent) numbered only 3,200.

>> *Spanish missions*

>> *Decline of Indian population*

The French Empire

Spain's North American colonies remained peripheral parts of its empire when compared with its possessions in Central and South America and the Caribbean. A greater rival to British power in North America—as well as in Europe and the Caribbean—was France. During the eighteenth century, the population and economy of Canada expanded. At the same time, French traders pushed into the Mississippi River valley southward from the Great Lakes and northward from Mobile, founded in 1702, and New Orleans, established in 1718. In the St. Lawrence River valley of French Canada, prosperous farming communities developed. By

>> *French expansion*

1750, the area had a population of about 55,000 colonists. Another 10,000 (about half Europeans, half African-American slaves) resided in Louisiana, mostly concentrated on the lower Mississippi River and along the Gulf Coast. By mid-century, sugar plantations had sprung up in the area between New Orleans and Baton Rouge. New Orleans already had a vibrant social life as well as an established community with churches, schools, and governmental buildings.

Small French population

Nonetheless, the population of French North America continued to be dwarfed by the British colonies. Around 1750, the 1.5 million British colonists (including slaves) greatly outnumbered the 65,000 French in North America. The giant Louisiana colony consisted of a core area around New Orleans, controlled by Europeans, and a vast hinterland dominated by Indians. Prejudice against emigration to North America remained widespread in France. A French novel written in 1731, known today as the basis for the nineteenth-century opera *Manon*, told the story of a prostitute punished by being transported to Louisiana and of her noble lover who followed her there. It expressed the popular view of the colony as a place of cruel exile for criminals and social outcasts. Nonetheless, by claiming control of a

A challenge to the British

large arc of territory and by establishing close trading and military relations with many Indian tribes, the French empire posed a real challenge to the British. French forts and trading posts ringed the British colonies. In present-day Mississippi and Alabama and in the western regions of Georgia and the Carolinas, French and British traders competed to form alliances with local Indians and control the trade in deerskins. The French were a presence on the New England and New York frontiers and in western Pennsylvania.

BATTLE FOR THE CONTINENT

The Middle Ground

For much of the eighteenth century, the western frontier of British North America was the flashpoint of imperial rivalries. The Ohio Valley became caught up in a complex struggle for power involving the French, British, rival Indian communities, and settlers and land companies pursuing their own interests. Here by mid-century resided numerous Indians, including Shawnees and Delawares who had been pushed out of Pennsylvania by advancing white settlement, Cherokees and Chickasaws from the southern colonies who looked to the region for new hunting grounds, and Iroquois seeking to exert control over the area's fur trade. On this **middle ground**, a borderland between European empires and Indian sovereignty, villages sprang up where members of numerous tribes lived side by side, along with European traders and the occasional missionary.

The Ohio Valley

By the mid-eighteenth century, Indians had learned that direct military confrontation with Europeans meant suicide, and that an alliance with a single European power exposed them to danger from others. The Indians of the Ohio Valley recognized that the imperial rivalry of Britain and France posed both threat and opportunity. As one Delaware spokesman remarked, it was impossible to know "where the Indians' land lay, for the French claimed all the land on one side of the Ohio River and the English on the other side." On the other hand, Indians sought (with some success) to play European empires off one another and to control the lucrative commerce with whites. The Iroquois were masters of balance-of-power diplomacy. The British accepted their sovereignty in the Ohio Valley, but it was challenged by the French and their Indian allies.

In 1750, few white settlers inhabited the Ohio Valley. The area was known more by rumor than by observation, and contemporary maps bore little resemblance to the actual geography. Nonetheless, many prominent colonists dreamed of establishing a new "empire" in what was then the West. Many others saw the West as a place where they could easily acquire land, and the freedom that went with it. Already, Scotch-Irish and German immigrants, Virginia planters, and land speculators were eyeing the region's fertile soil. In 1749, the government of Virginia awarded an immense land grant—half a million acres—to the Ohio Company, an example of the huge domains being parceled out to those with political connections. The company's members included the colony's royal governor, Robert Dinwiddie, and the cream of Virginia society—Lees, Carters, and the young George Washington. The land grant threatened the region's Indians as well as Pennsylvania land speculators, who also had claims in the area. It sparked the French to bolster their presence in the region. It was the Ohio Company's demand for French recognition of its land claims that inaugurated the **Seven Years' War** (known in the colonies as the **French and Indian War**), the first of the century's imperial wars to begin in the colonies and the first to result in a decisive victory for one combatant. It permanently altered the global balance of power.

A map of upstate New York presented to Governor William Tryon of colonial New York demonstrates that the area was considered the realm of the Six Iroquois Nations, whose domain also stretched into the Ohio Valley.

The Seven Years' War

Before 1688, England was a marginal power. Spain's empire was far more extensive, France had greater influence in Europe, and the Dutch dominated overseas trade and finance. Only in the eighteenth century, after numerous wars against its great rivals France and Spain, did Britain emerge as the world's leading empire and its center of trade and banking. The War of the Spanish Succession (known in the colonies as Queen Anne's War) lasted from 1702 to 1713; the War of Jenkins' Ear (named after a British seaman mistreated by the Spanish) from 1739 to 1742; and King George's War from 1740 to 1748. To finance these wars, Britain's public expenditures, taxes, and national debt rose enormously. The high rate of taxation inspired discontent at home, and would later help to spark the American Revolution.

The world's leading empire

By the 1750s, British possessions and trade reached around the globe. "Every part of the world affects us, in some way or another," remarked the duke of Newcastle. The existence of global empires implied that warfare among them would also be global. What became a worldwide struggle for imperial domination, which eventually spread to Europe, West Africa, and Asia, began in 1754 with British efforts to dislodge the French from forts they had constructed in western Pennsylvania. In the previous year, George Washington, then only twenty-one years old, had been dispatched by

THE
AMERICAN MAGAZINE,

PRÆVALEBIT ÆQUIOR.

AND
MONTHLY CHRONICLE for the BRITISH Colonies.
Vol. I. Nº. VI. FOR MARCH 1758.

This image from the cover of a magazine published in Pennsylvania in 1758 depicts an Englishman and a Frenchman attempting to trade with an Indian. The Frenchman offers a tomahawk and musket, the Englishman a Bible and cloth. Of course, the depictions of the two Europeans reflect pro-British stereotypes.

The global balance of power

the colony's governor on an unsuccessful mission to persuade French soldiers to abandon a fort they were building on lands claimed by the Ohio Company. In 1754, Washington returned to the area with two companies of soldiers. He hastily constructed Fort Necessity. After an ill-considered attempt to defend it against a larger French and Indian force, resulting in the loss of one-third of his men, Washington was forced to surrender. Soon afterward, an expedition led by General Edward Braddock against Fort Duquesne (today's Pittsburgh) was ambushed by French and Indian forces, leaving Braddock and two-thirds of his 3,000 soldiers dead or wounded.

For two years, the war went against the British. French and Indian forces captured British forts in northern New York. The southern backcountry was ablaze with fighting among British forces, colonists, and Indians. Inhumanity flourished on all sides. Indians killed hundreds of colonists in western Pennsylvania and pushed the line of settlement all the way back to Carlisle, only 100 miles west of Philadelphia. In Nova Scotia, the British rounded up around 5,000 local French residents, called Acadians, confiscated their land, and expelled them from the region, selling their farms to settlers from New England. Some of those expelled eventually returned to France; others ended up as far away as Louisiana, where their descendants came to be known as Cajuns.

As the British government raised huge sums of money and poured men and naval forces into the war, the tide of battle turned. Secretary of State William Pitt, who took office in 1757, devised a strategy of providing funds to Prussia to enable it to hold the line against France and its ally Spain in Europe, while the British struck at the French weak point, its colonies. By 1759, Britain—with colonial and Indian soldiers playing a major role—had captured the pivotal French outposts of Forts Duquesne, Ticonderoga (north of Albany), and Louisbourg on Cape Breton Island, which guarded the mouth of the St. Lawrence River. In September of that year, a French army was defeated on the Plains of Abraham near Quebec. British forces also seized nearly all the islands in the French Caribbean and established control of India. In Europe, meanwhile, Prussia managed to fend off the coalition of France, Russia, and Spain.

A World Transformed

"As long as the world has stood there has not been such a war," declared a British emissary to the Delaware Indians. Britain's victory fundamentally reshaped the world balance of power. In the Peace of Paris in 1763, France ceded Canada to Britain, receiving back in return the sugar islands of Guadeloupe and Martinique (far more lucrative colonies from the point of view of French authorities). As part of the reshuffling of imperial possessions, Spain ceded Florida to Britain in exchange for the return of the Philippines and Cuba (seized by the British during the war). Spain also acquired from France the vast Louisiana colony. France's 200-year-old North American empire had come to an end. With the exception of two tiny islands retained by France off the coast of Newfoundland, the entire continent east of the Mississippi River was now in British hands.

"Peace," remarked Prime Minister Pitt, "will be as hard to make as war." Eighteenth-century warfare, conducted on land and sea across the globe, was enormously expensive. The Seven Years' War put strains on all the participants. The war's cost produced a financial crisis in France that almost three decades later would help to spark the French Revolution. The British would try to recoup part of the cost of war by increasing taxes on their American colonies. "We no sooner leave fighting our neighbors, the French," commented the British writer Dr. Samuel Johnson, "but we must fall to quarreling among ourselves." In fact, the Peace of Paris was soon followed by open warfare in North America between the British and Native Americans.

The cost of war

Pontiac's Rebellion

Throughout eastern North America, the abrupt departure of the French in the aftermath of the Seven Years' War eliminated the balance-of-power diplomacy that had enabled groups like the Iroquois to maintain a significant degree of autonomy. Indians had fought on both sides in the war, although mainly as allies of the French. Their primary aim, however, was to maintain their independence from both empires. Indians hoped to preserve the middle ground, a borderland where various powers competed and none held sway, so that their own liberty could be maintained. As one British observer put it in 1764, the Six Nations and other Indians, "having never been conquered, either by the English or French, nor subject to the laws, consider themselves as a free people." Domination by any outside power, Indians feared, meant the loss of freedom. Without consulting them, the French had ceded land Indians claimed as their own, to British control. The Treaty of Paris left Indians more dependent than ever on the British and ushered in a period of confusion over land claims, control of the fur trade, and tribal relations in general. To Indians, it was clear that continued expansion of the British colonies posed a dire threat. One British army officer reported that Native Americans "say we mean to make slaves of them," by taking their land.

The British threat to the Indians

In 1763, in the wake of the French defeat, Indians of the Ohio Valley and Great Lakes launched a revolt against British rule. Although known as **Pontiac's Rebellion** after an Ottawa war leader, the rebellion owed at least as much to the teachings of **Neolin**, a Delaware religious prophet. (Like Bacon's Rebellion before it and Shays's Rebellion three decades later, the broad Indian uprising seems destined, misleadingly, to bear the name of a single individual.) During a religious vision, the Master of Life instructed Neolin that his people must reject European technology, free themselves from commercial ties with whites and dependence on alcohol, clothe themselves in the garb of their ancestors, and drive the British from their territory (although friendly French inhabitants could remain). Neolin combined this message with the relatively new idea of pan-Indian identity. All Indians, he preached, were a single people, and only through cooperation could they regain their lost independence. The common experience of dispossession, the intertribal communities that had developed in the Ohio country, and the mixing of Indian warriors in French armies had helped to inspire this sense of identity as Indians rather than members of individual tribes.

Neolin's message

The Proclamation Line

In the spring and summer of 1763, Ottawas, Hurons, and other Indians besieged Detroit, then a major British military outpost, seized nine other forts, and killed

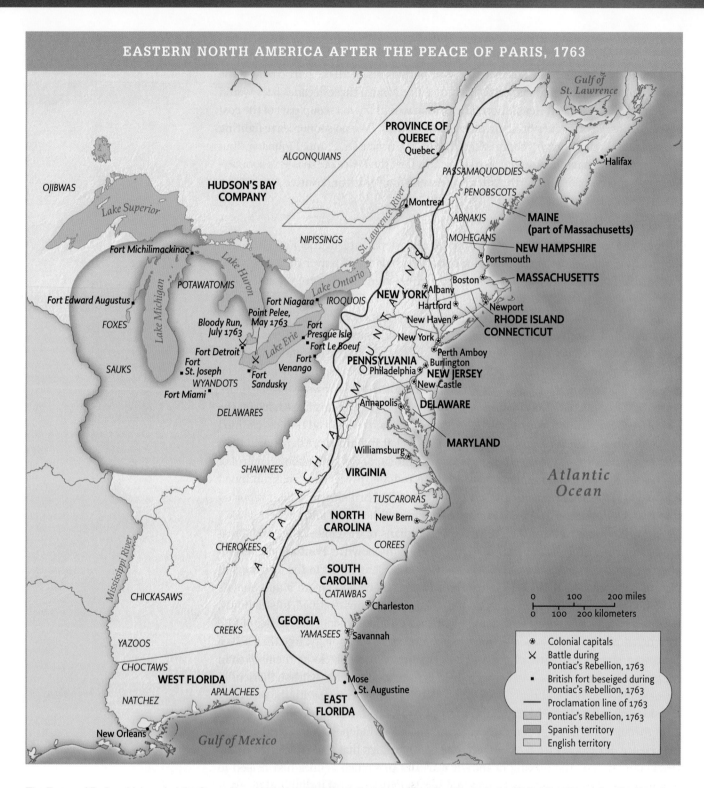

EASTERN NORTH AMERICA AFTER THE PEACE OF PARIS, 1763

Gulf of St. Lawrence

OJIBWAS

Lake Superior

HUDSON'S BAY COMPANY

ALGONQUIANS

PROVINCE OF QUEBEC
Quebec

PASSAMAQUODDIES

• Halifax

PENOBSCOTS

St. Lawrence River

• Montreal

ABNAKIS

MAINE
(part of Massachusetts)

NIPISSINGS

MOHEGANS

NEW HAMPSHIRE
• Portsmouth

Fort Michilimackinac

Lake Huron

Lake Ontario

Lake Michigan

POTAWATOMIS

Fort Niagara

IROQUOIS

NEW YORK
Albany

Boston

MASSACHUSETTS

Fort Edward Augustus

Point Pelee, May 1763

Hartford

Newport

RHODE ISLAND

FOXES

Bloody Run, July 1763

Fort Presque Isle

Lake Erie

New Haven

CONNECTICUT

Fort Detroit

Fort Le Boeuf

New York

Fort St. Joseph

Fort Venango

PENNSYLVANIA

Perth Amboy

SAUKS

WYANDOTS

Fort Sandusky

Philadelphia

Burlington

NEW JERSEY

Fort Miami

New Castle

DELAWARES

Annapolis

DELAWARE

MARYLAND

SHAWNEES

Williamsburg

APPALACHIAN MOUNTAINS

VIRGINIA

Atlantic Ocean

TUSCARORAS

NORTH CAROLINA

New Bern

Mississippi River

CHEROKEES

COREES

SOUTH CAROLINA

CATAWBAS

• Charleston

CHICKASAWS

CREEKS

GEORGIA

YAMASEES

Savannah

YAZOOS

CHOCTAWS

WEST FLORIDA

NATCHEZ

APALACHEES

Mose

St. Augustine

EAST FLORIDA

New Orleans

Gulf of Mexico

0   100   200 miles
0   100   200 kilometers

⊛ Colonial capitals
✕ Battle during Pontiac's Rebellion, 1763
▪ British fort beseiged during Pontiac's Rebellion, 1763
— Proclamation line of 1763
   Pontiac's Rebellion, 1763
   Spanish territory
   English territory

The Peace of Paris, which ended the Seven Years' War, left all of North America east of the Mississippi in British hands, ending the French presence on the continent.

hundreds of white settlers who had intruded onto Indian lands. British forces soon launched a counterattack, and over the next few years the tribes one by one made peace. But the uprising inspired the government in London to issue the **Proclamation of 1763**, prohibiting further colonial settlement west of the Appalachian Mountains. These lands were reserved exclusively for Indians. Moreover, the proclamation banned the sale of Indian lands to private individuals. Henceforth, only colonial governments could arrange such purchases.

Proclamation of 1763

The British aim was less to protect the Indians than to stabilize the situation on the colonial frontier and to avoid being dragged into an endless series of border conflicts. But the proclamation enraged both settlers and speculators hoping to take advantage of the expulsion of the French to consolidate their claims to western lands. They ignored the new policy. George Washington himself ordered his agents to buy up as much Indian land as possible, while keeping the transactions "a profound secret" because of their illegality. Failing to offer a viable solution to the question of westward expansion, the Proclamation of 1763 ended up further exacerbating settler-Indian relations.

Pennsylvania and the Indians

The Seven Years' War not only redrew the map of the world but produced dramatic changes within the American colonies as well. Nowhere was this more evident than in Pennsylvania, where the conflict shattered the decades-old rule of the Quaker elite and dealt the final blow to the colony's policy of accommodation with the Indians. During the war, with the frontier ablaze with battles between settlers and French and Indian warriors, western Pennsylvanians demanded that colonial authorities adopt a more aggressive stance. When the governor declared war on hostile Delawares, raised a militia, and offered a bounty for Indian scalps, many of the assembly's pacifist Quakers resigned their seats, effectively ending their control of Pennsylvania politics. The war deepened the antagonism of western farmers toward Indians and witnessed numerous indiscriminate assaults on Indian communities, both allies and enemies.

Frontier tensions

In December 1763, while Pontiac's Rebellion still raged, a party of fifty armed men, mostly Scotch-Irish farmers from the vicinity of the Pennsylvania town of Paxton, destroyed the Indian village of Conestoga, massacring half a dozen men, women, and children who lived there under the protection of Pennsylvania's governor. They then marched on Lancaster, where they killed fourteen additional Indians. Like participants in Bacon's Rebellion nearly a century earlier, they accused colonial authorities of treating Indians too leniently. They petitioned the legislature to remove all Indians from the colony. The Indians' "claim to freedom and independency," they insisted, threatened Pennsylvania's stability. When the Paxton Boys marched on Philadelphia in February 1764, intending to attack Moravian Indians who resided near the city, the governor ordered the expulsion of much of the Indian population. By the 1760s, Pennsylvania's Holy Experiment was at an end and with it William Penn's promise of "true friendship and amity" between colonists and the native population. No other large colony had a smaller Indian population or a more remorseless determination on the part of settlers to eliminate those who remained.

VOICES OF FREEDOM

From SCAROUYADY, SPEECH TO PENNSYLVANIA PROVINCIAL COUNCIL (1756)

The outbreak of the Seven Years' War inflamed relations between Native Americans and white settlers in the Pennsylvania backcountry. Scarouyady, an Oneida leader who wished to maintain harmony, told the colony's leaders that he approved of war against hostile tribes and hoped that a fort could be built to protect friendly Indians and keep armed whites in check. But the middle ground was rapidly disappearing.

You have . . . tried all amicable means with [the Delaware Indians] and with the Six Nations, but as all have proved ineffectual, you do right to strike them. You have had a great deal of patience; other people on losing a single man, would have armed and drove off the foe; but you have sat still while numbers of your people have been and now are murdered. . . . Your enemies have got great advantage by your inactivity; show them you are men.

You told us that you must now build a Fort at Shamokin; we are glad to hear it; it is a good thing. . . . The Fort at Shamokin is not a thing of little consequence; it is of the greatest importance to us as well as you. Your people are foolish; for want of this Fort, the Indians, who are your friends, can be of no service to you, having no place to go to where they can promise themselves protection. They cannot be called together; they can do nothing for you; they are not secure any where. At present your people cannot distinguish foes from friends; they think every Indian is against them; they blame us all without distinction, because they see nobody appear for them; the common people to a man entertain this notion, and insult us wherever we go. We bear their ill usage, though very irksome; but all this will be set right when you have built the Fort, and you will see that we in particular are sincere, and many others will come to your assistance. We desire when the fort is built, you will put into the command of so important a place some of your people; grave, solid, and sensible men, who are in repute amongst you, and in whom we can place a Confidence. . . . Do yourselves and us Justice, and bring your Enemies to a due Sense of themselves, and to offer just Terms, and then, and not till then, think of a Peace. This is our Advice.

From PONTIAC, SPEECHES
(1762 AND 1763)

Pontiac was a leader of the pan-Indian resistance to English rule known as Pontiac's Rebellion, which followed the end of the Seven Years' War. Neolin was a Delaware religious prophet who helped to inspire the rebellion.

———————————————

Englishmen, although you have conquered the French, you have not yet conquered us! We are not your slaves. These lakes, these woods, and mountains were left to us by our ancestors. They are our inheritance; and we will part with them to none. Your nation supposes that we, like the white people, cannot live without bread and pork and beef! But you ought to know that He, the Great Spirit and Master of Life, has provided food for us in these spacious lakes, and on these woody mountains.

[The Master of Life has said to Neolin:]

I am the Maker of heaven and earth, the trees, lakes, rivers, and all else. I am the Maker of all mankind; and because I love you, you must do my will. The land on which you live I have made for you and not for others. Why do you suffer the white man to dwell among you? My children, you have forgotten the customs and traditions of your forefathers. Why do you not clothe yourselves in skins, as they did, use bows and arrows and the stone-pointed lances, which they used? You have bought guns, knives, kettles and blankets from the white man until you can no longer do without them; and what is worse, you have drunk the poison firewater, which turns you into fools. Fling all these things away; live as your wise forefathers did before you. And as for these English—these dogs dressed in red, who have come to rob you of your hunting-grounds, and drive away the game—you must lift the hatchet against them. Wipe them from the face of the earth, and then you will win my favor back again, and once more be happy and prosperous.

QUESTIONS

1. *What aspects of white behavior does Scarouyady object to?*

2. *What elements of Indian life does Neolin criticize most strongly?*

3. *How do Scarouyady and Pontiac differ in the ways they address white audiences?*

Benjamin Franklin produced this famous cartoon in 1754, calling on Britain's North American colonies to unite against the French.

Stronger bonds with the British

Colonial Identities

Like the Indians, colonists emerged from the Seven Years' War with a heightened sense of collective identity. Before the war, the colonies had been largely isolated from one another. Outside of New England, more Americans probably traveled to England than from one colony to another. In 1751, Governor George Clinton of New York had called for a general conference on Indian relations, but only three colonies bothered to send delegates. The **Albany Plan of Union** of 1754, drafted by Benjamin Franklin at the outbreak of the Seven Years' War, envisioned the creation of a Grand Council composed of delegates from each colony, with the power to levy taxes and deal with Indian relations and the common defense. Rejected by the colonial assemblies, whose powers Franklin's proposal would curtail, the plan was never sent to London for approval.

Participation in the Seven Years' War created greater bonds among the colonies. But the war also strengthened colonists' pride in being members of the British empire. It has been said that Americans were never more British than in 1763. Colonial militiamen and British regulars fought alongside each other against the French. Tensions developed between the professional British military and the often undisciplined American citizen-soldiers, but the common experience of battle and victory also forged bonds between them. For much of the century, New Englanders had called for the conquest of Canada as a blow for "Protestant freedom" against "popish slavery." Now that this had been accomplished, British victory in the Seven Years' War seemed a triumph of liberty over tyranny. The defeat of the Catholic French reinforced the equation of British nationality, Protestantism, and freedom.

In fact, however, after 1763 Britain's global empire was not predominantly Protestant or British or free. It now included tens of thousands of French Catholics and millions of persons in India governed as subjects rather than as citizens. The English statesman Edmund Burke wondered whether British liberty could be reconciled with rule over this "vast, heterogeneous, intricate mass of interests." Burke was almost alone in seeing the newly expanded empire as a challenge to the principles of British freedom. But soon, the American colonists would come to believe that membership in the empire jeopardized their liberty. When they did, they set out on a road that led to independence.

SUGGESTED READING

BOOKS

- Anderson, Fred. *Crucible of War: The Seven Years' War and the Fate of Empire in British North America, 1754–1766* (2000). A general history of the Seven Years' War and its consequences.

- Beeman, Richard R. *Varieties of Political Experience in Eighteenth-Century America* (2004). Explores how political life differed from colony to colony, and what characteristics they had in common.

- Blackburn, Robin. *The American Crucible: Slavery, Emancipation, and Human Rights* (2011). A comprehensive history of the rise and fall of slavery in the Western Hemisphere and its centrality to European empires.

- Calloway, Colin G. *The Scratch of a Pen: 1763 and the Transformation of North America* (2006). Examines the impact of the Peace of Paris on North America, especially the Native American population.

- Colley, Linda. *Britons: Forging the Nation, 1707–1837* (1992). An influential study of the rise of a sense of national identity in Great Britain, relevant also for the American colonies.

- Gomez, Michael A. *Exchanging Our Country Marks: The Transformation of African Identities in the Colonial and Antebellum South* (1998). The most detailed study of the process by which Africans became African-Americans.

- Greene, Jack P. *The Quest for Power: The Lower Houses of Assembly in the Southern Royal Colonies, 1689–1776* (1963). A careful examination of how elected assemblies expanded their authority in the eighteenth-century South.

- Newman, Simon P. *A New World of Labor: The Development of Plantation Slavery in the British Atlantic* (2013). The most recent account of how slavery emerged and was consolidated in the British empire.

- Noll, Mark. *The Rise of Evangelicalism: The Age of Edwards, Whitefield, and the Wesleys* (2004). Explores the Great Awakening on both sides of the Atlantic and its impact on religious life.

- Rediker, Marcus. *The Slave Ship: A Human History* (2007). A fascinating and disturbing account of the Atlantic slave trade that focuses on the captains, sailors, and slaves aboard the slave ships.

- Smith, Barbara Clark. *The Freedoms We Lost: Consent and Resistance in Revolutionary America* (2010). Examines the ways colonial Americans participated in public life and sought to defend their concepts of freedom.

- Valerio-Jiménez, Omar S. *River of Hope: Forging Identity and Nation in the Rio Grande Borderlands* (2013). Traces the processes of cultural interaction and the establishment of national power in a major borderlands region.

- Weber, David J. *The Spanish Frontier in North America* (1992). The most comprehensive account of Spanish settlement in what is now the United States.

- White, Richard. *The Middle Ground: Indians, Empires, and Republics in the Great Lakes Region, 1650–1815* (1991). The book that developed the idea of a middle ground where Europeans and Indians both exercised authority.

WEBSITES

- Africans in America: www.pbs.org/wgbh/aia/
- Web de Anza: http://anza.uoregon.edu

CHAPTER REVIEW AND ONLINE RESOURCES

REVIEW QUESTIONS

1. How did Great Britain's position in North America change relative to the other European powers during the first three-quarters of the eighteenth century?

2. How did the ideas of republicanism and liberalism differ in eighteenth-century British North America?

3. Three distinct slave systems were well entrenched in Britain's mainland colonies. Describe the main characteristics of each system.

4. How and why did the colonists' sense of a collective British identity change during the years before 1764?

5. What ideas generated by the American Enlightenment and the Great Awakening prompted challenges to religious, social, and political authorities in the British colonies?

6. How were colonial merchants in British America involved in the Atlantic economy, and what was the role of the slave trade in that economy?

7. We often consider the impact of the slave trade only on the United States, but its impact extended much further. How did it affect West African nations and society, other regions of the New World, and the nations of Europe?

8. How was an African-American collective identity created in these years, and what role did slave rebellions play in that process?

KEY TERMS

Atlantic slave trade (p. 128)

Middle Passage (p. 130)

yeoman farmers (p. 138)

Stono Rebellion (p. 139)

republicanism (p. 141)

liberalism (p. 142)

salutary neglect (p. 145)

Enlightenment (p. 148)

Deism (p. 149)

Great Awakening (p. 149)

Father Junípero Serra (p. 154)

middle ground (p. 156)

Seven Years' War (p. 157)

French and Indian War (p. 157)

Pontiac's Rebellion (p. 159)

Neolin (p. 159)

Proclamation of 1763 (p. 161)

Albany Plan of Union (p. 164)

Go to 🐰 INQUIZITIVE

To see what you know—and learn what you've missed—with personalized feedback along the way.

Visit the *Give Me Liberty!* **Student Site** for primary source documents and images, interactive maps, author videos featuring Eric Foner, and more.

A NEW NATION, 1763-1840

PART 2

During the 1760s and 1770s, a dispute over taxation within the British empire escalated into a conflict that gave birth to a new nation, the United States of America. The American Revolution inaugurated an era of political upheaval throughout the Western world, known to historians ever since as the Age of Revolution. It helped to inspire popular uprisings in Europe, the Caribbean, and Latin America and forever changed the course of American development. Liberty emerged as the era's foremost rallying cry. The revolutionary generation insisted that the meaning of their struggle lay not only in political independence but also in the establishment of what the writer Thomas Paine called an asylum of liberty for all mankind.

The American Revolution not only broke the political bond with Great Britain but also inspired groups within American society to claim greater rights for themselves. Propertyless men demanded the right to vote. Women began to challenge their subordination to men. Indentured servants ran away from their masters. And slaves seized the opportunity to gain their freedom by fighting in the Continental army or by escaping to the British side.

By the time it had run its course, the Revolution had greatly expanded some realms of American freedom. It severed the connection between church and state, promoted the emergence of a lively public sphere in which ordinary men and, sometimes, women participated in political debate, and challenged the monopoly on political power by colonial elites. It set in motion the abolition of slavery in the northern states. On the other hand, for some Americans independence meant a loss of liberty. Many of those who had remained loyal to England were persecuted and forced to leave the country. The end of the British presence removed the last barrier to the westward expansion of the American population, making inevitable the dispossession of the remaining Indian population east of the Mississippi River. And the formation of a national government in which slaveowners occupied the presidency for most of the half-century after independence helped to consolidate the institution of slavery in the South.

Three processes set in motion by the Revolution gained strength in the early decades of the nineteenth century and profoundly affected Americans'

ideas about freedom. The first was the democratization of politics. Most members of the convention that drafted the nation's Constitution in 1787 assumed that men of property and education would dominate the new American government. But the democratic upsurge inspired by the Revolution, coupled with the swift emergence of political parties offering radically different programs for national development, encouraged a broad popular participation in politics. By the 1830s, a flourishing democratic system was firmly in place. Property qualifications for voting had been eliminated in nearly every state, two parties competed throughout the country, and voter turnout stood at record levels. Political democracy had become a defining element of American freedom.

Second, the development of steamboats, canals, and railroads brought rapid improvements in transportation and communication and created a broad market for farm products and manufactured goods. The "market revolution" opened up vast areas of the American interior to commercial farming and stimulated the early development of factory production. It offered new opportunities for personal advancement to many Americans while reducing others to what seemed an "unfree" situation—working for wages under the constant supervision of an employer. The market revolution also made possible the third major development of this era, the population's westward movement and the rise of the West as a distinct social and political region. The market revolution and westward shift of population also helped to reshape the idea of freedom, identifying it more and more closely with economic opportunity, physical mobility, and individual self-definition and fulfillment.

Many of the founding fathers had feared that economic growth, rapid territorial expansion, and the development of political parties would endanger the unity of the new republic. And between the coming of independence and 1840, the new nation faced a series of crises, as Americans divided according to political and regional loyalties and battled for advantage in the expanding economy. Political conflict often revolved around the relationship between government and the economy. Should the national government seek to promote economic development and direct its course by enacting a system of tariffs, internal improvements, and a national bank? Or should it stand aside and allow Americans to pursue economic self-interest without governmental interference? In the 1790s, the former view was represented by the Federalist Party, the latter by the Jeffersonian Republicans. In the 1830s, a similar division emerged between Whigs and Democrats. Advocates of both visions of the role of the national government insisted that theirs was the best program to promote American liberty.

American freedom also continued to be shaped by the presence of slavery. Rather than dying out, as some of the founders had hoped, slavery expanded rapidly in territorial extent and economic importance. Slavery helped to define the boundaries of American freedom. The privileges of voting, office-holding, and access to economic opportunity were increasingly restricted to whites. Women, too, were barred from these elements of freedom. Their role, according to the prevailing social values, was to remain in the "private sphere" of the home.

The contradiction embedded in American life from the earliest days of settlement—expanding freedom for some coexisting with and, indeed, depending on lack of freedom for others—continued to bedevil the new nation.

CHAPTER 5

THE AMERICAN REVOLUTION

★

1763–1783

On the night of August 26, 1765, a violent crowd of Bostonians assaulted the elegant home of Thomas Hutchinson, chief justice and lieutenant governor of Massachusetts. Hutchinson and his family were eating dinner when the rioters arrived. They barely had time to escape before the crowd broke down the front door and proceeded to destroy or carry off most of their possessions, including paintings, furniture, silverware, and notes for a history of Massachusetts Hutchinson was writing. By the time they departed, only the outer walls of the home remained standing.

The immediate cause of the riot was the **Stamp Act**, a recently enacted British tax that many colonists felt violated their liberty. Critics of the measure had spread a rumor that Hutchinson had written to London encouraging its passage (in fact, he privately opposed it). Only a few days earlier, Hutchinson had helped to disperse a crowd attacking a building owned by his relative Andrew Oliver, a merchant who had been appointed to help administer the new law. Both crowds were led by Ebenezer Mackintosh, a shoemaker who had fought against the French during the Seven Years' War and enjoyed a wide following among Boston's working people. Arrested after the destruction of Hutchinson's home, Mackintosh was released after the intervention of the Loyal Nine, a group of merchants and craftsmen who had taken the lead in opposing the Stamp Act. The violence had gone far beyond what the Loyal Nine intended, and they promised authorities that resistance to the Stamp Act would henceforth be peaceful. The riot, nonetheless, convinced Hutchinson that for Britain to rule America effectively, "there must be an abridgement of what are called English liberties." Whether colonists would accept such an abridgement, however, was very much in doubt.

The riot of August 26 was one small episode in a series of events that launched a half-century of popular protest and political upheaval throughout the Western world. The momentous era that came to be called the Age of Revolution began in British North America, spread to Europe and the Caribbean, and culminated in the Latin American wars for independence. In all these struggles, "Liberty" emerged as the foremost rallying cry for popular discontent. Rarely has the idea played so central a role in political debate and social upheaval.

If the attack on Hutchinson's home demonstrated the depths of feeling aroused by Britain's efforts to impose greater control over its empire, it also revealed that revolution is a dynamic process whose consequences no one can anticipate. The crowd's fury expressed resentments against the rich and powerful quite different from colonial leaders' objections to Parliament's attempt to tax the colonies. The Stamp Act crisis inaugurated not only a struggle for colonial liberty in relation to Great Britain but also a multisided battle to define and extend liberty within America.

THE CRISIS BEGINS

When George III assumed the throne of Great Britain in 1760, no one on either side of the Atlantic imagined that within two decades Britain's American colonies would separate from the empire. But the Seven Years' War, which left Britain with

FOCUS
QUESTIONS

What were the roots and significance of the Stamp Act controversy? –p. 171

What key events sharpened the divisions between Britain and the colonists in the late 1760s and early 1770s? –p. 178

What key events marked the move toward American independence? –p. 182

How were American forces able to prevail in the Revolutionary War? –p. 193

A French engraving depicts New Yorkers tearing down the statue of King George III in July 1776, after the approval of the Declaration of Independence. Slaves are doing the work, while whites look on. The statue was later melted down to make bullets for the Continental army.

an enormous debt and vastly enlarged overseas possessions to defend, led successive governments in London to seek ways to make the colonies share the cost of empire. Having studied the writings of British opposition thinkers who insisted that power inevitably seeks to encroach upon liberty, colonial leaders came to see these measures as part of a British design to undermine their freedom. Only recently they had gloried in their enjoyment of "British liberty," but they came to conclude that membership in the empire was a threat to freedom, rather than its foundation. This conviction set the colonies on the road to independence.

Consolidating the Empire

The Seven Years' War, to which the colonists contributed soldiers and economic resources, underscored for rulers in London how important the empire was to Britain's well-being and its status as a great power. Now, they believed, new regulations were needed to help guarantee the empire's continued strength and prosperity. Before 1763, Parliament had occasionally acted to forbid the issuance of paper money in America and to restrict colonial economic activities that competed with businesses at home. The Wool Act of 1699, Hat Act of 1732, and Iron Act of 1750 forbade colonial manufacture of these items. The Molasses Act of 1733 sought to curtail trade between New England and the French Caribbean by imposing a prohibitive tax on French-produced molasses used to make rum in American distilleries. And the Navigation Acts, discussed in Chapter 3, sought to channel key American exports like tobacco through British ports. The colonists frequently ignored all these measures.

As to internal affairs within the colonies, the British government frequently seemed uninterested. There was no point, one official said, in worrying about the behavior of colonists who "plant tobacco and Puritanism only, like fools." Beginning in the late 1740s, the Board of Trade, which was responsible for overseeing colonial affairs, attempted to strengthen imperial authority. It demanded that colonial laws conform to royal instructions and encouraged colonial assemblies to grant permanent salaries to royal governors. But the outbreak of the Seven Years' War suspended this initiative.

Having treated the colonists as allies during the war, Britain reverted in the mid-1760s to seeing them as subordinates whose main role was to enrich the mother country. During this period, the government in London concerned itself with the colonies in unprecedented ways, hoping to make British rule more efficient and systematic and to raise funds to help pay for the war and to finance the empire. Nearly all British political leaders supported the new laws that so enraged the colonists. Americans, Britons felt, should be grateful to the empire. To fight the Seven Years' War, Britain had borrowed from banks and individual investors more than £150 million (the equivalent of tens of trillions of dollars in today's money). Interest on the debt absorbed half the government's annual revenue. The tax burden in Britain had reached unprecedented heights. It seemed only reasonable that the colonies should help pay this national debt, foot part of the bill for continued British protection, and stop cheating the treasury by violating the Navigation Acts.

Nearly all Britons, moreover, believed that Parliament represented the entire empire and had a right to legislate for it. Millions of Britons, including the residents of major cities like Manchester and Birmingham, had no representatives in Parliament. But according to the widely accepted theory of **virtual representation**—which held that each member represented the entire empire, not just his own district—the interests of all who lived under the British crown were supposedly taken into account. When Americans began to insist that because they were unrepresented in Parliament, the British government could not tax the colonies, they won little support in the mother country. To their surprise, however, successive British governments found that the effective working of the empire required the cooperation of local populations. Time and again, British officials backed down in the face of colonial resistance, only to return with new measures to centralize control of the empire that only stiffened colonial resolve.

The British government had already alarmed many colonists by issuing **writs of assistance** to combat smuggling. These were general search warrants that allowed customs officials to search anywhere they chose for smuggled goods. In a celebrated court case in Boston in 1761, the lawyer James Otis insisted that the writs were "an instrument of arbitrary power, destructive to English liberty, and the fundamental principles of the [British] Constitution," and that Parliament therefore had no right to authorize them. ("American independence was then and there born," John Adams later remarked—a considerable exaggeration.) Many colonists were also outraged by the Proclamation of 1763 (mentioned in the previous chapter) barring further settlement on lands west of the Appalachian Mountains.

An engraving from a Massachusetts almanac published in 1774 depicts Lieutenant Governor Thomas Hutchinson, whose house had been destroyed by a mob nine years earlier. The devil carries a list of Hutchinson's "crimes." It was common in this period to use religious symbols to demonize political opponents.

Taxing the Colonies

In 1764, the **Sugar Act**, introduced by Prime Minister George Grenville, reduced the existing tax on molasses imported into North America from the French West Indies from six pence to three pence per gallon. But the act also established a new machinery to end widespread smuggling by colonial merchants. And to counteract the tendency of colonial juries to acquit merchants charged with violating trade regulations, it strengthened the admiralty courts, where accused smugglers could be judged without benefit of a jury trial. Thus, colonists saw the measure not as a welcome reduction in taxation but as an attempt to get them to pay a levy they would otherwise have evaded.

The Sugar Act of 1764

At the same time, a Revenue Act placed goods such as wool and hides, which had previously been traded freely with Holland, France, and southern Europe, on the enumerated list, meaning they had to be shipped through England. Together, these measures threatened the profits of colonial merchants and seemed certain to aggravate an already serious economic recession resulting from the end of the Seven Years' War. They were accompanied by the Currency Act, which reaffirmed the earlier ban on colonial assemblies issuing paper as "legal tender"—that is, money that individuals are required to accept in payment of debts.

The Stamp Act Crisis

The Sugar Act was an effort to strengthen the long-established (and long-evaded) Navigation Acts. The Stamp Act of 1765 represented a new departure in imperial

The Stamp Act of 1765

According to the doctrine of "virtual representation," the House of Commons represented all residents of the British empire, whether or not they could vote for members. In this 1775 cartoon criticizing the idea, a blinded Britannia, on the far right, stumbles into a pit. Next to her, two colonists complain of being robbed by British taxation. In the background, according to an accompanying explanation of the cartoon, stand the "Catholic" city of Quebec and the "Protestant town of Boston," the latter in flames.

Views of the British empire

policy. For the first time, Parliament attempted to raise money from direct taxes in the colonies rather than through the regulation of trade. The act required that all sorts of printed material produced in the colonies—such as newspapers, books, court documents, commercial papers, land deeds, almanacs—carry a stamp purchased from authorities. Its purpose was to help finance the operations of the empire, including the cost of stationing British troops in North America, without seeking revenue from colonial assemblies.

Whereas the Sugar Act had mainly affected residents of colonial ports, the Stamp Act managed to offend virtually every free colonist—rich and poor, farmers, artisans, and merchants. It was especially resented by members of the public sphere who wrote, published, and read books and newspapers and followed political affairs. The prospect of a British army permanently stationed on American soil also alarmed many colonists. And by imposing the stamp tax without colonial consent, Parliament directly challenged the authority of local elites who, through the assemblies they controlled, had established their power over the raising and spending of money. They were ready to defend this authority in the name of liberty.

Opposition to the Stamp Act was the first great drama of the revolutionary era and the first major split between colonists and Great Britain over the meaning of freedom. Nearly all colonial political leaders opposed the act. In voicing their grievances, they invoked the rights of the freeborn Englishman, which, they insisted, colonists should also enjoy. Opponents of the act drew on time-honored British principles such as a community's right not to be taxed except by its elected representatives. Liberty, they insisted, could not be secure where property was "taken away without consent."

Taxation and Representation

At stake were clashing ideas of the British empire itself. American leaders viewed the empire as an association of equals in which free inhabitants overseas enjoyed the same rights as Britons at home. Colonists in other outposts of the empire, such as India, the West Indies, and Canada, echoed this outlook. All, in the name of liberty, claimed the right to govern their own affairs. British residents of Calcutta, India, demanded the "rights inherent in Englishmen." The British government and its appointed representatives in America, by contrast, saw the empire as a system of unequal parts in which different principles governed different areas, and all were subject to the authority of Parliament. To surrender the right to tax the colonies would set a dangerous precedent for the empire as a whole. "In an empire, extended and diversified as that of Great Britain," declared Governor Francis Bernard of

Massachusetts in 1765, "there must be a supreme legislature, to which all other powers must be subordinate." Parliament, Bernard continued, was the "sanctuary of liberty"—a description with which many Americans were beginning to disagree.

Some opponents of the Stamp Act distinguished between "internal" taxes like the stamp duty, which they claimed Parliament had no right to impose, and revenue legitimately raised through the regulation of trade. But more and more colonists insisted that Britain had no right to tax them at all, since Americans were unrepresented in the House of Commons. **"No taxation without representation"** became their rallying cry. Virginia's House of Burgesses approved four resolutions offered by the fiery orator Patrick Henry. They insisted that the colonists enjoyed the same "liberties, privileges, franchises, and immunities" as residents of the mother country and that the right to consent to taxation was a cornerstone of "British freedom." (The House of Burgesses rejected as too radical three other resolutions, including Henry's call for outright resistance to unlawful taxation, but these were also reprinted in colonial newspapers.)

In October 1765, the Stamp Act Congress, with twenty-seven delegates from nine colonies, including some of the most prominent men in America, met in New York and endorsed Virginia's position. Its resolutions began by affirming the "allegiance" of all colonists to the "Crown of Great Britain" and their "due subordination" to Parliament. But they went on to insist that the right to consent to taxation was "essential to the freedom of a people." Soon, merchants throughout the colonies agreed to boycott British goods until Parliament repealed the Stamp Act. This was the first major cooperative action among Britain's mainland colonies. In a sense, by seeking to impose uniformity on the colonies rather than dealing with them individually as in the past, Parliament had inadvertently united America.

An engraving of James Otis graces the cover of the *Boston Almanack* for 1770. He is flanked by the ancient gods Hercules and Minerva (carrying a liberty cap).

Liberty and Resistance

No word was more frequently invoked by critics of the Stamp Act than "liberty." Throughout the colonies, opponents of the new tax staged mock funerals in which liberty's coffin was carried to a burial ground only to have the occupant miraculously revived at the last moment, whereupon the assembled crowd repaired to a tavern to celebrate. As the crisis continued, symbols of liberty proliferated. The large elm tree in Boston on which protesters had hanged an effigy of the stamp distributor Andrew Oliver to persuade him to resign his post came to be known as the Liberty Tree. Its image soon began to appear in prints and pamphlets throughout the colonies. Open-air meetings were held beneath the tree, and as a result the space came to be called Liberty Hall. In New York City, a pine mast erected in 1766 as a meeting place for opponents of the Stamp Act was called the Liberty Pole.

Colonial leaders resolved to prevent the new law's implementation, and by and large they succeeded. Even before the passage of the Stamp Act, a **Committee of Correspondence** in Boston communicated with other colonies to encourage opposition to the Sugar and Currency Acts. Now, such committees sprang up in other colonies, exchanging ideas and information about resistance. Initiated by

This teapot protesting the Stamp Act was produced in England and marketed in colonial America, illustrating the close political and economic connections between the two.

A British engraving from 1766 marking the repeal of the Stamp Act. A funeral procession on the banks of the River Thames in London includes Prime Minister George Grenville carrying a coffin noting that the act was born in 1765 and died a year later. Two large containers are labeled "Stamps from America"—stamps returned because no longer needed—and "black cloth from America," for use at the funeral. In the background, a warehouse contains goods to be "ship'd for America," now that the boycott of British imports has ended.

colonial elites, the movement against the Stamp Act quickly drew in a far broader range of Americans. The act, wrote John Adams, a Boston lawyer who drafted a set of widely reprinted resolutions against the measure, had inspired "the people, even to the lowest ranks," to become "more attentive to their liberties, more inquisitive about them, and more determined to defend them, than they were ever before known." Political debate, Adams added, pervaded the colonies—"our presses have groaned, our pulpits have thundered, our legislatures have resolved, our towns have voted."

Politics in the Streets

Opponents of the Stamp Act, however, did not rely solely on debate. Even before the law went into effect, crowds forced those chosen to administer it to resign and destroyed shipments of stamps. In New York City, processions involving hundreds of residents shouting "Liberty" paraded through the streets nearly every night in late 1765. They were organized by the newly created **Sons of Liberty**. While they enjoyed no standing among the colony's wealthy elite and carried little weight in municipal affairs, the Sons' leaders enjoyed a broad following among the city's craftsmen, laborers, and sailors.

Sons of Liberty

The Sons posted notices reading "Liberty, Property, and No Stamps" and took the lead in enforcing the boycott of British imports. Their actions were viewed with increasing alarm by the aristocratic Livingston and De Lancey families, who dominated New York politics. As the assault on Thomas Hutchinson's house in Boston demonstrated, crowds could easily get out of hand. In November 1765, a New York crowd reportedly composed of sailors, blacks, laborers, and youths hurled stones at Fort George at the tip of Manhattan Island. They then proceeded to destroy the home of Major Thomas James, a British officer who was said to have boasted that he would force the stamps down New Yorkers' throats.

Stunned by the ferocity of American resistance and pressured by London merchants and manufacturers who did not wish to lose their American markets, the British government retreated. In 1766, Parliament repealed the Stamp Act. But this concession was accompanied by the Declaratory Act, which rejected Americans' claims that only their elected representatives could levy taxes. Parliament, proclaimed this measure, possessed the power to pass laws for "the colonies and people of America . . . in all cases whatsoever." Since the debt-ridden British government continued to need money raised in the colonies, passage of the Declaratory Act promised further conflict.

Stamp Act repeal

The Regulators

The Stamp Act crisis was not the only example of violent social turmoil during the 1760s. Many colonies experienced contentious internal divisions as well. As population moved westward, the conflicting land claims of settlers, speculators, colonial governments, and Indians sparked fierce disputes. Rural areas had a long tradition of resistance by settlers and small farmers against the claims of land speculators and large proprietors. As in the Stamp Act crisis, "Liberty" was their rallying cry, but in this case liberty had less to do with imperial policy than with secure possession of land.

Beginning in the mid-1760s, a group of wealthy residents of the South Carolina backcountry calling themselves **Regulators** protested the underrepresentation of western settlements in the colony's assembly and the legislators' failure to establish local governments that could regularize land titles and suppress bands of outlaws. The lack of courts in the area, they claimed, had led to a breakdown of law and order, allowing "an infernal gang of villains" to commit "shocking outrages" on persons and property. They added: "We are *Free-men*—British subjects—Not Born Slaves."

South Carolina Regulators

A parallel movement in North Carolina mobilized small farmers, who refused to pay taxes, kidnapped local officials, assaulted the homes of land speculators, merchants, and lawyers, and disrupted court proceedings. Here, the complaint was not a lack of government, but corrupt county authorities. These local officials, the Regulators claimed, threatened inexpensive access to land and the prosperity of ordinary settlers through high taxes and court fees. Demanding the democratization of local government, the Regulators condemned the "rich and powerful" (the colony's elite) who used their political authority to prosper at the expense of "poor industrious" farmers. At their peak, the Regulators numbered around 8,000 armed farmers. The region remained in turmoil until 1771, when, in the "battle of Alamance," the farmers were suppressed by the colony's militia.

North Carolina Regulators

The Tenant Uprising

Also in the mid-1760s, tenants on the Livingston, Philipse, and Cortland manors along the Hudson River north of New York City stopped paying rent and began seizing land. Like opponents of the Stamp Act, they called themselves the Sons of Liberty. The original Sons, however, opposed their uprising, and it was soon suppressed by British and colonial troops. Meanwhile, small farmers in the Green Mountains took up arms to protect their holdings against intrusions by New York landlords. The legal situation there was complex. The area was part of New York, but during the 1750s the governor of New Hampshire had issued land grants to New England families, pocketing a fortune in fees. When New Yorkers tried to enforce their own title to the area, the settlers' leader, Ethan Allen, insisted that land should belong to the person who worked it. Outsiders, he claimed, were trying to "enslave a free people." In the mid-1770s, Allen and his Green Mountain Boys gained control of the region, which later became the state of Vermont.

Ethan Allen and the Green Mountain Boys

The emerging rift between Britain and America eventually superimposed itself on conflicts within the colonies. But the social divisions revealed in the Stamp Act riots and backcountry uprisings made some members of the colonial elite fear that opposition to British measures might unleash turmoil at home. As a result, they were more reluctant to challenge British authority when the next imperial crisis arose.

THE ROAD TO REVOLUTION

The Townshend Crisis

In 1767, the government in London decided to impose a new set of taxes on Americans, known as the **Townshend Acts**. They were devised by the Chancellor of the Exchequer (the cabinet's chief financial minister), Charles Townshend. In opposing the Stamp Act, some colonists had seemed to suggest that they would not object if Britain raised revenue by regulating trade. Taking them at their word, Townshend persuaded Parliament to impose new taxes on goods imported into the colonies and to create a new board of customs commissioners to collect them and suppress smuggling. He intended to use the new revenues to pay the salaries of American governors and judges, thus freeing them from dependence on colonial assemblies. Although many merchants objected to the new enforcement procedures, opposition to the Townshend duties developed more slowly than in the case of the Stamp Act. Leaders in several colonies nonetheless decided in 1768 to reimpose the ban on importing British goods.

Taxes on imports

The Townshend crisis led to the writing of one of the most important statements of the American position, *Letters from a Farmer in Pennsylvania* by John Dickinson (a lawyer, not a farmer, although he grew up on his family's tobacco plantation in Maryland). First published in a Philadelphia newspaper in 1767 and 1768 and then widely circulated in pamphlet form, the essays argued for reconciliation with the mother country, with the colonists enjoying all the traditional rights of Englishmen. Dickinson's learned presentation—he offered quotations from writers ranging from Shakespeare to such eighteenth-century figures as David Hume, William Blackstone, and Montesquieu—demonstrated that Enlightenment ideas were by now familiar in the colonies. It also showed that at this point, many American leaders still assumed that political debate should take place among the educated elite.

Dickinson's Letters

Homespun Virtue

The boycott began in Boston and soon spread to the southern colonies. Reliance on American rather than British goods, on homespun clothing rather than imported finery, became a symbol of American resistance. It also reflected, as the colonists saw it, a virtuous spirit of self-sacrifice as compared with the self-indulgence and luxury many Americans were coming to associate with Britain. Women who spun and wove at home so as not to purchase British goods were hailed as Daughters of Liberty.

Daughters of Liberty

The idea of using homemade rather than imported goods especially appealed to Chesapeake planters, who found themselves owing increasing amounts of money to British merchants. Nonimportation, wrote George Washington, reflecting Virginia planters' concern about their growing burden of debt, gave "the extravagant man" an opportunity to "retrench his expenses" by reducing the purchase of British luxuries, without having to advertise to his neighbors that he might be in financial distress. In this way, Washington continued, Virginians could "maintain the liberty which we have derived from our ancestors," while reducing their "considerable" debts. Virginia's leaders also announced a temporary ban on the importation of slaves, but smaller planters in the Piedmont region away from the coast, where the institution was expanding, ignored this restriction.

Nonimportation

Urban artisans, who welcomed an end to competition from imported British manufactured goods, strongly supported the boycott. Philadelphia and New York merchants at first were reluctant to take part, although they eventually agreed to go along. Nonimportation threatened their livelihoods and raised the prospect of unleashing further lower-class turmoil. As had happened during the Stamp Act crisis, the streets of American cities filled with popular protests against the new duties. Extralegal local committees attempted to enforce the boycott of British goods.

The Boston Massacre

Boston once again became the focal point of conflict. Royal troops had been stationed in the city in 1768 after rioting that followed the British seizure of the ship *Liberty* for violating trade regulations. The sloop belonged to John Hancock, one of the city's most prominent merchants. The soldiers, who competed for jobs on Boston's waterfront with the city's laborers, became more and more unpopular. On March 5, 1770, a fight between a snowball-throwing crowd of Bostonians and British troops escalated into an armed confrontation that left five Bostonians dead. One of those who fell in what came to be called the **Boston Massacre** was **Crispus Attucks**, a sailor of mixed Indian-African-white ancestry. Attucks would later be remembered as the "first martyr of the American Revolution." The commanding officer and eight soldiers were put on trial in Massachusetts. Ably defended by John Adams, who viewed lower-class crowd actions as a dangerous method of opposing British policies, seven were found not guilty, while two were convicted of manslaughter. But Paul Revere, a member of the Boston Sons of Liberty and a silversmith and engraver, helped to stir up indignation against the British army by producing a widely circulated (and quite inaccurate) print of the Boston Massacre depicting a line of British soldiers firing into an unarmed crowd.

Royal soldiers in Boston

By 1770, as merchants' profits shriveled and many members of the colonial elite found they could not do without British goods, the nonimportation movement was

The Boston Massacre. Less than a month after the Boston Massacre of 1770, in which five colonists died, Paul Revere produced this engraving of the event. Although it inaccurately depicts what was actually a disorganized brawl between residents of Boston and British soldiers, this image became one of the most influential pieces of political propaganda of the revolutionary era.

William Hogarth's depiction of John Wilkes holding a liberty cap. Wilkes's publication *North Briton* bitterly attacked the king and prime minister, for which Wilkes was arrested, tried, and acquitted by a London jury. He became a popular symbol of freedom on both sides of the Atlantic.

collapsing. The value of British imports to the colonies declined by about one-third during 1769, but then rebounded to its former level. British merchants, who wished to remove a possible source of future interruption of trade, pressed for repeal of the Townshend duties. When the British ministry agreed, leaving in place only a tax on tea, and agreed to remove troops from Boston, American merchants quickly abandoned the boycott.

Wilkes and Liberty

Once again, an immediate crisis had been resolved. Nonetheless, many Americans concluded that Britain was succumbing to the same pattern of political corruption and decline of liberty that afflicted other countries. The overlap of the Townshend crisis with a controversy in Britain over the treatment of John Wilkes reinforced this sentiment. A radical journalist known for scandalous writings about the king and ministry, Wilkes had been elected to Parliament from London but was expelled from his seat. "Wilkes and Liberty" became a popular rallying cry on both sides of the Atlantic. In addition, rumors circulated in the colonies that the Anglican Church in England planned to send bishops to America. Among members of other Protestant denominations, the rumors—strongly denied in London—sparked fears that bishops would establish religious courts like those that had once persecuted Dissenters. The conviction that the British government had set itself on a course dangerous to liberty underpinned colonial resistance when the next crisis arose.

The Tea Act

The next crisis underscored how powerfully events in other parts of Britain's global empire affected the American colonies. The East India Company, a giant trading monopoly, effectively governed recently acquired British possessions in India. Numerous British merchants, bankers, and other individuals had invested heavily in its stock. A classic speculative bubble ensued, with the price of stock in the company rising sharply and then collapsing. To rescue the company and its investors, the British government decided to help it market its enormous holdings of Chinese tea in North America.

The East India Company

Tea, once a preserve of the wealthy, had become a drink consumed by all social classes in England and the colonies. To further stimulate its sales and bail out the East India Company, the British government, now headed by Frederick Lord North, offered the company a series of rebates and tax exemptions. These enabled it to dump low-priced tea on the American market, undercutting both established merchants and smugglers. Money raised through the taxation of imported tea would be used to help defray the costs of colonial government, thus threatening, once again, the assemblies' control over finance.

Tea tax

The tax on tea was not new. But many colonists insisted that to pay it on this large new body of imports would acknowledge Britain's right to tax the colonies. As tea shipments arrived, resistance developed in the major ports. On December 16, 1773, a group of colonists disguised as Indians boarded three ships at anchor in Boston Harbor and threw more than 300 chests of tea into the water. The event became known as the **Boston Tea Party**. The loss to the East India Company was around £10,000 (the equivalent of more than $4 million today).

The Intolerable Acts

The British government, declared Lord North, must now demonstrate "whether we have, or have not, any authority in that country." Its response to the Boston Tea Party was swift and decisive. Parliament closed the port of Boston to all trade until the tea was paid for. It radically altered the Massachusetts Charter of 1691 by curtailing town meetings and authorizing the governor to appoint members to the council—positions previously filled by election. Parliament also empowered military commanders to lodge soldiers in private homes. These measures, called the Coercive or **Intolerable Acts** by Americans, united the colonies in opposition to what was widely seen as a direct threat to their political freedom.

At almost the same time, Parliament passed the Quebec Act. This extended the southern boundary of that Canadian province to the Ohio River and granted legal toleration to the Roman Catholic Church in Canada. With an eye to the growing tensions in colonies to the south, the act sought to secure the allegiance of Quebec's Catholics by offering rights denied to their coreligionists in Britain, including practicing their faith freely and holding positions in the civil service. The act not only threw into question land claims in the Ohio country but persuaded many colonists that the government in London was conspiring to

The Bostonians Paying the Excise-Man, a 1774 engraving, shows colonists pouring tea down the throat of a tax collector, who has been covered with tar and feathers. A noose hangs menacingly from the Liberty Tree. In the background is the Boston Tea Party.

strengthen Catholicism—dreaded by most Protestants—in its American empire. Fears of religious and political tyranny mingled in the minds of many colonists. Especially in New England, the cause of liberty became the cause of God. A gathering of 1,000 residents of Farmington, Connecticut, in May 1774 adopted resolutions proclaiming that, as "the sons of freedom," they would resist every attempt "to take away our liberties and properties and to enslave us forever." They accused the British ministry of being "instigated by the devil."

The Mitred Minuet, a British cartoon from 1774, shows four Roman Catholic bishops dancing around a copy of the Quebec Act. On the left, British officials Lord Bute, Lord North, and Lord Mansfield look on, while the devil oversees the proceedings.

THE COMING OF INDEPENDENCE

The Continental Congress

Opposition to the Intolerable Acts now spread to small towns and rural areas that had not participated actively in previous resistance. In September 1774, in the town of Worcester, Massachusetts, 4,600 militiamen from thirty-seven towns (half the adult male population of the entire county) lined both sides of Main Street as the British-appointed officials walked the gauntlet between them. In the same month, a convention of delegates from Massachusetts towns approved a series of resolutions (called the Suffolk Resolves for the county in which Boston is located) that urged Americans to refuse obedience to the new laws, withhold taxes, and prepare for war.

> *Suffolk Resolves*

To coordinate resistance to the Intolerable Acts, a **Continental Congress** convened in Philadelphia that month, bringing together the most prominent political leaders of twelve mainland colonies (Georgia did not take part). From Massachusetts came the "brace of Adamses"—John and his more radical cousin Samuel. Virginia's seven delegates included George Washington, Richard Henry Lee, and the renowned orator Patrick Henry. Henry's power as a speaker came from a unique style that combined moral appeals with blunt directness. "The distinctions between Virginians, Pennsylvanians, New Yorkers, and New Englanders," Henry declared, "are no more. I am not a Virginian, but an American." In March 1775, Henry concluded a speech urging a Virginia convention to begin military preparations with a legendary credo: "Give me liberty, or give me death!"

> *"Give me liberty, or give me death!"*

The Continental Association

Before it adjourned at the end of October 1774 with an agreement to reconvene the following May if colonial demands had not been met, the Congress endorsed the Suffolk Resolves and adopted the Continental Association, which called for an almost complete halt to trade with Great Britain and the West Indies (at South Carolina's insistence, exports of rice to Europe were exempted). The

Association also encouraged domestic manufacturing and denounced "every species of extravagance and dissipation." Congress authorized local Committees of Safety to oversee its mandates and to take action against "enemies of American liberty," including businessmen who tried to profit from the sudden scarcity of goods.

The Committees of Safety began the process of transferring effective political power from established governments whose authority derived from Great Britain to extralegal grassroots bodies reflecting the will of the people. By early 1775, some 7,000 men were serving on local committees throughout the colonies, a vast expansion of the "political nation." The committees became training grounds where small farmers, city artisans, propertyless laborers, and others who had heretofore had little role in government discussed political issues and exercised political power. In Philadelphia, the extralegal committees of the 1760s that oversaw the boycott of British goods had been composed almost entirely of prominent lawyers and merchants. But younger merchants, shopkeepers, and artisans dominated the committee elected in November 1774 to enforce the Continental Association. They were determined that resistance to British measures not be dropped as it had been in 1770. When the New York assembly refused to endorse the association, local committees continued to enforce it anyway.

Benjamin Franklin designed this four-dollar bill for the new nation. It depicts a wild boar—an animal he claimed was inoffensive until aroused.

The Sweets of Liberty

By 1775, talk of liberty pervaded the colonies. The past few years had witnessed an endless parade of pamphlets with titles like *A Chariot of Liberty* and *Oration on the Beauties of Liberty* (the latter, a sermon delivered in Boston by Joseph Allen in 1772, became the most popular public address of the years before independence). Sober men spoke longingly of the "sweets of liberty." While sleeping, Americans dreamed of liberty. One anonymous essayist reported a "night vision" of the word written in the sun's rays. Commented a British emigrant who arrived in Maryland early in 1775: "They are all liberty mad."

"Liberty mad"

The right to resist oppressive authority and the identification of liberty with the cause of God, so deeply ingrained by the imperial struggles of the eighteenth century, were now invoked against Britain itself, by colonists of all backgrounds. The first mass meeting in the history of Northampton County, Pennsylvania, whose population was overwhelmingly of German ancestry, gathered in 1774. By the following year, a majority of the county's adult population had joined militia associations. Many German settlers, whose close-knit communities had earlier viewed with some suspicion "the famous English liberty" as a byword for selfish individualism, now claimed all the "rights and privileges of natural-born subjects of his majesty."

As the crisis deepened, Americans increasingly based their claims not simply on the historical rights of Englishmen but on the more abstract language of natural rights and universal freedom. The First Continental Congress defended its actions

Natural rights

A Summary View of the Rights of British America

by appealing to the "principles of the English constitution," the "liberties of free and natural-born subjects within the realm of England," and the "immutable law of nature." John Locke's theory of natural rights that existed prior to the establishment of government offered a powerful justification for colonial resistance. Americans, declared Thomas Jefferson in *A Summary View of the Rights of British America* (written in 1774 to instruct Virginia's delegates to the Continental Congress), were "a free people claiming their rights, as derived from the laws of nature, and not as the gift of their chief magistrate." Americans, Jefferson insisted, still revered the king. But he demanded that empire henceforth be seen as a collection of equal parts held together by loyalty to a constitutional monarch, not a system in which one part ruled over the others.

The Outbreak of War

By the time the Second Continental Congress convened in May 1775, war had broken out between British soldiers and armed citizens of Massachusetts. On April 19, a force of British soldiers marched from Boston toward the nearby town of Concord seeking to seize arms being stockpiled there. Riders from Boston, among them Paul Revere, warned local leaders of the troops' approach. Militiamen took up arms and tried to resist the British advance. Skirmishes between Americans and British soldiers took place at Lexington and again at Concord, known as the **Battles of Lexington and Concord**. By the time the British retreated to the safety of Boston, some forty-nine Americans and seventy-three members of the Royal Army lay dead.

"The shot heard 'round the world"

What the philosopher Ralph Waldo Emerson would later call "the shot heard 'round the world" began the American War of Independence. It reverberated throughout the colonies. When news of the skirmish reached Lemuel Roberts, a poor New York farmer, he felt his "bosom glow" with the "call of liberty." Roberts set

The Battle of Concord, as depicted in a 1775 engraving by Amos Doolittle, a New Haven silversmith. Under musket fire from colonials, the British retreat across Concord's North Bridge. In his poem "Concorde Hymn" (1837), Ralph Waldo Emerson immortalized the moment: "By the rude bridge that arched the flood, Their flag to April's breeze unfurled, Here once the embattled farmers stood, And fired the shot heard 'round the world."

off for Massachusetts to enlist in the army. In May 1775, Ethan Allen and the Green Mountain Boys, together with militiamen from Connecticut led by Benedict Arnold, surrounded Fort Ticonderoga in New York and forced it to surrender. The following winter, Henry Knox, George Washington's commander of artillery, arranged for some of the Ticonderoga cannon to be dragged hundreds of miles to the east to reinforce the siege of Boston, where British forces were ensconced. On June 17, 1775, two months after Lexington and Concord,

In March 1776, James Pike, a soldier in the Massachusetts militia, carved this scene on his powder horn to commemorate the battles of Lexington and Concord. At the center stands the Liberty Tree.

the British had dislodged colonial militiamen from Breed's Hill, although only at a heavy cost in casualties. (The battle came to be named the **Battle of Bunker Hill**, after the nearby Bunker Hill.) But the arrival of American cannon in March 1776 and their entrenchment above the city made the British position in Boston untenable. The British army under the command of Sir William Howe was forced to abandon the city. Before leaving, Howe's forces cut down the original Liberty Tree.

Meanwhile, the Second Continental Congress authorized the raising of a **Continental army**, printed money to pay for it, and appointed George Washington its commander. Washington, who had gained considerable fighting experience during the Seven Years' War, was not only the colonies' best-known military officer but also a prominent Virginian. John Adams, who proposed his name, recognized that having a southerner lead American forces would reinforce colonial unity. In response, Britain declared the colonies in a state of rebellion, dispatched thousands of troops, and ordered the closing of all colonial ports.

Raising the Continental army

Independence?

By the end of 1775, the breach with Britain seemed irreparable. But many colonists shied away from the idea of independence. Pride in membership in the British empire was still strong, and many political leaders, especially in colonies that had experienced internal turmoil, feared that a complete break with the mother country might unleash further conflict. Anarchy from below, in their view, was as much a danger as tyranny from above. Many advocates of independence, one opponent warned, would find it "very agreeable" to divide the property of the rich among the poor.

Authority and independence

Such fears affected how colonial leaders responded to the idea of independence. The elites of Massachusetts and Virginia, who felt supremely confident of their ability to retain authority at home, tended to support a break with Britain. Massachusetts had borne the brunt of the Intolerable Acts. Southern leaders not only were highly protective of their political liberty but also were outraged by a proclamation issued in November 1775 by the earl of Dunmore, the British governor and military commander in Virginia. **Lord Dunmore's proclamation** offered freedom to any slave who escaped to his lines and bore arms for the king.

In New York and Pennsylvania, however, the diversity of the population made it difficult to work out a consensus on how far to go in resisting British measures. Here opposition to previous British laws had unleashed demands by small farmers

Thomas Paine, advocate of American independence, in a 1791 portrait.

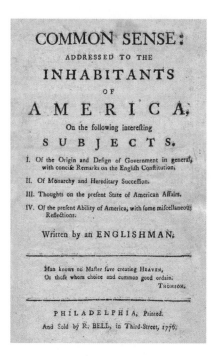

The cover of *Common Sense*, Thomas Paine's influential pamphlet denouncing the idea of hereditary rule and calling for American independence.

and urban artisans for a greater voice in political affairs. As a result, many established leaders drew back from further resistance. Joseph Galloway, a Pennsylvania leader and delegate to the Second Continental Congress who worked to devise a compromise between British and colonial positions, warned that independence would be accompanied by constant disputes within America. He even predicted a war between the northern and southern colonies. Americans, Galloway declared, could only enjoy "true liberty"—self-government and security for their persons and property—by remaining within the empire.

Common Sense

As 1776 dawned, America presented the unusual spectacle of colonists at war against the British empire but still pleading for their rights within it. Even as fighting raged, Congress in July 1775 had addressed the Olive Branch Petition to George III, reaffirming Americans' loyalty to the crown and hoping for a "permanent reconciliation." Ironically, it was a recent emigrant from England, not a colonist from a family long established on American soil, who grasped the inner logic of the situation and offered a vision of the broad significance of American independence. An English craftsman and minor government official, Thomas Paine had emigrated to Philadelphia late in 1774. He quickly became associated with a group of advocates of the American cause, including John Adams and Dr. Benjamin Rush, a leading Philadelphia physician. It was Rush who suggested to Paine that he write a pamphlet supporting American independence.

Its author listed only as "an Englishman," **Common Sense** appeared in January 1776. The pamphlet began not with a recital of colonial grievances but with an attack on the "so much boasted Constitution of England" and the principles of hereditary rule and monarchical government. Rather than being the most perfect system of government in the world, Paine wrote, the English monarchy was headed by "the royal brute of England," and the English constitution was composed in large part of "the base remains of two ancient tyrannies . . . monarchical tyranny in the person of the king [and] aristocratical tyranny in the persons of the peers." "Of more worth is one honest man to society, and in the sight of God," he continued, "than all the crowned ruffians that ever lived." Far preferable than monarchy would be a democratic system based on frequent elections, with citizens' rights protected by a written constitution.

Turning to independence, Paine drew on the colonists' experiences to make his case. "There is something absurd," he wrote, "in supposing a Continent to be perpetually governed by an island." Within the British empire, America's prospects were limited; liberated from the Navigation Acts and trading freely with the entire world, its "material eminence" was certain. Paine tied the economic hopes of the new nation to the idea of commercial freedom. With independence, moreover, the colonies could for the first time insulate themselves from involvement in the endless imperial wars of Europe. Britain had "dragged" its American colonies into conflicts with countries like Spain and France, which "never were . . . our enemies as *Americans*, but as our being the subjects of Great Britain." Membership in the British empire, Paine insisted, was a burden to the colonies, not a benefit.

Toward the close of the pamphlet, Paine moved beyond practical considerations to outline a breathtaking vision of the historical importance of the American

Revolution. "The cause of America," he proclaimed in stirring language, "is in great measure, the cause of all mankind." The new nation would become the home of freedom, "an asylum for mankind."

Paine's Impact

Few of Paine's ideas were original. What made *Common Sense* unique was his mode of expressing them and the audience he addressed. Previous political writings had generally been directed toward the educated elite. "When I mention the public," declared John Randolph of Virginia in 1774, "I mean to include the rational part of it. The ignorant vulgar are unfit . . . to manage the reins of government." Just as evangelical ministers had shattered the trained clergy's monopoly on religious preaching, Paine pioneered a new style of political writing, one designed to expand dramatically the public sphere where political discussion took place. He wrote clearly and directly, and he avoided the complex language and Latin phrases common in pamphlets aimed at educated readers. His style stood in marked contrast to previous political pamphlets, such as John Dickinson's *Letters from a Farmer in Pennsylvania*. *Common Sense* quickly became one of the most successful and influential pamphlets in the history of political writing, selling, by Paine's estimate, some 150,000 copies. Paine directed that his share of the profits be used to buy supplies for the Continental army.

Paine's writing style

In February 1776, the Massachusetts political leader Joseph Hawley read *Common Sense* and remarked, "Every sentiment has sunk into my well prepared heart." The hearts of Hawley and thousands of other Americans had been prepared for Paine's arguments by the extended conflict over Britain's right to tax the colonies, the outbreak of war in 1775, and the growing conviction that Britain was a corrupt society where liberty was diminishing. The intensification of fighting in the winter of 1775–1776, when Americans unsuccessfully invaded Canada while the British burned Falmouth (now Portland), Maine, and bombarded Norfolk, Virginia, gave added weight to the movement for independence. In the spring of 1776, scores of American communities adopted resolutions calling for a separation from Britain. Only six months elapsed between the appearance of *Common Sense* and the decision by the Second Continental Congress to sever the colonies' ties with Great Britain.

The move to independence

The Declaration of Independence

On July 2, 1776, the Congress formally declared the United States an independent nation. Two days later, it approved the Declaration of Independence, written by Thomas Jefferson and revised by the Congress before approval. (See the Appendix for the full text.) Most of the Declaration consists of a lengthy list of grievances directed against King George III, ranging from quartering troops in colonial homes to imposing taxes without the colonists' consent. Britain's aim, it declared, was to establish "absolute tyranny" over the colonies. One clause in Jefferson's draft, which condemned the inhumanity of the slave trade and criticized the king for overturning colonial laws that sought to restrict the importation of slaves, was deleted by the Congress at the insistence of Georgia and South Carolina.

Grievances against the king

VOICES OF FREEDOM

From SAMUEL SEABURY, *AN ALARM TO THE LEGISLATURE OF THE PROVINCE IN NEW-YORK* (1775)

An Anglican minister and graduate of Yale College, Samuel Seabury was a devoted loyalist, who in 1774 and 1775 published several pamphlets opposing the revolutionary movement. He remained in the United States after the War of Independence and became the new nation's first Episcopal bishop.

———————

The unhappy contention we have entered into with our parent state, would inevitably be attended with many disagreeable circumstances, with many and great inconveniences to us, even were it conducted on our part, with propriety and moderation. What then must be the case, when all proper and moderate measures are rejected? . . . When every scheme that tends to peace, is branded with ignominy; as being the machination of slavery! When nothing is called FREEDOM but SEDITION! Nothing LIBERTY but REBELLION!

I will not presume to encroach so far upon your time, as to attempt to point out the causes of our unnatural contention with Great Britain. . . . Nor will I attempt to trace out the progress of that infatuation, which hath so deeply, so miserably, infected the Colonies. . . . Most, if not all the measures that have been adopted, have been illegal in their beginning, tyrannical in their operation. . . . A Committee, chosen in a tumultuous, illegal manner, usurped

the most despotic authority over the province. They entered into contracts, compacts, combinations, treaties of alliance, with the other colonies, without any power from the legislature of the province. They agreed with the other Colonies to send Delegates to meet in convention at Philadelphia, to determine upon the rights and liberties of the good people of this province, unsupported by any Law. . . .

The state to which the Grand Congress, and the subordinate Committees, have reduced the colonies, is really deplorable. They have introduced a system of the most oppressive tyranny that can possibly be imagined;—a tyranny, not only over the actions, but over the words, thoughts, and minds, of the good people of this province. People have been threatened with the vengence of a mob, for speaking in support of order and good government. . . .

Behold, Gentlemen, behold the wretched state to which we are reduced! A foreign power is brought in to govern this province. Laws made at Philadelphia, by factious men from New-England, New-Jersey, Pennsylvania, Maryland, Virginia, and the Carolinas, are imposed upon us by the most imperious menaces. Money is levied upon us without the consent of our representatives. . . . Mobs and riots are encouraged, in order to force submission to the tyranny of the Congress.

From THOMAS PAINE, *COMMON SENSE* (1776)

A recent emigrant from England, Thomas Paine in January 1776 published *Common Sense*, a highly influential pamphlet that in stirring language made the case for American independence.

In the following pages I offer nothing more than simple facts, plain arguments, and common sense. . . .

Male and female are the distinctions of nature, good and bad the distinctions of heaven; but how a race of men came into the world so exalted above the rest, and distinguished like some new species, is worth enquiring into, and whether they are the means of happiness or of misery to mankind. . . . One of the strongest *natural* proofs of the folly of hereditary right in kings, is, that nature disapproves it, otherwise she would not so frequently turn it into ridicule, by giving mankind an *ass for a lion*. . . .

The sun never shined on a cause of greater worth. 'Tis not the affair of a city, a country, a province, or a kingdom, but of a continent—of at least one eighth part of the habitable globe. 'Tis not the concern of a day, a year, or an age; posterity are virtually involved in the context, and will be more or less affected, even to the end of time, by the proceedings now. Now is the seed time of continental union, faith and honor. . . .

I challenge the warmest advocate for reconciliation to show a single advantage that this continent can reap by being connected with Great Britain. . . . But the injuries and disadvantages which we sustain by that connection, are without number. . . . Any submission to, or dependence on, Great Britain, tends directly to involve this Continent in European wars and quarrels, and set us at variance with nations who would otherwise seek our friendship, and against whom we have neither anger nor complaint.

O ye that love mankind! Ye that dare oppose, not only the tyranny, but the tyrant, stand forth! Every spot of the old world is overrun with oppression. Freedom hath been hunted round the globe. Asia, and Africa, have long expelled her. Europe regards her like a stranger, and England hath given her warning to depart. O! Receive the fugitive, and prepare in time an asylum for mankind.

QUESTIONS

1. *Why does Seabury believe the Continental Congress and local committees are undermining Americans' liberties?*

2. *What does Paine see as the global significance of the American struggle for independence?*

3. *How do the two writers differ in their view of the main threats to American freedom?*

An early draft, with corrections, of the Declaration of Independence, in Thomas Jefferson's handwriting. Note how the elimination of unnecessary words added to the document's power—"all men are created equal and independent" became "all men are created equal," and "inherent and inalienable" rights became "inalienable" (in the final version, this would be changed to "unalienable").

Jefferson's preamble

The Declaration's enduring impact came not from the complaints against George III but from Jefferson's preamble, especially the second paragraph, which begins, "We hold these truths to be self-evident, that all men are created equal, that they are endowed by their Creator with certain unalienable Rights, that among these are Life, Liberty, and the pursuit of Happiness." By "unalienable rights," Jefferson meant rights so basic, so rooted in human nature itself (or in what John Locke had called the state of nature), that no government could take them away.

Jefferson then went on to justify the breach with Britain. Government, he wrote, derives its powers from "the consent of the governed." When a government threatens its subjects' natural rights, the people have the authority "to alter or to abolish it." The Declaration of Independence is ultimately an assertion of the right of revolution.

The Declaration and American Freedom

The **Declaration of Independence** changed forever the meaning of American freedom. It completed the shift from the rights of Englishmen to the rights of mankind as the object of American independence. In Jefferson's language, "the Laws of Nature and of Nature's God," not the British constitution or the heritage of the freeborn Englishman, justified independence. No longer a set of specific rights, no longer a privilege to be enjoyed by a corporate body or people in certain social circumstances, liberty had become a universal entitlement.

Jefferson's argument (natural rights, the right to resist arbitrary authority, etc.) drew on the writings of John Locke, who, as explained in the previous chapter, saw government as resting on a "social contract," violation of which destroyed the legitimacy of authority. But when Jefferson substituted the "pursuit of happiness" for property in the familiar Lockean triad that opens the Declaration, he tied the new nation's star to an open-ended, democratic process whereby individuals develop their own potential and seek to realize their own life goals. Individual self-fulfillment, unimpeded by government, would become a central element of American freedom. Tradition would no longer rule the present, and Americans could shape their society as they saw fit.

America as a Symbol of Liberty, a 1775 engraving from the cover of the *Pennsylvania Magazine*, edited by Thomas Paine soon after his arrival in America. The shield displays the colony's coat of arms. The female figure holding a liberty cap is surrounded by weaponry of the patriotic struggle, including a cartridge box marked "liberty," hanging from a tree (*right*).

An Asylum for Mankind

A distinctive definition of nationality resting on American freedom was born in the Revolution. From the beginning, the idea of "American exceptionalism"—the belief that the United States has a special mission to serve as a refuge from tyranny, a symbol of freedom, and a model for the rest of the world—has occupied a central place in American nationalism. The new nation declared itself, in the words of Virginia leader James Madison, the "workshop of liberty to the Civilized World." Paine's remark in *Common Sense*, "we have it in our power to begin the world over again," and his description of the new nation as an "asylum for mankind" expressed a sense that the Revolution was an event of global historical importance. Countless sermons, political tracts, and newspaper articles of the time repeated this idea. Unburdened by the institutions—monarchy, aristocracy, hereditary privilege—that oppressed the peoples of the Old World, America and America alone was the place where the principle of universal freedom could take root. This was why Jefferson addressed the Declaration to "the opinions of mankind," not just the colonists themselves or Great Britain.

American nationality

First to add his name to the Declaration of Independence was the Massachusetts merchant John Hancock, president of the Second Continental Congress, with a signature so large, he declared, according to legend, that King George III could read it without his spectacles.

The Global Declaration of Independence

Even apart from the Declaration of Independence, 1776 was a momentous year in North America. Spain established Mission Dolores, the first European settlement at San Francisco, in an effort to block Russian advances on the Pacific coast. In San Diego, local Indians rebelled, unsuccessfully, against Spanish rule. The Lakota Sioux, migrating westward from Minnesota, settled in the Black Hills of North

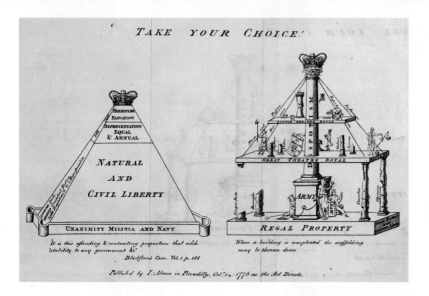

TAKE YOUR CHOICE!

Inspired by the American Revolution, the British reformer John Cartwright published an appeal for the annual election of Parliament as essential to liberty in Britain. He included an engraving contrasting the principles of reform, on the left, with despotism, on the right.

Other declarations of independence

Dakota, their homeland for the next century. All these places and peoples would eventually become part of the United States, but, of course, no one knew this in 1776.

Meanwhile, the struggle for independence reverberated around the globe. The American colonists were less concerned with securing human rights for all mankind than with winning international recognition in their struggle for independence from Britain. But Jefferson hoped that this rebellion would become "the signal of arousing men to burst the chains . . . and to assume the blessings and security of self-government." And for more than two centuries, the Declaration has remained an inspiration not only to generations of Americans denied the enjoyment of their natural rights, but to colonial peoples around the world seeking independence. The Declaration quickly appeared in French and German translations, although not, at first, in Spanish, since the government feared it would inspire dangerous ideas among the peoples of Spain's American empire.

In the years since 1776, numerous anticolonial movements have modeled their own declarations of independence on America's. The first came in Flanders (part of today's Belgium, then part of the Austrian empire), where rebels in 1790 echoed Jefferson's words by declaring that their province "is and of rights ought to be, a Free and Independent State." Today, more than half the countries in the world, in places as far-flung as China (issued after the revolution of 1911) and Vietnam (1945), have such declarations. Many of these documents, like Jefferson's, listed grievances against an imperial power to justify revolution. Few of these documents, however, have affirmed the natural rights—life, liberty, and the pursuit of happiness—Jefferson invoked. Over time, the Declaration in a global context has become an assertion of the right of various groups to form independent states, rather than a list of the rights of citizens that their governments could not abridge.

But even more than the specific language of the Declaration, the principle that legitimate political authority rests on the will of "the people" has been adopted around the world. In 1780, even as the American War of Independence raged, a Jesuit-educated Indian of Peru took the name of the last Inca ruler, Túpac Amaru, and led an uprising against Spanish rule. By the time it was suppressed in 1783, some 10,000 Spanish and 100,000 Indians had perished. In the Dutch, French, and Spanish empires, where European governments had been trying to tighten their control much as the British had done in North America, local elites demanded greater autonomy, often drawing on the constitutional arguments of American patriots. The idea that "the people" possess rights was quickly internationalized. Slaves in the Caribbean, colonial subjects in India, and indigenous inhabitants of Latin America could all speak this language, to the dismay of those who exercised power over them.

SECURING INDEPENDENCE

The Balance of Power

Declaring Americans independent was one thing; winning independence another. The newly created American army confronted the greatest military power on earth. Viewing the Americans as traitors, Britain resolved to crush the rebellion. On the surface, the balance of power seemed heavily weighted in Britain's favor. It had a well-trained army (supplemented by hired soldiers from German states like Hesse), the world's most powerful navy, and experienced military commanders. The Americans had to rely on local militias and an inadequately equipped Continental army. Washington himself felt that militiamen were too "accustomed to unbounded freedom" to accept the "proper degree of subordination" necessary in soldiers. Moreover, many Americans were not enthusiastic about independence, and some actively supported the British.

On the other hand, many American soldiers did not lack military experience, having fought in the Seven Years' War or undergone intensive militia training in the early 1770s. They were fighting on their own soil for a cause that inspired devotion and sacrifice. During the eight years of war from 1775 to 1783, some 200,000 men bore arms in the American army (whose soldiers were volunteers) and militias (where service was required of every able-bodied man unless he provided a substitute). As the war progressed, enlistment waned among propertied Americans and the Continental army increasingly drew on young men with limited economic prospects—landless sons of farmers, indentured servants, laborers, and African-Americans. The patriots suffered dearly for the cause. Of the colonies' free white male population aged sixteen to forty-five, one in twenty died in the War of Independence, the equivalent of nearly 3 million deaths in today's population. But so long as the Americans maintained an army in the field, the idea of independence remained alive no matter how much territory the British occupied.

Despite British power, to conquer the thirteen colonies would be an enormous and expensive task, and it was not at all certain that the public at home wished to pay the additional taxes that a lengthy war would require. The British, moreover, made a string of serious mistakes. From the outset the British misjudged the degree of support for independence among the American population, as well as the capacity of American citizen-soldiers. "These people," admitted the British general Thomas Gage, "show a spirit and conduct against us that they never showed against the French [in the Seven Years' War], and everybody has judged them from their former appearance and behavior, which has led many into great mistakes." Moreover, European rivals, notably France, welcomed the prospect of a British defeat. If the Americans could forge an alliance with France, a world power second only to Britain, it would go a long way toward equalizing the balance of forces.

> **Military power**

The Yankee Doodle Intrenchments near Boston, a 1776 British cartoon depicting the American revolutionaries as unimposing citizen soldiers egged on—according to the accompanying text—by a thieving commander and a reckless Puritan minister. The British greatly underestimated Americans' fighting ability in the War of Independence. One member of Parliament in 1775 claimed the colonists "were neither soldiers, nor could be made so," as they were naturally cowardly and "incapable of any sort of order or discipline."

American Foot Soldiers, Yorktown Campaign, a 1781 watercolor by a French officer, includes a black soldier from the First Rhode Island Regiment, an all-black unit of 250 men.

Blacks in the Revolution

At the war's outset, George Washington refused to accept black recruits. But he changed his mind after Lord Dunmore's 1775 proclamation, which offered freedom to slaves who joined the British cause. Some 5,000 blacks enlisted in state militias and the Continental army and navy. Since individuals drafted into the militia were allowed to provide a substitute, slaves suddenly gained considerable bargaining power. Not a few acquired their freedom by agreeing to serve in place of an owner or his son. In 1778, Rhode Island, with a higher proportion of slaves in its population than any other New England state, formed a black regiment and promised freedom to slaves who enlisted, while compensating the owners for their loss of property. Blacks who fought under George Washington and in other state militias did so in racially integrated companies (although invariably under white officers). They were the last black American soldiers to do so officially until the Korean War (except for the few black and white soldiers who fought alongside each other in irregular units at the end of World War II).

Except for South Carolina and Georgia, the southern colonies also enrolled free blacks and slaves to fight. They were not explicitly promised freedom, but many received it individually after the war ended. And in 1783, the Virginia legislature emancipated slaves who had "contributed towards the establishment of American liberty and independence" by serving in the army.

Dunmore's regiment

Fighting on the side of the British also offered opportunities for freedom. Before his forces were expelled from Virginia, 800 or more slaves had escaped from their owners to join Lord Dunmore's Ethiopian Regiment, wearing, according to legend, uniforms that bore the motto "Liberty to Slaves." During the war, blacks fought with the British in campaigns in New York, New Jersey, and South Carolina. Other escaped slaves served the Royal Army as spies, guided their troops through swamps, and worked as military cooks, laundresses, and construction workers. George Washington himself saw seventeen of his slaves flee to the British, some of whom signed up to fight the colonists. "There is not a man of them, but would leave us, if they believed they could make their escape," his cousin Lund Washington reported. "Liberty is sweet."

The First Years of the War

Had the British commander, Sir William Howe, prosecuted the war more vigorously at the outset, he might have nipped the rebellion in the bud by destroying Washington's army. But while Washington suffered numerous defeats in the first years of the war, he generally avoided direct confrontations with the British and managed to keep his army intact. Having abandoned Boston, Howe attacked New York City in the summer of 1776. Washington's army had likewise moved from Massachusetts to Brooklyn to defend the city. Howe pushed American forces

War in New York

back and almost cut off Washington's retreat across the East River. Washington managed to escape to Manhattan and then north to Peekskill, where he crossed the Hudson River to New Jersey. But the 3,000 men he had left behind at Fort Washington on Manhattan Island were captured by Howe.

Howe pursued the American army but never managed to inflict a decisive defeat. Demoralized by successive failures, however, many American soldiers simply went home. Once 28,000 men, Washington's army dwindled to fewer than 3,000. Indeed, Washington feared that without a decisive victory, it would melt away entirely. To restore morale and regain the initiative, he launched successful surprise attacks on **Hessian** soldiers at Trenton, New Jersey, on December 26, 1776, and on a British force at Princeton on January 3, 1777. Shortly before crossing the Delaware River to attack the Hessians, Washington had Thomas Paine's inspiring essay *The American Crisis* read to his troops. "These are the times that try men's souls," Paine wrote. "The summer soldier and the sunshine patriot will, in this crisis, shrink from the service of their country; but he that stands it *now*, deserves the love and thanks of man and woman."

> *Battles of New Jersey*

The Battle of Saratoga

In the summer of 1777, a second British army, led by General John Burgoyne, advanced south from Canada hoping to link up with Howe and isolate New England. But in July, Howe instead moved his forces from New York City to attack Philadelphia. In September, the Continental Congress fled to Lancaster, in central Pennsylvania, and Howe occupied the City of Brotherly Love. Not having been

> *Howe and Burgoyne*

Triumphant Entry of the Royal Troops into New York, an engraving showing the army of Sir William Howe occupying the city in 1776. New York City would remain in British hands for the duration of the War of Independence.

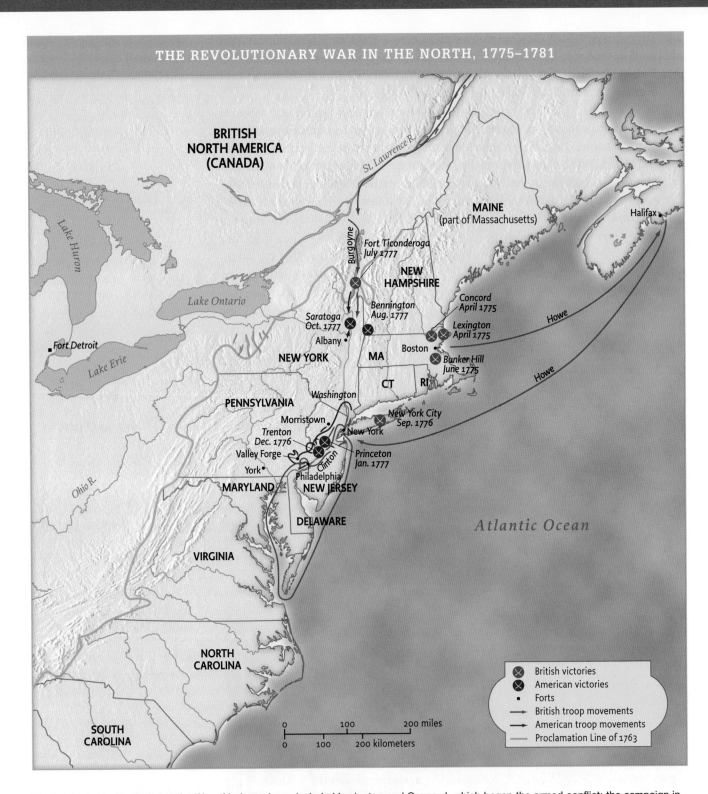

THE REVOLUTIONARY WAR IN THE NORTH, 1775–1781

BRITISH NORTH AMERICA (CANADA)

St. Lawrence R.

MAINE
(part of Massachusetts)

Halifax

Lake Huron

Lake Ontario

Burgoyne

Fort Ticonderoga
July 1777

NEW HAMPSHIRE

Bennington
Aug. 1777

Concord
April 1775

Howe

Fort Detroit

Lake Erie

Saratoga
Oct. 1777

Albany

Lexington
April 1775

NEW YORK

MA

Boston

Howe

Bunker Hill
June 1775

CT   RI

PENNSYLVANIA

Washington

Morristown

New York City
Sep. 1776

Trenton
Dec. 1776

New York

Valley Forge

Clinton

Princeton
Jan. 1777

York

Philadelphia

MARYLAND

NEW JERSEY

Atlantic Ocean

Ohio R.

DELAWARE

VIRGINIA

NORTH CAROLINA

⊗ British victories
⊗ American victories
■ Forts
→ British troop movements
→ American troop movements
— Proclamation Line of 1763

SOUTH CAROLINA

0   100   200 miles
0   100   200 kilometers

Key battles in the North during the War of Independence included Lexington and Concord, which began the armed conflict; the campaign in New York and New Jersey; and Saratoga, sometimes called the turning point of the war.

informed of Burgoyne's plans, Howe had unintentionally abandoned him. American forces blocked Burgoyne's way, surrounded his army, and on October 17, 1777, forced him to surrender at the **Battle of Saratoga**. The victory provided a significant boost to American morale.

During the winter of 1777–1778, the British army, now commanded by Sir Henry Clinton, was quartered in Philadelphia. (In the Revolution, as in most eighteenth-century wars, fighting came to a halt during the winter.) British officers took part in an elegant social life complete with balls and parties. Most notable was the great *Meschianza*, an extravaganza that included a regatta, a procession of medieval knights, and a jousting tournament. Meanwhile, Washington's army remained encamped at Valley Forge, where they suffered terribly from the frigid weather. Men who had other options simply went home. By the end of that difficult winter, recent immigrants and African-Americans made up half the soldiers at Valley Forge and most of the rest were landless or unskilled laborers.

But Saratoga helped to persuade the French that American victory was possible. In 1778, American diplomats led by Benjamin Franklin concluded a Treaty of Amity and Commerce in which France recognized the United States and agreed to supply military assistance. Still smarting from their defeat in the Seven Years' War, the French hoped to weaken Britain, their main European rival, and perhaps regain some of their lost influence and territory in the Western Hemisphere. Soon afterward, Spain also joined the war on the American side. French assistance would play a decisive part in the war's end. At the outset, however, the French fleet showed more interest in attacking British outposts in the West Indies than in directly aiding the Americans. And the Spanish confined themselves to regaining control of Florida, which they had lost to the British in the Seven Years' War. Nonetheless, French and Spanish entry transformed the War of Independence into a global conflict. By putting the British on the defensive in places ranging from Gibraltar to the West Indies, it greatly complicated their military prospects.

Alliance with France

The War in the South

In 1778, the focus of the war shifted to the South. Here the British hoped to exploit the social tensions between backcountry farmers and wealthy planters that had surfaced in the Regulator movements, to enlist the support of the numerous colonists in the region who remained loyal to the crown, and to disrupt the economy by encouraging slaves to escape. In December 1778, British forces occupied Savannah, Georgia. In May 1780, Clinton captured Charleston, South Carolina, and with it an American army of 5,000 men.

The year 1780 was arguably the low point of the struggle for independence. Congress was essentially bankrupt, and the army went months without being paid. The British seemed successful in playing upon social conflicts within the colonies, as thousands of southern Loyalists joined up with British forces (fourteen regiments from Savannah alone) and tens of thousands of slaves sought freedom by fleeing to British lines. In August, Lord Charles Cornwallis routed an American army at Camden, South Carolina. The following month one of

Setbacks in 1780

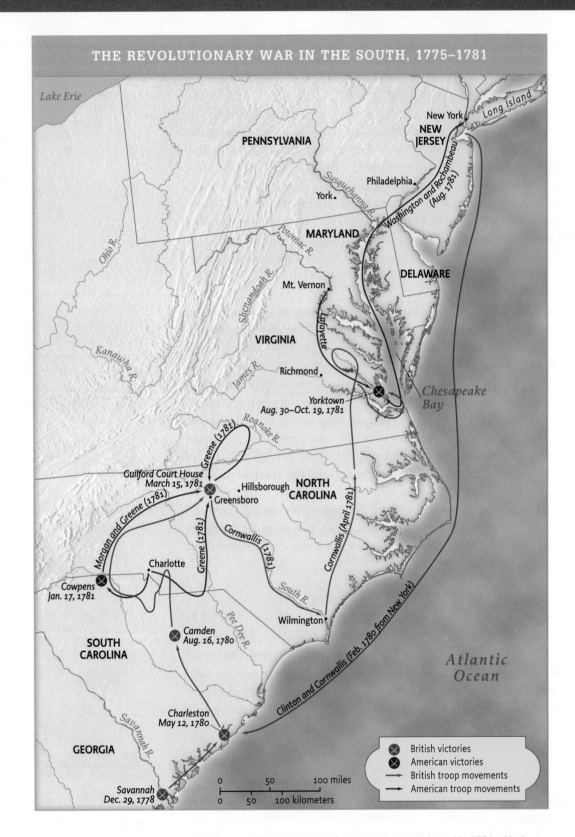

THE REVOLUTIONARY WAR IN THE SOUTH, 1775–1781

Lake Erie

PENNSYLVANIA

New York

NEW JERSEY

Long Island

Philadelphia

York

Susquehanna R.

MARYLAND

DELAWARE

Potomac R.

Ohio R.

Washington and Rochambeau (Aug. 1781)

Mt. Vernon

Shenandoah R.

VIRGINIA

Kanawha R.

Lafayette

James R.

Richmond

Chesapeake Bay

Yorktown
Aug. 30–Oct. 19, 1781

Greene (1781)

Roanoke R.

Guilford Court House
March 15, 1781

Hillsborough

NORTH
CAROLINA

Morgan and Greene (1781)

Greensboro

Cornwallis (April 1781)

Cornwallis (1781)

Greene (1781)

Charlotte

South R.

Cowpens
Jan. 17, 1781

Camden
Aug. 16, 1780

Pee Dee R.

Wilmington

SOUTH
CAROLINA

Clinton and Cornwallis (Feb. 1780 from New York)

Atlantic
Ocean

Charleston
May 12, 1780

Savannah R.

GEORGIA

Savannah
Dec. 29, 1778

⊗	British victories
⊗	American victories
→	British troop movements
→	American troop movements

0   50   100 miles
0   50   100 kilometers

After 1777, the focus of the War of Independence shifted to the South, where it culminated in 1781 with the British defeat at Yorktown.

Washington's ablest commanders, **Benedict Arnold**, defected and almost succeeded in turning over to the British the important fort at West Point on the Hudson River. On January 1, 1781, 1,500 disgruntled Pennsylvania soldiers stationed near Morristown, New Jersey, killed three officers and marched toward Philadelphia, where Congress was meeting. Their mutiny ended when the soldiers were promised discharges or bounties for reenlistment. Harsher treatment awaited a group of New Jersey soldiers who also mutinied. On Washington's orders, two of their leaders were executed.

But the British failed to turn these advantages into victory. British commanders were unable to consolidate their hold on the South. Wherever their forces went, American militias harassed them. Hit-and-run attacks by militiamen under Francis Marion, called the "swamp fox" because his men emerged from hiding places in swamps to strike swiftly and then disappear, eroded the British position in South Carolina. A bloody civil war engulfed North and South Carolina and Georgia, with patriot and Loyalist militias inflicting retribution on each other and plundering the farms of their opponents' supporters. The brutal treatment of civilians by British forces under Colonel Banastre Tarleton persuaded many Americans to join the patriot cause.

A British cartoon from 1779, *The Horse America Throwing His Master*, lampoons King George III for being unable to keep control of the colonies. In the background, a French officer carries a flag adorned with the fleur-de-lys, a symbol of that country, the colonists' ally. Powerful satirical attacks on public authorities, including the king, were commonplace in eighteenth-century Britain.

Victory at Last

In January 1781, American forces under Daniel Morgan dealt a crushing defeat to Tarleton at Cowpens, South Carolina. Two months later, at Guilford Courthouse, North Carolina, General Nathanael Greene, while conducting a

A 1781 French engraving showing the surrender of Lord Charles Cornwallis's army at Yorktown, ending the War of Independence. The French fleet sits just offshore.

This portrait of John Adams by the noted American artist John Singleton Copley was painted in London soon after the signing of the Treaty of Paris of 1783, which secured American independence. Adams, who helped to negotiate the treaty, points to a map and globe depicting the new nation. Copley hoped to display the painting in London but British audiences had no desire to see a work celebrating American independence.

campaign of strategic retreats, inflicted heavy losses on Cornwallis, the British commander in the South. Cornwallis moved into Virginia and encamped at Yorktown, located on a peninsula that juts into Chesapeake Bay. Brilliantly recognizing the opportunity to surround Cornwallis, Washington rushed his forces, augmented by French troops under the Marquis de Lafayette, to block a British escape by land. Meanwhile, a French fleet controlled the mouth of the Chesapeake, preventing supplies and reinforcements from reaching Cornwallis's army.

Imperial rivalries had helped to create the American colonies. Now, the rivalry of European empires helped to secure American independence. Taking land and sea forces together, more Frenchmen than Americans participated in the decisive **Battle of Yorktown**. On October 19, 1781, Cornwallis surrendered his army of 8,000 men. When the news reached London, public support for the war evaporated and peace negotiations soon began. Given its immense military prowess, Britain abandoned the struggle rather quickly. Many in Britain felt the West Indies were more valuable economically than the mainland colonies. In any event, British merchants expected to continue to dominate trade with the United States, and did so for many years.

Two years later, in September 1783, American and British negotiators concluded the **Treaty of Paris**. The American delegation—John Adams, Benjamin Franklin, and John Jay—achieved one of the greatest diplomatic triumphs in the country's history. They not only won recognition of American independence but also gained control of the entire region between Canada and Florida east of the Mississippi River and the right of Americans to fish in Atlantic waters off of Canada (a matter of considerable importance to New Englanders). At British insistence, the Americans agreed that colonists who had remained loyal to the mother country would not suffer persecution and that Loyalists' property that had been seized by local and state governments would be restored.

Until independence, the thirteen colonies had formed part of Britain's American empire, along with Canada and the West Indies. But Canada rebuffed repeated calls to join the War of Independence, and leaders of the West Indies, fearful of slave uprisings, also remained loyal to the crown. With the Treaty of Paris, the United States of America became the Western Hemisphere's first independent nation. Its boundaries reflected not so much the long-standing unity of a geographical region, but the circumstances of its birth.

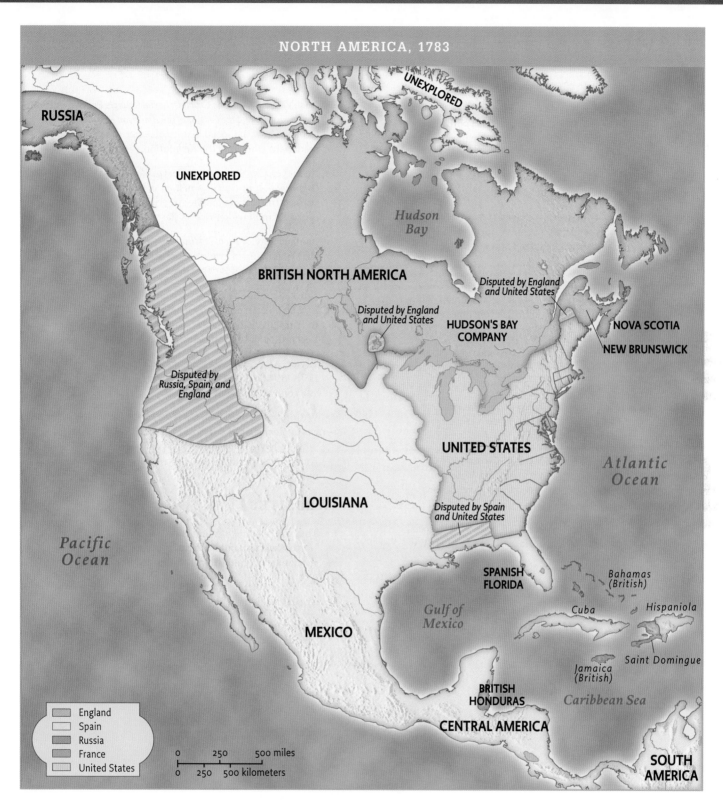

NORTH AMERICA, 1783

RUSSIA

UNEXPLORED

UNEXPLORED

Hudson Bay

BRITISH NORTH AMERICA

Disputed by England and United States

Disputed by England and United States

HUDSON'S BAY COMPANY

NOVA SCOTIA

NEW BRUNSWICK

Disputed by Russia, Spain, and England

UNITED STATES

Atlantic Ocean

Pacific Ocean

LOUISIANA

Disputed by Spain and United States

SPANISH FLORIDA

Bahamas (British)

Cuba

Hispaniola

MEXICO

Gulf of Mexico

Jamaica (British)

Saint Domingue

BRITISH HONDURAS

Caribbean Sea

CENTRAL AMERICA

SOUTH AMERICA

England
Spain
Russia
France
United States

0   250   500 miles
0   250   500 kilometers

The newly independent United States occupied only a small part of the North American continent in 1783.

SUGGESTED READING

BOOKS

- Armitage, David. *The Declaration of Independence: A Global History* (2007). Traces the international impact of the Declaration of Independence in the years since it was written.

- Bailyn, Bernard. *The Ideological Origins of the American Revolution* (1967; 2nd. ed., 1992). A classic study of the ideas that shaped the movement for independence.

- Bloch, Ruth. *Visionary Republic: Millennial Themes in American Thought, 1756–1800* (1988). Explores how the religious vision of a more perfect society contributed to the coming of the Revolution.

- Breen, T. H. *Marketplace of Revolution: How Consumer Politics Shaped American Independence* (2004). An examination of how the colonists' very dependence on British consumer goods led them to resent interference with trade.

- Countryman, Edward. *The American Revolution* (rev. ed., 2002). A brief summary of the Revolution's causes, conduct, and consequences.

- Ferling, John. *Independence: The Struggle to Set America Free* (2011). A recent history of the Revolution, covering its military, political, and social aspects.

- Foner, Eric. *Tom Paine and Revolutionary America* (1976). Examines the ideas of the era's greatest pamphleteer of revolution and how they contributed to the struggle for independence.

- Gross, Robert. *The Minutemen and Their World* (1976). A social history of the militia of Concord, Massachusetts, where the War of Independence began.

- Maier, Pauline. *American Scripture: Making the Declaration of Independence* (1997). The most detailed study of the writing of the Declaration and of previous calls for independence within the colonies.

- Nash, Gary. *The Urban Crucible: Social Change, Political Consciousness, and the Origins of the American Revolution* (1979). Explores how the social history of American cities contributed to the coming of the Revolution.

- Neimeyer, Charles. *America Goes to War: A Social History of the Continental Army* (1995). A history of Washington's army that stresses the role of nonelite Americans in the fighting and the impact of military service on the soldiers.

- Raphael, Ray. *A People's History of the American Revolution* (2001). A study of grassroots resistance to Britain before and during the War of Independence.

- Saunt, Claudio. *West of the Revolution: An Uncommon History of 1776* (2014). An account of events in North America among Indians, Spanish colonists, and others in the year of the Declaration of Independence.

- Taylor, Alan. *American Revolutions: A Continental History, 1750–1804* (2015). An excellent new history of the Revolution as a continental event.

- Withington, Anne. *Toward a More Perfect Union: Virtue and the Formation of American Republics* (1991). Considers how the boycotts of British goods promoted the idea of America's superior virtue, contributing to the movement for independence.

WEBSITES

- The American Revolution and Its Era: Maps and Charts of North America and the West Indies: http://memory.loc.gov/ammem/gmdhtml/armhtml/armhome.html

- The Coming of the American Revolution: www.masshist.org/revolution/

- Declaring Independence: www.loc.gov/exhibits/declara/declara1.html

CHAPTER REVIEW AND ONLINE RESOURCES

REVIEW QUESTIONS

1. What was the ideal of "homespun virtue," and how did it appeal to different groups in the colonies?

2. Patrick Henry proclaimed that he was not a Virginian, but rather an American. What unified the colonists and what divided them at the time of the Revolution?

3. Discuss the ramifications of using slaves in the British and Continental armies. Why did the British authorize the use of slaves? Why did the Americans? How did the slaves benefit?

4. Why did the colonists reach the conclusion that membership in the empire threatened their freedoms, rather than guaranteed them?

5. How did new ideas of liberty contribute to tensions between the social classes in the American colonies?

6. Why did people in other countries believe that the American Revolution (or the Declaration of Independence) was important to them or their own countries?

7. Summarize the difference of opinion between British officials and colonial leaders over the issues of taxation and representation.

8. How did the actions of the British authorities help to unite the American colonists during the 1760s and 1770s?

KEY TERMS

Stamp Act (p. 171)
virtual representation (p. 173)
writs of assistance (p. 173)
Sugar Act (p. 173)
"no taxation without representation" (p. 175)
Committee of Correspondence (p. 175)
Sons of Liberty (p. 176)
Regulators (p. 177)
Townshend Acts (p. 178)
Boston Massacre (p. 179)
Crispus Attucks (p. 179)
Boston Tea Party (p. 181)
Intolerable Acts (p. 181)
Continental Congress (p. 182)
Battles of Lexington and Concord (p. 184)
Battle of Bunker Hill (p. 185)
Continental army (p. 185)
Lord Dunmore's proclamation (p. 185)
Common Sense (p. 186)
Declaration of Independence (p. 190)
Hessians (p. 195)
Battle of Saratoga (p. 197)
Benedict Arnold (p. 199)
Battle of Yorktown (p. 200)
Treaty of Paris (p. 200)

Go to INQUIZITIVE

To see what you know—and learn what you've missed—with personalized feedback along the way.

Visit the *Give Me Liberty!* Student Site for primary source documents and images, interactive maps, author videos featuring Eric Foner, and more.

CHAPTER 6

THE REVOLUTION WITHIN

Born in Massachusetts in 1744, Abigail Adams became one of the revolutionary era's most articulate and influential women. At a time when educational opportunities for girls were extremely limited, she taught herself by reading books in the library of her father, a Congregational minister. In 1764, she married John Adams, a young lawyer about to emerge as a leading advocate of resistance to British taxation and, eventually, of American independence. During the War of Independence, with her husband away in Philadelphia and Europe serving the American cause, she stayed behind at their Massachusetts home, raising their four children and managing the family's farm. The letters they exchanged form one of the most remarkable correspondences in American history. She addressed John as "Dear friend," and signed her letters "Portia"—after Brutus's devoted wife in Shakespeare's play *Julius Caesar*. Though denied an official role in politics, Abigail Adams was a keen observer of public affairs. She kept her husband informed of events in Massachusetts and offered opinions on political matters. Later, when Adams served as president, he relied on her advice more than on members of his cabinet.

In March 1776, a few months before the Second Continental Congress declared American independence, Abigail Adams wrote her best-known letter to her husband. She began by commenting indirectly on the evils of slavery. How strong, she wondered, could the "passion for Liberty" be among those "accustomed to deprive their fellow citizens of theirs?" She went on to urge Congress, when it drew up a "Code of Laws" for the new republic, to "remember the ladies." All men, she warned, "would be tyrants if they could." Women, she playfully suggested, "will not hold ourselves bound by any laws in which we have no voice or representation."

It was the leaders of colonial society who initiated resistance to British taxation. But, as Abigail Adams's letter illustrates, the struggle for American liberty emboldened other colonists to demand more liberty for themselves. All revolutions enlarge the public sphere, inspiring previously marginalized groups to express their own dreams of freedom. At a time when so many Americans— slaves, indentured servants, women, Indians, apprentices, propertyless men— were denied full freedom, the struggle against Britain threw into question many forms of authority and inequality.

Abigail Adams did not believe in female equality in a modern sense. She accepted the prevailing belief that a woman's primary responsibility was to her family. But she resented the "absolute power" husbands exercised over their wives. "Put it out of the power of husbands," she wrote, "to use us as they will"—a discreet reference to men's legal control over the bodies of their wives, and their right to inflict physical punishment on them. Her letter is widely remembered today. Less familiar is John Adams's response, which illuminated how the Revolution had unleashed challenges to all sorts of inherited ideas of deference and authority: "We have been told that our struggle has loosened the bands of government everywhere; that children and apprentices were disobedient; that schools and colleges were grown turbulent; that Indians slighted their guardians, and negroes grew insolent to their masters." To John Adams, this upheaval, including his wife's claim to greater freedom, was an affront to the natural order of things. To others, it formed the essence of the American Revolution.

FOCUS QUESTIONS

How did equality become a stronger component of American freedom after the Revolution? *-p. 206*

How did the expansion of religious liberty after the Revolution reflect the new American ideal of freedom? *-p. 210*

How did the definition of economic freedom change after the Revolution, and who benefited from the changes? *-p. 215*

How did the Revolution diminish the freedoms of both Loyalists and Native Americans? *-p. 218*

What was the impact of the Revolution on slavery? *-p. 223*

How did the Revolution affect the status of women? *-p. 229*

Excelsior (Latin for "ever upward"), a large oil painting by an unknown artist, is probably an early representation of the coat of arms of New York, adopted in 1778 as one part of the transition from colony to state. It contains numerous symbols of liberty, independence, and optimism for the future—including a cap of liberty, the sunrise, an eagle atop a world globe, Justice with her scales, and an olive branch of peace.

Abigail Adams, a portrait by Gilbert Stuart, painted over several years beginning in 1800. Stuart told a friend that, as a young woman, Adams must have been a "perfect Venus."

DEMOCRATIZING FREEDOM

The Dream of Equality

The American Revolution took place at three levels simultaneously. It was a struggle for national independence, a phase in a century-long global battle among European empires, and a conflict over what kind of nation an independent America should be.

With its wide distribution of property, lack of a legally established hereditary aristocracy, and established churches far less powerful than in Britain, colonial America was a society with deep democratic potential. But it took the struggle for independence to transform it into a nation that celebrated equality and opportunity. The Revolution unleashed public debates and political and social struggles that enlarged the scope of freedom and challenged inherited structures of power within America. In rejecting the crown and the principle of hereditary aristocracy, many Americans also rejected the society of privilege, patronage, and fixed status that these institutions embodied. To be sure, the men who led the Revolution from start to finish were by and large members of the American elite. The lower classes did not rise to power as a result of independence. Nonetheless, the idea of liberty became a revolutionary rallying cry, a standard by which to judge and challenge homegrown institutions as well as imperial ones.

Jefferson's seemingly straightforward assertion in the Declaration of Independence that "all men are created equal" announced a radical principle whose full implications no one could anticipate. In both Britain and its colonies, a well-ordered society was widely thought to depend on obedience to authority—the power of rulers over their subjects, husbands over wives, parents over children, employers over servants and apprentices, slaveholders over slaves. Inequality had been fundamental to the colonial social order; the Revolution challenged it in many ways. Henceforth, American freedom would be forever linked with the idea of equality—equality before the law, equality in political rights, equality of economic opportunity, and, for some, equality of condition. "Whenever I use the words *freedom* or *rights*," wrote Thomas Paine, "I desire to be understood to mean a perfect equality of them. . . . The floor of Freedom is as level as water."

Expanding the Political Nation

With liberty and equality as their rallying cries, previously marginalized groups advanced their demands. Long-accepted relations of dependency and restrictions on freedom suddenly appeared illegitimate—a process not intended by most of the leading patriots. In political, social, and religious life, Americans challenged the previous domination by a privileged few. In the end, the Revolution did not undo the obedience to which male heads of household were entitled from their wives and children, and, at least in the southern states, their slaves. For free men, however, the democratization of freedom was dramatic. Nowhere was this more evident than in challenges to the traditional limitation of political participation to those who owned property.

In the political thought of the eighteenth century, "democracy" had several meanings. One, derived from the writings of Aristotle, defined democracy as a system in which the entire people governed directly. However, this was thought to mean mob rule. Another definition viewed democracy as the condition of primitive societies, which was not appropriate for the complex modern world. Yet another understanding revolved less around the structure of government than the principle that a government served the interests of the people rather than an elite. In the wake of the American Revolution, the term came into wider use to express the popular aspirations for greater equality inspired by the struggle for independence.

"We are all, from the cobbler up to the senator, become politicians," declared a Boston letter writer in 1774. Throughout the colonies, election campaigns became freewheeling debates on the fundamentals of government. Universal male suffrage, religious toleration, and even the abolition of slavery were discussed not only by the educated elite but by artisans, small farmers, and laborers, now emerging as a self-conscious element in politics. In many colonies-turned-states, the militia, composed largely of members of the "lower orders," became a "school of political democracy." Its members demanded the right to elect all their officers and to vote for public officials whether or not they met age and property qualifications. They thereby established the tradition that service in the army enabled excluded groups to stake a claim to full citizenship.

A pewter mug made by William Will, an important craftsman in Philadelphia, in the late 1770s. It depicts Captain Peter Ickes, a Pennsylvania militia officer, with the popular slogan "Liberty or Death."

The Revolution in Pennsylvania

The Revolution's radical potential was more evident in Pennsylvania than in any other state. Elsewhere, the established leadership either embraced independence by the spring of 1776 or split into pro-British and pro-independence factions (in New York, for example, the Livingstons and their supporters ended up as patriots, the De Lanceys as Loyalists). But in Pennsylvania nearly the entire prewar elite opposed independence, fearing that severing the tie with Britain would lead to rule by the "rabble" and to attacks on property.

The vacuum of political leadership opened the door for the rise of a new pro-independence grouping, based on the artisan and lower-class communities of Philadelphia, and organized in extralegal committees and the local militia. Their leaders included Thomas Paine (the author of *Common Sense*), Benjamin Rush (a local physician), Timothy Matlack (the son of a local brewer), and Thomas Young (who had already been involved in the Sons of Liberty in Albany and Boston). As a group, these were men of modest wealth who stood outside the merchant elite, had little political influence before 1776, and believed strongly in democratic reform. They formed a temporary alliance with supporters of independence in the Second Continental Congress (then meeting in Philadelphia), who disapproved of their strong belief in equality but hoped to move Pennsylvania toward a break with Britain.

As the public sphere expanded far beyond its previous boundaries, equality became the rallying cry of Pennsylvania's radicals. They particularly attacked property qualifications for voting. "God gave mankind freedom by nature,"

Pro-independence leaders

Americans have frequently defined the idea of freedom in relation to its opposite, which in the eighteenth century meant the highly unequal societies of the Old World. This engraving, *The Coronation of Louis XVI of France*, reveals the splendor of the royal court but also illustrates the world of fixed, unequal classes and social privilege repudiated by American revolutionaries.

declared the anonymous author of the pamphlet *The People the Best Governors*, "and made every man equal to his neighbors." The people, therefore, were "the best guardians of their own liberties," and every free man should be eligible to vote and hold office. In June 1776, a broadside (a printed sheet posted in public places) warned citizens to distrust "great and over-grown rich men" who were inclined "to be framing distinctions in society." Three months after independence, Pennsylvania adopted a new state constitution that sought to institutionalize democracy by concentrating power in a one-house legislature elected annually by all men over age twenty-one who paid taxes. It abolished the office of governor, dispensed with property qualifications for officeholding, and provided that schools with low fees be established in every county. It also included clauses guaranteeing "freedom of speech, and of writing," and religious liberty.

The New Constitutions

New state constitutions

Like Pennsylvania, every state adopted a new constitution in the aftermath of independence. Nearly all Americans now agreed that their governments must be republics, meaning that their authority rested on the consent of the governed, and that there would be no king or hereditary aristocracy. The essence of a **republic**, Paine wrote, was not the "particular form" of government, but its object: the "public good." But as to how a republican government should be structured so as to promote the public good, there was much disagreement.

Pennsylvania's new constitution reflected the belief that since the people had a single set of interests, a single legislative house was sufficient to represent it. In part to counteract what he saw as Pennsylvania's excessive radicalism, John Adams in 1776 published *Thoughts on Government*, which insisted that the new constitutions should create balanced governments whose structure would reflect the division of society between the wealthy (represented in the upper house) and ordinary men (who would control the lower). A powerful governor and judiciary would ensure that neither class infringed on the liberty of the other. Adams's call for

Balanced governments

two-house legislatures was followed by every state except Pennsylvania, Georgia, and Vermont. But only his own state, Massachusetts, gave the governor an effective veto over laws passed by the legislature. Americans had long resented efforts by appointed governors to challenge the power of colonial assemblies. They preferred power to rest with the legislature.

The Right to Vote

The issue of requirements for voting and officeholding proved far more contentious. Conservative patriots struggled valiantly to reassert the rationale for the old voting restrictions. It was ridiculous, wrote one pamphleteer, to think that "every silly clown and illiterate mechanic [artisan]" deserved a voice in government. To John Adams, as conservative on the internal affairs of America as he had been radical on independence, freedom and equality were opposites. Men without property, he believed, had no "judgment of their own," and the removal of property qualifications, therefore, would "confound and destroy all distinctions, and prostrate all ranks to one common level."

Voting restrictions

The provisions of the new state constitutions reflected the balance of power between advocates of internal change and those who feared excessive democracy. The least democratization occurred in the southern states, whose highly deferential political traditions enabled the landed gentry to retain their control of political affairs. In Virginia and South Carolina, the new constitutions retained property qualifications for voting and authorized the gentry-dominated legislature to choose the governor. Maryland combined a low property qualification for voting with high requirements for officeholding, including £5,000—a fortune—for the governor.

The most democratic new constitutions moved much of the way toward the idea of voting as an entitlement rather than a privilege, but they generally stopped short of universal **suffrage**, even for free men. Vermont's constitution of 1777 was the only one to sever voting completely from financial considerations, eliminating not only property qualifications but also the requirement that voters pay taxes. Pennsylvania's constitution no longer required ownership of property, but it retained the taxpaying qualification. As a result, it enfranchised nearly all of the state's free male population but left a small number, mainly paupers and domestic servants, still barred from voting. Nonetheless, even with the taxpaying requirement, it represented a dramatic departure from the colonial practice of restricting the suffrage to those who could claim to be economically independent. It elevated "personal liberty," in the words of one essayist, to a position more important than property ownership in defining the boundaries of the political nation.

John Dickinson's copy of the Pennsylvania constitution of 1776, with handwritten proposals for changes. Dickinson, one of the more conservative advocates of independence, felt the new state constitution was far too democratic. He crossed out a provision that all "free men" should be eligible to hold office, and another declaring the people not bound by laws that did not promote "the common good."

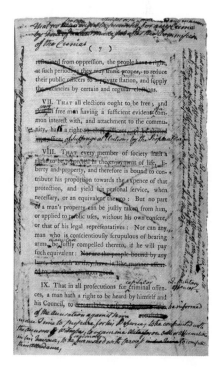

Democratizing Government

Overall, the Revolution led to a great expansion of the right to vote. By the 1780s, with the exceptions of Virginia, Maryland, and New York, a large majority of the adult white male population could meet voting requirements. New Jersey's new state constitution, of 1776, granted the suffrage to all "inhabitants" who met a property qualification. Until the state added the word "male" (along with "white") in 1807, property-owning women, mostly widows, did cast ballots. The new constitutions also expanded the number of legislative seats, with the result that numerous men of

Silk Flag displayed at the Rejoycing for PEACE in New Haven Apr. 24th 1783.

VIRTVS LIBERTY INDEPEN-

Ezra Stiles, the president of Yale College, drew this sketch of a flag in his diary on April 24, 1783, shortly after Congress ratified the Treaty of Paris. Thirteen stars surround the coat of arms of Pennsylvania. The banner text illustrates the linkage among virtue, liberty, and American independence.

lesser property assumed political office. The debate over the suffrage would, of course, continue for many decades. For white men, the process of democratization did not run its course until the Age of Jackson; for women and non-whites, it would take much longer.

Even during the Revolution, however, in the popular language of politics, if not in law, freedom and an individual's right to vote had become interchangeable. "The suffrage," declared a 1776 petition of disenfranchised North Carolinians, was "a right essential to and inseparable from freedom." Without it, Americans could not enjoy "equal liberty." A proposed new constitution for Massachusetts was rejected by a majority of the towns in 1778, partly because it contained a property qualification for voting. "All men were born equally free and independent," declared the town of Lenox. How could they defend their "life and liberty and property" without a voice in electing public officials? A new draft, which retained a substantial requirement for voting in state elections but allowed virtually all men to vote for town officers, was approved in 1780. And every state except South Carolina provided for annual legislative elections, to ensure that representatives remained closely accountable to the people. Henceforth, political freedom would mean not only, as in the past, a people's right to be ruled by their chosen representatives but also an individual's right to political participation.

TOWARD RELIGIOUS TOLERATION

As remarkable as the expansion of political freedom was the Revolution's impact on American religion. Religious toleration, declared one Virginia patriot, was part of "the common cause of Freedom." In Britain, Dissenters—Protestants who belonged to other denominations than the Anglican Church—had long invoked the language of liberty in seeking repeal of the laws that imposed various disabilities on non-Anglicans. (Few, however, included Catholics in their ringing calls for religious freedom.) We have already seen that Rhode Island and Pennsylvania had long made a practice of toleration. But freedom of worship before the Revolution arose more from the reality of religious pluralism than from a well-developed theory of religious liberty. Apart from Rhode Island, New England had little homegrown experience of religious pluralism. Indeed, authorities in England had occasionally pressed the region's rulers to become more tolerant. Before the Revolution, most colonies supported religious institutions with public funds and discriminated in voting and officeholding against Catholics, Jews, and even Dissenting Protestants. On the very eve of independence, Baptists who refused to pay taxes to support local

Religious pluralism

Congregational ministers were still being jailed in Massachusetts. "While our country are pleading so high for liberty," the victims complained, "yet they are denying of it to their neighbors."

Catholic Americans

The War of Independence weakened the deep tradition of American anti-Catholicism. The First Continental Congress denounced the Quebec Act of 1774, which, as noted in the previous chapter, allowed Canadian Catholics to worship freely, as part of a plot to establish "popery" in North America. But a year later, when the Second Continental Congress decided on an ill-fated invasion of Canada, it invited the inhabitants of Quebec to join in the struggle against Britain, assuring them that Protestants and Catholics could readily cooperate. In 1778, the United States formed an alliance with France, a Catholic nation. Benedict Arnold justified his treason, in part, by saying that an alliance with "the enemy of the protestant faith" was too much for him to bear. But the indispensable assistance provided by France to American victory strengthened the idea that Catholics had a role to play in the newly independent nation. This represented a marked departure from the traditional notion that the full rights of Englishmen only applied to Protestants. When America's first Roman Catholic bishop, John Carroll of Maryland, visited Boston in 1791, he received a cordial welcome.

Anti-Catholicism weakened

The Founders and Religion

The end of British rule immediately threw into question the privileged position enjoyed by the Anglican Church in many colonies. In Virginia, for example, back-country Scotch-Irish Presbyterian farmers demanded relief from taxes supporting the official Anglican Church. "The free exercise of our rights of conscience," one patriotic meeting resolved, formed an essential part of "our liberties."

Many of the leaders of the Revolution considered it essential for the new nation to shield itself from the unruly passions and violent conflicts that religious differences had inspired during the past three centuries. Men like Thomas

A 1771 image of New York City lists some of the numerous churches visible from the New Jersey shore, illustrating the diversity of religions practiced in the city.

Another image illustrating religious diversity, this one of Watertown, Connecticut, around 1836, with the Congregational and Episcopal churches facing each other on the town green.

Enlightenment views of religion

Jefferson, John Adams, James Madison, and Alexander Hamilton believed religion necessary as a foundation of public morality. But they viewed religious doctrines through the Enlightenment lens of rationalism and skepticism. They believed in a benevolent Creator but not in supernatural interventions into the affairs of men. Jefferson wrote a version of the Bible and a life of Jesus that insisted that while Jesus had lived a deeply moral life, he was not divine and performed no miracles. In discussing the natural history of the Blue Ridge Mountains in his book *Notes on the State of Virginia*, he rejected the biblical account of creation in favor of a prolonged process of geological change.

Separating Church and State

The drive to separate church and state brought together Deists like Jefferson, who hoped to erect a "wall of separation" that would free politics and the exercise of the intellect from religious control, with members of evangelical sects, who sought to protect religion from the corrupting embrace of government. Religious leaders continued to adhere to the traditional definition of Christian liberty—submitting to God's will and leading a moral life—but increasingly felt this could be achieved without the support of government. Christ's kingdom, as Isaac Backus, the Baptist leader, put it, was "not of this world."

Disestablishing churches

The movement toward religious freedom received a major impetus during the revolutionary era. Throughout the new nation, states disestablished their established churches—that is, deprived them of public funding and special legal privileges—although in some cases they appropriated money for the general support of Protestant denominations. The seven state constitutions that began with declarations of rights all declared a commitment to "the free exercise of religion."

Limits to religious freedom

To be sure, every state but New York—whose constitution of 1777 established complete religious liberty—kept intact colonial provisions barring Jews from voting and holding public office. Seven states limited officeholding to Protestants. Massachusetts retained its Congregationalist establishment well into the nineteenth century. Its new constitution declared church attendance compulsory while guaranteeing freedom of individual worship. It would not end public financial support for religious institutions until 1833. Throughout the country, however, Catholics gained the right to worship without persecution. Maryland's constitution of 1776 restored to the large Catholic population the civil and political rights that had been denied them for nearly a century.

Jefferson and Religious Liberty

In Virginia, Thomas Jefferson drew up a **Bill for Establishing Religious Freedom**, which was introduced in the House of Burgesses in 1779 and adopted, after considerable controversy, in 1786. "I have sworn upon the altar of God," he would write in 1800, "eternal hostility against every form of tyranny over the mind of man." Jefferson viewed established churches as a major example of such despotism and, as his statement reveals, believed that religious liberty served God's will. Jefferson's bill, whose preamble declared that God "hath created the mind free," eliminated religious requirements for voting and officeholding and government financial support for churches, and barred the state from "forcing" individuals to adopt one or another religious outlook. Late in life, Jefferson would list this measure, along with the Declaration of Independence and the founding of the

Bill for Establishing Religious Freedom

In Side of the Old Lutheran Church in 1800, York, Pa. A watercolor by a local artist depicts the interior of one of the numerous churches that flourished after independence. While the choir sings, a man chases a dog out of the building and another man stokes the stove. The institutionalization of religious liberty was one of the most important results of the American Revolution.

University of Virginia, as the three accomplishments (leaving out his two terms as president) for which he wished to be remembered.

Religious liberty became the model for the revolutionary generation's definition of "rights" as private matters that must be protected from governmental interference. In an overwhelmingly Christian (though not necessarily churchgoing) nation, the separation of church and state drew a sharp line between public authority and a realm defined as "private." It also offered a new justification for the idea of the United States as a beacon of liberty. In successfully opposing a Virginia tax for the general support of Christian churches, James Madison insisted that one reason for the complete separation of church and state was to reinforce the principle that the new nation offered "asylum to the persecuted and oppressed of every nation and religion."

Protecting rights from governmental interference

The Revolution and the Churches

Diversity of American Christianity

Thus, the Revolution enhanced the diversity of American Christianity and expanded the idea of religious liberty. But even as the separation of church and state created the social and political space that allowed all kinds of religious institutions to flourish, the culture of individual rights of which that separation was a part threatened to undermine church authority.

One example was the experience of the Moravian Brethren, who had emigrated from Germany to North Carolina on the eve of independence. To the dismay of the Moravian elders, younger members of the community, like so many other Americans of the revolutionary generation, insisted on asserting "their alleged freedom and human rights." Many rejected the community's tradition of arranged marriages, insisting on choosing their own husbands and wives. To the elders, the idea of individual liberty—which they called, disparagingly, "the American freedom"—was little more than "an opportunity for temptation," a threat to the spirit of self-sacrifice and communal loyalty essential to Christian liberty.

But despite such fears, the Revolution did not end the influence of religion on American society—quite the reverse. American churches, in the words of one Presbyterian leader, learned to adapt to living at a time when "a spirit of liberty prevails." Thanks to religious freedom, the early republic witnessed an amazing proliferation of religious denominations. The most well-established churches— Anglican, Presbyterian, and Congregationalist—found themselves constantly challenged by upstarts like Free-Will Baptists and Universalists. Today, even as debate continues over the proper relationship between spiritual and political authority, more than 1,300 religions are practiced in the United States.

Proliferation of religious denominations

Christian Republicanism

Despite the separation of church and state, colonial leaders were not hostile to religion. Indeed, religious and secular language merged in the struggle for independence, producing an outlook scholars have called Christian Republicanism. Proponents of evangelical religion and of republican government both believed that in the absence of some kind of moral restraint (provided by religion and government), human nature was likely to succumb to corruption and vice. Both believed that personal virtue was the foundation of a free society and that, by the same token, freedom—religious and political—was necessary for the development of virtue. Samuel Adams, for example, believed the new nation would become a "Christian Sparta," in which Christianity and personal self-discipline underpinned both personal and national progress. American religious leaders interpreted the American Revolution as a divinely sanctioned event, part of God's plan to promote the development of a good society. Rather than being so sinful that it would have to be destroyed before Christ returned, as many ministers had previously preached, the world, the Revolution demonstrated, could be perfected.

Most leaders of the Revolution were devout Christians, and even Deists who attended no organized church believed religious values reinforced the moral qualities necessary for a republic to prosper. Public authority continued to support religious values, in laws barring non-Christians from office and in the continued prosecution of blasphemy and breaches of the Sabbath. Pennsylvania's new democratic constitution required citizens to acknowledge the existence of God, and it directed the legislature to enact "laws for the prevention of vice and immorality." In the nineteenth century, Pennsylvania's lawmakers took this mandate so seriously that the state became as famous for its laws against swearing and desecrating the Sabbath as it had been in colonial times for religious freedom.

Patriot leaders worried about the character of future citizens, especially how to encourage the quality of "virtue," the ability to sacrifice self-interest for the public good. Some, like Jefferson, John Adams, and Benjamin Rush, put forward plans for the establishment of free, state-supported public schools. These would instruct future citizens in what Adams called "the principles of freedom," equipping them for participation in the now-expanded public sphere and for the wise election of representatives. A broad diffusion of knowledge was essential for a government based on the will of the people to survive. No nation, Jefferson wrote, could "expect to be ignorant and free."

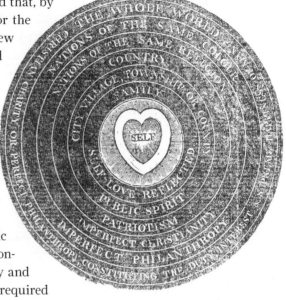

Circle of the Social and Benevolent Affections, an engraving in *The Columbian Magazine*, 1789, illustrates various admirable qualities radiating outward from the virtuous citizen, including love for one's family, community, nation, and all humanity. Affection only for those of the same religion or "colour" is labeled "imperfect."

Plans for public schools

DEFINING ECONOMIC FREEDOM

Toward Free Labor

In economic as well as political and religious affairs, the Revolution rewrote the definition of freedom. In colonial America, slavery was one part of a broad spectrum of kinds of unfree labor. In the generation after independence, with the rapid decline of indentured servitude and apprenticeship and the transformation of paid domestic service into an occupation for blacks and white females, the halfway houses between slavery and freedom disappeared, at least for white men. The decline of these forms of labor had many causes. Wage workers became more available as indentured servants completed their terms of required labor, and considerable numbers of servants and apprentices took advantage of the turmoil of the Revolution to escape from their masters.

Decline of unfree labor

View from Bushongo Tavern, an engraving from *The Columbian Magazine*, 1788, depicts the landscape of York County, Pennsylvania, exemplifying the kind of rural independence many Americans thought essential to freedom.

The lack of freedom inherent in apprenticeship and servitude increasingly came to be seen as incompatible with republican citizenship. Ebenezer Fox, a young apprentice on a Massachusetts farm, later recalled how he and other youths "made a direct application of the doctrines we heard daily, in relation to the oppression of the mother country, to our own circumstance. . . . I thought that I was doing myself a great injustice by remaining in bondage, when I ought to go free." Fox became one of many apprentices during the Revolution who decided to run away—or, as he put it, to "liberate myself." On the eve of the battles of Lexington and Concord in 1775, Fox and a friend set off for Rhode Island. After briefly working as a sailor, Fox, still a teenager, joined the Continental army.

In 1784, a group of "respectable" New Yorkers released a newly arrived shipload of indentured servants on the grounds that their status was "contrary to . . . the idea of liberty this country has so happily established." By 1800, indentured servitude had all but disappeared from the United States. This development sharpened the distinction between freedom and slavery, and between a northern economy relying on what would come to be called "free labor" (that is, working for wages or owning a farm or shop) and a southern economy ever more heavily dependent on the labor of slaves.

Sharpened distinction between freedom and slavery

The Soul of a Republic

Americans of the revolutionary generation were preoccupied with the social conditions of freedom. Could a republic survive with a sizable dependent class of citizens? "A general and tolerably equal distribution of landed property," proclaimed the educator and newspaper editor Noah Webster, "is the whole basis of national freedom." "Equality," he added, was "the very soul of a republic." Even a conservative like John Adams, who distrusted the era's democratic upsurge, hoped that every member of society could acquire land, "so that the multitude may be possessed of small estates" and the new nation could avoid the emergence of fixed and unequal social classes. At the Revolution's radical edge, some patriots believed that government had a responsibility to limit accumulations of property in the name of

Social conditions of freedom

equality. To most free Americans, however, "equality" meant equal opportunity, rather than equality of condition. Many leaders of the Revolution nevertheless assumed that in the exceptional circumstances of the New World, with its vast areas of available land and large population of independent farmers and artisans, the natural workings of society would produce justice, liberty, and equality.

Equal opportunity rather than equality of condition

Like many other Americans of his generation, Thomas Jefferson believed that to lack economic resources was to lack freedom. His proudest achievements included laws passed by Virginia abolishing entail (the limitation of inheritance to a specified line of heirs to keep an estate within a family) and primogeniture (the practice of passing a family's land entirely to the eldest son). These measures, he believed, would help to prevent the rise of a "future aristocracy." To the same end, Jefferson proposed to award fifty acres of land to "every person of full age" who did not already possess it, another way government could enhance the liberty of its subjects. Of course, the land Jefferson hoped would secure American liberty would have to come from Indians.

Abolishing entail and primogeniture

The Politics of Inflation

The Revolution thrust to the forefront of politics debates over whether local or national authorities should take steps to bolster household independence and protect Americans' livelihoods by limiting price increases. Economic dislocations sharpened the controversy. To finance the war, Congress issued hundreds of millions of dollars in paper money. Coupled with wartime disruption of agriculture and trade and the hoarding of goods by some Americans hoping to profit from shortages, this produced an enormous **inflation** as prices rapidly rose. The country, charged a letter to a Philadelphia newspaper in 1778, had been "reduced to the brink of ruin by the infamous practices of monopolizers."

Between 1776 and 1779, more than thirty incidents took place in which crowds confronted merchants accused of holding scarce goods off the market. Often, they seized stocks of food and sold them at the traditional "just price," a form of protest common in eighteenth-century England. In one such incident, a crowd of 100 Massachusetts women accused an "eminent, wealthy, stingy merchant" of hoarding coffee, opened his warehouse, and carted off the goods. "A large concourse of men," wrote Abigail Adams, "stood amazed, silent spectators of the whole transaction."

A cartoon from 1777 illustrates discontent with rising prices. One soldier identifies "extortioners" as "the worst enemies of the country." Another complains about serving "my country for sixteen pence per day."

The Debate over Free Trade

In 1779, with inflation totally out of control (in one month, prices in Philadelphia jumped 45 percent), Congress urged states to adopt measures to fix wages and prices. The policy embodied the belief that the task of republican government was to promote the public good, not individuals' self-interest. Bitter comments appeared in the Philadelphia press about the city's elite expending huge sums on "public dinners and other extravaganzas" while many in the city were "destitute of the necessities of life." But when a Committee of Safety tried to enforce price controls, it met spirited opposition from merchants and other advocates of a free market.

Against the traditional view that men should sacrifice for the public good, believers in **free trade** argued that economic development arose from economic self-interest. Just as Newton had revealed the inner workings of the natural

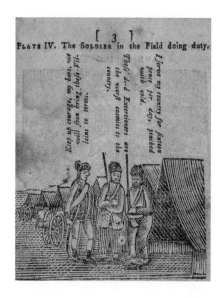

universe, so the social world also followed unchanging natural laws, among them that supply and demand regulated the prices of goods. Adam Smith's great treatise on economics, ***The Wealth of Nations***, published in England in 1776, was beginning to become known in the United States. Smith's argument that the "invisible hand" of the free market directed economic life more effectively and fairly than governmental intervention offered intellectual justification for those who believed that the economy should be left to regulate itself.

Smith's The Wealth of Nations

Advocates of independence had envisioned America, released from the British Navigation Acts, trading freely with all the world. Opponents of price controls advocated free trade at home as well. "Let trade be as free as air," wrote one merchant. "Natural liberty" would regulate prices. Here were two competing conceptions of economic freedom—one based on the traditional view that the interests of the community took precedence over the property rights of individuals, the other insisting that unregulated economic freedom would produce social harmony and public gain. After 1779, the latter view gained ascendancy. State and federal efforts to regulate prices ceased. But the clash between these two visions of economic freedom would continue long after independence had been achieved.

Economic freedom

"Yield to the mighty current of American freedom." So a member of the South Carolina legislature implored his colleagues in 1777. The current of freedom swept away not only British authority but also the principle of hereditary rule, the privileges of established churches, long-standing habits of deference and hierarchy, and old limits on the political nation. Yet in other areas, the tide of freedom encountered obstacles that did not yield as easily to its powerful flow.

THE LIMITS OF LIBERTY

Colonial Loyalists

Not all Americans shared in the democratization of freedom brought on by the American Revolution. **Loyalists**—those who retained their allegiance to the crown—experienced the conflict and its aftermath as a loss of liberty. Many leading Loyalists had supported American resistance in the 1760s but drew back at the prospect of independence and war. Loyalists included some of the most prominent Americans and some of the most humble. Altogether, an estimated 20 to 25 percent of free Americans remained loyal to the British, and nearly 20,000 fought on their side. At some points in the war, Loyalists serving with the British outnumbered Washington's army.

An estimated 20 to 25 percent of Americans were Loyalists.

There were Loyalists in every colony, but they were most numerous in New York, Pennsylvania, and the backcountry of the Carolinas and Georgia. Some were wealthy men whose livelihoods depended on close working relationships with Britain—lawyers, merchants, Anglican ministers, and imperial officials. Many feared anarchy in the event of an American victory. "Liberty," one wrote, "can have no existence without obedience to the laws."

The struggle for independence heightened existing tensions between ethnic groups and social classes within the colonies. Some Loyalist ethnic minorities, like Highland Scots in North Carolina, feared that local majorities would infringe

Social bases of loyalism

on their freedom to enjoy cultural autonomy. In the South, many backcountry farmers who had long resented the domination of public affairs by wealthy planters sided with the British. So did tenants on the New York estates of patriot landlords like the Livingston family. Robert Livingston had signed the Declaration of Independence. When the army of General Burgoyne approached Livingston's manor in 1777, tenants rose in revolt, hoping the British would confiscate his land and distribute it among themselves. Their hopes were dashed by Burgoyne's defeat at Saratoga. In the South, numerous slaves sided with the British, hoping an American defeat would bring them freedom.

A 1780 British cartoon commenting on the "cruel fate" of American Loyalists. Pro-independence colonists are likened to savage Indians.

The Loyalists' Plight

The War of Independence was in some respects a civil war among Americans. "This country," wrote a German colonel fighting with the British, "is the scene of the most cruel events. Neighbors are on opposite sides, children are against their fathers." Freedom of expression is often a casualty of war, and many Americans were deprived of basic rights in the name of liberty. After Dr. Abner Beebe, of East Haddam, Connecticut, spoke "very freely" in favor of the British, a mob attacked his house and destroyed his gristmill. Beebe himself was "assaulted, stripped naked, and hot pitch [tar] was poured upon him." The new state governments, or crowds of patriots, suppressed newspapers thought to be loyal to Britain.

Pennsylvania arrested and seized the property of Quakers, Mennonites, and Moravians—pacifist denominations who refused to bear arms because of their religious beliefs. With the approval of Congress, many states required residents to take oaths of allegiance to the new nation. Those who refused were denied the right to vote and in many cases forced into exile. "The flames of discord," wrote one British observer, "are sprouting from the seeds of liberty." Some wealthy Loyalists saw their land confiscated and sold at auction. Twenty-eight estates belonging to New Hampshire governor John Wentworth and his family were seized, as were the holdings of great New York Loyalist landlords like the De Lancey and Philipse families. Most of the buyers of this land were merchants, lawyers, and established landowners. Unable to afford the purchase price, tenants had no choice but to continue to labor for the new owners.

Loyalists after independence

The Revolution as a Borderlands Conflict

When the war ended, as many as 60,000 Loyalists were banished from the United States or emigrated voluntarily—mostly to Britain, Canada, or the West Indies—rather than live in an independent United States. So many Loyalists went to Nova Scotia, in Canada, that a new province, New Brunswick, was created to accommodate them. For those Loyalists who remained in the United States, hostility proved to be short-lived. In the Treaty of Paris of 1783, as noted in Chapter 5,

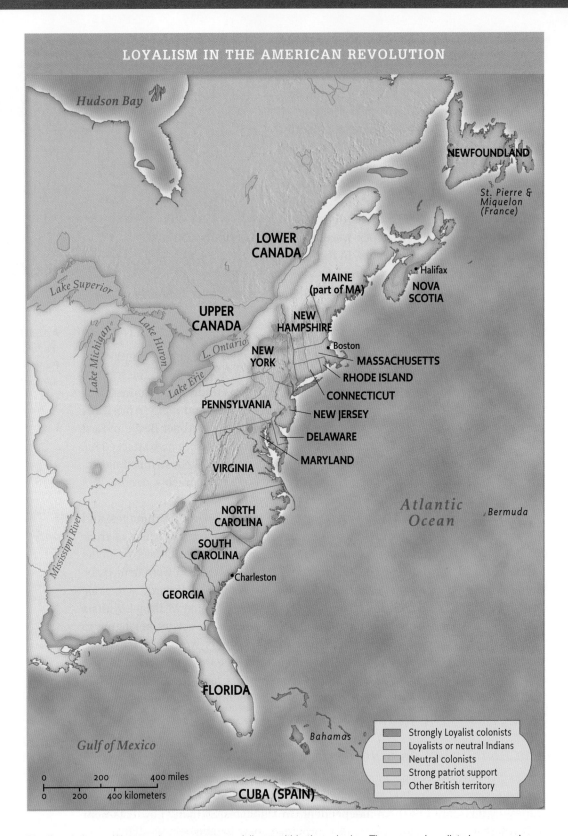

LOYALISM IN THE AMERICAN REVOLUTION

Hudson Bay

NEWFOUNDLAND

St. Pierre &
Miquelon
(France)

LOWER
CANADA

Lake Superior

MAINE
(part of MA)

•Halifax

NOVA
SCOTIA

UPPER
CANADA

NEW
HAMPSHIRE

Lake Michigan

Lake Huron

L. Ontario

NEW
YORK

•Boston

Lake Erie

MASSACHUSETTS

RHODE ISLAND

CONNECTICUT

PENNSYLVANIA

NEW JERSEY

DELAWARE

MARYLAND

VIRGINIA

Atlantic
Ocean

•Bermuda

NORTH
CAROLINA

Mississippi River

SOUTH
CAROLINA

•Charleston

GEORGIA

FLORIDA

Gulf of Mexico

Bahamas

Strongly Loyalist colonists
Loyalists or neutral Indians
Neutral colonists
Strong patriot support
Other British territory

0   200   400 miles
0   200   400 kilometers

CUBA (SPAIN)

The Revolutionary War was, in some ways, a civil war within the colonies. There were Loyalists in every colony;
they were most numerous in New York and North and South Carolina.

Americans pledged to end the persecution of Loyalists by state and local governments and to restore property seized during the war. American leaders believed the new nation needed to establish an international reputation for fairness and civility. States soon repealed their test oaths for voting and officeholding. Loyalists who did not leave the country were quickly reintegrated into American society, although despite the promise of the Treaty of Paris, confiscated Loyalist property was not returned.

Reintegration of Loyalists

The Loyalists' exile had a profound impact on the future development of North America. The War of Independence severed the British colonies of Nova Scotia and Quebec from the southern thirteen that formed the United States. Despite rejecting American independence, many Loyalists who settled in Canada brought with them not only a loyalty to the British crown but also a commitment to self-rule. They went on to agitate for responsible government in their new homeland. Their ideas would help to inspire rebellions in Canada in 1837 that helped close out the Age of Revolution the American revolt had launched. Although crushed by the British, the rebellions led eventually to the creation in 1867 of a single government for the Canadian provinces.

Thus, the American Revolution transformed the old boundary separating New England and New York from Quebec as provinces of the British empire into an international border. The consequences were profound. Without this development, Canada would not have been a refuge to slaves who left with the British when they evacuated the newly independent United States, or to those who escaped across the border later in the nineteenth century. Nor would Irish nationalists have been shielded from British law during and after the Civil War when they congregated in upstate New York and launched raids across the northern border as a way of striking a blow against British rule of their homeland. In Canada, the loyalist exiles would long be viewed as national founding fathers, and Canadians would often define their identity in opposition to their powerful neighbor to the south, even though goods and ideas always flowed easily across the border (today, each country is the other's largest trading partner).

Canada–United States border

The Indians' Revolution

Another region where the Revolution took on the character of a borderlands conflict as much as a struggle for independence was the trans-Appalachian West. Here, where British authority remained weak even after the expulsion of the French in the Seven Years' War and Indians enjoyed considerable authority, the patriots' victory marked a decisive shift of power away from native tribes and toward white settlers. The destruction of the "middle ground" would not be completed until after the War of 1812, but it received a major impetus from American independence.

Despite the Proclamation of 1763, discussed in Chapter 4, colonists had continued to move westward during the 1760s and early 1770s, leading Indian tribes to complain of intrusions on their land. Lord Dunmore, Virginia's royal governor, observed in 1772 that he had found it impossible "to restrain the Americans. . . . They do not conceive that government has any right to forbid their taking possession of a vast tract of country" or to force them to honor treaties with Indians.

Indian lands in the West

Kentucky, the principal hunting ground of southern Cherokees and numerous Ohio Valley Indians, became a flash point of conflict among settlers, land speculators, and Native Americans, with the faraway British government seeking in vain to impose order. Many patriot leaders, including George Washington, Patrick Henry, and Thomas Jefferson, were deeply involved in western land speculation. Washington himself had acquired more than 60,000 acres of land in western Pennsylvania after the Seven Years' War by purchasing land vouchers (a form of soldiers' wages) from his men at discount rates. Indeed, British efforts to restrain land speculation west of the line specified by the Proclamation of 1763 had been one of the many grievances of Virginia's revolutionary generation.

Indians' allegiances during the War of Independence

About 200,000 Native Americans lived east of the Mississippi River in 1790. Like white Americans, Indians divided in allegiance during the War of Independence. Some, like the Stockbridge tribe in Massachusetts, suffered heavy losses fighting the British. Many tribes tried to maintain neutrality, only to see themselves break into pro-American and pro-British factions. Most of the Iroquois nations sided with the British, but the Oneida joined the Americans. Despite strenuous efforts to avoid conflict, members of the Iroquois Confederacy for the first time faced each other in battle. (After the war, the Oneida submitted to Congress claims for losses suffered during the war, including sheep, hogs, kettles, frying pans, plows, and pewter plates—evidence of how fully they had been integrated into the market economy.) In the South, younger Cherokee leaders joined the British while older chiefs tended to favor the Americans. Other southern tribes like the Choctaw and Creek remained loyal to the crown.

Savage warfare

Among the grievances listed by Jefferson in the Declaration of Independence was Britain's enlisting "savages" to fight on its side. But in the war that raged throughout the western frontier, savagery was not confined to either combatant. In the Ohio country, the British encouraged Indian allies to burn frontier farms and settlements. For their part, otherwise humane patriot leaders ignored the traditional rules of warfare when it came to Indians. William Henry Drayton, a leader of the patriot cause in South Carolina and the state's chief justice in 1776, advised officers marching against the Cherokees to "cut up every Indian cornfield, burn every Indian town," and enslave all Indian captives. Three years later, Washington dispatched an expedition, led by General John Sullivan, against hostile Iroquois, with the aim of "the total destruction and devastation of their settlements and the capture of as many prisoners of every age and sex as possible." After his campaign ended, Sullivan reported that he had burned forty Indian towns, destroyed thousands of bushels of corn, and uprooted a vast number of fruit trees and vegetable gardens. Many Iroquois communities faced starvation.

White Freedom, Indian Freedom

Independence created governments democratically accountable to voters who coveted Indian land. Indeed, to many patriots, access to Indian land was one of the fruits of American victory. Driving the Indians from the Ohio Valley, wrote Jefferson, would "add to the Empire of Liberty an extensive and fertile country." But liberty for whites meant loss of liberty for Indians. "The whites were no sooner free themselves," a Pequot, William Apess, would later write, than they turned on "the poor Indians." Independence offered the opportunity to complete the process of dispossessing Indians of their rich lands in upstate New York, the Ohio Valley,

A loss of freedom for Indians

and the southern backcountry. The only hope for the Indians, Jefferson wrote, lay in their "removal beyond the Mississippi." Even as the war raged, Americans forced defeated tribes like the Cherokee to cede most of their land. The practice, which had begun early in the colonial era, continued in the new nation.

American independence, a group of visiting Indians told the Spanish governor at St. Louis, was "the greatest blow that could have been dealt us." The Treaty of Paris marked the culmination of a century in which the balance of power in eastern North America shifted away from the Indians and toward white Americans. The displacement of British power to Canada, coming twenty years after the departure of the French, left Indians with seriously diminished options for white support. Some Indian leaders, like **Joseph Brant**, a young Mohawk in upstate New York, hoped to create an Indian confederacy lying between Canada and the new United States. He sided with the British to try to achieve this goal. But in the Treaty of Paris, the British abandoned their Indian allies, agreeing to recognize American sovereignty over the entire region east of the Mississippi River, completely ignoring the Indian presence.

> *The Treaty of Paris and Indian peoples*

Like other Americans, they appropriated the language of the Revolution and interpreted it according to their own experiences and for their own purposes. The Iroquois, declared one spokesman, were "a free people subject to no power on earth." Creeks and Choctaws denied having done anything to forfeit their "independence and natural rights." When Massachusetts established a system of state "guardianship" over previously self-governing tribes, a group of Mashpees petitioned the legislature, claiming for themselves "the rights of man" and complaining of this "infringement of freedom." "Freedom" had not played a major part in Indians' vocabulary before the Revolution. By the early nineteenth century, dictionaries of Indian languages for the first time began to include the word. But there seemed to be no permanent place for the descendants of the continent's native population in a new nation bent on creating an empire in the West.

> *Indians in the new nation*

SLAVERY AND THE REVOLUTION

While Indians experienced American independence as a real threat to their own liberty, African-Americans saw in the ideals of the Revolution and the reality of war an opportunity to claim freedom. When the United States declared its independence in 1776, the slave population had grown to 500,000, about one-fifth of the new nation's inhabitants. Slave-owning and slave trading were accepted routines of colonial life. Advertisements announcing the sale of slaves and seeking the return of runaways filled colonial newspapers. Sometimes, the same issues of patriotic newspapers that published accounts of the activities of the Sons of Liberty or arguments against the Stamp Act also contained slave sale notices.

Advertisement for newly arrived slaves, in a Savannah newspaper, 1774. Even as colonists defended their own liberty against the British, the buying and selling of slaves continued.

TO BE SOLD, on WEDNESDAY 3d AUGUST next,
By COWPER & TELFAIRS,
A CARGO
Of 170 prime young likely healthy
GUINEA SLAVES,
Just imported, in the Bark Friends, William Ross Master, directly from Angola.
Savannah, July 25, 1774.

The Language of Slavery and Freedom

Slavery played a central part in the language of revolution. Apart from "liberty," it was the word most frequently invoked in the era's legal and political literature. Eighteenth-century writers frequently juxtaposed freedom and slavery as "the two extremes of happiness and misery in society." Yet in debates over British rule, slavery was primarily a political category, shorthand for the denial of one's personal and political rights by arbitrary government. Those who lacked a voice in public affairs, declared a 1769 petition demanding an expansion of the right to vote in Britain, were "enslaved." By the eve of independence, the contrast between Britain, "a kingdom of slaves," and America, a "country of free men," had become a standard part of the language of resistance. Such language was employed without irony even in areas where half the population in fact consisted of slaves. South Carolina, one writer declared in 1774, was a "sacred land" of freedom, where it was impossible to believe that "slavery shall soon be permitted to erect her throne."

Liberty Displaying the Arts and Sciences. This 1792 painting by Samuel Jennings is one of the few visual images of the early republic explicitly linking slavery with tyranny and liberty with abolition. The female figure offers books to newly freed slaves. Other forms of knowledge depicted include a globe and an artist's palette. Beneath her left foot lies a broken chain. In the background, free slaves enjoy some leisure time.

Colonial writers of the 1760s occasionally made a direct connection between slavery as a reality and slavery as a metaphor. Few were as forthright as James Otis of Massachusetts, whose pamphlets did much to popularize the idea that Parliament lacked the authority to tax the colonies and regulate their commerce. Freedom, Otis insisted, must be universal: "What man is or ever was born free if every man is not?" Otis wrote of blacks not as examples of the loss of rights awaiting free Americans, but as flesh and blood British subjects "entitled to all the civil rights of such."

Otis was hardly typical of patriot leaders. But the presence of hundreds of thousands of slaves powerfully affected the meaning of freedom for the leaders of the American Revolution. In a famous speech to Parliament warning against attempts to intimidate the colonies, the British statesman Edmund Burke suggested that familiarity with slavery made colonial leaders unusually sensitive to threats to their own liberties. Where freedom was a privilege, not a common right, he observed, "those who are free are by far the most proud and jealous of their freedom." On the other hand, many British observers could not resist pointing out the colonists' apparent hypocrisy. "How is it," asked Dr. Samuel Johnson, "that we hear the loudest yelps for liberty from the drivers of negroes?"

Obstacles to Abolition

The contradiction between freedom and slavery seems so self-evident that it is difficult today to appreciate the power of the obstacles to **abolition**. At the time of the Revolution, slavery was already an old institution in America. It existed in every colony and formed the basis of the economy and social structure from Maryland southward. At least 40 percent of Virginia's population and even higher proportions in Georgia and South Carolina were slaves.

Virtually every founding father owned slaves at one point in his life, including not only southern planters but also northern merchants, lawyers, and farmers. (John Adams and Tom Paine were notable exceptions.) Thomas Jefferson owned more than 100 slaves when he wrote of mankind's unalienable right to liberty, and everything he cherished in his own manner of life, from lavish entertainments to the leisure that made possible the pursuit of arts and sciences, ultimately rested on slave labor.

Slavery entrenched

Some patriots, in fact, argued that slavery for blacks made freedom possible for whites. Owning slaves offered a route to the economic autonomy widely deemed necessary for genuine freedom, a point driven home by a 1780 Virginia law that rewarded veterans of the War of Independence with 300 acres of land—and a slave. South Carolina and Georgia promised every white military volunteer a slave at the war's end.

So, too, the Lockean vision of the political community as a group of individuals contracting together to secure their natural rights could readily be invoked to defend bondage. Nothing was more essential to freedom, in this view, than the right of self-government and the protection of property against outside interference. These principles suggested that for the government to seize property—including slave property—against the owner's will would be an infringement on liberty. To require owners to give up their slave property would reduce *them* to slavery.

The Cause of General Liberty

Nonetheless, by imparting so absolute a value to liberty and defining freedom as a universal entitlement rather than a set of rights specific to a particular place or people, the Revolution inevitably raised questions about the status of slavery in the new nation. Before independence, there had been little public discussion of the institution, even though enlightened opinion in the Atlantic world had come to view slavery as morally wrong and economically inefficient, a relic of a barbarous past.

Freedom as universal

As early as 1688, a group of German Quakers issued a "protest" regarding the rights of blacks, declaring it as unjust "to have them slaves, as it is to have other white ones." Samuel Sewall, a Boston merchant, published *The Selling of Joseph* in 1700, the first antislavery tract printed in America. All "the sons of Adam," Sewall insisted, were entitled to "have equal right unto liberty." During the course of the eighteenth century, antislavery sentiments had spread among Pennsylvania's Quakers, whose belief that all persons possessed the divine "inner light" made them particularly receptive. But it was during the revolutionary era that slavery for the first time became a focus of public debate. The Pennsylvania patriot Benjamin Rush in 1773 called upon "advocates for American liberty" to "espouse the cause of . . . general liberty" and warned that slavery was one of those "national crimes" that one day would bring "national punishment." Although a slaveholder himself, in private Jefferson condemned slavery as a system that every day imposed on its victims "more misery, than ages of that which [the colonists] rose in rebellion to oppose."

Early antislavery

Petitions for Freedom

The Revolution inspired widespread hopes that slavery could be removed from American life. Most dramatically, slaves themselves appreciated that by defining freedom as a universal right, the leaders of the Revolution had devised a weapon that could be used against their own bondage. The language of liberty

> WHEREAS the NEGROES in the counties of Briftol and Worcefter, the 24th of March laft, petitioned the Committees of Correfpondence for the county of Worcefter (then convened in Worcefter) to affift them in obtaining their freedom. THEREFORE,
>
> *In County Convention, June 14th, 1775.*
>
> RESOLVED, That we abhor the enflaving of any of the human race, and particularly of the NEGROES in this country. And that whenever there fhall be a door opened, or opportunity prefent, for any thing to be done toward the emancipating the NEGROES; we will ufe our influence and endeavour that fuch a thing may be effected, *Atteft.* WILLIAM HENSHAW, Clerk.

A 1775 notice in *The Massachusetts Spy* reporting a resolution of the Committees of Correspondence of Worcester County that advocated the abolition of slavery.

African-American efforts for freedom

Lemuel Haynes

A portrait of the poet Phillis Wheatley (1753–1784).

echoed in slave communities, North and South. Living amid freedom but denied its benefits, slaves appropriated the patriotic ideology for their own purposes. The most insistent advocates of freedom as a universal entitlement were African-Americans, who demanded that the leaders of the struggle for independence live up to their self-proclaimed creed. As early as 1766, white Charlestonians had been shocked when their opposition to the Stamp Act inspired a group of blacks to parade about the city crying "Liberty."

The first concrete steps toward emancipation in revolutionary America were **freedom petitions**—arguments for liberty presented to New England's courts and legislatures in the early 1770s by enslaved African-Americans. How, one such petition asked, could America "seek release from English tyranny and not seek the same for disadvantaged Africans in her midst?" Some slaves sued in court for being "illegally detained in slavery." The turmoil of war offered other avenues to freedom. Many slaves ran away from their masters and tried to pass as freeborn. The number of fugitive-slave advertisements in colonial newspapers rose dramatically in the 1770s and 1780s. As one owner put it in accounting for his slave Jim's escape, "I believe he has nothing in view but freedom."

In 1776, the year of American independence, **Lemuel Haynes**, a black member of the Massachusetts militia and later a celebrated minister, urged that Americans "extend" their conception of freedom. If liberty were truly "an innate principle" for all mankind, Haynes insisted, "even an African [had] as equally good a right to his liberty in common with Englishmen." Blacks sought to make white Americans understand slavery as a concrete reality—the denial of all the essential elements of freedom—not merely as a metaphor for the loss of political self-determination. Petitioning for their freedom in 1773, a group of New England slaves exclaimed, "We have no property! We have no wives! No children! We have no city! No country!"

Most slaves of the revolutionary era were only one or two generations removed from Africa. They did not need the ideology of the Revolution to persuade them that freedom was a birthright—their experience and that of their parents and grandparents suggested as much. "My love of freedom," wrote the black poet Phillis Wheatley in 1783, arose from the "cruel fate" of being "snatch'd from Afric's" shore. Brought as a slave to Boston in 1761, Wheatley learned to read and published her first poem in a New England newspaper in 1765, when she was around twelve years old. The fact that a volume of her poems had to be printed with a testimonial from prominent citizens, including patriot leader John Hancock, affirming that she was in fact the author, illustrates that many whites found it difficult to accept the idea of blacks' intellectual ability. Yet by invoking the Revolution's ideology of liberty to demand their own rights and by defining freedom as a universal entitlement, blacks demonstrated how American they had become, even as they sought to redefine what American freedom in fact meant.

British Emancipators

As noted in the previous chapter, some 5,000 slaves fought for American independence and many thereby gained their freedom. Yet far more slaves obtained liberty from the British. Lord Dunmore's proclamation of 1775, and the Philipsburg Proclamation of General Henry Clinton issued four years later, offered sanctuary to slaves, except those owned by Loyalists, who escaped to British lines. Numerous signers of the Declaration of Independence lost slaves as a result. Thirty of Thomas Jefferson's slaves ran away to the British, as did slaves owned by Patrick Henry and James Madison. All told, tens of thousands of slaves, including one-quarter of all the slaves in South Carolina and one-third of those in Georgia, deserted their owners and fled to British lines. This was by far the largest exodus from the plantations until the outbreak of the Civil War.

Bedford Basin near Halifax, a watercolor by the Canadian artist Robert Petley, depicts a family of black Loyalists in Nova Scotia. Thousands of slaves gained their freedom by departing with the British after the War of Independence. Over 3,000 settled in Nova Scotia, where many were able to acquire land.

Some of these escaped slaves were recaptured as the tide of battle turned in the patriots' favor. But at the war's end, some 20,000 were living in three enclaves of British control—New York, Charleston, and Savannah. George Washington insisted they must be returned. Sir Guy Carleton, the British commander in New York, replied that to do so would be "a dishonorable violation of the public faith," since they had been promised their freedom. In the end, more than 15,000 black men, women, and children accompanied the British out of the country. They ended up in Nova Scotia, England, and Sierra Leone, a settlement for former slaves from the United States established by the British on the coast of West Africa. Some were re-enslaved in the West Indies. A number of their stories were indeed remarkable. Harry Washington, an African-born slave of George Washington, had run away from Mount Vernon in 1771 but was recaptured. In 1775, he fled to join Lord Dunmore and eventually became a corporal in a black British regiment, the Black Pioneers. He eventually ended up in Sierra Leone, where in 1800 he took part in an unsuccessful uprising by black settlers against the British-appointed government.

The issue of compensation for the slaves who departed with the British poisoned relations between Britain and the new United States for decades to come. Finally, in 1827, Britain agreed to make payments to 1,100 Americans who claimed they had been improperly deprived of their slave property.

Escaped slaves

Voluntary Emancipations

For a brief moment, the revolutionary upheaval appeared to threaten the continued existence of slavery. During the War of Independence, nearly every state prohibited or discouraged the further importation of slaves from Africa. The war left much of the plantation South in ruins. During the 1780s, a considerable number of slaveholders, especially in Virginia and Maryland, voluntarily

The Book of Negroes, compiled by British commanders when they evacuated New York City in 1783, lists some 3,000 African-Americans who had sought their freedom behind British lines and departed with the British army. Many ended up in Nova Scotia; some eventually made their way to Sierra Leone in West Africa. This page includes an entry for Deborah, formerly a slave of George Washington (at the bottom).

A photograph from around 1851 of Caesar, who had been a slave in New York State until the institution was finally ended in 1827.

emancipated their slaves. In 1796, Robert Carter III, a member of one of Virginia's wealthiest families, provided for the gradual emancipation of the more than 400 slaves he owned. In the same year, Richard Randolph, a member of another prominent Virginia family, drafted a will that condemned slavery as an "infamous practice," provided for the freedom of about ninety slaves, and set aside part of his land for them to own.

Farther south, however, the abolition process never got under way. When the British invaded South Carolina during the war, John Laurens, whose father Henry was Charleston's leading merchant and revolutionary-era statesman, proposed to "lead a corps of emancipated blacks in the defense of liberty." South Carolina's leaders rejected the idea. They would rather lose the war than lose their slaves.

Abolition in the North

Between 1777 (when Vermont drew up a constitution that banned slavery) and 1804 (when New Jersey acted), every state north of Maryland took steps toward emancipation, the first time in recorded history that legislative power had been invoked to eradicate slavery. But even here, where slavery was peripheral to the economy, the method of abolition reflected how property rights impeded emancipation. Generally, abolition laws did not free living slaves. Instead, they provided for the liberty of any child born in the future to a slave mother, but only after he or she had served the mother's master until adulthood as compensation for the owner's future economic loss. Children born to slave mothers in Pennsylvania after passage of the state's emancipation act of 1780 had to serve the owner for twenty-eight years, far longer than had been customary for white indentured servants. These laws gave indentured servitude, rapidly declining among whites, a new lease on life in the case of northern blacks.

Abolition in the North was a slow, drawn-out process. For slaves alive when the northern laws were passed, hopes for freedom rested on their own ability to escape and the voluntary actions of their owners. And many northern slaveholders proved reluctant indeed when it came to liberating their slaves. New York City, where one-fifth of the white families owned at least one slave in 1790, recorded only seventy-six such voluntary acts between 1783 and 1800. The first national census, in 1790, recorded 21,000 slaves still living in New York and 11,000 in New Jersey. New Yorker John Jay, chief justice of the United States, owned five slaves in 1800. As late as 1830, the census revealed that there were still 3,500 slaves in the North. The last slaves in Connecticut did not become free until 1848. In 1860, eighteen elderly slaves still resided in New Jersey.

Free Black Communities

All in all, the Revolution had a contradictory impact on American slavery and, therefore, on American freedom. Gradual as it was, the abolition of slavery in the

North drew a line across the new nation, creating the dangerous division between free and slave states. Abolition in the North, voluntary manumissions in the Upper South, and the escape of thousands from bondage created, for the first time in American history, a sizable **free black** population (many of whose members took new family names like Freeman or Freeland).

On the eve of independence, virtually every black person in America had been a slave. Now, free communities, with their own churches, schools, and leaders, came into existence. They formed a standing challenge to the logic of slavery, a haven for fugitives, and a springboard for further efforts at abolition. In 1776, fewer than 10,000 free blacks resided in the United States. By 1810, their numbers had grown to nearly 200,000, most of them living in Maryland and Virginia. In all the states except Virginia, South Carolina, and Georgia, free black men who met taxpaying or property qualifications enjoyed the right to vote under new state constitutions. As the widespread use of the term "citizens of color" suggests, the first generation of free blacks, at least in the North, formed part of the political nation.

A tray painted by an unknown artist in the early nineteenth century portrays Lemuel Haynes, a celebrated black preacher and critic of slavery.

For many Americans, white as well as black, the existence of slavery would henceforth be recognized as a standing affront to the ideal of American freedom, a "disgrace to a free government," as a group of New Yorkers put it. In 1792, when Samuel Jennings of Philadelphia painted *Liberty Displaying the Arts and Sciences*, he included among the symbols of freedom a slave's broken chain, graphically illustrating how freedom had become identified not simply with political independence, but with emancipation. Nonetheless, the stark fact is that slavery survived the War of Independence and, thanks to the natural increase of the slave population, continued to grow. The national census of 1790 revealed that despite all those who had become free through state laws, voluntary emancipation, and escape, the number of slaves in the United States had grown to 700,000—200,000 more than in 1776.

Growth in slave numbers

DAUGHTERS OF LIBERTY

Revolutionary Women

The revolutionary generation included numerous women who contributed to the struggle for independence. Deborah Sampson, the daughter of a poor Massachusetts farmer, disguised herself as a man and in 1782, at age twenty-one, enlisted in the Continental army. Sampson displayed remarkable courage, participating in several battles and extracting a bullet from her own leg so as not to have a doctor discover her identity. Ultimately, her commanding officer learned her secret but

Deborah Sampson

VOICES OF FREEDOM

From ABIGAIL ADAMS TO JOHN ADAMS, BRAINTREE, MASS. (MARCH 31, 1776)

From their home in Massachusetts, Abigail Adams maintained a lively correspondence with her husband while he was in Philadelphia serving in the Continental Congress. In this letter, she suggests some of the limits of the patriots' commitment to liberty.

———————————

I wish you would write me a letter half as long as I write you, and tell me if you may where your fleet have gone? What sort of defense Virginia can make against our common enemy? Whether it is so situated as to make an able defense? . . . I have sometimes been ready to think that the passion for Liberty cannot be equally strong in the breasts of those who have been accustomed to deprive their fellow creatures of theirs. Of this I am certain, that it is not founded upon that generous and Christian principle of doing to others as we would that others should do unto us. . . .

I long to hear that you have declared an independency, and by the way in the new Code of Laws which I suppose it will be necessary for you to make I desire you would Remember the Ladies, and be more generous and favorable to them than your ancestors. Do not put such unlimited power into the hands of the husbands. Remember all men would be tyrants if they could. If particular care and attention is not paid to the Ladies we are determined to foment a Rebellion, and will not hold ourselves bound by any such laws in which we have no voice, or representation.

That your sex are naturally tyrannical is a truth so thoroughly established as to admit of no dispute, but such of you as wish to be happy willingly give up the harsh title of Master for the more tender and endearing one of Friend. Why then, not put it out of the power of the vicious and the lawless to use us with cruelty and indignity with impunity? Men of sense in all ages abhor those customs which treat us only as the vassals of your sex. Regard us then as beings placed by providence under your protection and in imitation of the Supreme Being make use of that power only for our happiness.

From PETITIONS OF SLAVES TO THE MASSACHUSETTS LEGISLATURE (1773 AND 1777)

Many slaves saw the struggle for independence as an opportunity to assert their own claims to freedom. Among the first efforts toward abolition were petitions by Massachusetts slaves to their legislature.

———————————

The efforts made by the legislative of this province in their last sessions to free themselves from slavery, gave us, who are in that deplorable state, a high degree of satisfaction. We expect great things from men who have made such a noble stand against the designs of their *fellow-men* to enslave them. We cannot but wish and hope Sir, that you will have the same grand object, we mean civil and religious liberty, in view in your next session. The divine spirit of *freedom*, seems to fire every breast on this continent. . . .

* * *

Your petitioners apprehend that they have in common with all other men a natural and unalienable right to that freedom which the great parent of the universe hath bestowed equally on all mankind and which they have never forfeited by any compact or agreement whatever but [they] were unjustly dragged by the hand of cruel power from their dearest friends and . . . from a populous, pleasant, and plentiful country and in violation of laws of nature and of nations and in defiance of all the tender feelings of humanity brought here . . . to be sold like beast[s] of burden . . . among a people professing the mild religion of Jesus. . . .

In imitation of the laudable example of the good people of these states your petitioners have long and patiently waited the event of petition after petition by them presented to the legislative body. . . . They cannot but express their astonishment that it has never been considered that every principle from which America has acted in the course of their unhappy difficulties with Great Britain pleads stronger than a thousand arguments in favor of your petitioners [and their desire] to be restored to the enjoyment of that which is the natural right of all men.

QUESTIONS

1. *What does Abigail Adams have in mind when she refers to the "unlimited power" husbands exercise over their wives?*

2. *How do the slaves employ the principles of the Revolution for their own aims?*

3. *What do these documents suggest about the boundaries of freedom in the era of the American Revolution?*

A cartoon produced in London in 1775, *A Society of Patriotic Ladies* satirizes a group of women in Edenton, North Carolina, who signed a pledge to boycott British goods. They are depicted as fashionable but grotesque, and as forsaking their female responsibilities. The women on the right wields a gavel while a neglected child sits on the floor and is licked by a dog. Inadvertently, the cartoon makes the point that many colonial women devoted themselves to the patriotic cause.

kept it to himself, and she was honorably discharged at the end of the war. Years later, Congress awarded her a soldier's pension. Other patriotic women participated in crowd actions against merchants accused of seeking profits by holding goods off the market until their prices rose, contributed homespun goods to the army, and passed along information about British army movements.

In Philadelphia, Esther Reed, the wife of patriot leader Joseph Reed, and Sarah Franklin Bache, the daughter of Benjamin Franklin, organized a Ladies' Association to raise funds to assist American soldiers. They issued public broadsides calling for the "women of America" to name a "Treasuress" in each county in the United States who would collect funds and forward them to the governor's wife or, if he were unmarried, to "Mistress Washington." Referring to themselves as "brave Americans" who had been "born for liberty," the Ladies' Association illustrated how the Revolution was propelling women into new forms of public activism.

Within American households, women participated in the political discussions unleashed by independence. "Was not every fireside," John Adams later recalled, "a theater of politics?" Adams's own wife, Abigail Adams, as has been mentioned, was a shrewd analyst of public affairs. Mercy Otis Warren—the sister of James Otis and wife of James Warren, a founder of the Boston Committee of Correspondence—was another commentator on politics. She promoted the revolutionary cause in poems and dramas and later published a history of the struggle for independence.

Gender and Politics

Gender, nonetheless, formed a boundary limiting those entitled to the full blessings of American freedom. Lucy Knox, the wife of General Henry Knox, wrote her husband during the war that when he returned home he should not consider himself "commander in chief of your own house, but be convinced that there is such a thing as equal command." But the winning of independence did not alter

The 1781 cipher book (a notebook for mathematics exercises) of Martha Ryan, a North Carolina girl, contains images of ships and a port town and the patriotic slogan "Liberty or Death," illustrating how women shared in the political culture of the revolutionary era.

the family law inherited from Britain. The principle of **coverture** (described in Chapter 1) remained intact in the new nation. The husband still held legal authority over the person, property, and choices of his wife. The words "to have and to hold" appeared both in deeds conveying land from one owner to another, and in common marriage vows. Despite the expansion of democracy, politics remained overwhelmingly a male realm.

For men, political freedom meant the right to self-government, the power to consent to the individuals and political arrangements that ruled over them. For women, however, the marriage contract superseded the social contract. A woman's relationship to the larger society was mediated through her relationship with her husband. In both law and social reality, women lacked the essential qualification of political participation—autonomy based on ownership of property or control of one's own person. Since the common law included women within the legal status of their husbands, women could not be said to have property in themselves in the same sense as men.

Men took pride in qualities like independence and masculinity that distinguished them from women and still considered control over their families an element of freedom. Among the deprivations of slavery cited by a group of black male petitioners in 1774 was that it prevented their wives from "submitting themselves to husbands in all things," as the natural order of the universe required. Many women who entered public debate felt the need to apologize for their forthrightness. A group of Quaker women who petitioned Congress during the War of Independence protesting the mistreatment of men who would not take an oath of loyalty hoped the lawmakers would "take no offense at the freedom of women."

Most men considered women to be naturally submissive and irrational, and therefore unfit for citizenship. While public debate in the revolutionary era viewed men's rights as natural entitlements, discussions of women's roles emphasized duty and obligations, not individual liberty. Their rights were nonpolitical, deriving from their roles as wives and mothers.

Overall, the republican citizen was, by definition, male. In a notable case, a Massachusetts court returned to James Martin confiscated property previously owned by his mother, who had fled the state during the Revolution with her Loyalist husband. Like other states, Massachusetts seized the land of those who had supported the British. But, the court ruled, it was unreasonable to expect a wife to exercise independent political judgment. To rebel against the king was one thing, but one could hardly ask Mrs. Martin to rebel against her husband. Therefore, the court reasoned, she should not have been punished for taking the British side.

Portrait of John and Elizabeth Lloyd Cadwalader and Their Daughter Anne. This 1772 portrait of a prominent Philadelphia businessman and his family by the American artist Charles Willson Peale illustrates the emerging ideal of the "companionate" marriage, which is based on affection rather than male authority.

Women as unfit for citizenship

Republican Motherhood

The Revolution nonetheless did produce an improvement in status for many women. According to the ideology of **republican motherhood** that emerged as a result of independence, women played an indispensable role by training future citizens. The "foundation of national morality," wrote John Adams, "must be laid in private families." Even though republican motherhood ruled out direct female involvement in politics, it encouraged the expansion of educational opportunities for women, so that they could impart political wisdom to their children. Women, wrote Benjamin Rush, needed to have a "suitable education," to enable them to "instruct their sons in the principles of liberty and government."

"Companionate" marriage

The idea of republican motherhood reinforced the trend, already evident in the eighteenth century, toward the idea of "companionate" marriage, a voluntary union held together by affection and mutual dependency rather than male authority. In her letter to John Adams quoted earlier, Abigail Adams recommended that men should willingly give up "the harsh title of Master for the more tender and endearing one of Friend."

The structure of family life itself was altered by the Revolution. In colonial America, those living within the household often included indentured servants, apprentices, and slaves. After independence, southern slaves remained, rhe-

Modern household

torically at least, members of the owner's "family." In the North, however, with the rapid decline of various forms of indentured servitude and apprenticeship, a more modern definition of the household as consisting of parents and their children took hold. Hired workers, whether domestic servants or farm laborers, were not considered part of the family.

Like slaves, some free women adapted the rhetoric of the Revolution to their own situation. Ann Baker Carson later recalled how she became estranged from the tyrannical husband she had married at age sixteen. "I was an American," she wrote. "A land of liberty had given me birth. I felt myself his equal." She left the marriage rather than continue as a "female slave." But unlike the case of actual slaves, the subordination of women did not become a major source of public debate until long after American independence.

The Arduous Struggle for Liberty

The Revolution changed the lives of virtually every American. As a result of the long struggle against British rule, the public sphere, and with it the right to vote, expanded markedly. Bound labor among whites declined dramatically, religious groups enjoyed greater liberty, blacks mounted a challenge to slavery in which many won their freedom, and women in some ways enjoyed a higher status. On the other hand, for Indians, many Loyalists, and the majority of slaves, American independence meant a deprivation of freedom.

Significance of the Revolution

A new nation, which defined itself as an embodiment of freedom, had taken its place on the world stage. "Not only Britain, but all Europe are spectators of the conflict, the arduous struggle for liberty," wrote Ezra Stiles, a future president of Yale College, in 1775. "We consider ourselves as laying the foundation of a glorious future empire, and acting a part for the contemplation of the ages."

Like Stiles, many other Americans were convinced that their struggle for independence had worldwide significance. American independence, indeed, formed part of a larger set of movements that transformed the Atlantic world. The year 1776 saw not only Paine's *Common Sense* and Jefferson's Declaration but also the publication in England of Adam Smith's *The Wealth of Nations*, which attacked the British policy of closely regulating trade, and Jeremy Bentham's *Fragment on Government,* which criticized the nature of British government.

America Triumphant and Britannia in Distress. An elaborate allegory representing American independence as a triumph of liberty, from an almanac published in Boston in 1781. An accompanying key explains the symbolism: (1) America [on the right] holds an olive branch of peace and invites all nations to trade with her. (2) News of America's triumph is broadcast around the world. (3) Britain, seated next to the devil, laments the loss of trade with America. (4) The British flag falls from a fortress. (5) European ships in American waters. (6) Benedict Arnold, the traitor, hangs himself in New York City [in fact, Arnold died of natural causes in London in 1801].

The winds of change were sweeping across the Atlantic world. The ideals of the American Revolution helped to inspire countless subsequent struggles for social equality and national independence, from the French Revolution, which exploded in 1789, to the uprising that overthrew the slave system in Haiti in the 1790s, to the Latin American wars for independence in the early nineteenth century, and numerous struggles of colonial peoples for nationhood in the twentieth. But within the new republic, the debate over who should enjoy the blessings of liberty would continue long after independence had been achieved.

SUGGESTED READING

BOOKS

- Berkin, Carol. *Revolutionary Mothers: Women in the Struggle for American Independence* (2005). Presents profiles of women who took part in the movement for independence.

- Boulton, Terry. *Taming Democracy: "The People," the Founders, and the Troubled Ending of the American Revolution* (2007). Argues that the democratic impulse unleashed by the War of Independence was to some extent reversed by the events of the 1780s.

- Calloway, Colin. *The American Revolution in Indian Country* (1995). Examines how the Revolution affected Indians in each region of the United States.

- Davis, David Brion. *The Problem of Slavery in the Age of Revolution* (1975). An influential study of the emergence of slavery as a major public issue in the Atlantic world.

- Doerflinger, Thomas M. *A Vigorous Spirit of Enterprise: Merchants and Economic Development in Revolutionary Philadelphia* (1986). Explores how Philadelphia merchants participated in and reacted to the upheavals of the revolutionary era.

- Frey, Sylvia R. *Water from the Rock: Black Resistance in a Revolutionary Age* (1991). A study of the many ways blacks sought to gain freedom for themselves during the Revolution.

- Hatch, Nathan O. *The Democratization of American Christianity* (1989). A comprehensive account of the Revolution's impact on religion, and its aftermath.

- Holton, Woody. *Forced Founders: Indians, Debtors, Slaves and the Making of the American Revolution in Virginia* (1999). Explores how the struggles of those outside Virginia's elite contributed to the movement for independence.

- Jasanoff, Maya. *Liberty's Exiles: American Loyalists in the Revolutionary World* (2011). A study of Americans who remained loyal to Great Britain during the War of Independence.

- Kruman, Marc. *Between Authority and Liberty: State Constitution Making in Revolutionary America* (1997). The most detailed account of how state constitutions were changed during the era.

- Nash, Gary. *The Unknown American Revolution: The Unruly Birth of Democracy and the Struggle to Create America* (2005). Emphasizes the role of ordinary Americans in the struggle for independence.

- Schama, Simon. *Rough Crossing: Britain, the Slaves and the American Revolution* (2006). A detailed look at the experience of the thousands of slaves who escaped to British lines and their fate after the end of the War of Independence.

- Taylor, Alan. *The Divided Ground: Indians, Settlers, and the Northern Borderland of the American Revolution* (2006). Examines the Revolution and its consequence in the Iroquois region of upstate New York.

- Wood, Gordon. *The Radicalism of the American Revolution* (1992). An influential work that sees the Revolution as transforming a hierarchical society into a democratic one.

WEBSITES

- Creating the United States: www.loc.gov/exhibits/creating-the-united-states

- The Geography of Slavery in Virginia: www2.vcdh.virginia.edu/gos/

- Religion and the Founding of the American Republic: www.loc.gov/exhibits/religion/religion.html

CHAPTER REVIEW AND ONLINE RESOURCES

REVIEW QUESTIONS

1. For the lower classes, colonial society had been based on inequality, deference, and obedience. How did the American Revolution challenge that social order?

2. Why did the Revolution cause more radical changes in Pennsylvania than elsewhere, and how was this radicalism demonstrated in the new state constitution?

3. How did ideas of political freedom affect people's ideas about economic rights and relationships?

4. What role did the founders foresee for religion in American government and society?

5. What was the impact of the American Revolution on Native Americans?

6. What were the most important features of the new state constitutions?

7. How did popular views of property rights prevent slaves from enjoying all the freedoms of the social contract?

8. How did revolutionary America see both improvements and limitations in women's roles and rights?

KEY TERMS

republic (p. 208)

suffrage (p. 209)

Bill for Establishing Religious Freedom (p. 213)

inflation (p. 217)

free trade (p. 217)

The Wealth of Nations (p. 218)

Loyalists (p. 218)

Joseph Brant (p. 223)

abolition (p. 224)

freedom petitions (p. 226)

Lemuel Haynes (p. 226)

free blacks (p. 229)

coverture (p. 233)

republican motherhood (p. 233)

Go to INQUIZITIVE

To see what you know—and learn what you've missed—with personalized feedback along the way.

Visit the *Give Me Liberty!* **Student Site** for primary source documents and images, interactive maps, author videos featuring Eric Foner, and more.

CHAPTER 7

FOUNDING A NATION

★

1783–1791

During June and July of 1788, civic leaders in cities up and down the Atlantic coast organized colorful pageants to celebrate the ratification of the United States Constitution. For one day, Benjamin Rush commented of Philadelphia's parade, social class "forgot its claims," as thousands of marchers—rich and poor, businessman and apprentice—joined in a common public ceremony. New York's Grand Federal Procession was led by farmers, followed by the members of every craft in the city from butchers and coopers (makers of wooden barrels) to bricklayers, blacksmiths, and printers. Lawyers, merchants, and clergymen brought up the rear. The parades testified to the strong popular support for the Constitution in the nation's cities. And the prominent role of skilled artisans reflected how the Revolution had secured their place in the American public sphere. Elaborate banners and floats gave voice to the hopes inspired by the new structure of government. "May commerce flourish and industry be rewarded," declared Philadelphia's mariners and shipbuilders.

Throughout the era of the Revolution, Americans spoke of their nation as a "rising empire," destined to populate and control the entire North American continent. While Europe's empires were governed by force, America's would be different. In Jefferson's phrase, it would be "an empire of liberty," bound together by a common devotion to the principles of the Declaration of Independence. Already, the United States exceeded in size Great Britain, Spain, and France combined. As a new nation, it possessed many advantages, including physical isolation from the Old World (a significant asset between 1789 and 1815, when European powers were almost constantly at war), a youthful population certain to grow much larger, and a broad distribution of property ownership and literacy among white citizens.

On the other hand, while Americans dreamed of economic prosperity and continental empire, the nation's prospects at the time of independence were not entirely promising. Control of its vast territory was by no means secure. Nearly all of the 3.9 million Americans recorded in the first national census of 1790 lived near the Atlantic coast. Large areas west of the Appalachian Mountains remained in Indian hands. The British retained military posts on American territory near the Great Lakes, and there were fears that Spain might close the port of New Orleans to American commerce on the Mississippi River.

Away from navigable waterways, communication and transportation were primitive. The country was overwhelmingly rural—fewer than one American in thirty lived in a place with 8,000 inhabitants or more. The population consisted of numerous ethnic and religious groups and some 700,000 slaves, making unity difficult to achieve. No republican government had ever been established over so vast a territory or with so diverse a population. Local loyalties outweighed national patriotism. "We have no Americans in America," commented John Adams. It would take time for consciousness of a common nationality to sink deep roots.

Today, with the United States the most powerful country on earth, it is difficult to recall that in 1783 the future seemed precarious indeed for the fragile nation seeking to make its way in a world of hostile great powers. Profound

FOCUS
QUESTIONS

What were the achievements and problems of the Confederation government? *–p. 240*

What major disagreements and compromises molded the final content of the Constitution? *–p. 247*

How did Anti-Federalist concerns raised during the ratification process lead to the creation of the Bill of Rights? *–p. 254*

How did the definition of citizenship in the new republic exclude Native Americans and African-Americans? *–p. 263*

The Federal Ship Hamilton, an engraving depicting the centerpiece of the Grand Federal Procession in New York City in 1788 that celebrated the ratification of the Constitution. The ship carried over thirty seamen and fired several thirteen-gun salutes during the parade, one for each state. Alexander Hamilton was one of the era's key nationalists and an author of *The Federalist*, which made the argument for ratification.

questions needed to be answered. What course of development should the United States follow? How could the competing claims of local self-government, sectional interests, and national authority be balanced? Who should be considered full-fledged members of the American people, entitled to the blessings of liberty? These issues became the focus of heated debate as the first generation of Americans sought to consolidate their new republic.

AMERICA UNDER THE CONFEDERATION

The Articles of Confederation

The first written constitution of the United States was the **Articles of Confederation**, drafted by Congress in 1777 and ratified by the states four years later. The Articles sought to balance the need for national coordination of the War of Independence with widespread fear that centralized political power posed a danger to liberty. It explicitly declared the new national government to be a "perpetual union." But it resembled less a blueprint for a common government than a treaty for mutual defense—in its own words, a "firm league of friendship" among the states. Under the Articles, the thirteen states retained their individual "sovereignty, freedom, and independence." The national government consisted of a one-house Congress, in which each state, no matter how large or populous, cast a single vote. There was no president to enforce the laws and no judiciary to interpret them. Major decisions required the approval of nine states rather than a simple majority.

The only powers specifically granted to the national government by the Articles of Confederation were those essential to the struggle for independence— declaring war, conducting foreign affairs, and making treaties with other governments. Congress had no real financial resources. It could coin money but lacked the power to levy taxes or regulate commerce. Its revenue came mainly from contributions by the individual states. To amend the Articles required the unanimous consent of the states, a formidable obstacle to change. Various amendments to strengthen the national government were proposed during the seven years (1781–1788) when the Articles of Confederation were in effect, but none received the approval of all the states.

The Articles made energetic national government impossible. But Congress in the 1780s did not lack for accomplishments. The most important was establishing national control over land to the west of the thirteen states and devising rules for its settlement. Disputes over access to western land almost prevented ratification of the Articles in the first place. Citing their original royal charters, which granted territory running all the way to the "South Sea" (the Pacific Ocean), states like Virginia, the Carolinas, and Connecticut claimed immense tracts of western land. Land speculators, politicians, and prospective settlers from states with clearly defined boundaries insisted that such land must belong to the nation at large. Only after the land-rich states, in the interest of national unity, ceded their western claims to the central government did the Articles win ratification.

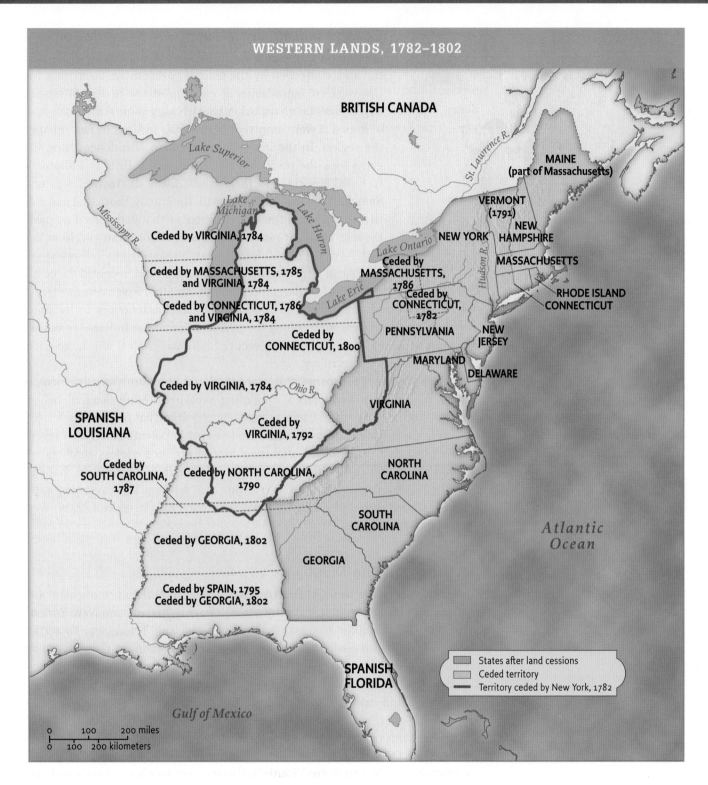

WESTERN LANDS, 1782–1802

BRITISH CANADA

Lake Superior

Lake Michigan

Lake Huron

Mississippi R.

St. Lawrence R.

MAINE (part of Massachusetts)

VERMONT (1791)

NEW HAMPSHIRE

NEW YORK

Lake Ontario

Ceded by VIRGINIA, 1784

Ceded by MASSACHUSETTS, 1785 and VIRGINIA, 1784

Ceded by CONNECTICUT, 1786 and VIRGINIA, 1784

Lake Erie

Ceded by MASSACHUSETTS, 1786

Ceded by CONNECTICUT, 1782

MASSACHUSETTS

RHODE ISLAND
CONNECTICUT

Hudson R.

Ceded by CONNECTICUT, 1800

PENNSYLVANIA

NEW JERSEY

MARYLAND

DELAWARE

Ceded by VIRGINIA, 1784

Ohio R.

VIRGINIA

SPANISH LOUISIANA

Ceded by VIRGINIA, 1792

Ceded by SOUTH CAROLINA, 1787

Ceded by NORTH CAROLINA, 1790

NORTH CAROLINA

SOUTH CAROLINA

Ceded by GEORGIA, 1802

GEORGIA

Atlantic Ocean

Ceded by SPAIN, 1795
Ceded by GEORGIA, 1802

SPANISH FLORIDA

Gulf of Mexico

States after land cessions
Ceded territory
Territory ceded by New York, 1782

0   100   200 miles
0   100   200 kilometers

The creation of a nationally controlled public domain from western land ceded by the states was one of the main achievements of the federal government under the Articles of Confederation.

A design for the Great Seal of the United States produced by a committee of Congress in 1782 includes symbols of liberty, war, and peace, a shield with thirteen stars, and an eagle, all below a Latin phrase meaning "In Defense of Liberty." On the reverse (illustrated at upper right) is an unfinished pyramid with thirteen steps and the Eye of Providence.

Indian land

Rapid settlement in frontier areas

Congress and the West

Establishing rules for the settlement of this national domain—the area controlled by the federal government, stretching from the western boundaries of existing states to the Mississippi River—was by no means easy. Although some Americans spoke of it as if it were empty, over 100,000 Indians in fact inhabited the region. In the immediate aftermath of independence, Congress took the position that by aiding the British, Indians had forfeited the right to their lands. Little distinction was made among tribes that had sided with the enemy, those that had aided the patriots, and those in the interior that had played no part in the war at all. At peace conferences at Fort Stanwix, New York, in 1784 and Fort McIntosh near Pittsburgh the following year, American representatives demanded and received large surrenders of Indian land north of the Ohio River. Similar treaties soon followed with the Cherokee, Choctaw, and Chickasaw tribes in the South, although here Congress guaranteed the permanency of the Indians' remaining, much-reduced holdings. The treaties secured national control of a large part of the country's western territory.

When it came to disposing of western land and regulating its settlement, the Confederation government faced conflicting pressures. Many leaders believed that the economic health of the new republic required that farmers have access to land in the West. But they also saw land sales as a potential source of revenue and worried that unregulated settlement would produce endless conflicts with the Indians. Land companies, which lobbied Congress vigorously, hoped to profit by purchasing real estate and reselling it to settlers. The government, they insisted, should step aside and allow private groups to take control of the West's economic development.

Settlers and the West

The arrival of peace meanwhile triggered a large population movement from settled parts of the original states into frontier areas like upstate New York and across the Appalachian Mountains into Kentucky and Tennessee. To settlers, the right to take possession of western lands and use them as they saw fit was an essential element of American freedom. When a group of Ohioans petitioned Congress in 1785, assailing landlords and speculators who monopolized available acreage and asking that preference in land ownership be given to "actual settlements," their motto was "Grant us Liberty." Indeed, settlers paid no heed to Indian land titles and urged the government to set a low price on public land or give it away. They frequently occupied land to which they had no legal title. By the 1790s, Kentucky courts were filled with lawsuits over land claims, and many settlers lost land they thought they owned. Eventually, disputes over land forced many early settlers (including the parents of Abraham Lincoln) to leave Kentucky for opportunities in other states.

At the same time, however, like British colonial officials before them, many leaders of the new nation feared that an unregulated flow of population across the

Appalachian Mountains would provoke constant warfare with Indians. Moreover, they viewed frontier settlers as disorderly and lacking in proper respect for authority—"our debtors, loose English people, our German servants, and slaves," Benjamin Franklin had once called them. Establishing law and order in the West and strict rules for the occupation of land there seemed essential to attracting a better class of settlers to the West and avoiding discord between the settled and frontier parts of the new nation.

The Land Ordinances

A series of measures approved by Congress during the 1780s defined the terms by which western land would be marketed and settled. Drafted by Thomas Jefferson, the **Ordinance of 1784** established stages of self-government for the West. The region would be divided into districts initially governed by Congress and eventually admitted to the Union as member states. By a single vote, Congress rejected a clause that would have prohibited slavery throughout the West. A second resolution, the **Ordinance of 1785**, regulated land sales in the region north of the Ohio River, which came to be known as the Old Northwest. Land would be surveyed by the government and then sold in "sections" of a square mile (640 acres) at $1 per acre. In each township, one section would be set aside to provide funds for public education. The system promised to control and concentrate settlement and raise money for Congress. But settlers violated the rules by pressing westward before the surveys had been completed.

Like the British before them, American officials found it difficult to regulate the thirst for new land. The minimum purchase price of $640, however, put public land out of the financial reach of most settlers. They generally ended up buying

Western settlement and self-government

Price of land

An engraving from *The Farmers' and Mechanics' Almanac* shows farm families moving west along a primitive road.

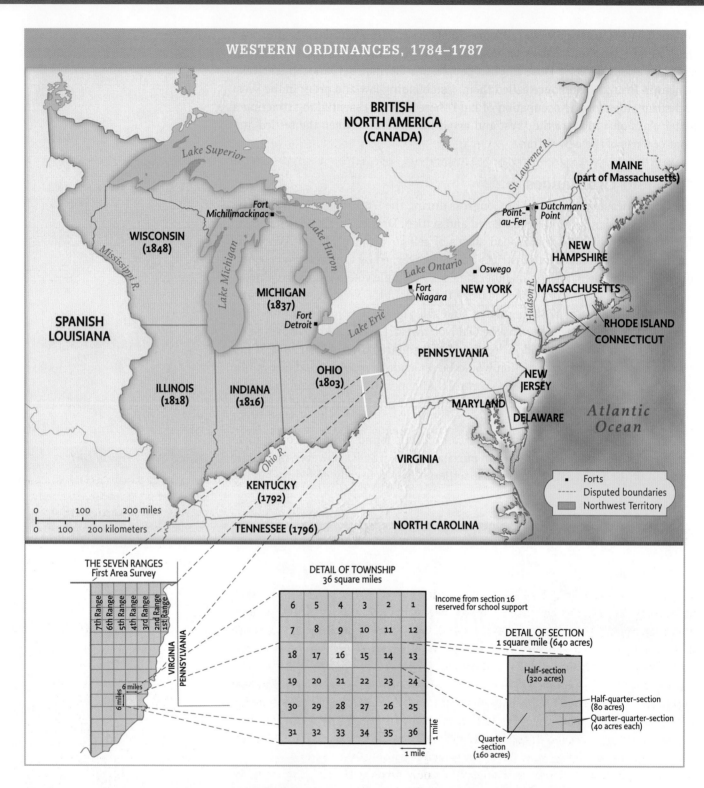

WESTERN ORDINANCES, 1784–1787

BRITISH NORTH AMERICA (CANADA)

Lake Superior

MAINE (part of Massachusetts)

Fort Michilimackinac

Point-au-Fer
Dutchman's Point

WISCONSIN (1848)

Lake Huron

NEW HAMPSHIRE

Lake Michigan

Lake Ontario
Oswego

Mississippi R.

MICHIGAN (1837)

Fort Niagara

NEW YORK

Hudson R.

MASSACHUSETTS

SPANISH LOUISIANA

Fort Detroit

Lake Erie

RHODE ISLAND
CONNECTICUT

PENNSYLVANIA

NEW JERSEY

OHIO (1803)

ILLINOIS (1818)

INDIANA (1816)

MARYLAND

DELAWARE

Atlantic Ocean

Ohio R.

VIRGINIA

KENTUCKY (1792)

0   100   200 miles
0   100   200 kilometers

■ Forts
---- Disputed boundaries
▨ Northwest Territory

TENNESSEE (1796)

NORTH CAROLINA

THE SEVEN RANGES
First Area Survey

7th Range | 6th Range | 5th Range | 4th Range | 3rd Range | 2nd Range | 1st Range

VIRGINIA
PENNSYLVANIA

6 miles

DETAIL OF TOWNSHIP
36 square miles

6	5	4	3	2	1
7	8	9	10	11	12
18	17	16	15	14	13
19	20	21	22	23	24
30	29	28	27	26	25
31	32	33	34	35	36

Income from section 16 reserved for school support

1 mile

DETAIL OF SECTION
1 square mile (640 acres)

Half-section (320 acres)

Half-quarter-section (80 acres)

Quarter-quarter-section (40 acres each)

Quarter-section (160 acres)

1 mile

A series of ordinances in the 1780s provided for both the surveying and sale of lands in the public domain north of the Ohio River and the eventual admission of states carved from the area as equal members of the Union.

smaller parcels from speculators and land companies. In 1787, Congress decided to sell off large tracts to private groups, including 1.5 million acres to the Ohio Company, organized by New England land speculators and army officers. (This was a different organization from the Ohio Company of the 1750s, mentioned in Chapter 4.) For many years, national land policy benefited private land companies and large buyers more than individual settlers. And for decades, actual and prospective settlers pressed for a reduction in the price of government-owned land, a movement that did not end until the Homestead Act of 1862 offered free land in the public domain.

A final measure, the **Northwest Ordinance of 1787**, called for the eventual establishment of from three to five states north of the Ohio River and east of the Mississippi. Thus was enacted the basic principle of what Jefferson called the **empire of liberty**—rather than ruling over the West as a colonial power, the United States would admit the area's population as equal members of the political system. Territorial expansion and self-government would grow together.

"Empire of liberty"

The Northwest Ordinance pledged that "the utmost good faith" would be observed toward local Indians and that their land would not be taken without consent. This was the first official recognition that Indians continued to own their land. Congress realized that allowing settlers and state government simply to seize Indian lands would produce endless, expensive military conflicts on the frontier. "It will cost much less," one congressman noted, "to conciliate the good opinion of the Indians than to pay men for destroying them." But national land policy assumed that whether through purchase, treaties, or voluntary removal, the Indian presence would soon disappear. The Ordinance also prohibited slavery in the Old Northwest, a provision that would have far-reaching consequences when the sectional conflict between North and South developed. But for years, owners brought slaves into the area, claiming that they had voluntarily signed long-term labor contracts.

The Confederation's Weaknesses

Whatever the achievements of the Confederation government, in the eyes of many influential Americans they were outweighed by its failings. Both the national government and the country at large faced worsening economic problems. To finance the War of Independence, Congress had borrowed large sums of money by selling interest-bearing bonds and paying soldiers and suppliers in notes to be redeemed in the future. Lacking a secure source of revenue, it found itself unable to pay either interest or the debts themselves. With the United States now outside the British empire, American ships were barred from trading with the West Indies. Imported goods, however, flooded the market, undercutting the business of many craftsmen, driving down wages, and draining money out of the country.

Some American businessmen looked for new areas with which to trade. In 1784, financed by leading New York and Philadelphia merchants, the *Empress of China* set sail for Canton, the first ship to do so flying the American flag. It carried furs, wine, Spanish silver dollars, and American ginseng. It returned the following year with silk, tea, and Chinese porcelain, a glazed ceramic widely admired for its beauty and resistance to heat and water (and commonly known simply as "China").

A Bankruptcy Scene. Creditors repossess the belongings of a family unable to pay its debts, while a woman weeps in the background. Popular fears of bankruptcy led several states during the 1780s to pass laws postponing the collection of debts.

One set had been ordered by George Washington for his home in Mount Vernon, Virginia. The investors turned a large profit. The voyage demonstrated the feasibility of trade with Asia, but for the moment, this could not compensate for the loss of nearby markets in the British West Indies.

With Congress unable to act, the states adopted their own economic policies. Several imposed tariff duties on goods imported from abroad. Indebted farmers, threatened with the loss of land because of failure to meet tax or mortgage payments, pressed state governments for relief, as did urban craftsmen who owed money to local merchants. In order to increase the amount of currency in circulation and make it easier for individuals to pay their debts, several states printed large sums of paper money. Others enacted laws postponing debt collection. Creditors considered such measures attacks on their property rights. In a number of states, legislative elections produced boisterous campaigns in which candidates for office denounced creditors for oppressing the poor and importers of luxury goods for undermining republican virtue.

Shays's Rebellion

Uprising in Massachusetts

In late 1786 and early 1787, crowds of debt-ridden farmers closed the courts in western Massachusetts to prevent the seizure of their land for failure to pay taxes. They called themselves "regulators"—a term already used by protesters in the Carolina backcountry in the 1760s. The uprising came to be known as **Shays's Rebellion**, a name affixed to it by its opponents, after Daniel Shays, one of the leaders and a veteran of the War for Independence. Massachusetts had firmly resisted pressure to issue paper money or in other ways assist needy debtors. The participants in Shays's Rebellion believed they were acting in the spirit of the Revolution. They modeled their tactics on the crowd activities of the 1760s and 1770s and employed liberty trees and liberty poles as symbols of their cause. They received no sympathy from Governor James Bowdoin, who dispatched an army headed by former revolutionary war general Benjamin Lincoln. The rebels were dispersed in January 1787, and more than 1,000 were arrested. Without adherence to the rule of law, Bowdoin declared, Americans would descend into "a state of anarchy, confusion and slavery."

Observing Shays's Rebellion from Paris where he was serving as ambassador, Thomas Jefferson refused to be alarmed. "A little rebellion now and then is a good thing," he wrote to a friend. "The tree of liberty must be refreshed from time to time with the blood of patriots and tyrants." But the uprising was the culmination of a series of events in the 1780s that persuaded an influential group of Americans that the national government must be strengthened so that it could develop uniform economic policies and protect property owners from infringements on their rights by local majorities. The actions of state legislatures (most of them elected annually by an expanded voting population), followed by Shays's Rebellion, produced fears that the Revolution's democratic impulse had gotten out of hand.

"Abuses of liberty"

Among proponents of stronger national authority, liberty had lost some of its luster. The danger to individual rights, they came to believe, now arose not from a tyrannical central government, but from the people themselves. "Liberty," declared James Madison, "may be endangered by the abuses of liberty as well as the abuses of power." To put it another way, private liberty, especially the secure enjoyment of property rights, could be endangered by public liberty—unchecked power in the hands of the people.

Nationalists of the 1780s

Madison, a diminutive, colorless Virginian and the lifelong disciple and ally of Thomas Jefferson, thought deeply and creatively about the nature of political freedom. He was among the group of talented and well-organized men who spearheaded the movement for a stronger national government. Another was Alexander Hamilton, who had come to North America as a youth from the West Indies, served at the precocious age of twenty as an army officer during the War of Independence, and married into a prominent New York family. Hamilton was perhaps the most vigorous proponent of an "energetic" government that would enable the new nation to become a powerful commercial and diplomatic presence in world affairs. Genuine liberty, he insisted, required "a proper degree of authority, to make and exercise the laws." Men like Madison and Hamilton were nation-builders. They came to believe during the 1780s that Americans were squandering the fruits of independence and that the country's future greatness depended on enhancing national authority.

James Madison, "father of the Constitution," in a miniature portrait painted by Charles Willson Peale in 1783. Madison was only thirty-six years old when the Constitutional Convention met.

The concerns voiced by critics of the Articles found a sympathetic hearing among men who had developed a national consciousness during the Revolution. Nationalists included army officers, members of Congress accustomed to working with individuals from different states, and diplomats who represented the country abroad. In the army, John Marshall (later a chief justice of the Supreme Court) developed "the habit of considering America as my country, and Congress as my government." Influential economic interests also desired a stronger national government. Among these were bondholders who despaired of being paid so long as Congress lacked a source of revenue, urban artisans seeking tariff protection from foreign imports, merchants desiring access to British markets, and all those who feared that the states were seriously interfering with property rights. While these groups did not agree on many issues, they all believed in the need for a stronger national government.

In September 1786, delegates from six states met at Annapolis, Maryland, to consider ways for better regulating interstate and international commerce. The delegates proposed another gathering, in Philadelphia, to amend the Articles of Confederation. Shays's Rebellion greatly strengthened the nationalists' cause. "The late turbulent scenes in Massachusetts," wrote Madison, underscored the need for a new constitution. "No respect," he complained, "is paid to the federal authority." Without a change in the structure of government, either anarchy or monarchy was the likely outcome, bringing to an end the experiment in republican government. Every state except Rhode Island, which had gone the furthest in developing its own debtor relief and trade policies, sent delegates to the Philadelphia convention. When they assembled in May 1787, they decided to scrap the Articles of Confederation entirely and draft a new constitution for the United States.

Alexander Hamilton, another youthful leader of the nationalists of the 1780s, was born in the West Indies in 1755. This life-size portrait was commissioned by five New York merchants and painted by John Trumbull in 1792, when Hamilton was secretary of the Treasury.

A NEW CONSTITUTION

The fifty-five men who gathered for the **Constitutional Convention** included some of the most prominent Americans. Thomas Jefferson and John Adams, serving as diplomats in Europe, did not take part. But among the delegates were George Washington (whose willingness to lend his prestige to the gathering and to serve as presiding officer was an enormous asset), George Mason (author of Virginia's Declaration of Rights of 1776), and Benjamin Franklin (who had returned to Philadelphia after helping to negotiate the Treaty of Paris of 1783, and was now eighty-one years old). John Adams described the convention as a gathering of men of "ability, weight, and experience." He might have added, "and wealth." Although a few, like Alexander Hamilton, had risen from humble origins, most had been born into propertied families. They earned their livings as lawyers, merchants, planters, and large farmers.

At a time when fewer than one-tenth of 1 percent of Americans attended college, more than half the delegates had college educations. A majority had participated in interstate meetings of the 1760s and 1770s, and twenty-two had served in the army during the Revolution. Their shared social status and political experiences bolstered their common belief in the need to strengthen national authority and curb what one called "the excesses of democracy." To ensure free and candid debate, the deliberations took place in private. Madison, who believed the outcome would have great consequences for "the cause of liberty throughout the world," took careful notes. They were not published, however, until 1840, four years after he became the last delegate to pass away.

The Structure of Government

It quickly became apparent that the delegates agreed on many points. The new Constitution would create a legislature, an executive, and a national judiciary. Congress would have the power to raise money without relying on the states. States would be prohibited from infringing on the rights of property. And the government would represent the people. Hamilton's proposal for a president and Senate serving life terms, like the king and House of Lords of England, received virtually no support. The "rich and well-born," Hamilton told the convention, must rule, for the masses "seldom judge or determine right." Most delegates, however, hoped to find a middle ground between the despotism of monarchy and aristocracy and what they considered the excesses of popular self-government. "We had been too democratic," observed George Mason, but he warned against the danger of going to "the opposite extreme." The key to stable, effective republican government was finding a way to balance the competing claims of liberty and power.

Differences quickly emerged over the proper balance between the federal and state governments and between the interests of large and small states. Early in the proceedings, Madison presented what came to be called the **Virginia Plan**. It proposed the creation of a two-house legislature with a state's population determining its representation in each. Smaller states, fearing that populous Virginia, Massachusetts, and Pennsylvania would dominate the new government,

A fifty-dollar note issued by the Continental Congress during the War of Independence. Congress's inability to raise funds to repay such paper money in gold or silver was a major reason why nationalists desired a stronger federal government.

The Philadelphia State House (now called Independence Hall), where the Declaration of Independence was signed in 1776 and the Constitutional Convention took place in 1787.

rallied behind the **New Jersey Plan**. This called for a single-house Congress in which each state cast one vote, as under the Articles of Confederation. In the end, a compromise was reached—a two-house Congress consisting of a Senate in which each state had two members, and a House of Representatives apportioned according to population. Senators would be chosen by state legislatures for six-year terms. They were thus insulated from sudden shifts in public opinion. Representatives were to be elected every two years directly by the people.

A two-house Congress

The Limits of Democracy

Under the Articles of Confederation, no national official had been chosen by popular vote. Thus, the mode of choosing the House of Representatives represented an expansion of democracy. Popular election of at least one part of the political regime, Madison declared, was "essential to every plan of free government." The Constitution, moreover, imposed neither property nor religious qualifications for voting, leaving it to the states to set voting rules.

Overall, however, the new structure of government was less than democratic. The delegates sought to shield the national government from the popular enthusiasms that had alarmed them during the 1780s and to ensure that the right kind of men held office. The people would remain sovereign, but they would choose among the elite to staff the new government. The delegates assumed that the Senate would be composed of each state's most distinguished citizens. They made the House of Representatives quite small (initially 65 members, at a time when the Massachusetts assembly had 200), on the assumption that only prominent individuals could win election in large districts.

Less-than-democratic structure

Nor did the delegates provide for direct election of either federal judges or the president. Members of the Supreme Court would be appointed by the president for life terms. The president would be chosen either by members of an electoral college or by the House of Representatives. The number of electors for each state was determined by adding together its allocation of senators and representatives. Electors would be prominent, well-educated individuals better qualified than ordinary voters to choose the head of state.

Indirect elections

The actual system of election seemed a recipe for confusion. Each elector was to cast votes for two candidates for president, with the second-place finisher becoming vice president. If no candidate received a majority of the electoral ballots—as the delegates seem to have assumed would normally be the case—the president would be chosen from among the top three finishers by the House of Representatives, with each state casting one vote. The Senate would then elect the vice president. The delegates devised this extremely cumbersome system of indirect election because they did not trust ordinary voters to choose the president and vice president directly.

The Division and Separation of Powers

Hammered out in four months of discussion and compromise, the Constitution is a spare document of only 4,000 words that provides only the briefest outline of the new structure of government. (See the Appendix for the full text.) It embodies two basic political principles—**federalism**, sometimes called the **division of powers**, and the system of **checks and balances** between the different branches of the national government, also known as the **separation of powers**.

Federalism

Federalism refers to the relationship between the national government and the states. Compared to the Articles of Confederation, the Constitution significantly strengthened national authority. It charged the president with enforcing the law and commanding the military. It empowered Congress to levy taxes, borrow money, regulate commerce, declare war, deal with foreign nations and Indians, and promote the "general welfare." Madison proposed to allow Congress to veto state laws, but this proved too far-reaching for most delegates. The Constitution did, however, declare national legislation the "supreme Law of the Land." And it included strong provisions to prevent the states from infringing on property rights. They were barred from issuing paper money, impairing contracts, interfering with interstate commerce, and levying their own import or export duties. On the other hand, most day-to-day affairs of government, from education to law enforcement, remained in the hands of the states. This principle of divided sovereignty was a recipe for debate, which continues to this day, over the balance of power between the national government and the states.

Checks and balances

The "separation of powers," or the system of "checks and balances," refers to the way the Constitution seeks to prevent any branch of the national government from dominating the other two. To prevent an accumulation of power dangerous to liberty, authority within the government is diffused and balanced against itself. Congress enacts laws, but the president can veto them, and a two-thirds majority is required to pass legislation over his objection. Federal judges are nominated by the president and approved by the Senate, but to ensure their independence, the judges then serve for life. The president can be impeached by the House and removed from office by the Senate for "high crimes and misdemeanors."

The Debate over Slavery

The structure of government was not the only source of debate at the Constitutional Convention. As Madison recorded, "the institution of slavery and its implications" divided the delegates at many sessions. Those who gathered in Philadelphia included numerous slaveholders, as well as some dedicated advocates of abolition. Madison, like Jefferson a Virginia slaveholder who detested slavery, told the convention that the "distinction of color" had become the basis for "the most oppressive dominion ever exercised by man over man." Yet he later assured the Virginia ratifying convention that the Constitution offered slavery "better security than any that now exists."

The words "slave" and "slavery" do not appear in the original Constitution—a concession to the sensibilities of delegates who feared they would "contaminate the glorious fabric of American liberty." As Luther Martin of Maryland wrote, his fellow delegates "anxiously sought to avoid the admission of expressions which might be odious to the ears of Americans." But, he continued, they were "willing to admit into their system those *things* which the *expressions signified*." The document prohibited Congress from abolishing the importation of slaves from abroad for twenty years. It required states to return to their owners fugitives from bondage. And the **three-fifths clause** provided that three-fifths of the slave population would be counted in determining each state's representation in the House of Representatives and its electoral votes for president.

South Carolina's delegates had come to Philadelphia determined to defend slavery, and they had a powerful impact on the final document. They originated the fugitive slave clause and the electoral college. They insisted on strict limits on the power of Congress to levy taxes within the states, fearing future efforts to raise revenue by taxing slave property. They threatened disunion if the Atlantic slave trade were prohibited immediately, as the New England states and Virginia, with its abundance of native-born slaves, demanded. Their threats swayed many delegates. Gouverneur Morris, one of Pennsylvania's delegates, declared that he was being forced to decide between offending the southern states and doing injustice to "human nature." For the sake of national unity, he said, he would choose the latter.

This advertisement by a slave-trading company appeared in a Richmond, Virginia newspaper only a few months after the signing of the Constitution. The company seeks to buy 100 slaves to sell to purchasers in states further south. Slavery was a major subject of debate at the Constitutional Convention.

South Carolina's influence

Slavery in the Constitution

The Constitution's slavery clauses were compromises, efforts to find a middle ground between the institution's critics and defenders. Taken together, however, they embedded slavery more deeply than ever in American life and politics. The slave trade clause allowed a commerce condemned by civilized society—one that had been suspended during the War of Independence—to continue until 1808. On January 1, 1808, the first day that Congress was allowed under the Constitution, it prohibited the further importation of slaves. But in the interim, partly to replace slaves who had escaped to the British and partly to provide labor for the expansion

The slave trade clause

of slavery to fertile land away from the coast, some 170,000 Africans were brought to the new nation as slaves. South Carolina and Georgia imported 100,000. This number represented more than one-quarter of all the slaves brought to mainland North America after 1700.

Fugitive slave clause

The fugitive slave clause accorded slave laws "extraterritoriality"—that is, the condition of bondage remained attached to a person even if he or she escaped to a state where slavery had been abolished. In the famous *Somerset* case of 1772, the lawyer for a West Indian slave brought to Britain had obtained his client's freedom by invoking the memorable words, "the air of England is too pure for a slave to breathe" (that is, the moment any person sets foot on British soil, he or she becomes free). Yet the new federal Constitution required all the states, North and South, to recognize and help police the institution of slavery. For slaves, there was no "free air" in America. Nonetheless, the clause was strikingly ambiguous. It did not say who was responsible for apprehending a fugitive slave—the states, the federal government, or the owner himself—or what judicial procedures would be employed to return him or her to bondage. As time went on, these questions would become a major source of conflict between the North and the South.

Three-fifths clause

The Constitution gave the national government no power to interfere with slavery in the states. And the three-fifths clause allowed the white South to exercise far greater power in national affairs than the size of its free population warranted. The clause greatly enhanced the number of southern votes in the House of Representatives and therefore in the electoral college (where, as noted above, the number of electors for each state was determined by adding together its number of senators and representatives). Of the first sixteen presidential elections, between 1788 and 1848, all but four placed a southern slaveholder in the White House.

Even the initial failure to include a Bill of Rights resulted, in part, from the presence of slavery. As South Carolina delegate Charles C. Pinckney explained, "such bills generally begin with declaring that all men are by nature born free," a declaration that would come "with a very bad grace, when a large part of our property consists in men who are actually born slaves."

But some slaveholders detected a potential threat buried in the Constitution. Patrick Henry, who condemned slavery but feared abolition, warned that, in time of war, the new government might take steps to arm and liberate the slaves. "May Congress not say," he asked, "that every black man must fight? Did we not see a little of this [in the] last war?" What Henry could not anticipate was that the war that eventually destroyed slavery would be launched by the South itself to protect the institution.

The preamble to the Constitution, as printed in a Pennsylvania newspaper two days after the Constitutional Convention adjourned.

The Signing of the Constitution, by mid-nineteenth-century American artist Thomas Prichard Rossiter, depicts the conclusion of the Constitutional Convention of 1787. Among the founding fathers depicted are James Wilson, signing the document at the table in the center, and George Washington, presiding from the dais with an image of the sun behind him.

The Final Document

Gouverneur Morris put the finishing touches on the final draft of the new Constitution, trying to make it, he explained, "as clear as our language would permit." For the original preamble, which began, "We the people of the States of New Hampshire, Massachusetts," etc., he substituted the far more powerful "We the people of the United States." He added a statement of the Constitution's purposes, including to "establish justice," promote "the general welfare," and "secure the blessings of liberty"—things the Articles of Confederation, in the eyes of most of the delegates, had failed to accomplish.

The last session of the Constitutional Convention took place on September 17, 1787. Benjamin Franklin urged the delegates to put aside individual objections and approve the document, whatever its imperfections. "The older I grow," he remarked, "the more apt I am to . . . pay more respect to the judgment of others." Of the forty-five delegates who remained in Philadelphia, thirty-nine signed the Constitution. It was then sent to the states for ratification.

The Constitution created a new framework for American development. By assigning to Congress power over tariffs, interstate commerce, the coining of money, patents, rules for bankruptcy, and weights and measures, and by prohibiting states from interfering with property rights, it made possible a national economic market. It created national political institutions, reduced the powers of the states, and sought to place limits on popular democracy. "The same enthusiasm, *now* pervades all classes in favor of *government*," observed Benjamin Rush, "that actuated us in favor of *liberty* in the years 1774 and 1775." Whether "all classes" truly agreed may be doubted, for the ratification process unleashed a nationwide debate over the best means of preserving American freedom.

Effects of the Constitution

THE RATIFICATION DEBATE AND
THE ORIGIN OF THE BILL OF RIGHTS

The Federalist

Even though the Constitution provided that it would go into effect when nine states, not all thirteen as required by the Articles of Confederation, had given their approval, ratification was by no means certain. Each state held an election for delegates to a special ratifying convention. A fierce public battle ensued, producing hundreds of pamphlets and newspaper articles and spirited campaigns to elect delegates. To generate support, Hamilton, Madison, and Jay composed a series of eighty-five essays that appeared in newspapers under the pen name Publius and were gathered as a book, ***The Federalist***, in 1788. Hamilton wrote fifty, Madison thirty, and Jay the remainder. Today, the essays are regarded as among the most important American contributions to political thought. At the time, however, they represented only one part of a much larger national debate over ratification, reflected in innumerable pamphlets, newspaper articles, and public meetings.

Again and again, Hamilton and Madison repeated that rather than posing a danger to Americans' liberties, the Constitution in fact protected them. Hamilton's essays sought to disabuse Americans of their fear of political power. Government, he insisted, was an expression of freedom, not its enemy. Any government could become oppressive, but with its checks and balances and division of power, the Constitution made political tyranny almost impossible. Hamilton insisted that he was "as zealous an advocate for liberty as any man whatever." But "want of power" had been the fatal flaw of the Articles. At the New York ratifying con-

A national debate

This satirical engraving by Amos Doolittle (who created the image of the Battle of Concord in Chapter 5) depicts some of the issues in the debate over the ratification of the Constitution. The wagon in the center is carrying Connecticut and sinking into the mud under the weight of debts and paper money as "Federals" and "Antifederals" try to pull it out. Federals call for the state to "comply with Congress" (that is, to pay money requisitioned by the national government); the Antifederals reply, "Tax luxury" and "Success to Shays," a reference to Shays's Rebellion. Underneath the three merchant ships is a phrase criticizing the tariffs that states were imposing on imports from one another (which the Constitution prohibited).

In this late-eighteenth-century engraving, Americans celebrate the signing of the Constitution beneath a temple of liberty.

vention, Hamilton assured the delegates that the Constitution had created "the perfect balance between liberty and power."

"Extend the Sphere"

Madison, too, emphasized how the Constitution was structured to prevent abuses of authority. But in several essays, especially *Federalist* nos. 10 and 51, he moved beyond such assurances to develop a strikingly new vision of the relationship between government and society in the United States. Madison identified the essential dilemma, as he saw it, of the new republic—government must be based on the will of the people, yet the people had shown themselves susceptible to dangerous enthusiasms. Most worrisome, they had threatened property rights, whose protection was the "first object of government." The problem of balancing democracy and respect for property would only grow in the years ahead because, he warned, economic development would inevitably increase the numbers of poor. What was to prevent them from using their political power to secure "a more equal distribution" of wealth by seizing the property of the rich?

The answer, Madison explained, lay not simply in the way power balanced power in the structure of government, but in the nation's size and diversity. Previous republics had existed only in small territories—the Dutch republic, or Italian city-states of the Renaissance. But, argued Madison, the very size of the United States was a source of stability, not, as many feared, weakness. "Extend the sphere," he wrote. In a nation as large as the United States, so many distinct interests—economic, regional, and political—would arise, that no single one would

Madison's Federalist *no. 10*

America's size and diversity

In New York City's Grand Federal Procession of 1788, celebrating the ratification of the Constitution, members of each trade and occupation marched together. This document illustrates the variety of crafts in the pre-industrial city.

ever be able to take over the government and oppress the rest. Every majority would be a coalition of minorities, and thus "the rights of individuals" would be secure.

Madison's writings did much to shape the early nation's understanding of its new political institutions. In arguing that the size of the republic helped to secure Americans' rights, they reinforced the tradition that saw continuous westward expansion as essential to freedom. And in basing the preservation of freedom on the structure of government and size of the republic, not the character of the people, his essays represented a major shift away from the "republican" emphasis on a virtuous citizenry devoted to the common good as the foundation of proper government. Madison helped to popularize the "liberal" idea that men are generally motivated by self-interest, and that the good of society arises from the clash of these private interests.

The Anti-Federalists

Opponents of ratification, called **Anti-Federalists**, insisted that the Constitution shifted the balance between liberty and power too far in the direction of the latter. Anti-Federalists lacked the coherent leadership of the Constitution's defenders. They included state politicians fearful of seeing their influence diminish, among them such revolutionary heroes as Samuel Adams, John Hancock, and Patrick Henry. Small farmers, many of whom supported the state debtor-relief measures of the 1780s that the Constitution's supporters deplored, also saw no need for a stronger central government. Some opponents of the Constitution denounced the document's protections for slavery; others warned that the powers of Congress were so broad that it might enact a law for abolition.

Anti-Federalists repeatedly predicted that the new government would fall under the sway of merchants, creditors, and others hostile to the interests of ordinary Americans. Repudiating Madison's arguments in *Federalist* nos. 10 and 51, Anti-Federalists insisted that "a very extensive territory cannot be governed on the principles of freedom." Popular self-government, they claimed, flourished best in small communities, where rulers and ruled interacted daily. Only men of wealth, "ignorant of the sentiments of the middling and lower class of citizens," would have the resources to win election to a national government. The result of the Constitution, warned Melancton Smith of New York, a member of Congress under the Articles of Confederation, would be domination of the "common people" by the "well-born." "This," Smith predicted, "will be a government of oppression."

Liberty was the Anti-Federalists' watchword. America's happiness, they insisted, "arises from the freedom of our institutions and the limited nature of our government," both threatened by the new Constitution. Maryland Anti-Federalists had caps manufactured bearing the word "Liberty," to wear to the polls when members of the state's ratification convention were elected. To the vision of the United States as an energetic great power, Anti-Federalists counterposed a way of life grounded in local, democratic institutions. "What is Liberty?" asked James Lincoln of South Carolina. "The power of governing yourselves. If you adopt this constitution, have you this power? No."

Anti-Federalists also pointed to the Constitution's lack of a **Bill of Rights**, which left unprotected rights such as trial by jury and freedom of speech and the press.

Banner of the Society of Pewterers. A banner carried by one of the many artisan groups that took part in New York City's Grand Federal Procession of 1788 celebrating the ratification of the Constitution. The banner depicts artisans at work in their shop and some of their products. The words "Solid and Pure," and the inscription at the upper right, link the quality of their pewter to their opinion of the new frame of government and hopes for the future. The inscription reads:

"The Federal Plan Most Solid and Secure Americans Their Freedom Will Endure All Arts Shall Flourish in Columbia's Land And All Her Sons Join as One Social Band"

The absence of a Bill of Rights, declared Patrick Henry, was "the most absurd thing to mankind that ever the world saw." State constitutions had bills of rights, yet the states, Henry claimed, were now being asked to surrender most of their powers to the federal government, with no requirement that it respect Americans' basic liberties.

In general, pro-Constitution sentiment flourished in the nation's cities and in rural areas closely tied to the commercial marketplace. The Constitution's most energetic supporters were men of substantial property. But what George Bryan of Pennsylvania, a supporter of ratification, called the "golden phantom" of prosperity also swung urban artisans, laborers, and sailors behind the movement for a government that would use its "energy and power" to revive the depressed economy. Anti-Federalism drew its support from small farmers in more isolated rural areas such as the Hudson Valley of New York, western Massachusetts, and the southern backcountry.

> Social bases of support and opposition

In the end, the supporters' energy and organization, coupled with their domination of the colonial press, carried the day. Ninety-two newspapers and magazines existed in the United States in 1787. Of these, only twelve published a significant number of Anti-Federalist pieces. Madison also won support for the new Constitution by promising that the first Congress would enact a Bill of Rights. By mid-1788, the required nine states had ratified. Although there was strong dissent in Massachusetts, New York, and Virginia, only Rhode Island and North Carolina voted against ratification, and they subsequently had little choice but to join the new government. Anti-Federalism died. But as with other movements in American history that did not immediately achieve their goals—for example, the Populists of the late nineteenth century—some of the Anti-Federalists' ideas eventually entered the political mainstream. To this day, their belief that a too-powerful central government is a threat to liberty continues to influence American political culture.

> Ratification

After the Grand Federal Procession, hundreds of marchers enjoyed a celebratory banquet. The ten tables represented the states that had ratified by July 1788 when the procession took place.

The Bill of Rights

Ironically, the parts of the Constitution Americans most value today—the freedoms of speech, the press, and religion; protection against unjust criminal procedures; equality before the law—were not in the original document. All of these but the last (which was enshrined in the Fourteenth Amendment after the Civil War) were contained in the first ten amendments, known as the Bill of Rights. Madison was so convinced that the balances of the Constitution would protect liberty that he believed a Bill of Rights "redundant or pointless." Amendments restraining federal power, he believed, would have no effect on the danger to liberty posed by unchecked majorities in the states, and no list of rights could ever anticipate the numerous ways that Congress might operate in the future. "Parchment barriers" to the abuse of authority, he observed, would prove least effective when most needed. Madison's prediction would be amply borne out at future times of popular hysteria, such as during the Red Scare following World War I and the McCarthy era of the 1950s, when all branches of government joined in trampling on freedom of expression, and during World War II, when hatred of a foreign enemy led to the internment of more than 100,000 Japanese-Americans, most of them citizens of the United States.

Nevertheless, every new state constitution contained some kind of declaration of citizens' rights, and large numbers of Americans—Federalist and Anti-Federalist alike—believed the new national Constitution should also have one. Indeed, many delegates at state conventions had refused to vote for ratification unless promised that a Bill of Rights would be added to the Constitution. In order to "conciliate the minds of the people," as Madison put it, he presented to Congress a series of amendments that became the basis of the Bill of Rights, which was ratified by the states in 1791. The First Amendment prohibited Congress from legislating with regard to religion or infringing on freedom of speech, freedom of the press, or the right of assembly. The Second upheld the people's right to "keep and bear arms" in conjunction with "a well-regulated militia." Others prohibited abuses such as arrests without warrants

Madison's objections

First Amendment rights

and forcing a person accused of a crime to testify against himself and reaffirmed the right to trial by jury.

In a sense, the Bill of Rights offered a definition of the "unalienable rights" Jefferson had mentioned in the Declaration of Independence—rights inherent in the human condition. Not having been granted by government in the first place, they could not be rescinded by government. In case any had been accidentally omitted, the Ninth Amendment declared that rights not specifically mentioned in the Constitution were "retained by the people." Its suggestion that the Constitution was not meant to be complete opened the door to future legal recognition of rights not grounded in the actual text (such as the right to privacy). The Tenth Amendment, meant to answer fears that the federal government would ride roughshod over the states, affirmed that powers not delegated to the national government or prohibited to the states continued to reside with the states.

> *Ninth Amendment rights*

The roots and even the specific language of some parts of the Bill of Rights lay far back in English history. The Eighth Amendment, prohibiting excessive bail and cruel and unusual punishments, incorporates language that originated in a declaration by the House of Lords in 1316 and was repeated centuries later in the English Bill of Rights and the constitutions of a number of American states.

Other provisions reflected the changes in American life brought about by the Revolution. The most remarkable of these was constitutional recognition of religious freedom. Unlike the Declaration of Independence, which invokes the blessing of divine providence, the Constitution is a purely secular document that contains no reference to God and bars religious tests for federal officeholders. The First Amendment prohibits the federal government from legislating on the subject of religion—a complete departure from British and colonial precedent. Under the Constitution it was and remains possible, as one critic complained, for "a papist, a Mohomatan, a deist, yea an atheist" to become president of the United States. Madison was so adamant about separating church and state that he even opposed the appointment of chaplains to serve Congress and the military.

> *Right to religious freedom*

An engraving and a poem, published in 1788 in an American newspaper, after New York became the eleventh state to ratify the new Constitution. North Carolina would ratify in 1789 and Rhode Island in 1790.

Today, when Americans are asked to define freedom, they instinctively turn to the Bill of Rights and especially the First Amendment, with its guarantees of freedom of speech, the press, and religion. Yet the Bill of Rights aroused little enthusiasm on ratification and for decades was all but ignored. Not until the twentieth century would it come to be revered as an indispensable expression of American freedom. Nonetheless, the Bill of Rights subtly affected the language of liberty. Applying only to the federal government, not the states, it reinforced the idea that concentrated national power posed the greatest threat to freedom. And it contributed to the long process whereby freedom came to be discussed in the vocabulary of rights.

The CENTINEL   VOL IX

REDEUNT SATURNIA REGNA.

On the erection of the *Eleventh* PILLAR of the great National DOME, we beg leave most sincerely to felicitate " OUR DEAR COUNTRY"

Rise it will.

The foundation good—it may yet be SAVED.

The FEDERAL EDIFICE.

ELEVEN STARS, in quick succeffion rise——
ELEVEN COLUMNS ftrike our wond'ring eyes,
Soon o'er the *whole*, fhall fwell the beauteous DOME,
COLUMBIA's boaft—and FREEDOM's hallow'd home.
  Here fhall the ARTS in glorious fplendour fhine !
And AGRICULTURE give her ftores divine !
COMMERCE refin'd, difpenfe us more than gold,
And this new world, teach WISDOM to the old——
RELIGION here fhall fix her bleft abode,
Array'd in *mildnefs*, like its parent GOD !
JUSTICE and LAW, fhall endlefs PEACE maintain,
And *the* " SATURNIAN AGE," *return again.*

VOICES OF FREEDOM

From DAVID RAMSAY, *THE HISTORY OF THE AMERICAN REVOLUTION* (1789)

A member of the Continental Congress from South Carolina, David Ramsay published his history of the Revolution the year after the Constitution was ratified. In this excerpt, he lauds the principles of representative government and the right of future amendment, embodied in the state constitutions and adopted in the national one, as unique American political principles and the best ways of securing liberty.

───────────────

The world has not hitherto exhibited so fair an opportunity for promoting social happiness. It is hoped for the honor of human nature, that the result will prove the fallacy of those theories that mankind are incapable of self government. The ancients, not knowing the doctrine of representation, were apt in their public meetings to run into confusion, but in America this mode of taking the sense of the people, is so well understood, and so completely reduced to system, that its most populous states are often peaceably convened in an assembly of deputies, not too large for orderly deliberation, and yet representing the whole in equal proportion. These popular branches of legislature are miniature pictures of the community, and from their mode of election are likely to be influenced by the same interests and feelings with the people whom they represent. . . .

In no age before, and in no other country, did man ever possess an election of the kind of government, under which he would choose to live. The constituent parts of the ancient free governments were thrown together by accident. The freedom of modern European governments was, for the most part, obtained by concessions, or liberality of monarchs, or military leaders. In America alone, reason and liberty concurred in the formation of constitutions. . . . In one thing they were all perfect. They left the people in the power of altering and amending them, whenever they pleased. In this happy peculiarity they placed the science of politics on a footing with the other sciences, by opening it to improvements from experience, and the discoveries of future ages. By means of this power of amending American constitutions, the friends of mankind have fondly hoped that oppression will one day be no more.

From JAMES WINTHROP, ANTI-FEDERALIST ESSAY SIGNED "AGRIPPA" (1787)

A local official in Middlesex, Massachusetts, James Winthrop published sixteen public letters between November 1787 and February 1788 opposing ratification of the Constitution.

It is the opinion of the ablest writers on the subject, that no extensive empire can be governed upon republican principles, and that such a government will degenerate into a despotism, unless it be made up of a confederacy of smaller states, each having the full powers of internal regulation. This is precisely the principle which has hitherto preserved our freedom. No instance can be found of any free government of considerable extent which has been supported upon any other plan. Large and consolidated empires may indeed dazzle the eyes of a distant spectator with their splendor, but if examined more nearly are always found to be full of misery.... It is under such tyranny that the Spanish provinces languish, and such would be our misfortune and degradation, if we should submit to have the concerns of the whole empire managed by one empire. To promote the happiness of the people it is necessary that there should be local laws; and it is necessary that those laws should be made by the representatives of those who are immediately subject to [them]....

It is impossible for one code of laws to suit Georgia and Massachusetts. They must, therefore, legislate for themselves. Yet there is, I believe, not one point of legislation that is not surrendered in the proposed plan. Questions of every kind respecting property are determinable in a continental court, and so are all kinds of criminal causes. The continental legislature has, therefore, a right to make rules in all cases.... No rights are reserved to the citizens.... This new system is, therefore, a consolidation of all the states into one large mass, however diverse the parts may be of which it is composed....

A bill of rights ... serves to secure the minority against the usurpation and tyranny of the majority.... The experience of all mankind has proved the prevalence of a disposition to use power wantonly. It is therefore as necessary to defend an individual against the majority in a republic as against the king in a monarchy.

QUESTIONS

1. *Why does Ramsay feel that the power to amend the Constitution is so important a political innovation?*

2. *Why does Winthrop believe that a Bill of Rights is essential in the Constitution?*

3. *How do Ramsay and Winthrop differ concerning how the principle of representation operates in the United States?*

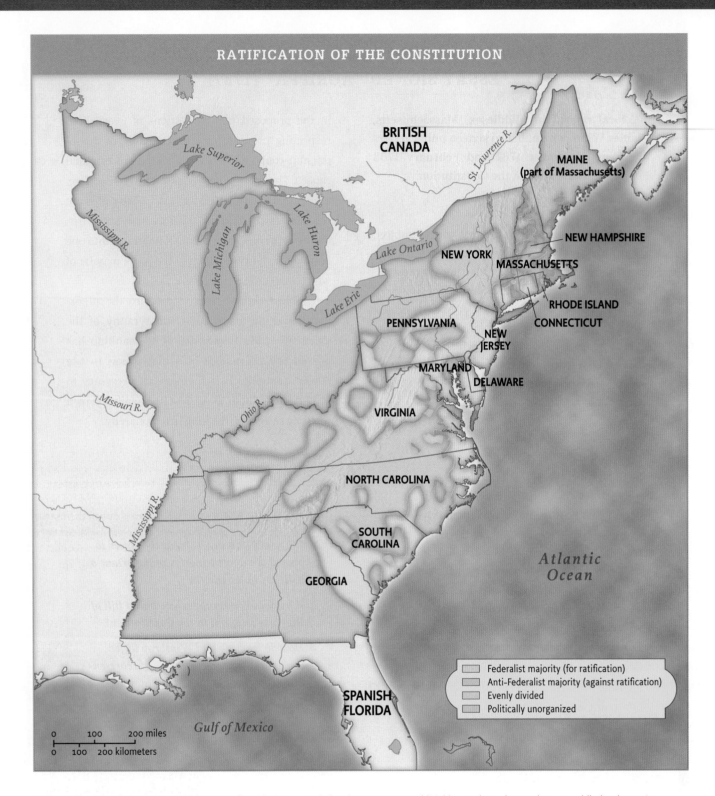

RATIFICATION OF THE CONSTITUTION

BRITISH CANADA

Lake Superior

Lake Michigan

Lake Huron

Lake Ontario

Lake Erie

St. Lawrence R.

MAINE
(part of Massachusetts)

NEW HAMPSHIRE

NEW YORK

MASSACHUSETTS

RHODE ISLAND

CONNECTICUT

PENNSYLVANIA

NEW JERSEY

MARYLAND

DELAWARE

Mississippi R.

Missouri R.

Ohio R.

VIRGINIA

NORTH CAROLINA

SOUTH CAROLINA

GEORGIA

Mississippi R.

Atlantic Ocean

SPANISH FLORIDA

Gulf of Mexico

- Federalist majority (for ratification)
- Anti-Federalist majority (against ratification)
- Evenly divided
- Politically unorganized

| 0 | 100 | 200 miles |
| 0 | 100 | 200 kilometers |

Federalists—those who supported the new Constitution—tended to be concentrated in cities and nearby rural areas, while backcountry farmers were more likely to oppose the new frame of government.

Among the most important rights were freedom of speech and the press, vital building blocks of a democratic public sphere. Once an entitlement of members of Parliament and colonial assemblies, free speech came to be seen as a basic right of citizenship. Although the legal implementation remained to be worked out, and serious infringements would occur at many points in American history, the Bill of Rights did much to establish freedom of expression as a cornerstone of the popular understanding of American freedom.

"WE THE PEOPLE"

National Identity

The colonial population had been divided by ethnicity, religion, class, and status and united largely by virtue of their allegiance to Britain. The Revolution created not only a new nation but also a new collective body, the American people, whose members were to enjoy freedom as citizens in a new political community. Since government in the United States rested on the will of the people, it was all the more important to identify who the people were.

The Constitution opens with the words "We the People," describing those who, among other things, are to possess "the Blessings of Liberty" as a birthright and pass them on to "Posterity." (Abraham Lincoln would later cite these words to argue that since the nation had been created by the people, not the states, the states could not dissolve it.) Although one might assume that the "people" of the United States included all those living within the nation's borders, the text made clear that this was not the case. The Constitution identifies three populations inhabiting the United States: Indians, treated as members of independent tribes and not part of the American body politic; "other persons"—that is, slaves; and the "people." Only the third were entitled to American freedom.

Every nation confronts the task of defining its identity. Historians have traditionally distinguished between "civic nationalism," which envisions the nation as a community open to all those devoted to its political institutions and social values, and "ethnic nationalism," which defines the nation as a community of descent based on a shared ethnic heritage, language, and culture. At first glance, the United States appears to conform to the civic model. It lacked a clear ethnic identity or long-established national boundaries—the political principles of the Revolution held Americans together. To be an American, all one had to do was commit oneself to an ideology of liberty, equality, and democracy. From the outset, however, American nationality combined both civic and ethnic definitions. For most of our history, American citizenship has been defined by blood as well as by political allegiance.

Indians in the New Nation

The early republic's policies toward Indians and African-Americans illustrate the conflicting principles that shaped American nationality. American leaders agreed that the West should not be left in Indian hands, but they disagreed about the Indians' ultimate fate. The government hoped to encourage the westward expansion of white settlement, which implied one of three things: the removal of the Indian population to lands even

> *The American people*

> *Exclusion of Indians and slaves*

A medal issued to Red Jacket, a Seneca chief, during his visit to Philadelphia (then the national capital) in 1792. It depicts George Washington offering an Indian a peace pipe. The agricultural scene in the background was intended to suggest that Indians should take up farming.

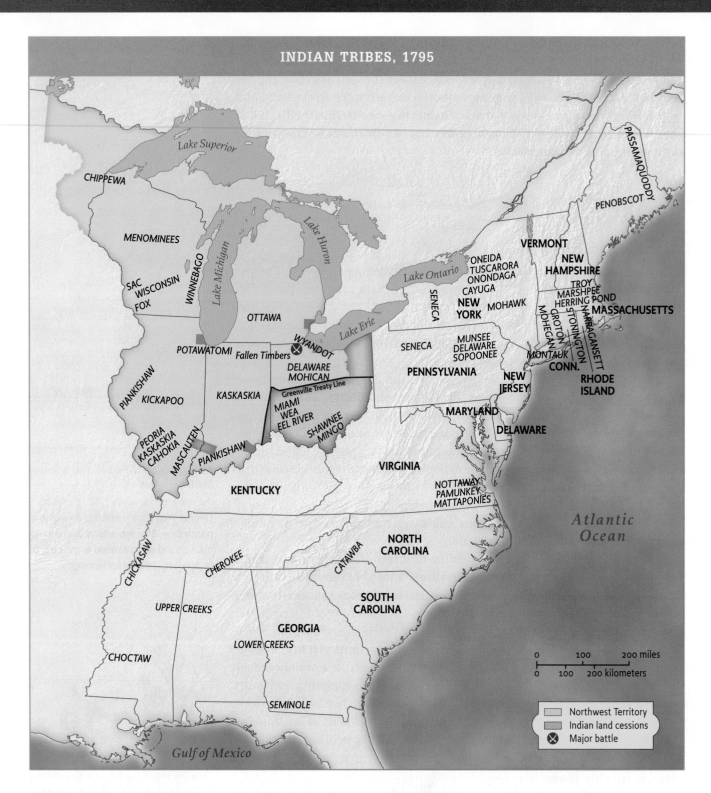

INDIAN TRIBES, 1795

CHIPPEWA

MENOMINEES

SAC
WISCONSIN
FOX

WINNEBAGO

OTTAWA

POTAWATOMI   Fallen Timbers

PIANKISHAW

KICKAPOO

KASKASKIA

PEORIA
KASKASKIA
CAHOKIA

MASCAUTEN

PIANKISHAW

WYANDOT

DELAWARE
MOHICAN

Greenville Treaty Line

MIAMI
WEA
EEL RIVER

SHAWNEE
MINGO

KENTUCKY

CHICKASAW

CHEROKEE

UPPER CREEKS

CHOCTAW

LOWER CREEKS

SEMINOLE

Gulf of Mexico

Lake Superior

Lake Michigan

Lake Huron

Lake Erie

Lake Ontario

SENECA

NEW
YORK

ONEIDA
TUSCARORA
ONONDAGA
CAYUGA

MOHAWK

SENECA

MUNSEE
DELAWARE
SOPOONEE

PENNSYLVANIA

MARYLAND

DELAWARE

VIRGINIA

NOTTAWAY
PAMUNKEY
MATTAPONIES

NORTH
CAROLINA

CATAWBA

SOUTH
CAROLINA

GEORGIA

PASSAMAQUODDY

PENOBSCOT

VERMONT

NEW
HAMPSHIRE

TROY
MARSHPEE
HERRING POND

MASSACHUSETTS

CROTON
MOHEGAN

STONINGTON

NARRAGANSETT

MONTAUK

CONN.

RHODE
ISLAND

NEW
JERSEY

Atlantic
Ocean

0   100   200 miles

0   100   200 kilometers

☐ Northwest Territory
☐ Indian land cessions
⊗ Major battle

By 1795, the Indian population had declined significantly from the early colonial era, but the area west of the Appalachian Mountains was still known as "Indian country."

farther west, their total disappearance, or their incorporation into white "civilization" with the expectation that they might one day become part of American society.

Many white Americans, probably most, deemed Indians savages unfit for citizenship. Indian tribes had no representation in the new government, and the Constitution excluded Indians "not taxed" from being counted in determining each state's number of congressmen. The treaty system gave them a unique status within the American political system. But despite this recognition of their sovereignty, treaties were essentially ways of transferring land from Indians to the federal government or the states. Often, a treaty was agreed to by only a small portion of a tribe, but the whole tribe was then forced to accept its legitimacy.

The treaty system

During Washington's administration, Secretary of War Henry Knox hoped to deal with Indians with a minimum of warfare and without undermining the new nation's honor. He recognized, he said in 1794, that American treatment of the continent's native inhabitants had been even "more destructive to the Indian" than Spain's conduct in Mexico and Peru. His conciliatory policy had mixed results. Congress forbade the transfer of Indian land without federal approval. But several states ignored this directive and continued to negotiate their own agreements.

Open warfare continued in the Ohio Valley. In 1791, Little Turtle, leader of the Miami Confederacy, inflicted a humiliating defeat on American forces led by Arthur St. Clair, the American governor of the Northwest Territory. With 630 dead, this was the costliest loss ever suffered by the United States Army at the hands of Indians. In 1794, 3,000 American troops under Anthony Wayne defeated Little Turtle's forces at the Battle of Fallen Timbers. This led directly to the **Treaty of Greenville** of 1795, in which twelve Indian tribes ceded most of Ohio and Indiana to the federal

War in the Ohio Valley

The signing of the Treaty of Greenville of 1795, painted by an unknown member of General Anthony Wayne's staff. In the treaty, a group of tribes ceded most of the area of the current states of Ohio and Indiana, along with the site that became the city of Chicago, to the United States.

The Plan of Civilization. Painted circa 1800 by an unidentified artist, this work depicts Hawkins explaining the advantages of settled agriculture as part of a plan to promote "civilization" among Native Americans. Having served in the Continental army during the War of Independence and as a senator from North Carolina, Hawkins was appointed in 1795 Superintendent of Indian Affairs for the southeastern United States. He supplied the Creeks, Cherokees, and Choctaws with agricultural training and farm implements and married a Creek woman.

government. The treaty also established the **annuity system**—yearly grants of federal money to Indian tribes that institutionalized continuing government influence in tribal affairs and gave outsiders considerable control over Indian life.

Many prominent figures, however, rejected the idea that Indians were innately inferior to white Americans. Thomas Jefferson believed that Indians merely lived at a less advanced stage of civilization. Indians could become full-fledged members of the republic by abandoning communal landholding and hunting in favor of small-scale farming. Once they "possessed property," Jefferson told one Indian group, they could "join us in our government" and, indeed, "mix your blood with ours."

To pursue the goal of assimilation, Congress in the 1790s authorized President Washington to distribute agricultural tools and livestock to Indian men and spinning wheels and looms to Indian women. To whites, the adoption of American gender norms, with men working the land and women tending to their homes, would be a crucial sign that the Indians were becoming "civilized." But the American notion of civilization required so great a transformation of Indian life that most tribes rejected it. To Indians, freedom meant retaining tribal autonomy and identity, including the ability to travel widely in search of game. "Since our acquaintance with our brother white people," declared a Mohawk speaker at a 1796 treaty council, "that which we call freedom and liberty, becomes an entire stranger to us." There was no room for Indians who desired to retain their traditional way of life in the American empire of liberty.

Tribal identity

Blacks and the Republic

By 1790, the number of African-Americans far exceeded the Indian population within the United States. The status of free blacks was somewhat indeterminate. Nowhere does the original Constitution define who in fact are citizens of the United

States. The individual states were left free to determine the boundaries of liberty. The North's **gradual emancipation** acts assumed that former slaves would remain in the country, not be colonized abroad. Northern statesmen like Hamilton, Jay, and Franklin worked for abolition, and some helped to establish schools for black children. During the era of the Revolution, free blacks enjoyed at least some of the legal rights accorded to whites, including, in most states, the right to vote. Some cast ballots in the election of delegates to conventions that ratified the Constitution. The large majority of blacks, of course, were slaves, and slavery rendered them all but invisible to those imagining the American community. Slaves, as Edmund Randolph, the nation's first attorney general, put it, were "not . . . constituent members of our society," and the language of liberty did not apply to them.

One of the era's most widely read books, ***Letters from an American Farmer***, published in France in 1782 by Hector St. John de Crèvecoeur, strikingly illustrated this process of exclusion. Born in France, Crèvecoeur had taken part in the unsuccessful defense of Quebec during the Seven Years' War. Instead of returning home, he came to New York City in 1759. As a trader and explorer, he visited most of the British mainland colonies, as well as the Ohio and Mississippi Valleys. Crèvecoeur eventually married the daughter of a prominent New York landowner and lived with his own family on a farm in Orange County. Seeking to remain neutral during the War of Independence, he suffered persecution by both patriots and the British, and eventually returned to France.

In *Letters from an American Farmer*, Crèvecoeur popularized the idea, which would become so common in the twentieth century, of the United States as a melting pot. "Here," he wrote, "individuals of all nations are melted into a new one." The American left behind "all his ancient prejudices and manners [and received] new ones from the new mode of life he has embraced." Crèvecoeur was well aware of what he called "the horrors of slavery." But when he posed the famous question, "What then is the American, this new man?" he answered, "A mixture of English, Scotch, Irish, French, Dutch, Germans, and Swedes. . . . He is either a European, or the descendant of a European." This at a time when fully one-fifth of the population (the highest proportion in U.S. history) consisted of Africans and their descendants.

Like Crèvecoeur, many white Americans excluded blacks from their conception of the American people. The Constitution empowered Congress to create a uniform system by which immigrants became citizens, and the Naturalization Act of 1790 offered the first legislative definition of American nationality. With no debate, Congress restricted the process of becoming a citizen from abroad to "free white persons."

The law initiated a policy that some historians, with only partial accuracy, call **open immigration**. For Europeans, the process was indeed open. Only in the last quarter of the nineteenth century were groups of whites, beginning with prostitutes, convicted felons, lunatics, and persons likely to become a "public

STATE	TOTAL POPULATION	SLAVES	FREE BLACKS
New England:			
New Hampshire	141,899	158	630
Vermont*	85,341	0	271
Massachusetts	378,556	0	5,369
Connecticut	237,655	2,764	2,771
Rhode Island	69,112	948	3,484
Maine**	96,643	0	536
Middle States:			
New York	340,241	21,324	4,682
New Jersey	184,139	11,423	2,762
Pennsylvania	433,611	3,737	6,531
South:			
Delaware	59,096	8,887	3,899
Maryland	319,728	103,036	8,043
Virginia	747,610	292,627	12,866
North Carolina	395,005	100,572	5,041
South Carolina	249,073	107,094	1,801
Georgia	82,548	29,264	398
Kentucky*	73,677	12,430	114
Tennessee*	35,691	3,417	361
Total	3,929,625	697,681	59,559

TABLE 7.1 Total Population and Black Population of the United States, 1790

*Vermont, Kentucky, and Tennessee were territories that had not yet been admitted as states.
**Maine was part of Massachusetts in 1790.

Crèvecoeur

This painting by artist Gilbert Stuart, best known for his portraits of George Washington, is thought to depict Hercules, Washington's slave and the chief cook at his estate at Mount Vernon, Virginia. As president, Washington brought Hercules to Philadelphia, then the nation's capital, in violation of Pennsylvania's 1780 emancipation law, which freed any slave who resided in the state for six months. In 1797, as Washington and his family were preparing to return home at the end of his term in office, Hercules escaped. Washington died two years later; his will freed his slaves, including Hercules.

Benjamin Banneker

Jefferson's vision of American society

charge," barred from entering the country. For the first century of the republic, virtually the only white persons in the entire world ineligible to claim American citizenship were those unwilling to renounce hereditary titles of nobility, as required in an act of 1795. And yet, the word "white" in the Naturalization Act excluded a large majority of the world's population from emigrating to the "asylum for mankind" and partaking in the blessings of American freedom. For eighty years, no non-white immigrant could become a naturalized citizen. Africans were allowed to do so in 1870, but not until the 1940s did persons of Asian origin become eligible. (Native Americans were granted American citizenship in 1924.)

Jefferson, Slavery, and Race

Man's liberty, John Locke had written, flowed from "his having reason." To deny liberty to those who were not considered rational beings did not seem to be a contradiction. White Americans increasingly viewed blacks as permanently deficient in the qualities that made freedom possible—the capacity for self-control, reason, and devotion to the larger community. These were the characteristics that Jefferson, in a famous comparison of the races in his book **Notes on the State of Virginia**, published in 1785, claimed blacks lacked, partly due to natural incapacity and partly because the bitter experience of slavery had (quite understandably, he felt) rendered them disloyal to the nation. Jefferson was reluctant to "degrade a whole race of men from the rank in the scale of beings which their Creator may perhaps have given them." He therefore voiced the idea "as a suspicion only" that blacks "are inferior to the whites in the endowments both of body and mind." Yet this "unfortunate" circumstance, he went on, "is a powerful obstacle to the emancipation of these people."

Jefferson was obsessed with the connection between heredity and environment, race and intelligence. His belief that individuals' abilities and achievements are shaped by social conditions inclined him to hope that no group was fixed permanently in a status of inferiority. He applied this principle, as has been noted, to Indians, whom he believed naturally the equal of whites in intelligence. In the case of blacks, however, he could not avoid the "suspicion" that nature had permanently deprived them of the qualities that made republican citizenship possible. Benjamin Banneker, a free African-American from Maryland who had taught himself the principles of mathematics, sent Jefferson a copy of an astronomical almanac he had published, along with a plea for the abolition of slavery. Jefferson replied, "Nobody wishes more than I do to see such proofs as you exhibit, that nature has given to our black brethren, talents equal to the other colors of men." To his friend Joel Barlow, however, Jefferson suggested that a white person must have helped Banneker with his calculations.

"Nothing is more certainly written in the book of fate," wrote Jefferson, "than that these people are to be free." Yet he felt that America should have a homogeneous citizenry with common experiences, values, and inborn abilities. Black Americans, Jefferson affirmed, should eventually enjoy the natural rights enumerated in the Declaration of Independence, but in Africa or the Caribbean, not in the United States. He foresaw Indians merging with whites into a single people, but he was horrified by the idea of miscegenation between blacks and whites. Unlike Indians, blacks, he believed, were unfit for economic independence and political

RUN away from the subscriber in *Albemarle*, a Mulatto slave called *Sandy*, about 35 years of age, his stature is rather low, inclining to corpulence, and his complexion light; he is a shoemaker by trade, in which he uses his left hand principally, can do coarse carpenters work, and is something of a horse jockey; he is greatly addicted to drink, and when drunk is insolent and disorderly, in his conversation he swears much, and in his behaviour is artful and knavish. He took with him a white horse, much scarred with traces, of which it is expected he will endeavour to dispose; he also carried his shoemakers tools, and will probably endeavour to get employment that way. Whoever conveys the said slave to me, in *Albemarle*, shall have 40 s. reward, if taken up within the county, 4 l. if elsewhere within the colony, and 10 l. if in any other colony, from
THOMAS JEFFERSON.

Thomas Jefferson, future author of the Declaration of Independence and in private a sharp critic of slavery, placed this advertisement in a Virginia newspaper in 1769, seeking the return of a runaway slave. Sandy was in fact recaptured, and Jefferson sold him in 1773.

self-government. Freeing the slaves without removing them from the country would endanger the nation's freedom.

Jefferson reflected the divided mind of his generation. Some prominent Virginians assumed that blacks could become part of the American nation. Edward Coles, an early governor of Illinois, brought his slaves from Virginia, freed them, and settled them on farms. Washington, who died in 1799, provided in his will that his 277 slaves would become free after the death of his wife, Martha. (Feeling uncomfortable living among men and women who looked forward to her death, she emancipated them the following year.) Jefferson thought of himself as a humane owner. Believing the slave trade immoral, Jefferson tried to avoid selling slaves to pay off his mounting debts. But his will provided for the freedom of only five, all relatives of his slave Sally Hemings, with whom he appears to have fathered one or more children. When he died in 1826, Jefferson owed so much money that his property, including the majority of his more than 200 slaves, was sold at auction, thus destroying the slave community he had tried to keep intact.

Jefferson as slaveholder

Principles of Freedom

Even as the decline of apprenticeship and indentured servitude narrowed the gradations of freedom among the white population, the Revolution widened the divide between free Americans and those who remained in slavery. Race, one among many kinds of legal and social inequality in colonial America, now emerged as a convenient justification for the existence of slavery in a land that claimed to be committed to freedom. Blacks' "natural faculties," Alexander Hamilton noted in 1779, were "probably as good as ours." But the existence of slavery, he added, "makes us fancy many things that are founded neither in reason nor experience."

Emergence of race

"We the people" increasingly meant only white Americans. "Principles of freedom, which embrace only half mankind, are only half systems," declared the anonymous author of a Fourth of July speech in Hartford, Connecticut, in 1800. "Declaration of Independence," he wondered, "where art thou now?" The answer came from a Richmond newspaper: "Tell us not of principles. Those principles have been annihilated by the existence of slavery among us."

SUGGESTED READING

BOOKS

- Amar, Akhil Reed. *Bill of Rights: Creation and Reconstruction* (1998). Presents the history of the Bill of Rights from its ratification through the Reconstruction era.

- Berkin, Carol. *A Brilliant Solution: Inventing the American Constitution* (2002). A lively account of the proceedings of the Constitutional Convention.

- Cornell, Saul. *The Other Founders: Anti-Federalism and the Dissenting Tradition in America, 1788–1828* (1999). A careful examination of the ideas of those who opposed ratification of the Constitution.

- Dowd, Gregory E. *A Spirited Resistance: The North American Indian Struggle for Unity, 1745–1815* (1992). Contains an important discussion of the place of Indians in the new American nation.

- Holton, Woody. *Unruly Americans and the Origins of the Constitution* (2007). Argues that the political activities of ordinary Americans helped to shape the Constitution.

- Kettner, James T. *The Development of American Citizenship, 1608–1870* (1978). Traces the development of the definition of American citizenship from early colonization to the aftermath of the Civil War.

- Levy, Leonard. *The Establishment Clause: Religion and the First Amendment* (1994). A historical account of one of the key components of the Bill of Rights.

- MacLeod, Duncan J. *Slavery, Race, and the American Revolution* (1974). A British scholar's interpretation of the role of race and slavery in the revolutionary era.

- Maier, Pauline. *Ratification: The People Debate the Constitution, 1787–1788* (2010). The most complete account of the state-by-state debates over ratification of the Constitution.

- McMillin, James A. *The Final Victims: Foreign Slave Trade to North America, 1783–1810* (2004). A study of the last phase of the American slave trade, as made possible by the new Constitution.

- Nash, Gary. *The Forgotten Fifth: African Americans in the Age of Revolution* (2006). A comprehensive survey of the Revolution's impact on blacks, slave and free.

- Nedelsky, Jennifer. *Private Property and the Limits of American Constitutionalism* (1990). Analyzes how the protection of private property shaped the writing of the Constitution.

- Rakove, Jack. *Original Meanings: Politics and Ideas in the Making of the Constitution* (1996). An influential interpretation of the ideas that went into the drafting of the Constitution.

- Richards, Leonard L. *Shays's Rebellion: The American Revolution's Final Battle* (2002). The most recent study of the uprising that helped to produce the Constitution.

- Wood, Gordon S. *The Creation of the American Republic, 1776–1789* (1969). Presents the evolution of American political ideas and institutions from the Declaration of Independence to the ratification of the Constitution.

WEBSITES

- Creating the United States: www.loc.gov/exhibits/creating-the-united-states

- Explore the Constitution: http://constitutioncenter.org

- The Presidency: http://americanhistory.si.edu/presidency/home.html

CHAPTER REVIEW AND ONLINE RESOURCES

REVIEW QUESTIONS

1. How did the limited central government created by the Articles of Confederation reflect the issues behind the Revolution and fears for individual liberties?

2. What were the ideas and motivations that pushed Americans to expand west?

3. What events and ideas led to the belief in 1786 and 1787 that the Articles of Confederation were not working well?

4. The Constitution has been described as a "bundle of compromises." Which compromises were the most significant in shaping the direction of the new nation and why?

5. What were the major arguments in support of the Constitution given by the Federalists?

6. What were the major arguments against the Constitution put forth by the Anti-Federalists?

7. How accurate was Hector St. John de Crèvecoeur's description of America as a melting pot?

KEY TERMS

Articles of Confederation (p. 240)

Ordinance of 1784 (p. 243)

Ordinance of 1785 (p. 243)

Northwest Ordinance of 1787 (p. 245)

empire of liberty (p. 245)

Shays's Rebellion (p. 246)

Constitutional Convention (pp. 247)

Virginia Plan (p. 248)

New Jersey Plan (p. 249)

federalism (p. 250)

division of powers (p. 250)

checks and balances (p. 250)

separation of powers (p. 250)

three-fifths clause (p. 251)

The Federalist (p. 254)

Anti-Federalists (p. 256)

Bill of Rights (p. 256)

Treaty of Greenville (p. 265)

annuity system (p. 266)

gradual emancipation (p. 267)

Letters from an American Farmer (p. 267)

open immigration (p. 267)

Notes on the State of Virginia (p. 268)

Go to 🐰 INQUIZITIVE

To see what you know—and learn what you've missed—with personalized feedback along the way.

Visit the *Give Me Liberty!* **Student Site** for primary source documents and images, interactive maps, author videos featuring Eric Foner, and more.

CHAPTER 8

SECURING THE REPUBLIC

★

1791–1815

UNDER ☆ MY ☆ ☆ WINGS ☆ ☆ EVERY ☆ ☆ THING ☆ ☆ PROSPERS ☆

On April 30, 1789, in New York City, the nation's temporary capital, George Washington became the first president under the new Constitution. All sixty-nine electors had awarded him their votes. Dressed in a plain suit of "superfine American broad cloth" rather than European finery, Washington took the oath of office on the balcony of Federal Hall before a large crowd that reacted with "loud and repeated shouts" of approval. He then retreated inside to deliver his inaugural address before members of Congress and other dignitaries.

Washington's speech expressed the revolutionary generation's conviction that it had embarked on an experiment of enormous historical importance, whose outcome was by no means certain. "The preservation of the sacred fire of liberty and the destiny of the republican model of government," Washington proclaimed, depended on the success of the American experiment in self-government. Most Americans seemed to agree that freedom was the special genius of American institutions. In a resolution congratulating Washington on his inauguration, the House of Representatives observed that he had been chosen by "the freest people on the face of the earth." When the time came to issue the nation's first coins, Congress directed that they bear the image not of the head of state (as would be the case in a monarchy) but "an impression emblematic of liberty," with the word itself prominently displayed.

American leaders believed that the success of the new government depended, above all, on maintaining political harmony. They were especially anxious to avoid the emergence of organized political parties, which had already appeared in several states. Parties were considered divisive and disloyal. "They serve to organize faction," Washington would later declare, and to substitute the aims of "a small but artful" minority for the "will of the nation." The Constitution makes no mention of political parties, and the original method of electing the president assumes that candidates will run as individuals, not on a party ticket (otherwise, the second-place finisher would not have become vice president). Nonetheless, national political parties quickly arose. Originating in Congress, they soon spread to the general populace. Instead of harmony, the 1790s became, in the words of one historian, an "age of passion," with each party questioning the loyalty of the other and lambasting its opponent in the most extreme terms. Political rhetoric became inflamed because the stakes seemed so high—nothing less than the legacy of the Revolution, the new nation's future, and the survival of American freedom.

POLITICS IN AN AGE OF PASSION

President Washington provided a much-needed symbol of national unity. Having retired to private life after the War of Independence (despite some army officers' suggestion that he set himself up as a dictator), he was a model of self-sacrificing republican virtue. His vice president, John Adams, was widely respected as one of the main leaders in the drive for independence. Washington brought into his cabinet some of the new nation's most prominent political leaders, including Thomas

FOCUS QUESTIONS

What issues made the politics of the 1790s so divisive? –p. 273

How did competing views of freedom and global events promote the political divisions of the 1790s? –p. 284

What were the achievements and failures of Jefferson's presidency? –p. 290

What were the causes and significant results of the War of 1812? –p. 297

New Orleans in 1803, at the time of the Louisiana Purchase. The painting shows a view of the city from a nearby plantation. The town houses of merchants and plantation owners line the broad promenade along the waterfront. At the lower center, a slave goes about his work. An eagle holds aloft a banner that suggests the heady optimism of the young republic: Under My Wings Every Thing Prospers.

Jefferson as secretary of state and Alexander Hamilton to head the Treasury Department. He also appointed a Supreme Court of six members, headed by John Jay of New York. But harmonious government proved short-lived.

Hamilton's Program

Political divisions first surfaced over the financial plan developed by Secretary of the Treasury Hamilton in 1790 and 1791. Hamilton's immediate aims were to establish the nation's financial stability, bring to the government's support the country's most powerful financial interests, and encourage economic development. His long-term goal was to make the United States a major commercial and military power. Hamilton's model was Great Britain. The goal of national greatness, he believed, could never be realized if the government suffered from the same weaknesses as under the Articles of Confederation.

Hamilton's program had five parts. The first step was to establish the new nation's credit-worthiness—that is, to create conditions under which persons would loan money to the government by purchasing its bonds, confident that they would be repaid. Hamilton proposed that the federal government assume responsibility for paying off at its full face value the national debt inherited from the War of Independence, as well as outstanding debts of the states. Second, he called for the creation of a new national debt. The old debts would be replaced by new interest-bearing bonds issued to the government's creditors. This would give men of economic substance a stake in promoting the new nation's stability, since the stronger and more economically secure the federal government, the more likely it would be to pay its debts.

The third part of Hamilton's program called for the creation of a **Bank of the United States**, modeled on the Bank of England, to serve as the nation's main financial agent. A private corporation rather than a branch of the government, it would hold public funds, issue bank notes that would serve as currency, and make loans to the government when necessary, all the while returning a tidy profit to its stockholders. Fourth, to raise revenue, Hamilton proposed a tax on producers of whiskey. Finally, in a Report on Manufactures delivered to Congress in December 1791, Hamilton called for the imposition of a tariff (a tax on imported foreign goods) and government subsidies to encourage the development of factories that could manufacture products currently purchased from abroad. Privately, Hamilton promoted an unsuccessful effort to build an industrial city at present-day Paterson, New Jersey. He also proposed the creation of a national army to deal with uprisings like Shays's Rebellion.

The Emergence of Opposition

Hamilton's vision of a powerful commercial republic won strong support from American financiers, manufacturers, and merchants. But it alarmed those who believed the new nation's destiny lay in charting a different path of development. Hamilton's plans hinged on close ties with Britain, America's main trading partner. To James Madison and Thomas Jefferson, the future lay in westward expansion, not connections with Europe. They had little desire to promote manufacturing or urban growth or to see economic policy shaped in the interests of bankers and business leaders. Their goal was a republic of independent farmers marketing grain, tobacco, and other products freely to the entire world. Free trade, they believed, not a system of government favoritism through tariffs and subsidies, would promote American prosperity while fostering greater social equality. Jefferson and Madison quickly concluded that the greatest threat to American freedom lay in the alliance of a powerful central government with an emerging class of commercial capitalists, such as Hamilton appeared to envision.

To Jefferson, Hamilton's system "flowed from principles adverse to liberty, and was calculated to undermine and demolish the republic." Hamilton's plans for a standing army seemed to his critics a bold threat to freedom. The national bank and assumption of state debts, they feared, would introduce into American politics the same corruption that had undermined British liberty, and enrich those already wealthy at the expense of ordinary Americans. During the 1780s, speculators had bought up at great discounts (often only a few cents on the dollar) government bonds and paper notes that had been used to pay those who fought in the Revolution or supplied the army. Under Hamilton's plan, speculators would reap a windfall by being paid at face value while the original holders received nothing. Because transportation was so poor, moreover, many backcountry farmers were used to distilling their grain harvest into whiskey, which could then be carried more easily to market. Hamilton's whiskey tax seemed to single them out unfairly in order to enrich bondholders.

The Jefferson–Hamilton Bargain

At first, opposition to Hamilton's program arose almost entirely from the South, the region that had the least interest in manufacturing development and the least diversified economy. It also had fewer holders of federal bonds than the Middle States and New England. (Virginia had pretty much paid off its war debt; it did not see why it should be taxed to benefit states like Massachusetts that had failed to do so.) Hamilton insisted that all his plans were authorized by the Constitution's ambiguous clause empowering Congress to enact laws for the "general welfare." As a result, many southerners who had supported the new Constitution now became "strict constructionists," who insisted that the federal government could only exercise powers specifically listed in the document. Jefferson, for example, believed the new national bank unconstitutional, since the right of Congress to create a bank was not mentioned in the Constitution.

Opposition in Congress threatened the enactment of Hamilton's plans. Behind-the-scenes negotiations followed. They culminated at a famous dinner in 1790 at which Jefferson brokered an agreement whereby southerners accepted Hamilton's fiscal program (with the exception of subsidies to manufacturers) in exchange for the establishment of the permanent national capital on the Potomac River between Maryland and Virginia. Southerners hoped that the location would enhance their own power in the government while removing it from the influence of the northern financiers and merchants with whom Hamilton seemed to be allied. Major Pierre Charles L'Enfant, a French-born veteran of the War of Independence, designed a grandiose plan for the "federal city" modeled on the great urban centers of Europe, with wide boulevards, parks, and fountains. The job of surveying was done, in

An early American coin, bearing an image of liberty and the word itself, as directed by Congress in a 1792 law. The first U.S. coin to feature a real person rather than an idealized image of liberty was the Lincoln penny, issued in 1909 for the centennial of his birth.

Liberty and Washington, painted by an unknown artist around 1800, depicts a female figure of liberty placing a wreath on a bust of the first president. She carries an American flag and stands on a royal crown, which has been thrown to the ground. In the background is a liberty cap. Washington had died in 1799 and was now immortalized as a symbol of freedom, independence, and national pride.

The prominent Connecticut artist Amos Doolittle created this engraving, *A Display of the United States of America*, in 1794, during George Washington's second term as president. Washington is at the center with the motto "The protector of his country and the supporter of the rights of mankind." He is surrounded by the seals of the original thirteen states, plus the seal of Vermont in the lower right corner. The seals contain various images of commerce and liberty.

Edmond Genet

Jay's Treaty

part, by Benjamin Banneker, the free African-American scientist mentioned in the previous chapter. When it came to constructing public buildings in the nation's new capital, most of the labor was done by slaves.

The Impact of the French Revolution

Political divisions began over Hamilton's fiscal program, but they deepened in response to events in Europe. When the French Revolution began in 1789, nearly all Americans welcomed it, inspired in part by the example of their own rebellion. John Marshall later recalled, "I sincerely believed human liberty to depend in a great measure on the success of the French Revolution." But in 1793, the Revolution took a more radical turn with the execution of King Louis XVI along with numerous aristocrats and other foes of the new government, and war broke out between France and Great Britain.

Events in France became a source of bitter conflict in America. Jefferson and his followers believed that despite its excesses the Revolution marked a historic victory for the idea of popular self-government, which must be defended at all costs. Enthusiasm for France inspired a rebirth of symbols of liberty. Liberty poles and caps reappeared on the streets of American towns and cities. To Washington, Hamilton, and their supporters, however, the Revolution raised the specter of anarchy. America, they believed, had no choice but to draw closer to Britain.

American leaders feared being divided into parties "swayed by rival European powers," in the words of John Quincy Adams. But the rivalry between Britain and France did much to shape early American politics. The "permanent" alliance between France and the United States, which dated to 1778, complicated the situation. No one advocated that the United States should become involved in the European war, and Washington in April 1793 issued a proclamation of American neutrality. But that spring the French Revolution's American admirers organized tumultuous welcomes for Edmond Genet, a French envoy seeking to arouse support for his beleaguered government. When Genet began commissioning American ships to attack British vessels under the French flag, the Washington administration asked for his recall. (Deeming the situation in France too dangerous, he decided to remain in America and married the daughter of George Clinton, the governor of New York.)

Meanwhile, the British seized hundreds of American ships trading with the French West Indies and resumed the hated practice of **impressment**—kidnapping sailors, including American citizens of British origin, to serve in their navy. Sent to London to present objections, while still serving as chief justice, John Jay negotiated an agreement in 1794 that produced the greatest public controversy of Washington's presidency. **Jay's Treaty** contained no

British concessions on impressment or the rights of American shipping. Britain did agree to abandon outposts on the western frontier, which it was supposed to have done in 1783. In return, the United States guaranteed favored treatment to British imported goods. In effect, the treaty canceled the American-French alliance and recognized British economic and naval supremacy as unavoidable facts of life. Critics of the administration charged that it aligned the United States with monarchical Britain in its conflict with republican France. Ultimately, Jay's Treaty sharpened political divisions in the United States and led directly to the formation of an organized opposition party.

Political Parties

By the mid-1790s, two increasingly coherent parties had appeared in Congress, calling themselves **Federalists and Republicans**. (The latter had no connection with today's Republican Party, which was founded in the 1850s.) Both parties laid claim to the language of liberty, and each accused its opponent of engaging in a conspiracy to destroy it.

The Federalists, supporters of the Washington administration, favored Hamilton's economic program and close ties with Britain. Prosperous merchants, farmers, lawyers, and established political leaders (especially outside the South) tended to support the Federalists. Their outlook was generally elitist, reflecting the traditional eighteenth-century view of society as a fixed hierarchy and of public office as reserved for men of economic substance—the

Philadelphia, Auguft, 1793.

ALL able bodied feamen who are willing to engage in the caufe of Liberty, and in the fervice of the French Republic, will pleafe to apply to the French Conful, at No. 132, North Second-ftreet.

Particular attention will be paid to the generous and intrepid natives of Ireland, who, it is prefumed, will act like thofe warlike troops from that oppreffed country, who took refuge in France about a century ago, and performed prodigies of valor under the old government of that country.

Thefe, and volunteers from any other country, will be received into prefent pay, and comfortable accommodations.

N. B. The Republic has, at this prefent time, in her fervice, officers and foldiers from every civilized country in Europe, and natives of America, who, in imitation of the heroes from France in the American revolution are a glory to themfelves, and an honour to the country which gave them birth.

A recruiting poster seeking "able bodied seamen" willing to volunteer to fight for revolutionary France and "the cause of Liberty," issued in Philadelphia by Edmond Genet, a French envoy. Genet thought Irish immigrants in the United States would be especially willing to serve France in its war with Great Britain.

Infant Liberty Nursed by Mother Mob, a Federalist cartoon from 1807, illustrates the party's fear that the spirit of liberty was degenerating into anarchy. In the background, a mob assaults a building, while in the foreground a pile of books burns.

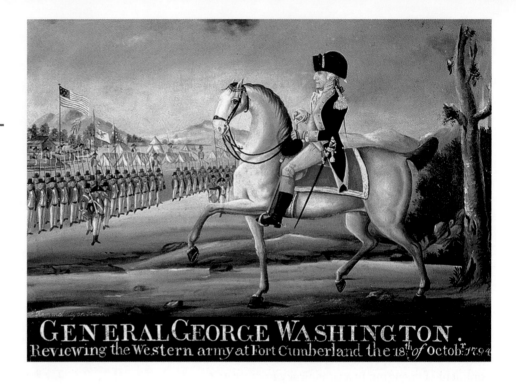

A 1794 painting by the Baltimore artist and sign painter Frederick Kemmelmeyer depicting President George Washington as commander-in-chief of the army dispatched to put down the Whiskey Rebellion.

GENERAL GEORGE WASHINGTON.
Reviewing the Western army at Fort Cumberland the 18th of octobr 1794

"rich, the able, and the well-born," as Hamilton put it. Freedom, Federalists insisted, did not mean the right to stand up in opposition to the government. Federalists feared that the "spirit of liberty" unleashed by the American Revolution was degenerating into anarchy and "licentiousness." When the New York Federalist leader Rufus King wrote an essay on the "words . . . with wrong meaning" that had "done great harm" to American society, his first example was "Liberty."

The Whiskey Rebellion

The Federalists may have been the only major party in American history forthrightly to proclaim democracy and freedom dangerous in the hands of ordinary citizens. The **Whiskey Rebellion** of 1794, which broke out when backcountry Pennsylvania farmers sought to block collection of the new tax on distilled spirits, reinforced this conviction. The "rebels" invoked the symbols of 1776, displaying liberty poles and banners reading "Liberty or Death." "The citizens of the western country," one group wrote to the president, "consider [the tax] as repugnant to liberty, [and] an invasion of those privileges which the revolution bestowed upon them." But Washington dispatched 13,000 militiamen to western Pennsylvania (a larger force than he had commanded during the Revolution). He accompanied them part of the way to the scene of the disturbances, the only time in American history that the president has actually commanded an army in the field. The "rebels" offered no resistance. His vigorous response, Washington wrote, was motivated in part by concern for "the impression" the restoration of public order "will make on others"—the "others" being Europeans who did not believe the American experiment in self-government could survive.

Venerate the Plough, a medal of the Philadelphia Society for the Promotion of Agriculture, 1786. Americans like Jefferson and Madison believed that farmers were the most virtuous citizens and therefore agriculture must remain the foundation of American life.

VENERATE THE PLOUGH

The Republican Party

Republicans, led by Madison and Jefferson, were more sympathetic to France than the Federalists and had more faith in democratic self-government. They drew their support from an unusual alliance of wealthy southern planters and ordinary farmers throughout the country. Enthusiasm for the French Revolution increasingly drew urban artisans into Republican ranks as well. Republicans preferred what a New Hampshire editor called the "boisterous sea of liberty" to the "calm of despotism." They were far more critical than the Federalists of social and economic inequality, and more accepting of broad democratic participation as essential to freedom.

> *The "boisterous sea of liberty"*

Each emerging party considered itself the representative of the nation and the other an illegitimate "faction." As early as 1792, Madison composed an imaginary dialogue between spokesmen for the two groups. The Federalist described ordinary people as "stupid, suspicious, licentious" and accused the Republican of being "an accomplice of atheism and anarchy." The latter called the Federalist an opponent of liberty and "an idolater of tyranny."

In real life, too, political language became more and more heated. Federalists denounced Republicans as French agents, anarchists, and traitors. Republicans called their opponents monarchists intent on transforming the new national government into a corrupt, British-style aristocracy. Each charged the other with betraying the principles of the War of Independence and of American freedom. Washington himself received mounting abuse. When he left office, a Republican newspaper declared that his name had become synonymous with "political iniquity" and "legalized corruption." One contemporary complained that the American press, "one of the great safeguards of free government," had become "the most scurrilous in the civilized world."

An Expanding Public Sphere

The debates of the 1790s produced not only one of the most intense periods of partisan warfare in American history but also an enduring expansion of the public sphere, and with it the democratic content of American freedom. More and more citizens attended political meetings and became avid readers of pamphlets and newspapers. The establishment of nearly 1,000 post offices made possible the wider circulation of personal letters and printed materials. The era witnessed the rapid growth of the American press—the number of newspapers rose from around 100 to 260 during the 1790s, and reached nearly 400 by 1810.

Hundreds of "obscure men" wrote pamphlets and newspaper essays and formed political organizations. The decade's democratic ferment was reflected in writings like *The Key of Liberty* by William Manning, a self-educated Massachusetts

A print shop in the early republic. The increasing number of newspapers played a major role in the expansion of the public sphere.

farmer who had fought at the battle of Concord that began the War of Independence. Although not published until many years later, Manning's work, addressed to "friends to liberty and free government," reflected the era's popular political thought. The most important division in society, Manning declared, was between the "few" and the "many." He called for the latter to form a national political association to prevent the "few" from destroying "free government" and "tyrannizing over" the people.

The Democratic-Republican Societies

Inspired by the Jacobin clubs of Paris, supporters of the French Revolution and critics of the Washington administration in 1793 and 1794 formed nearly fifty **Democratic-Republican societies**. The Republican press publicized their meetings, replete with toasts to French and American liberty. The declaration of the Democratic Society of Addison County, Vermont, was typical: "That all men are naturally free, and possess equal rights. That all legitimate government originates in the voluntary social compact of the people."

Federalists saw the societies as another example of how liberty was getting out of hand. The government, not "self-created societies," declared the president, was the authentic voice of the American people. Forced to justify their existence, the societies developed a defense of the right of the people to debate political issues and organize to affect public policy. To the societies, "free inquiry" and "free communication" formed the first line of defense of "the unalienable rights of free men." Political liberty meant not simply voting at elections but constant involvement in public affairs. "We make no apology for thus associating ourselves," declared the Addison County society. "Political freedom" included the right to "exercise watchfulness and inspection, upon the conduct of public officers." Blamed by Federalists for helping to inspire the Whiskey Rebellion, the societies disappeared by the end of 1795. But much of their organization and outlook was absorbed into the emerging Republican Party. They helped to legitimize the right of "any portion of the people," regardless of station in life, to express political opinions and take an active role in public life.

The Republicans also gained support from immigrants from the British Isles, where war with France inspired a severe crackdown on dissent. Thomas Paine had returned to Britain in 1787. Five years later, after publishing *The Rights of Man*, a defense of the French Revolution and a stirring call for democratic change at home, he was forced to flee to France one step ahead of the law. But his writings inspired the emergence of a mass movement for political and social change, which authorities brutally suppressed.

The Rights of Women

The democratic ferment of the 1790s inspired renewed discussion about women's rights. In 1792, Mary Wollstonecraft published in England her extraordinary pamphlet, *A Vindication of the Rights of Woman*. Inspired by Paine's *Rights of Man*, she asserted that the "rights of humanity" should not be "confined to the male

An engraving from *The Lady's Magazine and Repository of Entertaining Knowledge*, published in Philadelphia in 1792. A woman identified as the "Genius of the Ladies Magazine" kneels before Liberty, presenting a petition for the "Rights of Women." In the foreground are symbols of the arts, science, and literature—knowledge that should be available to women as well as men.

Mary Wollstonecraft, author of the pioneering work *A Vindication of the Rights of Woman*, in a 1797 portrait.

line." Wollstonecraft did not directly challenge traditional gender roles. Her call for greater access to education and to paid employment for women rested on the idea that this would enable single women to support themselves and married women to perform more capably as wives and mothers. But she did "drop a hint," as she put it, that women "ought to have representation" in government. Within two years, American editions of Wollstonecraft's work had appeared, along with pamphlets defending and attacking her arguments. A short-lived women's rights magazine was published in 1795 in New York City. For generations, Wollstonecraft's writings would remain an inspiration to women seeking greater rights. "She is alive and active," the British novelist Virginia Woolf wrote in the 1920s, "she argues and experiments, we hear her voice and trace her influence even now among the living."

The expansion of the public sphere offered new opportunities to women. Increasing numbers began expressing their thoughts in print. Hannah Adams of Massachusetts became the first American woman to support herself as an author, publishing works on religious history and the history of New England. Other women took part in political discussions, read newspapers, and listened to orations, even though outside of New Jersey none could vote.

Judith Sargent Murray, one of the era's most accomplished American women, wrote essays for the *Massachusetts Magazine* under the pen name "The Gleaner." Murray's father, a prosperous Massachusetts merchant, had taken an enlightened view of his daughter's education. Although Judith could not attend college because of her sex, she studied alongside her brother with a tutor preparing the young man for admission to Harvard. In her essay "On the Equality of the Sexes," written in 1779 and published in 1790, Murray insisted that women had as much right as men to exercise all their talents and should be allowed equal educational opportunities to enable them to do so. Women's apparent mental inferiority to men, she insisted, simply reflected the fact that they had been denied "the opportunity of acquiring knowledge." "The idea of the incapability of women," she maintained, was "totally inadmissable in this enlightened age."

Women and the Republic

Were women part of the new body politic? Until after the Civil War, the word "male" did not appear in the Constitution. Women were counted fully in determining representation in Congress, and there was nothing explicitly limiting the rights outlined in the Constitution to men. A few contributors to the pamphlet debate on women's rights admitted that, according to the logic of democracy, women ought to have a voice in government. The Constitution's use of the word "he" to describe officeholders, however, reflected an assumption so widespread that it scarcely required explicit defense: politics was a realm for men. The time had not yet arrived for a broad assault on gender inequality. But like the activities of

Wollstonecraft's A Vindication of the Rights of Woman

An 1804 embroidery by sixteen-year-old Mary Green of Worcester, Massachusetts, based on *Liberty in the Form of the Goddess of Youth*, a widely reprinted engraving linking liberty and nationhood. Atop the American flag sits a liberty cap. At the goddess's feet lie symbols of Old World monarchy, including the key to the Bastille (the Paris prison stormed by a crowd at the outset of the French Revolution) and a broken royal scepter.

VOICES OF FREEDOM

From JUDITH SARGENT MURRAY, "ON THE EQUALITY OF THE SEXES" (1790)

A prominent writer of plays, novels, and poetry, Judith Sargent Murray of Massachusetts was one of the first women to demand equal educational opportunities for women.

Is it upon mature consideration we adopt the idea, that nature is thus partial in her distributions? Is it indeed a fact, that she hath yielded to one half of the human species so unquestionable a mental superiority? I know that to both sexes elevated understandings, and the reverse, are common. But, suffer me to ask, in what the minds of females are so notoriously deficient, or unequal. . . .

Are we deficient in reason? We can only reason from what we know, and if an opportunity of acquiring knowledge hath been denied us, the inferiority of our sex cannot fairly be deduced from thence. . . . Will it be said that the judgment of a male of two years old, is more sage than that of a female's of the same age? I believe the reverse is generally observed to be true. But from that period what partiality! How is the one exalted,

and the other depressed, by the contrary modes of education which are adopted! The one is taught to aspire, and the other is early confined and limited. As their years increase, the sister must be wholly domesticated, while the brother is led by the hand through all the flowery paths of science. Grant that their minds are by nature equal, yet who shall wonder at the *apparent* superiority. . . . At length arrived at womanhood, the uncultivated fair one feels a void, which the employments allotted her are by no means capable of filling. . . . She herself is most unhappy; she feels the want of a cultivated mind. . . . Should it . . . be vociferated, "Your domestic employments are sufficient"—I would calmly ask, is it reasonable, that a candidate for immortality, for the joys of heaven, an intelligent being, who is to spend an eternity in contemplating the works of Deity, should at present be so degraded, as to be allowed no other ideas, than those which are suggested by the mechanism of a pudding, or the sewing the seams of a garment? . . .

Yes, ye lordly, ye haughty sex, our souls are by nature *equal* to yours.

From ADDRESS OF THE DEMOCRATIC-REPUBLICAN SOCIETY OF PENNSYLVANIA (DECEMBER 18, 1794)

The creation of around fifty Democratic-Republican societies in 1793 and 1794 reflected the expansion of the public sphere. The Pennsylvania society issued an address defending itself against critics who questioned its right to criticize the administration of George Washington.

The principles and proceedings of our Association have lately been caluminated [tarred by malicious falsehoods]. We should think ourselves unworthy to be ranked as Freemen, if awed by the name of any man, however he may command the public gratitude for past services, we could suffer in silence so sacred a right, so important a principle, as the freedom of opinion to be infringed, by attack on Societies which stand on that constitutional basis.

Freedom of thought, and a free communication of opinions by speech through the medium of the press, are the safeguards of our Liberties. . . . By the freedom of opinion, cannot be meant the right of thinking merely; for of this right the greatest Tyrant cannot deprive his meanest slave; but, it is freedom in the communication of sentiments [by] speech or through the press. This liberty is an imprescriptable [unlimitable] right, independent of any Constitution or social compact; it is as complete a right as that which any man has to the enjoyment of his life. These principles are eternal—they are recognized by our Constitution; and that nation is already enslaved that does not acknowledge their truth. . . .

If freedom of opinion, in the sense we understand it, is the right of every Citizen, by what mode of reasoning can that right be denied to an assemblage of Citizens? . . . The Society are free to declare that they never were more strongly impressed with . . . the importance of associations . . . than at the present time. The germ of an odious Aristocracy is planted among us—it has taken root. . . . Let us remain firm in attachment to principles. . . . Let us be particularly watchful to preserve inviolate the freedom of opinion, assured that it is the most effectual weapon for the protection of our liberty.

QUESTIONS

1. *How does Murray answer the argument that offering education to women will lead them to neglect their "domestic employments"?*

2. *Why does the Democratic-Republican Society insist on the centrality of "free communication of opinions" in preserving American liberty?*

3. *How do these documents reflect expanding ideas about who should enjoy the freedom to express one's ideas in the early republic?*

the Democratic-Republican societies, the discussion of women's status helped to popularize the language of rights in the new republic.

The men who wrote the Constitution did not envision the active and continuing involvement of ordinary citizens in affairs of state. But the rise of political parties seeking to mobilize voters in hotly contested elections, the emergence of the "self-created societies," the stirrings of women's political consciousness, and even armed uprisings like the Whiskey Rebellion broadened and deepened the democratization of public life set in motion by the American Revolution.

THE ADAMS PRESIDENCY

Washington's Farewell Address

In 1792, Washington won unanimous reelection. Four years later, he decided to retire from public life, in part to establish the precedent that the presidency is not a life office. In his Farewell Address (mostly drafted by Hamilton and published in the newspapers rather than delivered orally; see the Appendix for excerpts from the speech), Washington defended his administration against criticism, warned against the party spirit, and advised his countrymen to steer clear of international power politics by avoiding "permanent alliances with any portion of the foreign world."

The Election of 1796

George Washington's departure unleashed fierce party competition over the choice of his successor. In this, the first contested presidential election, two tickets presented themselves: John Adams, with Thomas Pinckney of South Carolina for vice president, representing the Federalists, and Thomas Jefferson, with Aaron Burr of New York, for the Republicans. In a majority of the sixteen states (Vermont, Kentucky, and Tennessee had been added to the original thirteen during Washington's presidency), the legislature chose presidential electors. But in the six states where the people voted for electors directly, intense

The first contested presidential election

campaigning took place. Adams received seventy-one electoral votes to Jefferson's sixty-eight. Because of factionalism among the Federalists, Pinckney received only fifty-nine votes, so Jefferson, the leader of the opposition party, became vice president. Voting fell almost entirely along sectional lines: Adams carried New England, New York, and New Jersey, while Jefferson swept the South, along with Pennsylvania.

In 1797, John Adams assumed leadership of a divided nation. Brilliant but austere, stubborn, and self-important, he was disliked even by those who honored his long career of service to the cause of independence. His presidency was beset by crises.

On the international front, the country was nearly dragged into the ongoing European war. As a neutral nation, the United States claimed the right to trade nonmilitary goods with both Britain and France, but both countries seized American ships with impunity. In 1797, American diplomats were sent to Paris to negotiate a treaty to replace the old alliance of 1778. French officials presented them with a demand for bribes before negotiations could proceed. When Adams made public the envoys' dispatches, the French officials were designated by the last three letters of the alphabet. This **XYZ affair** poisoned America's relations with its former ally. By 1798, the United States and France were engaged in a "quasi-war" at sea, with French ships seizing American vessels in the Caribbean and a newly enlarged American navy harassing the French. In effect, the United States had become a military ally of Great Britain. But despite pressure from Hamilton, who desired a declaration of war, Adams in 1800 negotiated peace with France.

Adams was less cautious in domestic affairs. Unrest continued in many rural areas. In 1799, farmers in southeastern Pennsylvania obstructed the assessment of a tax on land and houses that Congress had imposed to help fund an expanded army and navy. A crowd led by John Fries, a local militia leader and auctioneer, released arrested men from prison. No shots were fired in what came to be called Fries's Rebellion, but Adams dispatched units of the federal army to the area. The army arrested Fries for treason and proceeded to terrorize his supporters, tear down liberty poles, and whip Republican newspaper editors. Adams pardoned Fries in 1800, but the area, which had supported his election in 1796, never again voted Federalist.

A New Display of the United States, an 1803 engraving by Amos Doolittle, depicts President John Adams surrounded by shields of sixteen states (the original thirteen plus Kentucky, Tennessee, and Vermont), with the population and number of senators and representatives of each. At the top, an eagle holds an arrow, an olive branch, and a banner reading "Millions for Our Defence Not a Cent for Tribute," a motto that originated during the XYZ affair of 1798 when French officials demanded bribes before entering into negotiations to avoid war with the United States.

The "Reign of Witches"

But the greatest crisis of the Adams administration arose over the **Alien and Sedition Acts** of 1798. Confronted with mounting opposition, some of it voiced by immigrant pamphleteers and editors, Federalists moved to silence their critics. A new Naturalization Act extended from five to fourteen years the residency requirement for immigrants seeking American citizenship. The Alien Act allowed the deportation of persons from abroad deemed "dangerous" by federal authorities. The Sedition Act (which was set to expire in 1801, by which time Adams hoped to have been reelected) authorized the prosecution of virtually any public assembly or publication critical of the government. While more lenient than many such measures in Europe (it did not authorize legal action before publication and allowed for trials by jury), the new law meant that opposition editors could be prosecuted for almost any political comment they printed. The main target was the Republican press, seen by Federalists as a group of upstart workingmen (most editors had started out as printers) whose persistent criticism of the administration fomented popular rebelliousness and endangered "genuine liberty."

The Alien and Sedition Acts

Congressional Pugilists, a 1798 cartoon depicting a fight on the floor of Congress between Connecticut Federalist Roger Griswold and Matthew Lyon, a Republican from Vermont. Lyon would soon be jailed under the Sedition Act for criticizing the Adams administration in his newspaper.

Opposition to the Sedition Act

The passage of these measures launched what Jefferson—recalling events in Salem, Massachusetts, a century earlier—termed a "reign of witches." Eighteen individuals, including several Republican newspaper editors, were charged under the Sedition Act. Ten were convicted for spreading "false, scandalous, and malicious" information about the government. Matthew Lyon, a member of Congress from Vermont and editor of a Republican newspaper, *The Scourge of Aristocracy*, received a sentence of four months in prison and a fine of $1,000. (Lyon had been the first former printer and most likely the first former indentured servant elected to Congress.) In Massachusetts, authorities indicted several men for erecting a liberty pole bearing the inscription "No Stamp Act, no Sedition, no Alien Bill, no Land Tax; Downfall to the Tyrants of America."

The Virginia and Kentucky Resolutions

The Alien and Sedition Acts failed to silence the Republican press. Some newspapers ceased publication, but new ones, with names like *Sun of Liberty* and *Tree of Liberty*, entered the field. The Sedition Act thrust freedom of expression to the center of discussions of American liberty. Madison and Jefferson mobilized opposition, drafting resolutions adopted by the Virginia and Kentucky legislatures. The **Virginia and Kentucky resolutions** attacked the Sedition Act as an unconstitutional violation of the First Amendment. Virginia's, written by Madison, called on the federal courts to protect free speech. The original version of Jefferson's Kentucky resolution went further, asserting that states could nullify laws of Congress that violated the Constitution—that is, states could unilaterally prevent the enforcement of such laws within their borders. The legislature prudently deleted this passage. The resolutions were directed against assaults on freedom of expression by the federal government, not the states. Jefferson took care to insist that the states "fully possessed" the authority to punish "seditious" speech, even if the national government did not. Indeed, state-level prosecutions of newspapers for seditious libel did not end when the Sedition Act expired in 1801.

No other state endorsed the Virginia and Kentucky resolutions. Many Americans, including many Republicans, were horrified by the idea of state action that might endanger the Union. But the "crisis of freedom" of the late 1790s strongly reinforced the idea that "freedom of discussion" was an indispensable attribute of American liberty and of democratic government. Free speech, as Massachusetts Federalist Harrison Gray Otis noted, had become the people's "darling privilege." The broad revulsion against the Alien and Sedition Acts contributed greatly to Jefferson's election as president in 1800.

The "Revolution of 1800"

"Jefferson and Liberty" became the watchword of the Republican campaign. By this time, Republicans had developed effective techniques for mobilizing voters, such as printing pamphlets, handbills, and newspapers and holding mass meetings to promote their cause. The Federalists, who viewed politics as an activity for a small group of elite men, found it difficult to match their opponents' mobilization. Nonetheless, they still dominated New England and enjoyed considerable support in the Middle Atlantic states. Jefferson triumphed, with seventy-three electoral votes to Adams's sixty-five.

Before assuming office, Jefferson was forced to weather an unusual constitutional crisis. Each party arranged to have an elector throw away one of his two votes for president, so that its presidential candidate would come out a vote ahead of the vice presidential. But the designated Republican elector failed to do so. As a result, both Jefferson and his running mate, Aaron Burr, received seventy-three electoral votes. With no candidate having a majority, the election was thrown into the House of Representatives that had been elected in 1798, where the Federalists enjoyed a slight majority. For thirty-five ballots, neither man received a majority of the votes. Finally, Hamilton intervened. He disliked Jefferson but believed him enough of a statesman to recognize that the Federalist financial system could not be dismantled. Burr, he warned, was obsessed with power, "an embryo Caesar."

Hamilton's support for Jefferson tipped the balance. To avoid a repetition of the crisis, Congress and the states soon adopted the Twelfth Amendment to the Constitution, requiring electors to cast separate votes for president and vice president. The election of 1800 also set in motion a chain of events that culminated four years later when Burr killed Hamilton in a duel. Burr appears to have subsequently engaged in a plot to form a new nation in the West from land detached from the United States and the Spanish empire. Acquitted of treason in 1807, he went into exile in Europe, eventually returning to New York, where he practiced law until his death in 1836.

The events of the 1790s demonstrated that a majority of Americans believed ordinary people had a right to play an active role in politics, express their opinions freely, and contest the policies of their government. His party, wrote Samuel Goodrich, a prominent Connecticut Federalist, was overthrown because democracy had become "the watchword of popular liberty." To their credit, Federalists never considered resistance to the election result. Adams's acceptance of defeat established the vital precedent of a peaceful transfer of power from a defeated party to its successor.

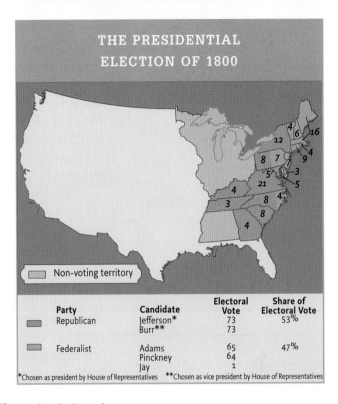

THE PRESIDENTIAL ELECTION OF 1800

Non-voting territory

Party	Candidate	Electoral Vote	Share of Electoral Vote
Republican	Jefferson*	73	53%
	Burr**	73	
Federalist	Adams	65	47%
	Pinckney	64	
	Jay	1	

*Chosen as president by House of Representatives   **Chosen as vice president by House of Representatives

An 1800 campaign banner, with a portrait of Thomas Jefferson and the words "John Adams is no more."

Slavery and Politics

Slavery's role in Jefferson's election

Lurking behind the political battles of the 1790s lay the potentially divisive issue of slavery. Jefferson, after all, received every one of the South's forty-one electoral votes. He always referred to his victory as the **Revolution of 1800** and saw it not simply as a party success but as a vindication of American freedom, securing for posterity the fruits of independence. Yet the triumph of "Jefferson and Liberty" would not have been possible without slavery. Had three-fifths of the slaves not been counted in apportionment, John Adams would have been reelected in 1800.

The issue of slavery would not disappear. The very first Congress under the new Constitution received petitions calling for emancipation. One bore the weighty signature of Benjamin Franklin, who in 1787 had agreed to serve as president of the Pennsylvania Abolition Society. The blessings of liberty, Franklin's petition insisted, should be available "without distinction of color to all descriptions of people."

Keeping slavery out of politics

A long debate followed, in which speakers from Georgia and South Carolina vigorously defended the institution and warned that behind northern criticism of slavery they heard "the trumpets of civil war." Madison found their forthright defense of slavery an embarrassment. But he concluded that the slavery question was so divisive that it must be kept out of national politics. He opposed Congress's even receiving a petition from North Carolina slaves on the grounds that they were not part of the American people and had "no claim" on the lawmakers' "attention." In 1793, to implement the Constitution's fugitive slave clause, Congress enacted a law providing for local officials to facilitate the return of escaped slaves.

The Haitian Revolution

Events during the 1790s underscored how powerfully slavery defined and distorted American freedom. The same Jeffersonians who hailed the French Revolution as a step in the universal progress of liberty reacted in horror against the slave revolution that began in 1791 in Saint Domingue, the jewel of the French overseas empire situated not far from the southern coast of the United States. Toussaint L'Ouverture, an educated slave on a sugar plantation, forged the rebellious slaves into an army able to defeat British forces seeking to seize the island and then an expedition hoping to reestablish French authority. The slave uprising led to the establishment of Haiti as an independent nation in 1804.

Reactions to the Haitian Revolution

Although much of the country was left in ruins by years of warfare, the **Haitian Revolution** affirmed the universality of the revolutionary era's creed of liberty. It inspired hopes for freedom among slaves in the United States. Throughout the nineteenth century, black Americans would look to Toussaint as a hero and celebrate the winning of Haitian independence. During the 1820s, several thousand free African-Americans emigrated to Haiti, whose government promised newcomers political rights and economic opportunity they did not enjoy in the United States.

Among white Americans, the response to the Haitian Revolution was different. Thousands of refugees from Haiti poured into the United States, fleeing the upheaval. Many spread tales of the massacres of slaveowners and the burning of their plantations, which reinforced white Americans' fears of slave insurrection at home. To most whites, the rebellious slaves seemed not men and women seeking liberty in the tradition of 1776, but a danger to American institutions. That the slaves had resorted to violence was widely taken to illustrate blacks' unfitness for republican freedom. Ironically, the Adams administration, which hoped that American merchants could replace their French counterparts in the island's lucrative sugar trade, encouraged the independence of black Haiti. When Jefferson became president, on the other hand, he sought to quarantine and destroy the hemisphere's second independent republic.

Gabriel's Rebellion

The momentous year of 1800 witnessed not only the "revolution" of Jefferson's election but also an attempted real one, a plot by slaves in Virginia itself to gain their freedom. It was organized by a Richmond blacksmith, Gabriel, and his brothers Solomon, also a blacksmith, and Martin, a slave preacher. The conspirators planned to march on the city, which had recently become the state capital, from surrounding plantations. They would kill some white inhabitants and hold the rest, including Governor James Monroe, hostage until their demand for the abolition of slavery was met. Gabriel hoped that "poor white people" would join the insurrection, and he ordered that Quakers and Methodists (many of whom were critics of slavery) and "French people" (whose country was engaged in the "quasi-war" with the United States described earlier) be spared. On the night when the slaves were to gather, a storm washed out the roads to Richmond. The plot was soon discovered and the leaders arrested. Twenty-six slaves, including Gabriel, were hanged and dozens more transported out of the state.

Blacks in 1800 made up half of Richmond's population. One-fifth were free. A black community had emerged in the 1780s and 1790s, and the conspiracy was rooted in its institutions. Gabriel gathered recruits at black Baptist churches, funerals, barbecues, and other gatherings. In cities like Richmond, many skilled slave craftsmen, including Gabriel himself, could read and write and enjoyed the privilege of hiring themselves out to employers—that is, negotiating their own labor arrangements, with their owner receiving their "wages." Their relative autonomy helps account for slave artisans' prominent role in the conspiracy.

Gabriel's Rebellion was a product of its age. Gabriel himself had been born in 1776. Like other Virginians, the participants in the conspiracy spoke the language of liberty forged in the American Revolution and reinvigorated during the 1790s. The rebels even planned to carry a banner emblazoned with the slogan, reminiscent of Patrick Henry, "Death or Liberty." "We have as much right," one conspirator declared, "to fight for our liberty as any men." Another likened himself to George Washington, who had rebelled against established authority to "obtain the liberty of [his] countrymen."

If Gabriel's conspiracy demonstrated anything, commented the prominent Virginian George Tucker, it was that slaves possessed "the love of freedom" as fully as other men. Gabriel's words, he added, reflected "the advance of knowledge" among Virginia's slaves, including knowledge of the American language of liberty. When slaves escaped to join Lord Dunmore during the War of Independence, he wrote, "they sought freedom merely as a good; now they also claim it as a right."

Toussaint L'Ouverture, leader of the slave revolution in Saint Domingue (modern-day Haiti). Painted in 1800 as part of a series of portraits of French military leaders, it depicts him as a courageous general.

The black community in Richmond

The slaves' "love of freedom"

Tucker believed Virginians should emancipate their slaves and settle them outside of the state. The legislature, however, moved in the opposite direction. It tightened controls over the black population—making it illegal for them to congregate on Sundays without white supervision—and severely restricted the possibility of masters voluntarily freeing their slaves. Any slave freed after 1806 was required to leave Virginia or be sold back into slavery. The door to manumission, thrown open during the American Revolution, had been slammed shut.

Tightening control over blacks in Virginia

JEFFERSON IN POWER

The first president to begin his term in Washington, D.C., Jefferson assumed office on March 4, 1801. The city, with its unpaved streets, impoverished residents, and unfinished public buildings, scarcely resembled L'Enfant's grand plan. At one point, part of the roof of the Capitol collapsed, narrowly missing the vice president. The capital's condition seemed to symbolize Jefferson's intention to reduce the importance of the national government in American life.

Inauguration

Jefferson's inaugural address was conciliatory toward his opponents. "Every difference of opinion," he declared, "is not a difference of principle. . . . We are all Republicans, we are all Federalists." He went on to expound the policies his administration would follow—economy in government, unrestricted trade, freedom of religion and the press, friendship to all nations but "entangling alliances" with none. America, "the world's best hope," would flourish if a limited government allowed its citizens to be "free to regulate their own pursuits."

Pierre Charles L'Enfant's 1791 plan for Washington, D.C., includes broad avenues that crisscross the city and that are named for the thirteen states, and a long mall stretching from the Potomac River to the Capitol building, slightly to the right of center.

Jefferson hoped to dismantle as much of the Federalist system as possible. Among his first acts as president was to pardon all those imprisoned under the Sedition Act. During his eight years as president, he reduced the number of government employees and slashed the army and navy. He abolished all taxes except the tariff, including the hated tax on whiskey, and paid off part of the national debt. He aimed to minimize federal power and eliminate government oversight of the economy. His policies ensured that the United States would not become a centralized state on a European model, as Hamilton had envisioned.

Minimizing federal power

Judicial Review

Nonetheless, as Hamilton predicted, it proved impossible to uproot national authority entirely. Jefferson distrusted the unelected judiciary and always believed in the primacy of local self-government. But during his presidency, and for many years thereafter, Federalist John Marshall headed the Supreme Court. Marshall had served John Adams as secretary of state and was appointed by the president to the Court shortly before Jefferson took office. A strong believer in national supremacy, Marshall established the Court's power to review laws of Congress and the states.

The first landmark decision of the Marshall Court came in 1803, in the case of **Marbury v. Madison**. On the eve of leaving office, Adams had appointed a number of justices of the peace for the District of Columbia. Madison, Jefferson's secretary of state, refused to issue commissions (the official documents entitling them to assume their posts) to these "midnight judges." Four, including William Marbury, sued for their offices. Marshall's decision declared unconstitutional the section of the Judiciary Act of 1789 that allowed the courts to order executive officials to deliver judges' commissions. It exceeded the power of Congress as outlined in the Constitution and was therefore void. Marbury, in other words, may have been entitled to his commission, but the Court had no power under the Constitution to order Madison to deliver it. On the immediate issue, therefore, the administration got its way. But the cost, as Jefferson saw it, was high. The Supreme Court had assumed the right to determine whether an act of Congress violates the Constitution—a power known as "judicial review."

Marbury v. Madison

Seven years later, in *Fletcher v. Peck*, the Court extended judicial review to state laws. In 1794, four land companies had paid nearly every member of the state legislature, Georgia's two U.S. senators, and a number of federal judges to secure their right to purchase land in present-day Alabama and Mississippi claimed by Georgia. They then sold the land to individual buyers at a large profit. Two years later, many of the corrupt lawmakers were defeated for reelection and the new legislature rescinded the land grant and subsequent sales. Whatever the circumstances of the legislature's initial action, Marshall declared, the Constitution forbade Georgia from taking any action that impaired a contract. Therefore, the individual purchasers could keep their land and the legislature could not repeal the original grant.

Fletcher v. Peck

The Louisiana Purchase

But the greatest irony of Jefferson's presidency involved his greatest achievement, the **Louisiana Purchase**. This resulted not from astute American diplomacy but because the rebellious slaves of Saint Domingue defeated forces sent by the ruler of France, Napoleon Bonaparte, to reconquer the island. Moreover, to take advantage of the sudden opportunity to purchase Louisiana, Jefferson had to abandon his conviction that the federal government was limited to powers specifically mentioned in the Constitution, since the document said nothing about buying territory from a foreign power.

A vast territory

This vast Louisiana Territory, which stretched from the Gulf of Mexico to Canada and from the Mississippi River to the Rocky Mountains, had been ceded by France to Spain in 1762 as part of the reshuffling of colonial possessions at the end of the Seven Years' War. France secretly reacquired it in 1800. Soon after taking office, Jefferson learned of the arrangement. He had long been concerned about American access to the port of New Orleans, which lay within Louisiana at the mouth of the Mississippi River. The right to trade through New Orleans, essential to western farmers, had been acknowledged in the Treaty of San Lorenzo (also known as Pinckney's Treaty) of 1795 between the United States and Spain. But Jefferson feared that the far more powerful French might try to interfere with American commerce. He dispatched envoys to France offering to purchase the city. Needing money for military campaigns in Europe and with his dreams of American empire in ruins because of his inability to reestablish control over Saint Domingue, Napoleon offered to sell the entire Louisiana Territory. The cost, $15 million (the equivalent of perhaps $250 million in today's money), made the Louisiana Purchase one of history's greatest real-estate bargains.

U.S. doubled in size

In a stroke, Jefferson had doubled the size of the United States and ended the French presence in North America. Federalists were appalled. "We are to give money, of which we have too little," one declared, "for land, of which we already have too much." Jefferson admitted that he had "done an act beyond the Constitution." But he believed the benefits justified his transgression. Farmers, Jefferson had written, were "the chosen people of God," and the country would remain "virtuous" as long as it was "chiefly agricultural." Madison, in *Federalist* no. 10, had explained that the large size of the republic made self-government possible. Now, Jefferson believed, he had ensured the agrarian character of the United States and its political stability for centuries to come.

White Hall Plantation, painted around 1800, depicts a Louisiana plantation and the dynamism of the region's economy on the eve of its acquisition by the United States. Black oarsmen man a boat carrying bales of cotton for sale in New Orleans.

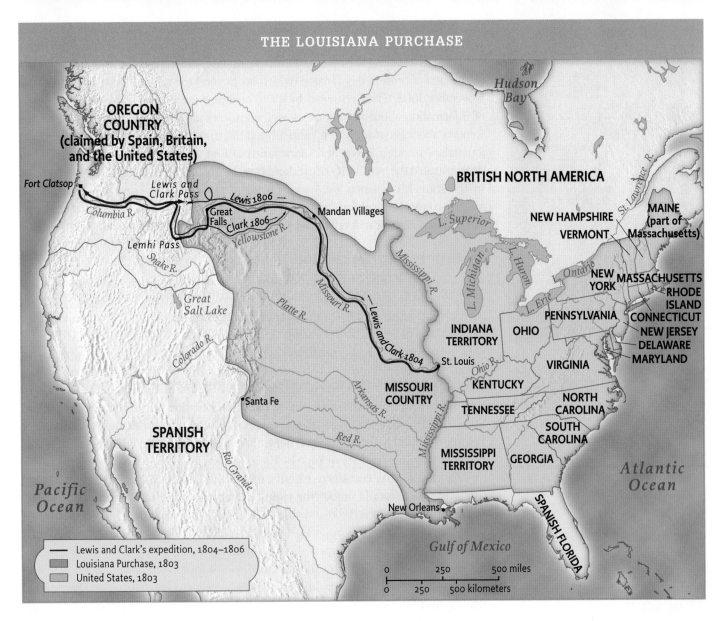

THE LOUISIANA PURCHASE

Legend:
— Lewis and Clark's expedition, 1804–1806
Louisiana Purchase, 1803
United States, 1803

The Louisiana Purchase of 1803 doubled the land area of the United States.

Lewis and Clark

Within a year of the purchase, Jefferson dispatched an expedition led by Meriwether Lewis and William Clark, two Virginia-born veterans of Indian wars in the Ohio Valley, to explore the new territory. Their objectives were both scientific and commercial—to study the area's plants, animal life, and geography, and to discover how the region could be exploited economically. Jefferson hoped the **Lewis and Clark expedition** would establish trading relations with western Indians and locate a water route to the Pacific Ocean—an updated version of the old dream of a Northwest Passage that could facilitate commerce with Asia.

In the spring of 1804, Lewis and Clark's fifty-member "corps of discovery" set out from St. Louis on the most famous exploring party in American history. They spent the winter in the area of present-day North Dakota and then resumed their journey

Scientific and commercial objectives

A page from William Clark's journal of the Lewis and Clark expedition, depicting a salmon. Among their tasks was to record information about the West's plants, animal life, and geography.

in April 1805. They were now accompanied by a fifteen-year-old Shoshone Indian woman, Sacajawea, the wife of a French fur trader, who served as their guide and interpreter. After crossing the Rocky Mountains, the expedition reached the Pacific Ocean in the area of present-day Oregon (which lay beyond the nation's new boundaries) in November 1805. They returned in 1806, bringing with them an immense amount of information about the region as well as numerous plant and animal specimens. Reports about geography, plant and animal life, and Indian cultures filled their daily journals. Although Lewis and Clark failed to find a commercial route to Asia, they demonstrated the possibility of overland travel to the Pacific coast. They found Indians in the trans-Mississippi West accustomed to dealing with European traders and already connected to global markets. The success of their journey helped to strengthen the idea that American territory was destined to reach all the way to the Pacific.

Incorporating Louisiana

The only part of the Louisiana Purchase with a significant non-Indian population in 1803 was the region around New Orleans. When the United States took control, the city had around 8,000 inhabitants, including nearly 3,000 slaves and 1,300 free persons of color. Incorporating this diverse population into the United States was by no means easy. French and Spanish law accorded free blacks, many of whom were the offspring of unions between white military officers and slave women, nearly all the rights of white citizens. Slaves in Louisiana, as in Florida and Texas under Spanish rule, enjoyed legal protections unknown in the United States. Spain made it easy for slaves to obtain their freedom through purchase or voluntary emancipation by the owners. Slave women had the right to go to court for protection against cruelty or rape by their owners.

The treaty that transferred Louisiana to the United States promised that all free inhabitants would enjoy "the rights, advantages, and immunities of citizens." Spanish and French civil codes, unlike British and American law, recognized women as co-owners of family property. Under American rule, Louisiana retained this principle of "community property" within marriage. But free blacks suffered a steady decline in status. And the local legislature soon adopted one of the most sweeping slave codes in the South, forbidding blacks to "ever consider themselves the equal of whites" and limiting the practice of manumission and access to the courts. Louisiana's slaves had enjoyed far more freedom under the rule of tyrannical Spain than as part of the liberty-loving United States.

> *Louisiana slavery*

The Barbary Wars

Among other things, the Louisiana Purchase demonstrated that despite its vaunted isolation from the Old World, the United States continued to be deeply affected by events throughout the Atlantic world. At a time when Americans still relied on British markets to purchase their farm produce and British suppliers for imported manufactured goods, European wars directly influenced the livelihood of American farmers, merchants, and artisans. Jefferson hoped to avoid foreign entanglements, but he found it impossible as president to avoid being drawn into the continuing wars of Europe. Even as he sought to limit the power of the national government, foreign relations compelled him to expand it. The first war fought by the United States was to protect American commerce in a dangerous world.

> *The first war fought by the U.S.*

Only a few months after taking office, Jefferson employed the very navy whose expansion by John Adams he had strongly criticized. The Barbary states on the northern coast of Africa had long preyed on shipping in the Mediterranean and Atlantic, receiving tribute from several countries, including the United States, to protect their vessels. Between 1785 and 1796, pirates captured thirteen American ships and held more than 100 sailors as "slaves," paralyzing American trade with the Mediterranean. The federal government paid hundreds of thousands of dollars in ransom and agreed to annual sums to purchase peace. In 1801, Jefferson refused demands for increased payments and the pasha of Tripoli, in modern-day Libya, declared war on the United States. The naval conflict lasted until 1804, when an American squadron won a victory at Tripoli harbor (a victory commemorated in the official hymn of the Marine Corps, which mentions fighting on "the shores of Tripoli"). The treaty ending the war guaranteed the freedom of American commerce, but Tripoli soon resumed harassing American ships. Only after the War of 1812 and one final American show of force did Barbary interference with American shipping end.

> *Defending American shipping*

The **Barbary Wars** were the new nation's first encounter with the Islamic world. In the 1790s, as part of an attempt to establish peaceful relations, the federal government declared that the United States was "not, in any sense, founded on the Christian religion." But the conflicts helped to establish a long-lasting pattern in which Americans viewed Muslims as an exotic people whose way of life did not adhere to Western standards. In the eyes of many Americans, Islam joined monarchy and aristocracy as forms of Old World despotism that stood as opposites to freedom.

The Embargo

Far more serious in its impact on the United States was warfare between Britain and France, which resumed in 1803 after a brief lull. According to international

The Attack Made on Tripoli, a print from 1805, celebrates the bombardment of Tripoli (in present-day Libya) by the U.S. Navy as part of the Barbary Wars, the first American encounter with the Islamic world.

O-Grab-Me, or, the American Snapping-Turtle, a cartoon criticizing Jefferson's Embargo (spelled backward as o-grab-me), which banned all American shipping to foreign ports.

law, neutral nations had a right to trade nonmilitary goods with countries at war. By 1806, however, each combatant had declared the other under blockade, seeking to deny trade with America to its rival. Engaged in a life-and-death struggle with Napoleon, Britain needed thousands of new sailors each year. The Royal Navy resumed the practice of impressment. By the end of 1807, it had seized more than 6,000 American sailors (claiming they were British citizens and deserters), including men from the U.S. warship *Chesapeake*, which the British frigate *Leopard* bombarded and boarded in American waters off the coast of Maryland.

To Jefferson, the economic health of the United States required freedom of trade with which no foreign government had a right to interfere. American farmers needed access to markets in Europe and the Caribbean. As colonial patriots had done in the 1760s and 1770s, he decided to use trade as a weapon. In December 1807, he persuaded Congress to enact the **Embargo Act**, a ban on all American vessels sailing for foreign ports. For a believer in limited government, this was an amazing exercise of federal power.

Enforcement of the Embargo brought back memories of the Intolerable Acts of 1774, with the navy sealing off ports and seizing goods without warrants and the army arresting accused smugglers. Jefferson hoped it would lead Europeans to stop their interference with American shipping and also reduce the occasion for impressment. In 1808, American exports plummeted by 80 percent. Unfortunately, neither Britain nor France, locked in a death struggle, took much notice. But the Embargo devastated the economies of American port cities. Just before his term ended, in March 1809, Jefferson signed the Non-Intercourse Act, banning trade only with Britain and France but providing that if either side rescinded its edicts against American shipping, commerce with that country would resume.

Domestic effects of the Embargo

Madison and Pressure for War

Jefferson left office at the lowest point of his career. He had won a sweeping reelection in 1804, receiving 162 electoral votes to only 14 for the Federalist candidate, Charles C. Pinckney. With the exception of Connecticut, he even carried the Federalist stronghold of New England. Four years later, his handpicked successor, James Madison, also won an easy victory. The Embargo, however, had failed to achieve its diplomatic aims and was increasingly violated by American shippers and resented by persons whose livelihoods depended on trade. In 1810, Madison adopted a new policy. Congress enacted a measure known as Macon's Bill No. 2, which allowed trade to resume but provided that if either France or Britain ceased interfering with American rights, the president could reimpose an embargo on the other. With little to lose, since Britain controlled the seas, the French emperor Napoleon announced that he had repealed his decrees against neutral shipping. But the British continued to attack American vessels and, with their navy hard-pressed for manpower,

Macon's Bill No. 2

stepped up the impressment of American sailors. In the spring of 1812, Madison reimposed the embargo on trade with Britain.

Meanwhile, a group of younger congressmen, mostly from the West, were calling for war with Britain. Known as the War Hawks, this new generation of political leaders had come of age after the winning of independence and were ardent nationalists. Their leaders included Henry Clay of Kentucky, elected Speaker of the House of Representatives in 1810, and John C. Calhoun of South Carolina. The War Hawks spoke passionately of defending the national honor against British insults, but they also had more practical goals in mind, notably the annexation of Canada. "Agrarian cupidity [greed], not maritime rights," declared Congressman John Randolph of Virginia, "urges the war. We have heard but one word . . . Canada! Canada! Canada!" Randolph exaggerated, for many southern War Hawks also pressed for the conquest of Florida, a haven for fugitive slaves owned by Britain's ally Spain. Members of Congress also spoke of the necessity of upholding the principle of free trade and liberating the United States once and for all from European infringements on its independence. Unimpeded access to overseas markets was essential if the agrarian republic were to prosper.

War Hawks

THE "SECOND WAR OF INDEPENDENCE"

The growing crisis between the United States and Britain took place against the background of deteriorating Indian relations in the West, which also helped propel the United States down the road to war. Jefferson had long favored the removal beyond the Mississippi River of Indian tribes who refused to cooperate in "civilizing" themselves. The Louisiana Purchase made this policy more feasible. "The acquisition of Louisiana," he wrote, "will, it is hoped, put in our power the means of inducing all the Indians on this side [of the Mississippi River] to transplant themselves to the other side." Jefferson enthusiastically pursued efforts to purchase Indian lands west of the Appalachian Mountains. He encouraged traders to lend money to Indians, in the hope that accumulating debt would force them to sell some of their holdings, thus freeing up more land for "our increasing numbers." On the other hand, the government continued President Washington's policy of promoting settled farming among the Indians. Benjamin Hawkins, a friend of Jefferson who served as American agent for Indian affairs south of the Ohio River, also encouraged the expansion of African-American slavery among the tribes as one of the elements of advancing civilization.

Indian relations in the West

The Indian Response

By 1800, nearly 400,000 American settlers lived west of the Appalachian Mountains. They far outnumbered the remaining Indians, whose seemingly irreversible decline in power led some Indians to rethink their opposition to assimilation. Among the Creek and Cherokee, a group led by men of mixed Indian-white ancestry like Major Ridge and John Ross enthusiastically endorsed the federal policy of promoting "civilization." Many had established businesses as traders and slaveowning farmers with the help of their white fathers. Their views, in turn, infuriated "nativists," who wished to root out European influences and resist further white encroachment on Indian lands.

Debating assimilation

The period from 1800 to 1812 was an "age of prophecy" among the Indians. Movements for the revitalization of Indian life arose among the Creeks, Cherokees, Shawnees, Iroquois, and other tribes. Handsome Lake of the Seneca, who had overcome an earlier addiction to alcohol, preached that Indians must refrain from fighting, gambling, drinking, and sexual promiscuity. He believed Indians could regain their autonomy without directly challenging whites or repudiating all white ways, and he urged his people to take up farming and attend school.

War Party at Fort Douglas, a watercolor by the Swiss-born Canadian artist Peter Rindisbacher. Painted in 1823, it depicts an incident during the War of 1812 when Indian allies of Great Britain fired rifles into the air to greet their commander, Captain Andrew Bulger, pictured on the far right.

Tecumseh's Vision

A more militant message was expounded by two Shawnee brothers, **Tecumseh and Tenskwatawa**. Tecumseh was a chief who had refused to sign the Treaty of Greenville in 1795, and Tenskwatawa was a religious prophet who called for complete separation from whites, the revival of traditional Indian culture, and resistance to federal policies. White people, Tenskwatawa preached, were the source of all evil in the world, and Indians should abandon American alcohol, clothing, food, and manufactured goods. His followers gathered at Prophetstown, located on the Wabash River in Indiana.

Tecumseh meanwhile traversed the Mississippi Valley, seeking to revive Neolin's pan-Indian alliance of the 1760s (discussed in Chapter 4). The alternative to resistance was extermination. "Where today are the Pequot?" he asked. "Where are the Narragansett, the Mohican, the Pocanet, and other powerful tribes of our people? They have vanished before the avarice [greed] and oppression of the white man, as snow before the summer sun." Indians, he proclaimed, must recognize that they were a single people and unite in claiming "a common and equal right in the land." He repudiated chiefs who had sold land to the federal government: "Sell a country! Why not sell the air, the great sea, as well as the earth? Did not the Great Spirit make them all for the use of his children?" In 1810, Tecumseh called for attacks on American frontier settlements. In November 1811, while he was absent, American forces under William Henry Harrison destroyed Prophetstown in the Battle of Tippecanoe.

Tenskwatawa (the Prophet), in a portrait by the American artist Charles Bird King, who painted numerous Indian leaders.

The War of 1812

In 1795, James Madison had written that war is the greatest enemy of "true liberty." "War," he explained, "is the parent of armies; from these proceed debts and taxes, and armies, and debts, and taxes are the known instruments for bringing the many under the domination of the few." Nonetheless, Madison became a war president. Reports that the British were encouraging Tecumseh's efforts contributed to the coming of the **War of 1812**. In June 1812, with assaults on American shipping continuing, Madison asked Congress for a declaration of war. American nationality, the president declared, was at stake—would Americans remain "an independent people" or become "colonists and vassals" of Great Britain? The vote revealed a deeply divided country. Both Federalists and Republicans representing the states from New Jersey northward, where most of the mercantile and financial resources of the country were concentrated, voted against war. The South and West were strongly in favor. The bill passed the House by a vote of 79–49 and the Senate by 19–13. It was the first time the United States declared war on another country, and was approved by the smallest margin of any declaration of war in American history.

In retrospect, it seems remarkably foolhardy for a disunited and militarily unprepared nation to go to war with one of the world's two major powers. And with the expiration in 1811 of the charter of the Bank of the United States and the refusal of northern merchants and bankers to loan money, the federal government found it increasingly difficult to finance the war. Before the conflict ended, it was essentially bankrupt. Fortunately for the United States, Great Britain at the outset was preoccupied with the struggle in Europe. But it easily repelled two feeble American invasions of Canada and imposed a blockade that all but destroyed American commerce. In 1814, having finally defeated Napoleon, Britain invaded the United States. Its forces seized Washington, D.C., and burned the Capitol and the White House, while the government fled for safety.

Americans did enjoy a few military successes. In August 1812, the American frigate *Constitution* defeated the British warship *Guerriere*. Commodore Oliver H. Perry defeated a British naval force in September 1813 on Lake Erie (a startling result considering that Britain prided itself on having the world's most powerful navy—although the Americans outgunned them on the Great Lakes). In the following year, a British assault on Baltimore was repulsed when **Fort McHenry** at the entrance to the harbor withstood a British bombardment. This was the occasion when Francis Scott Key composed "The Star-Spangled Banner," an ode to the "land of the free and home of the brave" that became the national anthem during the 1930s.

Like the War of Independence, the War of 1812 was a two-front struggle—against the British and against the Indians. The war produced significant victories over western Indians who sided with the British. In 1813, pan-Indian forces led by Tecumseh (who had been commissioned a general in the British army) were defeated, and he himself was killed, at the Battle of the Thames, near Detroit, by an American force led by William Henry

The lid of a chest decorated with scenes from the War of 1812. Images of Hope, on the left, and Liberty flank a picture of the naval battle in which the USS *Constitution* defeated a British warship. Liberty holds a paper that reads, "Free Trade and Sailors Rights," two of the issues that drew the United States into the war.

An engraving depicting the burning of Washington, D.C., by the British during the War of 1812, from an 1817 book by the antislavery Philadelphia physician Jesse Torrey. Torrey suggests that the event is divine punishment for the practice of slave trading in the nation's capital. The image includes children among the group of chained slaves at the right to emphasize the breakup of slave families. At the top is a heavenly image of liberty.

The bombardment of Fort McHenry in Baltimore harbor in September 1814 was of minor military importance, but it is remembered as the inspiration for Francis Scott Key's poem, "The Star-Spangled Banner."

A VIEW of the BOMBARDMENT of Fort McHenry, near Baltimore, by the British fleet taken from the Observation...

Harrison. In March 1814, an army of Americans and pro-assimilation Cherokees and Creeks under the command of Andrew Jackson defeated hostile Creeks known as the Red Sticks at the Battle of Horseshoe Bend in Alabama, killing more than 800 of them. "The power of the Creeks is forever broken," Jackson wrote, and he dictated terms of surrender that required the Indians, hostile and friendly alike, to cede more than half their land, more than 23 million acres in all, to the federal government.

Jackson then proceeded to New Orleans, where he engineered the war's greatest American victory, fighting off a British invasion in January 1815. Although a slaveholder, Jackson recruited the city's free men of color into his forces, appealing to them as "sons of freedom" and promising them the same pay and land bounties as white recruits. Jackson and Harrison would ride their reputations as military heroes all the way to the White House. Colonel Richard M. Johnson, who claimed to have actually killed Tecumseh, would later be elected vice president.

Battle of New Orleans

With neither side wishing to continue the conflict, the United States and Britain signed the Treaty of Ghent, ending the war. Although the treaty was signed in December 1814, ships carrying news of the agreement did not reach America until after the **Battle of New Orleans** had been fought. The treaty restored the previous status quo. No territory exchanged hands, nor did any provisions relate to impressment or neutral shipping rights. Considering that the war had not been a military success for the United States, the Treaty of Ghent was about as good an outcome as could be expected.

Treaty of Ghent

The Treaty of Ghent produced an unusual episode in American diplomacy. As in the War of Independence, thousands of slaves found freedom by escaping to British forces during the War of 1812. The peace treaty specified that they must be returned, but the British refused to hand them over to their former owners. After five years of inconclusive negotiations, both countries agreed to international arbitration of the dispute—by one of the world's leading despots, Czar Nicholas I of Russia. He ruled in

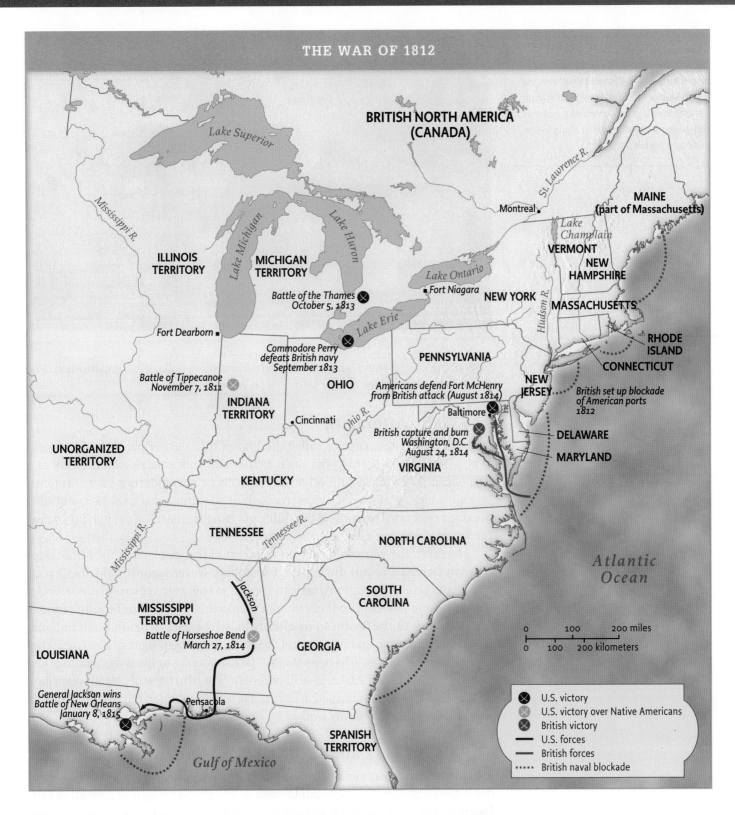

THE WAR OF 1812

BRITISH NORTH AMERICA (CANADA)

Lake Superior

St. Lawrence R.

Montreal

MAINE (part of Massachusetts)

Lake Champlain

VERMONT

NEW HAMPSHIRE

ILLINOIS TERRITORY

MICHIGAN TERRITORY

Lake Michigan

Lake Huron

Lake Ontario

Fort Niagara

NEW YORK

Hudson R.

MASSACHUSETTS

RHODE ISLAND

CONNECTICUT

Battle of the Thames
October 5, 1813 ⊗

Lake Erie

Fort Dearborn ■

Commodore Perry
defeats British navy
September 1813 ⊗

PENNSYLVANIA

NEW JERSEY

British set up blockade
of American ports
1812

Battle of Tippecanoe
November 7, 1811 ⊗

OHIO

Americans defend Fort McHenry
from British attack (August 1814)

INDIANA TERRITORY

Ohio R.

• Cincinnati

Baltimore ⊗

British capture and burn
Washington, D.C.
August 24, 1814 ⊗

DELAWARE

MARYLAND

UNORGANIZED TERRITORY

KENTUCKY

VIRGINIA

Mississippi R.

TENNESSEE

Tennessee R.

NORTH CAROLINA

Atlantic Ocean

Mississippi R.

Jackson

MISSISSIPPI TERRITORY

Battle of Horseshoe Bend
March 27, 1814 ⊗

SOUTH CAROLINA

GEORGIA

0   100   200 miles

0   100   200 kilometers

LOUISIANA

General Jackson wins
Battle of New Orleans
January 8, 1815 ⊗

Pensacola

SPANISH TERRITORY

Gulf of Mexico

⊗ U.S. victory
⊗ U.S. victory over Native Americans
⊗ British victory
— U.S. forces
— British forces
····· British naval blockade

Although the British burned the nation's capital, the War of 1812 essentially was a military draw.

The Hornet and Peacock, or, John Bull in Distress, a watercolor by Amos B. Doolittle from 1813, celebrates a victory by the American warship *Hornet* over the British vessel *Peacock* during the War of 1812. Britain is represented as a half-bull, half-peacock creature being stung in the neck by a hornet.

favor of the United States, and Britain paid a few million dollars in compensation. The freed slaves themselves mostly settled in Nova Scotia, Canada.

The War's Aftermath

A number of contemporaries called the War of 1812 the Second War of Independence. Despite widespread opposition to the conflict, it confirmed the ability of a republican government to conduct a war without surrendering its institutions. Jackson's victory at New Orleans not only made him a national hero but also became a celebrated example of the ability of virtuous citizens of a republic to defeat the forces of despotic Europe.

Moreover, the war completed the conquest of the area east of the Mississippi River, which had begun during the Revolution. Never again would the British or Indians pose a threat to American control of this vast region. The war broke the remaining power of Indians in the Old Northwest and significantly reduced their holdings in the South. In its aftermath, white settlers poured into Indiana, Michigan, Alabama, and Mississippi, bringing with them their distinctive forms of social organization. "I have no doubt," Jackson wrote to his wife, "but in a few years the banks of the Alabama will present a beautiful view of elegant mansions and extensive rich and productive farms." He did not mention that those mansions would be built and the farms worked by slaves.

American control east of the Mississippi

The War of 1812 and the Canadian Borderland

Like the American Revolution, the War of 1812 had a profound impact along the border between the United States and Canada, further solidifying it as a dividing line. Much of the fighting took place on this porous border in the long-contested region near Detroit and on the Great Lakes. A great deal of trade had developed between Vermont and Quebec, and across the lakes, which became a flourishing smuggling business during Jefferson's Embargo. When war broke out, Canadians began to see

American traders as spies. The unsuccessful American attacks on Canada during the war (some led by Irish immigrants resentful at British rule over their country of birth) strengthened anti-Americanism even among Canadians not connected to revolutionary-era Loyalists. To be sure, as in so many borderland regions, many people had family ties on both sides and the exchange of goods and ideas continued after the war ended. But far more Americans now turned their sights toward the western frontier rather than Canada. For both Canadians and Americans, the war reaffirmed a sense of national identity, and both came to see the conflict as a struggle for freedom—for the United States, freedom from dependence on Great Britain; for Canada, freedom from domination by the United States.

Britain's defeat of Napoleon inaugurated a long period of peace in Europe. With diplomatic affairs playing less and less of a role in American public life, Americans' sense of separateness from the Old World grew ever stronger. The war also strengthened a growing sense of nationalism in Canada, based in part on separateness from the United States. As in 1775, Canadians did not rise up to welcome an army from the south, but instead repelled the invading American forces, to the puzzlement of Americans who could not understand why they did not

This colorful painting by the artist John Archibald Woodside from around the time of the War of 1812 contains numerous symbols of freedom, among them the goddess of liberty with her liberty cap, a broken chain at the sailor's feet, the fallen crown (under his left foot), a broken royal scepter, and the sailor himself, since English interference with American shipping was one of the war's causes.

wish to become part of the empire of liberty. Each side developed stereotypes of the other that resonate to this day: Americans saw Canadians as monarchical, European, and lacking in an understanding of liberty; Canadians viewed Americans as a people unusually prone to violence.

The End of the Federalist Party

Jefferson and Madison succeeded in one major political aim—the elimination of the Federalist Party. At first, the war led to a revival of Federalist fortunes. With antiwar sentiment at its peak in 1812, Madison had been reelected by the relatively narrow margin of 128 electoral votes to 89 over his Federalist opponent, DeWitt Clinton of New York. But then came a self-inflicted blow. In December 1814, a group of New England Federalists gathered at Hartford, Connecticut, to give voice to their party's long-standing grievances, especially the domination of the federal government by Virginia presidents and their own region's declining influence as new western states entered the Union. They called for amending the Constitution to eliminate the three-fifths clause that strengthened southern political power, and to require a two-thirds vote of Congress for the admission of new states, declarations of war, and laws restricting trade. Contrary to later myth, the **Hartford Convention** did not call for secession or disunion. But it affirmed the right of a state to "interpose" its authority if the federal government violated the Constitution.

The Hartford Convention had barely adjourned before Jackson electrified the nation with his victory at New Orleans. "Rising Glory of the American Republic," one newspaper exulted. In speeches and sermons, political and religious leaders alike proclaimed that Jackson's triumph revealed, once again, that a divine hand oversaw America's destiny. The Federalists could not free themselves from the charge of lacking patriotism. Within a few years, their party no longer existed. Its stance on the war was only one cause of the party's demise. The urban commercial and financial interests it championed represented a small minority in an expanding agricultural nation. Their elitism and distrust of popular self-government placed Federalists more and more at odds with the new nation's democratic ethos. Yet in their dying moments Federalists had raised an issue—southern domination of the national government—that would long outlive their political party. And the country stood on the verge of a profound economic and social transformation that strengthened the very forces of commercial development that Federalists had welcomed and many Republicans feared.

SUGGESTED READING

BOOKS

- Appleby, Joyce. *Capitalism and a New Social Order: The Republican Vision of the 1790s* (1984). Explores how the Jeffersonians sought simultaneously to expand economic enterprise and equality of opportunity.

- Dowd, Gregory. *A Spirited Resistance: The North American Indian Struggle for Unity, 1745–1815* (1992). Places the efforts of Tecumseh and Tenskwatawa in the context of the long effort to forge pan-Indian unity.

- Egerton, Douglas R. *Gabriel's Rebellion: The Virginia Slave Conspiracies of 1800 and 1802* (1993). The most comprehensive account of one of the most important slave conspiracies in American history.

- Elkins, Stanley, and Eric L. McKitrick. *The Age of Federalism* (1993). A detailed account of the politics of the 1790s.

- Hofstadter, Richard. *The Idea of a Party System: The Rise of Legitimate Opposition in the United States, 1780–1840* (1969). Considers how Americans began by rejecting the idea of organized political parties and ended up accepting their legitimacy.

- Kerber, Linda K. *Women of the Republic: Intellect and Ideology in Revolutionary America* (1980). A study of prevailing ideas about women's place in the new republic.

- Lambert, Frank. *The Barbary Wars: American Independence in the Atlantic World* (2005). An account of the first foreign military conflict conducted by the newly independent United States.

- McCoy, Drew. *The Elusive Republic: Political Economy in Jeffersonian America* (1980). An influential study of the economic and political outlooks and policies of Federalists and Jeffersonians.

- Miller, John C. *Crisis in Freedom: The Alien and Sedition Acts* (1952). Examines how the Adams administration sought to use the power of the federal government to stifle dissent and the free press.

- Ronda, James P. *Lewis and Clark among the Indians* (1984). An account of the most famous exploring party in American history.

- Rothman, Adam. *Slave Country: American Expansion and the Origins of the Deep South* (2005). A pioneering study of how the United States secured control of what are now the Gulf states, opening the door for the expansion of slavery.

- Smelser, Marshall. *The Democratic Republic, 1801–1815* (1968). Still the best narrative history of the presidencies of Jefferson and Madison.

- Sugden, John. *Tecumseh's Last Stand* (1985). Relates the rise and fall of the era's most prominent Indian leader.

- Taylor, Alan. *The Civil War of 1812* (2010). An account of the War of 1812 that stresses how divided Americans were during the conflict.

- Waldstreicher, David. *In the Midst of Perpetual Fetes: The Making of American Nationalism, 1776–1820* (1997). Explores how Americans celebrated and thought about their nation's independence in the years of the early republic.

WEBSITE

- Rivers, Edens, Empires: Lewis and Clark and the Revealing of America: www.loc.gov/exhibits/lewisandclark /lewisandclark.html

CHAPTER REVIEW AND ONLINE RESOURCES

REVIEW QUESTIONS

1. Identify the major parts of Hamilton's financial plan, who supported these proposals, and why they created such passionate opposition.

2. How did the French Revolution and ensuing global struggle between Great Britain and France shape early American politics?

3. How did the United States become involved in foreign affairs in this period?

4. How did the expansion of the public sphere and a new language of rights offer opportunities to women?

5. What caused the demise of the Federalists?

6. What impact did the Haitian Revolution have on the United States?

7. How did the Louisiana Purchase affect the situation of Native Americans in that region?

8. Whose status was changed the most by the War of 1812—that of Great Britain, the United States, or Native Americans?

KEY TERMS

Bank of the United States (p. 274)

impressment (p. 276)

Jay's Treaty (p. 276)

Federalists and Republicans (p. 277)

Whiskey Rebellion (p. 278)

Democratic-Republican societies (p. 280)

Judith Sargent Murray (p. 281)

XYZ affair (p. 285)

Alien and Sedition Acts (p. 285)

Virginia and Kentucky resolutions (p. 286)

Revolution of 1800 (p. 288)

Haitian Revolution (p. 288)

Gabriel's Rebellion (p. 289)

Marbury v. Madison (p. 291)

Louisiana Purchase (p. 291)

Lewis and Clark expedition (p. 293)

Barbary Wars (p. 295)

Embargo Act (p. 296)

Tecumseh and Tenskwatawa (p. 298)

War of 1812 (p. 298)

Fort McHenry (p. 299)

Battle of New Orleans (p. 300)

Hartford Convention (p. 303)

Go to 🐰 INQUIZITIVE

To see what you know—and learn what you've missed—with personalized feedback along the way.

Visit the *Give Me Liberty!* **Student Site** for primary source documents and images, interactive maps, author videos featuring Eric Foner, and more.

CHAPTER 9

THE MARKET REVOLUTION

★

1800–1840

In 1824, the Marquis de Lafayette visited the United States. Nearly fifty years had passed since, as a youth of twenty, the French nobleman fought at Washington's side in the War of Independence. Now, his thirteen-month tour became a triumphant Jubilee of Liberty. Since 1784, when he had last journeyed to the United States, the nation's population had tripled to nearly 12 million, its land area had more than doubled, and its political institutions had thrived. Lafayette's tour demonstrated how profoundly the nation had changed. The thirteen states of 1784 had grown to twenty-four, and he visited every one—a journey that would have been almost impossible forty years earlier. Lafayette traveled up the Mississippi and Ohio Rivers by steamboat, a recent invention that was helping to bring economic development to the trans-Appalachian West, and crossed upstate New York via the Erie Canal, the world's longest man-made waterway, which linked the region around the Great Lakes with the Atlantic coast via the Hudson River.

Americans in the first half of the nineteenth century were fond of describing liberty as the defining quality of their new nation, the unique genius of its institutions. The poet Walt Whitman wrote of his countrymen's "deathless attachment to freedom." Likenesses of the goddess of liberty, a familiar figure in eighteenth-century British visual imagery, became even more common in the United States, appearing in paintings and sculpture and on folk art from weather vanes to quilts and tavern signs. Never, declared President Andrew Jackson in his farewell address in 1837, had any population "enjoyed so much freedom and happiness as the people of these United States." The celebration of freedom could be found in sermons, newspaper editorials, and political pronouncements in every region of the country. In *Democracy in America*, the French historian and politician Alexis de Tocqueville wrote of the "holy cult of freedom" he encountered on his own visit to the United States during the early 1830s.

Even as Lafayette, Tocqueville, and numerous other visitors from abroad toured the United States, however, Americans' understandings of freedom were changing. Three historical processes unleashed by the Revolution accelerated after the War of 1812: the spread of market relations, the westward movement of the population, and the rise of a vigorous political democracy. (The first two will be discussed in this chapter, the third in Chapter 10.) All powerfully affected the development of American society. They also helped to reshape the idea of freedom, identifying it ever more closely with economic opportunity, physical mobility, and participation in a vibrantly democratic political system.

But American freedom also continued to be shaped by the presence of slavery. Lafayette, who had purchased a plantation in the West Indies and freed its slaves, once wrote, "I would never have drawn my sword in the cause of America if I could have conceived that thereby I was founding a land of slavery." Yet slavery was moving westward with the young republic. The same steamboats and canals that enabled millions of farm families to send their goods to market also facilitated the growth of slave-based cotton plantations in the South. And slavery drew a strict racial boundary around American democracy, making voting, officeholding, and participation in the public sphere privileges for whites

What were the main elements of the market revolution? *–p. 308*

How did the market revolution spark social change? *–p. 318*

How did the meanings of American freedom change in this period? *–p. 329*

How did the market revolution affect the lives of workers, women, and African-Americans? *–p. 337*

Conestoga Wagon on the Pennsylvania Turnpike, by the English-born American artist Thomas Birch, depicts a rural scene in 1816. Named for a Pennsylvania town, the Conestoga Wagon was large enough to carry a family and up to six tons of goods. It was used by many of the families who moved west in the aftermath of the War of 1812.

alone. In several southern cities, public notices warned "persons of color" to stay away from the ceremonies honoring Lafayette. Half a century after the winning of independence, the coexistence of liberty and slavery, and their simultaneous expansion, remained the central contradiction of American life.

A NEW ECONOMY

In the first half of the nineteenth century, an economic transformation known to historians as the market revolution swept over the United States. Its catalyst was a series of innovations in transportation and communication. American technology had hardly changed during the colonial era. No important alterations were made in sailing ships, no major canals were built, and manufacturing continued to be done by hand, with skills passed on from artisan to journeyman and apprentice. At the dawn of the nineteenth century, most roads were little more than rutted paths through the woods. Transporting goods thirty miles inland by road cost as much as shipping the same cargo from England. In 1800, it took fifty days to move goods from Cincinnati to New York City, via a flatboat ride down the Mississippi River to New Orleans and then a journey by sail along the Gulf and Atlantic coasts.

To be sure, the market revolution represented an acceleration of developments already under way in the colonial era. As noted in previous chapters, southern planters were marketing the products of slave labor in the international market as early as the seventeenth century. By the eighteenth, many colonists had been drawn into Britain's commercial empire. Consumer goods like sugar and tea, and market-oriented tactics like the boycott of British goods, had been central to the political battles leading up to independence.

Nonetheless, as Americans moved across the Appalachian Mountains, and into interior regions of the states along the Atlantic coast, they found themselves more and more isolated from markets. In 1800, American farm families produced at home most of what they needed, from clothing to farm implements. What they could not make themselves, they obtained by bartering with their neighbors or purchasing from local stores and from rural craftsmen like blacksmiths and shoemakers. Those farmers not located near cities or navigable waterways found it almost impossible to market their produce.

The early life of Abraham Lincoln was typical of those who grew up in the pre-market world. Lincoln was born in Kentucky in 1809 and seven years later moved with his family to Indiana, where he lived until 1831. His father occasionally took pork down the Ohio and Mississippi Rivers to market in New Orleans, and Lincoln himself at age nineteen traveled by flatboat to that city to sell the goods of a local merchant. But essentially, the Lincoln family was self-sufficient. They hunted game for much of their food and sewed most of their clothing at home. They relied little on cash; Lincoln's father sometimes sent young Abraham to work for neighbors as a way of settling debts. As an adult, however, Lincoln embraced the market revolution. In the Illinois legislature in the 1830s, he eagerly promoted the improvement of rivers to facilitate access to markets. As a lawyer, he eventually came to represent the Illinois Central Railroad, which opened large areas of Illinois to commercial farming.

Roads and Steamboats

In the first half of the nineteenth century, in rapid succession, the **steamboat**, canal, railroad, and telegraph wrenched America out of its economic past. These innovations opened new land to settlement, lowered transportation costs, and made it far easier for economic enterprises to sell their products. They linked farmers to national and world markets and made them major consumers of manufactured goods. Americans, wrote Tocqueville, had "annihilated space and time."

The first advance in overland transportation came through the construction of toll roads, or "turnpikes," by localities, states, and private companies. Between 1800 and 1830, the New England and Middle Atlantic states alone chartered more than 900 companies to build new roads. In 1806, Congress authorized the construction of the paved National Road from Cumberland, Maryland, to the Old Northwest. It reached Wheeling, on the Ohio River, in 1818 and by 1838 extended to Illinois, where it ended.

Because maintenance costs were higher than expected and many towns built "shunpikes"—short detours that enabled residents to avoid tollgates—most private toll roads never turned a profit. Even on the new roads, horse-drawn wagons remained an inefficient mode of getting goods to market, except over short distances. It was improved water transportation that most dramatically increased the speed and lowered the expense of commerce.

Robert Fulton, a Pennsylvania-born artist and engineer, had experimented with steamboat designs while living in France during the 1790s. He even launched a steamboat on the Seine River in Paris in 1803. But not until 1807, when Fulton's ship the *Clermont* navigated the Hudson River from New York City to Albany, was the steamboat's technological and commercial feasibility demonstrated. The invention made possible upstream commerce (that is, travel against the current) on the country's major rivers as well as rapid transport across the Great Lakes and, eventually, the Atlantic Ocean. By 1811, the first steamboat had been introduced on the Mississippi River; twenty years later some 200 plied its waters.

A watercolor from 1829 by John William Hill depicts the Erie Canal five years after it opened. Boats carrying passengers and goods traverse the waterway, along whose banks farms and villages have sprung up.

Upstream commerce

The Erie Canal

The completion in 1825 of the 363-mile **Erie Canal** across upstate New York (a remarkable feat of engineering at a time when America's next-largest canal was only twenty-eight miles long) allowed goods to flow between the Great Lakes and New York City. Almost instantaneously, the canal attracted an influx of farmers migrating from New England, giving birth to cities like Buffalo, Rochester, and Syracuse along its path. Its water, wrote the novelist Nathaniel Hawthorne after a trip on the canal, served as a miraculous "fertilizer," for "it causes towns with their masses of brick and stone, their churches and theaters, their business . . . to spring up."

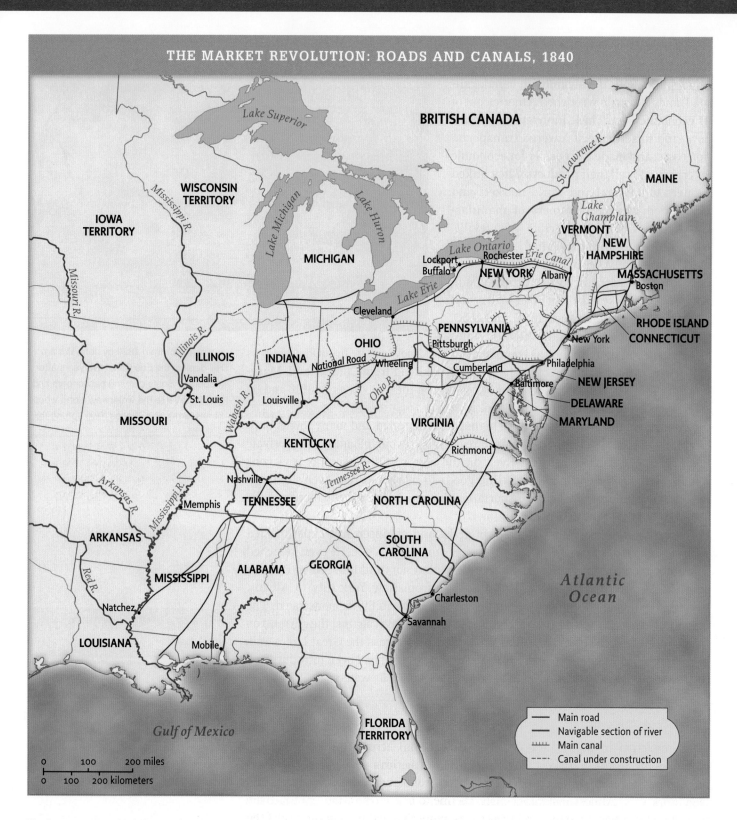

THE MARKET REVOLUTION: ROADS AND CANALS, 1840

The improvement of existing roads and building of new roads and canals sharply reduced transportation times and costs and stimulated the growth of the market economy.

A view of New York City, in 1849, by the noted lithographer Nathaniel Currier. Steamships and sailing vessels of various sizes crowd the harbor of the nation's largest city and busiest port.

New York governor DeWitt Clinton, who oversaw the construction of the state-financed canal, predicted that it would make New York City "the granary of the world, the emporium of commerce, the seat of manufactures, the focus of great moneyed operations." And, indeed, the canal gave New York City primacy over competing ports in access to trade with the Old Northwest. In its financing by the state government, the Erie Canal typified the developing transportation infrastructure. With the federal government generally under the control of political leaders hostile to federal funding for internal improvements, the burden fell on the states. Between 1787 and 1860, the federal government spent about $60 million building roads and canals and improving harbors; the states spent nearly ten times that sum.

The completion of the Erie Canal set off a scramble among other states to match New York's success. Several borrowed so much money to finance elaborate programs of canal construction that they went bankrupt during the economic depression that began in 1837. By then, however, more than 3,000 miles of canals had been built, creating a network linking the Atlantic states with the Ohio and Mississippi Valleys and drastically reducing the cost of transportation.

Railroads and the Telegraph

Canals connected existing waterways. The railroad opened vast new areas of the American interior to settlement, while stimulating the mining of coal for fuel and the manufacture of iron for locomotives and rails. Work on the Baltimore and Ohio, the nation's first commercial railroad, began in 1828. Five years later, the South Carolina Canal and Railroad, which stretched from Charleston across the state to Hamburg, became the first long-distance line to begin operation. By 1860, the railroad network had grown to 30,000 miles, more than the total in the rest of the world combined.

At the same time, the telegraph made possible instantaneous communication throughout the nation. The device was invented during the 1830s by Samuel F. B.

The cover of a periodical published in Philadelphia depicts the integrated, diversified economy promoted by the market revolution. The top two images depict farmers, factory workers, and craftsmen; at the bottom, a canal boat and a railroad illustrate how goods are transported.

An 1884 watercolor, *Locomotive DeWitt Clinton*, recalls the early days of rail travel, and also depicts modes of transportation on canal and river. The train is driven by a steam-powered locomotive and the cars strongly resemble horse-drawn stagecoaches.

Samuel F. B. Morse

Morse, an artist and amateur scientist living in New York City, and was put into commercial operation in 1844. Using Morse code, messages could be sent over electric wires, with each letter and number represented by its own pattern of electrical pulses. Within sixteen years, some 50,000 miles of telegraph wire had been strung. Initially, the telegraph was a service for businesses, and especially newspapers, rather than individuals. It helped speed the flow of information and brought uniformity to prices throughout the country.

The Rise of the West

Improvements in transportation and communication made possible the rise of the West as a powerful, self-conscious region of the new nation. Between 1790 and 1840, some 4.5 million people crossed the Appalachian Mountains—more than the entire U.S. population at the time of Washington's first inauguration. Most of this migration took place after the War of 1812, which unleashed a flood of land-hungry settlers moving from eastern states. In the six years following the end of the war in 1815, six new states entered the Union (Indiana, Illinois, Missouri, Alabama, Mississippi, and Maine—the last an eastern frontier for New England).

Migration west

Few Americans moved west as lone pioneers. More frequently, people traveled in groups and, once they arrived in the West, cooperated with each other to clear land, build houses and barns, and establish communities. One stream of migration, including both small farmers and planters with their slaves, flowed out of the South to create the new Cotton Kingdom of Alabama, Mississippi, Louisiana, and Arkansas. Many farm families from the Upper South crossed into southern Ohio, Indiana, and Illinois. A third population stream moved from New England across New York to the Upper Northwest—northern Ohio, Indiana, and Illinois, and Michigan and Wisconsin.

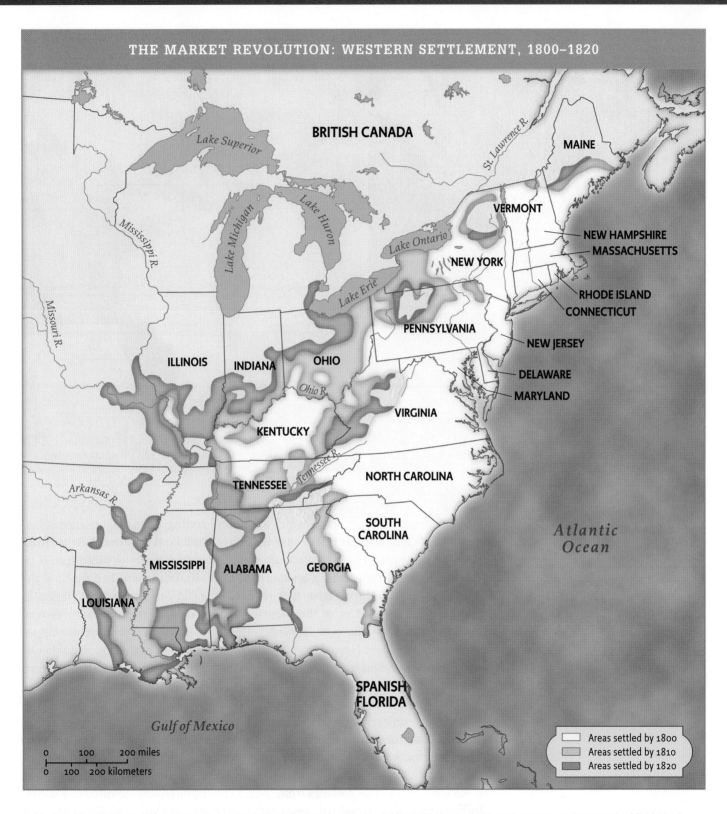

THE MARKET REVOLUTION: WESTERN SETTLEMENT, 1800–1820

Areas settled by 1800
Areas settled by 1810
Areas settled by 1820

In the first two decades of the nineteenth century, the westward movement of the population brought settlement to and across the Mississippi River. Before canals—and later, railroads—opened previously landlocked areas to commercial farming, settlement was concentrated near rivers.

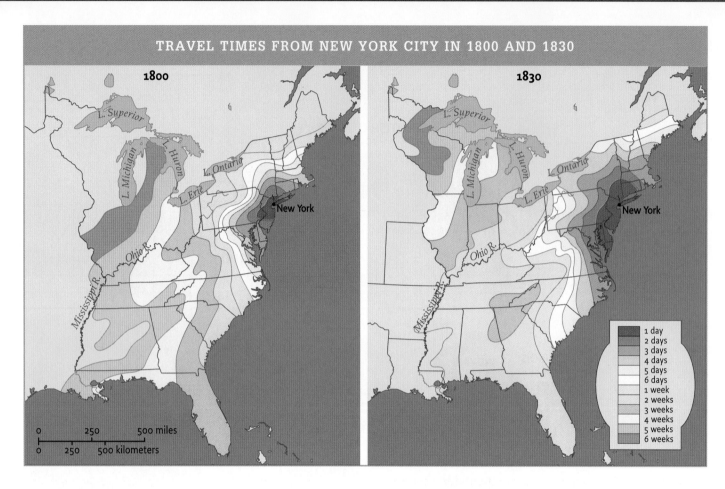

TRAVEL TIMES FROM NEW YORK CITY IN 1800 AND 1830

1800

1830

L. Superior
L. Michigan
L. Huron
L. Ontario
L. Erie
New York
Ohio R.
Mississippi R.

1 day	
2 days	
3 days	
4 days	
5 days	
6 days	
1 week	
2 weeks	
3 weeks	
4 weeks	
5 weeks	
6 weeks	

0   250   500 miles
0   250   500 kilometers

These maps illustrate how the transportation revolution of the early nineteenth century made possible much more rapid travel within the United States.

Regional cultures in the West

Expansion into Florida

Some western migrants became "squatters," setting up farms on unoccupied land without a clear legal title. Those who purchased land acquired it either from the federal government, at the price, after 1820, of $1.25 per acre payable in cash, or from land speculators on long-term credit. By 1840, settlement had reached the Mississippi River and two large new regions—the Old Northwest and Old Southwest—had entered the Union. The West became the home of regional cultures very much like those the migrants had left behind. Upstate New York and the Upper Northwest resembled New England, with its small towns, churches, and schools, while the Lower South replicated the plantation-based society of the southern Atlantic states.

As population moved west, the nation's borders expanded. National boundaries made little difference to territorial expansion—in Florida, and later in Texas and Oregon, American settlers rushed in to claim land under the jurisdiction of foreign countries (Spain, Mexico, and Britain) or Indian tribes, confident that American sovereignty would soon follow in their wake. Nor did the desire of local inhabitants to remain outside the American republic deter the nation's expansion. Florida, for example, fell into American hands despite the resistance of local Indians and Spain's rejection of American offers to buy the area. In 1810, American residents of West Florida rebelled and seized Baton Rouge, and the United States soon annexed the area. The drive for the acquisition of East Florida was spurred by Georgia and

Alabama planters who wished to eliminate a refuge for fugitive slaves and hostile Seminole Indians. Andrew Jackson led troops into the area in 1818. While on foreign soil, he created an international crisis by executing two British traders and a number of Indian chiefs. Although Jackson withdrew, Spain, aware that it could not defend the territory, sold it to the United States in the Adams-Onís Treaty of 1819 negotiated by John Quincy Adams.

Successive censuses told the remarkable story of western growth. In 1840, by which time the government had sold to settlers and land companies nearly 43 million acres of land, 7 million Americans—two-fifths of the total population—lived beyond the Appalachian Mountains. Between 1810 and 1830, Ohio's population grew from 231,000 to more than 900,000. It reached nearly 2 million in 1850, when it ranked third among all the states. The careers of the era's leading public figures reflected the westward movement. Andrew Jackson, Henry Clay, and many other statesmen had been born in states along the Atlantic coast but made their mark in politics after moving west.

Western growth

An Internal Borderland

Before the War of 1812, the Old Northwest was a prime example of a borderland, a meeting-ground of Native Americans and various people of English, French, and American descent, where cultural boundaries remained unstable and political authority uncertain. The American victory over the British and Indians erased any doubt over who would control the region. But a new, internal borderland region quickly developed.

Because the Northwest Ordinance of 1787 prohibited slavery in the Old Northwest, the Ohio River came to mark a boundary between free and slave societies. But for many years it was easier for people and goods to travel between the slave state Kentucky and the southern counties of Ohio, Indiana, and Illinois than to

Ohio river as boundary

A watercolor by the artist Edwin Whitefield depicts a squatter's cabin in the Minnesota woods.

the northern parts of those states. The region stretching northward from the Ohio River retained much of the cultural flavor of the Upper South. Its food, speech, settlement patterns, family ties, and economic relations had more in common with Kentucky and Tennessee than with the northern counties of their own states, soon to be settled by New Englanders. Until the 1850s, farmers in the southern counties of Ohio, Indiana, and Illinois were far more likely to ship their produce southward via the Ohio and Mississippi Rivers than northward or to the East. The large concentration of people of southern ancestry would make Indiana and Illinois key political battlegrounds as the slavery controversy developed.

The Cotton Kingdom

Although the market revolution and westward expansion occurred simultaneously in the North and the South, their combined effects heightened the nation's sectional divisions. In some ways, the most dynamic feature of the American economy in the first thirty years of the nineteenth century was the rise of the **Cotton Kingdom**. The early industrial revolution, which began in England and soon spread to parts of the North, centered on factories producing cotton textiles with water-powered spinning and weaving machinery. These factories generated an immense demand for cotton, a crop the Deep South was particularly suited to growing because of its climate and soil fertility. Until 1793, the marketing of cotton had been slowed by the laborious task of removing seeds from the plant itself. But in that year, Eli Whitney, a Yale graduate working in Georgia as a private tutor, invented the **cotton gin**. A fairly simple device consisting of rollers and brushes, the gin quickly separated the seed from the cotton. It made possible the growing and selling of cotton on a large scale.

Coupled with rising demand for cotton and the opening of new lands in the West to settlement, Whitney's invention revolutionized American slavery. An institution that many Americans had expected to die out because its major crop, tobacco, exhausted the soil, now embarked on a period of unprecedented expansion. In the first decade of the nineteenth century, cotton plantations spread into the South Carolina upcountry (the region inland from the Atlantic coast previously dominated by small farms), a major reason why the state reopened the African slave trade between 1803 and 1808. After the War of 1812, the federal government moved to consolidate American control over the Deep South, forcing defeated Indians to cede land, encouraging white settlement, and acquiring Florida. With American sovereignty came the expansion of slavery. Settlers from the older southern states flooded into the region. Planters monopolized the most fertile land, while poorer farmers were generally confined to less productive and less accessible areas in the "hill country" and piney woods. After Congress prohibited the Atlantic slave trade in 1808—the earliest date allowed by the Constitution—a massive trade in slaves developed

TABLE 9.1   Population Growth of Selected Western States, 1800–1850 (Excluding Indians)

STATE	1810	1830	1850
Alabama	9,000	310,000	772,000
Illinois	12,000	157,000	851,000
Indiana	25,000	343,000	988,000
Louisiana	77,000	216,000	518,000
Mississippi	31,000	137,000	607,000
Missouri	20,000	140,000	682,000
Ohio	231,000	938,000	1,980,000

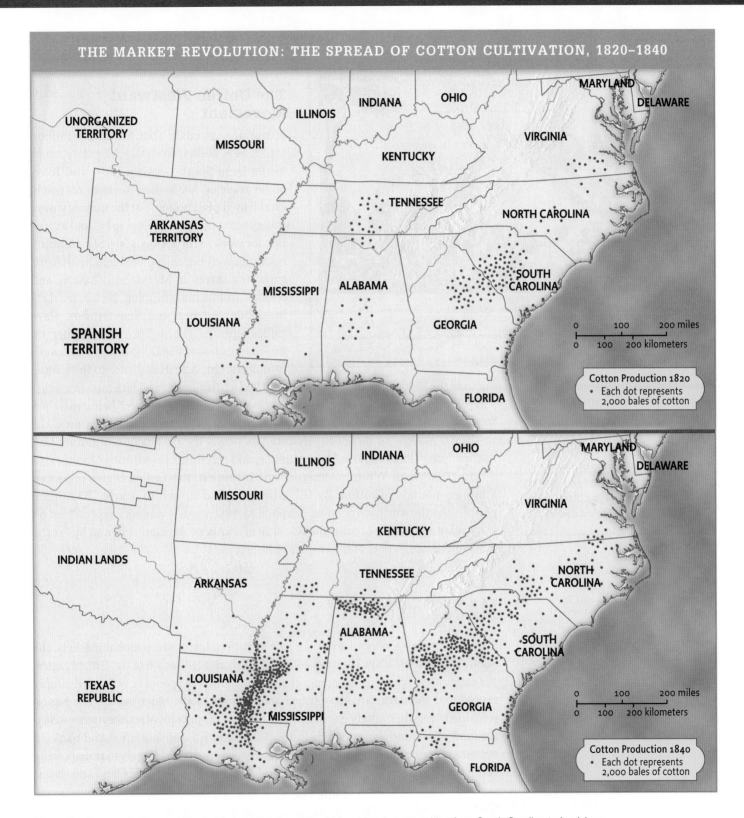

THE MARKET REVOLUTION: THE SPREAD OF COTTON CULTIVATION, 1820–1840

Cotton Production 1820
• Each dot represents 2,000 bales of cotton

Cotton Production 1840
• Each dot represents 2,000 bales of cotton

Maps of cotton production graphically illustrate the rise of the Cotton Kingdom stretching from South Carolina to Louisiana.

within the United States, supplying the labor force required by the new Cotton Kingdom.

The Unfree Westward Movement

Historians estimate that around 1 million slaves were shifted from the older slave states to the Deep South between 1800 and 1860. Some traveled with their owners to newly established plantations, but the majority were transported by slave traders to be sold at auction for work in the cotton fields. Slave trading became a well-organized business, with firms gathering slaves in Maryland, Virginia, and South Carolina and shipping them to markets in Mobile, Natchez, and New Orleans. Slave coffles—groups chained to one another on forced marches to the Deep South—became a common sight. A British visitor to the United

Slave Trader, Sold to Tennessee, a watercolor sketch by the artist Lewis Miller from the mid-1850s. Miller depicts a group of slaves being marched from Virginia to Tennessee. Once Congress voted to prohibit the further importation of slaves into the country, slaveowners in newly opened areas of the country had to obtain slaves from other parts of the United States.

States in the 1840s encountered what he called a "disgusting and hideous spectacle," a file of "about two hundred slaves, manacled and chained together," being marched from Virginia to Louisiana. A source of greater freedom for many whites, the westward movement meant to African-Americans the destruction of family ties, the breakup of long-standing communities, and receding opportunities for liberty.

In 1793, when Whitney designed his invention, the United States produced 5 million pounds of cotton. By 1820, the crop had grown to nearly 170 million pounds. As the southern economy expanded westward, it was cotton produced on slave plantations that became the linchpin of southern development and by far the most important export of the empire of liberty.

MARKET SOCIETY

Since cotton was produced solely for sale in national and international markets, the South was in some ways the most commercially oriented region of the United States. Yet rather than spurring economic change, the South's expansion westward simply reproduced the agrarian, slave-based social order of the older states. The region remained overwhelmingly rural. In 1860, roughly 80 percent of southerners worked the land—the same proportion as in 1800. The South's transportation and banking systems remained adjuncts of the plantation economy, geared largely to transporting cotton and other staple crops to market and financing the purchase of land and slaves.

Economic expansion with little change in the South

Commercial Farmers

In the North, however, the market revolution and westward expansion set in motion changes that transformed the region into an integrated economy of commercial farms and manufacturing cities. As in the case of Lincoln's family, the initial pioneer stage of settlement reinforced the farmer's self-sufficiency, for the tasks of felling trees, building cabins, breaking the soil, and feeding the family left little time for agriculture geared to the market. But as the Old Northwest became a more settled society, bound by a web of transportation and credit to eastern centers of commerce and banking, farmers found themselves drawn into the new market economy. They increasingly concentrated on growing crops and raising livestock for sale, while purchasing at stores goods previously produced at home.

Economic development in the North

Western farmers found in the growing cities of the East a market for their produce and a source of credit. Loans originating with eastern banks and insurance companies financed the acquisition of land and supplies and, in the 1840s and 1850s, the purchase of fertilizer and new agricultural machinery to expand production. The steel plow, invented by John Deere in 1837 and mass-produced by the 1850s, made possible the rapid subduing of the western prairies. The reaper, a horse-drawn machine that greatly increased the amount of wheat a farmer could harvest, was invented by Cyrus McCormick in 1831 and produced in large quantities soon afterward. Tens of thousands were in use on the eve of the Civil War. Between 1840 and 1860, America's output of wheat nearly tripled. Unlike cotton, however, the bulk of the crop was consumed within the country. Eastern farmers, unable to grow wheat and corn as cheaply as their western counterparts, increasingly concentrated on producing dairy products, fruits, and vegetables for nearby urban centers.

Technology and western farming

The Growth of Cities

From the beginning, cities formed part of the western frontier. Western cities like Cincinnati and St. Louis that stood at the crossroads of inter-regional trade experienced extraordinary growth. Cincinnati was known as **Porkopolis**, after its

Western cities

A painting of Cincinnati, self-styled Queen City of the West, from 1835. Steamboats line the Ohio River waterfront.

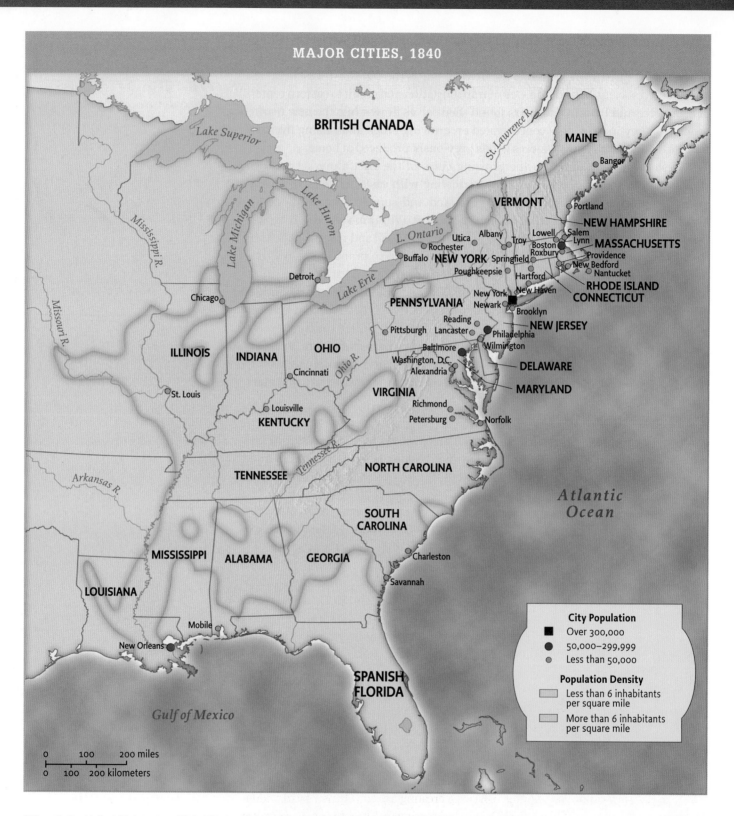

MAJOR CITIES, 1840

BRITISH CANADA

Lake Superior

Lake Michigan

Lake Huron

L. Ontario

Lake Erie

St. Lawrence R.

Mississippi R.

Missouri R.

MAINE
• Bangor

VERMONT
• Portland

NEW HAMPSHIRE

Albany • Lowell • Salem
Utica • Troy • Boston • Lynn **MASSACHUSETTS**
Rochester • Roxbury
Buffalo • **NEW YORK** Springfield Providence
Poughkeepsie New Bedford
Hartford Nantucket
New Haven **RHODE ISLAND**
New York **CONNECTICUT**
Newark
Brooklyn

Detroit

Chicago •

PENNSYLVANIA

NEW JERSEY

Reading
Pittsburgh • Lancaster
Philadelphia
Wilmington

ILLINOIS **INDIANA** **OHIO**

Ohio R.

Cincinnati •

St. Louis •

Baltimore
Washington, D.C.
Alexandria

DELAWARE

MARYLAND

VIRGINIA
Richmond •
Petersburg • Norfolk •

Louisville •

KENTUCKY

Tennessee R.

Arkansas R.

TENNESSEE

NORTH CAROLINA

Atlantic Ocean

SOUTH CAROLINA

MISSISSIPPI **ALABAMA** **GEORGIA**

Charleston •

Savannah •

LOUISIANA

Mobile •

New Orleans •

SPANISH FLORIDA

Gulf of Mexico

City Population
■ Over 300,000
● 50,000–299,999
○ Less than 50,000

Population Density
Less than 6 inhabitants per square mile
More than 6 inhabitants per square mile

0   100   200 miles
0   100   200 kilometers

Although the United States was still predominantly agricultural, by 1840 major cities had arisen in the northern and northwestern states. The South lagged far behind in urban growth. Most cities were located on navigable waterways—either the Atlantic coast or inland rivers—or on rivers that provided water power for early factories.

slaughterhouses, where hundreds of thousands of pigs were butchered each year and the meat was shipped to eastern consumers. The greatest of all the western cities was Chicago. In the early 1830s, it was a tiny settlement on the shore of Lake Michigan. By 1860, thanks to the railroad, Chicago had become the nation's fourth-largest city, where farm products from throughout the Northwest were gathered to be sent east.

Like rural areas, urban centers witnessed dramatic changes due to the market revolution. The number of cities with populations exceeding 5,000 rose from 12 in 1820 to nearly 150 three decades later, by which time the urban population numbered more than 6 million. Urban merchants, bankers, and master craftsmen took advantage of the economic opportunities created by the expanding market among commercial farmers. The drive among these businessmen to increase production and reduce labor costs fundamentally altered the nature of work. Traditionally, skilled artisans had manufactured goods at home, where they controlled the pace and intensity of their own labor. Now, entrepreneurs gathered artisans into large workshops in order to oversee their work and subdivide their tasks. Craftsmen who traditionally produced an entire pair of shoes or piece of furniture saw the labor process broken down into numerous steps requiring far less skill and training. They found themselves subjected to constant supervision by their employers and relentless pressure for greater output and lower wages.

The Factory System

In some industries, most notably textiles, the factory superseded traditional craft production altogether. Factories gathered large groups of workers under central supervision and replaced hand tools with power-driven machinery. Samuel Slater, an immigrant from England, established America's first factory in 1790 at Pawtucket, Rhode Island. Since British law made it illegal to export the plans for industrial machinery, Slater, a skilled mechanic, built from memory a power-driven spinning jenny, one of the key inventions of the early industrial revolution.

Spinning factories such as Slater's produced yarn, which was then sent to traditional hand-loom weavers and farm families to be woven into cloth. This "outwork" system, in which rural men and women earned money by taking in jobs from factories, typified early industrialization. Before shoe production was fully mechanized, for example, various parts of the shoe were produced in factories, then stitched together in nearby homes, and then returned to the factories for finishing. Eventually, however, the entire manufacturing process in textiles, shoes, and many other products was brought under a single factory roof.

The cutoff of British imports because of the Embargo of 1807 and the War of 1812 stimulated the establishment of the first large-scale American factory utilizing power looms for weaving cotton cloth. This was constructed in 1814 at Waltham, Massachusetts, by a group of merchants who came to be called the Boston Associates. In the 1820s, they expanded their enterprise by creating an entirely new factory town (incorporated as the city of Lowell in 1836) on the Merrimack River, twenty-seven miles from Boston. Here they built a group of modern textile factories that brought together all phases of production from the spinning of thread to the weaving and finishing of cloth. By 1850, Lowell's fifty-two mills employed more than 10,000 workers. Across

A trade card depicts the interior of a chair-manufacturing workshop in New York City. The owner stands at the center, dressed quite differently from his employees. The men are using traditional hand tools; furniture manufacturing had not yet been mechanized.

The Lowell mills

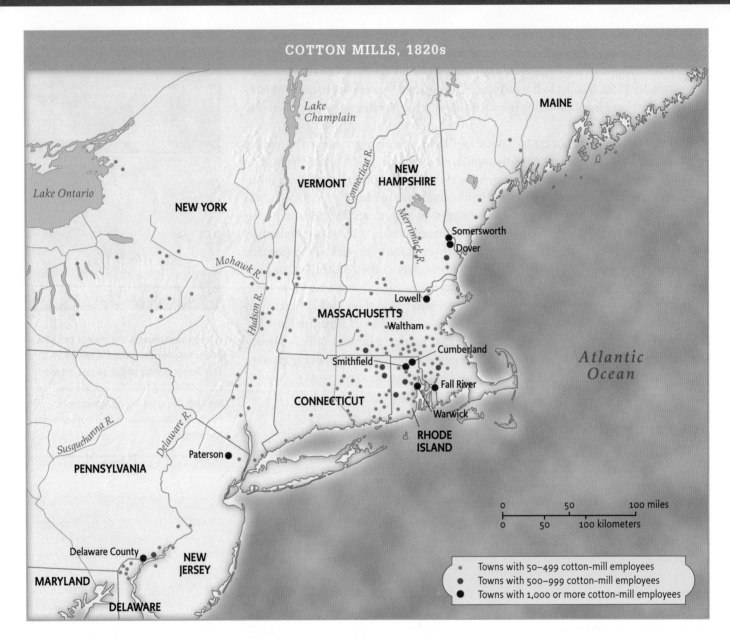

COTTON MILLS, 1820s

MAINE

Lake Champlain

VERMONT

NEW HAMPSHIRE

Connecticut R.

Merrimack R.

Somersworth

Dover

Lake Ontario

NEW YORK

Mohawk R.

Hudson R.

Lowell

MASSACHUSETTS

Waltham

Cumberland

Smithfield

Fall River

CONNECTICUT

Warwick

RHODE ISLAND

Susquehanna R.

Delaware R.

Paterson

PENNSYLVANIA

Atlantic Ocean

0   50   100 miles
0   50   100 kilometers

Delaware County

NEW JERSEY

MARYLAND

DELAWARE

• Towns with 50–499 cotton-mill employees
● Towns with 500–999 cotton-mill employees
● Towns with 1,000 or more cotton-mill employees

The early industrial revolution was concentrated in New England, where factories producing textiles from raw cotton sprang up along the region's many rivers, taking advantage of water power to drive their machinery.

Factory production

New England, small industrial cities sprang up patterned on Waltham and Lowell. Massachusetts soon became the second most industrialized region of the world, after Great Britain.

The earliest factories, including those at Pawtucket, Waltham, and Lowell, were located along the "fall line," where waterfalls and river rapids could be harnessed to provide power for spinning and weaving machinery. By the 1840s, steam power made it possible for factory owners to locate in towns like New Bedford nearer to the coast, and in large cities like Philadelphia and Chicago with their immense local markets. In 1850, manufacturers produced in factories not only textiles but also a wide variety of other goods, including tools, firearms, shoes, clocks, ironware, and agricultural machinery. What came to be called the **American system of manufactures** relied on the mass production of interchangeable parts that could be rapidly assembled into standardized finished products. This technique was first perfected in the manufacture

Mill on the Brandywine, an 1830 watercolor of a Pennsylvania paper mill. Because it relied on water power, much early manufacturing took place in the countryside.

of clocks by Eli Terry, a Connecticut craftsman, and in small-arms production by Eli Whitney, who had previously invented the cotton gin. More impressive, in a way, than factory production was the wide dispersion of mechanical skills throughout northern society. Every town, it seemed, had its sawmill, paper mill, iron works, shoemaker, hatmaker, tailor, and a host of other such small enterprises.

The early industrial revolution was largely confined to New England and a few cities outside it. Lacking a strong internal market, and with its slaveholding class generally opposed to industrial development, the South lagged in factory production. And outside New England, most northern manufacturing was still done in small-scale establishments employing a handful of workers, not in factories. In Cincinnati, for example, most workers in 1850 still labored in small unmechanized workshops.

The Industrial Worker

The market revolution helped to change Americans' conception of time itself. Farm life continued to be regulated by the rhythms of the seasons. But in cities, clocks became part of daily life, and work time and leisure time came to be clearly marked off from one another. In artisan workshops of the colonial and early national eras, bouts of intense work alternated with periods of leisure. Artisans would set down their tools to enjoy a drink at a tavern or attend a political discussion. As the market revolution accelerated, work in factories, workshops, and even for servants in Americans' homes took place for a specified number of hours per day. In colonial America, an artisan's pay was known as his "price," since it was linked to the goods he produced. In the nineteenth century, pay increasingly became a "wage," paid according to an hourly or daily rate. The increasing reliance on railroads, which operated

A broadside from 1853 illustrates the long hours of work (from 5 AM to 6:30 PM with brief breaks for meals) in the textile mills of Holyoke, Massachusetts. Factory labor was strictly regulated by the clock.

Women at work tending machines in the Lowell textile mills.

Young women workers from the Amoskeag textile mills in Manchester, New Hampshire, photographed in 1854.

according to fixed schedules, also made Americans more conscious of arranging their lives according to "clock time."

Closely supervised work tending a machine for a period determined by a clock seemed to violate the independence Americans considered an essential element of freedom. Consequently, few native-born men could be attracted to work in the early factories. Employers turned instead to those who lacked other ways of earning a living.

The "Mill Girls"

Although some factories employed entire families, the early New England textile mills relied largely on female and child labor. At Lowell, the most famous center of early textile manufacturing, young unmarried women from Yankee farm families dominated the work-force that tended the spinning machines. To persuade parents to allow their daughters to leave home to work in the mills, Lowell owners set up boarding houses with strict rules regulating personal behavior. They also established lecture halls and churches to occupy the women's free time.

The constant supervision of the workers' private lives seems impossibly restrictive from a modern point of view. But this was the first time in history that large numbers of women left their homes to participate in the public world. Most valued the opportunity to earn money independently at a time when few other jobs were open to women. Home life, Lucy Larcom later recalled, was narrow and confining, while living and working at Lowell gave the **mill girls** a "larger, firmer idea of womanhood," teaching them "to go out of themselves and enter into the lives of others. . . . It was like a young man's pleasure in entering upon business for himself." But women like Larcom did not become a permanent class of factory workers. They typically remained in the factories for only a few years, after which they left to return home, marry, or move west. Larcom herself migrated to Illinois, where she became a teacher and writer. The shortage of industrial labor continued, easing only when large-scale immigration began in the 1840s and 1850s.

The Growth of Immigration

Economic expansion fueled a demand for labor, which was met, in part, by increased immigration from abroad. Between 1790 and 1830, immigrants contributed only marginally to American population growth. But between 1840 and 1860, over 4 million people (more than the entire population of 1790) entered the United States, the majority from Ireland and Germany. About 90 percent headed for the northern states, where job opportunities were most abundant and the new arrivals would not have to compete with slave labor. Immigrants were virtually unknown in the slave states, except in cities on the periphery of the South, such as New Orleans, St. Louis, and Baltimore. In the North, however, they became a visible presence in both urban and rural areas. In 1860, the 814,000 residents of New York City, the major port of entry, included more than 384,000 immigrants, and one-third of the population of Wisconsin was foreign-born.

Numerous factors inspired this massive flow of population across the Atlantic. In Europe, the modernization of agriculture and the industrial revolution disrupted

Currency issued by a bank in Sanford, Maine, is embellished with images of women textile workers, illustrating their centrality to the state's economy. Before the Civil War, there was no national currency and banks issued their own paper money.

centuries-old patterns of life, pushing peasants off the land and eliminating the jobs of traditional craft workers. The introduction of the oceangoing steamship and the railroad made long-distance travel more practical. The Cunard Line began regular sailings with inexpensive fares from Britain to Boston and New York City in the 1840s. Beginning around 1840, emigration from Europe accelerated, not only to the United States but to Canada and Australia as well. Frequently, a male family member emigrated first; he would later send back money for the rest of the family to follow.

Irish and German Newcomers

To everyone discontented in Europe, commented the *New York Times*, "thoughts come of the New Free World." America's political and religious freedoms attracted Europeans who chafed under the continent's repressive governments and rigid social hierarchies, including political refugees from the failed revolutions of 1848. "In America," wrote a German newcomer, "there aren't any masters, here everyone is a free agent."

The largest number of immigrants, however, were refugees from disaster—Irish men and women fleeing the Great Famine of 1845–1851, when a blight destroyed the potato crop on which the island's diet rested. An estimated 1 million persons starved to death and another million emigrated in those years, most of them to the United States. Lacking industrial skills and capital, these impoverished agricultural laborers and small farmers ended up filling the low-wage unskilled jobs native-born Americans sought to avoid. Male Irish immigrants built America's railroads, dug canals, and worked as common laborers, servants, longshoremen, and factory operatives. Irish women frequently went to work as servants in the homes of native-born Americans, although some preferred factory work to domestic service. "It's the freedom that we want when the day's work is done," one Irish woman explained. "Our day is ten hours long, but when it's done it's done"; however, servants were on call at any time. By the end of the 1850s, the Lowell textile mills had largely replaced Yankee farm women with immigrant Irish families. Four-fifths of Irish immigrants remained in the Northeast. In Boston, New York, and smaller industrial cities, they congregated in overcrowded urban ghettos notorious for poverty, crime, and disease.

The second-largest group of immigrants, Germans, included a considerably larger number of skilled craftsmen than the Irish. Germans also settled in tightly knit neighborhoods in eastern cities, but many were able to move to the West, where they established themselves as craftsmen, shopkeepers, and farmers. The "German

> *The Great Famine of 1845–1851*

TABLE 9.2 Total Number of Immigrants by Five-Year Period	
YEARS	**NUMBER OF IMMIGRANTS**
1841–1845	430,000
1846–1850	1,283,000
1851–1855	1,748,000
1856–1860	850,000

Although our image of the West emphasizes the lone pioneer, many migrants settled in tightly knit communities and worked cooperatively. This painting by Olof Krans, who came to the United States from Sweden with his family in 1850 at the age of twelve, shows a group of women preparing to plant corn at the immigrant settlement of Bishop Hill, Illinois.

triangle," as the cities of Cincinnati, St. Louis, and Milwaukee were sometimes called, attracted large German populations. A vibrant German-language culture, with its own schools, newspapers, associations, and churches, developed wherever large numbers of Germans settled. "As one passes along the Bowery," one observer noted of a part of New York City known as Kleindeutschland (Little Germany), "almost everything is German."

Some 40,000 Scandinavians also emigrated to the United States in these years, most of whom settled on farms in the Old Northwest. The continuing expansion of industry and the failure of the Chartist movement of the 1840s, which sought to democratize the system of government in Britain, also inspired many English workers to emigrate to the United States.

The Rise of Nativism

Immigrants from England (whose ranks included the actor Junius Brutus Booth, father of John Wilkes Booth) were easily absorbed, but those from Ireland encountered intense hostility. As Roman Catholics, they faced discrimination in a largely Protestant society in which the tradition of "anti-popery" still ran deep. The Irish influx greatly enhanced the visibility and power of the Catholic Church, previously a minor presence in most parts of the country. During the 1840s and 1850s, Archbishop John Hughes of New York City made the church a more assertive institution. Hughes condemned the use of the Protestant King James Bible in New York City's public schools, pressed Catholic parents to send their children to an expanding network of parochial schools, and sought government funding to pay for them. He aggressively sought to win converts from Protestantism.

Many Protestants found such activities alarming. Catholicism, they feared, threatened American institutions and American freedom. In 1834, Lyman Beecher, a prominent Presbyterian minister (and father of the religious leader Henry Ward Beecher

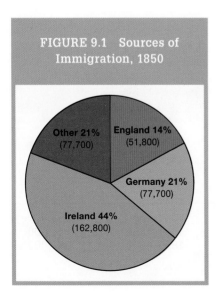

FIGURE 9.1 Sources of Immigration, 1850

Other 21% (77,700)
England 14% (51,800)
Germany 21% (77,700)
Ireland 44% (162,800)

Riot in Philadelphia, an 1844 lithograph, depicts street battles between nativists and Irish Catholics that left fifteen persons dead. The violence originated in a dispute over the use of the Protestant King James Bible in the city's public schools.

and the writers Harriet Beecher Stowe and Catharine Beecher), delivered a sermon in Boston, soon published as "A Plea for the West." Beecher warned that Catholics were seeking to dominate the American West, where the future of Christianity in the world would be worked out. His sermon inspired a mob to burn a Catholic convent in the city.

The idea of the United States as a refuge for those seeking economic opportunity or as an escape from oppression has always coexisted with suspicion of and hostility to foreign newcomers. American history has witnessed periods of intense anxiety over immigration. The Alien Act of 1798 reflected fear of immigrants with radical political views. During the early twentieth century, as will be discussed below, there was widespread hostility to the "new immigration" from southern and eastern Europe. In the early twenty-first century, the question of how many persons should be allowed to enter the United States, and under what circumstances, remains a volatile political issue.

Opposition to immigration

The Irish influx of the 1840s and 1850s thoroughly alarmed many native-born Americans. Those who feared the impact of immigration on American political and social life were called "nativists." They blamed immigrants for urban crime, political corruption, and a fondness for intoxicating liquor, and they accused them of undercutting native-born skilled laborers by working for starvation wages. The Irish were quickly brought into the urban political machines of the Democratic Party, whose local bosses provided jobs and poor relief to struggling newcomers. Nativists contended that the Irish, supposedly unfamiliar with American conceptions of liberty and subservient to the Catholic Church, posed a threat to democratic institutions, social reform, and public education. Stereotypes similar to those directed at blacks flourished regarding the Irish as well—childlike, lazy, and slaves of their passions, they were said to be unsuited for republican freedom.

Nativists

Nativism would not become a national political movement until the 1850s, as we will see in Chapter 13. But in the 1840s, New York City and Philadelphia witnessed violent anti-immigrant riots. Appealing mainly to skilled native-born workers who feared that immigrants were taking their jobs and undercutting their wages, a nativist candidate was elected New York City's mayor in 1844.

An engraving depicts the ruins of the Ursuline Convent in Charlestown, Massachusetts, burned by a mob in 1834 after a sermon by the Reverend Lyman Beecher, who warned that Catholics were conspiring to dominate the American West.

The Transformation of Law

American law increasingly supported the efforts of entrepreneurs to participate in the market revolution, while shielding them from interference by local governments and liability for some of the less desirable results of economic growth. The corporate form of business organization became central to the new market economy. A corporate firm enjoys special privileges and powers granted in a charter from the government, among them that investors and directors are not personally liable for the company's debts. Unlike companies owned by an individual, family, or limited partnership, in other words, a corporation can fail without ruining its directors and stockholders. Corporations were therefore able to raise far more capital than the traditional forms of enterprise. By the 1830s, many states had replaced the granting of charters through specific acts of legislation with "general incorporation laws," allowing any company to obtain a corporate charter if it paid a specified fee.

Corporations

Many Americans distrusted corporate charters as a form of government-granted special privilege. But the courts upheld their validity, while opposing efforts by established firms to limit competition from newcomers. In ***Dartmouth College v. Woodward*** (1819), John Marshall's Supreme Court defined corporate charters issued by state legislatures as contracts, which future lawmakers could not alter or rescind. Five years later, in ***Gibbons v. Ogden***, the Court struck down a monopoly the New York legislature had granted for steamboat navigation. And in 1837, with Roger B. Taney now the chief justice, the Court ruled that the Massachusetts legislature did not infringe the charter of an existing company that had constructed a bridge over the Charles River when it empowered a second company to build a competing bridge. The community, Taney declared, had a legitimate interest in promoting transportation and prosperity.

Court decisions on the economy

Local judges, meanwhile, held businessmen blameless for property damage done by factory construction (such as the flooding of upstream farmlands and the disruption of fishing when dams were built to harness water power). Numerous court decisions also affirmed employers' full authority over the workplace and invoked the old common law of conspiracy to punish workers who sought to strike for higher wages. Not until 1842, in **Commonwealth v. Hunt**, did Massachusetts chief justice Lemuel Shaw decree that there was nothing inherently illegal in workers organizing a union or a strike.

THE FREE INDIVIDUAL

By the 1830s, the market revolution and westward expansion had produced a society that amazed European visitors: energetic, materialistic, and seemingly in constant motion. Arriving in Chicago in 1835, the British writer Harriet Martineau found the streets "crowded with land speculators, hurrying from one sale to another.... As the gentlemen of our party walked the streets, store-keepers hailed them from their doors, with offers of farms, and all manner of land-lots, advising them to speculate before the price of land rose higher." Alexis de Tocqueville was struck by Americans' restless energy and apparent lack of attachment to place. "No sooner do you set foot on American soil," he observed, "than you find yourself in a sort of tumult. All around you, everything is on the move." Westward migration and urban development created a large mobile population no longer tied to local communities who sought to seize the opportunities offered by economic change. "In the United States," wrote Tocqueville, "a man builds a house in which to spend his old age, and sells it before the roof is on; he plants a garden and [rents] it just as the trees are coming into bearing; he brings a field into tillage and leaves other men to gather the crops."

> *An energetic society*

The West and Freedom

Westward expansion and the market revolution profoundly affected the lives of all Americans. They reinforced some older ideas of freedom and helped to create new ones. American freedom, for example, had long been linked with the availability of land in the West. A New York journalist, John L. O'Sullivan, first employed the phrase "**manifest destiny**," meaning that the United States had a divinely appointed mission, so obvious as to be beyond dispute, to occupy all of North America. Americans, he proclaimed, had a far better title to western lands than could be provided by any international treaty, right of discovery, or long-term settlement. Their right to the continent was provided by the nation's divinely inspired mission to extend the area of freedom. Other peoples' claims, O'Sullivan wrote, must give way to "our manifest destiny to overspread and to possess the whole of the continent which Providence has given us for the development of the great experiment in liberty." Those who stood in the way of expansion—European powers like Great Britain and Spain, Native Americans, Mexicans—were by definition obstacles to the progress of freedom.

O'Sullivan wrote these words in 1845, but the essential idea was familiar much earlier. As the population moved across the Appalachian Mountains, so did the linkage between westward expansion and freedom. "The Goddess

A song written in 1845 offers a satire of the widely held image of the West as "the land of the free," a place where the "humblest" American can achieve economic success. The pictures surrounding the text offer a somewhat different image of westerners, and the verses go on to complain about illness and hardship. But the opening words reflect the ways in which Americans have always viewed the West.

TO THE WEST!

To the west! to the west! to the land of the free,
Where the mighty Missouria rolls down to the sea,
Where a man is a man if he is willing to toil,
And the humblest may gather the fruits of the soil,
Where children are blessings, and he who hath most
Has aid to his fortune, and riches to boast;
Where the young may exult, and the aged may rest,
Away, far away, to the land of the west.

CHORUS.

To the west! to the west! to the land of the free,
Where the mighty Missouria rolls down to the sea,
Where the young may exult and the aged may rest,
Away, far away, to the land of the west!

Westward expansion and freedom

of Liberty," declared Senator John Breckinridge of Kentucky, was not "governed by geographical limits." A sense of spatial openness, of the constant opportunity to pick up and move when the pursuit of happiness seemed to demand it, became more and more a central component of American freedom. Freedom in the United States, wrote the French historian Michel Chevalier, one of the many Europeans who visited the country in the 1830s, was a "practical idea" as much as a "mystical one"—it meant "a liberty of action and motion which the American uses to expand over the vast territory that Providence has given him and to subdue it to his uses."

In national myth and ideology, the West would long remain, as the writer Wallace Stegner would later put it, "the last home of the freeborn American." The settlement and economic exploitation of the West promised to prevent the United States from following down the path of Europe and becoming a society with fixed social classes and a large group of wage-earning poor. In the West, land was more readily available and oppressive factory labor far less common than in the East. With population and the price of land rising dramatically in the older states and young men's prospects for acquiring a farm or setting up an independent artisan shop declining, the West still held out the chance to achieve economic independence, the social condition of freedom.

The West and economic independence

The Transcendentalists

The restless, competitive world of the market revolution strongly encouraged the identification of American freedom with the absence of restraints on self-directed individuals seeking economic advancement and personal development. The "one important revolution" of the day, the philosopher Ralph Waldo Emerson wrote in the 1830s, was "the new value of the private man." The opportunity for personal growth offered a new definition of Jefferson's pursuit of happiness, one well suited to a world in which territorial expansion and the market revolution had shattered traditional spatial and social boundaries and made moving from place to place and status to status common features of American life.

In a widely reprinted 1837 address, "The American Scholar," Emerson called on the person engaged in writing and thinking to "feel all confidence in himself, . . . to never defer to the popular cry," and to find and trust his own "definition of freedom." In Emerson's definition, rather than a preexisting set of rights or privileges, freedom was an open-ended process of self-realization by which individuals could remake themselves and their own lives. The keynote of the times, he declared, was "the new importance given to the single person" and the "emancipation" of the individual, the "American idea."

Emerson was perhaps the most prominent member of a group of New England intellectuals known as the **transcendentalists**, who insisted on the primacy of individual judgment over existing social traditions and institutions. Emerson's Concord, Massachusetts, neighbor, the writer Henry David Thoreau, echoed his call for individual self-reliance. "Any man more right than his neighbors," Thoreau wrote, "is a majority of one."

Individualism

Ironies abounded in the era's "individualism" (a term that first entered the language in the 1820s). For even as the market revolution promoted commercial connections between far-flung people, the idea of the "sovereign individual"

The daguerreotype, an early form of photography, required the sitter to remain perfectly still for twenty seconds or longer. The philosopher Ralph Waldo Emerson, depicted here, did not like the result. He complained in his journal that in his "zeal not to blur the image," every muscle had become "rigid" and his face was fixed in a frown as "in madness, or in death."

proclaimed that Americans should depend on no one but themselves. Of course, personal independence had long been associated with American freedom. But eighteenth-century thinkers generally saw no contradiction between private happiness and self-sacrificing public virtue, defined as devotion to the common good. Now, Tocqueville observed, individualism led "each member of the community to sever himself from the mass of his fellows and to draw apart with his family and his friends . . . [leaving] society at large to itself." Americans increasingly understood the realm of the self—which came to be called "privacy"—as one with which neither other individuals nor government had a right to interfere. As will be discussed in the next chapter, individualism also helped to inspire the expansion of democracy. Ownership of one's self rather than ownership of property now made a person capable of exercising the right to vote.

Looking back from the 1880s, Emerson would recall the era before the Civil War as a time when "social existence" gave way to "the enlargement and independency of the individual, . . . driven to find all his resources, hopes, rewards, society, and deity within himself." In his own life, Thoreau illustrated Emerson's point about the primacy of individual conscience in matters political, social, and personal, and the need to find one's own way rather than following the crowd. Thoreau became persuaded that modern society stifled individual judgment by making men "tools of their tools," trapped in stultifying jobs by their obsession with acquiring wealth. Even in "this comparatively free country," he wrote, most persons were so preoccupied with material things that they had no time to contemplate the beauties of nature.

To escape this fate, Thoreau retreated for two years to a cabin on Walden Pond near Concord, where he could enjoy the freedom of isolation from the "economical and moral tyranny" he believed ruled American society. He subsequently published *Walden* (1854), an account of his experiences and a critique of how the market revolution was, in his opinion, degrading both Americans' values and the natural environment. An area that had been covered with dense forest in his youth, he observed,

The sketch of Henry David Thoreau's cabin on Walden Pond illustrates his belief that Americans could enjoy what he called "absolute freedom" by rejecting market society and retreating into the wilderness. Only in this way, he insisted, could they preserve both individual independence and the natural environment.

Thomas Cole's 1846 painting *A Pic-Nic Party* exemplifies the work of the Hudson River School, a group of artists fascinated by the glory of nature. Cole portrays nature and civilization coexisting in harmony, although the prominence of the stump in the foreground, the remains of a tree felled by an axe, suggests that man poses a danger to the natural environment.

VOICES OF FREEDOM

From RECOLLECTIONS OF HARRIET L. NOBLE (1824)

One of countless women who took part in the westward movement after the War of 1812, Harriet L. Noble later described her family's migration from New York to Michigan, then a sparsely populated territory, and the burdens pioneer life placed on women.

———————————————

My husband was seized with the mania, and accordingly made preparation to start and . . . we started about the 20th of September, 1824, for Michigan. . . . As we approached Detroit, the "Cantonment" with the American flag floating on its walls, was decidedly the most interesting of any part of the town; for a city it was certainly the most filthy, irregular place I had ever seen. . . . I said to myself, "if this be a Western city, give me a home in the woods." . . .

We passed two log houses between this and Ann Arbor. About the middle of the afternoon we found ourselves at our journey's end—but what a prospect? There were some six or seven log huts occupied by as many inmates as could be crowded into them. . . . We lived in this way until our husbands got a log house raised and the roof on. . . . We sold out and bought again ten miles west of Ann Arbor, a place which suited us better. . . . My husband and myself were four days

building it. I suppose most of my lady friends would think a woman quite out of "her legitimate sphere" in turning mason, but I was not at all particular what kind of labor I performed, so we were only comfortable and provided with the necessaries of life. . . .

I am not of a desponding disposition, nor often low-spirited, and having left New York to make Michigan my home, I had no idea of going back, or being very unhappy. Yet the want of society, of church privileges, and in fact almost every thing that makes life desirable, would often make me sad in spite of all effort to the contrary. . . .

When I look back upon my life, and see the ups and downs, the hardships and privations I have been called upon to endure, I feel no wish to be young again. I was in the prime of life when I came to Michigan—only twenty-one, and my husband was thirty-three. Neither of us knew the reality of hardship. Could we have known what it was to be pioneers in a new country, we should never have had the courage to come, but I am satisfied that with all the disadvantages of raising a family in a new country, there is a consolation in knowing that our children are prepared to brave the ills of life, I believe, far better than they would have been had we never left New York.

From "FACTORY LIFE AS IT IS, BY AN OPERATIVE" (1845)

Beginning in the 1830s, young women who worked in the cotton textile factories in Lowell, Massachusetts, organized to demand shorter hours of work and better labor conditions. In this pamphlet from 1845, a factory worker details her grievances as well as those of female domestic workers, the largest group of women workers.

Philanthropists of the nineteenth century!—shall not the operatives of our country be permitted to speak for themselves?. . . Shall tyranny and cruel oppression be allowed to rivet the chains of physical and mental slavery on the millions of our country who are the real producers of all its improvements and wealth, and they fear to speak out in noble self-defense? Shall they fear to appeal to the sympathies of the people, or the justice of this far-famed republican nation? God forbid!

Much has been written and spoken in woman's behalf, especially in America; and yet a large class of females are, and have been, destined to a state of servitude as degrading as unceasing toil can make it. I refer to the female operatives of New England—the free states of our union—the states where no colored slave can breathe the balmy air, and exist as such—but yet there are those, a host of them, too, who are in fact nothing more nor less than slaves in every sense of the word! Slaves to a system of labor which requires them to toil from five until seven o'clock, with one hour only to attend to the wants of nature, allowed—slaves to the will and requirements of the "powers that be," however they may infringe on the rights or conflict with the feelings of the operative—slaves to ignorance—and how can it be otherwise? What time has the operative to bestow on moral, religious or intellectual culture? How can our country look for aught but ignorance and vice, under the existing state of things? When the whole system is exhausted by unremitting labor

during twelve and thirteen hours per day, can any reasonable being expect that the mind will retain its vigor and energy? Impossible! Common sense will teach every one the utter impossibility of improving the mind under these circumstances, however great the desire may be for knowledge.

Again, we hear much said on the subject of benevolence among the wealthy and so called, Christian part of community. Have we not cause to question the sincerity of those who, while they talk benevolence in the parlor, compel their help to labor for a mean, paltry pittance in the kitchen? And while they manifest great concern for the souls of the heathen in distant lands, care nothing for the bodies and intellects of those within their own precincts? . . .

In the strength of our united influence we will soon show these drivelling cotton lords, this mushroom aristocracy of New England, who so arrogantly aspire to lord it over God's heritage, that our rights cannot be trampled upon with impunity; that we WILL not longer submit to that arbitrary power which has for the last ten years been so abundantly exercised over us.

QUESTIONS

1. *In what ways did the experience of moving west alter traditional expectations of women's roles?*

2. *Why does the female factory worker compare her conditions with those of slaves?*

3. *What do these documents suggest about how different kinds of women were affected by economic change in the first part of the nineteenth century?*

This 1819 engraving depicts a ceremony of Anabaptists, one of the numerous religious groups that flourished in nineteenth-century America. Anabaptists reject infant baptism in favor of the baptism of adults who have professed religious belief.

had been so transformed by woodcutters and farmers that it had become almost completely devoid of trees and wild animals. In one famous passage, Thoreau noted how his enjoyment of nature was disturbed by the distant sound of a locomotive whistle—a symbol of how it seemed impossible to escape the market revolution. Thoreau appealed to Americans to "simplify" their lives rather than become obsessed with the accumulation of wealth. Genuine freedom, he insisted, lay within.

The Second Great Awakening

The popular religious revivals that swept over the country during the **Second Great Awakening** added a religious underpinning to the celebration of personal self-improvement, self-reliance, and self-determination. These revivals, which began at the turn of the century, were originally organized by established religious leaders alarmed by low levels of church attendance in the young republic (perhaps as few as 10 percent of white Americans regularly attended church during the 1790s). But they quickly expanded far beyond existing churches. They peaked in the 1820s and early 1830s, when the Reverend Charles Grandison Finney held months-long revival meetings in upstate New York and New York City.

Charles Grandison Finney ▶

The son of Connecticut farmers, Finney had been inspired to preach after attending a religious revival in 1821. Like the evangelists (traveling preachers) of the first Great Awakening of the mid-eighteenth century, discussed in Chapter 4, Finney warned of hell in vivid language while offering the promise of salvation to converts who abandoned their sinful ways. He became a national celebrity after his success in Oneida County in upstate New York. After Finney's preaching, according to one report, the area had been "completely overthrown by the Holy Ghost" so that "the theater has been deserted, the tavern sanctified . . . and far higher and purer enjoyment has been found in exercises of devotion."

The Second Great Awakening spread to all regions of the country and democratized American Christianity, making it a truly mass enterprise. At the time of independence, fewer than 2,000 Christian ministers preached in the United States. In 1845, they numbered 40,000. Evangelical denominations like the Methodists and Baptists enjoyed explosive growth in membership, and smaller sects proliferated. By the 1840s, Methodism, with more than 1 million members, had become the country's largest denomination. Deism, a form of religious belief hostile to organized churches, had been prominent among the generation of the founding fathers. It now waned, and Christianity became even more central to American culture. Americans, wrote Tocqueville, "combine the notions of Christianity and of liberty so intimately in their minds that it is impossible to make them conceive the one without the other."

Growing denominations

New religious prophets seemed to appear regularly in early-nineteenth-century America, determined, in novelist Herman Melville's phrase, to "gospelize the world anew." At large camp meetings, especially prominent on the frontier, fiery revivalist preachers rejected the idea that man is a sinful creature with a preordained fate, promoting instead the doctrine of human free will. At these gatherings, rich and poor, male and female, and in some instances whites and blacks worshiped alongside one another and pledged to abandon worldly sins in favor of the godly life.

Camp meetings

The Awakening's Impact

Even more than its predecessor of several decades earlier, the Second Great Awakening stressed the right of private judgment in spiritual matters and the possibility of universal salvation through faith and good works. Every person, Finney insisted,

Das neue Jerusalem (The New Jerusalem), an early-nineteenth-century watercolor, in German, illustrates the narrow gateway to heaven and the fate awaiting sinners in hell. These were common themes of preachers in the Second Great Awakening.

was a "moral free agent"—that is, a person free to choose between a Christian life and sin. Sinners could experience a "change of heart" and embrace spiritual freedom, defined, in the words of evangelical minister Jonathan Blanchard, as "Christ ruling in and over rational creatures who are obeying him freely and from choice."

Mass religion

Revivalist ministers seized the opportunities offered by the market revolution to spread their message. They raised funds, embarked on lengthy preaching tours by canal, steamboat, and railroad, and flooded the country with mass-produced, inexpensive religious tracts. The revivals' opening of religion to mass participation and their message that ordinary Americans could shape their own spiritual destinies resonated with the spread of market values.

The Awakening and market society

To be sure, evangelical preachers can hardly be described as cheerleaders for a market society. They regularly railed against greed and indifference to the welfare of others as sins. Finney called selfishness—an extreme form of individualism encouraged by the scramble for wealth produced by the market revolution—"the law of Satan's empire," not God's. Yet the revivals thrived in areas caught up in the rapid expansion of the market economy, such as the region of upstate New York along the path of the Erie Canal. Most of Finney's converts here came from the commercial and professional classes. Evangelical ministers promoted what might be called a controlled **individualism** as the essence of freedom. In stressing the importance of industry, sobriety, and self-discipline as examples of freely chosen moral behavior, evangelical preachers promoted the very qualities necessary for success in a market culture.

The Emergence of Mormonism

The Second Great Awakening illustrated how the end of governmental support for established churches promoted religious pluralism. Competition among religious groups kept religion vibrant and promoted the emergence of new denominations. Among the most successful of the religions that sprang up, hoping to create a Kingdom of God on earth, was the **Church of Jesus Christ of Latter-Day Saints**, or Mormons. The Mormons were founded in the 1820s by Joseph Smith, a farmer in upstate New York who as a youth began to experience religious visions. He claimed to have been led by an angel to a set of golden plates covered with strange writing. Smith translated and published them as *The Book of Mormon*, after a fourth-century prophet.

Depending on one's point of view, *The Book of Mormon* is either a divinely inspired holy book or an impressive work of American literature. It tells the story of three families who traveled from the ancient Middle East to the Americas, where they eventually evolved into Native American tribes. Jesus Christ plays a prominent role in the book, appearing to one of the family groups in the

In this 1846 photograph the massive Mormon temple in Nauvoo, Illinois, towers over the ramshackle wooden buildings of this town along the Mississippi River.

Western Hemisphere after his death and resurrection. Thus, the word of God had been transmitted not only to people in the Biblical Middle East, but also directly to inhabitants of North America. The second coming of Christ would take place in the New World, where Smith was God's prophet. Smith mortgaged his farm to help pay for an edition of 5,000 copies, which appeared in 1830.

Mormonism emerged in a center of the Second Great Awakening, upstate New York. The church founded by Smith responded to the disruptions caused by the market revolution. It was self-consciously democratic, admitting anyone, regardless of wealth or occupation, who accepted Smith's message. (African-Americans could join, but could not enter the priesthood—a policy not overturned until 1978.) Like Jesus, Smith condemned the selfishness of the rich—in the ideal ancient society described in *The Book of Mormon* "there was no poor among them." At a time when paper money seemed to have little intrinsic worth, gold remained an unchallenged standard of value, which may help to explain the appeal of a religious text written on golden plates.

Gradually, however, Smith began to receive visions that led to more controversial doctrines, notably polygamy, which allows one man to have more than one wife. By the end of his life, Smith had married no fewer than thirty women. Along with the absolute authority Smith exercised over his followers, this doctrine outraged the Mormons' neighbors. Mobs drove Smith and his followers out of New York, Ohio, and Missouri before they settled in 1839 in Nauvoo, Illinois, where they hoped to await the Second Coming of Christ. There, five years later, Smith was arrested on the charge of inciting a riot that destroyed an anti-Mormon newspaper. While in jail awaiting trial, Smith was murdered by a group of intruders. In 1847, his successor as Mormon leader, Brigham Young, led more than 2,000 followers across the Great Plains and Rocky Mountains to the shores of the Great Salt Lake in present-day Utah, seeking a refuge where they could practice their faith undisturbed. (The area was then part of Mexico; the United States annexed it in 1848.) By 1852, the number of Mormons in various settlements in Utah had reached 16,000. The experience of expulsion helped to shape Mormon theology. Their distinctive practice of posthumous baptism, in which modern members of the church retrospectively baptize long-dead ancestors, seeks to unite across generations families separated not only by death but also by migration. The practice has also led the church to gather and make publicly available an enormous library of genealogical records from around the world—a goldmine for scholars of every religion.

The Mormons' experience revealed the limits of religious toleration in nineteenth-century America but also the opportunities offered by religious pluralism. Today, Mormons constitute the fourth largest church in the United States and *The Book of Mormon* has been translated into over 100 languages.

A democratic church

Controversial doctrines

Pat Lyon at the Forge, an 1826–1827 painting of a prosperous blacksmith. Proud of his accomplishments as a self-made man who had achieved success through hard work and skill rather than inheritance, Lyon asked the artist to paint him in his shop wearing his work clothes.

THE LIMITS OF PROSPERITY

Liberty and Prosperity

As the market revolution progressed, the right to compete for economic advancement became a touchstone of American freedom. Official imagery linked the goddess of liberty ever more closely to emblems of material wealth. New Jersey, whose official seal, adopted in 1776, had paired liberty with Ceres, the Roman goddess of agriculture, in 1821 added the motto "Liberty and Prosperity." The state seal of Arkansas, admitted to the Union in 1836, pictured liberty atop an image of a steamboat and two overflowing horns of plenty.

John Jacob Astor

Many enterprising Americans seized the opportunities offered by the market revolution to enrich themselves. John Jacob Astor, the son of a poor German butcher who emigrated to the United States at the end of the War of Independence, earned large profits in the early nineteenth century by shipping furs to China and importing teas and silk. Astor invested his wealth in Manhattan real estate, which was rapidly rising in value, and built Astor House, which quickly became the nation's most famous hotel. He died in 1848 the richest man in the United States, leaving a fortune of perhaps $10 million, the equivalent of hundreds of millions of dollars today.

The "self-made man"

Astor's story seemed to exemplify the opportunities open to the "self-made man," a term that came into use during his lifetime. According to this idea, those who achieved success in America did so not as a result of hereditary privilege or government favoritism as in Europe, but through their own intelligence and hard work. In the extent of his wealth, of course, Astor was hardly typical. But the market revolution and the quickening of commercial life enriched numerous bankers, merchants, industrialists, and planters. It produced a new middle class—an army of clerks, accountants, and other office employees who staffed businesses in Boston, New York, and elsewhere. It created new opportunities for farmers who profited from the growing demand at home and abroad for American agricultural products, and for skilled craftsmen like Thomas Rodgers, a machine builder who established a successful locomotive factory in Paterson, New Jersey. New opportunities for talented men opened in professions like law, medicine, and teaching. By the early 1820s, there were an estimated 10,000 physicians in the United States.

Race and Opportunity

The market revolution affected the lives of all Americans. But not all were positioned to take advantage of its benefits. Most blacks, of course, were slaves, but even free blacks found themselves excluded from the new economic opportunities. The 220,000 blacks living in the free states on the eve of the Civil War (less than 2 percent of the North's population) suffered discrimination in every phase of their lives. Although virtually every northern county east of the Mississippi River reported some black residents, the majority of blacks lived in the poorest, unhealthiest sections of cities like New York, Philadelphia, and Cincinnati. And even these neighborhoods were subjected to occasional violent assault by white mobs, like the armed bands that attacked blacks and destroyed their homes and businesses in Cincinnati in 1829.

Barred from schools and other public facilities, free blacks laboriously constructed their own institutional life, centered on mutual aid and educational societies, as well as independent churches, most notably the African Methodist Episcopal Church. Richard Allen of Philadelphia, a Methodist preacher, had been spurred to found it after being forcibly removed from his former church for praying at the altar rail, a place reserved for whites.

While many white Americans could look forward to a life of economic accumulation and individual advancement, large numbers of free blacks experienced

Juliann Jane Tillman, a preacher in the African Methodist Episcopal Church, in an 1844 engraving. Many Protestant denominations allowed women to preach, although their presence also aroused much criticism.

downward mobility. At the time of abolition, because of widespread slave owner-ship among eighteenth-century artisans, a considerable number of northern blacks possessed craft skills. But it became more and more difficult for blacks to utilize these skills once they became free. Although many white artisans criticized slavery, most viewed the freed slaves as low-wage competitors and sought to bar them from skilled employment. "They are leaders in the cause of equal rights for themselves," a black editor commented of New York City's artisans in the 1830s.

Hostility from white craftsmen, however, was only one of many obstacles that kept blacks confined to the lowest ranks of the labor market. White employers refused to hire them in anything but menial positions, and white customers did not wish to be served by them. The result was a rapid decline in economic status, until by mid-century, the vast majority of northern blacks labored for wages in unskilled jobs and as domestic servants. The state census of 1855 revealed 122 black barbers and 808 black servants in New York City, but only 1 lawyer and 6 doctors. Nor could free blacks take advantage of the opening of the West to improve their economic status, a central component of American freedom. Federal law barred them from access to public land, and by 1860 four states—Indiana, Illinois, Iowa, and Oregon—prohibited them from entering their territory altogether.

> *Downward mobility of free blacks*

The Cult of Domesticity

Women, too, found many of the opportunities opened by the market revolution closed to them. As the household declined as a center of economic production, many women saw their traditional roles undermined by the availability of mass-produced goods previously made at home. Some women, as noted above, followed work as it moved from household to factory. Others embraced a new definition of femininity, which glorified not a woman's contribution to the family's economic well-being, but her ability to create a private environment shielded from the competitive tensions of the market economy. Woman's "place" was in the home, a site increasingly emptied of economically productive functions as work moved from the household to workshops and factories. Her role was to sustain nonmarket values like love, friendship, and mutual obligation, providing men with a shelter from the competitive marketplace.

The earlier ideology of "republican motherhood," which allowed women a kind of public role as mothers of future citizens, subtly evolved into the mid-nineteenth-century **cult of domesticity**. "Virtue," which in the eighteenth century was a political characteristic of men essential to the success of republican government, came to be redefined as a personal moral quality associated more and more closely with women. "Virtue" for a woman meant not only sexual innocence

The Industrious Man, a lithograph from a book produced for children by the American Sunday School Union in the 1840s, depicts an ideal family scene. The father, a laborer, returns home carrying his lunch pail to find his wife and children awaiting him in a comfortable although hardly extravagant home. The scene exemplifies the idea of separate spheres according to which men worked outside the home and women's role was to fulfill their family responsibilities.

but also beauty, frailty, and dependence on men. "In whatever situation of life a woman is placed from her cradle to her grave," declared *The Young Lady's Book*, one of numerous popular magazines addressed to female audiences of the 1820s and 1830s, "a spirit of obedience and submission, pliability of temper, and humility of mind, are required from her." These magazines carried articles such as "Woman, a Source of Comfort," "Woman, a Being to Come Home To," and "Woman—Man's Best Friend."

With more and more men leaving the home for work, women did exercise considerable power over personal affairs within the family. The rapid decline in the American birthrate during the nineteenth century (from an average of seven children per woman in 1800 to four in 1900) cannot be explained except by the conscious decision of millions of women to limit the number of children they bore. But the idea of domesticity minimized women's even indirect participation in the outside world. For both sexes, freedom meant fulfilling their respective "inborn" qualities. Men were rational, aggressive, and domineering, while women were nurturing, selfless, ruled by the emotions, and thus less fitted for public life. If submission to the will of another increasingly seemed inadmissible for free men, it remained a condition natural to women and expected of them. Men moved freely between the public and private "spheres"; women were supposed to remain cloistered in the private realm of the family.

Men and women's "inborn" qualities

Women and Work

Prevailing ideas concerning gender bore little relation to the experience of those women who worked for wages at least some time in their lives. They did so despite severe disadvantages. Women could not compete freely for employment, since only low-paying jobs were available to them. Married women still could not sign independent contracts or sue in their own name, and not until after the Civil War did they, not their husbands, control the wages they earned. Nonetheless, for poor city dwellers and farm families, the labor of all family members was essential to economic survival. Thousands of poor women found jobs as

Life and Age of Woman and *Life and Age of Man*, popular lithographs from 1848, depict the stages of life of the two sexes. The ideal man achieves military and then commercial success, while the woman's life focuses on marriage and motherhood. The woman seems to show signs of aging more rapidly than the man.

domestic servants, factory workers, and seamstresses. Early industrialization enhanced the availability of paid work for northern women, as the spread of the putting-out system in such industries as shoemaking, hatmaking, and clothing manufacture allowed women laboring at home to contribute to family income even as they retained responsibility for domestic chores.

For the expanding middle class, however, it became a badge of respectability for wives to remain at home, outside the disorderly new market economy, while husbands conducted business in their offices, shops, and factories. In larger cities, where families of different social classes had previously lived alongside one another, fashionable middle-class neighborhoods populated by merchants, factory owners, and professionals like lawyers and doctors began to develop. Work in middle-class homes was done by domestic servants, the largest employment category for women in nineteenth-century America. The freedom of the middle-class woman—defined in part as freedom from labor—rested on the employment of other women within her household.

Even though most women were anything but idle, in a market economy where labor increasingly meant work that created monetary value, it became more and more difficult to think of labor as encompassing anyone but men. Lydia Maria Child wrote a popular book, *The Frugal Housewife*, published in 1829, that sought to prepare women for the ups and downs of the market revolution (one chapter was entitled "How to Endure Poverty"). Child supported her family by her writing and became a prominent advocate of antislavery and of greater rights for women. Her diary reveals that in a single year she also sewed thirty-six pieces of clothing, prepared more than 700 meals, and spent much time supervising household help.

By any reasonable definition, Child worked—at home and as a writer. But discussions of labor rarely mentioned housewives, domestic servants, and female outworkers, except as an indication of how the spread of capitalism was degrading men. The idea that the male head of household should command a **family wage** that enabled him to support his wife and children became a popular definition of social justice. It sank deep roots not only among middle-class Americans but among working-class men as well. Capitalism, said the newspaper *Workingman's Advocate*, tore women from their role as "happy and independent mistresses" of the domestic sphere and forced them into the labor market, thereby undermining the natural order of the household and the authority of its male head.

The Early Labor Movement

As this complaint suggests, many Americans experienced the market revolution not as an enhancement of the power to shape their own lives, but as a loss of freedom. The period between the War of 1812 and 1840 witnessed a sharp economic downturn in 1819, a full-fledged depression starting in 1837, and numerous ups and downs in between, during which employment was irregular and numerous businesses failed. For every aspiring American who rode the tide of economic progress, another seemed to sink beneath the waves. The economic transformation produced an explosive growth in the nation's output and trade and a rise in the

A woman with a sewing machine, in an undated photograph. It is not clear if she is sewing for herself and family, or for income as a seamstress.

A "family wage"

Growing inequality

No More Grinding the Poor—But Liberty and the Rights of Man, a labor movement cartoon of the 1830s. The devil and a millionaire conspire to buy an election with money (in the box at the lower left), while an honest workingman hands his ballot to a female figure of liberty. The worker's motto is "Liberty, Equity, Justice, and The Rights of Man."

general standard of living. But especially in the growing cities of the Northeast, it significantly widened the gap between wealthy merchants and industrialists on the one hand and impoverished factory workers, unskilled dockworkers, and seamstresses laboring at home on the other. In Massachusetts, the most industrialized state in the country, the richest 5 percent of the population owned more than half the wealth. Inequality was even more pronounced in Philadelphia, where the top 1 percent possessed more wealth than the rest of the population combined. Bankruptcy was a common fact of life, and men unable to pay their debts filled the prisons of major cities.

Alarmed at the erosion of traditional skills and the threat of being reduced to the status of dependent wage earners, skilled craftsmen in the late 1820s created the world's first Workingmen's Parties, short-lived political organizations that sought to mobilize lower-class support for candidates who would press for free public education, an end to imprisonment for debt, and legislation limiting work to ten hours per day. In the 1830s, a time of rapidly rising prices, union organization spread and strikes became commonplace. Along with demands for higher wages and shorter hours, the early labor movement called for free homesteads for settlers on public land and an end to the imprisonment of union leaders for conspiracy.

Labor issues

Labor actions

The "Liberty of Living"

But over and above these specific issues, workers' language of protest drew on older ideas of freedom linked to economic autonomy, public-spirited virtue, and social equality. The conviction of twenty New York tailors in 1835 under the common law of conspiracy for combining to seek higher wages inspired a public procession marking the "burial of liberty." Such actions and language were not confined to male workers. The young mill women of Lowell walked off their jobs in 1834 to protest a reduction in wages and again two years later when employers raised rents at their boardinghouses. They carried banners affirming their rights as "daughters of free men," and, addressing the factory owners, they charged, "the oppressive hand of avarice [greed] would enslave us." Freedom, Noah Webster's *American Dictionary* declared in 1828, was "a state of exemption from the power or control of another." The labor movement asked how many wage earners truly enjoyed such "exemption."

Some labor spokesmen, like Langdon Byllesby of Philadelphia, went so far as to describe wage labor itself as the "very essence of slavery," since dependence on another person for one's economic livelihood was incompatible with freedom.

> *Labor and freedom*

Rooted in the traditions of the small producer and the identification of freedom with economic independence, labor's critique of the market economy directly challenged the idea that individual improvement—Emerson's "self-trust, self-reliance, self-control, self-culture"—offered an adequate response to social inequality. "Wealth and labor," wrote Orestes Brownson in his influential essay "The Laboring Classes" (1840), were at war. Workers' problems, he went on, must be understood as institutional, not individual. They had their root in "the constitution of society," and their solution required not a more complete individualism, but a "radical change [in] existing social arrangements" so as to produce "equality between man and man."

"We are free," wrote Peter Rödel, an immigrant German shoemaker, "but not free enough. . . . We want the liberty of living." Here lay the origins of the idea,

The Shoemakers' Strike in Lynn—Procession in the Midst of a Snow-Storm, of Eight Hundred Women Operatives, an engraving from *Frank Leslie's Illustrated Newspaper*, March 17, 1860. The striking women workers carry a banner comparing their condition to that of slaves.

which would become far more prominent in the late nineteenth and twentieth centuries, that economic security—a standard of life below which no person would fall—formed an essential part of American freedom.

Thus, the market revolution transformed and divided American society and its conceptions of freedom. It encouraged a new emphasis on individualism and physical mobility among white men, while severely limiting the options available to women and African-Americans. It opened new opportunities for economic freedom for many Americans, while leading others to fear that their traditional economic independence was being eroded. In a democratic society, it was inevitable that the debate over the market revolution and its consequences for freedom would be reflected in American politics.

SUGGESTED READING

BOOKS

- Bergmann, William H. *The American National State and the Early West* (2014). Demonstrates how governmental action was crucial to early western development.

- Boydston, Jeanne. *Home and Work: Housework, Wages, and the Ideology of Work in the Early Republic* (1990). Examines how the market revolution affected ideas relating to women's work.

- Deyle, Steven. *Carry Me Back: The Domestic Slave Trade in American Life* (2005). The most comprehensive history of the internal slave trade, by which millions of slaves were transported to the Deep South.

- Dublin, Thomas. *Women at Work: The Transformation of Work in Lowell, Massachusetts, 1826–1860* (1975). A pioneering study of the working and nonworking lives of Lowell "factory girls."

- Faragher, John M. *Sugar Creek: Life on the Illinois Prairie* (1986). Traces the growth of a frontier community from early settlement to market society.

- Harris, Leslie. *In the Shadow of Slavery: African-Americans in New York City, 1626–1863* (2003). A study that emphasizes the exclusion of African-Americans from the economic opportunities offered by the market revolution.

- Haselby, Sam. *The Origins of American Religious Nationalism* (2015). Explores how the battle between frontier evangelists and more traditional New England ministers shaped religion and politics in the early republic.

- Howe, Daniel W. *What Hath God Wrought: The Transformation of America, 1815–1848* (2007). A comprehensive account of social and political changes in this era, emphasizing the significance of the communications revolution.

- Johnson, Paul E. *A Shopkeeper's Millennium: Society and Revivals in Rochester, New York, 1815–1837* (1978). Explores the impact of religious revivals on a key city of upstate New York.

- Larson, John L. *The Market Revolution in America: Liberty, Ambition, and the Eclipse of the Common Good* (2010). The most recent account of the market revolution and its impact on American society and values.

- Miller, Kerby A. *Exiles and Emigrants: Ireland and the Irish Exodus to North America* (1985). An examination of Irish immigration over the course of American history.

- Rockman, Seth. *Scraping By: Wage Labor, Slavery, and Survival in Early Baltimore* (2009). A pioneering study of the status of free laborers in a major city in a slave-based economy.

- Ryan, Mary P. *Cradle of the Middle Class: The Family in Oneida County, New York, 1790–1865* (1981). Examines how economic change helped to produce a new kind of middle-class family structure centered on women's dominance of the household.

- Stansell, Christine. *City of Women: Sex and Class in New York, 1789–1860* (1986). Considers how gender conventions and economic change shaped the lives of working-class women.

- Wilentz, Sean. *Chants Democratic: New York City and the Rise of the American Working Class, 1788–1850* (1984). A study of the early labor movement in one of its key centers in antebellum America.

WEBSITES

- American Transcendentalism: www.vcu.edu/engweb /transcendentalism/
- The First West: The Ohio Valley to 1820: http://loc.gov /ammem/award99/icuhtml/fawhome.html
- Women in America, 1820–1842: http://xroads.virginia .edu/~hyper/detoc/fem/home.htm

CHAPTER REVIEW AND ONLINE RESOURCES

REVIEW QUESTIONS

1. Identify the major transportation improvements in this period and explain how they influenced the market economy.

2. How did state and local governments promote the national economy in this period?

3. How did the market economy and westward expansion intensify the institution of slavery?

4. How did westward expansion and the market revolution drive each other?

5. What role did immigrants play in the new market society?

6. How did changes in the law promote development in the economic system?

7. As it democratized American Christianity, the Second Great Awakening both took advantage of the market revolution and criticized its excesses. Explain.

8. How did the market revolution change women's work and family roles?

9. Give some examples of the rise of individualism in these years.

KEY TERMS

steamboats (p. 309)

Erie Canal (p. 309)

Cotton Kingdom (p. 316)

cotton gin (p. 316)

Porkopolis (p. 319)

American system of manufactures (p. 322)

mill girls (p. 324)

nativism (p. 327)

Dartmouth College v. Woodward (p. 328)

Gibbons v. Ogden (p. 328)

Commonwealth v. Hunt (p. 329)

manifest destiny (p. 329)

transcendentalists (p. 330)

Second Great Awakening (p. 334)

individualism (p. 336)

Church of Jesus Christ of Latter-Day Saints (p. 336)

cult of domesticity (p. 339)

family wage (p. 341)

Go to 🐰 INQUIZITIVE

To see what you know—and learn what you've missed—with personalized feedback along the way.

Visit the *Give Me Liberty!* **Student Site** for primary source documents and images, interactive maps, author videos featuring Eric Foner, and more.

CHAPTER 10

DEMOCRACY IN AMERICA

★

1815–1840

The inauguration of Andrew Jackson on March 4, 1829, made it clear that something had changed in American politics. The swearing-in of the president had previously been a small, dignified event. Jackson's inauguration attracted a crowd of some 20,000 people who poured into the White House after the ceremony, ruining furniture and breaking china and glassware in the crush. It was "the reign of King Mob," lamented Justice Joseph Story of the Supreme Court.

Jackson aroused powerful feelings, pro and con. His supporters viewed his election as the advent of genuine democracy, the coming to power of the "common man." Philip Hone, a New York political leader who kept a detailed diary for more than thirty years, recorded that Jackson was "the most popular man we have ever known." Hone had voted for President John Quincy Adams in 1828, but he recognized that Jackson's democratic bearing and beliefs "suit [the people] exactly." Jackson's critics, on the other hand, considered him a tyrant. They called him King Andrew I, and when they organized politically they borrowed their name, the Whig Party, from the opponents of royal power in eighteenth-century England.

The 1830s and 1840s have been called the Age of Jackson, or the period of Jacksonian Democracy. No one individual can capture the full complexity of any period of history, but Andrew Jackson's career did embody the major developments of his era—the market revolution, the westward movement, the expansion of slavery, and the growth of democracy. He was a symbol of the self-made man. Unlike previous presidents, Jackson rose to prominence from a humble background, reflecting his era's democratic opportunities. Born in 1767 on the South Carolina frontier, he had been orphaned during the American Revolution. Early on, Jackson displayed the courage and impetuousness for which he would later become famous. While still a youth, he served as a courier for patriotic forces during the War of Independence. Captured and imprisoned, he was almost killed when a British officer struck him with a sword after Jackson refused an order to polish the officer's boots.

As a young man, Jackson moved to Tennessee, where he studied law, became involved in local politics, and in the 1790s won election to the House of Representatives and the Senate, and became a judge on the state supreme court. His military campaigns against the British and Indians helped to consolidate American control over the Deep South, making possible the rise of the Cotton Kingdom. He himself acquired a large plantation in Tennessee. But more than anything else, to this generation of Americans Andrew Jackson symbolized one of the most crucial features of national life—the triumph of political democracy.

Americans pride themselves on being the world's oldest democracy. New Zealand, whose constitution of 1893 gave women and Maoris (the native population) the right to vote, may have a better claim. Even in the nineteenth century, when democracy meant male suffrage, some Latin American nations extended the right to vote to free blacks and the descendants of the indigenous population well before the United States did. Europe lagged far behind. Britain did not achieve universal male suffrage until the 1880s. France instituted it in 1793,

FOCUS QUESTIONS

What were the social bases for the flourishing democracy of the early mid-nineteenth century? –p. 348

What efforts were made in this period to strengthen the economic integration of the nation, and what major crises hindered these efforts? –p. 353

What were the major areas of conflict between nationalism and sectionalism? –p. 359

In what ways did Andrew Jackson embody the contradictions of democratic nationalism? –p. 367

How did the Bank War influence the economy and party competition? –p. 378

Justice's Court in the Back Woods, an 1852 painting by Tompkins Harrison Matteson, depicts the expansion of the public sphere to include ordinary Americans. A court is in session in a local tavern. The justice of the peace, who presides, is a shoemaker who has set aside his tools but still wears his leather work apron. A lawyer appeals to the jury, composed of average (male) citizens. The case has to do with an assault. The plaintiff, his head bandaged, leans on the table at the right, while a woman consoles the defendant on the far left.

abandoned it in 1799, reintroduced it in 1848, and abandoned it again a few years later. More to the point, perhaps, democracy became a central part of the definition of American nationality and the American idea of freedom.

THE TRIUMPH OF DEMOCRACY

Property and Democracy

The market revolution and territorial expansion were intimately connected with a third central element of American freedom—political democracy. The challenge to property qualifications for voting, begun during the American Revolution, reached its culmination in the early nineteenth century. Not a single state that entered the Union after the original thirteen required ownership of property to vote. In the older states, constitutional conventions during the 1820s and 1830s reconsidered democracy's economic basis. Even as the expansion of industry and commercial agriculture increased the number of wage earners in cities and older rural areas, men who could not meet property requirements insisted that they were as fit as others to exercise the rights of citizens. Their insistent pressure did much to democratize American politics.

Owning property, declared a petition by "Non-Freeholders" (landless men) of Richmond to the Virginia constitutional convention of 1829, did not necessarily mean the possession of "moral or intellectual endowments" superior to those of the poor. "They alone deserve to be called free," they continued, "who participate in the formation of their political institutions." By this time, only North Carolina, Rhode Island, and Virginia still retained property requirements. The large slaveholders who dominated Virginia politics successfully resisted demands for changes in voting qualifications in 1829, but a subsequent constitutional convention, in 1850, eliminated the property requirement. Although the speed of the process varied from state to state, by 1860 all but one had ended property requirements for voting (though several continued to bar persons accepting poor relief, on the grounds that they lacked genuine independence). The personal independence necessary in the citizen now rested not on ownership of property, but on ownership of one's self—a reflection of the era's individualism.

The Dorr War

The lone exception to the trend toward democratization was Rhode Island, which required voters to own real estate valued at $134 or rent property for at least $7 per year. A center of factory production, Rhode Island had a steadily growing population of propertyless wage earners unable to vote. Leaders of the state's labor movement complained repeatedly about the absence of "free suffrage." In October 1841, proponents of democratic reform organized a People's Convention, which drafted a new state constitution. It enfranchised all adult white men while eliminating blacks entirely (although in a subsequent referendum, blacks' right to vote was restored). When the reformers ratified their constitution in an extralegal referendum and proceeded to inaugurate Thomas Dorr, a prominent Rhode Island lawyer, as governor, President John Tyler dispatched federal troops to the state. The movement collapsed, and Dorr subsequently served nearly two years in prison for treason. **The Dorr War** demonstrated the passions aroused by the continuing exclusion of any group of white men from voting. And the legislature soon eliminated the property qualification for native-born men, black as well as white, although it retained it for immigrants until 1888.

Tocqueville on Democracy

By 1840, more than 90 percent of adult white men were eligible to vote. A flourishing democratic system had been consolidated. American politics was boisterous, highly partisan, and sometimes violent, and it engaged the energies of massive numbers of citizens. In a country that lacked more traditional bases of nationality—a powerful and menacing neighbor, historic ethnic, religious, and cultural unity—democratic political institutions came to define the nation's sense of its own identity.

Alexis de Tocqueville, the French writer who visited the United States in the early 1830s, returned home to produce **Democracy in America** in 1833, a classic account of a society in the midst of a political transformation. Tocqueville had come to the United States to study prisons. But he soon realized that to understand America, one must understand democracy (which as a person of aristocratic background he rather disliked). His key insight was that democracy by this time meant far more than either the right to vote or a particular set of political institutions. It was a "habit of the heart," a culture that encouraged individual initiative, belief in equality, and an active public sphere populated by numerous voluntary organizations that sought to improve society. Democracy, Tocqueville saw, had become an essential attribute of American freedom.

As Tocqueville recognized, the rise of democracy represented a profound political transformation. The idea that sovereignty belongs to the mass of ordinary citizens was a new departure in Western thought. As long ago as Aristotle, political philosophers had warned that democracy inevitably degenerated into anarchy and tyranny. For centuries, doctrines of divine right and hierarchical authority had dominated political thought. The founders of the republic, who believed that government must rest on the consent of the governed, also sought to shield political authority from excessive influence by ordinary people (hence the Electoral College, Supreme Court, and other undemocratic features of the Constitution). Nonetheless, thanks to persistent pressure from those originally excluded from political participation, democracy—for white males—triumphed by the Age of Jackson.

Democracy reinforced a sense of equality among those who belonged to the political nation, and it deepened the divide separating them from those who did not. Participation in elections and the pageantry surrounding them—parades, bonfires, mass meetings, party conventions—helped to define the "people" of the United States. The right to vote increasingly became the emblem of American citizenship. In law, voting was still, strictly speaking, a privilege rather than a right, subject to regulation by the individual states. But Noah Webster's *American Dictionary* noted that according to common usage and understanding in America (but not in Europe), the term "citizen" had become

An anti-Jackson cartoon from 1832 portrays Andrew Jackson as an aspiring monarch, wielding the veto power while trampling on the Constitution.

Dorr Liberation Stock, a certificate indicating that a person has helped to finance Thomas Dorr's appeal to the U.S. Supreme Court of his conviction for treason against the state of Rhode Island because of his role in the Dorr War. The Court ruled against him, and Dorr served two years in prison.

Independence Day Celebration in Centre Square, an 1819 painting by John Lewis Krimmel, a German-American artist, depicts a gathering to celebrate the Fourth of July in Philadelphia. On the left, beneath a portrait of George Washington, is a depiction of a naval battle from the War of 1812; on the right, beneath the state flag of Pennsylvania, is an image of the Battle of New Orleans. The celebration, an example of rising American nationalism, includes men and women, soldiers, merchants, and ordinary citizens, but is entirely white except for a young black boy in the lower left.

synonymous with the right to vote. Suffrage, said one advocate of democratic reform, was "the first mark of liberty, the only true badge of the freeman."

The Information Revolution

The market revolution and political democracy produced a large expansion of the public sphere and an explosion in printing sometimes called the "information revolution." The application of steam power to newspaper printing led to a great increase in output and the rise of the mass-circulation "penny press," priced at one cent per issue instead of the traditional six. Newspapers like the *New York Sun* and *New York Herald* introduced a new style of journalism, appealing to a mass audience by emphasizing sensationalism, crime stories, and exposés of official misconduct. By 1840, according to one estimate, the total weekly circulation of newspapers in the United States, whose population was 17 million, exceeded that of Europe, with 233 million people.

Thanks to low postal rates, many newspapers circulated far beyond their places of publication. Indeed, by the 1830s, newspapers accounted for most postal traffic, outstripping private letters. The emergence of organized political parties also spurred newspaper publication. Each major party needed to have newspapers supporting its views in every part of the country, and government printing contracts were essential to most newspapers' survival. The publication of all sorts of magazines, travel guides, advice manuals, religious titles, and other reading materials also rose dramatically.

The reduction in the cost of printing also made possible the appearance of "alternative" newspapers in the late 1820s and early 1830s, including *Freedom's*

Journal (the first black newspaper), *Philadelphia Mechanic's Advocate* and other labor publications, the abolitionist weekly *The Liberator*, and *Cherokee Phoenix*, the first Native American newspaper.

The growth of the reading public, yet another facet of the democratization of American life, opened the door for the rise of a new generation of women writers. Lydia Maria Child, Catharine Maria Sedgwick, Catharine Beecher, and others published stories, poetry, essays, and guides to domestic life. By the 1830s, moreover, through participation in religious and reform movements, thousands of women would establish a public presence, as will be described in Chapter 12. Nonetheless, once New Jersey added the word "male" to its voting requirements in 1807, women everywhere, whether married or single, propertied or dependent, were denied the right to vote.

Women writers

The Limits of Democracy

By the 1830s, the time of Andrew Jackson's presidency, the axiom that "the people" ruled had become a universally accepted part of American politics. Those who opposed this principle, wrote Tocqueville, "hide their heads." But the very centrality of democracy to the definition of both freedom and nationality made it all the more necessary to define the boundaries of the political nation. As older economic exclusions fell away, others survived and new ones were added. The vigorous public life of antebellum America was simultaneously expansive and exclusive, and its limits were as essential to its nature as its broad scope. Democracy in America could absorb native-born poor white men as well as waves of immigrants, yet it erected impenetrable barriers to the participation of women and non-white men—groups also excluded, as noted in the previous chapter, from full participation in the market revolution.

The "principle of universal suffrage," declared the *United States Magazine and Democratic Review* in 1851, meant that "white males of age constituted the political nation." How could the word "universal" be reconciled with barring blacks and women from political participation? As democracy triumphed, the intellectual grounds for exclusion shifted from economic dependency to natural incapacity. Gender and racial differences were widely understood as part of a single, natural hierarchy of innate endowments. A boundary drawn by nature itself was not really exclusion at all. "How did woman first become subject to man, as she now is all over the world?" asked the *New York Herald* in 1852. "By her nature, her sex, just as the negro is and always will be, to the end of time, inferior to the white race, and, therefore, doomed to subjection." In the colonial era, women had been seen as a threat to the political order because they were prone to be swayed by passion (unlike men, supposedly governed by reason). In the nineteenth century, women came to be seen as too pure to risk contamination in the rough-and-tumble world of politics. Nature, men insisted, did not intend women for roles outside the home. Paradoxically, therefore, while freedom for white men involved an open-ended process of personal transformation, developing to the fullest the potential inherent within each human being, the limits of American democracy rested on the belief that the character and abilities of non-whites and women were forever fixed by nature.

The debate over which people are and are not qualified to take part in American democracy lasted well into the twentieth century. Not until 1920 was the Constitution amended to require states to allow women to vote. The Voting Rights Act of 1965 swept away restrictions on black voting imposed by many southern states.

The American Woman's Home, a guide to domestic life by the sisters Catharine Beecher and Harriet Beecher Stowe. Even though works like this were meant to instruct middle-class women on how to meet their domestic responsibilities, their popularity allowed talented women to take on a new public role as writers.

Jim Crow, a piece of sheet music from 1829. Minstrel shows were a form of nineteenth-century entertainment in which white actors impersonated blacks. One of the most popular characters was Jim Crow, the happy, childlike plantation slave created by the performer Thomas D. Rice. Years later, "Jim Crow" would come to mean the laws and customs of southern segregation.

Race and the vote

Disenfranchising free blacks

Even today, controversy persists over the voting rights of immigrants, persons who have served prison terms, and the poor.

The political world of the nineteenth century, so crucial an arena for the exercise of American freedom, was in part defined in contrast to the feminine sphere of the home. The "most rabid Radical," Ralph Waldo Emerson remarked in his journal in 1841, was likely to be conservative "in relation to the theory of Marriage." Beyond the right to "decent treatment" by her husband and to whatever property the law allowed her to control, declared the *New York Herald*, a woman had "no rights . . . with which the public have any concern."

A Racial Democracy

If the exclusion of women from political freedom continued a long-standing practice, the increasing identification of democracy and whiteness marked something of a departure. Tocqueville noted that by the 1830s, "equality" had become an American obsession. In contrast to the highly stratified societies of Europe, white Americans of all social classes dressed the same, traveled in the same stagecoaches and railroad cars, and stayed in the same hotels. Yet at the same time, blacks were increasingly considered a group apart.

Racist imagery became the stock-in-trade of popular theatrical presentations like minstrel shows, in which white actors in blackface entertained the audience by portraying African-Americans as stupid, dishonest, and altogether ridiculous. With the exception of Herman Melville, who portrayed complex, sometimes heroic black characters in works like *Moby-Dick* and *Benito Cereno* (the latter a fictionalized account of a shipboard slave rebellion), American authors either ignored blacks entirely or presented them as stereotypes—happy slaves prone to superstition or long-suffering but devout Christians. Meanwhile, the somewhat tentative thinking of the revolutionary era about the status of non-whites flowered into an elaborate ideology of racial superiority and inferiority, complete with "scientific" underpinnings. These developments affected the boundaries of the political nation.

In the revolutionary era, only Virginia, South Carolina, and Georgia explicitly confined the vote to whites, although elsewhere, custom often made it difficult for free blacks to exercise the **franchise**. As late as 1800, no northern state barred blacks from voting. But every state that entered the Union after that year, with the single exception of Maine, limited the right to vote to white males. And, beginning with Kentucky in 1799 and Maryland two years later, states that had allowed blacks to vote rescinded the privilege.

Race and Class

In 1821, the same New York constitutional convention that removed property qualifications for white voters raised the requirement for blacks to $250, a sum beyond the reach of nearly all of the state's black residents. North Carolina disenfranchised free blacks in 1835, and Pennsylvania, home of an articulate, economically successful black community in Philadelphia, did the same three years later. One delegate to the Pennsylvania constitutional convention refused to sign the completed document because of its provision limiting suffrage to whites. This was Thaddeus Stevens, who would later become a leader in the drive for equal rights for African-Americans after the Civil War. By 1860, blacks could vote on the same basis as whites in only five New England states, which contained only 4 percent of the nation's free black population. A delegate to the Pennsylvania convention of 1837 described the United States as "a political community of white persons."

Despite racial inequalities, many whites of the revolutionary generation had thought of African-Americans as "citizens of color," potential members of the body politic. But in the nineteenth century, the definition of the political nation became more and more associated with race. The federal government barred free blacks from service in state militias and the army (although the navy did enroll some black sailors). No state accorded free blacks what today would be considered full equality before the law. In Illinois, for example, blacks could not vote, testify or sue in court, serve in the militia, or attend public schools. Blacks were aliens, not Americans, "intruders among us," declared a political leader in Minnesota.

In effect, race had replaced class as the boundary between those American men who were entitled to enjoy political freedom and those who were not. Even as this focus on race limited America's political community as a whole, it helped to solidify a sense of national identity among the diverse groups of European origin. In a country where the right to vote had become central to the meaning of freedom, it is difficult to overstate the importance of the fact that white male immigrants could vote in some states almost from the moment they landed in America, while nearly all free blacks (and, of course, slaves), whose ancestors had lived in the country for centuries, could not vote at all.

> *Race replaces class as a voting qualification*

NATIONALISM AND ITS DISCONTENTS

The American System

The War of 1812, which the United States and Great Britain—the world's foremost military power—fought to a draw, inspired an outburst of nationalist pride. But the war also revealed how far the United States still was from being a truly integrated nation. With the Bank of the United States having gone out of existence when its charter expired in 1811, the country lacked a uniform currency and found it almost impossible to raise funds for the war effort. Given the primitive state of transportation, it proved very difficult to move men and goods around the country. One shipment of supplies from New England had taken seventy-five days to reach New Orleans. With the coming of peace, the manufacturing enterprises that sprang up while trade with Britain had been suspended faced intense competition from low-cost imported goods. A younger generation of Republicans, including Henry Clay and John C. Calhoun, who had led the call for war in 1812, believed these "infant industries" deserved national protection. While retaining their Jeffersonian belief in an agrarian republic, they insisted that agriculture must be complemented by a manufacturing sector if the country were to become economically independent of Britain.

> *"Infant industries"*

In 1806, Congress, as noted in the previous chapter, had approved using public funds to build a paved National Road from Cumberland, Maryland, to the Ohio Valley. Two years later, Albert Gallatin, Jefferson's secretary of the treasury, outlined a plan for the federal government to tie the vast nation together by constructing

An image from a broadside from the campaign of 1824, promoting the American System of government-sponsored economic development. The illustrations represent industry, commerce, and agriculture. The ship at the center is named the *John Quincy Adams*. Its flag, "No Colonial Subjection," suggests that without a balanced economy, the United States will remain economically dependent on Great Britain.

roads and canals up and down the eastern seaboard, and by connecting the Atlantic coast with the Great Lakes and Ohio and Mississippi Rivers. Gallatin's proposal fell victim to regional rivalries and fears of excessive national power. But the idea revived after the War of 1812.

In his annual message (now known as the State of the Union address) to Congress in December 1815, President James Madison put forward a blueprint for government-promoted economic development that came to be known as the **American System**, a label coined by Henry Clay. (It should not be confused with the "American system of manufactures" mentioned in the previous chapter, which referred to a way of mass-producing goods with interchangeable parts, not a political program for economic growth.) The plan rested on three pillars: a new national bank, a tariff on imported manufactured goods to protect American industry, and federal financing of improved roads and canals. The last was particularly important to those worried about the dangers of disunity. "Let us bind the nation together, with a perfect system of roads and canals," John C. Calhoun implored Congress in 1815. "Let us conquer space." When believers in strict construction of the Constitution objected, Calhoun replied: "If we are restricted in the use of money to the enumerated powers, on what principle can the purchase of Louisiana be justified?"

Government-sponsored internal improvements, as the construction of roads and canals was called, proved to be the most controversial part of the plan. Congress enacted an internal improvements program drafted by Calhoun only to be astonished when the president, on the eve of his retirement from office in March 1817, vetoed the bill. Since calling for its enactment, Madison had become convinced that allowing the national government to exercise powers not mentioned in the Constitution would prove dangerous to individual liberty and southern interests. A constitutional amendment would be necessary, he declared, before the federal government could build roads and canals. The other two parts of his plan, however, became law. The **tariff of 1816** offered protection to goods that could be produced in the United States, especially cheap cotton textiles, while admitting tax-free those that could not be manufactured at home. Many southerners supported the tariff, believing that it would enable their region to develop a

Madison's blueprint for economic development

Internal improvements

manufacturing base to rival New England's. And in 1816, a new Bank of the United States was created, with a twenty-year charter from Congress.

Banks and Money

The Second Bank of the United States soon became the focus of public resentment. Like its predecessor, it was a private, profit-making corporation that served as the government's financial agent, issuing paper money, collecting taxes, and paying the government's debts. It was also charged with ensuring that paper money issued by local banks had real value. The number of local banks had risen to more than 200—a sign of the accelerating market revolution. They promoted economic growth by helping to finance manufacturing and commerce and extending loans to farmers for the purchase of land, tools, consumer goods, and, in the South, slaves. They also printed paper money.

Second Bank of the United States

Today, only the federal government issues paper money, and the total is determined by the Federal Reserve Bank, not the amount of gold held at the repository at Fort Knox. But in the nineteenth century, paper money consisted of notes promising to pay the bearer on demand a specified amount of "specie" (gold or silver). The value of the currency issued by individual banks depended on their reputation for stability. Since banks often printed far more money than the specie in their vaults, the value of paper currency fluctuated wildly. No one knew if the notes issued by many banks had any value. Public confidence was essential to a bank's success. (In Herman Melville's satirical novel *The Confidence Man* written in 1857, a man on a steamboat must decide whether a three-dollar bill is genuine or counterfeit.) The Bank of the United States was supposed to prevent the overissuance of money. Because it held all the funds of the federal government, it accumulated a large amount of paper money issued by local banks, which had been used to purchase public land. The Bank of the United States could demand payment in gold and silver from a local bank in exchange for that bank's paper money. This prospect was supposed to prevent local banks from acting improperly, for if it could not provide the specie when asked, it would have to suspend operations.

Paper money

The Panic of 1819

But instead of effectively regulating the currency and loans issued by local banks, the Bank of the United States participated in a speculative fever that swept the country after the end of the War of 1812. The resumption of trade with Europe created a huge overseas market for American cotton and grain. Coupled with the rapid expansion of settlement into the West, this stimulated demand for loans to purchase land, which local banks and branches of the Bank of the United States were only too happy to meet by printing more money. The land boom was especially acute in the South, where the Cotton Kingdom was expanding.

Early in 1819, as European demand for American farm products returned to normal levels, the economic bubble burst. During the resulting **Panic of 1819**, the demand for land plummeted, and speculators lost millions as the price of western land fell. At this time, loans tended to be of short duration and banks could demand repayment at any time. The Bank of the United States, followed by state banks, began asking for payments from those to whom it had loaned money. Farmers and businessmen who could not repay declared bankruptcy, and unemployment rose in eastern cities.

An economic bubble

The Politics of the Panic

Panic of 1819

The Panic of 1819 lasted little more than a year, but it severely disrupted the political harmony of the previous years. Those suffering from the economic downturn pressed the state and national governments for assistance. To the consternation of creditors, many states, especially in the West, responded by suspending the collection of debts. Kentucky went even further, establishing a state bank that flooded the state with paper money that creditors were required to accept in repayment of loans. This eased the burden on indebted farmers, but injured those who had loaned them the money. Overall, the Panic deepened many Americans' traditional distrust of banks. It undermined the reputation of the Second Bank of the United States, which was widely blamed for causing the Panic. Several states retaliated against the national bank by taxing its local branches.

McCulloch v. Maryland

These tax laws produced another of John Marshall's landmark Supreme Court decisions, in the case of ***McCulloch v. Maryland*** (1819). Reasserting his broad interpretation of governmental powers, Marshall declared the Bank a legitimate exercise of congressional authority under the Constitution's clause that allowed Congress to pass "necessary and proper" laws. Marshall's interpretation of the Constitution directly contradicted the "strict construction" view that limited Congress to powers specifically granted in the Constitution. Marshall acknowledged that the Constitution nowhere mentions the right of lawmakers to issue corporate charters. But, he wrote, where the aim of legislation—in this case to promote the "general welfare"—was legitimate, "all means which are . . . not prohibited . . . are constitutional." Maryland, the chief justice continued, could not tax the Bank. "The power to tax," Marshall remarked, "involves the power to destroy," and the states lacked the authority to destroy an agency created by the national government.

The Missouri Controversy

In 1816, James Monroe handily defeated Federalist candidate Rufus King, becoming the last of the Virginia presidents. By 1820, the Federalists fielded electoral tickets in only two states, and Monroe carried the entire country. (One elector, William Plumer of New Hampshire, however, cast his vote for John Quincy Adams, whom he deemed more qualified than Monroe to be president. The legend later arose that Plumer voted as he did because he wished George Washington to remain the only president elected unanimously.) Monroe's two terms in office were years of one-party government, sometimes called the **Era of Good Feelings**. Plenty of bad feelings, however, surfaced during his presidency. In the absence of two-party competition, politics was organized along lines of competing sectional interests.

Missouri statehood

Even as political party divisions faded and John Marshall aligned the Supreme Court with the aggressive nationalism of Clay, Calhoun, and others, the troublesome issue of slavery again threatened to disrupt the nation's unity. In 1819, Congress considered a request from Missouri, an area carved out of the Louisiana Purchase, to form a constitution in preparation for admission to the Union as a state. Missouri's slave population already exceeded 10,000. James Tallmadge, a Republican congressman from New York, moved that the introduction of more slaves be prohibited and that children of those already in Missouri be freed at age twenty-five.

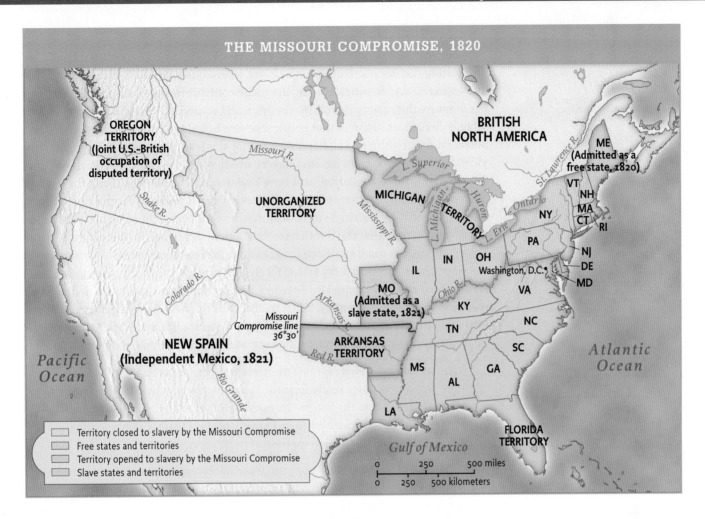

THE MISSOURI COMPROMISE, 1820

Territory closed to slavery by the Missouri Compromise
Free states and territories
Territory opened to slavery by the Missouri Compromise
Slave states and territories

Tallmadge's proposal sparked two years of controversy, during which Republican unity shattered along sectional lines. His restriction passed the House, where most northern congressmen supported it over the objections of southern representatives. It died in the Senate, however. When Congress reconvened in 1820, Senator Jesse Thomas of Illinois proposed a compromise with three parts. Missouri would be authorized to draft a constitution without Tallmadge's restriction. Maine, which prohibited slavery, would be admitted to the Union to maintain the sectional balance between free and slave states. And slavery would be prohibited in all remaining territory within the Louisiana Purchase north of latitude 36°30′ (Missouri's southern boundary). Congress adopted Thomas's plan as the **Missouri Compromise**.

A year later, Missouri presented to Congress its new constitution, which not only protected slavery but prohibited free blacks from entering the state. Since some northern states still considered blacks citizens, this seemed to violate the federal Constitution's "comity" clause, which requires each state to recognize the rights of citizens of other states. Henry Clay engineered a second Missouri Compromise, according to which Congress accepted the state's constitution as written, but instructed Missouri that it could not deprive the citizens of any states of their rights under the U.S. Constitution. Missouri, however, largely ignored this provision.

The Missouri Compromise temporarily settled the question of the expansion of slavery by dividing the Louisiana Purchase into free and slave areas.

Slavery and the Missouri constitution

The Slavery Question

Slavery and party politics

Thomas Jefferson, who had drafted the clause of the Northwest Ordinance of 1787 prohibiting slavery north of the Ohio River, strenuously opposed efforts to keep the institution out of Missouri. He saw the entire controversy as an attempt by Federalists to revive their party by setting northern and southern Republicans against each other. Jefferson was correct that political power, not moral scruples, motivated most northern congressmen. But Republicans, not the few remaining Federalists, provided the bulk of the votes against slavery in Missouri. By 1820, New York had surpassed Virginia in population, and New York Republicans were among the leading advocates of emancipation in Missouri. Twenty-eight years of Virginia presidents, interrupted only by the single term of John Adams of Massachusetts, had persuaded many northerners that the South exercised undue influence in Washington. More slave states meant more southern congressmen and electoral votes.

Westward expansion of slavery

The Missouri controversy raised for the first time what would prove to be a fatal issue—the westward expansion of slavery. The sectional division it revealed aroused widespread feelings of dismay. "This momentous question," wrote Jefferson, "like a fire bell in the night, awakened and filled me with terror. I considered it at once as the knell of the union." John Quincy Adams wrote of the debate in his diary:

> [It] disclosed a secret: it revealed the basis for a new organization of parties. . . . Here was a new party really formed . . . terrible to the whole Union, but portentously terrible to the South—threatening in its progress the emancipation of all their slaves, threatening in its immediate effect that southern domination which has swayed the Union for the last twenty years.

The "dissolution of the Union" over the issue of slavery, Adams mused, disastrous as that might be, would result in civil war and the "extirpation of slavery from this whole continent." It would take more than forty years for Adams's prediction to be fulfilled. For the moment, the slavery issue faded once again from national debate.

The House of Representatives in 1822, in a painting by Samuel F. B. Morse (who also invented the telegraph). By this time, most adult white men could vote for members of the House, a far wider franchise than was known in Europe at the time.

NATION, SECTION, AND PARTY

The United States and the Latin American Wars of Independence

Between 1810 and 1822, Spain's Latin American colonies rose in rebellion and established a series of independent nations, including Mexico, Venezuela, Ecuador, and Peru. By 1825, Spain's once vast American empire had been reduced to the islands of Cuba and Puerto Rico. The uprisings inspired a wave of sympathy in the United States. In 1822, the Monroe administration became the first government to extend diplomatic recognition to the new Latin American republics.

Parallels existed between the Spanish-American revolutions and the one that had given birth to the United States. In both cases, the crisis of empire was precipitated by programs launched by the imperial country aimed in large measure at making the colonies contribute more to its finances. The government in Spain had been trying to strengthen its hold on the empire since the late eighteenth century. A French army under Napoleon occupied Spain in 1808 and overthrew the monarchy, inspiring assertions of local control throughout Spanish America. A new constitution adopted by Spain in 1812 granted greater local rights in Spain and the colonies. When the king was restored in 1814, he repudiated the constitution and moved to reassert control over the colonies. As had happened in British North America, local elites demanded status and treatment equal to residents of the imperial power. The Spanish-American declarations of independence borrowed directly from that of the United States. The first, issued in 1811, even before the restoration of the monarchy in Spain, declared that the "United Provinces" of Venezuela now enjoyed "among the sovereign nations of the earth the rank which the Supreme Being and nature has assigned us"—language strikingly similar to Jefferson's.

Unlike the British empire, Spain's dissolved into seventeen different nations. The Spanish empire was too vast and disconnected for a common sense of nationhood to emerge. The Spanish government had imposed severe restrictions on printing, thereby making communication between the various parts of the empire more difficult than in the British colonies. The first printing press in Bogotá, a major city in South America, was not established until the 1770s. Nonetheless, imported books had circulated widely, spreading the era's revolutionary ideas.

In some ways, the new Latin American constitutions were more democratic than that of the United States. Most sought to implement the transatlantic ideals of rights and freedom by creating a single national "people" out of the diverse populations that made up the Spanish empire. To do so, they extended the right to vote to Indians and free blacks. The Latin American wars of independence, in which black soldiers participated on both sides, also set in motion the gradual abolition of slavery. But the Latin American wars of independence lasted longer—sometimes more than a decade—and were more destructive than the one in the United States had been. In some countries, independence was followed by civil war. As a result, it proved far more difficult for the new Latin American republics to achieve economic development than for the United States.

The new Latin American republics

Latin American constitutions

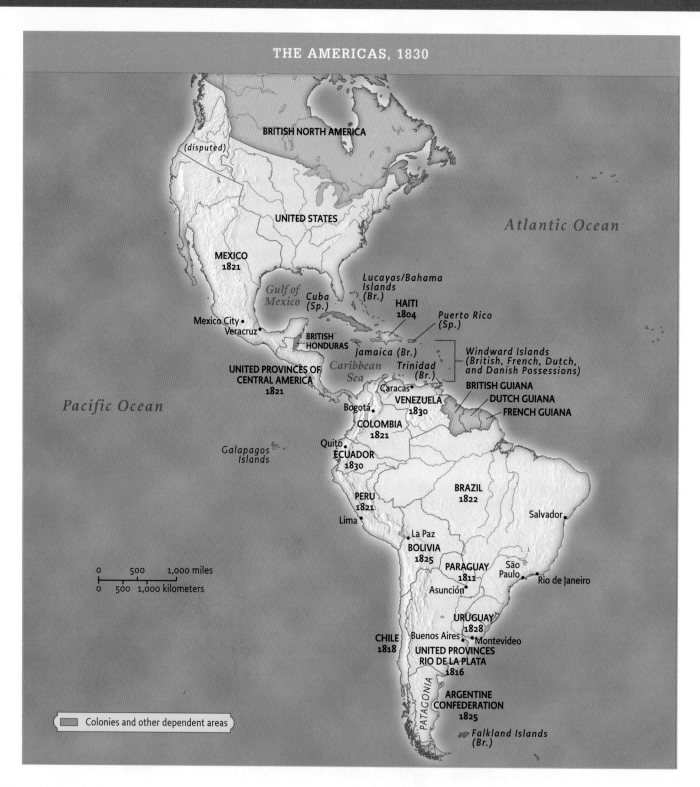

THE AMERICAS, 1830

BRITISH NORTH AMERICA

(disputed)

UNITED STATES

Atlantic Ocean

MEXICO
1821

Gulf of Mexico

Mexico City •
Veracruz •

Cuba (Sp.)

Lucayas/Bahama Islands (Br.)

HAITI
1804

Puerto Rico (Sp.)

BRITISH HONDURAS

Jamaica (Br.)

Caribbean Sea

Trinidad (Br.)

Windward Islands (British, French, Dutch, and Danish Possessions)

UNITED PROVINCES OF CENTRAL AMERICA
1821

Caracas •

BRITISH GUIANA
DUTCH GUIANA
FRENCH GUIANA

Pacific Ocean

Bogotá •

VENEZUELA
1830

COLOMBIA
1821

Galapagos Islands

Quito •

ECUADOR
1830

BRAZIL
1822

PERU
1821

Salvador •

Lima •

La Paz •

BOLIVIA
1825

PARAGUAY
1811

São Paulo •

Rio de Janeiro •

0   500   1,000 miles
0   500 1,000 kilometers

Asunción •

URUGUAY
1828

CHILE
1818

Buenos Aires •
Montevideo •

UNITED PROVINCES RIO DE LA PLATA
1816

PATAGONIA

ARGENTINE CONFEDERATION
1825

Falkland Islands (Br.)

Colonies and other dependent areas

This map depicts the Western Hemisphere after most of Spain's colonies achieved their independence.

The Monroe Doctrine

John Quincy Adams, who was serving as James Monroe's secretary of state, was devoted to consolidating the power of the national government at home and abroad. Adams feared that Spain would try to regain its Latin American colonies. In 1823, he drafted a section of the president's annual message to Congress that became known as the **Monroe Doctrine**. It expressed three principles. First, the United States would oppose any further efforts at colonization by European powers in the Americas (a statement aimed not only against Spain but also at France, which had designs on Cuba, and at Russia, which was seeking to expand its holdings on the Pacific coast). Second, the United States would abstain from involvement in the wars of Europe. Finally, Monroe warned European powers not to interfere with the newly independent states of Latin America.

The Monroe Doctrine is sometimes called America's diplomatic declaration of independence. For many decades, it remained a cornerstone of American foreign policy. Based on the assumption that the Old and New Worlds formed separate political and diplomatic systems, it claimed for the United States the role of dominant power in the Western Hemisphere. For Adams, the commercial implications were as important as the political ones. In 1823, Latin America was a major market for British goods, and British citizens were heavily involved in mining, banking, and commercial enterprises there. Adams hoped that the United States could eventually assume Britain's economic role.

America's diplomatic declaration of independence

The Election of 1824

The Monroe Doctrine reflected a rising sense of American nationalism. But sectionalism seemed to rule domestic politics. As the election of 1824 approached, only Andrew Jackson could claim truly national support. Jackson's popularity rested not on any specific public policy—few voters knew his views—but on military victories over the British at the Battle of New Orleans, and over the Creek and Seminole Indians. Other candidates included John Quincy Adams, Secretary of the Treasury William H. Crawford of Georgia, and Henry Clay of Kentucky. Adams's support was concentrated in New England and, more generally, in the North, where

Sectionalism and domestic politics

The White House in 1826, during the presidency of John Quincy Adams, as painted by a British diplomat, Anthony St. John Baker. The stone wall, erected by Thomas Jefferson, was removed after the Civil War.

VOICES OF FREEDOM

From THE MEMORIAL OF THE NON-FREEHOLDERS OF THE CITY OF RICHMOND (1829)

By the 1820s, as political democracy expanded, only North Carolina, Rhode Island, and Virginia still required property qualifications for voting for white men. When Virginia held a constitutional convention in 1829–1830, "non-freeholders" of Richmond—men who did not possess enough property—petitioned for the right to vote. The major slaveholders who dominated Virginia politics resisted their demand; not until 1850 did the state eliminate the property qualification.

———————————

Your memorialists . . . belong to that class of citizens, who, not having the good fortune to possess a certain portion of land, are, for that cause only, debarred from the enjoyment of the right of suffrage. . . . Comprising a very large part, probably a majority of male citizens of mature age, they have been passed by, like aliens or slaves, as if . . . unworthy of a voice, in the measures involving their future political destiny. . . .

The existing regulation of the suffrage . . . creates an odious distinction between members of the same community; robs of all share, in the enactment of the laws, a large portion of the citizens, . . . and vests in a favored class, not in consideration of their public services, but of their private possessions, the highest of all privileges. . . . [We] cannot discern in the possession of land any evidence of peculiar merit, or superior title [to] moral or intellectual endowments. . . . Such possession no more proves him who has it, wiser or better, than it proves him taller or stronger, than him who has it not. . . .

Let us concede that the right of suffrage is a social right; that it must of necessity be regulated by society. . . . For obvious reasons, by almost universal consent, women and children, aliens and slaves, are excluded. . . . But the exclusion of these classes for reasons peculiarly applicable to them, is no argument for excluding others. . . .

They alone deserve to be called free, or have a guarantee for their rights, who participate in the formation of their political institutions, and in control of those who make and administer the law.

From APPEAL OF FORTY THOUSAND CITIZENS THREATENED WITH DISFRANCHISEMENT (1838)

In many states, the expansion of political democracy for white men went hand in hand with the elimination of democratic participation for blacks. In 1837, a constitutional convention in Pennsylvania stripped black men of the right to vote. A large gathering in Philadelphia issued a protest to "fellow citizens" of Pennsylvania.

———————————

Fellow Citizens:—We appeal to you from the decision of the "Reform Convention," which has stripped us of a right peaceably enjoyed during forty seven years under the Constitution of this commonwealth. We honor Pennsylvania and her noble institutions too much to part with our birth-right, as her free citizens, without a struggle. To all her citizens the right of suffrage is valuable in proportion as she is free; but surely there are none who can so ill afford to spare it as ourselves.

Was it the intention of the people of this commonwealth that the Convention to which the Constitution was committed for revision and amendment, should tear up and cast away its first principles? Was it made the business of the Convention to deny "that all men are born equally free," by making political rights depend upon the skin in which a man is born? or to divide what our fathers bled to unite, to wit, TAXATION and REPRESENTATION?... It is the safeguard of the strongest that he lives under a government which is obliged to respect the voice of the weakest. When you have taken from an individual his right to vote, you have made the government, in regard to him, a mere despotism; and you have taken a step towards making it a despotism to all.... When a distinct class of the community, already sufficiently the objects of prejudice, are wholly, and for

ever, disfranchised and excluded, to the remotest posterity, from the possibility of a voice in regard to the laws under which they are to live—it is the same thing as if their abode were transferred to the dominions of the Russian Autocrat, or of the Grand Turk. They have lost their check upon oppression, their wherewith to buy friends, their panoply of manhood; in short, they are thrown upon the mercy of a despotic majority....

It was said in the Convention, that this government belongs to the Whites. We have already shown this to be false, as to the past. Those who established our present government designed it equally for all. It is for you to decide whether it shall be confined to the European complexion in future. Why should you exclude us from a fair participation in the benefits of the republic?... We put it to the conscience of every Pennsylvanian, whether there is, or ever has been, in the commonwealth, either a political party or religious sect which has less deserved than ourselves to be thus disfranchised.... If we are bad citizens let them apply the proper remedies.... Fair protection is all that we aspire to.

QUESTIONS

1. *What "obvious reasons" exclude women, children, non-citizens, and slaves from the right to vote?*

2. *How do the Philadelphia memorialists link their claims to the legacy of the American Revolution?*

3. *How similar are the definitions of political freedom in the two documents?*

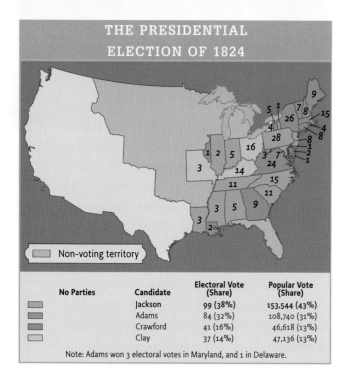

THE PRESIDENTIAL ELECTION OF 1824

Non-voting territory

No Parties	**Candidate**	**Electoral Vote (Share)**	**Popular Vote (Share)**
	Jackson	99 (38%)	153,544 (43%)
	Adams	84 (32%)	108,740 (31%)
	Crawford	41 (16%)	46,618 (13%)
	Clay	37 (14%)	47,136 (13%)

Note: Adams won 3 electoral votes in Maryland, and 1 in Delaware.

Republican leaders insisted the time had come for the South to relinquish the presidency. Crawford represented the South's Old Republicans, who wanted the party to reaffirm the principles of states' rights and limited government. Clay was one of the era's most popular politicians, but his support in 1824 lay primarily in the West. A caucus of Republican congressmen traditionally chose the party's nominee for president. The caucus selected Crawford, but this did not deter the other candidates, a sign that at a time of expanding democracy a small group of officials could no longer determine who ran for office.

Jackson received 153,544 votes and carried states in all the regions outside of New England. But with four candidates in the field, none received a majority of the electoral votes. As required by the Constitution, Clay, who finished fourth, was eliminated, and the choice among the other three fell to the House of Representatives. Sincerely believing Adams to be the most qualified candidate and the one most likely to promote the American System, and probably calculating that the election of Jackson, a westerner, would impede his own presidential ambitions, Clay gave his support to Adams, helping to elect him. He soon became secretary of state in Adams's cabinet. The charge that he had made a "corrupt bargain"—bartering critical votes in the presidential contest for a public office—clung to Clay for the rest of his career, making it all but impossible for him to reach the White House. The election of 1824 laid the groundwork for a new system of political parties. Supporters of Jackson and Crawford would soon unite in a new organization, the Democratic Party, determined to place Jackson in the White House in 1828. The alliance of Clay and Adams became the basis for the Whig Party of the 1830s.

The Nationalism of John Quincy Adams

John Quincy Adams enjoyed one of the most distinguished pre-presidential careers of any American president. The son of John Adams, he had witnessed the Battle of Bunker Hill at age eight and at fourteen had worked as private secretary and French interpreter for an American envoy in Europe. He had gone on to serve as ambassador to Prussia, the Netherlands, Britain, and Russia, and as senator from Massachusetts. Although elected as a Federalist, Adams cast one of New England's few votes in favor of Jefferson's embargo policy, arguing that his region must rise above sectional self-interest to defend the national good. Given the intense political passions of the time, he had been forced to resign his seat as a result of his vote, and he soon abandoned the Federalist Party.

Adams was not an engaging figure. He described himself as "a man of cold, austere, and foreboding manners." But he had a clear vision of national greatness. At home, he strongly supported the American System of government-sponsored economic development. Abroad, he hoped to encourage American commerce throughout the world and, as illustrated by his authorship of the Monroe Doctrine, enhance American influence in the Western Hemisphere. As Monroe's secretary of state, he

A vision of national greatness

had been the only cabinet member to oppose reprimanding Andrew Jackson for his violent incursion into Florida. In 1819, as noted in the previous chapter, Adams negotiated a treaty by which the United States acquired Florida from Spain. He also concluded an agreement with Great Britain fixing the Canadian-American border at the 49th parallel, the northern boundary of the Louisiana Purchase. An ardent expansionist, Adams was certain that the United States would eventually, and peacefully, absorb Canada, Cuba, and at least part of Mexico. Indeed, he once said, the "proper domain" of the United States was "the entire continent of North America."

"Liberty Is Power"

Adams held a view of federal power far more expansive than most of his contemporaries. In his first message to Congress, in December 1825, he set forth a comprehensive program for an activist national state. "The spirit of improvement is abroad in the land," Adams announced, and the federal government should be its patron. He called for legislation promoting agriculture, commerce, manufacturing, and "the mechanical and elegant arts." His plans included the establishment of a national university, an astronomical observatory, and a naval academy. At a time when many Americans felt that governmental authority posed the greatest threat to freedom, Adams astonished many listeners with the bold statement "Liberty is power." The United States, the freest nation on earth, would also, he predicted, become the mightiest.

Adams's proposals alarmed all believers in strict construction of the Constitution. His administration spent more on internal improvements than his five predecessors combined, and it enacted a steep increase in tariff rates in 1828. But the rest of Adams's ambitious ideas received little support in Congress. Not until the twentieth century would the kind of national economic and educational planning envisioned by Adams be realized. Some of his proposals, like the adoption by the United States of the metric system of weights and measures used by nearly every other nation in the world, and the building of a national university, have yet to be implemented.

John Quincy Adams in an 1843 daguerreotype.

Martin Van Buren and the Democratic Party

Adams's program handed his political rivals a powerful weapon. With individual liberty, states' rights, and limited government as their rallying cries, Jackson's supporters began to organize for the election of 1828 almost as soon as Adams assumed office. Martin Van Buren, a senator from New York, oversaw the task. The clash between Adams and Van Buren demonstrated how democracy was changing the nature of American politics. Adams typified the old politics—he was the son of a president and, like Jefferson and Madison, a man of sterling intellectual accomplishments. Van Buren represented the new political era. The son of a tavern keeper, he was a talented party manager, not a person of great vision or intellect.

The new politics

But Van Buren did have a compelling idea. Rather than being dangerous and divisive, as the founding generation had believed, political parties, he insisted, were a necessary and indeed desirable element of political life. Party competition provided a check on those in power and offered voters a real choice in elections.

Political parties as desirable

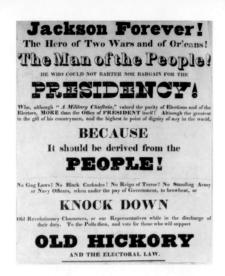

A broadside from the 1828 campaign illustrates how Andrew Jackson's supporters promoted him as a military hero and "man of the people."

And by bringing together political leaders from different regions in support of common candidates and principles, national parties could counteract the sectionalism that had reared its head during the 1820s. Like many of his contemporaries, Van Buren had been alarmed when politics divided along sectional lines in the Missouri debates and again in the election of 1824. He attributed this in part to a loss of discipline within the ruling Republican Party. "Party attachment," Van Buren wrote to Virginia editor Thomas Ritchie, "in former times furnished a complete antidote for sectional prejudices by producing counteracting feelings. It was not until that defense had been broken down that the clamor against southern influence and African slavery could be made effectual in the North." National political parties, Van Buren realized, formed a bond of unity in a divided nation. He set out to reconstruct the Jeffersonian political alliance between "the planters of the South and the plain republicans [the farmers and urban workers] of the North."

The Election of 1828

By 1828, Van Buren had established the political apparatus of the Democratic Party, complete with local and state party units overseen by a national committee and a network of local newspapers devoted to the party. Adams, for his part, disdained political organization. Despite Clay's urging, he refused to dismiss federal office-holders who campaigned for Jackson and did little to promote his own reelection.

Apart from a general commitment to limited government, Jackson's supporters made few campaign promises, relying on their candidate's popularity and the workings of party machinery to get out the vote. The 1828 election campaign was scurrilous. Jackson's supporters accused Adams of having had a series of mistresses while serving as a diplomat in Europe. They praised their candidate's frontier manliness and ridiculed Adams's intellectual attainments. ("Vote for Andrew Jackson who can fight, not John Quincy Adams who can write," declared one campaign slogan.) Jackson's opponents condemned him as a murderer for having executed army deserters and killing men in duels. They questioned the morality of his wife, Rachel, because she had married Jackson before her divorce from her first husband had become final. Jackson always believed his opponents' slanders had contributed to his wife's death shortly after the election.

By 1828, voters, not the legislature, chose presidential electors in every state except South Carolina, a fact that helped to encourage vigorous campaigning and high turnout. Nearly 57 percent of the eligible electorate cast ballots, more than double the percentage four years earlier. Jackson won a resounding victory, with around 650,000 votes to 500,000 for Adams. He carried the entire South and West, along with Pennsylvania. Jackson's election was the first to demonstrate how the advent of universal white male voting, organized by national political parties, had transformed American politics. For better or worse, the United States had entered the Age of Jackson.

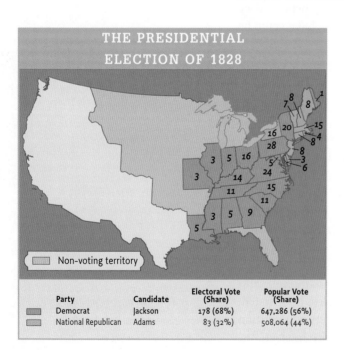

THE PRESIDENTIAL ELECTION OF 1828

Non-voting territory

	Party	Candidate	Electoral Vote (Share)	Popular Vote (Share)
	Democrat	Jackson	178 (68%)	647,286 (56%)
	National Republican	Adams	83 (32%)	508,064 (44%)

THE AGE OF JACKSON

Andrew Jackson was a man of many contradictions. Although he had little formal education (Adams called him "a barbarian who could not write a sentence of grammar"), Jackson was capable of genuine eloquence in his public statements. He was a self-proclaimed champion of the common man, but his vision of democracy excluded any role for Indians, who he believed should be pushed west of the Mississippi River, and African-Americans, who should remain as slaves or be freed and sent abroad. Although he rose from modest beginnings on the South Carolina frontier to become one of the richest men in Tennessee, he had an abiding suspicion of banks and paper money, and he shared the fears of many Americans that the market revolution was a source of moral decay rather than progress. A strong nationalist, Jackson nonetheless believed that the states, not Washington, D.C., should be the focal point of governmental activity. He opposed federal efforts to shape the economy or interfere in individuals' private lives.

Jackson's background

The Party System

By the time of Jackson's presidency, politics had become more than a series of political contests—it was a spectacle, a form of mass entertainment, a part of Americans' daily lives. Every year witnessed elections to some office—local, state, or national—and millions took part in the parades and rallies organized by the parties. Politicians were popular heroes with mass followings and popular nicknames. Jackson was Old Hickory, Clay Harry of the West, and Van Buren the Little Magician (or, to his critics, the Sly Fox). Thousands of Americans willingly

Politics and public life

Stump Speaking. In this painting from the 1850s, George Caleb Bingham depicts a candidate in a county election addressing a group of voters, an illustration of grassroots democracy in action. One of the listeners appears about to question or challenge the speaker. A founder of the Whig Party in Missouri, Bingham himself ran for office several times and was elected to the state legislature in 1848.

attended lengthy political orations and debates. An audience of 100,000 was said to have gathered on a Massachusetts hillside to hear a speech by the great Whig orator Daniel Webster.

Professional politicians

"Politics," one newspaper editor remarked, "seems to enter into everything." Indeed, party machines, headed by professional politicians, reached into every neighborhood, especially in cities. They provided benefits like jobs to constituents and ensured that voters went to the polls on election day. Party functionaries were rewarded with political offices. Government posts, Jackson declared, should be open to the people, not reserved for a privileged class of permanent bureaucrats. He introduced the principle of rotation in office (called the **spoils system** by opponents) into national government, making loyalty to the party the main qualification for jobs like postmaster and customs official.

Large national conventions where state leaders gathered to hammer out a platform now chose national candidates. Newspapers played a greater and greater role in politics. Nearly 400 were published in 1830, compared to 90 in 1790. Every significant town, it seemed, had its Democratic and Whig papers whose job was not so much to report the news as to present the party's position on issues of the day. Jackson's Kitchen Cabinet—an informal group of advisers who helped to write his speeches and supervise communication between the White House and local party officials—mostly consisted of newspaper editors.

Democrats and Whigs

There was more to party politics, however, than spectacle and organization. Jacksonian politics revolved around issues spawned by the market revolution and the continuing tension between national and sectional loyalties. The cen-

Procession of Victuallers, a lithograph commemorating a parade of butchers through the streets of Philadelphia in 1821. Their banner, "We Feed the Hungry," illustrates the belief among members of the "producing classes" that their work led to practical benefits for society, unlike the activities of "nonproducers" like bankers.

tral elements of political debate were the government's stance toward banks, tariffs, currency, and internal improvements, and the balance of power between national and local authority. Although both parties were coalitions of groups with varied, sometimes contradictory approaches to the issues of the day, the market revolution did much to determine their views and makeup. Democrats tended to be alarmed by the widening gap between social classes. They warned that "nonproducers"—bankers, merchants, and speculators—were seeking to use connections with government to enhance their wealth to the disadvantage of the "producing classes" of farmers, artisans, and laborers. They believed the government should adopt a hands-off attitude toward the economy and not award special favors to entrenched economic interests.

> *Democrats on the issues*

"All bank charters, all acts of incorporation," declared a Democratic newspaper, "are calculated to enhance the power of wealth, produce inequalities among the people and to subvert liberty." If the national government removed itself from the economy, ordinary Americans could test their abilities in the fair competition of the self-regulating market. The Democratic Party attracted aspiring entrepreneurs who resented government aid to established businessmen, as well as large numbers of farmers and city workingmen suspicious of new corporate enterprises. Poorer farming regions isolated from markets, like the lower Northwest and the southern backcountry, tended to vote Democratic.

Whigs united behind the American System, believing that via a protective tariff, a national bank, and aid to internal improvements, the federal government could guide economic development. They were strongest in the Northeast, the most rapidly modernizing region of the country. Most established businessmen and bankers supported their program of government-promoted economic growth, as did farmers in regions near rivers, canals, and the Great Lakes, who benefited from economic changes or hoped to do so. The counties of upstate New York along the Erie Canal, for example, became a Whig stronghold, while more isolated rural communities tended to vote Democratic. Many slaveholders supported the Democrats, believing states' rights to be slavery's first line of defense. But like well-to-do merchants and industrialists in the North, the largest southern planters generally voted Whig.

> *Whigs on the issues*

Public and Private Freedom

The party battles of the Jacksonian era reflected the clash between "public" and "private" definitions of American freedom and their relationship to governmental power, a persistent tension in the nation's history. For Democrats, liberty was a private entitlement best secured by local governments and endangered by powerful national authority. "The limitation of power, in every branch of our government," wrote a Democratic newspaper in 1842, "is the only safeguard of liberty." A "splendid" government was always "built upon the ruins of popular rights."

> *The Democrats: power a threat to liberty*

Under Jackson, even as democracy expanded, the power of the national government waned. Weak national authority, in the Democratic view, was essential to both private freedom and states' rights—"the freedom of the individual in the social union, [and] the freedom of the State in the Federative Union." Ralph Waldo Emerson called antebellum Americans "fanatics in freedom," whose obsession

County Election, another painting by George Caleb Bingham depicting American democracy in action. In this 1852 work, a voter takes an oath while party workers dispense liquor, seek to persuade voters, and keep track of who has cast ballots. The banner on the pole reads, "The Will of the People the Supreme Law." The slogan is meant to be ironic. Bingham includes a number of Democratic politicians he accused of cheating him in a recent election.

expressed itself in hatred of "tolls, taxes, turnpikes, banks, hierarchies, governors, yea, almost laws." Democrats regularly condemned the faraway federal government as the greatest "danger to liberty" in America and identified government-granted privilege as the root cause of social inequality. During Jackson's presidency, Democrats reduced expenditures, lowered the tariff, killed the national bank, and refused pleas for federal aid to internal improvements. By 1835, Jackson even managed to pay off the national debt. As a result, states replaced the federal government as the country's main economic actors, planning systems of canals and roads and chartering banks and other corporations.

Politics and Morality

Morality: public or private

Democrats, moreover, considered individual morality a private matter, not a public concern. They opposed attempts to impose a unified moral vision on society, such as "temperance" legislation, which restricted or outlawed the production and sale of liquor, and laws prohibiting various kinds of entertainment on Sundays. As noted in Chapter 9, Catholic Irish and German immigrants who began arriving in significant numbers in the 1830s flocked to the Democratic Party. One reason was that they did not wish to have Protestant moral standards enforced by the government. "In this country," declared the New York *Journal of Commerce* in 1848, "liberty is understood to be the *absence* of government from private affairs." The test of public policies was not whether they enhanced the common good, but the extent to which they allowed scope for "free agency"—that is, for individuals to make decisions, pursue their interests, and cultivate their unique talents without outside interference.

The Whigs: power allied with liberty

Whigs, for their part, insisted that liberty and power reinforced each other. An activist national government could enhance the realm of freedom. Liberty, Whigs believed, required a prosperous and moral America. The government should create the conditions for balanced and regulated economic development, thereby promoting a prosperity in which all classes and regions would share. Like the Federalists before them, wealthy Whigs tended to view society as a hierarchy of social classes, in contrast to the disorderly world of unrestrained individual competition embraced by many Democrats. But unlike most Federalists, they insisted that in the United States class status was not fixed, since any individual could achieve upward mobility.

Whigs, moreover, rejected the premise that the government must not interfere in private life. To function as free—that is, self-directed and self-disciplined—moral agents, individuals required certain character traits, which government could help to instill. The role of government, declared one New York Whig, was not simply to stand aside but actively to "promote the welfare of the people." Many evangelical Protestants supported the Whigs, convinced that via public education, the building of schools and asylums, temperance legislation, and the like, democratic governments could inculcate the "principles of morality." And during the Jacksonian era, popularly elected local authorities enacted numerous laws, ordinances, and regulations that tried to shape public morals by banning prostitution and the consumption of alcohol, and regulating other kinds of personal behavior.

> *Shaping public morals*

South Carolina and Nullification

Andrew Jackson, it has been said, left office with many more principles than he came in with. Elected as a military hero backed by an efficient party machinery, he was soon forced to define his stance on public issues. Despite his commitment to states' rights, Jackson's first term was dominated by a battle to uphold the supremacy of federal over state law. The tariff of 1828, which raised taxes on imported manufactured goods made of wool as well as on raw materials like iron, had aroused considerable opposition in the South, nowhere more than in South Carolina, where it was called the **tariff of abominations**. The state's leaders no longer believed it possible or desirable to compete with the North in industrial development. Insisting that the tariff on imported manufactured goods raised the prices paid by southern consumers to benefit the North, the legislature threatened to "nullify" it—that is, declare it null and void within their state.

> *The South and the "tariff of abominations"*

John C. Calhoun, who evolved from a nationalist into the most prominent spokesman for state sovereignty and the right of nullification.

The state with the largest proportion of slaves in its population (55 percent in 1830), South Carolina was controlled by a tightly knit group of large planters. They maintained their grip on power by a state constitution that gave plantation counties far greater representation in the legislature than their population warranted, as well as through high property qualifications for officeholders. They had been thoroughly alarmed by the Missouri crisis and by the steady strengthening of national authority by John Marshall's Supreme Court. Behind their economic complaints against the tariff lay the conviction that the federal government must be weakened lest it one day take action against slavery.

Calhoun's Political Theory

John C. Calhoun soon emerged as the leading theorist of nullification. As the South began to fall behind the rest of the country in population, Calhoun had evolved from the nationalist of 1812 into a powerful defender of southern sectionalism. Having

A cartoon published in 1833, at the height of the nullification controversy, shows John C. Calhoun climbing steps, including those marked "nullification," "treason," and "civil war," toward the goal of "despotism." He is flanked by James H. Hammond and Robert Y. Haynes, two of South Carolina's political leaders. On the right, President Andrew Jackson threatens to hang them.

South Carolina Exposition and Protest

been elected vice president in 1828, Calhoun at first remained behind the scenes, secretly drafting the ***Exposition and Protest*** in which the South Carolina legislature justified nullification. The document drew on the arguments in the Virginia and Kentucky resolutions of 1798 (discussed in Chapter 8). The national government, Calhoun insisted, had been created by an agreement among sovereign states, each of which retained the right to prevent the enforcement within its borders of acts of Congress that exceeded the powers specifically spelled out in the Constitution.

Almost from the beginning of Jackson's first term, Calhoun's influence in the administration waned, while Secretary of State Martin Van Buren emerged as the president's closest adviser. One incident that helped set Jackson against Calhoun occurred a few weeks after the inauguration. Led by Calhoun's wife, Floride, Washington society women ostracized Peggy Eaton, the wife of Jackson's secretary of war, because she was the daughter of a Washington tavern keeper and, allegedly, a woman of "easy virtue." Van Buren, a widower, stood by her, as did Jackson, who identified criticism of Peggy Eaton with the abuse his own wife had suffered during the campaign of 1828.

Far weightier matters soon divided Jackson and Calhoun. Debate over nullification raged in Washington. In a memorable exchange in the Senate in January 1830 that came to be known as the **Webster-Hayne debate**, Daniel Webster responded to South Carolina senator Robert Y. Hayne, a disciple of Calhoun. The people, not the states, declared Webster, created the Constitution, making the federal government sovereign. He called nullification illegal, unconstitutional, and treasonous. Webster's ending was widely hailed throughout the country—"Liberty *and* Union, now and forever, one and inseparable." A few weeks later, at a White House dinner, Jackson delivered a toast while fixing his gaze on Calhoun: "Our Federal Union—it must be

Webster-Hayne debate

preserved." Calhoun's reply came immediately: "The Union—next to our liberty most dear." By 1831, Calhoun had publicly emerged as the leading theorist of states' rights.

The Nullification Crisis

Nullification was not a purely sectional issue. South Carolina stood alone during the **nullification crisis**, and several southern states passed resolutions condemning its action. Nonetheless, the elaboration of the compact theory of the Constitution gave the South a well-developed political philosophy to which it would turn when sectional conflict became more intense. Calhoun denied that nullification was a step toward disunion. On the contrary, the only way to ensure the stability of a large, diverse nation was for each state to be assured that national actions would never trample on its rights or vital interests. According to Calhoun's theory of the "concurrent majority," each major interest, including slaveholders, should have a veto over all measures that affected it.

The "concurrent majority"

To Jackson, however, nullification amounted to nothing less than disunion. He dismissed Calhoun's constitutional arguments out of hand: "Can anyone of common sense believe the absurdity, that a faction of any state, or a state, has a right to secede and destroy this union, and the liberty of the country with it?" The issue came to a head in 1832, when a new tariff was enacted. Despite a reduction in rates, South Carolina declared the tax on imported goods null and void in the state after the following February. In response, Jackson persuaded Congress to pass a Force Act authorizing him to use the army and navy to collect customs duties.

The politics of nullification

To avert a confrontation, Henry Clay, with Calhoun's assistance, engineered the passage of a new tariff, in 1833, further reducing duties. South Carolina then rescinded the ordinance of nullification, although it proceeded to "nullify" the **Force Act**. Calhoun abandoned the Democratic Party for the Whigs, where, with Clay and Webster, he became part of a formidable trio of political leaders (even though the three agreed on virtually nothing except hostility toward Jackson). It is perhaps ironic that Andrew Jackson, a firm believer in states' rights and limited

An 1834 print portrays the United States as a Temple of Liberty. At the center, a figure of liberty rises from the flames, holding the Bill of Rights and a staff with a liberty cap. Justice and Minerva (Roman goddess of war and wisdom) flank the temple, above which flies a banner, "The Union Must and Shall Be Preserved."

government, did more than any other individual to give an emotional aura to the idea of Union and to offer an example of willingness to go to war, if necessary, to preserve what he considered the national government's legitimate powers.

Indian Removal

The nullification crisis underscored Jackson's commitment to the sovereignty of the nation. His exclusion of Indians from the era's assertive democratic nationalism led to the final act in the centuries-long conflict between white Americans and Indians east of the Mississippi River. The last Indian resistance to the advance of white settlement in the Old Northwest came in 1832, when federal troops and local militiamen routed the Sauk leader Black Hawk, who, with about 1,000 followers, attempted to reclaim ancestral land in Illinois. One of the Illinois militiamen was the young Abraham Lincoln, although, as he later remarked, he saw no action, except against mosquitoes.

Black Hawk

In the slave states, the onward march of cotton cultivation placed enormous pressure on remaining Indian holdings. "Extending the area of slavery," proclaimed Thomas Hart Benton, who represented Missouri in the Senate for thirty years, required "converting Indian soil into slave soil." During the 1820s, Missouri forced its Indian population to leave the state. Soon, the policy of expulsion was enacted in the older slave states. One of the early laws of Jackson's administration, the **Indian Removal Act** of 1830, provided funds for uprooting the so-called Five Civilized Tribes—the Cherokee, Chickasaw, Choctaw, Creek, and Seminole—with a population of around 60,000 living in North Carolina, Georgia, Florida, Alabama, and Mississippi.

Indian Removal Act of 1830

The law marked a repudiation of the Jeffersonian idea that "civilized" Indians could be assimilated into the American population. These tribes had made great efforts to become everything republican citizens should be. The Cherokee had taken the lead, establishing schools, adopting written laws and a constitution modeled on that of the United States, and becoming successful farmers, many of whom owned slaves. But in his messages to Congress, Jackson repeatedly referred to them as "savages" and supported Georgia's effort to seize Cherokee land and nullify the tribe's laws.

"Free citizens of the Cherokee nation" petitioned Congress for aid in remaining "in peace and quietude upon their ancient territory." In good American fashion, Cherokee leaders also went to court to protect their rights, guaranteed in treaties with the federal government. Their appeals forced the Supreme Court to clarify the unique status of American Indians.

A lithograph from 1836 depicts Sequoia, with the alphabet of the Cherokee language that he developed. Because of their written language and constitution, the Cherokee were considered by many white Americans to be a "civilized tribe."

The Supreme Court and the Indians

In a crucial case involving Indians in 1823, *Johnson v. M'Intosh*, the Court had proclaimed that Indians were not in fact owners of their land, but merely had a "right of occupancy." Chief Justice John Marshall, himself a speculator in western lands, claimed that from the early colonial era, Indians had lived as nomads and hunters, not farmers. Entirely inaccurate as history, the decision struck a serious blow against Indian efforts to retain their lands. In *Cherokee Nation v. Georgia* (1831), Marshall described Indians as "wards" of the federal government. They deserved

INDIAN REMOVALS, 1830–1840

The removal of the so-called Five Civilized Tribes from the Southeast all but ended the Indian presence east of the Mississippi River.

paternal regard and protection, but they lacked the standing as citizens that would allow the Supreme Court to enforce their rights. The justices could not, therefore, block Georgia's effort to extend its jurisdiction over the tribe.

Marshall, however, believed strongly in the supremacy of the federal government over the states. In 1832, in **Worcester v. Georgia**, the Court seemed to change its mind, holding that Indian nations were a distinct people with the right to maintain a separate political identity. They must be dealt with by the federal government, not the states, and Georgia's actions violated the Cherokees' treaties with Washington. But despite its strong assertion of national supremacy in the nullification crisis, Jackson refused to recognize the validity of the *Worcester* ruling. "John Marshall has made his decision," he supposedly declared, "now let him enforce it."

Worcester v. Georgia

With legal appeals exhausted, one faction of the tribe agreed to cede their lands, but the majority, led by John Ross, who had been elected "principal chief" under the Cherokee constitution, adopted a policy of passive resistance. Federal soldiers forcibly removed them during the presidency of Jackson's successor, Martin

Hiding in a Mangrove Swamp, a painting showing Seminole Indians in the Florida Everglades avoiding American sailors during the Second Seminole War.

Seminole resistance

Van Buren. The army herded 18,000 men, women, and children into stockades and then forced them to move west. At least one-quarter perished during the winter of 1838–1839 on the **Trail of Tears**, as the removal route from Georgia to the area of present-day Oklahoma came to be called. (In the Cherokee language, it was called "the trail on which we cried.") Among the Cherokees removed were 1,500 slaves, most of them owned by white men who had married Indian women or the "mixed-blood" descendants of these unions.

During the 1830s, most of the other southern tribes bowed to the inevitable and departed peacefully. But the Seminoles of sparsely settled Florida resisted. Osceola, one of the leaders of Seminole resistance to removal, was a Red Stick who had survived Andrew Jackson's assault on hostile Creeks during the War of 1812. The Indians were assisted by escaped slaves. As early as colonial times, Florida had been a refuge for fugitive slaves from South Carolina and Georgia, to whom Spanish officials offered freedom. The administration of George Washington attempted to persuade the Seminoles to expel the fugitives, but they refused. Georgia sent the militia into Florida to recapture them, but it was driven out by Seminole and African-American fighters. In the Second Seminole War, which lasted from 1835 to 1842 (the first had preceded American acquisition of Florida in 1819), some 1,500 American soldiers and the same number of Seminoles were killed, and perhaps 3,000 Indians and 500 blacks were forced to move to the

The Trapper and His Family (1845), by the artist Charles Deas, depicts a white pioneer who married an Indian woman.

Bull Dance, an 1832 painting of a ceremony of the Mandan tribe by George Catlin, who created dozens of works depicting Indians in the trans-Mississippi West. Each participant in the dance wears an entire buffalo skin, complete with head, horns, hooves, and tail. At the time, millions of buffalo inhabited the West, providing food and hides for Native Americans. Catlin saw himself as recording a vanishing way of life.

West. A small number of Seminoles managed to remain in Florida, a tiny remnant of the once sizable Indian population east of the Mississippi River.

In 1831, William Apess, a descendant of Metacom, or King Philip, who had battled New England colonists in the 1670s, published *A Son of the Forest*, the first significant autobiography by a Native American. The son of a white man and an Indian woman, Apess had served with American forces in an unsuccessful attack on Canada during the War of 1812. He later converted to Methodism and became a revivalist preacher. His book appealed for harmony between white Americans and Indians. "How much better it would be if the whites would act like civilized people [and] give every one his due," Apess wrote. "What do they, the Indians, want? You have only to look at the unjust laws made for them and say, 'They want what I want.'"

> *William Apess*

Removal was the alternative to the coexistence championed by Apess. It power-fully reinforced the racial definition of American nationhood and freedom. At the time of independence, Indians had been a familiar presence in many parts of the United States. John Adams once recalled how, when he was young, local Indians "were frequent visitors in my father's house," and how he would visit a nearby Indian family, "where I never failed to be treated with whortleberries, blackberries, strawberries or apples, plums, peaches, etc." By 1840, in the eyes of most whites east of the Mississippi River, they were simply a curiosity, a relic of an earlier period of American history. Although Indians still dominated the trans-Mississippi West, as American settlement pushed relentlessly westward it was clear that their days of freedom there also were numbered.

> *Effects of Indian removal*

THE BANK WAR AND AFTER

Biddle's Bank

The central political struggle of the Age of Jackson was the president's war on the Bank of the United States. The Bank symbolized the hopes and fears inspired by the market revolution. The expansion of banking helped to finance the nation's economic development. But many Americans, including Jackson, distrusted bankers as "nonproducers" who contributed nothing to the nation's wealth but profited from the labor of others. The tendency of banks to overissue paper money, whose deterioration in value reduced the real income of wage earners, reinforced this conviction. Jackson himself had long believed that "hard money"—gold and silver—was the only honest currency. Nonetheless, when he assumed office there was little reason to believe that the **Bank War** would become the major event of his presidency.

Nicholas Biddle

Heading the Bank was Nicholas Biddle of Pennsylvania, who during the 1820s had effectively used the institution's power, discussed earlier in this chapter, to curb the overissuing of money by local banks and to create a stable currency throughout the nation. A snobbish, aristocratic Philadelphian, Biddle was as strong-willed as Jackson and as unwilling to back down in a fight. In 1832, he told a congressional committee that his Bank had the ability to "destroy" any state bank. He hastened to add that he had never "injured" any of them. But Democrats wondered whether any institution, public or private, ought to possess such power. Many called it the Monster Bank, an illegitimate union of political authority and entrenched economic privilege. The issue of the Bank's future came to a head in 1832. Although the institution's charter would not expire until 1836, Biddle's allies persuaded Congress to approve a bill extending it for another twenty years. Jackson saw the tactic as a form of blackmail—if he did not sign the bill, the Bank would use its considerable resources to oppose his reelection. "The Bank," he told Van Buren, "is trying to destroy me, but I will kill it."

The Downfall of Mother Bank, a Democratic cartoon celebrating the destruction of the Second Bank of the United States. President Andrew Jackson topples the building by brandishing his order removing federal funds from the Bank. Led by Nicholas Biddle, with the head of a demon, the Bank's corrupt supporters flee, among them Henry Clay, Daniel Webster, and newspaper editors allegedly paid by the institution.

Jackson's veto message is perhaps the central document of his presidency. Its argument resonated with popular values. In a democratic government, Jackson insisted, it was unacceptable for Congress to create a source of concentrated power and economic privilege unaccountable to the people. "It is to be regretted," he declared, "that the rich and powerful too often bend the acts of government to their selfish purposes." Exclusive privileges like the Bank's charter widened the gap between the wealthy and "the humble members of society—the farmers, mechanics, and laborers." Jackson presented himself as the defender of these "humble" Americans.

Jackson's veto of the bank bill

The Bank War reflected how Jackson enhanced the power of the presidency during his eight years in office, proclaiming himself the symbolic representative of all the people. He was the first president to use the veto power as a major weapon and to appeal directly to the public for political support, over the head of Congress. Whigs denounced him for usurping the power of the legislature. They insisted that Congress, not the president, represented the will of the people and that the veto power, while created by the Constitution, should be used only in extraordinary circumstances. But Jackson's effective appeal to democratic popular sentiments helped him win a sweeping reelection victory in 1832 over the Whig candidate, Henry Clay. His victory ensured the death of the Bank of the United States. (Ironically, Jackson's image today adorns the twenty-dollar bill issued by the Federal Reserve Bank, in some respects a successor of the Bank of the United States.)

Enhancing the power of the presidency

The Pet Banks and the Economy

What, however, would take the Bank's place? Two very different groups applauded Jackson's veto—state bankers who wished to free themselves from Biddle's regulations and issue more paper currency (called **soft money**), **and hard money** advocates who opposed all banks, whether chartered by the states or the federal government, and believed that gold and silver formed the only reliable currency.

During Jackson's second term, state bankers were in the ascendancy. Not content to wait for the charter of the Bank of the United States to expire in 1836, Jackson authorized the removal of federal funds from its vaults and their deposit in local banks. Not surprisingly, political and personal connections often determined the choice of these **pet banks**. The director of the Maine Bank of Portland, for example, was the brother-in-law of Levi Woodbury, a member of Jackson's cabinet. A justice of the Supreme Court recommended the Planters Bank of Savannah. Two secretaries of the treasury refused to transfer federal money to the pet banks, since the law creating the Bank had specified that government funds could not be removed except for a good cause as communicated to Congress. Jackson finally appointed Attorney General Roger B. Taney, a loyal Maryland Democrat, to the treasury post, and he carried out the order. When John Marshall died in 1835, Jackson rewarded Taney by appointing him chief justice.

Jackson's "pet banks"

Without government deposits, the Bank of the United States lost its ability to regulate the activities of state banks. They issued more and more paper money, partly to help finance the rapid expansion of industrial development in New England, agriculture in the South and West, and canal and railroad systems planned by the states. The value of bank notes in circulation rose from $10 million in 1833 to $149 million in 1837.

Consequences of the removal of federal deposits

The Times, an 1837 engraving that blames Andrew Jackson's policies for the economic depression. The Custom House is idle, while next door a bank is mobbed by worried depositors. Beneath Jackson's hat, spectacles, and clay pipe (with the ironic word "glory"), images of hardship abound.

Prices rose dramatically, and even though wages also increased, they failed to keep pace. As a result, workers' "real wages"—the actual value of their pay—declined. Numerous labor unions emerged, which attempted to protect the earnings of urban workers. Speculators hastened to cash in on rising land prices. Using paper money, they bought up huge blocks of public land, which they resold to farmers or to eastern purchasers of lots in entirely nonexistent western towns. States projected tens of millions of dollars in internal improvements.

The Panic of 1837

The Specie Circular and its results

Inevitably, the speculative boom collapsed. The government sold 20 million acres of federal land in 1836, ten times the amount sold in 1830, nearly all of it paid for in paper money, often of questionable value. In July 1836, the Jackson administration issued the Specie Circular, declaring that henceforth it would accept only gold and silver as payment for public land. At the same time, the Bank of England, increasingly suspicious about the value of American bank notes, demanded that American merchants pay their creditors in London in gold or silver. Then, an economic downturn in Britain dampened demand for American cotton, the country's major export.

Panic of 1837

Taken together, these events triggered an economic collapse in the United States, the **Panic of 1837**, followed by a depression that lasted to 1843. Prices fell by 25 percent in the first year of the downturn. Businesses throughout the country failed, and many farmers, unable to meet mortgage payments because of declining income, lost their land. Tens of thousands of urban workers saw their jobs disappear. The fledgling labor movement collapsed as strikes became impossible given the surplus of unemployed labor. By 1842, nine states had defaulted on their debts, mostly incurred to finance ambitious internal improvement projects. During the 1840s, states amended their constitutions to prohibit legislatures from borrowing money, issuing corporate charters, and buying stock in private enterprises. For the time being, the Jacksonians had succeeded in separating government—both federal and state—from the economy.

Van Buren in Office

The president forced to deal with the depression was Martin Van Buren, who had been elected in 1836 over three regional candidates put forward by the Whigs in an attempt to maximize the party's electoral vote and throw the election into the House of Representatives. Under Van Buren, the hard-money, anti-bank wing of the Democratic Party came to power. In 1837, the administration announced its intention to remove federal funds from the pet banks and hold them in the Treasury Department in Washington, under the control of government officials. Not until 1840 did Congress approve the new policy, known as the Independent Treasury, which completely separated the federal government from the nation's banking system. It would be repealed in 1841 when the Whigs returned to power, but it was reinstated under President James K. Polk in 1846. Making federal funds unavailable for banks to use for investment would have dampened future economic growth had not the discovery of gold in California in 1848 poured new money into the economy.

The Independent Treasury

The Independent Treasury split the Democratic Party. Business-oriented Democrats, often connected with the state banks, strongly opposed Van Buren's policy and shifted wholesale to the Whigs. Meanwhile, the party's "agrarian" wing—small farmers and urban laborers opposed to all banking and paper money and uncomfortable with the market revolution in general—rallied to Van Buren. Many advocates of state sovereignty who had joined the Whigs after the nullification crisis now returned to the Democratic fold, including Van Buren's old nemesis, John C. Calhoun.

The Election of 1840

Despite his reputation as a political magician, Van Buren found that without Jackson's personal popularity he could not hold the Democratic coalition together. In 1840, he also discovered that his Whig opponents had mastered the political

A political cartoon from the 1840 presidential campaign shows public opinion as the "almighty lever" of politics in a democracy. Under the gaze of the American eagle, "Loco-Foco" Democrats slide into an abyss, while the people are poised to lift William Henry Harrison, the Whig candidate, to victory.

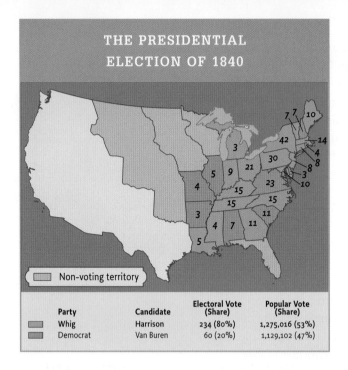

THE PRESIDENTIAL ELECTION OF 1840

Non-voting territory

	Party	Candidate	Electoral Vote (Share)	Popular Vote (Share)
	Whig	Harrison	234 (80%)	1,275,016 (53%)
	Democrat	Van Buren	60 (20%)	1,129,102 (47%)

Mass politics

techniques he had helped to pioneer. Confronting an unprecedented opportunity for victory because of the continuing economic depression, the Whigs abandoned their most prominent leader, Henry Clay, and nominated William Henry Harrison. Like Jackson when he first sought the presidency, Harrison's main claim to fame was military success against the British and Indians during the War of 1812.

The party nominated Harrison without a platform. In a flood of publications, banners, parades, and mass meetings, they promoted him as the "log cabin" candidate, the champion of the common man. This tactic proved enormously effective, even though it bore little relationship to the actual life of the wealthy Harrison. The Whigs also denounced Van Buren as an aristocrat who had squandered the people's hard-earned money on "expensive furniture, china, glassware, and gold spoons" for the White House. Harrison's running mate was John Tyler, a states'-rights Democrat from Virginia who had joined the Whigs after the nullification crisis and did not follow Calhoun back to the Democrats. On almost every issue of political significance, Tyler held views totally opposed to those of other Whigs. But party leaders hoped he could expand their base in the South.

By 1840, the mass democratic politics of the Age of Jackson had absorbed the logic of the marketplace. Selling candidates and their images was as important as the positions for which they stood. With two highly organized parties competing throughout the country, voter turnout soared to 80 percent of those eligible, a level at which it remained for the rest of the nineteenth century. Harrison won a sweeping victory. "We have taught them how to conquer us," lamented a Democratic newspaper.

His Accidency

Whig success proved short-lived. Immediately upon assuming office, Harrison contracted pneumonia. He died a month later, and John Tyler succeeded him. When the Whig majority in Congress tried to enact the American System into law, Tyler vetoed nearly every measure, including a new national bank and higher tariff. Most of the cabinet resigned, and his party repudiated him. Whig newspapers were soon calling the president "His Accidency" and "The Executive Ass."

Tyler's four years in office were nearly devoid of accomplishment. If the campaign that resulted in the election of Harrison and Tyler demonstrated how a flourishing system of democratic politics had come into existence, Tyler's lack of success showed that political parties had become central to American government. Without a party behind him, a president could not govern. But a storm was now gathering that would test the stability of American democracy and the statesmanship of its political leaders.

SUGGESTED READING

BOOKS

- Ashworth, John. *"Agrarians" and "Aristocrats": Party Ideology in the United States, 1837–1846* (1983). A careful study of political ideas in the last years of Jacksonian politics, stressing increasing class divisions between the parties.

- Balogh, Brian. *A Government Out of Sight: The Mystery of National Authority in Nineteenth-Century America* (2009). Examines the paradox of widespread belief in limited government yet frequent energetic use of federal authority.

- Cott, Nancy. *The Bonds of Womanhood: "Woman's Sphere" in New England, 1780–1835* (1977). A pioneering study of the emergence of the ideological separation between gender-defined "public" and "private" spheres.

- Forbes, Robert. *The Missouri Compromise and Its Aftermath: Slavery and the Meaning of America* (2007). Places the Missouri controversy in the context of the long national debate over slavery.

- Formisano, Ronald P. *The Transformation of Political Culture: Massachusetts Parties, 1790–1840s* (1983). A study of politics in one key state, stressing the importance of ethnocultural divisions in shaping political alignments.

- Freehling, William G. *Prelude to Civil War: The Nullification Controversy in South Carolina, 1816–1836* (1966). Still the standard account of the nullification crisis during Jackson's presidency.

- Howe, Daniel W. *The Political Culture of the American Whigs* (1979). Illuminates the key ideas that held the Whig Party together.

- Keyssar, Alexander. *The Right to Vote: The Contested History of Democracy in the United States* (2000). The most up-to-date history of the right to vote in America from the colonial era to the present.

- Kinsbrunner, Jay. *Independence in Spanish America: Civil Wars, Revolutions, and Underdevelopment* (2000). A history of the Latin American wars of independence and their aftermath.

- McFaul, James. *The Politics of Jacksonian Finance* (1972). A careful examination of party differences on currency and banking questions.

- Schlesinger, Arthur M., Jr. *The Age of Jackson* (1945). An influential account of Jacksonian ideas and politics, which shaped debate among a generation of historians.

- Starr, Paul. *Creation of the Media: Political Origins of Modern Communications* (2004). Contains an illuminating account of the "information revolution" in Jacksonian America.

- Wallace, Anthony. *The Long, Bitter Trail: Andrew Jackson and the Indians* (1993). A brief history of Jackson's Indian policies, especially Indian Removal in the southern states.

- Watson, Harry. *Liberty and Power: The Politics of Jacksonian America* (1990). A valuable brief account of the politics of the 1820s and 1830s.

- Wilentz, Sean. *The Rise of American Democracy: Jefferson to Lincoln* (2005). A comprehensive history of democratic ideas and politics from the American Revolution to the Civil War.

WEBSITES

- *Democracy in America*, Alexis de Tocqueville: http://xroads.virginia.edu/~hyper/detoc/home.html
- George Catlin and His Indian Gallery: http://americanart.si.edu/exhibitions/online/catlin/index.html
- Legacy: Spain and the United States in the Age of Independence, 1763–1848: http://latino.si.edu/SpainLegacy/Archive/index.html

CHAPTER REVIEW AND ONLINE RESOURCES

REVIEW QUESTIONS

1. What global changes prompted the Monroe Doctrine? What were its key provisions? How does it show America's growing international presence?

2. How did Andrew Jackson represent the major developments of the era: westward movement, the market revolution, and the expansion of democracy for some alongside the limits on it for others?

3. How did the expansion of white male democracy run counter to the ideals of the founders, who believed government should be sheltered from excessive influence by ordinary people?

4. What were the components of the American System, and how were they designed to promote the national economy under the guidance of the federal government?

5. How did the Missouri Compromise and the nullification crisis demonstrate increasing sectional competition and disagreements over slavery?

6. According to Martin Van Buren, why were political parties a desirable element of public life? What did he do to build the party system?

7. What were the major economic, humanitarian, political, and social arguments for and against Indian removal?

8. What were the key issues that divided the Democratic and Whig parties? Where did each party stand on those issues?

9. Explain the causes and effects of the Panic of 1837.

KEY TERMS

the Dorr War (p. 348)

Democracy in America (p. 349)

franchise (p. 352)

American System (p. 354)

tariff of 1816 (p. 354)

Panic of 1819 (p. 355)

McCulloch v. Maryland (p. 356)

Era of Good Feelings (p. 356)

Missouri Compromise (p. 357)

Monroe Doctrine (p. 361)

spoils system (p. 368)

tariff of abominations (p. 371)

Exposition and Protest (p. 372)

Webster-Hayne debate (p. 372)

nullification crisis (p. 373)

Force Act (p. 373)

Indian Removal Act (p. 374)

Worcester v. Georgia (p. 375)

Trail of Tears (p. 376)

Bank War (p. 378)

soft money and hard money (p. 379)

pet banks (p. 379)

Panic of 1837 (p. 380)

Go to 🐰 INQUIZITIVE

To see what you know—and learn what you've missed—with personalized feedback along the way.

Visit the *Give Me Liberty!* Student Site for primary source documents and images, interactive maps, author videos featuring Eric Foner, and more.

SLAVERY, FREEDOM, AND THE CRISIS OF THE UNION, 1840-1877

During the middle part of the nineteenth century, the United States confronted its greatest crisis, as the division between slave and free societies tore the country apart. A new nation emerged from the Civil War, with slavery abolished and the meaning of freedom transformed for all Americans.

Despite the hope of some of the founders that slavery might die out, the institution grew in size and economic importance as the nineteenth century progressed. Slavery expanded westward with the young republic, and the slave population grew to nearly 4 million by 1860. After the northern states abolished slavery, it became the "peculiar institution" of the South, the basis of a society growing ever more different from the rest of the country in economic structure and social values. Planters who dominated southern life also exerted enormous influence in national affairs. They developed a defense of slavery that insisted the institution was the foundation of genuine freedom for white citizens. Slaves, meanwhile, created their own semiautonomous culture that nurtured from one generation to the next their hope for liberation from bondage. Nonetheless, slavery was in some ways a national institution. Slave-grown cotton, a source of wealth to slaveowners, also provided the raw material for the North's growing textile industry and became the country's most important export.

During the 1820s and 1830s, numerous social movements arose that worked to reform American society. Their inspiration lay primarily in the Second Great Awakening, the religious revivals that swept both North and South and offered salvation to sinners and improvement to society at large. While some reform movements were national in scope, others existed only in the North. Most notable among the latter was a new, militant movement demanding the immediate abolition of slavery and the incorporation of blacks as equal citizens of the republic. The abolitionists helped to focus discussions of freedom on the sharp contradiction between liberty and slavery. They promoted an understanding of freedom as control over one's self and participation as an equal member in social and political life. They not only helped to place the issue of slavery squarely on the national agenda but also inspired the stirrings of protest among a number of northern women, whose work in the antislavery movement led them to resent their own lack of legal rights and educational and economic opportunities.

In the 1840s, the conflict between free and slave societies moved to the center stage of American politics. It did so as a result of the nation's territorial expansion. The acquisition of a vast new area of land in the aftermath of the Mexican War raised the question of whether slavery would be able to expand farther westward. By the 1850s, this issue had destroyed the Whig Party, weakened the Democrats, and led to the creation of an entirely new party, the Republicans, dedicated to confining slavery to the states where it already existed. Exalting the superiority of northern society, based on "free labor," to southern society, based on slavery, Republicans elected Abraham Lincoln as president in 1860, even though he did not receive a single vote in most of the southern states. In response, seven slave states seceded from the Union and formed a new nation, the Confederate States of America. When southern forces fired on Fort Sumter, an enclave of Union control in Charleston harbor, they inaugurated the Civil War, by far the bloodiest conflict in American history.

Begun as a struggle to preserve the Union, the Civil War eventually became a crusade for emancipation, which brought the nation what President Lincoln called "a new birth of freedom." The North's failure to achieve military victory in the first two years of the war, coupled with the actions of slaves who by the thousands abandoned the plantations to flee to Union lines, propelled the Lincoln administration down the road to emancipation. Although it freed few slaves on the day it was issued, January 1, 1863, Lincoln's Emancipation Proclamation proved to be the turning point of the Civil War, for it announced that, henceforth, the Union army would serve as an agent of freedom. And by authorizing, for the first time, the enlistment of black men into the Union army, the Proclamation raised the question of black citizenship in the postwar world.

The era of Reconstruction that followed the Civil War was a time of intense political and social conflict, in which the definition of freedom and the question of who was entitled to enjoy it played a central role. Former slaves claimed that freedom meant full incorporation into American society, with the same rights and opportunities whites enjoyed. They also demanded that the government guarantee them access to land, to provide an economic foundation for their freedom. Most southern whites believed that blacks should go back to work on the plantations, enjoying very few political and civil rights. Andrew Johnson, who succeeded Lincoln as president, shared their view. But the majority of northern Republicans came to believe that the emancipated slaves should enjoy the same legal rights as whites. In 1867, they granted black men in the South the right to vote. During Reconstruction, northern Republicans rewrote the laws and Constitution to incorporate the ideal of equal citizenship for all Americans, regardless of race. This was a dramatic expansion of the meaning of freedom.

In the South, Reconstruction witnessed a short-lived period in which former slaves voted and held office alongside whites, a remarkable experiment in interracial democracy. On the other hand, the former slaves failed to achieve the economic freedom they desired, since the North proved unwilling to distribute land. As a result, most former slaves, and increasing numbers of whites in the war-devastated South, found themselves confined to working as sharecroppers on land owned by others. But the genuine advances achieved during Reconstruction, such as improved access to education, exercise of political rights, and the creation of new black institutions like independent churches, produced a violent reaction by upholders of white supremacy. During the 1870s, the North retreated from its commitment to equality. In 1877, Reconstruction came to an end. Many of the rights guaranteed to the former slaves were violated in the years that followed.

Although Reconstruction only lasted from 1865 to 1877, the issues debated then forecast many of the controversies that would envelop American society in the decades that followed. The definition of American citizenship, the power of the federal government and its relationship to the states, the future of political democracy in a society marked by increasing economic inequality—all these were Reconstruction issues, and all reverberated in the Gilded Age and Progressive era that followed.

The Civil War era resolved the contradiction of the existence of slavery in a land that celebrated freedom. But just as the American Revolution left to nineteenth-century Americans the problem of slavery, the Civil War and Reconstruction left to future generations the challenge of bringing genuine freedom to the descendants of slavery.

CHAPTER 11

THE PECULIAR INSTITUTION

★

In an age of "self-made" men, no American rose more dramatically from humble origins to national and international distinction than Frederick Douglass. Born into slavery in 1818, he became a major figure in the crusade for abolition, the drama of emancipation, and the effort during Reconstruction to give meaning to black freedom.

Douglass was the son of a slave mother and an unidentified white man, possibly his owner. As a youth in Maryland, he gazed out at the ships in Chesapeake Bay, seeing them as "freedom's swift-winged angels." In violation of Maryland law, Douglass learned to read and write, initially with the assistance of his owner's wife and then, after her husband forbade her to continue, with the help of local white children. "From that moment," he later wrote, he understood that knowledge was "the pathway from slavery to freedom." Douglass experienced slavery in all its variety, from work as a house servant and as a skilled craftsman in a Baltimore shipyard to labor as a plantation field hand. When he was fifteen, Douglass's owner sent him to a "slave breaker" to curb his independent spirit. After numerous whippings, Douglass defiantly refused to allow himself to be disciplined again. This confrontation, he recalled, was "the turning-point in my career as a slave." It rekindled his desire for freedom. In 1838, having borrowed the free papers of a black sailor, he escaped to the North.

Frederick Douglass went on to become the most influential African-American of the nineteenth century and the nation's preeminent advocate of racial equality. "He who has endured the cruel pangs of slavery," he wrote, "is the man to advocate liberty." Douglass lectured against slavery throughout the North and the British Isles, and he edited a succession of antislavery publications. He published a widely read autobiography that offered an eloquent condemnation of slavery and racism. Indeed, his own accomplishments testified to the incorrectness of prevailing ideas about blacks' inborn inferiority. Douglass was also active in other reform movements, including the campaign for women's rights. During the Civil War, he advised Abraham Lincoln on the employment of black soldiers and became an early advocate of giving the right to vote to the emancipated slaves. Douglass died in 1895, as a new system of white supremacy based on segregation and disenfranchisement was being fastened upon the South.

Throughout his career, Douglass insisted that slavery could only be overthrown by continuous resistance. "Those who profess to favor freedom, and yet deprecate agitation," he declared, "are men who want crops without plowing up the ground, they want rain without thunder and lightning, they want the ocean without the awful roar of its many waters." In effect, Douglass argued that in their desire for freedom, the slaves were truer to the nation's underlying principles than the white Americans who annually celebrated the Fourth of July while allowing the continued existence of slavery.

FOCUS QUESTIONS

How did slavery shape social and economic relations in the Old South? *–p. 390*

What were the legal and material constraints on slaves' lives and work? *–p. 400*

How did family, gender, religion, and values combine to create distinct slave cultures in the Old South? *–p. 410*

What were the major forms of resistance to slavery? *–p. 415*

The Slave Auction, by the British artist Eyre Crowe, depicts a scene in an auction house. A slave sale is in progress, while on the right, slaves wait apprehensively for their turn to be sold. A child clings to her mother, perhaps for the last time, while potential buyers examine the seated women. Crowe entered the auction house in March 1853 after seeing an advertisement for a slave sale, and began sketching. When the white crowd realized what he was doing, they "rushed on him savagely and obliged him to quit," Crowe's traveling companion wrote to a friend. The painting is based on his sketches.

THE OLD SOUTH

When Frederick Douglass was born, slavery was already an old institution in America. Two centuries had passed since the first twenty Africans were landed in Virginia from a Dutch ship. After abolition in the North, slavery had become **the "peculiar institution"** of the South—that is, an institution unique to southern society. The Mason-Dixon Line, drawn by two surveyors in the eighteenth century to settle a boundary dispute between Maryland and Pennsylvania, eventually became the dividing line between slavery and freedom.

Despite the hope of some of the founders that slavery might die out, in fact the institution survived the crisis of the American Revolution and rapidly expanded westward. During the first forty years of Douglass's life, the number of slaves and the economic and political importance of slavery continued to grow. On the eve of the Civil War, the slave population had risen to nearly 4 million, its high rate of natural increase more than making up for the prohibition in 1808 of further slave imports from Africa. In the South as a whole, slaves made up one-third of the total population, and in the cotton-producing states of the Deep South, around half. By the 1850s, slavery had crossed the Mississippi River and was expanding rapidly in Arkansas, Louisiana, and eastern Texas. In 1860, one-third of the nation's cotton crop was grown west of the Mississippi.

Cotton Is King

In the nineteenth century, cotton replaced sugar as the world's major crop produced by slave labor. And although slavery survived in Brazil and the Spanish and French Caribbean, its abolition in the British empire in 1833 made the United States indisputably the center of New World slavery.

When measured by slavery's geographic extent, the numbers held in bondage, and the institution's economic importance both regionally and nationally, the Old South was the largest and most powerful slave society the modern world has known. Its strength rested on a virtual monopoly of cotton, the South's "white gold." Cotton had been grown for thousands of years in many parts of the globe. The conquistador Hernán Cortés was impressed by the high quality of woven cotton clothing worn by the Aztecs. But in the nineteenth century, cotton assumed an unprecedented role in the world economy.

Because the early industrial revolution centered on factories using cotton as the raw material to manufacture cloth, cotton became by far the most important commodity in international trade. And three-fourths of the world's cotton supply came from the southern United States. Throughout the world, hundreds of thousands of workers loaded, unloaded, spun, and wove cotton, and thousands of manufacturers and merchants owed their wealth to the cotton trade. Textile manufacturers in places as far-flung as Massachusetts, Lancashire in Great Britain, Normandy in France, and the suburbs of Moscow depended on a regular supply of American cotton.

Cotton sales earned the money from abroad that allowed the United States to pay for imported manufactured goods. On the eve of the Civil War, cotton represented well over half of the total value of American exports. In 1860, the economic investment represented by the slave population exceeded the value of the nation's factories, railroads, and banks combined.

The Second Middle Passage

As noted in Chapter 9, to replace the slave trade from Africa, which had been prohibited by Congress in 1808, a massive trade in slaves developed within the United States. More than 2 million slaves were sold between 1820 and 1860, a majority to local buyers but hundreds of thousands from older states to "importing" states of the Lower South, resulting in what came to be known as the **Second Middle Passage**. Slave trading was a visible, established business. The main commercial districts of southern cities contained the offices of slave traders, complete with signs reading "Negro Sales" or "Negroes Bought Here." Auctions of slaves took place at public slave markets, as in New Orleans, or at courthouses. Southern newspapers carried advertisements for slave sales, southern banks financed slave trading, southern ships and railroads carried slaves from buyers to sellers, and southern states and municipalities earned revenue by taxing the sale of slaves. The Cotton Kingdom could not have arisen without the internal slave trade, and the economies of older states like Virginia came increasingly to rely on the sale of slaves.

The internal slave trade

Slavery and the Nation

Slavery, Henry Clay proclaimed in 1816, "forms an exception . . . to the general liberty prevailing in the United States." But Clay, like many of his contemporaries, underestimated slavery's impact on the entire nation. The "free states" had ended slavery, but they were hardly unaffected by it. The Constitution, as we have seen, enhanced the power of the South in the House of Representatives and electoral college and required all states to return fugitives from bondage. Slavery shaped the lives of all Americans, white as well as black. It helped to determine where they

Slavery's influence

COTTON PRESSING IN LOUISIANA

"Cotton Processing in Louisiana," from *Ballou's Magazine* in 1856, illustrates how slaves were used to supply power for a partially mechanized work process.

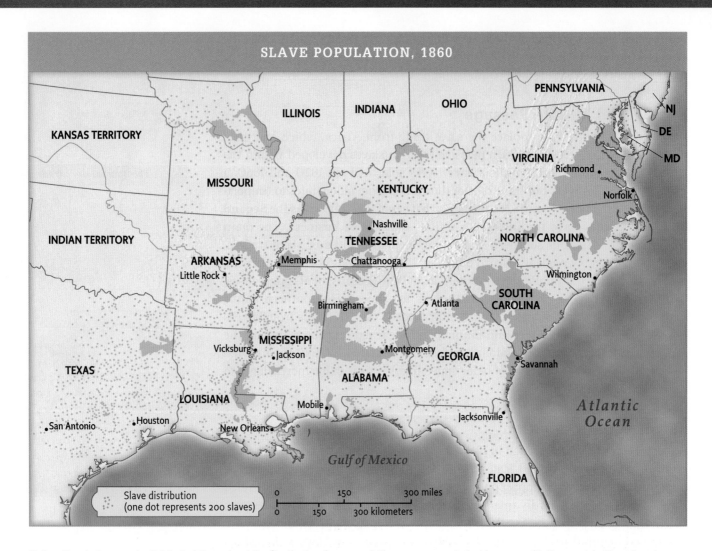

SLAVE POPULATION, 1860

Slave distribution
(one dot represents 200 slaves)

Rather than being evenly distributed throughout the South, the slave population was concentrated in areas with the most fertile soil and easiest access to national and international markets. By 1860, a significant percentage of the slave population had been transported from the Atlantic coast to the Deep South via the internal slave trade.

lived, how they worked, and under what conditions they could exercise their freedoms of speech, assembly, and the press.

Northern merchants and manufacturers participated in the slave economy and shared in its profits. Money earned in the cotton trade helped to finance industrial development and internal improvements in the North. Northern ships carried cotton to New York and Europe, northern bankers financed cotton plantations, northern companies insured slave property, and northern factories turned cotton into cloth. New York City's rise to commercial prominence depended as much on the establishment of shipping lines that gathered the South's cotton and transported it to Europe, as on the Erie Canal. The Lords of the Loom (New England's early factory owners) relied on cotton supplied by the Lords of the Lash (southern slaveowners). Northern manufacturers like Brooks

Slavery and the North

Brothers supplied cheap fabrics (called "Negro cloth") to clothe the South's slaves.

The Southern Economy

There was no single South before the Civil War. In the eight slave states of the Upper South, slaves and slaveowners made up a smaller percentage of the total population than in the seven Deep South states that stretched from South Carolina west to Texas. The Upper South had major centers of industry in Baltimore, Richmond, and St. Louis, and its economy was more diversified than that of the Deep South, which was heavily dependent on cotton. Not surprisingly, during the secession crisis of 1860–1861, the Deep South states were the first to leave the Union.

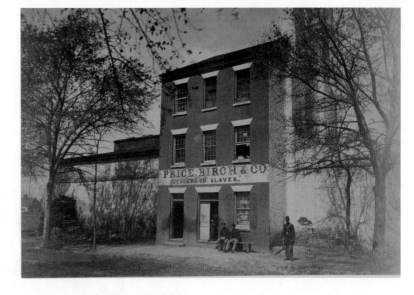

A slave dealer's place of business in Alexandria, Virginia, then part of the District of Columbia, the nation's capital. The buying and selling of slaves was a regularized part of the southern economy, and such businesses were a common sight in every southern city. This building contained a "slave pen" that typically contained over 300 slaves being kept before their sale.

Nonetheless, slavery led the South down a very different path of economic development than the North's, limiting the growth of industry, discouraging immigrants from entering the region, and inhibiting technological progress. The South did not share in the urban growth experienced by the rest of the country. Most southern cities were located on the region's periphery and served mainly as centers for gathering and shipping cotton. Southern banks existed primarily to help finance the plantations. They loaned money for the purchase of land and slaves, not manufacturing development. Southern railroads mostly consisted of short lines that brought cotton from the interior to coastal ports.

In the Cotton Kingdom, the only city of significant size was New Orleans. With a population of 168,000 in 1860, New Orleans ranked as the nation's sixth-largest city. As the gathering point for cotton grown along the Mississippi River and sugar from the plantations of southeastern Louisiana, it was the world's leading exporter of slave-grown crops. Unlike other cities with slavery (apart from St. Louis and Baltimore, on the periphery of the South), New Orleans also attracted large numbers of European immigrants. In 1860, 40 percent of its population was foreign-born. And New Orleans's rich French heritage and close connections with the Caribbean produced a local culture quite different from that of the rest of the United States, reflected in the city's distinctive music, dance, religion, and cuisine.

In 1860, the South produced less than 10 percent of the nation's manufactured goods. Many northerners viewed slavery as an obstacle to American economic progress. But as New Orleans showed, slavery and economic growth could go hand in hand. In general, the southern economy was hardly stagnant, and slavery proved very profitable for most owners. The profits produced by slavery for the South and the nation as a whole formed a powerful obstacle to abolition. Speaking of cotton, Senator James Henry Hammond of South Carolina declared, "No power on earth dares to make war upon it. **Cotton is king.**"

TABLE 11.1 Growth of the Slave Population	
YEARS	**SLAVE POPULATION**
1790	697,624
1800	893,602
1810	1,191,362
1820	1,538,022
1830	2,009,043
1840	2,487,355
1850	3,204,313
1860	3,953,760

This 1860 view of New Orleans captures the size and scale of the cotton trade in the South's largest city. More than 3,500 steamboats arrived in New Orleans in 1860.

TABLE 11.2 Slaveholding, 1850 (in Round Numbers)

NUMBER OF SLAVES OWNED	SLAVEHOLDERS
1	68,000
2–4	105,000
5–9	80,000
10–19	55,000
20–49	30,000
50–99	6,000
100–199	1,500
200 +	250

Plain Folk of the Old South

The foundation of the Old South's economy, slavery powerfully shaped race relations, politics, religion, and the law. Its influence was pervasive: "Nothing escaped," writes one historian, "nothing and no one." This was true despite the fact that the majority of white southerners—three out of four white families—owned no slaves. Since planters monopolized the best land, most small white farmers lived outside the plantation belt in hilly areas unsuitable for cotton production. They worked the land using family labor rather than slaves or hired workers.

Many southern farmers lived lives of economic self-sufficiency remote from the market revolution. They raised livestock and grew food for their families, purchasing relatively few goods at local stores. Those residing on marginal land in isolated hill areas and the Appalachian Mountains were often desperately poor and, since nearly all the southern states lacked systems of free public education, were more often illiterate than their northern counterparts. Not until the arrival of railroads and coal mining later in the nineteenth century would such areas become integrated into the market economy. Most yeoman farmers enjoyed a comfortable standard of living, and many owned a slave or two. But even successful small farmers relied heavily on home production to supply their basic needs. Unlike northern farmers, therefore, they did not provide a market for manufactured goods. This was one of the main reasons why the South did not develop an industrial base.

Some poorer whites resented the power and privileges of the great planters. Politicians like Andrew Johnson of Tennessee and Joseph Brown of Georgia rose to power as self-proclaimed spokesmen of the common man against the "slavocracy." But most poor whites made their peace with the planters in whose hands economic and social power was concentrated. Racism, kinship ties, common participation in a democratic political culture, and regional loyalty in the face of outside criticism all served to cement bonds between planters and the South's "plain folk." In the plantation regions, moreover, small farmers manned the slave patrols that kept a lookout for runaway slaves and those on the roads without permission. Non-slaveholders regularly elected slaveowners to public offices in the South. Like other white southerners, most small farmers believed their economic and personal freedom rested on slavery.

The Planter Class

Even among slaveholders, the planter was far from typical. In 1850, a majority of slaveholding families owned five or fewer slaves. Fewer than 40,000 families possessed the twenty or more slaves that qualified them as planters. Fewer than 2,000 families owned a hundred slaves or more. Nonetheless, the planter's values and aspirations dominated southern life. The plantation, wrote Frederick Douglass, was "a little nation by itself, with its own language, its own rules, regulations, and customs." These rules and customs set the tone for southern society.

An upcountry family, dressed in home-spun, in Cedar Mountain, Virginia. Many white families in the pre–Civil War South were largely isolated from the market economy. This photograph was taken in 1862 but reflects the prewar way of life.

Ownership of slaves provided the route to wealth, status, and influence. Planters not only held the majority of slaves, but they controlled the most fertile land, enjoyed the highest incomes, and dominated state and local offices and the leadership of both political parties. Small slaveholders aspired to move up into the ranks of the planter class. Those who acquired wealth almost always invested it in land and slaves. But as the price of a "prime field hand" rose from $1,000 in 1840 to $1,800 in 1860 (the latter figure equivalent to around $40,000 today), it became more and more difficult for poorer white southerners to become slaveholders.

Slavery, of course, was a profit-making system, and slaveowners kept close watch on world prices for their products and invested in enterprises such as railroads and canals. They paid careful attention to every detail of their operations, adopted the most modern business and accounting practices, and carefully monitored market conditions and their own profits. Their wives—the "plantation mistresses" idealized in southern lore for femininity, beauty, and dependence on men—were hardly idle. They cared for sick slaves, directed the domestic servants, and supervised the entire plantation when their husbands were away. Of course, owners' sexual exploitation of slave women produced deep resentment among their wives, who sometimes took it out on the slaves themselves.

Alexis de Tocqueville observed that "the northerner loves to make money, the southerner to spend it." Many of the richest planters squandered their wealth in a lifestyle complete with lavish entertainments and summer vacations in Newport and Saratoga. House slaves were so numerous in Charleston, wrote one visitor to the city, that "the Charlestonians are obliged to exercise their wits to devise sufficient variety to keep them employed." On the cotton frontier, many planters lived in crude log homes. But in the older slave states, and as settled society developed in

Louisa, a slave woman, with her charge in an 1858 photograph. The slave had been purchased at age twenty-two at a slave auction in New Orleans to serve as a nursemaid. Because of a death in the white family, the child was her legal owner.

A detail from *Norman's Chart of the Lower Mississippi River* (1858) shows slave plantations laid out so that each fronted on the river and, therefore, had easy access to the market.

Significance of paternalism

Dueling

the Deep South, they constructed elegant mansions adorned with white columns in the Greek Revival style of architecture.

The Paternalist Ethos

The slave plantation was deeply embedded in the world market, and planters sought to accumulate land, slaves, and profits. But planters' values glorified not the competitive capitalist marketplace, but a hierarchical, agrarian society in which slaveholding gentlemen took personal responsibility for the physical and moral well-being of their dependents—women, children, and slaves. "The master," wrote one planter, "as the head of the system, has a right to the obedience and labor of the slave, but the slave has also his mutual rights in the master; the right of protection, the right of counsel and guidance, the right of subsistence, the right of care and attention in sickness and old age."

This outlook, known as **paternalism** (from the Latin word for "father"), had been a feature of American slavery even in the eighteenth century. But it became more ingrained after the closing of the African slave trade in 1808, which narrowed the cultural gap between master and slave. Unlike the absentee planters of the West Indies, many of whom resided in Great Britain, southern slaveholders lived on their plantations and thus had year-round contact with their slaves.

The paternalist outlook both masked and justified the brutal reality of slavery. It enabled slaveowners to think of themselves as kind, responsible masters even as they bought and sold their human property—a practice at odds with the claim that slaves formed part of the master's "family." Some slaveowners tried to reform the system to eliminate its most oppressive features. The Reverend Charles C. Jones, a wealthy planter of Liberty County, Georgia, organized his neighbors to promote the religious instruction of slaves, improve slave housing, diet, and medical care, and discourage severe punishments. But even Jones believed his slaves so "degraded" and lacking in moral self-discipline that he could not contemplate an end to slavery.

The Code of Honor

As time went on, the dominant southern conception of the good society diverged more and more sharply from that of the egalitarian, competitive, individualistic North. In the South, for example, both upper- and lower-class whites adhered to a code of personal honor, in which men were expected to defend, with violence if necessary, their own reputation and that of their families. Although dueling was illegal, many prominent southerners took part in duels to avenge supposed insults. In 1826, Henry Clay and John Randolph, two of the most important southern political leaders, fought a duel with pistols after Clay took exception to criticisms by Randolph on the floor of Congress. Fortunately, each missed the other. Twenty years later, however, John H. Pleasants, editor of the *Richmond Whig*, died in a duel with the son of a rival newspaperman.

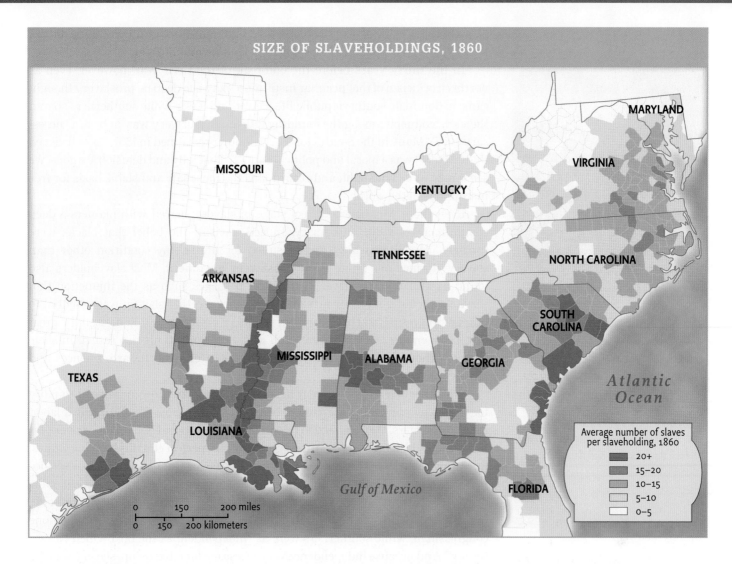

SIZE OF SLAVEHOLDINGS, 1860

Average number of slaves per slaveholding, 1860

- 20+
- 15–20
- 10–15
- 5–10
- 0–5

Just as southern men had a heightened sense of their own honor and masculinity, white southern women, even more than in the North, were confined within the "domestic circle." "A man loves his children," wrote George Fitzhugh, a Virginia lawyer and author of numerous books and articles on social issues, "because they are weak, helpless, and dependent. He loves his wife for similar reasons." As will be discussed in the next chapter, many northern women before the Civil War became part of a thriving female culture centered on voluntary religious and reform organizations. Few parallels existed in the South, and plantation mistresses often complained of loneliness and isolation.

Most southern slaveholders owned fewer than five slaves. The largest plantations were concentrated in coastal South Carolina and along the Mississippi River.

Women in southern ideology

The Proslavery Argument

Some southerners worried about their standing in the eyes of the world, especially how others viewed the intellectual life of their region. "We of the South," one wrote, "must, to Europe, continue to appear inferior to the North in intellectual cultivation." The free states outstripped the slave states in public education, in the number of colleges, and in newspapers, literary journals, and other publications.

A pre–Civil War engraving depicting the paternalist ideal. The old slave in the fore-ground says, "God Bless you massa! you feed and clothe us, . . . and when too old to work, you provide for us!" The master replies, "These poor creatures are a sacred legacy from my ancestors and while a dollar is left me, nothing shall be spared to increase their comfort and happiness."

Nonetheless, the life of the mind flourished in the Old South, and the region did not lack for novelists, political philosophers, scientists, and the like.

In the thirty years before the outbreak of the Civil War, however, even as northern criticism of the "peculiar institution" began to deepen, proslavery thought came to dominate southern public life. Fewer and fewer white southerners shared the view, common among the founding fathers, that slavery was, at best, a "necessary evil." "Many in the South," John C. Calhoun proclaimed in 1837, "once believed that [slavery] was a moral and political evil. . . . That folly and delusion are gone; we see it now in its true light, and regard it as the most safe and stable basis for free institutions in the world."

Even those who had no direct stake in slavery shared with planters a deep commitment to white supremacy. Indeed, racism—the belief that blacks were innately inferior to whites and unsuited for life in any condition other than slavery—formed one pillar of the **proslavery argument**. Most slaveholders also found legitimation for slavery in biblical passages such as the injunction that servants should obey their masters. Others argued that slavery was essential to human progress. Had not the ancient republics of Greece and Rome and the great European empires of the seventeenth and eighteenth centuries rested on slave labor? Without slavery, planters would be unable to cultivate the arts, sciences, and other civilized pursuits.

Still other defenders of slavery insisted that the institution guaranteed equality for whites by preventing the growth of a class doomed to a life of unskilled labor. Like northerners, they claimed to be committed to the ideal of freedom. Slavery for blacks, they declared, was the surest guarantee of "perfect equality" among whites, liberating them from the "low, menial" jobs like factory labor and domestic service performed by wage laborers in the North. Slavery made possible the considerable degree of economic autonomy (the social condition of freedom) enjoyed not only by planters but also by non-slaveholding whites. Because of slavery, claimed one congressman, white southerners were as "independent as the bird which cleaves the air." And because independence was necessary for citizenship, slavery was the "cornerstone of our republican edifice."

Slavery and white equality

Abolition in the Americas

American slaveowners were well aware of developments in slave systems elsewhere in the Western Hemisphere. As noted in Chapter 8, the slave revolution in Haiti sent shock waves of fear throughout the American South. White southerners observed carefully the results of the wave of emancipations that swept the hemisphere in the first four decades of the century. In these years, slavery was abolished in most of Spanish America and in the British empire.

In most Latin American nations, the end of slavery followed the pattern established earlier in the northern United States—gradual emancipation accompanied by some kind of recognition of the owners' legal right to property in slaves. These "laws of the free womb" allowed slaveholders to retain ownership of existing slaves while freeing their slaves' children after they worked for the mother's owner for a specified number of years. Such laws, wrote one official, "respected the past and corrected only the future." Abolition was far swifter in the British empire, where

"Laws of the free womb"

Parliament in 1833 mandated almost immediate emancipation, with a seven-year transitional period of "apprenticeship." This system produced so much conflict between former master and former slave that Britain decreed complete freedom in 1838. The law appropriated 20 million pounds to compensate the owners.

The experience of emancipation in other parts of the hemisphere strongly affected debates over slavery in the United States. Southern slaveowners judged the vitality of the Caribbean economy by how much sugar and other crops it produced for the world market. Since many former slaves preferred to grow food for their own families, defenders of slavery in the United States charged that British emancipation had been a failure. Abolitionists disagreed, pointing to the rising standard of living of freed slaves, the spread of education among them, and other improvements in their lives. In a hemispheric perspective, slavery was a declining institution. By 1840, slavery had been outlawed in Mexico, Central America, and Chile, and only small numbers of aging slaves remained in Venezuela, Colombia, and Peru. During the European revolutions of 1848, France and Denmark emancipated their colonial slaves. At mid-century, significant New World slave systems remained only in Cuba, Puerto Rico, Brazil—and the United States. Nonetheless, because of the rapid growth of the slave population in the Old South, there were more slaves in the hemisphere in 1860 than at any point prior to that.

A plate manufactured in England to celebrate emancipation in the British empire. After a brief period of apprenticeship, all slaves were freed on August 1, 1838. At the center, a family of former slaves celebrates outside their cabin.

Slavery and Liberty

Many white southerners declared themselves the true heirs of the American Revolution. They claimed to be inspired by "the same spirit of freedom and independence" that motivated the founding generation. Like their ancestors of the 1760s and 1770s, their political language was filled with contrasts between liberty and slavery and complaints that outsiders proposed to reduce them to "slaves" by interfering with their local institutions. Southern state constitutions enshrined the idea of equal rights for free men, and the South participated fully in the movement toward political democracy for whites.

Beginning in the 1830s, however, proslavery writers began to question the ideals of liberty, equality, and democracy so widely shared elsewhere in the nation. South Carolina, the only southern state where a majority of white families owned slaves, became the home of an aggressive defense of slavery that repudiated the idea that freedom and equality were universal entitlements. The language of the Declaration of Independence—that all men were created equal and entitled to liberty—was "the most false and dangerous of all political errors," insisted John C. Calhoun. Proslavery spokesmen returned to the older definition of freedom as a privilege, a "reward to be earned, not a blessing to be gratuitously lavished on all alike."

Repudiating freedom and equality for all

As the sectional controversy intensified after 1830, a number of southern writers and politicians came to defend slavery less as the basis of equality for whites than as the foundation of an organic, hierarchical society. Inequality and hence the submission of inferior to superior—black to white, female to male, lower classes to upper classes—was a "fundamental law" of human existence. A hierarchy of "ranks

Embracing hierarchy

and orders in human society," insisted John B. Alger, a Presbyterian minister in South Carolina, formed part of the "divine arrangement" of the world.

Slavery and Civilization

The Virginia writer George Fitzhugh took the argument to its most radical conclusion. Far from being the natural condition of mankind, Fitzhugh wrote, "universal liberty" was the exception, an experiment carried on "for a little while" in "a corner of Europe" and the northern United States. Taking the world and its history as a whole, slavery, "without regard to race and color," was "the general, . . . normal, natural" basis of "civilized society." Indeed, wrote Fitzhugh, slaveowners and slaves shared a "community of interest" unknown in "free society." Since they lacked economic cares, he contended, "the Negro slaves of the South are the happiest, and, in some degree, the freest people in the world." White workers in both the North and South, according to Fitzhugh, would fare better having individual owners, rather than living as "slaves" of the economic marketplace.

Abraham Lincoln would later observe that the essential function of the proslavery argument was to serve the interests of those who benefited from a system of extreme inequality. He imagined Dr. Frederick A. Ross, a leading proslavery clergyman, considering whether he should free his slave Sambo. God's view of the subject, Lincoln noted, was not entirely clear, and "no one thinks of asking Sambo's opinion." Therefore, it fell to Dr. Ross to decide the question. "If he decides that God wills Sambo to continue a slave," Lincoln wrote, "he thereby retains his own comfortable position; but if he decides that God wills Sambo to be free, he thereby has to walk out of the shade, take off his gloves, and [work] for his own bread." Under these circumstances, it was hardly surprising that Dr. Ross found the argument that Sambo should remain a slave very persuasive.

After 1830, southern writers, newspaper editors, politicians, and clergymen increasingly devoted themselves to spreading the defense of slavery. The majority of white southerners came to believe that freedom for whites rested on the power to command the labor of blacks. In the words of the Richmond *Enquirer*, "freedom is not possible without slavery."

George Fitzhugh

Lincoln's thoughts

A poster advertising the raffle of a horse and a slave, treated as equivalents, at a Missouri store.

LIFE UNDER SLAVERY

Slaves and the Law

For slaves, the "peculiar institution" meant a life of incessant toil, brutal punishment, and the constant fear that their families would be destroyed by sale. Under the law, slaves were property. Although they had a few legal rights (all states made it illegal to kill a slave except in self-defense, and slaves accused of serious crimes were entitled to their day in court, before all-white judges and juries), these were haphazardly enforced. Slaves could be sold or leased by their owners at will and lacked any voice in the governments that ruled over them. They could not testify in court against a white person, sign contracts or acquire property, own firearms, hold meetings unless a white person was present, or leave the farm or plantation without the permission of their owner. By the 1830s, it was against the law to teach a slave to read or write.

Not all of these laws were rigorously enforced. Some members of slaveholding families taught slave children to read (although rather few, since well over 90 percent of the slave population was illiterate in 1860). In the South Carolina rice fields, owners allowed some slaves to carry shotguns, in defiance of the law, to scare off birds feasting on rice seeds. It was quite common throughout the South for slaves to gather without white supervision at crossroads villages and country stores on Sunday, their day of rest. But the extent to which authorities enforced or bent the law depended on the decisions of the individual owners.

The slave, declared a Louisiana law, "owes to his master . . . a respect without bounds, and an absolute obedience." Not only did the owner have the legal right to what Alabama's legal code called the "time, labor, and services" of his slaves, but no aspect of their lives, from the choice of marriage partners to how they spent their free time, was immune from his interference. The entire system of southern justice, from the state militia and courts down to armed patrols in each locality, was designed to enforce the master's control over the person and labor of his slaves.

In one famous case, a Missouri court considered the "crime" of Celia, a slave who had killed her master in 1855 while resisting a sexual assault. State law deemed "any woman" in such circumstances to be acting in self-defense. But Celia, the court ruled, was not a "woman" in the eyes of the law. She was a slave, whose master had complete power over her person. The court sentenced her to death. However, since Celia was pregnant, her execution was postponed until the child was born, so as not to deprive her owner's heirs of their property rights.

Metal shackles, from around 1850. Slaves were shackled as a form of punishment, or to prevent escape when being transported from one place to another.

Conditions of Slave Life

As the nineteenth century progressed, some southern states enacted laws to prevent the mistreatment of slaves, and their material living conditions improved. Food supplies and wild game were abundant in the South, and many slaves supplemented the food provided by their owners (primarily cornmeal and pork or bacon) with chickens and vegetables they raised themselves, animals they hunted in the forests, and, not infrequently, items they stole from the plantation smokehouse. Compared with their counterparts in the West Indies and Brazil, American slaves enjoyed better diets, lower rates of infant mortality, and longer life expectancies. Many factors contributed to improving material conditions. One was the growing strength of the planters' paternalist outlook. Douglass himself noted that "not to give a slave enough to eat, is regarded as the most aggravated development of meanness, even among slaveholders." Most of the South, moreover, lies outside the geographical area where tropical diseases like malaria, yellow fever, and typhoid fever flourish, so health among all southerners was better than in the Caribbean. And with the price of slaves rising dramatically after the closing of the African slave trade, it made economic sense for owners to become concerned with the health and living conditions of their human property.

Improvements in the slaves' living conditions were meant to strengthen slavery, not undermine it. Even as the material lives of the majority of slaves improved,

A female slave drying cotton on a plantation in the South Carolina Sea Islands, 1862. Slave men, women, and children all worked in the cotton fields.

Slaves outside their cabin on a South Carolina plantation, probably photographed in the 1850s. They had brought their furniture outdoors to be included in the photo.

the South drew tighter and tighter the chains of bondage. If slaves in the United States enjoyed better health and diets than elsewhere in the Western Hemisphere, they had far less access to freedom. In Brazil, it was not uncommon for an owner to free slaves as a form of celebration—on the occasion of a wedding in the owner's family, for example—or to allow slaves to purchase their freedom. Although slavery in Brazil lasted until 1888, more than half the population of African descent was already free in 1850. (The comparable figure in the American South was well below 10 percent.) In the nineteenth-century South, more and more states set limits on voluntary manumission, requiring that such acts be approved by the legislature. "All the powers of earth," declared Abraham Lincoln in 1857, seemed to be "rapidly combining" to fasten bondage ever more securely upon American slaves. Few slave societies in history have so systematically closed off all avenues to freedom as the Old South did.

Free Blacks in the Old South

The existence of slavery helped to define the status of those blacks who did enjoy freedom. On the eve of the Civil War, nearly half a million free blacks lived in the United States, a majority in the South. Most were the descendants of slaves freed by southern owners in the aftermath of the Revolution or by the gradual emancipation laws of the northern states. Their numbers were supplemented by slaves who had been voluntarily liberated by their masters, who had been allowed to purchase their freedom, or who succeeded in running away.

When followed by "black" or "Negro," the word "free" took on an entirely new meaning. Whites defined their freedom, in part, by their distance from slavery. But among blacks, wrote Douglass, "the distinction between the slave and the free is not great." Northern free blacks, as noted in Chapter 10, generally could not vote and enjoyed few economic opportunities. Free blacks in the South could legally own property and marry and, of course, could not be bought and sold. But many regulations restricting the lives of slaves also applied to them. Free blacks had no voice in selecting public officials. Like slaves, they were prohibited from owning dogs, firearms, or liquor, and they could not strike a white person, even in self-defense. They were not allowed to testify in court against whites or serve on juries, and they had to carry at all times a certificate of freedom. Poor free blacks who required public assistance could be bound out to labor alongside slaves. "Free negroes," declared a South Carolina judge in 1848, "belong to a degraded caste of society" and should learn to conduct themselves "as inferiors."

As noted above, nineteenth-century Brazil had a large free black population. In the West Indies, many children of white owners and female slaves gained their

Restrictions on free blacks

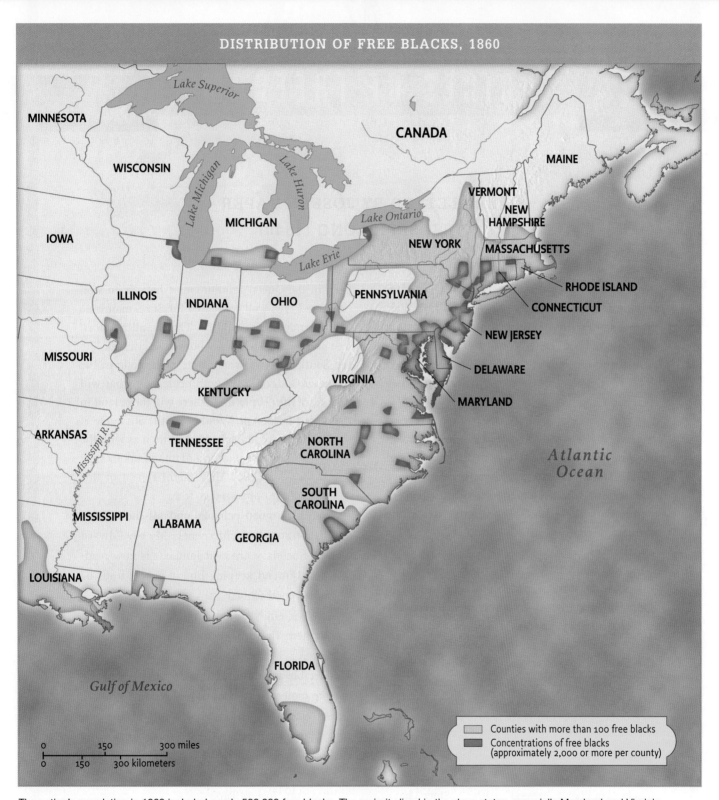

DISTRIBUTION OF FREE BLACKS, 1860

Counts legend:
- Counties with more than 100 free blacks
- Concentrations of free blacks (approximately 2,000 or more per county)

The nation's population in 1860 included nearly 500,000 free blacks. The majority lived in the slave states, especially Maryland and Virginia.

VOICES OF FREEDOM

From LETTER BY JOSEPH TAPER
TO JOSEPH LONG (1840)

No one knows how many slaves succeeded in escaping from bondage before the Civil War. Some settled in northern cities like Boston, Cincinnati, and New York. But because the Constitution required that fugitives be returned to slavery, many continued northward until they reached Canada.

One successful fugitive was Joseph Taper, a slave in Frederick County, Virginia, who in 1837 ran away to Pennsylvania with his wife and children. Two years later, learning that a "slave catcher" was in the neighborhood, the Tapers fled to Canada. In 1840, Taper wrote to a white acquaintance in Virginia recounting some of his experiences.

The biblical passage to which Taper refers reads: "And I will come near to you to judgment; and I will be a swift witness against the sorcerers, and against the adulterers, and against false swearers, and against those that oppress the hireling in his wages, the widow, and the fatherless, and that turn aside the stranger from his right, and fear not me, saith the Lord of hosts."

Dear sir,

I now take the opportunity to inform you that I am in a land of liberty, in good health. . . . Since I have been in the Queen's dominions I have been well contented, Yes well contented for Sure, man is as God intended he should be. That is, all are born free and equal. This is a wholesome law, not like the Southern laws which puts man made in the image of God, on level with brutes. O, what will become of the people, and where will they stand in the day of Judgment. Would that the 5th verse of the 3d chapter of Malachi were written as with the bar of iron, and the point of a diamond upon every oppressor's heart that they might repent of this evil, and let the oppressed go free. . . .

We have good schools, and all the colored population supplied with schools. My boy Edward who will be six years next January, is now reading, and I intend keeping him at school until he becomes a good scholar.

I have enjoyed more pleasure within one month here than in all my life in the land of bondage. . . . My wife and self are sitting by a good comfortable fire happy, knowing that there are none to molest [us] or make [us] afraid. God save Queen Victoria. The Lord bless her in this life, and crown her with glory in the world to come is my prayer,

Yours With much respect
most obt, Joseph Taper

From "SLAVERY AND THE BIBLE"
(1850)

White southerners developed an elaborate set of arguments defending slavery in the period before the Civil War. One pillar of proslavery thought was the idea that the institution was sanctioned by the Bible, as in this essay from the influential southern magazine *De Bow's Review*.

A very large party in the United States believe that holding slaves is morally wrong; this part founds its belief upon precepts taught in the Bible, and takes that book as the standard of morality and religion.

. . . We think we can show; that the Bible teaches clearly and conclusively that the holding of slaves is right; and if so, no deduction from general principles can make it wrong, if that book is true.

From the earliest period of time down to the present moment, slavery has existed in some form or under some name, in almost every country of the globe. It existed in every country known, even by name, to any one of the sacred writers, at the time of his writing; yet no one of them condemns it in the slightest degree. Would this have been the case had it been wrong in itself? Would not some of the host of sacred writers have spoken of this alleged crime, in such terms as to show, in a manner not to be misunderstood, that God wished all men to be equal?

. . . Abraham, the chosen servant of God, had his bond servants, whose condition was similar to, or worse than, that of our slaves. He considered them as his property, to be bought and sold as any other property which he owned.

. . . We find, that both the Old and New Testaments speak of slavery—that they do not condemn the relation, but, on the contrary, expressly allow it or create it; and they give commands and exhortations, which are based upon its legality and propriety. It can not, then, be wrong.

QUESTIONS

1. *How does Taper's letter reverse the rhetoric, common among white Americans, which saw the United States as a land of freedom and the British empire as lacking in liberty?*

2. *Why does De Bow feel that it is important to show that the Bible sanctions slavery?*

3. *How do Taper and De Bow differ in their understanding of the relationship of slavery and Christianity?*

freedom, becoming part of a "free colored" population sharply distinguished from both whites above them and slaves below. In the absence of a white lower middle class, free blacks in Jamaica and other Caribbean islands operated shops and worked as clerks in government offices.

In the United States, a society that equated "black" and "slave" and left little room for a mulatto group between them, free blacks were increasingly considered an undesirable group, a potential danger to the slave system. By the 1850s, most southern states prohibited free blacks from entering their territory and a few states even moved to expel them altogether, offering the choice of enslavement or departure. Nonetheless, a few free blacks managed to prosper within slave society. William Johnson, a Natchez barber, acquired enough money to purchase a plantation with fifteen slaves; he hunted with upper-class whites and loaned them money. But he suffered from the legal disadvantages common to his race. He could not, for example, testify against his debtors in court when they failed to pay. In Virginia, the slaves freed and given land by the will of Richard Randolph (noted in Chapter 6) established a vibrant community they called Israel Hill. Despite the legal restrictions on free blacks in the state, they prospered as farmers and skilled craftsmen.

Prosperous free blacks

The Upper and Lower South

Very few free blacks (around 37,000 persons, or less than 2 percent of the area's black population) lived in the Lower South in 1860. Like William Johnson, a majority of them resided in cities. Mississippi, an overwhelmingly rural state with no real urban centers, had fewer than 800 free blacks on the eve of the Civil War. In New Orleans and Charleston, on the other hand, relatively prosperous free black communities developed, mostly composed of mixed-race descendants of unions between white men and slave women. Some became truly wealthy—Antoine Dubuclet of Louisiana, for example, owned 100 slaves. Many free blacks in these cities acquired an education and worked as skilled craftsmen such as tailors, carpenters, and mechanics. They established churches for their communities and schools for their children. Some New Orleans free blacks sent their children to France for an education. These elite free blacks did everything they could to maintain a separation from the slave population. The Brown Fellowship Society of Charleston, for example, would not even allow dark-skinned free men to join. Even in these cities, however, most free blacks were poor unskilled laborers.

In the Upper South, where the large majority of southern free blacks lived, they generally worked for wages as farm laborers. Here, where tobacco had exhausted the soil, many planters shifted to grain production, which required less year-round labor. They sold off many slaves to the Lower South and freed others. By 1860, half the African-American population of Maryland was free. Planters hired

REGION	FREE BLACK POPULATION	PERCENTAGE OF TOTAL BLACK POPULATION
North	226,152	100%
South	261,918	6.2
Upper South	224,963	12.8
Lower South	36,955	1.5
Delaware	19,829	91.7
Washington, D.C.	11,131	77.8
Kentucky	10,684	4.5
Maryland	83,942	49.1
Missouri	3,572	3.0
North Carolina	30,463	8.4
Tennessee	7,300	2.6
Virginia	58,042	10.6
Alabama	2,690	0.6
Arkansas	144	0.1
Florida	932	1.5
Georgia	3,500	0.8
Louisiana	18,647	5.3
Mississippi	773	0.2
South Carolina	9,914	2.4
Texas	355	0.2

TABLE 11.3 Free Black Population, 1860

local free blacks to work alongside their slaves at harvest time. Free blacks in Virginia and Maryland were closely tied to the slave community and often had relatives in bondage. Some owned slaves, but usually these were free men who had purchased their slave wives and children but could not liberate them because the law required any slave who became free to leave the state. Overall, in the words of Willis A. Hodges, a member of a free Virginia family that helped runaways to reach the North, free blacks and slaves were "one man of sorrow."

"One man of sorrow"

Slave Labor

First and foremost, slavery was a system of labor; "from sunup to first dark," with only brief interruptions for meals, work occupied most of the slaves' time. Large plantations were diversified communities, where slaves performed all kinds of work. The 125 slaves on one plantation, for instance, included a butler, two waitresses, a nurse, a dairymaid, a gardener, ten carpenters, and two shoemakers. Other plantations counted among their slaves engineers, blacksmiths, and weavers, as well as domestic workers from cooks to coachmen.

Slaves cut wood to provide fuel for steamboats, worked in iron and coal mines, manned the docks in southern seaports, and laid railroad track. They were set to work by local authorities to construct and repair bridges, roads, and other facilities and by the federal government to build forts and other public buildings in the South. Businessmen, merchants, lawyers, and civil servants owned slaves, and by 1860 some 200,000 worked in industry, especially in the ironworks and tobacco factories of the Upper South. Reliance on unfree labor, moreover, extended well beyond the ranks of slaveholders, for, as noted earlier, many small farmers and manufacturers rented slaves from plantation owners. A few owners gave trusted slaves extensive responsibilities. Simon Gray's owner made him the head of a riverboat crew on the Mississippi. Gray supervised both white and slave workers, sold his owner's lumber at urban markets, and handled large sums of money.

Slaves were an ever-present part of southern daily life. In this 1826 portrait of the five children of Commodore John Daniel Daniels, a wealthy Baltimore shipowner, a young slave lies on the floor at their side, holding the soap for a game of blowing bubbles, while another hovers in the background, almost depicted as part of the room's design.

Gang Labor and Task Labor

Gray's experience, of course, was hardly typical. The large majority of slaves—75 percent of women and nearly 90 percent of men, according to one study—worked in the fields. The precise organization of their labor varied according to the crop and the size of the holding. On small farms, the owner often toiled side-by-side with his slaves. The largest concentration of slaves, however, lived and worked on plantations in the Cotton Belt, where men, women, and children labored in gangs, often under the direction of an overseer and perhaps a slave "driver" who assisted him. Among slaves, overseers had a reputation for meting out harsh treatment. "The requisite qualifications for an overseer," wrote Solomon Northup, a free black who spent twelve years in slavery after being kidnapped

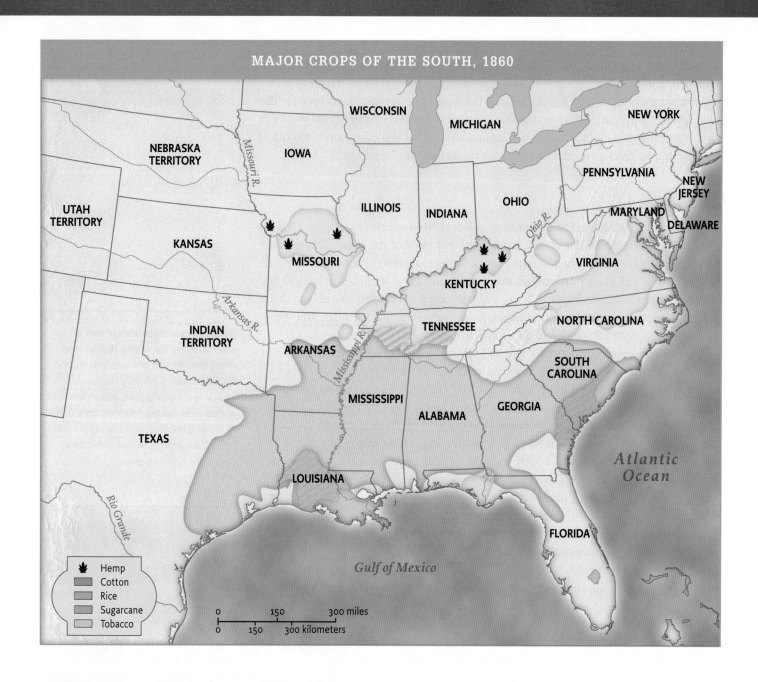

MAJOR CROPS OF THE SOUTH, 1860

Legend:
- Hemp
- Cotton
- Rice
- Sugarcane
- Tobacco

Cotton was the major agricultural crop of the South, and, indeed, the nation, but slaves also grew rice, sugarcane, tobacco, and hemp.

from the North, "are utter heartlessness, brutality, and cruelty. It is his business to produce large crops, no matter [what the] cost."

The 150,000 slaves who worked in the sugar fields of southern Louisiana also labored in large gangs. Conditions here were among the harshest in the South, for the late fall harvest season required round-the-clock labor to cut and process the sugarcane before it spoiled. On the rice plantations of South Carolina and Georgia, the system of task labor, which had originated in the colonial era, prevailed. With few whites willing to venture into the malaria-infested swamps, slaves were assigned daily tasks and allowed to set their own pace of work. Once a slave's task had been completed, he or she could spend the rest of the day hunting, fishing, or cultivating garden crops.

Slavery in the Cities

Skilled urban craftsmen also enjoyed considerable autonomy. Most city slaves were servants, cooks, and other domestic laborers. But owners sometimes allowed those with craft skills to "hire their own time." This meant that they could make work arrangements individually with employers, with most of the wages going to the slave's owner. Many urban slaves even lived on their own. But slaveholders increasingly became convinced that, as one wrote, the growing independence of skilled urban slaves "exerts a most injurious influence upon the relation of master and servant." For this reason, many owners in the 1850s sold city slaves to the countryside and sought replacements among skilled white labor.

During his time in Baltimore, Frederick Douglass "sought my own employment, made my own contracts, and collected my own earnings." Compared to conditions on the plantation, he concluded, "I was really well off." Douglass hastened to add, however, that his favored treatment in no way lessened his desire for freedom—"it was *slavery*, not its mere incidents, that I hated."

In this undated photograph, men, women, and children pick cotton under the watchful eye of an overseer. Unlike sugarcane, cotton does not grow to a great height, allowing an overseer to supervise a large number of slaves.

Maintaining Order

Slaveowners employed a variety of means in their attempts to maintain order and discipline among their human property and persuade them to labor productively. At base, the system rested on force. Masters had almost complete discretion in inflicting punishment, and rare was the slave who went through his or her life without experiencing a whipping. Josiah Henson, who escaped to the North and published an autobiography, wrote that he could never erase from his memory the traumatic experience of seeing his father brutally whipped for striking a white man. Any infraction of plantation rules, no matter how minor, could be punished by the lash. One Georgia planter recorded in his journal that he had whipped a slave "for not bringing over milk for my coffee, being compelled to take it without."

Detail from *Rice Culture on the Ogeechee*. Published in January 1867 in *Harper's Weekly*, this engraving illustrates work on a rice plantation divided into a checkerboard pattern by irrigation ditches. Although a white person is present, most slaves in the rice fields worked under the task system, without daily oversight.

Subtler means of control supplemented violence. Owners encouraged and exploited divisions among the slaves, especially between field hands and house servants. They created systems of incentives that rewarded good work with time off or even money payments. One Virginia slaveholder gave his slaves ten cents per day for good work and reported that this made them labor "with as much steadiness and cheerfulness as whites," thereby "saving all the expense of overseers." Probably the most powerful weapon wielded by slaveowners was the threat of sale, which separated slaves from their immediate families and from

A Public Whipping of Slaves in Lexington, Missouri, in 1856, an illustration from the abolitionist publication *The Suppressed Book about Slavery*. Whipping was a common form of punishment for slaves.

the communities that, despite overwhelming odds, African-Americans created on plantations throughout the South.

SLAVE CULTURE

Slaves never abandoned their desire for freedom or their determination to resist total white control over their lives. In the face of grim realities, they succeeded in forging a semi-independent culture, centered on the family and church. This enabled them to survive the experience of bondage without surrendering their self-esteem and to pass from generation to generation a set of ideas and values fundamentally at odds with those of their masters.

Slave culture drew on the African heritage. African influences were evident in the slaves' music and dances, style of religious worship, and the use of herbs by slave healers to combat disease. (Given the primitive nature of professional medical treatment, some whites sought out slave healers instead of trained physicians.) Unlike the plantation regions of the Caribbean and Brazil, where the African slave trade continued into the nineteenth century and the black population far outnumbered the white, most slaves in the United States were American-born and lived amid a white majority. Slave culture was a new creation, shaped by African traditions and American values and experiences.

Kitchen Ball at White Sulphur Springs, Virginia, an 1838 painting by the German-born American artist Christian Mayr. Fashionably dressed domestic slaves celebrate the wedding of a couple, dressed in white at the center.

The Slave Family

At the center of the slave community stood the family. On the sugar plantations of the West Indies, the number of males far exceeded that of females, the workers lived in barracks-type buildings, and settled family life was nearly impossible. The United States, where the slave population grew from natural increase rather than continued importation from Africa, had an even male-female ratio, making the creation of families far more possible. To be sure, the law did not recognize the legality of slave marriages. The master had to consent before a man and woman could "jump over the broomstick" (the slaves' marriage ceremony), and families stood in constant danger of being broken up by sale.

Nonetheless, most adult slaves married, and their unions, when not disrupted by sale, typically lasted for a lifetime. To solidify a sense of family continuity, slaves frequently named children after cousins, uncles, grandparents, and other relatives. Nor did the slave family simply mirror kinship patterns among whites. Slaves, for example, did not marry first cousins, a practice common among white southerners. Because of constant sales, the slave community had a significantly higher number of female-headed households than among whites, as well as families in which grandparents, other relatives, or even non-kin assumed responsibility for raising children.

The Threat of Sale

As noted above, the threat of sale, which disrupted family ties, was perhaps the most powerful disciplinary weapon slaveholders possessed. As the domestic slave trade expanded with the rise of the Cotton Kingdom, about one slave marriage in three in slave-selling states like Virginia was broken by sale. Many children were separated from their parents by sale. According to one estimate, at least 10 percent of the teenage slaves in the Upper South were sold in the interstate slave trade. Fear of sale permeated slave life, especially in the Upper South. "Mother, is Massa going to sell us tomorrow?" ran a line in a popular slave song. As a reflection of their paternalist responsibilities, some owners encouraged slaves to marry. Others, however, remained unaware of their slaves' family connections, and their interest in slave children was generally limited to the children's ability to work in the fields. The federal census broke down the white population by five-year age categories, but it divided slaves only once, at age ten, the point at which they became old enough to enter the plantation labor force.

Slave traders gave little attention to preserving family ties. A public notice, "Sale of Slaves and Stock," announced the 1852 auction of property belonging to a recently deceased Georgia planter. It listed thirty-six individuals ranging from an infant to a sixty-nine-year-old woman and ended with the proviso "Slaves will be sold separate, or in lots, as best suits the purchaser." Sales like this were a human tragedy. "My dear wife," a Georgia slave wrote in 1858, "I take the pleasure of writing you these few [lines] with much regret to inform you that I am sold. . . . Give my love to my father and mother and tell them good bye for me, and if

Slave marriages

A broadside advertising the public sale of slaves, along with horses, mules, and cattle, after the death of their owner. The advertisement notes that the slaves will be sold individually or in groups "as best suits the purchaser," an indication that families were likely to be broken up. The prices are based on each slave's sex, age, and skill.

Sale of Slaves and Stock.

The Negroes and Stock listed below, are a Prime Lot, and belong to the ESTATE OF THE LATE LUTHER McGOWAN, and will be sold on Monday, Sept. 22nd, 1852, at the Fair Grounds, in Savannah, Georgia, at 1:00 P. M. The Negroes will be taken to the grounds two days previous to the Sale, so that they may be inspected by prospective buyers.

On account of the low prices listed below, they will be sold for cash only, and must be taken into custody within two hours after sale.

No.	Name.	Age.	Remarks.	Price.
1	Lunesta	27	Prime Rice Planter,	$1,275.00
2	Violet	16	Housework and Nursemaid,	900.00
3	Lizzie	30	Rice, Unsound,	300.00
4	Minda	27	Cotton, Prime Woman,	1,200.00
5	Adam	28	Cotton, Prime Young Man,	1,100.00
6	Abel	41	Rice Hand, Eyesight Poor,	675.00
7	Tanney	22	Prime Cotton Hand,	950.00
8	Flementina	39	Good Cook, Stiff Knee,	400.00
9	Lanney	34	Prime Cottom Man,	1,000.00
10	Sally	10	Handy in Kitchen,	675.00
11	Maccabey	35	Prime Man, Fair Carpenter,	980.00
12	Dorcas Judy	25	Seamstress, Handy in House,	800.00
13	Happy	60	Blacksmith,	575.00
14	Mowden	15	Prime Cotton Boy,	700.00
15	Bills	21	Handy with Mules,	900.00
16	Theopolis	39	Rice Hand, Gets Fits,	575.00
17	Coolidge	29	Rice Hand and Blacksmith,	1,275.00
18	Bessie	69	Infirm, Sews,	250.00
19	Infant	1	Strong Likely Boy,	400.00
20	Samson	41	Prime Man, Good with Stock,	975.00
21	Callie May	27	Prime Woman, Rice,	1,000.00
22	Honey	14	Prime Girl, Hearing Poor,	850.00
23	Angelina	16	Prime Girl, House or Field,	1,000.00
24	Virgil	21	Prime Field Hand,	1,100.00
25	Tom	40	Rice Hand, Lame Leg,	750.00
26	Noble	11	Handy Boy,	900.00
27	Judge Lesh	55	Prime Blacksmith,	800.00
28	Booster	43	Fair Mason, Unsound,	600.00
29	Big Kate	37	Housekeeper and Nurse,	950.00
30	Melie Ann	19	Housework, Smart Yellow Girl,	1,250.00
31	Deacon	26	Prime Rice Hand,	1,000.00
32	Coming	19	Prime Cotton Hand,	1,000.00
33	Mabel	47	Prime Cotton Hand,	800.00
34	Uncle Tim	60	Fair Hand with Mules,	600.00
35	Abe	27	Prime Cotton Hand,	1,000.00
36	Tennes	29	Prime Rice Hand and Coachman,	1,250.00

There will also be offered at this sale, twenty head of Horses and Mules with harness, along with thirty head of Prime Cattle. Slaves will be sold separate, or in lots, as best suits the purchaser. Sale will be held rain or shine.

Virginian Luxuries. Originally painted on the back panel of a formal portrait, this image illustrates two "luxuries" of a Virginia slaveowner—the power to sexually abuse slave women and to whip slaves.

we shall not meet in this world I hope to meet in heaven. My dear wife for you and my children my pen cannot express the grief I feel to be parted from you all."

Gender Roles among Slaves

In some ways, gender roles under slavery differed markedly from those in the larger society. Slave men and women experienced, in a sense, the equality of powerlessness. The nineteenth century's "cult of domesticity," which defined the home as a woman's proper sphere, did not apply to slave women, who regularly worked in the fields. Slave men could not act as the economic providers for their families. Nor could they protect their wives from physical or sexual abuse by owners and overseers (a frequent occurrence on many plantations) or determine when and under what conditions their children worked.

When slaves worked "on their own time," however, more conventional gender roles prevailed. Slave men chopped wood, hunted, and fished, while women washed, sewed, and assumed primary responsibility for the care of children. Some planters allowed their slaves small plots of land on which to grow food to supplement the rations provided by the owner; women usually took charge of these "garden plots." But whatever its internal arrangements, the family was central to the slave community, allowing for the transmission of values, traditions, and survival strategies—in a word, of slave culture—from one generation to the next.

Slave Religion

A distinctive version of Christianity also offered solace to slaves in the face of hardship and hope for liberation from bondage. Some blacks, free and slave, had taken part in the Great Awakening of the colonial era, and even more were swept into the South's Baptist and Methodist churches during the religious revivals of the late eighteenth and early nineteenth centuries. As one preacher recalled of the great camp meeting that drew thousands of worshipers to Cane Ridge, Kentucky, in 1801, no distinctions were made "as to age, sex, color, or anything of a temporary nature; old and young, male and female, black and white, had equal privilege to minister the light which they received, in whatever way the Spirit directed."

The importance of religion

Even though the law prohibited slaves from gathering without a white person present, every plantation, it seemed, had its own black preacher. Usually the preacher was a "self-called" slave who possessed little or no formal education but whose rhetorical abilities and familiarity with the Bible made him one of the most respected members of the slave community. Especially in southern cities, slaves also worshiped in biracial congregations with white ministers, where they generally were required to sit in the back pews or in the balcony. Urban free blacks established their own churches, sometimes attended by slaves.

Religion and social control

To masters, Christianity offered another means of social control. Many required slaves to attend services conducted by white ministers, who preached that theft was immoral and that the Bible required servants to obey their masters. One slave later recalled being told in a white minister's sermon "how good God was in bringing us over to this country from dark and benighted Africa, and permitting us to listen to the sound of the gospel." Several slaves walked out of the service during a sermon by Charles C. Jones stressing that God had commanded servants to obey their masters and that they should not try to run away. One man came up to Jones at the end and said, "the doctrine is *one-sided.*"

The Gospel of Freedom

The slaves transformed the Christianity they had embraced, turning it to their own purposes. A blend of African traditions and Christian belief, slave religion was practiced in secret nighttime gatherings on plantations and in "praise meetings" replete with shouts, dances, and frequent emotional interchanges between the preacher and the congregation. One former slave later recalled typical secret religious gatherings: "We used to slip off into the woods in the old slave days on Sunday evening way down in the swamps to sing and pray to our own liking. We prayed for this day of freedom."

The biblical story of Exodus, in which God chose Moses to lead the enslaved Jews of Egypt into a promised land of freedom, played a central role in black Christianity. Slaves identified themselves as a chosen people, whom God in the fullness of time would deliver from bondage. At the same time, the figure of Jesus Christ represented to slaves a personal redeemer, one who truly cared for the oppressed. Slaves found other heroes and symbols in the Bible as well: Jonah, who overcame hard luck and escaped from the belly of a whale; David, who vanquished the more powerful Goliath; and Daniel, who escaped from the lion's den. And the Christian message of brotherhood and the equality of all souls before the Creator, in the slaves' eyes, offered an irrefutable indictment of the institution of slavery.

The "Negro church" on Rockville Plantation near Charleston, South Carolina, in an 1863 photograph. Few plantations had such a building; most slaves worshiped secretly or in biracial churches with white ministers.

The Desire for Liberty

If their masters developed an elaborate ideology defending the South's "peculiar institution," slave culture rested on a conviction of the unjustness of bondage and the desire for freedom. "Nobody," the British political philosopher Edmund Burke had written during the American Revolution, "will be argued into slavery." Whatever proslavery writers asserted and ministers preached, blacks thought of themselves as a working people unjustly deprived of the fruits of their labor by idle planters who lived in luxury. "We bake the bread / they give us the crust," said a line from one slave song.

Most slaves fully understood the impossibility of directly confronting the system. Their folktales had no figures equivalent to Paul Bunyan, the powerful, larger-than-life backwoodsman popular in white folklore. Slaves' folklore, such as the Brer Rabbit stories, glorified the weak hare who outwitted stronger foes like

Slaves' adaptation of Christianity

Slave culture

Plantation Burial, a painting from around 1860 by John Antrobus, an English artist who emigrated to New Orleans in 1850 and later married the daughter of a plantation owner. A slave preacher conducts a funeral service while black men, women, and children look on. This is a rare eyewitness depiction of black culture under slavery.

the bear and fox, rather than challenging them directly. Their religious songs, or spirituals, spoke of lives of sorrow ("I've been 'buked and I've been scorned"), while holding out hope for ultimate liberation ("Didn't my Lord deliver Daniel?"). When they sang, "I'm bound for the land of Canaan," slaves meant not only relief from worldly woes in an afterlife but also escaping to the North or, in God's good time, witnessing the breaking of slavery's chains.

"Freedom," declared a black minister after emancipation, "burned in the black heart long before freedom was born." Even the most ignorant slave, observed Solomon Northup, could not "fail to observe the difference between their own condition and the meanest white man's, and to realize the injustice of laws which place it within [the owner's] power not only to appropriate the profits of their industry, but to subject them to unmediated and unprovoked punishment without remedy."

Neighborhood networks

Owners attempted to prevent slaves from learning about the larger world. But slaves created neighborhood networks that transmitted information between plantations. Skilled craftsmen, preachers, pilots on ships, and other privileged slaves spread news of local and national events. Owners found that slaves knew more about political events than they expected. James Henry Hammond of South Carolina was "astonished and shocked" to find that his slaves understood the political views of the presidential candidates of 1844, Henry Clay and James K. Polk, and knew "most of what the abolitionists are doing."

The world of most rural slaves was bounded by their local communities and kin. They became extremely familiar with the local landscape, crops, and population, but had little knowledge of the larger world. Nonetheless, slaves could not remain indifferent to the currents of thought unleashed by the American Revolution or to the language of freedom in the society around them. "I am in a land of liberty," wrote Joseph Taper, a Virginia slave who escaped to Canada around 1840. "Here man is as God intended he should be . . . not like the southern laws which put man, made in the image of God, on level with brutes." The social and political agenda African-Americans would put forward in the Reconstruction era that followed emancipation—stressing civil and political equality, the strengthening of the black community, and autonomy in their working lives—flowed directly out of their experience in slavery.

RESISTANCE TO SLAVERY

Confronted with federal, state, and local authorities committed to preserving slavery, and outnumbered within the South as a whole by the white population, slaves could only rarely express their desire for freedom by outright rebellion. Compared to Brazil and the West Indies, which experienced numerous uprisings, involving hundreds or even thousands of slaves, revolts in the United States were smaller and less frequent. There was no parallel, of course, to the successful slave revolution in Haiti discussed in Chapter 8 or to the unsuccessful 1831 rebellion in Jamaica that appears to have involved as many as 20,000 slaves. This does not, however, mean that slaves in the United States placidly accepted the system under which they were compelled to live. Resistance to slavery took many forms in the Old South, from individual acts of defiance to occasional uprisings. These actions posed a constant challenge to the slaveholders' self-image as benign paternalists and their belief that slaves were obedient subjects grateful for their owners' care.

> Revolts and resistance

The top part of a typical broadside offering a reward for the capture of four runaway slaves. This was distributed in Mississippi County, Missouri, in 1852. The high reward for George, $1,000, suggests that he is an extremely valued worker.

Forms of Resistance

The most widespread expression of hostility to slavery was "day-to-day resistance" or "silent sabotage"—doing poor work, breaking tools, abusing animals, and in other ways disrupting the plantation routine. Frederick Law Olmsted, a northerner who toured the South in the 1850s, took note of "gates left open, rails removed from fences by the negroes, mules lamed and implements broken, a flat boat set adrift in the river, men ordered to cart rails for a new fence, depositing them so that a double expense of labor would be required to lay them." Many slaves made believe that they were ill to avoid work (although almost no slaves reported themselves sick on Sunday, their only day of rest). Then there was the theft of food, a form of resistance so common that one southern physician diagnosed it as a hereditary disease unique to blacks. Less frequent, but more dangerous, were serious crimes committed by slaves, including arson, poisoning, and armed assaults against individual whites.

Fugitive Slaves

Even more threatening to the stability of the slave system were slaves who ran away. As we have seen, war provided the opportunity for mass escapes. Thousands of slaves gained their freedom by running away to British lines during the War of Independence

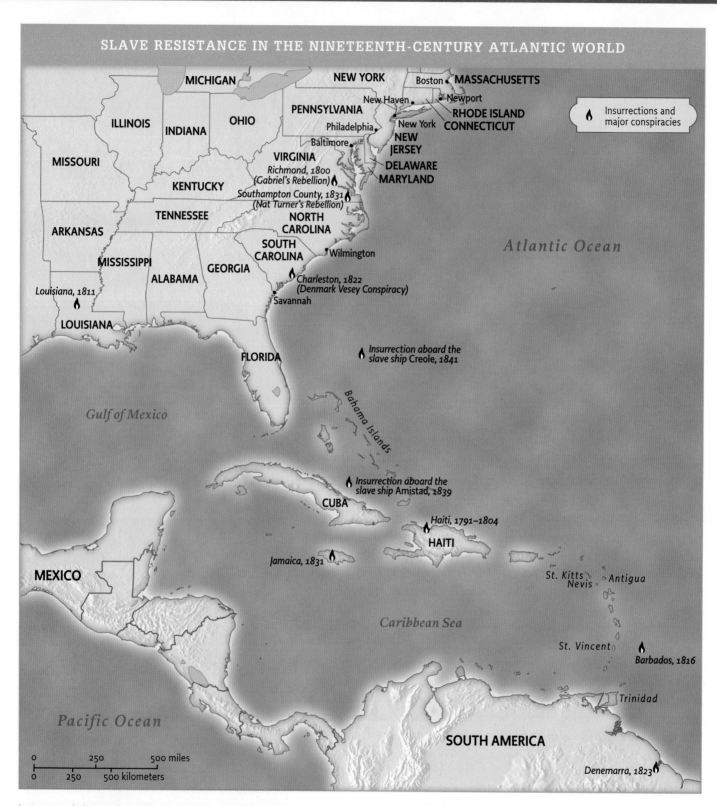

SLAVE RESISTANCE IN THE NINETEENTH-CENTURY ATLANTIC WORLD

MICHIGAN

NEW YORK

Boston **MASSACHUSETTS**

New Haven • Newport

ILLINOIS

INDIANA

OHIO

PENNSYLVANIA

New York **RHODE ISLAND**

CONNECTICUT

Philadelphia

MISSOURI

Baltimore

NEW JERSEY

DELAWARE

MARYLAND

VIRGINIA

Richmond, 1800
(Gabriel's Rebellion)

KENTUCKY

Southampton County, 1831
(Nat Turner's Rebellion)

TENNESSEE

NORTH CAROLINA

ARKANSAS

SOUTH CAROLINA

• Wilmington

MISSISSIPPI

ALABAMA

GEORGIA

Charleston, 1822
(Denmark Vesey Conspiracy)

Louisiana, 1811

Savannah

LOUISIANA

FLORIDA

Insurrection aboard the
slave ship Creole, 1841

Atlantic Ocean

| | Insurrections and major conspiracies |

Gulf of Mexico

Bahama Islands

Insurrection aboard the
slave ship Amistad, 1839

CUBA

Haiti, 1791–1804

HAITI

Jamaica, 1831

St. Kitts
Nevis Antigua

MEXICO

Caribbean Sea

St. Vincent

Barbados, 1816

Trinidad

Pacific Ocean

SOUTH AMERICA

| 0 | 250 | 500 miles |
| 0 | 250 | 500 kilometers |

Denemarra, 1823

Instances of slave resistance occurred throughout the Western Hemisphere, on land and at sea. This map shows the location of major events in the nineteenth century.

and War of 1812. Generally, however, formidable obstacles confronted the prospective **fugitive slave**. As Solomon Northup recalled, "Every white man's hand is raised against him, the patrollers are watching for him, the hounds are ready to follow in his track." Slaves had little or no knowledge of geography, apart from understanding that following the north star led to freedom. Not surprisingly, most of those who succeeded lived, like Frederick Douglass, in the Upper South, especially Maryland, Virginia, and Kentucky, which bordered on the free states. Douglass, who escaped at age twenty, was also typical in that the large majority of fugitives were young men. Most slave women were not willing to leave children behind, and to take them along on the arduous escape journey was nearly impossible.

In one of the most celebrated escapes of the antebellum years, Henry Brown, a slave in Richmond, had himself concealed in a crate and shipped to the antislavery office in Philadelphia. This lithograph from 1851 shows three white abolitionists, including J. Miller McKim, with a hatchet, as well as the African-American William Still, a leader of the underground railroad in the city, who holds the top of the crate as Brown emerges.

In the Deep South, fugitives tended to head for cities like New Orleans or Charleston, where they hoped to hide "in plain sight" among the growing communities of free blacks. Other escapees fled to remote areas like the Great Dismal Swamp of Virginia or the Florida Everglades, where the Seminole Indians offered refuge before they were forced to move west. Even in Tennessee, a study of newspaper advertisements for runaways finds that around 40 percent were thought to have remained in the local neighborhood and 30 percent to have headed to other locations in the South, while only 25 percent tried to reach the North.

The Underground Railroad

The **Underground Railroad**, a loose organization of sympathetic abolitionists who hid fugitives in their homes and sent them on to the next "station," assisted some runaway slaves. A few courageous individuals made forays into the South to liberate slaves. The best known was **Harriet Tubman**. Born in Maryland in 1820, Tubman escaped to Philadelphia in 1849 and during the next decade risked her life by making numerous trips back to her state of birth to lead relatives and other slaves to freedom. Recent scholarship suggests that she rescued about seventy-five men, women, and children from slavery. But most who managed to reach the North did so on their own initiative, sometimes showing remarkable ingenuity. William and Ellen Craft impersonated a sickly owner traveling with her slave. Henry "Box" Brown packed himself inside a crate and literally had himself shipped from Richmond, Virginia, to freedom in the North. When his crate was opened, Brown emerged "with a face radiant with joy," and launched into a "hymn of praise." But because fugitives were always vulnerable to recapture, Brown soon departed for England, where he became a fixture on the antislavery lecture circuit.

Rather than a single, centralized system with tunnels, codes, and clearly defined routes and stations, the underground railroad was a series of interlocking

Escapes to the North

local networks involving black and white abolitionists. These networks communicated with each other and together helped a substantial number of fugitives reach safety in the free states and Canada. One estimate is that around 30,000 fugitives managed to escape from the South in the three decades before the Civil War. The number was hardly sufficient to undermine the slave system, which counted nearly four million slaves in 1860, but enough to become a major source of consternation in the slave states.

Impact of escaped slaves on national politics

By the 1850s, slaves were using numerous means of escape, not simply running away on foot but hiding on boats with the help of sympathetic captains and sailors, taking an owner's horse and carriages, and boarding trains, as Frederick Douglass had done. They had many motives—brutality by the owners, fear of sale, or simply, as one said, because "I was tired of being a slave." Their actions had a profound impact on national politics. Running away undermined proslavery propaganda about contented slaves. The status of fugitives became a major irritant in diplomatic relations as successive administrations demanded, without success, that Canada and Mexico return escaped slaves. Efforts to recapture fugitives on northern soil showed that the power of slavery reached into the free states and forced many northerners who were not abolitionists to confront the question of the relationship between individual conscience and obedience to law.

The *Amistad*

In a few instances, large groups of slaves collectively seized their freedom. The most celebrated instance involved fifty-three slaves who in 1839 took control of **the *Amistad***, a ship transporting them from one port in Cuba to another, and tried to force the navigator to steer it to Africa. The *Amistad* wended its way up the Atlantic coast, until an American vessel seized it off the coast of Long Island. President Martin Van Buren favored returning the slaves to Cuba. But abolitionists brought their case to the Supreme Court, where former president John Quincy Adams argued that since they had been recently brought from Africa in violation of international treaties banning the slave trade, the captives should be freed. The Court accepted Adams's reasoning, and most of the captives made their way back to Africa.

Uprising on ship

The *Amistad* case had no legal bearing on slaves within the United States. But it may well have inspired a similar uprising in 1841, when 135 slaves being transported by sea from Norfolk, Virginia, to New Orleans seized control of the ship *Creole* and sailed for Nassau in the British Bahamas. Their leader had the evocative name Madison Washington. To the dismay of the Tyler administration, the British gave refuge to the *Creole* slaves.

Slave Revolts

Resistance to slavery occasionally moved beyond such individual and group acts of defiance to outright rebellion. The four largest conspiracies in American history occurred within the space of thirty-one years in the early nineteenth century. The first, organized by the Virginia slave Gabriel in 1800, was discussed in Chapter 8.

It was followed eleven years later by an uprising on sugar plantations upriver from New Orleans. Some 500 men and women, armed with sugarcane knives, axes, clubs, and a few guns, marched toward the city, destroying property as they proceeded and shouting, "Freedom or death." The white population along the route fled in panic to New Orleans. Within two days, the militia and regular army troops met the rebels and dispersed them in a pitched battle, killing sixty-six. Soon afterward, the principal leaders were executed. Captured rebels offered little explanation for their revolt other than the desire, as one put it, "to kill the white." But they seem to have been inspired by the recent success of the slave revolution in Haiti.

Uprising near New Orleans

The next major conspiracy was organized in 1822 by Denmark Vesey, a slave carpenter in Charleston, South Carolina, who had purchased his freedom after winning a local lottery. An outspoken, charismatic leader, he rebuked blacks who stepped off the city's sidewalks to allow whites to pass and took a leading role in the local African Methodist Church. **Denmark Vesey's conspiracy** reflected the combination of American and African influences then circulating in the Atlantic world and coming together in black culture. "He studied the Bible a great deal," recalled one of his followers, "and tried to prove from it that slavery and bondage is against the Bible." Vesey also quoted the Declaration of Independence, pored over newspaper reports of the debates in Congress regarding the Missouri Compromise, and made pronouncements like "all men had equal rights, blacks as well as whites." And he read to his co-conspirators accounts of the successful slave revolution in Haiti. The African heritage was present in the person of Vesey's lieutenant Gullah Jack, a religious "conjurer" from Angola who claimed to be able to protect the rebels against injury or death. The plot was discovered before it could reach fruition.

As in the case of many slave conspiracies, evidence about the Vesey plot is contradictory and disputed. Much of it comes from a series of trials in which the court operated in secret and failed to allow the accused to confront those who testified against them. South Carolina's governor, Thomas Bennett Jr., a number of whose slaves were among the accused, complained to Robert Y. Hayne, the state's attorney general, that the court proceedings violated "the rules which universally obtain among civilized nations." Hayne replied that to try a "free white man" under such circumstances would clearly violate his fundamental rights. But, he added, "slaves are not entitled to these rights," since "all the provisions of our constitution in favor of liberty are intended for freemen only." In the end, thirty-five slaves and free blacks, among them Vesey and three slaves belonging to the governor, were executed and an equal number banished from the state.

Secret trials

Nat Turner's Rebellion

The best known of all slave rebels was Nat Turner, a slave preacher and religious mystic in Southampton County, Virginia, who came to believe that God had chosen him to lead a black uprising. Turner traveled widely in the county conducting religious services. He told of seeing black and white angels fighting in the sky and the heavens running red with blood. Perhaps from a sense of irony, Turner

The most prominent slave revolt

An engraving depicting Nat Turner's slave rebellion of 1831, from a book published soon after the revolt.

initially chose July 4, 1831, for his rebellion only to fall ill on the appointed day. On August 22, he and a handful of followers marched from farm to farm assaulting the white inhabitants. Most of their victims were women and children, for many of the area's men were attending a religious revival across the border in North Carolina. By the time the militia put down the uprising, about eighty slaves had joined Turner's band, and some sixty whites had been killed. Turner was subsequently captured and, with seventeen other rebels, condemned to die. Asked before his execution whether he regretted what he had done, Turner responded, "Was not Christ crucified?"

Nat Turner's Rebellion was the last large-scale rebellion in southern history. Like Gabriel's and Vesey's conspiracies, Turner's took place outside the heart of the plantation South, where slavery was most rigidly policed. Because Turner began with only a handful of followers, he faced less chance of discovery or betrayal than Gabriel or Vesey. Nonetheless, his revolt demonstrated conclusively that in a region where whites outnumbered blacks and the white community was armed and united, slaves stood at a fatal disadvantage in any violent encounter. Only an outside force could alter the balance of power within the South.

Turner's rebellion sent shock waves through the entire South. "A Nat Turner," one white Virginian warned, "might be in any family." In the panic that followed the revolt, hundreds of innocent slaves were whipped and scores executed. For one last time, Virginia's leaders openly debated whether steps ought to be taken to do away with the "peculiar institution." "The blood of Turner and his innocent victims," declared a Richmond newspaper, "has opened the doors which have been shut for fifty years." But a proposal to commit the state to gradual emancipation and the removal of the black population from the state failed to win legislative approval. The measure gained overwhelming support in the western part of Virginia, where slaves represented less than 10 percent of the population, but it failed to win sufficient votes in the eastern counties where slavery was centered.

Instead of moving toward emancipation, the Virginia legislature of 1832 decided to fasten even more tightly the chains of bondage. New laws prohibited blacks, free or slave, from acting as preachers (a measure that proved impossible to enforce), strengthened the militia and patrol systems, banned free blacks from owning firearms, and prohibited teaching slaves to read. Other southern states followed suit. In the debate's aftermath, Thomas R. Dew, a professor at the College of William and Mary in Virginia, published an influential pamphlet pointing to the absurdity of deporting the bulk of the state's labor force. The state, he insisted, faced a stark choice—retain slavery, or free the slaves and absorb them into Virginia society. Few critics of slavery were willing to accept the latter alternative.

Shock waves through the South

Stronger controls

In some ways, 1831 marked a turning point for the Old South. In that year, Parliament debated a program for abolishing slavery throughout the British empire, underscoring the South's growing isolation in the Western world. Turner's rebellion, following only a few months after the appearance in Boston of William Lloyd Garrison's abolitionist journal, *The Liberator,* suggested that American slavery faced enemies both within and outside the South. The proslavery argument increasingly permeated southern intellectual and political life, while dissenting opinions were suppressed. Some states made membership in an abolitionist society a criminal offense, while mobs drove critics of slavery from their homes. The South's "great reaction" produced one of the most thoroughgoing suppressions of freedom of speech in American history. Even as reform movements arose in the North that condemned slavery as contrary to Christianity and to basic American values, and national debate over the peculiar institution intensified, southern society closed in defense of slavery.

A turning point

SUGGESTED READING

BOOKS

- Aptheker, Herbert. *American Negro Slave Revolts* (1943). Still the fullest account of slave rebellions in the United States.

- Baptist, Edward E. *The Half Has Never Been Told: Slavery and the Making of American Capitalism.* A study of the cotton kingdom, emphasizing the role of violence in ensuring labor productivity and the crucial role of slavery in the national economy.

- Beckert, Sven. *The Empire of Cotton* (2014). A history of one of the world's most important commodities, placing the old South in an international context.

- Berlin, Ira. *Slaves without Masters: The Free Negro in the Antebellum South* (1974). A careful study of the status of free blacks, stressing differences between the Upper and Lower South.

- Clinton, Catherine. *The Plantation Mistress: Woman's World in the Old South* (1982). Explores how the institution of slavery affected the lives of planters' wives and daughters.

- Davis, David Brion. *Inhuman Bondage: The Rise and Fall of Slavery in the New World* (2006). Places the history of slavery in the United States firmly in a hemispheric context.

- Foner, Eric. *Gateway to Freedom: The Hidden History of the Underground Railroad.* A study of the operations of the underground railroad, focusing on New York City, and of the fugitives it assisted.

- Genovese, Eugene D. *Roll, Jordan, Roll: The World the Slaves Made* (1974). A classic study of the paternalist ethos and the culture that developed under slavery.

- Gutman, Herbert G. *The Black Family in Slavery and Freedom* (1976). A pioneering examination of how slaves created and sustained families under the harsh conditions of slavery.

- Johnson, Walter. *Soul by Soul: Life inside the Antebellum Slave Market* (1999). Considers the operations of the New Orleans slave market as a window into slavery as a whole.

- Kaye, Anthony E. *Joining Places: Slave Neighborhoods in the Old South* (2007). Emphasizes the importance of the local networks established by slaves in Mississippi.

- Kolchin, Peter. *American Slavery, 1619–1877* (rev. ed., 2003). A careful, up-to-date survey of the history of slavery in North America from its beginning through emancipation.

- McCurry, Stephanie. *Masters of Small Worlds: Yeoman Households, Gender Relations, and the Political Culture of Antebellum South Carolina* (1995). Studies the lives of men and women in non-slaveholding families, to explore their links with the planter class.

- O'Brien, Michael. *Conjectures of Order: Intellectual Life and the American South* (2004). A comprehensive study of intellectual life in the Old South.

- Stevenson, Brenda. *Life in Black and White: Family and Community in the Slave South* (1996). Focusing on Virginia, an examination of how slaves adapted to the rise of the interstate slave trade.

WEBSITES

- Born in Slavery: Slave Narratives from the Federal Writers' Project: http://lcweb2.loc.gov/ammem/snhtml/snhome.html

- Documenting the American South: http://docsouth.unc.edu

- Gilder Lehrman Center for the Study of Slavery, Resistance, and Abolition: www.yale.edu/glc/index.htm

- Slaves and the Courts, 1740–1860: http://memory.loc.gov/ammem/sthtml/sthome.html

CHAPTER REVIEW AND ONLINE RESOURCES

REVIEW QUESTIONS

1. Given that most northern states had abolished slavery by the 1830s, how is it useful to think of slavery as a national—rather than regional—economic and political system?

2. While some poor southern whites resented the dominance of the "slavocracy," most supported the institution and accepted the power of the planter class. Why did the "plain folk" continue to support slavery?

3. How did the planters' paternalism serve to justify the system of slavery? How did it hide the reality of life for slaves?

4. Identify the basic elements of the proslavery defense and those points aimed especially at non-southern audiences.

5. Compare slaves in the Old South with those elsewhere in the world, focusing on health, diet, and opportunities for freedom.

6. Describe the difference between gang labor and task labor for slaves, and explain how slaves' tasks varied by region across the Old South.

7. How did enslaved people create community and a culture that allowed them to survive in an oppressive society?

8. Identify the different types of resistance to slavery. Which ones were the most common, the most effective, and the most demonstrative?

KEY TERMS

the "peculiar institution" (p. 390)

Second Middle Passage (p. 391)

"Cotton Is King" (p. 393)

paternalism (p. 396)

proslavery argument (p. 398)

fugitive slaves (p. 417)

Underground Railroad (p. 417)

Harriet Tubman (p. 417)

the *Amistad* (p. 418)

Denmark Vesey's conspiracy (p. 419)

Nat Turner's Rebellion (p. 420)

Go to 🐰 INQUIZITIVE

To see what you know—and learn what you've missed—with personalized feedback along the way.

Visit the *Give Me Liberty!* Student Site for primary source documents and images, interactive maps, author videos featuring Eric Foner, and more.

CHAPTER 12

AN
AGE OF REFORM

★

1820–1840

Among the many Americans who devoted their lives to the crusade against slavery, few were as selfless or courageous as Abby Kelley. Born in Massachusetts in 1811, she was educated at a Quaker boarding school in Rhode Island. As a teacher in Lynn, Massachusetts, she joined the Female Anti-Slavery Society and, like thousands of other northern women, threw herself into the abolitionist movement. In 1838, Kelley began to give public speeches about slavery. Her first lecture outside of Lynn was literally a baptism of fire. Enraged by reports that abolitionists favored "amalgamation" of the races—that is, sexual relations between whites and blacks—residents of Philadelphia stormed the meeting hall and burned it to the ground.

For two decades, Kelley traveled throughout the North, speaking almost daily in churches, public halls, and antislavery homes on "the holy cause of human rights." Her career illustrated the interconnections of the era's reform movements. In addition to abolitionism, she was active in pacifist organizations—which opposed the use of force, including war, to settle disputes—and was a pioneer in the early struggle for women's rights. "In striving to strike [the slave's] irons off," she wrote, women "found most surely that we were manacled ourselves." Kelley was not the first American woman to speak in public. But she covered more miles and gave more speeches than any other female orator. She forthrightly challenged her era's assumption that a woman's "place" was in the home. More than any other individual, remarked Lucy Stone, another women's rights advocate, Kelley "earned for us all the right of free speech."

Abby Kelley's private life was as unconventional as her public career. She enjoyed a long and happy marriage to Stephen S. Foster, a strong-willed abolitionist given to interrupting Sunday sermons to denounce ministers who failed to condemn slavery. She gave birth to a daughter in 1847 but soon returned to lecturing. When criticized for not devoting herself to the care of her infant, Kelley replied: "I have done it for the sake of the mothers whose babies are sold away from them. The most precious legacy I can leave my child is a free country."

THE REFORM IMPULSE

"In the history of the world," wrote Ralph Waldo Emerson in 1841, "the doctrine of reform has never had such hope as at the present hour." Abolitionism was only one of the era's numerous efforts to improve American society. During his visit in the early 1830s, Alexis de Tocqueville noted how in the absence of a powerful national government, Americans' political and social activities were organized through voluntary associations—churches, fraternal orders, political clubs, and the like. The reform impulse was part of this proliferation of voluntary groups. Americans established organizations that worked to prevent the manufacture and sale of liquor, end public entertainments and the delivery of the mail on Sunday, improve conditions in prisons, expand public education, uplift the condition of wage laborers, and reorganize society on the basis of cooperation rather than competitive individualism.

FOCUS QUESTIONS

What were the major movements and goals of antebellum reform? *–p. 425*

What were the different varieties of abolitionism? *–p. 435*

How did abolitionism challenge barriers to racial equality and free speech? *–p. 441*

What were the diverse sources of the antebellum women's rights movement and its significance? *–p. 446*

A Woman's Rights Quilt. Made by an unknown woman only a few years after the Seneca Falls Convention of 1848, this quilt embodies an unusual form of political expression. It includes scenes visualizing a woman engaged in various activities that violated the era's cult of domesticity, and it illustrates some of the demands of the early women's rights movement. The individual blocks show a woman driving her own buggy and a banner advocating "woman rights," another dressing to go out while her husband remains at home wearing an apron, and a third addressing a public meeting with a mixed male-female audience.

Nearly all these groups worked to convert public opinion to their cause. They sent out speakers, gathered signatures on petitions, and published pamphlets. Like Abby Kelley, many reformers were active in more than one crusade. Some reform movements, like restraining the consumption of liquor and alleviating the plight of the blind and insane, flourished throughout the nation. Others, including women's rights, labor unionism, and educational reform, were weak or nonexistent in the South, where they were widely associated with antislavery sentiment. Reform was an international crusade. Peace, temperance, women's rights, and antislavery advocates regularly crisscrossed the Atlantic to promote their ideas.

Reformers adopted a wide variety of tactics to bring about social change. Some relied on "moral suasion" to convert people to their cause. Others, like opponents of the "demon rum," sought to use the power of the government to force sinners to change their ways. Some reformers decided to withdraw altogether from the larger society and establish their own cooperative settlements. They hoped to change American life by creating "heavens on earth," where they could demonstrate by example the superiority of a collective way of life. Reformers never amounted to anything like a majority of the population, even in the North, but they had a profound impact on both politics and society.

Utopian Communities

About 100 reform communities were established in the decades before the Civil War. Historians call them "utopian" after Thomas More's sixteenth-century novel *Utopia*, an outline of a perfect society. (The word has also come to imply that such plans are impractical and impossible to realize.) These communities differed greatly in structure and motivation. Some were subject to the iron discipline of a single leader, while others operated in a democratic fashion. Most arose from religious conviction, but others were inspired by the secular desire to counteract the social and economic changes set in motion by the market revolution.

Nearly all the communities set out to reorganize society on a cooperative basis, hoping to restore social harmony to a world of excessive individualism and to narrow the widening gap between rich and poor. Through their efforts, the words "socialism" and "communism," meaning a social organization in which productive property is owned by the community rather than private individuals, entered the language of politics. Most **utopian communities** also tried to find substitutes for conventional gender relations and marriage patterns. Some prohibited sexual relations between men and women altogether; others allowed them to change partners at will. But nearly all insisted that the abolition of private property must be accompanied by an end to men's "property" in women.

The Shakers

Religious communities attracted those who sought to find a retreat from a society permeated by sin, "a refuge from the evils of this Sodom," as the founders of Zoar, in Ohio, put it. But the **Shakers**, the most successful of the religious communities, also had a significant impact on the outside world. At their peak during the 1840s, cooperative Shaker settlements, which stretched from Maine to Kentucky, included more than 5,000 members. The Shakers were founded in the late

An engraving of a Shaker dance, drawn by Benson Lossing, an artist who visited a Shaker community and reported on life there for *Harper's Magazine* in 1857.

eighteenth century by Mother Ann Lee, the daughter of an English blacksmith, who became a religious exhorter and claimed that Christ had directed her to emigrate with her followers to America. The first Shaker community was established in upstate New York in 1787.

God, the Shakers believed, had a "dual" personality, both male and female, and thus the two sexes were spiritually equal. Their work was deemed equally important (although each man was assigned a "sister" to take care of his washing and sewing). "Virgin purity" formed a pillar of the Shakers' faith. They completely abandoned traditional family life. Men and women lived separately in large dormitory-like structures and ate in communal dining rooms. Their numbers grew by attracting converts and adopting children from orphanages, rather than through natural increase. Numerous outsiders visited Shaker communities to observe the religious services that gave the group its name, in which men and women, separated by sex, engaged in frenzied dancing. Although they rejected the individual accumulation of private property, the Shakers proved remarkably successful economically. They were among the first to market vegetable and flower seeds and herbal medicines commercially and to breed cattle for profit. Their beautifully crafted furniture is still widely admired today.

Shaker beliefs

Oneida

Another influential and controversial community was **Oneida**, founded in 1848 in upstate New York by John Humphrey Noyes, the Vermont-born son of a U.S. congressman. Noyes took the revivalists' message that man could achieve moral perfection to an atypical extreme. He preached that he and his followers had become so perfect that they had achieved a state of complete "purity of heart," or sinlessness.

John Humphrey Noyes

In 1836, Noyes and his disciples formed a small community in Putney, Vermont. Like the Shakers, Noyes did away with private property and abandoned

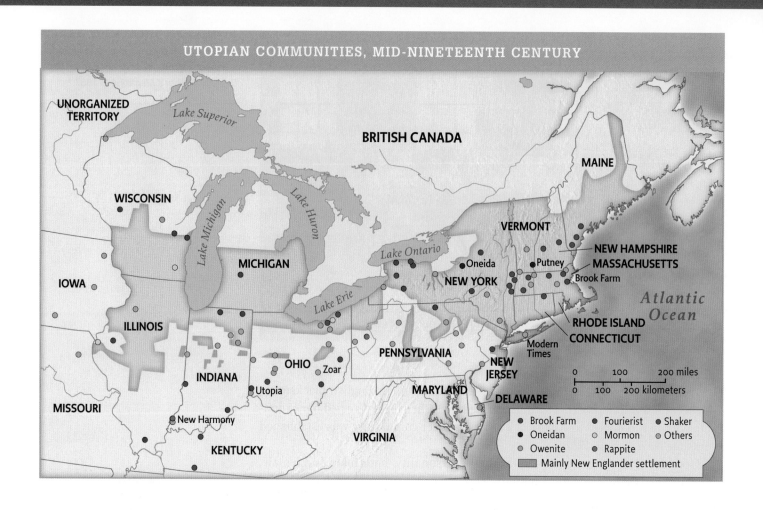

UTOPIAN COMMUNITIES, MID-NINETEENTH CENTURY

Brook Farm • Fourierist • Shaker
Oneidan • Mormon • Others
Owenite • Rappite
Mainly New Englander settlement

In the first half of the nineteenth century, dozens of utopian communities were established in the United States, where small groups of men and women attempted to establish a more perfect social order within the larger society.

"Complex marriage"

traditional marriage. But in contrast to Shaker celibacy, he taught that all members of his community formed a single "holy family" of equals. It became notorious for what Noyes called "complex marriage," whereby any man could propose sexual relations to any woman, who had the right to reject or accept his invitation, which would then be registered in a public record book. The great danger was "exclusive affections," which, Noyes felt, destroyed the harmony of the community.

After being indicted for adultery by local officials, Noyes in 1848 moved his community to Oneida, where it survived until 1881. Oneida was an extremely dictatorial environment. To become a member of the community, one had to demonstrate command of Noyes's religious teachings and live according to his rules. Members carefully observed each other's conduct and publicly criticized those who violated Noyes's regulations. By the 1860s, a committee was even determining which couples would be permitted to have children—an early example of "eugenics," as the effort to improve the human race by regulating reproduction came to be known.

Worldly Communities

To outside observers, utopian communities like Oneida seemed a case of "voluntary slavery." But because of their members' selfless devotion to the teachings and rules laid down by their leader, spiritually oriented communities often achieved remarkable longevity. The Shakers survived well into the twentieth century. Communities with a more worldly orientation tended to be beset by internal divisions and therefore lasted for much shorter periods.

In 1841, New England transcendentalists established **Brook Farm** not far from Boston, where they hoped to demonstrate that manual and intellectual labor could coexist harmoniously. They modeled the community in part on the ideas of the French social reformer Charles Fourier, who envisioned communal living and working arrangements, while retaining private property. Fourier's blueprint for "phalanxes," as he called his settlements, planned everything to the last detail, from the number of residents (2,000) to how much income would be generated by charging admission to sightseers. With leisure time devoted to music, dancing, dramatic readings, and intellectual discussion, Brook Farm was like an exciting miniature university. But it attracted mostly writers, teachers, and ministers, some of whom disliked farm labor. The novelist Nathaniel Hawthorne, a resident for a time, complained about having to shovel manure. Brook Farm disbanded after a few years, and Hawthorne offered a skeptical view of life there in his 1852 novel *The Blithedale Romance*.

> **Phalanxes**

The Owenites

The most important secular communitarian (meaning a person who plans or lives in a cooperative community) was Robert Owen, a British factory owner. Appalled by the degradation of workers in the early industrial revolution, Owen created a model factory village at New Lanark, Scotland, which combined strict rules of work discipline with comfortable housing and free public education. Around 1815, its 1,500 employees made New Lanark the largest center of cotton manufacturing in the world. Convinced that the "rich and the poor, the governors and the governed, have really but one interest," Owen promoted **communitarianism** as a peaceful means of ensuring that workers received the full value of their labor. In 1824, he purchased the Harmony community in Indiana—originally founded by the German Protestant religious leader George Rapp, who had emigrated to America with his followers at the beginning of the nineteenth century. Here, Owen established **New Harmony**, where he hoped to create a "new moral world."

"The character of man is, without a single exception, always formed for him," Owen declared. Individuals could be transformed by changing the circumstances in which they lived. In Owen's scheme, children would be removed at an early age from the care of their parents to be educated in schools where they would be trained to subordinate individual ambition to the common good. Owen also defended women's rights, especially access to education and the right to divorce. At New Harmony, he promised, women would no longer be "enslaved" to their husbands, and "false notions" about innate differences between the sexes would be abandoned.

Harmony eluded the residents of New Harmony. They squabbled about everything from the community's constitution to the distribution of property. Owen's settlement survived for only a few years, but it strongly influenced the labor movement, educational reformers, and women's rights advocates. Owen's vision resonated with the widely held American belief that a community of equals could be created in the New World.

The Crisis, a publication by the communitarian Robert Owen and his son, Robert Dale Owen. The cover depicts Owen's vision of a planned socialist community.

The DRUNKARD's PROGRESS,

OR THE DIRECT ROAD TO POVERTY, WRETCHEDNESS & RUIN.

The MORNING DRAM.

The GROG SHOP.

The CONFIRMED DRUNKARD.

CONCLUDING SCENE.

The Drunkard's Progress, an 1826 anti-liquor broadside illustrating how drinking leads a respectable man and his family to ruin.

Josiah Warren

Quite different from Owen's planned system were the short-lived secular communities founded by Josiah Warren, an early American anarchist (one who believes that all institutions that exercise power over individuals, including government, are illegitimate). At Utopia, Ohio, and Modern Times, New York, Warren established totally unregulated voluntary settlements. Like other communitarians, Warren tried to address the sources of labor unrest and women's inequality. In an attempt to solve the labor problem, he created stores where goods were exchanged according to the amount of work that had gone into producing them, thus preventing middlemen like bankers and merchants from sharing in the hard-earned income of farmers, laborers, and manufacturers. Marriage in Warren's communities was a purely voluntary arrangement, since no laws regulated personal behavior. In effect, Warren took American individualism to its logical extreme. Freedom, he declared, meant "allowing each individual to be absolute despot or sovereign" over himself.

Religion and Reform

Most Americans saw the ownership of property as the key to economic independence—and, therefore, to freedom—and marriage as the foundation of the social order. Few were likely to join communities that required them to surrender both. Far more typical of the reform impulse were movements that aimed at liberating men and women either from restraints external to themselves, such as slavery and war, or from forms of internal "servitude" like drinking, illiteracy, and a tendency toward criminality. Drinkers, proclaimed one reformer, could not be considered free: they were "chained to alcohol, bound to the demon rum." Many of these reform movements drew their inspiration from the religious revivalism of the Second Great Awakening, discussed in Chapter 9, and many of the leaders of reform movements had had transformative religious experiences. If, as the revivalist preachers maintained, God had created man as a "free moral agent," sinners could not only reform themselves but could also remake the world.

The revivals popularized the outlook known as **perfectionism**, which saw both individuals and society at large as capable of indefinite improvement. Regions like upstate New York and northern Ohio became known as "burned-over districts" because of the intense revivals they experienced in the 1820s and 1830s. Such areas became fertile soil for the era's reform movements and their vision of a society freed from sin. Under the impact of the revivals, older reform efforts moved in a new, radical direction. Temperance (which literally means moderation in the consumption of liquor) was transformed into a crusade to eliminate drinking entirely. Criticism of war became outright pacifism. And, as will be related below, critics of slavery now demanded not gradual emancipation but immediate and total abolition.

A temperance banner from around 1850 depicts a young man torn between a woman in white, who illustrates female purity, and a temptress, who offers him a drink of liquor.

The Temperance Movement

To members of the North's emerging middle-class culture, reform became a badge of respectability, an indication that individuals had taken control of their own lives and had become morally accountable human beings. The American Temperance Society, founded in 1826, directed its efforts to redeeming not only habitual drunkards but also the occasional drinker. It claimed by the 1830s to have persuaded hundreds of thousands of Americans to renounce liquor. By 1840, the consumption of alcohol per person had fallen to less than half the level of a decade earlier. (It had peaked in 1830 at seven gallons per person per year, compared to around two gallons today.) During the 1840s, the Washingtonian Society gathered reformed drinkers in "experience meetings," where they offered public testimony about their previous sins.

American Temperance Society

The **temperance movement** and other reform campaigns aroused considerable hostility. One person's sin is another's pleasure or cherished custom. Those Americans who enjoyed Sunday recreation or a stiff drink from time to time did not think they were any less moral than those who had been reborn at a religious camp meeting, had abandoned drinking, and devoted the Sabbath to religious observances.

Critics of Reform

Many Americans saw the reform impulse as an attack on their own freedom. Drinking was a prominent feature of festive celebrations and events like militia gatherings. As in the colonial era, taverns were popular meeting places for workingmen in early-nineteenth-century towns and cities, sites not only of drinking but also of political discussions, organizational meetings, and popular recreations. A "Liberty Loving Citizen" of Worcester, Massachusetts, wondered what gave one group of citizens the right to dictate to others how to conduct their personal lives.

Alcohol's social role

A German Beer Garden on Sunday Evening, an engraving from *Harper's Weekly*, October 15, 1858. German and Irish immigrants resented efforts of temperance reformers to prohibit the sale of alcoholic beverages.

American Catholics, their numbers growing because of Irish and German immigration, proved hostile to the reform impulse. Catholics understood freedom in ways quite different from Protestant reformers. They viewed sin as an inescapable burden of individuals and society. The perfectionist idea that evil could be banished from the world struck them as an affront to genuine religion, and they bitterly opposed what they saw as reformers' efforts to impose their own version of Protestant morality on their neighbors. While reformers spoke of man as a free moral agent, Catholics tended to place less emphasis on individual independence and more on the importance of communities centered on family and church. "Man," declared Archbishop John Hughes of New York, the nation's most prominent Catholic leader, was not an autonomous creature but "by his nature, a being of society."

Reformers and Freedom

Reformers had to reconcile their desire to create moral order with their quest to enhance personal freedom. They did this through a vision of freedom that was liberating and controlling at the same time. On the one hand, reformers insisted that their goal was to enable Americans to enjoy genuine liberty. In a world in which personal freedom increasingly meant the opportunity to compete for economic gain and individual self-improvement, they spoke of liberating Americans from various forms of "slavery" that made it impossible to succeed—slavery to drink, to poverty, to sin.

On the other hand, reformers insisted that self-fulfillment came through self-discipline. Their definition of the free individual was the person who internalized the practice of self-control. Philip Schaff, a German minister who emigrated to Pennsylvania in 1843, wrote that "true national freedom, in the American view," was "anything but an absence of restraint." Rather, it "rests upon a moral groundwork, upon the virtue of self-possession and self-control in individual citizens." In some ways, reformers believed, American society suffered from an excess of liberty—the anarchic "natural liberty" John Winthrop had warned against in the early days of Puritan Massachusetts, as opposed to the "Christian liberty" of the morally upright citizen.

Many religious groups in the East worried that settlers in the West and immigrants from abroad lacked self-control and led lives of vice, exhibited by drinking, violations of the Sabbath, and lack of Protestant devotion. They formed the American Tract Society, the American Bible Society, and other groups that flooded eastern cities and the western frontier with copies of the gospel and pamphlets promoting religious virtue. Between 1825 and 1835, the pamphlets distributed by the Tract Society amounted to more than 500 million pages. Both their understanding

Self-discipline

American Tract Society

of freedom and their ability to take advantage of the new printing technologies influenced the era's reform movements.

The Invention of the Asylum

The tension between liberation and control in the era's reform movements was vividly evident in the proliferation of new institutions that reformers hoped could remake human beings into free, morally upright citizens. In colonial America, crime had mostly been punished by whipping, fines, or banishment. The poor received relief in their own homes, orphans lived with neighbors, and families took care of mentally ill members.

During the 1830s and 1840s, Americans embarked on a program of institution building—jails for criminals, poorhouses for the destitute, asylums for the insane, and orphanages for children without families. These institutions differed in many respects, but they shared with communitarians and religious believers in "perfectionism" the idea that social ills once considered incurable could in fact be eliminated. The way to "cure" undesirable elements of society was to place afflicted persons and impressionable youths in an environment where their character could be transformed. Today, prisons and asylums have become overcrowded places where rehabilitating the inmates seems less important than simply holding them at bay, away from society. At the outset, however, these institutions were inspired by the conviction that those who passed through their doors could eventually be released to become productive, self-disciplined citizens.

Reform institutions

The Common School

The largest effort at institution building before the Civil War came in the movement to establish **common schools**—that is, tax-supported state school systems open to all children. In the early nineteenth century, most children were educated in locally supported schools, private academies, or charity schools, or at home, and many had

The New York House of Refuge, one of many institutions established in the 1820s and 1830s to address social ills by assisting and reforming criminals and the poor. Young boys and girls convicted of petty theft were assigned to the House of Refuge, where they performed supervised labor and received some educational instruction.

This daguerreotype from around 1850 depicts a classroom in a school for girls, presided over by a male teacher.

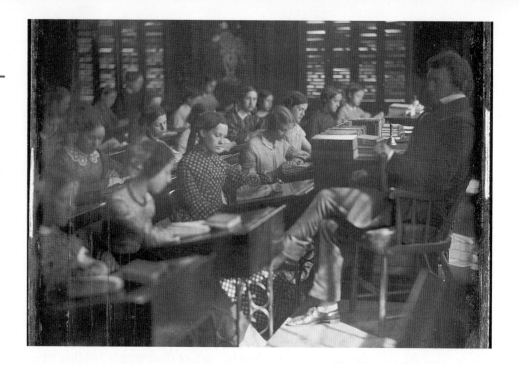

Horace Mann

no access to learning at all. School reform reflected the numerous purposes that came together in the era's reform impulse. Horace Mann, a Massachusetts lawyer and Whig politician who served as director of the state's board of education, was the era's leading educational reformer. His annual reports, widely read throughout the country, combined conservatism and radicalism, liberation and social control.

Mann hoped that universal public education could restore equality to a fractured society by bringing the children of all classes together in a common learning experience and equipping the less fortunate to advance in the social scale. Education would "equalize the conditions of men"—in effect, it would serve as industrial society's alternative to moving west to acquire a farm. This view of free public education as an avenue to social advancement was also shared by the early labor movement, which made the establishment of common schools one of its goals. At the same time, Mann argued that the schools would reinforce social stability by rescuing students from the influence of parents who failed to instill the proper discipline. To some extent, the schools' "silent curriculum"—obedience to authority, promptness in attendance, organizing one's day according to predetermined time periods that changed at the ringing of a bell—helped to prepare students for work in the new industrial economy.

Education and equality

The schools, Mann believed, were training free individuals—meaning persons who internalized self-discipline. But he encountered persistent opposition from parents who did not wish to surrender the moral education of their children to teachers and bureaucrats. Nonetheless, with labor organizations, factory owners, and middle-class reformers all supporting the idea, every northern state by 1860 had established tax-supported school systems for its children. The common school movement created the first real career opportunity for women, who quickly came to dominate the ranks of teachers. The South, where literate blacks were increasingly viewed as a danger to social order and planters had no desire to tax themselves to pay for education for poor white children, lagged far behind in

The rise of public education

public education. This was one of many ways in which North and South seemed to be growing apart.

THE CRUSADE AGAINST SLAVERY

Compared with drinking, Sabbath-breaking, and illiteracy, the greatest evil in American society at first appeared to attract the least attention from reformers. For many years, it seemed that the only Americans willing to challenge the existence of slavery were Quakers, slaves, and free blacks. After the antislavery impulse spawned by the Revolution died out, the slavery question faded from national life, with occasional eruptions like the Missouri controversy of 1819–1821.

Colonization

Before the 1830s, those white Americans willing to contemplate an end to bondage almost always coupled calls for abolition with the "colonization" of freed slaves—their deportation to Africa, the Caribbean, or Central America. In 1816, proponents of this idea founded the **American Colonization Society**, which promoted the gradual abolition of slavery and the settlement of black Americans in Africa. It soon established Liberia on the coast of West Africa, an outpost of American influence whose capital, Monrovia, was named for President James Monroe.

Colonization struck many observers as totally impractical. When the English writer Harriet Martineau visited the United States in the 1830s, she was amazed that former president James Madison endorsed the idea. "How such a mind as his" could be convinced that slavery would not end unless blacks were deported from the country she could not understand.

Nonetheless, numerous prominent political leaders of the Jacksonian era—including Henry Clay, John Marshall, Daniel Webster, and Jackson himself—supported the Colonization Society. Many northerners saw colonization as the only way to rid the nation of slavery. Southern supporters of colonization devoted most of their energy to persuading those African-Americans who were already free to leave the United States. Free blacks, they insisted, were a "degraded" group whose presence posed a danger to white society. Other colonizationists believed that slavery and racism were so deeply embedded in American life that blacks could never achieve equality if freed and allowed to remain in the country. Like Indian removal, colonization rested on the premise that America is fundamentally a white society.

Blacks and Colonization

In the decades before the Civil War, several thousand black Americans did emigrate to Liberia with the aid of the Colonization Society. Some were slaves emancipated by their owners on the condition that they depart, while others left voluntarily, motivated by a desire to spread Christianity in Africa or to enjoy rights denied them in the United States. Having experienced "the legal slavery of the South and the social slavery of the North," wrote one emigrant on leaving for Liberia, he knew he could "never be a free man in this country."

A pamphlet issued in 1848 by the American Colonization Society urging free blacks to emigrate to Liberia, in West Africa, and defending the society against "certain cavilings"—that is, abolitionist criticism.

The frontispiece of the 1848 edition of David Walker's *Appeal* and Henry Highland Garnet's *Address to the Slaves* depicts a black figure receiving "liberty" and "justice" from heaven.

An abolitionist banner. Antislavery organizations adopted the Liberty Bell as a symbol of their campaign to extend freedom to black Americans. Previously, the bell, forged in Philadelphia in the eighteenth century, had simply been known as the Old State House Bell.

But most African-Americans adamantly opposed the idea of colonization. In fact, the formation of the American Colonization Society galvanized free blacks to claim their rights as Americans. Early in 1817, some 3,000 free blacks assembled in Philadelphia for the first national black convention. Their resolutions insisted that blacks were Americans, entitled to the same freedom and rights enjoyed by whites. "We have no wish to separate from our present homes," they declared. In the years that followed, a number of black organizations removed the word "African" from their names to eliminate a possible reason for being deported from the land of their birth.

Militant Abolitionism

The abolitionist movement that arose in the 1830s differed profoundly from its genteel, conservative predecessor. Drawing on the religious conviction that slavery was an unparalleled sin and the secular one that it contradicted the values enshrined in the Declaration of Independence, a new generation of reformers rejected the traditional approach of gradual emancipation and demanded immediate abolition. Also unlike their predecessors, they directed explosive language against slavery and slaveholders and insisted that blacks, once free, should be incorporated as equal citizens of the republic rather than being deported. White abolitionists themselves were hardly free of the racism that pervaded American society. Nonetheless, nearly all abolitionists insisted that economic, civil, and political rights in the United States should be equally enjoyed without regard to race. Perfecting American society, they insisted, meant rooting out not just slavery, but racism in all its forms.

The first indication of the new spirit of abolitionism came in 1829 with the appearance of *An Appeal to the Coloured Citizens of the World* by David Walker, a free black who had been born in North Carolina and now operated a used-clothing store in Boston. A passionate indictment of slavery and racial prejudice, the *Appeal* called on black Americans to mobilize for abolition—by force if necessary—and warned whites that the nation faced divine punishment if it did not mend its sinful ways. Walker invoked the Bible and the Declaration of Independence, but he went beyond these familiar arguments to call on blacks to take pride in the achievements of ancient African civilizations and to claim all their rights as Americans. "Tell us no more about colonization," Walker wrote, addressing white readers, "for America is as much our country as it is yours." Like other reformers, Walker used both secular and religious language. He warned that God would wreak vengeance on the United States for violating the principles of justice and heaped scorn on ministers who defended slavery for violating the golden rule espoused by Jesus Christ ("Whatsoever ye would that men should do unto you, do yet even so unto them").

The Emergence of Garrison

Walker's language alarmed both slaveholders and many white critics of slavery. When free black sailors secretly distributed the pamphlet in the South, some southern states put a price on Walker's head. Walker, however, did not create an abolitionist organization, and he died in mysterious circumstances in 1830. Not until the appearance in 1831 of *The Liberator*, William Lloyd Garrison's weekly journal published in Boston, did the new breed of abolitionism find a permanent voice. "I will be as harsh as truth," Garrison announced, "and as uncompromising as justice. On this subject, I do not wish to think, or speak, or write, with moderation. . . . I will not equivocate—I will not excuse—I will not retreat a single inch—and I will be heard."

And heard he was, partly because southerners, outraged by his inflammatory rhetoric (one editorial called slaveowners "an adulterous and perverse generation, a brood of vipers"), reprinted Garrison's editorials in their own newspapers in order to condemn them, thus providing him with instant notoriety. Some of Garrison's ideas, such as his suggestion that the North abrogate the Constitution and dissolve the Union to end its complicity in the evil of slavery, were rejected by most abolitionists. But his call for the immediate abolition of slavery echoed throughout antislavery circles. Garrison's pamphlet *Thoughts on African Colonization* persuaded many foes of slavery that blacks must be recognized as part of American society, not viewed as aliens to be shipped overseas. Other antislavery publications soon emerged, but *The Liberator* remained the preeminent abolitionist journal.

William Lloyd Garrison, editor of *The Liberator* and probably the nation's most prominent abolitionist, in a daguerreotype from around 1850.

Spreading the Abolitionist Message

Beginning with a handful of activists, the abolitionist movement expanded swiftly throughout the North. Antislavery leaders took advantage of the rapid development of print technology and the expansion of literacy due to common school education to spread their message. Like radical pamphleteers of the American Revolution and evangelical ministers of the Second Great Awakening, they recognized the democratic potential in the production of printed material. Abolitionists seized upon the recently invented steam printing press to produce millions of copies of pamphlets, newspapers, petitions, novels, and broadsides. Between the formation of the **American Anti-Slavery Society** in 1833 and the end of the decade, some 100,000 northerners joined local groups devoted to abolition. Most were ordinary citizens—farmers, shopkeepers, craftsmen, and laborers, along with a few prominent businessmen like the merchants Arthur and Lewis Tappan of New York.

Antislavery printing

If Garrison was the movement's most notable propagandist, Theodore Weld, a young minister who had been converted by the evangelical preacher Charles G. Finney, helped to create its mass constituency. A brilliant orator, Weld trained a band of speakers who brought the abolitionist message into the heart of the rural and small-town North. Their methods were those of the revivals—fervent preaching, lengthy meetings, calls for individuals to renounce their immoral ways—and their message was a simple one: slavery was a sin. "In discussing the subject of slavery," wrote Weld, "I have always presented it

Theodore Weld

Pages from an abolitionist book for children. Abolitionists sought to convince young and old of the evils of slavery.

A is an Abolitionist—
A man who wants to free
The wretched slave—and give to all
An equal liberty.

B is a Brother with a skin
Of somewhat darker hue,
But in our Heavenly Father's sight,
He is as dear as you.

5

C is the Cotton-field, to which
This injured brother's driven,
When, as the white man's *slave*, he toils
From early morn till even.

D is the Driver, cold and stern,
Who follows, whip in hand,
To punish those who dare to rest,
Or disobey command.

as preeminently a moral question, arresting the conscience of the nation. As a question of politics and national economy, I have passed it with scarce a look or a word."

There was far more to Weld's moralistic approach than a concern for religious righteousness. Identifying slavery as a sin was essential to replacing the traditional strategies of gradual emancipation and colonization with immediate abolition. The only proper response to the sin of slavery, abolitionist speakers proclaimed, was the institution's immediate elimination. Weld also supervised the publication of abolitionist pamphlets, including his own *Slavery As It Is* (1839), a compilation of accounts of the maltreatment of slaves. Since Weld took all his examples from the southern press, they could not be dismissed as figments of the northern imagination.

Charity fairs

Abolitionists also pioneered modern ways of raising funds, especially charity fairs or "bazaars," where women sold clothing and embroidery made by local sewing circles and luxury items such as silks, porcelain, jewelry, and works of art dispatched by antislavery groups in the British Isles. Generally, fairs were held just before Christmas, and included a large assortment of dolls, toys, and other gifts for children. Indeed, abolitionists helped to establish the idea of a Christmas shopping season when people exchanged presents bought at commercial venues. With their slogan, "Buy for the Sake of the Slave," the fairs offered a foretaste of later consumer activism. The grandest of these fairs was the National Anti-Slavery Bazaar in Boston, organized by the wealthy and stylish reformer Maria Weston Chapman, which by the 1850s was raising several thousand dollars per year for the cause, but smaller versions proliferated throughout the North.

Slavery and Moral Suasion

Many southerners feared that the abolitionists intended to spark a slave insurrection, a belief strengthened by the outbreak of Nat Turner's Rebellion a few months after *The Liberator* made its appearance. Yet not only was Garrison completely unknown to Turner, but nearly all abolitionists, despite their militant language, rejected violence as a means of ending slavery. Many were pacifists or "non-resistants," who believed that coercion should be eliminated from all human relationships and institutions. Their strategy was **moral suasion** and their arena the public sphere. Slaveholders must be convinced of the sinfulness of their ways, and the North of its complicity in the peculiar institution.

Standing outside established institutions, abolitionists adopted the role of radical social critics. Among the first to appreciate the key role of public opinion in a mass democracy, they focused their efforts not on infiltrating the existing political parties, but on awakening the nation to the moral evil of slavery. Their language was deliberately provocative, calculated to seize public attention. "Slavery," said Garrison, "will not be overthrown without excitement, without a most tremendous excitement."

Social critics

Abolitionists and the Idea of Freedom

The abolitionist crusade both reinforced and challenged common understandings of freedom in Jacksonian America. Abolitionists helped to popularize the concept, fortified by the market revolution, that personal freedom derived not from the ownership of productive property such as land but from ownership of one's self and the ability to enjoy the fruits of one's labor. Abolitionists repudiated the idea of "wage slavery," which had been popularized by the era's labor movement and by southern defenders of slavery. Compared with the slave, the person working for wages, they insisted, was an embodiment of freedom: the free laborer could change jobs if he wished, accumulate property, and enjoy a stable family life. Only slavery, wrote the abolitionist William Goodell, deprived human beings of their "grand central right—the inherent right of self-ownership."

Slave Market of America, an engraving produced by the American Anti-Slavery Society in 1836, illustrates how abolitionists sought to identify their cause with American traditions, even as they mocked the nation's claim to be a "land of the free."

A rare photograph of an abolitionist meeting in New York State around 1850. Frederick Douglass is at the left of the woman at the center.

On the other hand, abolitionists argued that slavery was so deeply embedded in American life that its destruction would require fundamental changes in the North as well as the South. They insisted that the inherent, natural, and absolute right to personal liberty, regardless of race, took precedence over other forms of freedom, such as the right of citizens to accumulate and hold property or self-government by local political communities.

A New Vision of America

In a society in which the rights of citizenship had become more and more closely associated with whiteness, the antislavery movement sought to reinvigorate the idea of freedom as a truly universal entitlement. The origin of the idea of an American people unbounded by race lie not with the founders, who by and large made their peace with slavery, but with the abolitionists. The antislavery crusade viewed slaves and free blacks as members of the national community, a position summarized in the title of Lydia Maria Child's popular treatise of 1833, *An Appeal in Favor of That Class of Americans Called Africans*. Child's text insisted that blacks were fellow countrymen, not foreigners or a permanently inferior caste. They should no more be considered Africans than whites were Englishmen. The idea that birthplace alone, not race, should determine who was an American, later enshrined in the Fourteenth Amendment, represented a radical departure from the traditions of American life. Abolitionists also pioneered the modern idea that human rights took precedence over national sovereignty. They urged the United States to participate in the courts that brought together judges

Antislavery Picnic at Weymouth Landing, Massachusetts, a watercolor from 1845, depicts dozens of men, women, and children at an abolitionist gathering. Unlike most social events of the time, it includes both black and white participants. The artist, Susan Torrey Merritt, painted the tiny figures separately and then cut them out and pasted them on the paper. The red flag at the upper left proclaims Liberty, possibly an allusion to the antislavery Liberty Party.

from Britain and other countries to punish those who violated the ban on the Atlantic slave trade. These courts were perhaps the first example of transnational human rights enforcement. But with southerners exerting powerful influence in Washington, the United States did not join the court system until 1862, in the midst of the Civil War.

The crusade against slavery, wrote Angelina Grimké, who became a leading abolitionist speaker, was the nation's preeminent "school in which human rights are . . . investigated." Abolitionists debated the Constitution's relationship to slavery. William Lloyd Garrison burned the document, calling it a covenant with the devil; Frederick Douglass came to believe that it offered no national protection to slavery. But despite this difference of opinion, abolitionists developed an alternative, rights-oriented view of constitutional law, grounded in their universalistic understanding of liberty. Seeking to define the core rights to which all Americans were entitled—the meaning of freedom in concrete legal terms—abolitionists invented the concept of equality before the law regardless of race, one all but unknown in American life before the Civil War. Abolitionist literature also helped to expand the definition of cruelty. The graphic descriptions of the beatings, brandings, and other physical sufferings of the slaves helped to popularize the idea of bodily integrity as a basic right that slavery violated.

Despite being denounced by their opponents as enemies of American principles, abolitionists consciously identified their movement with the revolutionary heritage. The Declaration of Independence was not as fundamental to public oratory in the early republic as it would later become. Abolitionists seized upon it, interpreting the document's preamble as a condemnation of slavery. The Liberty Bell, later one of the nation's most venerated emblems of freedom, did not achieve that status until abolitionists adopted it as a symbol and gave it its name, as part of an effort to identify their principles with those of the founders. (Prior to the 1830s, it was simply the Old State House Bell, used at various times to mark the death of prominent citizens, summon students at the University of Pennsylvania to their classes, and celebrate patriotic holidays.) Of course, Americans of all regions and political beliefs claimed the Revolution's legacy. Mobs that disrupted abolitionist meetings invoked the "spirit of '76," as did southern defenders of slavery. Abolitionists never represented more than a small part of the North's population. But as the slavery controversy intensified, the belief spread far beyond abolitionist circles that slavery contradicted the nation's heritage of freedom.

BLACK AND WHITE ABOLITIONISM

Black Abolitionists

Blacks played a leading role in the antislavery movement. Even before the appearance of *The Liberator*, as we have seen, northern free blacks had organized in opposition to the Colonization Society. James Forten, a successful black sailmaker in Philadelphia, helped to finance *The Liberator* in its early years. As late as 1834,

One of many popular lithographs illustrating scenes from Harriet Beecher Stowe's novel *Uncle Tom's Cabin*, the most widely read of all antislavery writings. This depicts the slave Eliza escaping with her child across the ice floes of the Ohio River.

Harriet Beecher Stowe, author of the abolitionist novel *Uncle Tom's Cabin*.

An illustration from *Types of Mankind*, an 1854 book by the physicians and racial theorists Josiah C. Nott and George R. Gliddon, who argued that blacks formed a separate species, midway between whites and chimpanzees. Abolitionists sought to counter the pseudoscientific defenses of slavery and racism.

"Am I Not a Man and a Brother?"

northern blacks, attracted by Garrison's rejection of colonization and his demand for equal rights for black Americans, made up a majority of the journal's subscribers. Several blacks served on the board of directors of the American Anti-Slavery Society, and northern-born blacks and fugitive slaves quickly emerged as major organizers and speakers.

Frederick Douglass was only one among many former slaves who published accounts of their lives in bondage; these works convinced thousands of northerners of the evils of slavery. Indeed, the most effective piece of antislavery literature of the entire period, Harriet Beecher Stowe's novel ***Uncle Tom's Cabin***, was to some extent modeled on the autobiography of fugitive slave Josiah Henson. Serialized in 1851 in a Washington antislavery newspaper and published as a book the following year, *Uncle Tom's Cabin* sold more than 1 million copies by 1854, and it also inspired numerous stage versions. By portraying slaves as sympathetic men and women, and as Christians at the mercy of slaveholders who split up families and set bloodhounds on innocent mothers and children, Stowe's melodrama gave the abolitionist message a powerful human appeal.

Abolitionism and Race

The first racially integrated social movement in American history and the first to give equal rights for blacks a central place in its political agenda, abolitionism was nonetheless a product of its time and place. Racism, as we have seen, was pervasive in nineteenth-century America, North as well as South. White abolitionists could not free themselves entirely from this prejudice. They monopolized the key decision-making posts, charged black spokesman Martin R. Delany, relegating blacks to "a mere secondary, underling position." By the 1840s, black abolitionists sought an independent role within the movement, regularly holding their own conventions. The black abolitionist Henry Highland Garnet, who as a child had escaped from slavery in Maryland with his father, proclaimed at one such gathering in 1843 that slaves should rise in rebellion to throw off their shackles. His position was so at odds with the prevailing belief in moral suasion that the published proceedings entirely omitted the speech. Not until 1848 did Garnet's speech appear in print, along with David Walker's *Appeal*, in a pamphlet partially financed by a then-obscure abolitionist named John Brown.

What is remarkable, however, is not that white abolitionists reflected the prejudices of their society, but the extent to which they managed to rise above them. Defying overwhelming odds, abolitionists launched legal and political battles against racial discrimination in the North. They achieved occasional victories, such as the end of school segregation in Massachusetts in 1855. The abolitionist emblem—a portrait of a slave in chains coupled with the motto "Am I Not a Man and a Brother?"—challenged white Americans to face up to the reality that men and women no different from themselves were being held in bondage.

Most adamant in contending that the struggle against slavery required a redefinition of both freedom and Americanness were black members of the abolitionist crusade. Black abolitionists developed an understanding of freedom that went well beyond the usage of most of their white contemporaries. They worked to attack the intellectual foundations of racism, seeking to disprove pseudoscientific arguments for black inferiority. They challenged the prevailing image of Africa as a continent without civilization. Many black abolitionists called on free blacks to seek out skilled and dignified employment in order to demonstrate the race's capacity for advancement.

Slavery and American Freedom

At every opportunity, black abolitionists rejected the nation's pretensions as a land of liberty. Many free blacks dramatically reversed the common association of the United States with the progress of freedom. Black communities in the North devised an alternative calendar of "freedom celebrations" centered on January 1, the date in 1808 on which the slave trade became illegal, and August 1, the anniversary of West Indian emancipation, rather than July 4. (Many localities forcibly barred them from Independence Day festivities.) Thanks to its embrace of emancipation in the 1830s, declared a group of black abolitionists in Philadelphia, Britain had become a model of liberty and justice, while the United States remained a land of tyranny.

A photograph of Frederick Douglass, the fugitive slave who became a prominent abolitionist, taken between 1847 and 1852. As a fellow abolitionist noted at the time, "The very look and bearing of Douglass are an irresistible logic against the oppression of his race."

"The real battleground between liberty and slavery," wrote Samuel Cornish, "is prejudice against color." (Cornish, a Presbyterian minister, had helped to establish the nation's first black newspaper, *Freedom's Journal*, in New York City in 1827. The first editor, John B. Russwurm, closed the paper after two years and moved to Liberia, explaining, "we consider it a waste of mere words to talk of ever enjoying citizenship in this country.") Black abolitionists also identified the widespread poverty of the free black population as a consequence of slavery and insisted that freedom possessed an economic dimension. It must be part of the "great work" of the antislavery crusade, insisted Charles L. Reason, "to abolish not only chattel slavery, but that other kind of slavery, which, for generation after generation, dooms an oppressed people to a condition of dependence and pauperism."

Am I Not a Man and a Brother? The most common abolitionist depiction of a slave, this image not only presents African-Americans as unthreatening individuals seeking white assistance but also calls upon white Americans to recognize blacks as fellow men unjustly held in bondage.

The greatest oration on American slavery and American freedom was delivered in Rochester in 1852 by Frederick Douglass. Speaking just after the annual Independence Day celebration, Douglass posed the question, "What, to the Slave, is the Fourth of July?" (see the Appendix for excerpts from the speech). He answered that Fourth of July festivities revealed the hypocrisy of a nation that proclaimed its belief in liberty yet daily committed "practices more shocking and bloody" than any other country on earth. Like other abolitionists, however, Douglass also laid claim to the founders' legacy. The Revolution had left a "rich inheritance of justice, liberty, prosperity, and independence," from which subsequent generations had tragically strayed. Only by abolishing slavery and freeing the "great doctrines" of the Declaration of Independence from the "narrow bounds" of race could the United States recapture its original mission.

A broadside calling on "fellow citizens" to disrupt an 1837 lecture by "an abolitionist of the most revolting character."

Elijah P. Lovejoy

Gentlemen of Property and Standing

At first, abolitionism aroused violent hostility from northerners who feared that the movement threatened to disrupt the Union, interfere with profits wrested from slave labor, and overturn white supremacy. Led by **"gentlemen of property and standing"** (often merchants with close commercial ties to the South), mobs disrupted abolitionist meetings in northern cities. In 1835, a Boston crowd led William Lloyd Garrison through the streets with a rope around his neck. The editor barely escaped with his life. In the following year, a Cincinnati mob destroyed the printing press of James G. Birney, a former slaveholder who had been converted to abolitionism by Theodore Weld and had been forced to flee Kentucky for the North.

In 1837, antislavery editor Elijah P. Lovejoy became the movement's first martyr when he was killed by a mob in Alton, Illinois, while defending his press. A native of Maine and a Presbyterian minister, Lovejoy had begun his editorial career in the slave state of Missouri but had soon been forced to move to Illinois. His message, that "the system of Negro slavery is an awful evil and sin," won few converts in Alton, then the state's largest city, which enjoyed a flourishing trade with the South. Four times, mobs destroyed his printing press, only to see Lovejoy resume publication. The fifth attack ended in his death. In 1838, a mob in Philadelphia burned to the ground Pennsylvania Hall, which abolitionists had built to hold their meetings. Before starting the fire, however, the mob patriotically carried a portrait of George Washington to safety.

Elsewhere, crowds of southerners, with the unspoken approval of Andrew Jackson's postmaster general, Amos Kendall, burned abolitionist literature that they had removed from the mails. In 1836, when abolitionists began to flood Washington with petitions calling for emancipation in the nation's capital, the

"Immediate Emancipation Illustrated," an anti-abolitionist cartoon from 1833. Members of an antislavery society prepare to write a pamphlet calling for immediate abolition. The statue of the leopard is meant to remind viewers of the biblical phrase, "Can the Ethiopian change his skin, or the leopard his spots?"—that is, that blacks' condition is fixed by nature. On the left is a reminder of the Haitian revolution, with slaves massacring a white family. The emancipated slave has only one interest—food.

Destruction by Fire of Pennsylvania Hall, a lithograph depicting the burning of the abolitionist meeting hall by a Philadelphia mob in 1838.

House of Representatives adopted the notorious **gag rule**, which prohibited their consideration. The rule was repealed in 1844, thanks largely to the tireless opposition of former president John Quincy Adams, who from 1831 represented Massachusetts in the House.

The "gag rule"

Slavery and Civil Liberties

Far from stemming the movement's growth, however, mob attacks and attempts to limit abolitionists' freedom of speech convinced many northerners that slavery was incompatible with the democratic liberties of white Americans. In a speech after Lovejoy's murder, Theodore Weld commented on the contrast between Americans' self-confident claims to freedom and the reality of anti-abolitionist violence: "The empty name is everywhere—*free* government, *free* men, *free* speech, *free* schools, and *free* churches. Hollow counterfeits all! . . . The substance has gone." It was the murder of Lovejoy that led Wendell Phillips, who became one of the movement's greatest orators, to associate himself with the abolitionist cause. "We commenced the present struggle," announced abolitionist William Jay, "to obtain the freedom of the slave; we are compelled to continue it to preserve our own. We are now contending . . . for the liberty of speech, of the press, and of conscience."

Abolitionism and free speech

The abolitionist movement now broadened its appeal so as to win the support of northerners who cared little about the rights of blacks but could be convinced that slavery endangered their own cherished freedoms. The gag rule aroused considerable resentment in the North. "If the government once begins to discriminate as to what is orthodox and what heterodox in opinion," wrote the *New York Evening Post*, hardly a supporter of abolitionism, "farewell, a long farewell to our freedom."

For many years, the American public sphere excluded discussion of slavery. Tocqueville had noted that in a democracy, individual dissenters found it difficult to stand up against the overwhelming power of majority opinion. Americans valued free speech, he wrote, but he did "not know any country where, in general, less independence of mind and genuine freedom of discussion reign than in America." The fight for the right to debate slavery openly and without reprisal led abolitionists to elevate "free opinion"—freedom of speech and of the press and the right of petition—to a central place in what Garrison called the "gospel of freedom." In defending free speech, abolitionists claimed to have become custodians of the "rights of every freeman."

"Free opinion"

THE ORIGINS OF FEMINISM

The Rise of the Public Woman

"When the true history of the antislavery cause shall be written," Frederick Douglass later recalled, "women will occupy a large space in its pages." Much of the movement's grassroots strength derived from northern women, who joined by the thousands. Most were evangelical Protestants, New England Congregationalists, or Quakers convinced, as Martha Higginson of Vermont wrote, that slavery was "a disgrace in this land of Christian light and liberty." A few became famous, but most antislavery women remain virtually unknown to history. One such activist was Lucy Colman, whose mother sang her antislavery songs when she was a child. Colman's career illustrated how the era's reform movements often overlapped. She became an abolitionist lecturer, a teacher at a school for blacks in upstate New York, an advocate of women's rights, and an opponent of capital punishment.

Women abolitionists

The public sphere was open to women in ways government and party politics were not. Women's letters and diaries reveal a keen interest in political issues, from slavery to presidential campaigns. Long before they could vote, women circulated petitions, attended mass meetings, marched in political parades, delivered public lectures, and raised money for political causes. Women organized a petition campaign against the policy of Indian removal. Although unsuccessful, the experience helped to produce a generation of women who then turned their attention to abolitionism, temperance, and other reforms. Harriet Beecher (later the author of *Uncle Tom's Cabin*) participated in the movement against Indian removal—of which her sister, Catharine, was a major organizer. **Dorothea Dix**, a Massachusetts schoolteacher, was the leading advocate of more humane treatment of the insane, who at the time generally were placed in jails alongside debtors and hardened criminals. Thanks to her efforts, twenty-eight states constructed mental hospitals before the Civil War. In 1834, middle-class women in New York City organized the Female Moral Reform Society, which sought to redeem prostitutes from lives of sin and to protect the morality of single women. They attacked the era's sexual double standard by publishing lists of men who frequented prostitutes

Petition against Indian removal

or abused women. By 1840, the society had been replicated in hundreds of American communities.

Women and Free Speech

All these activities enabled women to carve out a place in the public sphere. But it was participation in abolitionism that inspired the early movement for women's rights. In working for the rights of the slave, not a few women developed a new understanding of their own subordinate social and legal status. The daughters of a prominent South Carolina slaveholder, Angelina and Sarah Grimké had been converted first to Quakerism and then to abolitionism while visiting Philadelphia. During the 1830s, they began to deliver popular lectures that offered a scathing condemnation of slavery from the perspective of those who had witnessed its evils firsthand.

Abolitionism and women's rights

The Grimké sisters were neither the first women to lecture in public nor the first to be feverishly condemned by self-proclaimed guardians of female modesty. Frances Wright, a Scottish-born follower of reformer Robert Owen, spoke at New York's Hall of Science in the late 1820s and early 1830s, on subjects ranging from communitarianism to slavery, women's rights, and the plight of northern laborers. One New York newspaper called Wright a "female monster" for "shamefully obtruding herself upon the public." Maria Stewart, a black Bostonian, in 1832 became the first American woman to lecture to mixed male and female audiences. She, too, received intense criticism. "I have made myself contemptible in the eyes of many," Stewart wrote. "This is the land of freedom," she added, "and we claim our rights," including the right to speak in public.

Stewart left Boston in 1833 and rarely lectured again. The Grimké sisters, however, used the controversy over their speeches as a springboard for a vigorous argument against the idea that taking part in assemblies, demonstrations, and lectures was unfeminine. Outraged by the sight of females sacrificing all "modesty and delicacy" by appearing on the public lecture platform, a group of Massachusetts clergymen denounced the sisters. In reply, they forthrightly defended not only the right of women to take part in political debate but also their right to share the social and educational privileges enjoyed by men. "Since I engaged in the investigation of the rights of the slave," declared Angelina Grimké, "I have necessarily been led to a better understanding of my own." Her sister Sarah proceeded to publish *Letters on the Equality of the Sexes* (1838), a powerful call for equal rights for women and a critique of the notion of separate spheres. The book raised numerous issues familiar even today, including what later generations would call "equal pay for equal work." Why, Sarah Grimké wondered, did male teachers invariably receive higher wages than women, and a male tailor earn "two or three times as much" as a female counterpart "although the work done by each may be equally good?"

The Grimké sisters

Women's Rights

The Grimkés were the first to apply the abolitionist doctrine of universal freedom and equality to the status of women. When the prominent writer Catharine Beecher

The May Session of the Woman's Rights Convention, a cartoon published in *Harper's Weekly*, June 11, 1859. A female orator addresses the audience of men and women, while hecklers in the balcony disrupt the proceedings.

reprimanded the sisters for stepping outside "the domestic and social sphere," urging them to accept the fact that "heaven" had designated man "the superior" and woman "the subordinate," Angelina Grimké issued a stinging answer. "I know nothing," she wrote, "of men's rights and women's rights. My doctrine, then is, that whatever it is morally right for man to do, it is morally right for woman to do." Like their predecessors Frances Wright and Maria Stewart, the Grimké sisters soon retired from the fray, unwilling to endure the intense criticism to which they were subjected. But their writings helped to spark the movement for women's rights, which arose in the 1840s.

Elizabeth Cady Stanton and Lucretia Mott, the key organizers of the Seneca Falls Convention of 1848, were veterans of the antislavery crusade. In 1840, they had traveled to London as delegates to the World Anti-Slavery Convention, only to be barred from participating because of their sex. The Seneca Falls Convention, a gathering on behalf of women's rights held in the upstate New York town where Stanton lived, raised the issue of woman's suffrage for the first time. Stanton, the principal author, modeled the Seneca Falls Declaration of Sentiments on the Declaration of Independence (see the Appendix for the full text). But the document added "women" to Jefferson's axiom "all men are created equal," and in place of a list of injustices committed by George III, it condemned the "injuries and usurpations on the part of man toward woman." The first to be listed was denying her the right to vote. As Stanton told the convention, only the vote would make woman "free as man is free," since in a democratic society, freedom was impossible without access to the ballot. The argument was simple and irrefutable: in the words of Lydia Maria Child, "either the theory of our government [the democratic principle that government rests on the will of the people] is *false*, or women have a right to vote."

Seneca Falls marked the beginning of the seventy-year struggle for **woman suffrage**. The vote, however, was hardly the only issue raised at the convention.

The Seneca Falls Convention

The Declaration of Sentiments condemned the entire structure of inequality that denied women access to education and employment, gave husbands control over the property and wages of their wives and custody of children in the event of divorce, deprived women of independent legal status after they married, and restricted them to the home as their "sphere of action." Equal rights became the rallying cry of the early movement for women's rights, and equal rights meant claiming access to all the prevailing definitions of freedom.

The Declaration of Sentiments

Feminism and Freedom

Like abolitionism, temperance, and other reforms, **feminism** was an international movement. Lacking broad backing at home, early feminists found allies abroad. "Women alone will say what freedom they want," declared an article in *The Free Woman*, a journal established in Paris in 1832. With their household chores diminished because of the availability of manufactured goods and domestic servants, many middle-class women chafed at the restrictions that made it impossible for them to gain an education, enter the professions, and in other ways exercise their talents. Whether married or not, early feminists insisted, women deserved the range of individual choices—the possibility of self-realization—that constituted the essence of freedom.

Margaret Fuller

Women, wrote Margaret Fuller, had the same right as men to develop their talents, to "grow . . . to live freely and unimpeded." The daughter of a Jeffersonian congressman, Fuller was educated at home, at first under her father's supervision (she learned Latin before the age of six) and later on her own. She became part of New England's transcendentalist circle (discussed in Chapter 9) and from 1840 to 1842 edited *The Dial*, a magazine that reflected the group's views. In 1844, Fuller became literary editor of the *New York Tribune*, the first woman to achieve so important a position in American journalism.

In *Woman in the Nineteenth Century*, published in 1845, Fuller sought to apply to women the transcendentalist idea that freedom meant a quest for personal development. "Every path" to self-fulfillment, she insisted, should be "open to woman as freely as to man." Fuller singled out Abby Kelley as a "gentle hero" for continuing to speak in public despite being denounced by men for venturing "out of her sphere." Fearing that marriage to an American would inevitably mean subordination to male dictation, Fuller traveled to Europe as a correspondent for the *Tribune*. There she married an Italian patriot. Along with her husband and baby, she died in a shipwreck in 1850 while returning to the United States.

An undated engraving of feminist writer Margaret Fuller (1810–1850).

Women and Work

Women also demanded the right to participate in the market revolution. At an 1851 women's rights convention, the black abolitionist Sojourner Truth insisted that the movement devote attention to the plight of poor and working-class women and repudiate the idea that

VOICES OF FREEDOM

From ANGELINA GRIMKÉ, LETTER IN *THE LIBERATOR* (AUGUST 2, 1837)

The daughters of a prominent South Carolina slaveholder, Angelina and Sarah Grimké became abolitionists after being sent to Philadelphia for education. In this article, Angelina Grimké explains how participation in the movement against slavery led her to a greater recognition of women's lack of basic freedoms.

———————————

Since I engaged in the investigation of the rights of the slave, I have necessarily been led to a better understanding of my own; for I have found the Anti-Slavery cause to be . . . the school in which human rights are more fully investigated, and better understood and taught, than in any other [reform] enterprise. . . . Here we are led to examine why human beings have any rights. It is because they are moral beings. . . . Now it naturally occurred to me, that if rights were founded in moral being, then the circumstance of sex could not give to man higher rights and responsibilities, than to woman. . . .

When I look at human beings as moral beings, all distinction in sex sinks to insignificance and nothingness; for I believe it regulates rights and responsibilities no more than the color of the skin or the eyes. My doctrine, then is, that whatever it is morally right for man to do, it is morally right for woman to do. . . . This regulation of duty by the mere circumstance of sex . . . has led to all that [numerous] train of evils flowing out of the anti-christian doctrine of masculine and feminine virtues. By this doctrine, man has been converted into the warrior, and clothed in sternness . . . whilst woman has been taught to lean upon an arm of flesh, to . . . be admired for her personal charms, and caressed and humored like a spoiled child, or converted into a mere drudge to suit the convenience of her lord and master. . . . It has robbed woman of . . . the right to think and speak and act on all great moral questions, just as men think and speak and act. . . .

The discussion of the wrongs of slavery has opened the way for the discussion of other rights, and the ultimate result will most certainly be . . . the letting of the oppressed of every grade and description go free.

From CATHARINE BEECHER, *AN ESSAY ON SLAVERY AND ABOLITIONISM* (1837)

Most men, and many women, did not approve of women taking part in public debate. The writer Catharine Beecher responded to the activities of the Grimké sisters by urging them to accept that "heaven" had designated man "the superior" and woman "the subordinate."

I have ... been informed, that you contemplate a tour, during the ensuing year, for the purpose of exerting your influence to form Abolition Societies among ladies of the non-slave-holding States. . . . The object I have in view, is to present some reasons why it seems unwise and inexpedient for ladies of the non-slave-holding States to unite themselves in Abolition Societies; and thus, at the same time, to exhibit the inexpediency of the course you propose to adopt. . . .

Heaven has appointed to one sex the superior, and to the other the subordinate station, and this without any reference to the character or conduct of either. It is therefore as much for the dignity as it is for the interest of females, in all respects to conform to the duties of this relation. . . . But while woman holds a subordinate relation in society to the other sex, it is not because it was designed that her duties or her influence should be any the less important, or all-pervading. But it was designed that the mode of gaining influence and of exercising power should be altogether different and peculiar. . . . Woman is to win every thing by peace and love; by making herself so much respected, esteemed and loved, that to yield to her opinions and to gratify her wishes, will be the free-will offering of the heart. But this is to be all accomplished in the domestic and social circle. . . . The moment woman begins to feel the promptings of ambition, or the thirst for power, her ægis of defence is gone. All the sacred protection of religion, all the generous promptings of chivalry, all the poetry of romantic gallantry, depend upon woman's retaining her place as dependent and defenceless, and making no claims, and maintaining no right but what are the gifts of honour, rectitude and love.

A woman may seek the aid of cooperation and combination among her own sex, to assist her in her appropriate offices of piety, charity, maternal and domestic duty; but whatever, in any measure, throws a woman into the attitude of a combatant, either for herself or others—whatever binds her in a party conflict—whatever obliges her in any way to exert coercive influences, throws her out of her appropriate sphere. . . . In this country, petitions to congress, in reference to the official duties of legislators, seem, IN ALL CASES, to fall entirely without the sphere of female duty. Men are the proper persons to make appeals to the rulers whom they appoint, and if their female friends, by arguments and persuasions, can induce them to petition, all the good that can be done by such measures will be secured.

QUESTIONS

1. *What consequences does Grimké believe follow from the idea of rights being founded in the individual's "moral being"?*

2. *How does Beecher believe women should exert power within American society?*

3. *How do the two definitions of women's freedom differ from one another?*

women were too delicate to engage in work outside the home. Born a slave in New York State around 1799, Truth did not obtain her freedom until slavery finally ended in the state in 1827. A listener at her 1851 speech (which was not recorded at the time) later recalled that Truth had spoken of her years of hard physical labor, flexed her arm to show her strength, and exclaimed, "and aren't I a woman?"

Although those who convened at Seneca Falls were predominantly from the middle class—no representatives of the growing number of "factory girls" and domestic servants took part—the participants rejected the identification of the home as a woman's "sphere." Women, wrote Pauline Davis in 1853, "must go *to work*" to emancipate themselves from "bondage." During the 1850s, some feminists tried to popularize a new style of dress, devised by Amelia Bloomer, consisting of a loose-fitting tunic and trousers. In her autobiography, published in 1898, Elizabeth Cady Stanton recalled that women who adopted Bloomer's attire were ridiculed by the press and insulted by "crowds of boys in the streets." They found that "the physical freedom enjoyed did not compensate for the persistent persecution and petty annoyances suffered at every turn." The target of innumerable male jokes, the "bloomer" costume attempted to make a serious point—that the long dresses, tight corsets, and numerous petticoats considered to be appropriate female attire were so confining that they made it almost impossible for women to claim a place in the public sphere or to work outside the home.

In one sense, feminism demanded an expansion of the boundaries of freedom rather than a redefinition of the idea. Women, in the words of one reformer, should enjoy "the rights and liberties that every 'free white male citizen' takes to himself as God-given." But even as it sought to apply prevailing notions of freedom to women, the movement posed a fundamental challenge to some of society's central beliefs—that the capacity for independence and rationality were male traits, that the world was properly divided into public and private realms, and that issues of

Woman's Emancipation, a satirical engraving from *Harper's Monthly*, August 1851, illustrating the much-ridiculed "bloomer" costume.

justice and freedom did not apply to relations within the family. In every realm of life, including the inner workings of the family, declared Elizabeth Cady Stanton, there could be "no happiness without freedom."

The Slavery of Sex

The dichotomy between freedom and slavery powerfully shaped early feminists' political language. Just as the idea of "wage slavery" enabled northern workers to challenge the inequalities of the market revolution, the concept of the "slavery of sex" empowered the women's movement to develop an all-encompassing critique of male authority and their own subordination. Feminists of the 1840s and 1850s pointed out that the law of marriage made nonsense of the description of the family as a "private" institution independent of public authority. When the abolitionists and women's rights activitists Lucy Stone and Henry Blackwell married, they felt obliged to repudiate New York's laws that clothed the husband "with legal powers which . . . no man should possess."

Feminist abolitionists did not invent the analogy between marriage and slavery. The English writer Mary Wollstonecraft had invoked it as early as the 1790s in *A Vindication of the Rights of Woman* (discussed in Chapter 8). But the analogy between free women and slaves gained prominence as it was swept up in the accelerating debate over slavery. "Woman is a slave, from the cradle to the grave," asserted Ernestine Rose. "Father, guardian, husband—master still. One conveys her, like a piece of property, over to the other." For their part, southern defenders of slavery frequently linked slavery and marriage as natural and just forms of inequality. Eliminating the former institution, they charged, would threaten the latter.

Marriage was not, literally speaking, equivalent to slavery. The married woman, however, did not enjoy the fruits of her own labor—a central element of freedom. Beginning with Mississippi in 1839, numerous states enacted married women's property laws, shielding from a husband's creditors property brought into a marriage by his wife. Such laws initially aimed not to expand women's rights as much as to prevent families from losing their property during the depression that began in 1837. But in 1860, New York enacted a more far-reaching measure, allowing married women to sign contracts, buy and sell property, and keep their own wages. In most states, however, property accumulated after marriage, as well as wages earned by the wife, still belonged to the husband.

"Social Freedom"

Influenced by abolitionism, women's rights advocates turned another popular understanding of freedom—self-ownership, or control over one's own person—in an entirely new direction. The emphasis in abolitionist literature on the violation of the slave woman's body by her master helped to give the idea of self-ownership a concrete reality that encouraged application to free women as well. The law of domestic relations presupposed the husband's right of sexual access to his wife and to inflict corporal punishment on her. Courts proved reluctant to intervene in cases of physical abuse so long as it was not "extreme" or "intolerable." "Women's Rights," declared a Boston meeting in 1859, included "freedom and equal rights in

Am I Not a Woman and a Sister?, an illustration from *The Liberator*, 1849. Identifying with the plight of the female slave enabled free women to see more clearly the inequalities they themselves faced.

Marriage and slavery

Self-ownership

the family." The demand that women should enjoy the rights to regulate their own sexual activity and procreation and to be protected by the state against violence at the hands of their husbands challenged the notion that claims for justice, freedom, and individual rights should stop at the household's door.

The issue of women's private freedom revealed underlying differences within the movement for women's rights. Belief in equality between the sexes and in the sexes' natural differences coexisted in antebellum feminist thought. Even as they entered the public sphere and thereby challenged some aspects of the era's "cult of domesticity" (discussed in Chapter 9), many early feminists accepted other elements. Allowing women a greater role in the public sphere, many female reformers argued, would bring their "inborn" maternal instincts to bear on public life, to the benefit of the entire society.

Women's private freedom

Even feminists critical of the existing institution of marriage generally refrained from raising in public the explosive issue of women's "private" freedom. The question frequently arose, however, in the correspondence of feminist leaders. "Social Freedom," Susan B. Anthony observed to Lucy Stone, "lies at the bottom of all—and until woman gets that, she must continue the slave of men in all other things." Women like Anthony, who never married, and Stone, who with her husband created their own definition of marriage, reflected the same dissatisfactions with traditional family life as the women who joined communitarian experiments. Not until the twentieth century would the demand that freedom be extended to intimate aspects of life inspire a mass movement. But the dramatic fall in the birthrate over the course of the nineteenth century suggests that many women were quietly exercising "personal freedom" in their most intimate relationships.

The Abolitionist Schism

The role of women in abolitionism

Even in reform circles, the demand for a greater public role for women remained extremely controversial. Massachusetts physician Samuel Gridley Howe pioneered humane treatment of the blind and educational reform, and he was an ardent abolitionist. But Howe did not support his wife's participation in the movement for female suffrage, which, he complained, caused her to "neglect domestic relations." When organized abolitionism split into two wings in 1840, the immediate cause was a dispute over the proper role of women in antislavery work. Abby Kelley's election to the business committee of the American Anti-Slavery Society sparked the formation of a rival abolitionist organization, the American and Foreign Anti-Slavery Society, which believed it wrong for a woman to occupy so prominent a position. The antislavery poet John Greenleaf Whittier compared Kelley to Eve, Delilah, and Helen of Troy, women who had sown the seeds of male destruction.

Behind the split lay the fear among some abolitionists that Garrison's radicalism on issues like women's rights, as well as his refusal to support the idea of abolitionists voting or running for public office, impeded the movement's growth. Determined to make abolitionism a political movement, the seceders formed the **Liberty Party**, which nominated James G. Birney as its candidate for president.

He received only 7,000 votes (about one-third of 1 percent of the total). In 1840, antislavery northerners saw little wisdom in "throwing away" their ballots on a third-party candidate.

While the achievement of most of their demands lay far in the future, the women's rights movement succeeded in making "the woman question" a permanent part of the transatlantic discussion of social reform. As for abolitionism, although it remained a significant presence in northern public life until emancipation was achieved, by 1840 the movement had accomplished its most important work. More than 1,000 local antislavery societies were now scattered throughout the North, representing a broad constituency awakened to the moral issue of slavery. The "great duty of freedom," Ralph Waldo Emerson had declared in 1837, was "to open our halls to discussion of this question." The abolitionists' greatest achievement lay in shattering the conspiracy of silence that had sought to preserve national unity by suppressing public debate over slavery.

This image appeared on the cover of the sheet music for "Get Off the Track!," a song popularized by the Hutchinson singers, who performed antislavery songs. The trains *Immediate Emancipation* (with *The Liberator* as its front wheel) and *Liberty Party* pull into a railroad station. *The Herald of Freedom* and *American Standard* were antislavery newspapers. The song's lyrics praised William Lloyd Garrison and criticized various politicians, among them Henry Clay. The chorus went: "Roll it along! Through the nation / Freedom's car, Emancipation."

SUGGESTED READING

BOOKS

- Bestor, Arthur E. *Backwoods Utopias: The Sectarian and Owenite Phases of Communitarian Socialism in America* (1948). An account of some of the numerous communitarian experiments in pre–Civil War America.

- Boylan, Anne M. *The Origins of Women's Activism: New York and Boston, 1797–1840* (2002). Considers how middle-class urban women organized numerous associations for social improvement and thereby gained a place in the public sphere.

- Goodman, Paul. *Of One Blood: Abolitionists and the Origins of Racial Equality* (1998). Explores the origins of racial egalitarianism in the movement against slavery.

- Jeffrey, Julie R. *The Great Silent Army of Abolitionism: Ordinary Women in the Antislavery Movement* (1998). The role of women as the grassroots foot soldiers of the abolitionist movement.

- Jones, Martha S. *All Bound Up Together: The Woman Question in African American Public Culture, 1830–1900* (2007). How African-American leaders and organizations debated the proper social role of women.

- Kaestle, Carl F. *Pillars of the Republic: Common Schools and American Society, 1780–1860* (1983). Surveys the movement to introduce free public education in the United States.

- Kantrowitz, Stephen. *More than Freedom: Fighting for Black Citizenship in a White Republic, 1829–1889* (2012). A study of the black abolitionists of Boston and their struggle for an expansive understanding of freedom.

- Kraditor, Aileen S. *Means and Ends in American Abolitionism* (1969). An influential discussion of the political strategies of Garrisonian abolitionists.

- McGreevy, John T. *Catholicism and American Freedom* (2003). Contains an illuminating discussion of how Catholics responded to Protestant-based reform movements.

- Nye, Russell B. *Fettered Freedom: Civil Liberties and the Slavery Controversy, 1830–1860* (1949). Examines the impact of mob activities and other violations of civil liberties on the growth of abolitionism.

- Sinha, Manisha. *The Slave's Cause: A History of Abolition* (2016). A comprehensive history of the antislavery movement from the colonial era through the Civil War.

- Tyrrell, Ian. *Sobering Up: From Temperance to Prohibition in Antebellum America, 1800–1860* (1979). Traces the movement against the sale and use of liquor and how it changed in the first part of the nineteenth century.

- Zboray, Ronald J. and Mary. *Voices Without Votes: Women and Politics in Antebellum New England* (2010). Shows how women took part in Jacksonian-era politics in ways other than voting.

WEBSITES

- Samuel J. May Anti-Slavery Collection: http://dlxs.library.cornell.edu/m/mayantislavery/

- Women and Social Movements in the United States, 1600–2000: http://asp6new.alexanderstreet.com/wam2/wam2.index.map.aspx

CHAPTER REVIEW AND ONLINE RESOURCES

REVIEW QUESTIONS

1. How did the utopian communities challenge existing ideas about property and marriage?

2. How did the supporters and opponents of temperance understand the meaning of freedom differently?

3. What were the similarities and differences between the common school and institutions like asylums, orphanages, and prisons that were created by reformers?

4. Why did so many prominent white Americans, from both the North and South, support the colonization of freed slaves?

5. How was the abolition movement affected by other social and economic changes such as the rise in literacy, new print technology, and ideas associated with the market revolution?

6. How was racism evident even in the abolitionist movement, and what steps did some abolitionists take to fight racism in American society?

7. How could antebellum women participate in the public sphere even though they were excluded from government and politics?

8. How did white women's participation in the abolitionist movement push them to a new understanding of their own rights and oppression?

9. How did advocates for women's rights in these years both accept and challenge existing gender beliefs and social roles?

10. To what degree was antebellum reform international in scope?

KEY TERMS

utopian communities (p. 426)

Shakers (p. 426)

Oneida (p. 427)

Brook Farm (p. 429)

communitarianism (p. 429)

New Harmony (p. 429)

perfectionism (p. 431)

temperance movement (p. 431)

common school (p. 433)

American Colonization Society (p. 435)

American Anti-Slavery Society (p. 437)

moral suasion (p. 439)

Uncle Tom's Cabin (p. 442)

"gentlemen of property and standing" (p. 444)

gag rule (p. 445)

Dorothea Dix (p. 446)

woman suffrage (p. 448)

feminism (p. 449)

Liberty Party (p. 454)

Go to INQUIZITIVE

To see what you know—and learn what you've missed—with personalized feedback along the way.

Visit the *Give Me Liberty!* **Student Site** for primary source documents and images, interactive maps, author videos featuring Eric Foner, and more.

CHAPTER 13

A HOUSE DIVIDED

★

1840–1861

In 1855, Thomas Crawford, one of the era's most prominent American sculptors, was asked to design a statue to adorn the Capitol's dome, still under construction in Washington, D.C. He proposed a statue of Freedom, a female figure wearing a liberty cap. Secretary of War Jefferson Davis of Mississippi, one of the country's largest slaveholders, objected to Crawford's plan. A familiar symbol in the colonial era, the liberty cap had fallen into disfavor among some Americans after becoming closely identified with the French Revolution. Davis's disapproval, however, rested on other grounds. Ancient Romans, he noted, regarded the cap as "the badge of the freed slave." Its use, he feared, might suggest that there was a connection between the slaves' longing for freedom and the liberty of freeborn Americans. Davis ordered the liberty cap replaced with a less controversial military symbol, a feathered helmet.

Crawford died in Italy, where he had spent most of his career, in 1857. Two years later, the colossal Statue of Freedom, which weighed 15,000 pounds, was transported to the United States in several pieces and assembled at a Maryland foundry under the direction of Philip Reed, a slave craftsman. In 1863, it was installed atop the Capitol, where it can still be seen today. By the time it was put in place, the country was immersed in the Civil War and Jefferson Davis had become president of the Confederate States of America. The dispute over the Statue of Freedom offers a small illustration of how, by the mid-1850s, nearly every public question was being swept up into the gathering storm over slavery.

FRUITS OF MANIFEST DESTINY

Continental Expansion

In the 1840s, slavery moved to the center stage of American politics. It did so not in the moral language or with the immediatist program of abolitionism, but as a result of the nation's territorial expansion. By 1840, with the completion of Indian removal, virtually all the land east of the Mississippi River was in white hands. The depression that began in 1837 sparked a large migration of settlers farther west. Some headed to Oregon, whose Willamette Valley was reputed to be one of the continent's most beautiful and fertile regions. Until the 1840s, the American presence in the area had been limited to a few fur traders and explorers. But between 1840 and 1845, some 5,000 emigrants made the difficult 2,000-mile journey by wagon train to Oregon from jumping-off places on the banks of the Missouri River. By 1860, nearly 300,000 men, women, and children braved disease, starvation, the natural barrier of the Rocky Mountains, and occasional Indian attacks to travel overland to Oregon and California.

During most of the 1840s, the United States and Great Britain jointly administered Oregon, and Utah was part of Mexico. This did not stop Americans from settling in either region. National boundaries meant little to those who moved west. The 1840s witnessed an intensification of the old belief that God intended the American nation to reach all the way to the Pacific Ocean. As noted in Chapter 9, the term that became a shorthand for this expansionist spirit was "manifest destiny."

FOCUS QUESTIONS

What were the major factors contributing to U.S. territorial expansion in the 1840s? *–p. 459*

Why did the expansion of slavery become the most divisive political issue in the 1840s and 1850s? *–p. 472*

What combination of issues and events fueled the creation of the Republican Party in the 1850s? *–p. 480*

What enabled Lincoln to emerge as president from the divisive party politics of the 1850s? *–p. 485*

What were the final steps on the road to secession? *–p. 495*

A lithograph from around 1860 depicts the town of Bridgewater, Massachusetts, home of a major iron works. A railroad speeds along in the foreground, while factory smokestacks dot the horizon. The tidy buildings in the center suggest that industrialization has not upset social harmony. Industrial development in the north widened the gap between the sections.

The original and final designs for Thomas Crawford's *Statue of Freedom* for the dome of the Capitol building. Secretary of War Jefferson Davis of Mississippi insisted that the liberty cap in the first design, a symbol of the emancipated slave in ancient Rome, be replaced.

The Mexican Frontier: New Mexico and California

Settlement of Oregon did not directly raise the issue of slavery. But the nation's acquisition of part of Mexico did. When Mexico achieved its independence from Spain in 1821, it was nearly as large as the United States and its population of 6.5 million was about two-thirds that of its northern neighbor. Mexico's northern provinces—California, New Mexico, and Texas—however, were isolated and sparsely settled outposts surrounded by Indian country. New Mexico's population at the time of Mexican independence consisted of around 30,000 persons of Spanish origin, 10,000 Pueblo Indians, and an indeterminate number of nomadic Indians—bands of Apaches, Comanches, Navajos, and Utes. With the opening in 1821 of the Santa Fe Trail linking that city with Independence, Missouri, the northern periphery of the new Mexican nation was quickly incorporated into the sphere of influence of the rapidly expanding western United States. New Mexico's commerce with the United States eclipsed trade with the rest of Mexico.

California's non-Indian population in 1821, some 3,200 missionaries, soldiers, and settlers, was vastly outnumbered by about 20,000 Indians living and working on land owned by religious missions and by 150,000 members of unsubdued tribes in the interior. In 1834, in the hope of reducing the power of the Catholic Church and attracting Mexican and foreign settlers to California, the Mexican government dissolved the great mission landholdings and emancipated Indians working for the friars. Most of the land ended up in the hands of a new class of Mexican cattle ranchers, the *Californios*, who defined their own identity in large measure against the surrounding Indian population. *Californios* referred to themselves as *gente de razón* (people capable of reason) as opposed to the *indios*, whom they called *gente sin razón* (people without reason). For the "common good," Indians were required to continue to work for the new landholders.

By 1840, California was already linked commercially with the United States. New England ships were trading with the region. California also attracted a small number of American newcomers. In 1846, Alfred Robinson, who had moved from Boston, published *Life in California*. "In this age of annexation," he wondered, "why not extend the 'area of freedom' by the annexation of California?"

Trade with California

The Texas Revolt

The first part of Mexico to be settled by significant numbers of Americans was Texas, whose non-Indian population of Spanish origin (called **Tejanos**) numbered only about 2,000 when Mexico became independent. In order to develop the region, the Spanish government had accepted an offer by Moses Austin, a Connecticut-born farmer, to colonize it with Americans. In 1820, Austin received a large land grant. He died soon afterward and his son Stephen continued the plan, now in independent Mexico, reselling land in smaller plots to American settlers at twelve cents per acre. Although settlers were required to become Mexican citizens, by 1830, the population of American origin had reached around 7,000, considerably exceeding the number of *Tejanos*.

American settlers in Texas

Alarmed that its grip on the area was weakening, the Mexican government in 1830 annulled existing land contracts and barred future emigration from the United States. Led by Stephen Austin, American settlers demanded greater autonomy within Mexico. Part of the area's tiny *Tejano* elite joined them. Mostly ranchers and large farmers, they had welcomed the economic boom that accompanied the settlers and had formed economic alliances with American traders. The issue of slavery further exacerbated matters. Mexico had abolished slavery, but local authorities allowed American settlers to bring slaves with them. When Mexico's ruler, General **Antonio López de Santa Anna**, sent an army in 1835 to

American Progress. This 1872 painting by John Gast, commissioned by the author of a travel guide to the Pacific coast, reflects the ebullient spirit of manifest destiny. A female figure descended from earlier representations of the goddess of liberty wears the star of empire and leads the movement westward while Indians retreat before her. Symbols of civilization abound: the eastern city in the upper right corner, railroads, fenced animals, stagecoaches, and telegraph wires and a "school book" held by the central figure.

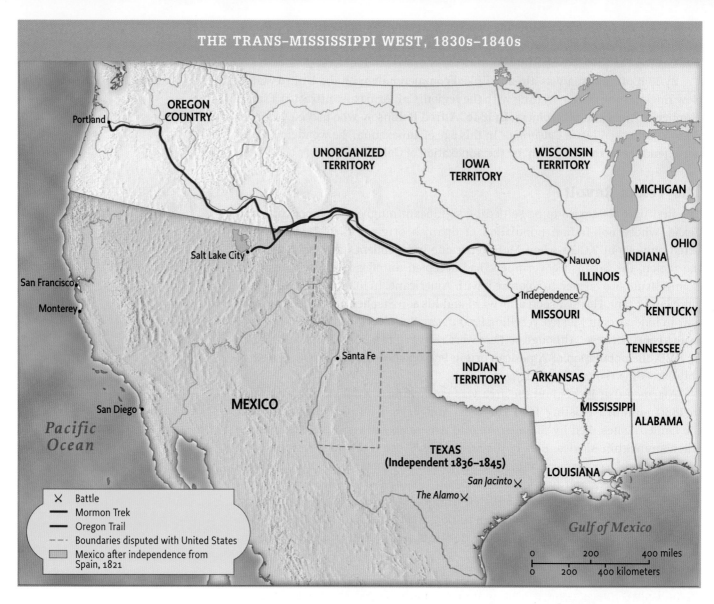

THE TRANS-MISSISSIPPI WEST, 1830s–1840s

Legend:
- ✕ Battle
- Mormon Trek
- Oregon Trail
- Boundaries disputed with United States
- Mexico after independence from Spain, 1821

Westward migration in the early and mid-1840s took American settlers across Indian country into the Oregon Territory, ownership of which was disputed with Great Britain. The Mormons migrated west to Salt Lake City, then part of Mexico.

The Republic of Texas

impose central authority, a local committee charged that his purpose was "to give liberty to our slaves and make slaves of ourselves."

The appearance of Santa Anna's army sparked the chaotic **Texas revolt**. The rebels formed a provisional government that soon called for Texan independence. On March 6, 1836, Santa Anna's army stormed the Alamo, a mission compound in San Antonio, killing its 187 American and *Tejano* defenders. "Remember the Alamo" became the Texans' rallying cry. In April, forces under Sam Houston, a former governor of Tennessee, routed Santa Anna's army at the Battle of San Jacinto and forced him to recognize Texan independence. Houston was soon elected the first president of the Republic of Texas. In 1837, the Texas Congress called for union with the United States. But fearing the political disputes certain to result from an attempt to add another slave state to the Union, President Martin Van Buren shelved the question. Settlers from the United States nonetheless poured into the region, many of them slaveowners taking up fertile cotton land. By 1845, the population of Texas had reached nearly 150,000.

A flag carried at the Battle of San Jacinto during the Texas revolt of 1836 portrays a female figure displaying the rallying cry "Liberty or Death."

The Election of 1844

Texas annexation remained on the political back burner until President John Tyler revived it in the hope of rescuing his failed administration and securing southern support for renomination in 1844. In April 1844, a letter by John C. Calhoun, whom Tyler had appointed secretary of state, was leaked to the press. It linked the idea of absorbing Texas directly to the goal of strengthening slavery in the United States. Some southern leaders, indeed, hoped that Texas could be divided into several states, thus further enhancing the South's power in Congress. Late that month, Henry Clay and former president Van Buren, the prospective Whig and Democratic candidates for president and two of the party system's most venerable leaders, met at Clay's Kentucky plantation. They agreed to issue letters rejecting immediate annexation on the grounds that it might provoke war with Mexico. Clay and Van Buren were reacting to the slavery issue in the traditional manner—by trying to keep it out of national politics.

Texas annexation

   Clay went on to receive the Whig nomination, but for Van Buren the letters proved to be a disaster. At the Democratic convention, southerners bent on annexation deserted Van Buren's cause, and he failed to receive the two-thirds majority necessary for nomination. The delegates then turned to the little-known James K. Polk, a former governor of Tennessee whose main assets were his support for annexation and his close association with Andrew Jackson, still the party's most popular figure. Like nearly all the presidents before him, Polk was a slaveholder. He owned substantial cotton plantations in Tennessee and Mississippi, where

James K. Polk

The plaza in San Antonio not long after the United States annexed Texas in 1845.

conditions were so brutal that only half of the slave children lived to the age of fifteen, and adults frequently ran away. To soothe injured feelings among northern Democrats over the rejection of Van Buren, the party platform called for not only the "reannexation" of Texas (implying that Texas had been part of the Louisiana Purchase and therefore once belonged to the United States) but also the "reoccupation" of all of Oregon. "Fifty-four forty or fight"—American control of Oregon all the way to its northern boundary at north latitude 54°40'—became a popular campaign slogan. But the bitterness of the northern Van Burenites over what they considered to be a betrayal on the part of the South would affect American politics for years to come.

Polk's election

Polk was the first "dark horse" candidate for president—that is, one whose nomination was completely unexpected. In the fall, he defeated Clay in an extremely close election. Polk's margin in the popular vote was less than 2 percent. Had not James G. Birney, running again as the Liberty Party candidate, received 16,000 votes in New York, mostly from antislavery Whigs, Clay would have been elected. In March 1845, only days before Polk's inauguration, Congress declared Texas part of the United States.

The Road to War

James K. Polk may have been virtually unknown, but he assumed the presidency with a clearly defined set of goals: to reduce the tariff, reestablish the independent Treasury system, settle the dispute over ownership of Oregon, and bring California into the Union. Congress soon enacted the first two goals, and the third was accomplished in an agreement with Great Britain dividing Oregon at the forty-ninth parallel. Many northerners were bitterly disappointed by this compromise, considering it a betrayal of Polk's campaign promise not to give up any part of Oregon without a fight. But the president secured his main objectives, the Willamette Valley and the magnificent harbor of Puget Sound.

Acquiring California proved more difficult. Polk dispatched an emissary to Mexico offering to purchase the region, but the Mexican government refused to negotiate. By the spring of 1846, Polk was planning for military action. In April, American soldiers under Zachary Taylor moved into the region between the Nueces River and the Rio Grande, land claimed by both countries on the disputed border between Texas and Mexico. This action made conflict with Mexican forces inevitable. When fighting broke out, Polk claimed that the Mexicans had "shed blood upon American soil" and called for a declaration of war.

The War and Its Critics

The **Mexican War** was the first American conflict to be fought primarily on foreign soil and the first in which American troops occupied a foreign capital. Inspired by the expansionist fervor of manifest destiny, a majority of Americans supported the war. They were convinced, as Herman Melville put it in his novel *White-Jacket* (1850), that since Americans "bear the ark of Liberties" for all mankind, "national selfishness is unbounded philanthropy . . . to the world." But a significant minority in the North dissented, fearing that far from expanding the "great empire of liberty," the administration's real aim was to acquire new land for the expansion of slavery. Ulysses S. Grant, who served with distinction in Mexico, later called the war "one of the most unjust ever waged by a stronger nation against a weaker nation." Henry David Thoreau was jailed in Massachusetts in 1846 for refusing to pay taxes as a protest against the war. Defending his action, Thoreau wrote an important essay, "On Civil Disobedience," which inspired such later advocates of nonviolent resistance to unjust laws as Martin Luther King Jr. "Under a government which imprisons unjustly," wrote Thoreau, "the true place of a just man is also a prison."

Among the war's critics was Abraham Lincoln, who had been elected to Congress in 1846 from Illinois. Like many Whigs, Lincoln questioned whether the Mexicans had actually inflicted casualties on American soil, as Polk claimed, and in 1847 he introduced a resolution asking the president to specify the precise "spot" where blood had first been shed. But Lincoln was also disturbed by Polk's claiming the right to initiate an invasion of Mexico. "Allow the president to invade a neighboring country whenever he shall deem it necessary to repel an invasion," he declared, "and you allow him to make war at pleasure." Lincoln's stance proved unpopular in Illinois. He had already agreed to serve only one term in Congress, but when Democrats captured his seat in 1848, many blamed the result on Lincoln's criticism of the war. But the concerns he raised regarding the president's power to "make war at pleasure" would continue to echo in the twentieth and twenty-first centuries.

> *Support for the war*

An image from a Mexican magazine depicts a Mexican soldier holding a flag emblazoned with the words "nation" and "liberty" and standing astride the American invader.

Combat in Mexico

More than 60,000 volunteers enlisted and did most of the fighting. Combat took place on three fronts. In June 1846, a band of American insurrectionists proclaimed California freed from Mexican control and named Captain John C. Frémont, head of a small scientific expedition in the West, its ruler. Their aim was California's incorporation into the United States, but for the moment they adopted a flag depicting a large bear as the symbol of the area's independence. A month later, the U.S. Navy sailed into Monterey and San Francisco harbors, raised the American flag, and put an end to the "bear flag republic." At almost the same time, 1,600 American troops under General Stephen W. Kearny occupied Sante Fe without resistance and then set out for southern California, where they helped to put down a Mexican uprising against American rule.

The bulk of the fighting occurred in central Mexico. In February 1847, Taylor defeated Santa Anna's army at the Battle of Buena Vista. When the Mexican government still refused to negotiate, Polk ordered American forces under Winfield Scott to march inland from the port of Veracruz toward Mexico City. Scott's forces routed Mexican defenders and in September occupied the country's capital. In February 1848, the two governments agreed to the Treaty of Guadalupe Hidalgo, which confirmed the annexation of Texas and ceded California and present-day New Mexico, Arizona, Nevada, and Utah to the United States. In exchange, the United States paid Mexico $15 million. The Mexican Cession, as the land annexed from Mexico was called, established the present territorial boundaries on the North American continent except for the **Gadsden Purchase**, a parcel of additional land bought from Mexico in 1853, and Alaska, acquired from Russia in 1867.

The Mexican War is only a footnote in most Americans' historical memory. Unlike other wars, few public monuments celebrate the conflict. Mexicans, however, regard the war (or "the dismemberment," as it is called in that country) as a central event of their national history and a source of continued resentment over a century and a half after it was fought. As the Mexican negotiators of 1848 complained, it was unprecedented to launch a war because a country refused to sell part of its territory to a neighbor.

With the end of the Mexican War, the United States absorbed half a million square miles of Mexico's territory, one-third of that nation's total area. A region that for centuries had been united was suddenly split in two, dividing families and severing trade routes. An estimated 75,000 to 100,000 Spanish-speaking Mexicans and more than 150,000 Indians inhabited the Mexican Cession. The Treaty of

War News from Mexico, an 1848 painting by Richard C. Woodville, shows how Americans received war news through the popular press.

"The dismemberment"

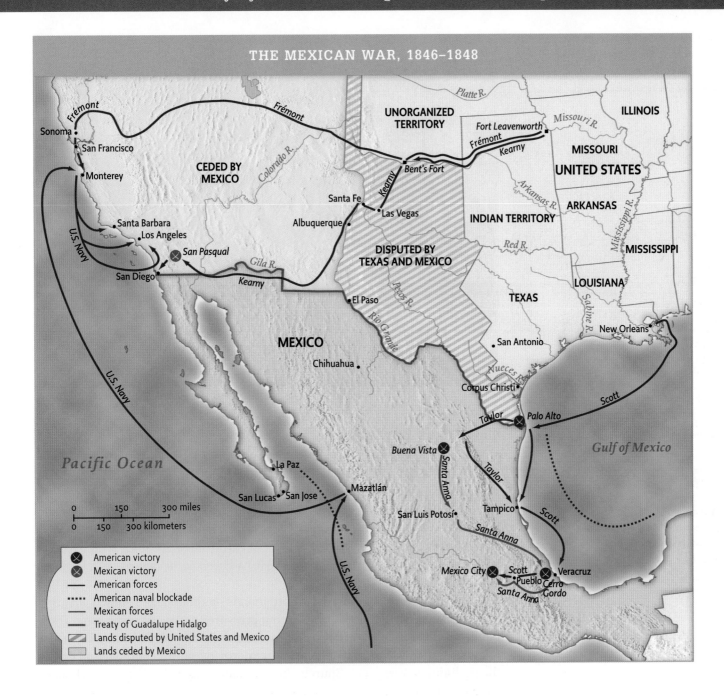

THE MEXICAN WAR, 1846–1848

Pacific Ocean

	American victory
	Mexican victory
	American forces
	American naval blockade
	Mexican forces
	Treaty of Guadalupe Hidalgo
	Lands disputed by United States and Mexico
	Lands ceded by Mexico

Guadalupe Hidalgo guaranteed to "male citizens" of the area "the free enjoyment of their liberty and property" and "all the rights" of Americans—a provision designed to protect the property of large Mexican landowners in California. Thus, in the first half of the nineteenth century, some residents of the area went from being Spaniards to Mexicans to Americans. Although not newcomers, they had to adjust to a new identity as if they were immigrants. As to Indians whose homelands and hunting grounds suddenly became part of the United States, the treaty referred to them only as "savage tribes" whom the United States must prevent from launching incursions into Mexico across the new border.

The Mexican War was the first in which an American army invaded another country and occupied its capital. As a result of the war, the United States acquired a vast new area in the modern-day Southwest.

A scene on a California ranch in 1849, with *Californios* (on horseback) and Native Americans at work.

The Texas Borderland

After achieving independence in 1836, Texas became a prime example of a western borderland. *Anglos* (white settlers from the East) and *Tejanos* had fought together to achieve independence, but soon relations between them soured. *Anglos* in search of land and resources expelled some Mexicans, including former allies, now suspected of loyalty to Mexico. Juan Seguín, a *Tejano*, had played an active role in the revolt and served for a time as mayor of San Antonio. In 1842, still mayor, he was driven from the town by vigilantes. He had become, he lamented, "a foreigner in my native land."

Tensions between Anglos *and* Tejanos

This was a problem inherent to borderlands—as boundaries shifted, longtime residents suddenly became aliens. Facing pressures to Americanize, some *Tejano* families sent their children to English-language schools established by Protestant missionaries from the East. But most refused to convert from Catholicism, despite the declining power of the Church after Texas became part of the United States. Increasingly, *Tejanos* were confined to unskilled agricultural or urban labor. Some *Tejanos* used their ambiguous identities to their own advantage. Women seeking divorces took advantage of new American laws, more liberal than those in Mexico. During the Civil War, some *Tejano* men avoided the Confederate draft by claiming to be citizens of Mexico.

Disputed territory

Meanwhile, in southern Texas, the disputed territory between the Nueces River and the Rio Grande, claimed by both Texas and Mexico but actually controlled by Comanche Indians, became a site of continual conflict. Authority in the area remained contested until Texas became part of the much more powerful United States and even then, Comanche power would not be broken until the 1860s and 1870s.

Race and Manifest Destiny

The spirit of manifest destiny gave a new stridency to ideas about racial superiority. During the 1840s, territorial expansion came to be seen as proof of the innate superiority of the "Anglo-Saxon race" (a mythical construct defined largely by its opposites: blacks, Indians, Hispanics, and Catholics). "*Race*," declared John L. O'Sullivan's *Democratic Review*, was the "key" to the "history of nations."

"Race" in the mid-nineteenth century was an amorphous notion involving color, culture, national origin, class, and religion. Newspapers, magazines, and scholarly works popularized the link between American freedom and the supposedly innate liberty-loving qualities of Anglo-Saxon Protestants. The annexation of Texas and conquest of much of Mexico became triumphs of civilization, progress, and liberty over the tyranny of the Catholic Church and the innate incapacity of "mongrel races." Indeed, calls by some expansionists for the United States to annex all of Mexico failed in part because of fear that the nation could not assimilate its large non-white Catholic population, supposedly unfit for citizenship in a republic.

The imposition of the American system of race relations proved detrimental to many inhabitants of the newly acquired territories. Texas had already demonstrated as much. Mexico had abolished slavery and declared persons of Spanish, Indian, and African origin equal before the law. The Texas Constitution adopted after independence not only included protections for slavery but also denied civil rights to Indians and persons of African origin. Only whites were permitted to purchase land, and the entrance of free blacks into the state was prohibited altogether. "Every privilege dear to a free man is taken away," one free black resident of Texas complained.

Local circumstances affected racial definitions in the former Mexican territories. Texas defined "Spanish" Mexicans, especially those who occupied important social positions, as white. Many New Mexicans, too, emphasized their "Spanish" heritage, hoping to acquire the freedoms that came with statehood. But the residents of New Mexico of both Mexican and Indian origin were long deemed "too Mexican" for democratic self-government. With white migration lagging, Congress did not allow New Mexico to become a state until 1912.

A portrait from 1838 of Juan Seguín. Born in San Antonio, Seguín played an active role in the Texas Revolution, but later was forced by vigilantes to flee the city (where he was serving as mayor) for refuge in Mexico.

Gold-Rush California

California had a non-Indian population of fewer than 15,000 when the Mexican War ended. For most of the 1840s, five times as many Americans emigrated to Oregon as to California. But this changed dramatically after January 1848, when gold was discovered in the foothills of the Sierra Nevada Mountains at a sawmill owned by the Swiss immigrant Johann A. Sutter. A mania for gold spread throughout the world, fanned by newspaper accounts of instant wealth acquired by early migrants. By ship and land, newcomers poured into California, in what came to be called the **gold rush**. The non-Indian population rose to 200,000 by 1852 and more than 360,000 eight years later.

California's gold-rush population was incredibly diverse. Experienced miners flooded in from Mexico and South America. Tens of thousands of Americans who had never seen a mine arrived from the East, and from overseas came Irish, Germans, Italians, and Australians. Nearly 25,000 Chinese landed between 1849 and 1852,

Emigration to California

Painted in 1850 by William S. Jewett, *The Promised Land—The Grayson Family* portrays a family that traveled overland from Missouri to California in 1846, two years before the gold rush. The husband, Andrew J. Grayson, commissioned the painting and gave the artist detailed instructions about the setting and the family's clothing (which is typical of domestic scenes of the period but seems inappropriate for the difficult overland journey). The painting suggests that the West was empty before the arrival of settlers from the East.

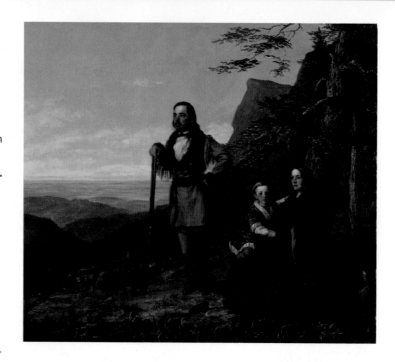

The gold rush brought thousands of fortune seekers, from nearly every corner of the globe, to California.

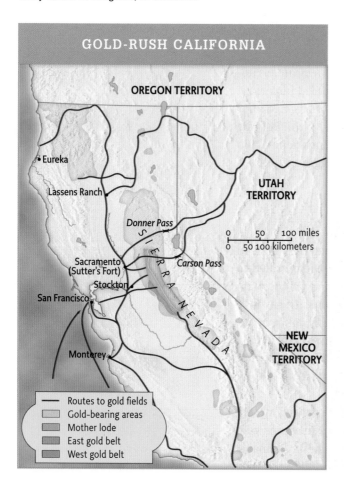

GOLD-RUSH CALIFORNIA

OREGON TERRITORY

• Eureka

Lassens Ranch

UTAH TERRITORY

Donner Pass

Sacramento (Sutter's Fort)

Carson Pass

Stockton

San Francisco

SIERRA NEVADA

NEW MEXICO TERRITORY

Monterey

0 50 100 miles
0 50 100 kilometers

— Routes to gold fields
Gold-bearing areas
Mother lode
East gold belt
West gold belt

almost all of them young men who had signed long-term labor contracts with Chinese merchants, who in turn leased them to mining and railroad companies and other employers. San Francisco, a town of 1,000 in 1848, became the gateway to the *El Dorado* of northern California. By 1850, it had 30,000 residents and had become perhaps the world's most racially and ethnically diverse city. Unlike farming frontiers settled by families, most of the gold-rush migrants were young men. Women played many roles in western mining communities, running restaurants and boardinghouses and working as laundresses, cooks, and prostitutes. But as late as 1860, California's male population outnumbered females by nearly three to one.

California and the Boundaries of Freedom

As early surface mines quickly became exhausted, they gave way to underground mining that required a large investment of capital. This economic development worsened conflicts among California's many racial and ethnic groups engaged in fierce competition for gold. The law was very fragile in gold-rush California. In 1851 and 1856, "committees of vigilance" took control of San Francisco, sweeping aside established courts to try and execute those accused of crimes. White miners organized extralegal groups that expelled "foreign miners"—Mexicans, Chileans, Chinese, French, and American Indians—from areas with gold. The state legislature imposed a tax of twenty dollars per month on foreign miners, driving many of them from the state.

California would long remain in the American imagination a place of infinite opportunity, where newcomers could start their lives anew. But the boundaries of freedom there were tightly drawn. The state constitution of 1850 limited voting and the right to testify in court to whites, excluding Indians, Asians, and the state's few blacks (who numbered only 962). California landowners who claimed Spanish descent or had intermarried with American settlers were deemed to be white. But with land titles derived from Mexican days challenged in court, many sold out to newcomers from the East.

For California's Indians, the gold rush and absorption into the United States proved to be disastrous. Gold seekers overran Indian communities. Miners, ranchers, and vigilantes murdered thousands of Indians. Determined to reduce the native population, state officials paid millions in bounties to private militias that launched attacks on the state's Indians. Although California was a free state, thousands of Indian children, declared orphans or vagrants by local courts, were bought and sold as slaves. By 1860, California's Indian population, nearly 150,000 when the Mexican War ended, had been reduced to around 30,000.

Limits set by the state constitution

The gold rush's toll on Indians

Opening Japan

The Mexican War ended with the United States in possession of the magnificent harbors of San Diego and San Francisco, long seen as jumping-off points for trade with the Far East. Between 1848 and 1860 American trade with China tripled. In 1850, New York businessman Asa Whitney submitted

A photograph from 1852 depicts miners at work in California. Chinese and white miners labor side by side searching for gold.

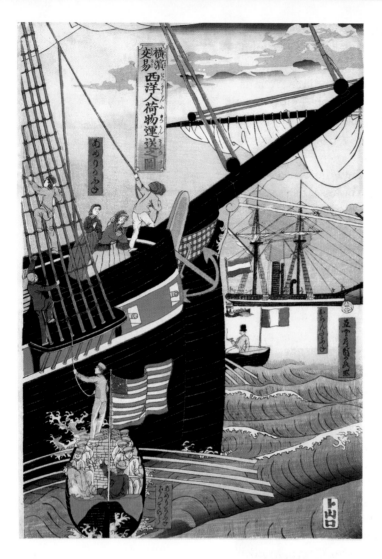

Transportation of Cargo by Westerners at the Port of Yokohama, 1861, by the Japanese artist Utagawa Sadahide, depicts ships in port, including an American one on the left, eight years after Commodore Perry's first voyage to Japan.

a plan to Congress for a transcontinental railroad that would speed eastern goods to Asian markets by eliminating the long and expensive sea route around South America. In a sense, he saw East Asia as a commercial extension of the American West. One congressman wrote in response to Whitney's proposal, "In the Bay of San Francisco will converge the commerce of Asia and the model republic."

In the 1850s, the United States took the lead in opening Japan, a country that had closed itself to nearly all foreign contact for more than two centuries. In 1853 and 1854, American warships under the command of **Commodore Matthew Perry** (the younger brother of Oliver Perry, a hero of the War of 1812) sailed into Tokyo Harbor. Perry, who had been sent by President Millard Fillmore to negotiate a trade treaty, demanded that the Japanese deal with him. Alarmed by European intrusions into China and impressed by Perry's armaments as well as a musical pageant he presented that included a blackface minstrel show, Japanese leaders agreed to do so. In 1854, they opened two ports to American shipping. Two years later, Townsend Harris, a merchant from New York City, arrived as the first American consul (and, according to some accounts, the inspiration for Puccini's great opera, *Madama Butterfly*, about an American who marries and then abandons a Japanese woman). Harris persuaded the Japanese to allow American ships into additional ports and to establish full diplomatic relations between the two countries. As a result, the United States acquired refueling places on the route to China. And Japan soon launched a process of modernization that transformed it into the region's major military power.

A DOSE OF ARSENIC

Victory over Mexico added more than 1 million square miles to the United States—an area larger than the Louisiana Purchase. But the acquisition of this vast territory raised the fatal issue that would disrupt the political system and plunge the nation into civil war—whether slavery should be allowed to expand into the West. Events soon confirmed Ralph Waldo Emerson's prediction that if the United States gobbled up part of Mexico, "it will be as the man who swallows arsenic. . . . Mexico will poison us."

Already, the bonds of union were fraying. In 1844 and 1845, the Methodists and Baptists, the two largest evangelical churches, divided into northern and southern branches. But it was the entrance of the slavery issue into the heart of American

Slavery in the West

politics as the result of the Mexican War that eventually dissolved perhaps the strongest force for national unity—the two-party system.

The Wilmot Proviso

Before 1846, the status of slavery in all parts of the United States had been settled, either by state law or by the Missouri Compromise, which determined slavery's status in the Louisiana Purchase. The acquisition of new land reopened the question of slavery's expansion. The divisive potential of this issue became clear in 1846, when Congressman David Wilmot of Pennsylvania proposed a resolution prohibiting slavery from all territory acquired from Mexico. Party lines crumbled as every northerner, Democrat and Whig alike, supported what came to be known as the **Wilmot Proviso**, while nearly all southerners opposed it. The measure passed the House, where the more populous North possessed a majority, but failed in the Senate, with its even balance of free and slave states. The proviso, said one newspaper, "as if by magic, brought to a head the great question that is about to divide the American people."

> *Sectional division caused by the proviso*

In 1848, opponents of slavery's expansion organized the **Free Soil Party** and nominated Martin Van Buren for president and Charles Francis Adams, the son of John Quincy Adams, as his running mate. Democrats nominated Lewis Cass of Michigan, who proposed that the decision on whether to allow slavery should be left to settlers in the new territories (an idea later given the name "popular sovereignty"). Van Buren was motivated in part by revenge against the South for jettisoning him in 1844. But his campaign struck a chord among northerners opposed to the expansion of slavery, and he polled some 300,000 votes, 14 percent of the northern total. Victory in 1848 went to the Whig candidate, Zachary Taylor, a hero of the Mexican War and a Louisiana sugar planter. But the fact that a former president and the son of another abandoned their parties to run on a Free Soil platform showed that antislavery sentiment had spread far beyond abolitionist ranks. "Antislavery," commented Senator William H. Seward of New York, "is at length a respectable element in politics."

> *"Popular sovereignty"*

The Free Soil Appeal

The Free Soil position had a popular appeal in the North that far exceeded the abolitionists' demand for immediate emancipation and equal rights for blacks. While Congress possessed no constitutional power to abolish slavery within a state, well-known precedents existed for keeping territories (areas that had not yet entered the Union as states) free from slavery. Congress had done this in 1787 in the Northwest Ordinance and again in the Missouri Compromise of 1820–1821. Many northerners had long resented what they considered southern domination of the federal government. The idea of preventing the creation of new slave states appealed to those who favored policies, such as the protective tariff and government aid to internal improvements, that the majority of southern political leaders opposed.

For thousands of northerners, moreover, the ability to move to the new western territories held out the promise of economic betterment. The depression

> *Economic betterment in the West*

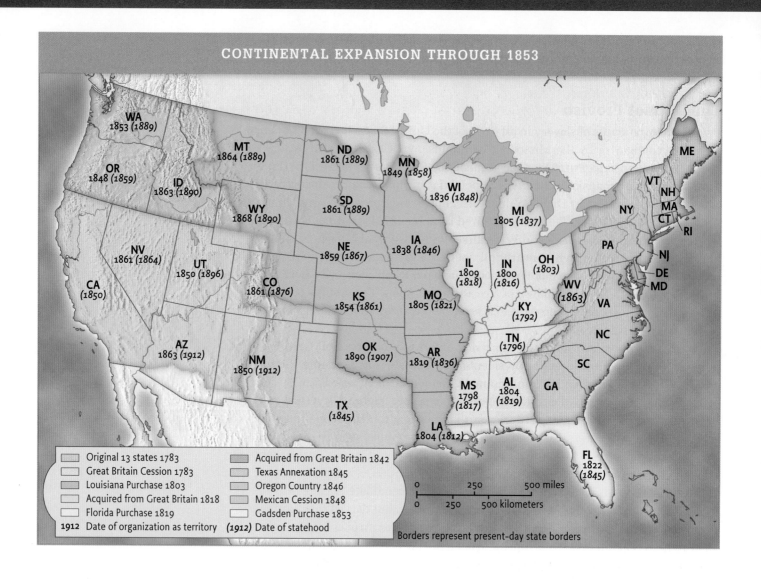

CONTINENTAL EXPANSION THROUGH 1853

WA 1853 (1889)
OR 1848 (1859)
MT 1864 (1889)
ID 1863 (1890)
ND 1861 (1889)
MN 1849 (1858)
WI 1836 (1848)
MI 1805 (1837)
ME
VT
NH
MA
CT
RI
NY
PA
NV 1861 (1864)
UT 1850 (1896)
WY 1868 (1890)
SD 1861 (1889)
IA 1838 (1846)
NE 1859 (1867)
IL 1809 (1818)
IN 1800 (1816)
OH (1803)
NJ
DE
MD
CA (1850)
CO 1861 (1876)
KS 1854 (1861)
MO 1805 (1821)
KY (1792)
WV (1863)
VA
AZ 1863 (1912)
NM 1850 (1912)
OK 1890 (1907)
AR 1819 (1836)
TN (1796)
NC
SC
TX (1845)
MS 1798 (1817)
AL 1804 (1819)
GA
LA 1804 (1812)
FL 1822 (1845)

Original 13 states 1783
Great Britain Cession 1783
Louisiana Purchase 1803
Acquired from Great Britain 1818
Florida Purchase 1819
1912 Date of organization as territory

Acquired from Great Britain 1842
Texas Annexation 1845
Oregon Country 1846
Mexican Cession 1848
Gadsden Purchase 1853
(1912) Date of statehood

0   250   500 miles
0   250   500 kilometers

Borders represent present-day state borders

By 1853, with the Gadsden Purchase, the present boundaries of the United States in North America, with the exception of Alaska, had been created.

of the early 1840s had reinforced the traditional equation of landownership with economic freedom. The labor movement promoted access to western land as a way of combating unemployment and low wages in the East. "Freedom of the soil," declared George Henry Evans, the editor of a pro-labor newspaper, offered the only alternative to permanent economic dependence for American workers.

Such views merged easily with opposition to the expansion of slavery. If slave plantations were to occupy the fertile lands of the West, northern migration would be effectively blocked. The term "free soil" had a double meaning. The Free Soil platform of 1848 called both for barring slavery from western territories and for the federal government to provide free homesteads to settlers in the new territories. Unlike abolitionism, the "free soil" idea also appealed to the racism so widespread in northern society. Wilmot himself insisted that his controversial proviso was motivated not by "morbid sympathy for the slaves" but to advance "the cause and rights of the free white man," in part by preventing him from having to compete with "black labor."

To white southerners, the idea of barring slavery from territory acquired from Mexico seemed a violation of their equal rights as members of the Union.

Appeal of the "free soil" to northern racism

Southerners had fought and died to win these territories; surely they had a right to share in the fruits of victory. A majority of slaves in 1848 lived in states that had not even existed when the Constitution was adopted. Many older plantation areas already suffered from soil exhaustion. Just as northerners believed westward expansion essential to their economic well-being, southern leaders became convinced that slavery must expand or die. Moreover, the admission of new free states would overturn the delicate political balance between the sections and make the South a permanent minority. Southern interests would not be secure in a Union dominated by non-slaveholding states.

The views of southern leaders

Crisis and Compromise

In world history, the year 1848 is remembered as the "springtime of nations," a time of democratic uprisings against the monarchies of Europe and demands by ethnic minorities for national independence. American principles of liberty and self-government appeared to be triumphing in the Old World. The Chartist movement in Great Britain organized massive demonstrations in support of democratic reforms. The French replaced their monarchy with a republic. Hungarians proclaimed their independence from Austrian rule. Patriots in Italy and Germany, both divided into numerous states, demanded national unification. But the revolutionary tide receded. Chartism faded away. In France, the Second Republic was soon succeeded by the reign of Emperor Napoleon III. Revolts in Budapest, Rome, and other cities were crushed. Would their own experiment in self-government, some Americans wondered, suffer the same fate as the failed revolutions of Europe?

Developments in Europe

With the slavery issue appearing more and more ominous, established party leaders moved to resolve differences between the sections. Some disputes were of long standing, but the immediate source of controversy arose from the acquisition of new lands after the Mexican War. In 1850, California asked to be admitted to the Union as a free state. Many southerners opposed the measure, fearing that it would upset the sectional balance in Congress. Senator Henry Clay offered a plan with four main provisions that came to be known as the Compromise of 1850. California would enter the Union as a free state. The slave trade, but not slavery itself, would be abolished in the nation's capital. A stringent new law would allow southerners to reclaim runaway slaves. And the status of slavery in the remaining territories acquired from Mexico would be left to the decision of the local white inhabitants. The United States would also agree to pay off the massive debt Texas had accumulated while independent.

The Compromise of 1850

The Great Debate

In the Senate debate on the Compromise, the divergent sectional positions received eloquent expression. Powerful leaders spoke for and against compromise. Daniel Webster of Massachusetts announced his willingness to abandon the Wilmot Proviso and accept a new fugitive slave law if this were the price of sectional peace. John C. Calhoun, again representing South Carolina, was too ill to speak. A colleague read his remarks rejecting the very idea of compromise. Slavery, Calhoun insisted, must be protected by the national government and extended into all the new territories. The North must yield or the Union could not survive. William

Arguments for and against the Compromise of 1850

Senator Daniel Webster of Massachusetts in a daguerreotype from 1850, the year his speech in support of the Compromise of 1850 contributed to its passage.

H. Seward of New York also opposed compromise. To southerners' talk of their constitutional rights, Seward responded that a "higher law" than the Constitution condemned slavery—the law of morality. Here was the voice of abolitionism, now represented in the U.S. Senate.

President Zachary Taylor, like Andrew Jackson a southerner but a strong nationalist, was alarmed by talk of disunion. He accused southern leaders in Congress of holding California hostage to their own legislative aims and insisted that all Congress needed to do was admit California to the Union. But Taylor died suddenly of an intestinal infection on July 9, 1850. His successor, Millard Fillmore of New York, threw his support to Clay's proposals. Fillmore helped to break the impasse in Congress and secure adoption of the **Compromise of 1850**.

The Fugitive Slave Issue

For one last time, political leaders had removed the dangerous slavery question from congressional debate. The new **Fugitive Slave Act**, however, made further controversy inevitable. The law allowed special federal commissioners to determine the fate of alleged fugitives without benefit of a jury trial or even testimony by the accused individual. It prohibited local authorities from interfering with the capture of fugitives and required individual citizens to assist in such capture when called upon by federal agents. Thus, southern leaders, usually strong defenders of states' rights and local autonomy, supported a measure that brought federal agents into communities throughout the North, armed with the power to override local law enforcement and judicial procedures to secure the return of runaway slaves. The security of slavery was more important to them than states'-rights consistency.

The fugitive slave issue affected all the free states, not just those that bordered on the South. Slave catchers, for example, entered California attempting to apprehend fugitives from Texas and New Mexico who hoped to reach freedom in British Columbia. The issue drew into politics individuals like Ralph Waldo Emerson, who, although antislavery, had previously remained aloof from the abolitionist crusade. Emerson and others influenced by transcendentalism viewed the Fugitive Slave Act as a dangerous example of how a government doing the bidding of the South could override an individual's ability to act according to his conscience—the foundation, for Emerson, of genuine freedom.

During the 1850s, federal tribunals heard more than 300 cases and ordered 157 fugitives returned to the South, many at the government's expense. But the law further widened sectional divisions and reinvigorated the underground railroad. In a series of dramatic confrontations, fugitives, aided by abolitionist allies, violently resisted recapture. A large crowd in 1851 rescued the escaped slave Jerry from jail in Syracuse, New York, and spirited him off to Canada. In the same year, an owner who attempted to recapture a fugitive was killed in Christiana, Pennsylvania. Later in the decade, Margaret Garner, a Kentucky slave who had escaped with her family to Ohio, killed her own young daughter rather than see her returned to slavery by federal marshals. (At the end of the twentieth century, this incident would become the basis for Toni Morrison's celebrated novel *Beloved*.)

Less dramatically, the men and women involved in the Underground Railroad redoubled their efforts to assist fugitives. Thanks to the consolidation of the railroad network in the North, it was now possible for escaping slaves who reached the free

Ralph Waldo Emerson

Resisting recapture

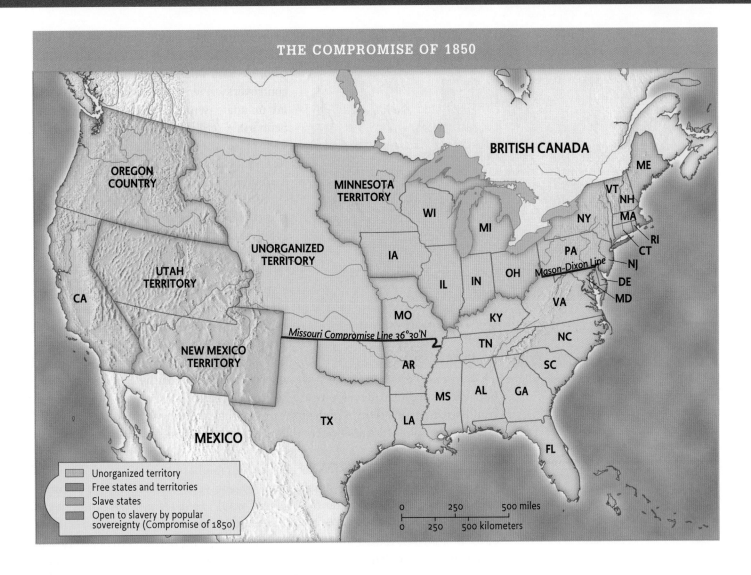

THE COMPROMISE OF 1850

Legend:
- Unorganized territory
- Free states and territories
- Slave states
- Open to slavery by popular sovereignty (Compromise of 1850)

states to be placed on trains that would take them to safety in Canada in a day or two. In 1855 and 1856, Sydney Howard Gay, an abolitionist editor in New York City and a key Underground Railroad operative, recorded in a notebook the arrival of over 200 fugitives—men, women, and children—a majority of whom had been sent by train from Philadelphia. Gay dispatched them to upstate New York and Canada.

Overall several thousand fugitives and freeborn blacks, worried that they might be swept up in the stringent provisions of the Fugitive Slave Act, fled to safety in Canada. The sight of so many refugees seeking liberty in a foreign land challenged the familiar image of the United States as an asylum for freedom. "Families are separating," reported a Toronto newspaper in October 1850, "leaving their homes, and flying in all directions to seek in Canada, under the British flag, the protection denied to them in the free republic."

The Compromise of 1850 attempted to settle issues arising from the acquisition of territory from Mexico by admitting California as a free state and providing that the status of slavery in Utah and New Mexico would be determined by the settlers.

Douglas and Popular Sovereignty

At least temporarily, the Compromise of 1850 seemed to restore sectional peace and party unity. In the 1852 presidential election, Democrat Franklin Pierce won

THE FUGITIVE SLAVE LAW.....HAMLET IN CHAINS.

An engraving from the *National Anti-Slavery Standard*, October 17, 1850, depicts James Hamlet, the first person returned to slavery under the Fugitive Slave Act of 1850, in front of City Hall in New York. Flags fly from the building, emblazoned with popular American maxims violated by Hamlet's rendition. By the time this appeared in print, New Yorkers had raised the money to purchase Hamlet's freedom and he was back in the city.

Appeal of the Independent Democrats

a sweeping victory over the Whig Winfield Scott on a platform that recognized the Compromise as a final settlement of the slavery controversy. Pierce received a broad popular mandate, winning 254 electoral votes to Scott's 42. Yet his administration turned out to be one of the most disastrous in American history. It witnessed the collapse of the party system inherited from the Age of Jackson.

In 1854, the old political order finally succumbed to the disruptive pressures of sectionalism. Early in that year, Illinois senator Stephen A. Douglas introduced a bill to provide territorial governments for Kansas and Nebraska, located within the Louisiana Purchase. With Calhoun, Clay, and Webster (the "great triumvirate") all having died between 1850 and 1852, Douglas, although only forty-one, saw himself as the new leader of the Senate. A strong believer in western development, he hoped that a transcontinental railroad could be constructed through Kansas or Nebraska. But he feared that this could not be accomplished unless formal governments had been established in these territories. Southerners in Congress, however, seemed adamant against allowing the organization of new free territories that might further upset the sectional balance. Douglas hoped to satisfy them by applying the principle of **popular sovereignty**, whereby the status of slavery would be determined by the votes of local settlers, not Congress. To Douglas, popular sovereignty embodied the idea of local self-government and offered a middle ground between the extremes of North and South. It was a principle on which all parts of the Democratic Party could unite, and which might enable him to capture the presidential nomination in 1856 to succeed the ineffectual Pierce.

The Kansas-Nebraska Act

Unlike the lands taken from Mexico, Kansas and Nebraska lay in the nation's heartland, directly in the path of westward migration. Slavery, moreover, was prohibited there under the terms of the Missouri Compromise, which Douglas's bill would repeal. In response, a group of antislavery congressmen issued the *Appeal of the Independent Democrats*. Written by two abolitionists from Ohio—Congressman Joshua Giddings and Senator Salmon P. Chase—the *Appeal* proved to be one of the most effective pieces of political persuasion in American history. It arraigned Douglas's bill as a "gross violation of a sacred pledge," part and parcel of "an atrocious plot" to convert free territory into a "dreary region of despotism, inhabited by masters and slaves." It helped to convince millions of northerners that southern leaders aimed at nothing less than extending their peculiar institution throughout the West.

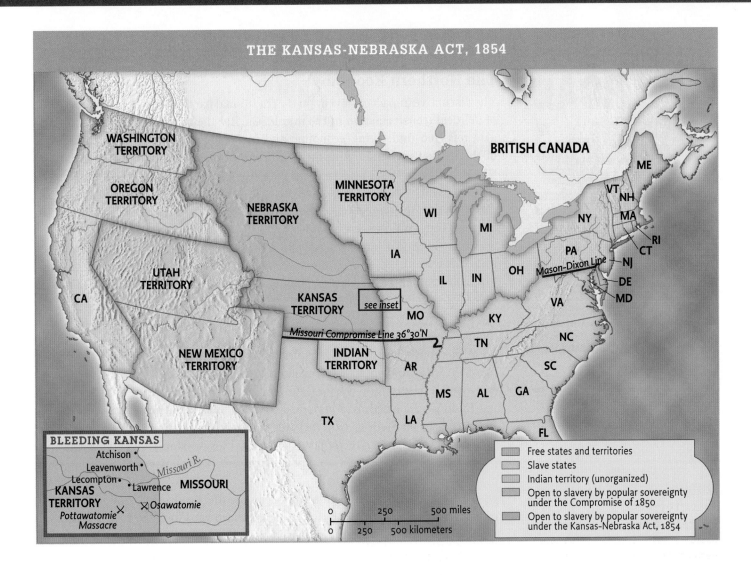

THE KANSAS-NEBRASKA ACT, 1854

WASHINGTON TERRITORY

OREGON TERRITORY

NEBRASKA TERRITORY

MINNESOTA TERRITORY

BRITISH CANADA

ME

VT
NH

WI

MI

NY

MA

UTAH TERRITORY

CA

IA

IL

IN

OH

PA

Mason-Dixon Line

NJ

RI
CT

DE
MD

KANSAS TERRITORY

see inset

MO

KY

VA

Missouri Compromise Line 36°30'N

NEW MEXICO TERRITORY

INDIAN TERRITORY

AR

TN

NC

SC

MS

AL

GA

TX

LA

FL

BLEEDING KANSAS
Atchison •
Leavenworth •
Lecompton • • Lawrence   **MISSOURI**
KANSAS TERRITORY
Pottawatomie   ✕ *Osawatomie*
Massacre
Missouri R.

Free states and territories
Slave states
Indian territory (unorganized)
Open to slavery by popular sovereignty under the Compromise of 1850
Open to slavery by popular sovereignty under the Kansas-Nebraska Act, 1854

0   250   500 miles
0   250   500 kilometers

Thanks to Douglas's energetic leadership, the **Kansas-Nebraska Act** became law. But it shattered the Democratic Party's unity. Even as Congress debated, protest meetings sprang up throughout the North. Fearing that the bill's unpopularity among their constituents would harm their chances for reelection, half the northern Democrats in the House cast negative votes. Loyalty to Pierce, Douglas, and their party led the other half to support the measure. It is difficult to think of a piece of legislation in American history that had a more profound impact on national life. In the wake of the bill's passage, American politics underwent a profound reorganization. During the next two years, the Whig Party, unable to develop a unified response to the political crisis, collapsed. From a region divided between the two parties, the South became solidly Democratic. Most northern Whigs, augmented by thousands of disgruntled Democrats, joined a new organization, the Republican Party, dedicated to preventing the further expansion of slavery.

The Kansas-Nebraska Act opened a vast area in the nation's heartland to the possible spread of slavery by repealing the Missouri Compromise and providing that settlers would determine the status of slavery in these territories.

ILLINIOS CENTRAL
RAILROAD.

OPEN FROM LASALLE TO BLOOMINGTON.

Arrangements commencing May 23, 1853.

Passenger Trains leave as follows, daily,
(Sundays excepted):

Bloomington,	8.00 A.M.	La Salle,	2.00 P.M.
Hudson,	8.35 "	Tonica,	2.35 "
Kappa,	8.54 "	Wenona,	3.15 "
Panola,	9.24 "	Minonk,	3.50 "
Minonk,	9.54 "	Panola,	4.30 "
Wenona,	10.40 "	Kappa,	5.00 "
Tonica,	11.25 "	Hudson,	5.20 "
LaSalle, arr.	12.00 "	Bloomington, arr.	6.00 "

*Stopping at these places on signal to take or leave passengers.

A Freight Train, with Passenger Car attached, will leave La Salle on Mondays, Wednesdays and Fridays at 8.30, A. M. arriving at Bloomington 2.30, P. M. stopping at all stations.
Returning, leaves Bloomington on Tuesday, Thursday and Saturday at 5 A. M. arriving at La Salle at 11 A. M.
Stages, it is expected, will soon run in connection with the Cars between Bloomington, Springfield, Decatur and Urbana.

Chicago, May 23.   **R. B. MASON, Sup't.**

An 1853 broadside for one section of the Illinois Central Railroad. One of the most important new lines of the 1850s, the Illinois Central opened parts of the Old Northwest to settlement and commercial agriculture, and it helped to cement Chicago's place as the region's foremost city.

Northern industrial production

Hostility to immigrants

THE RISE OF THE REPUBLICAN PARTY

The Northern Economy

The disruptive impact of slavery on the traditional parties was the immediate cause of political transformation in the mid-1850s. But the rise of the Republican Party also reflected underlying economic and social changes, notably the completion of the market revolution and the beginning of mass immigration from Europe. The period from 1843, when prosperity returned, to 1857, when another economic downturn hit, witnessed explosive economic growth, especially in the North. The catalyst was the completion of the railroad network. From 5,000 miles in 1848, railroad track mileage grew to 30,000 by 1860, with most of the construction occurring in Ohio, Illinois, and other states of the Old Northwest. Four great trunk railroads now linked eastern cities with western farming and commercial centers. The railroads completed the reorientation of the Northwest's trade from the South to the East. As late as 1850, most western farmers still shipped their produce down the Mississippi River. Ten years later, however, railroads transported nearly all their crops to the East, at a fraction of the previous cost. By 1860, for example, 60 million bushels of wheat were passing through Buffalo on their way to market in eastern cities and abroad. The economic integration of the Northwest and Northeast created the groundwork for their political unification in the Republican Party.

By 1860, the North had become a complex, integrated economy, with eastern industrialists marketing manufactured goods to the commercial farmers of the West, while residents of the region's growing cities consumed the food westerners produced. Northern society stood poised between old and new ways. The majority of the population still lived not in large cities but in small towns and rural areas, where the ideal of economic independence—owning one's own farm or shop—still lay within reach. Yet the majority of the northern workforce no longer labored in agriculture, and the industrial revolution was spreading rapidly.

Two great areas of industrial production had arisen. One, along the Atlantic coast, stretched from Boston to Philadelphia and Baltimore. A second was centered on or near the Great Lakes, in inland cities like Buffalo, Cleveland, Pittsburgh, and Chicago. Driven by railroad expansion, coal mining and iron manufacturing were growing rapidly. Chicago, the Old Northwest's major rail center and the jumping-off place for settlers heading for the Great Plains, had become a complex manufacturing center, producing 5,000 reapers each year, along with barbed wire, windmills, and prefabricated "balloon frame" houses, all of which facilitated further western settlement. New York City by 1860 had become the nation's preeminent financial, commercial, and manufacturing center. Although the southern economy was also growing and the continuing expansion of cotton production brought wealth to slaveholders, the South did not share in these broad economic changes.

The Rise and Fall of the Know-Nothings

As noted in Chapter 9, nativism—hostility to immigrants, especially Catholics—emerged as a local political movement in the 1840s. But in 1854, with the party system in crisis, it burst on the national political scene with the sudden appearance of the American, or Know-Nothing, Party (so called because it began as a secret

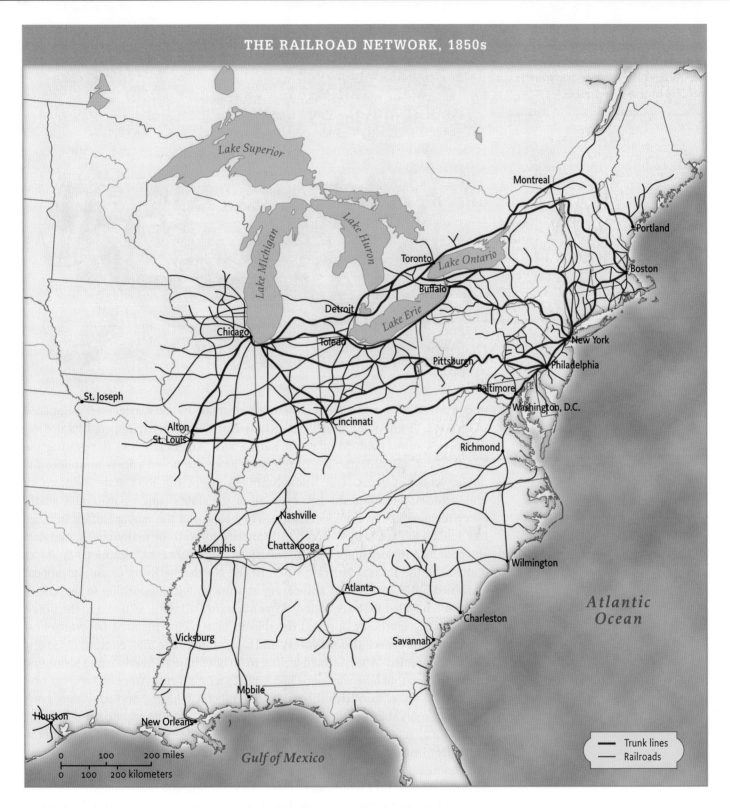

THE RAILROAD NETWORK, 1850s

Trunk lines
Railroads

The rapid expansion of the railroad network in the 1850s linked the Northeast and Old Northwest in a web of commerce. The South's rail network was considerably less developed, accounting for only 30 percent of the nation's track mileage.

Lagonda Agricultural Works, a color lithograph from 1859 advertising an Ohio manufacturer of agricultural machinery, in this case a horse-drawn reaper.

organization whose members, when asked about its existence, were supposed to respond, "I know nothing"). The **Know-Nothing Party** trumpeted its dedication to reserving political office for native-born Americans and to resisting the "aggressions" of the Catholic Church, such as its supposed efforts to undermine public school systems. The Know-Nothings swept the 1854 state elections in Massachusetts, electing the governor, all of the state's congressmen, and nearly every member of the state legislature. They captured the mayor's office in cities like Philadelphia, Chicago, and San Francisco as well. In many states, nativists emerged as a major component of victorious "anti-Nebraska" coalitions of voters opposed to the Kansas-Nebraska Act. In the North, the Know-Nothings' appeal combined anti-Catholic and antislavery sentiment, with opposition to the sale of liquor often added to the equation. After all, most Catholics, as noted in the previous chapter, vigorously opposed the reform movements inspired by evangelical Protestantism, especially antislavery and temperance. The 1854 elections, said one observer, revealed "a deep seated feeling in favor of human freedom and also a fine determination that hereafter none but Americans shall rule America."

Nativism and anti-slavery

Despite severe anti-Irish discrimination in jobs, housing, and education, however, it is remarkable how little came of demands that immigrants be barred from the political nation. All European immigrants benefited from being white. During the 1850s, free blacks found immigrants pushing them out of even the jobs as servants and common laborers previously available to them. The newcomers had the good fortune to arrive after white male suffrage had become the norm and automatically received the right to vote. Even as New England states sought to reduce immigrant political power (Massachusetts and Connecticut made literacy a voting requirement, and Massachusetts mandated a two-year waiting period between becoming a naturalized citizen and voting), western states desperate for labor allowed

Immigrant suffrage

immigrants to vote well before they became citizens. In a country where the suffrage had become essential to understandings of freedom, it is significant that many white male immigrants could vote almost from the moment they landed in America, while non-whites, whose ancestors had lived in the country for centuries, could not.

The Free Labor Ideology

By 1856, it was clear that the Republican Party—a coalition of antislavery Democrats, northern Whigs, Free Soilers, and Know-Nothings opposed to the further expansion of slavery—would become the major alternative to the Democratic Party in the North. Republicans managed to convince most northerners that **the Slave Power**, as they called the South's proslavery political leadership, posed a more immediate threat to their liberties and aspirations than "popery" and immigration. The party's appeal rested on the idea of "free labor." In Republican hands, the antithesis between "free society" and "slave society" coalesced into a comprehensive worldview that glorified the North as the home of progress, opportunity, and freedom.

Free labor

The defining quality of northern society, Republicans declared, was the opportunity it offered each laborer to move up to the status of landowning farmer or independent craftsman, thus achieving the economic independence essential to freedom. Slavery, by contrast, spawned a social order consisting of degraded slaves, poor whites with no hope of advancement, and idle aristocrats. The struggle over the territories was a contest about which of two antagonistic labor systems would dominate the West and, by implication, the nation's future. If slavery were to spread into the West, northern free laborers would be barred, and their chances for social advancement severely diminished. Slavery, Republicans insisted, must be kept out of the territories so that free labor could flourish. The Republican platform of 1856 condemned slavery as one of the "twin relics of barbarism" in the United States (the other being Mormon polygamy).

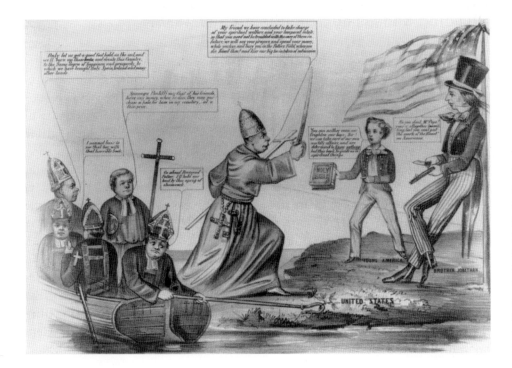

The Propagation Society—More Free than Welcome, an anti-Catholic cartoon from the 1850s, illustrates the nativist fear that the Catholic Church poses a threat to American society. Pope Pius IX, cross in hand, steps ashore from a boat that also holds five bishops. Addressing "Young America," who holds a Bible, he says that he has come to "take charge of your spiritual welfare." A bishop adds, "I cannot bear to see that boy, with that horrible book."

SOUTHERN CHIVALRY — ARGUMENT versus CLUB'S.

A contemporary print denounces South Carolina congressman Preston S. Brooks's assault on Massachusetts senator Charles Sumner in May 1856. The attack on the floor of the Senate was in retaliation for Sumner's speech accusing Senator Andrew P. Butler (Brooks's distant cousin) of having taken "the harlot slavery" as his mistress.

To southern claims that slavery was the foundation of liberty, Republicans responded with the rallying cry "freedom national"—meaning not abolition, but ending the federal government's support of slavery. Under the banner of free labor, northerners of diverse backgrounds and interests rallied in defense of the superiority of their own society. Republicans acknowledged that some northern laborers, including most Irish immigrants, were locked into jobs as factory workers and unskilled laborers and found it extremely difficult to rise in the social scale. But Republicans concluded that it was their "dependent nature"—a lack of Protestant, middle-class virtues—that explained the plight of the immigrant poor.

Republicans were not abolitionists—they focused on preventing the spread of slavery, not attacking it where it existed. Nonetheless, many party leaders viewed the nation's division into free and slave societies as an "irrepressible conflict," as Senator William H. Seward of New York put it in 1858, that eventually would have to be resolved. These "two systems" of society, Seward insisted, were "incompatible" within a single nation. The market revolution, Seward argued, by drawing the entire nation closer together in a web of transportation and commerce, heightened the tension between freedom and slavery. The United States, he predicted, "must and will, sooner or later, become either entirely a slaveholding nation, or entirely a free-labor nation."

Bleeding Kansas and the Election of 1856

Their free labor outlook, which resonated so effectively with deeply held northern values, helps to explain the Republicans' rapid rise to prominence. But dramatic events in 1855 and 1856 also fueled the party's growth. When Kansas held elections in 1854 and 1855, hundreds of proslavery Missourians crossed the border to cast fraudulent ballots. President Franklin Pierce recognized the legitimacy of the resulting proslavery legislature and replaced the territorial governor, Andrew H. Reeder of Pennsylvania, when he dissented. Settlers from free states soon established a rival government, and a sporadic civil war broke out in Kansas in which some 200 persons eventually lost their lives. In one incident, in May 1856, a proslavery mob attacked the free-soil stronghold of Lawrence, burning public buildings and pillaging private homes.

Kansas elections

Brooks and Sumner

"**Bleeding Kansas**" seemed to discredit Douglas's policy of leaving the decision on slavery up to the local population, thus aiding the Republicans. The party also drew strength from an unprecedented incident in the halls of Congress. South Carolina representative Preston Brooks, wielding a gold-tipped cane, beat the antislavery senator Charles Sumner of Massachusetts unconscious after Sumner delivered a denunciation of "The Crime against Kansas." Many southerners applauded Brooks, sending him canes emblazoned with the words "Hit him again!"

In the election of 1856, the Republican Party chose as its candidate John C. Frémont and drafted a platform that strongly opposed the further expansion of slavery. Stung by the northern reaction to the Kansas-Nebraska Act, the Democrats nominated James Buchanan, who had been minister to Great Britain in 1854 and thus had no direct connection with that divisive measure. The Democratic platform endorsed the principle of popular sovereignty as the only viable solution to the slavery controversy. Meanwhile, the Know-Nothings presented ex-president Millard Fillmore as their candidate. Frémont outpolled Buchanan in the North, carrying eleven of sixteen free states—a remarkable achievement for an organization that had existed for only two years. But Buchanan won the entire South and the key northern states of Illinois, Indiana, and Pennsylvania, enough to ensure his victory. Fillmore carried only Maryland. But he ran well among former Whig voters in the Upper South and more conservative areas of the North, who were reluctant to join the Democrats but feared Republican victory might threaten the Union.

The 1856 election returns made starkly clear that parties had reoriented themselves along sectional lines. One major party had been destroyed, another had been seriously weakened, and a new one had arisen, devoted entirely to the interests of the North.

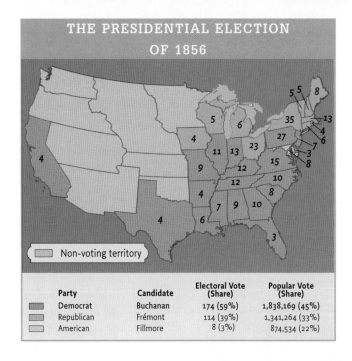

THE PRESIDENTIAL ELECTION OF 1856

Non-voting territory

Party	Candidate	Electoral Vote (Share)	Popular Vote (Share)
Democrat	Buchanan	174 (59%)	1,838,169 (45%)
Republican	Frémont	114 (39%)	1,341,264 (33%)
American	Fillmore	8 (3%)	874,534 (22%)

THE EMERGENCE OF LINCOLN

The final collapse of the party system took place during the administration of a president who epitomized the old political order. Born during George Washington's presidency, James Buchanan had served in Pennsylvania's legislature, in both houses of Congress, and as secretary of state under James K. Polk. A staunch believer in the Union, he committed himself to pacifying inflamed sectional emotions. Few presidents have failed more disastrously in what they set out to accomplish.

The Dred Scott Decision

Even before his inauguration, Buchanan became aware of an impending Supreme Court decision that held out the hope of settling the slavery controversy once and for all. This was the case of ***Dred Scott v. Sandford***. During the 1830s, Scott had accompanied his owner, Dr. John Emerson of Missouri, to Illinois, where slavery had been prohibited by the Northwest Ordinance of 1787 and by state law, and to Wisconsin Territory, where it was barred by the Missouri Compromise. After returning to Missouri, Scott sued for his freedom, claiming that residence on free soil had made him free.

The Dred Scott decision, one of the most famous—or infamous—rulings in the long history of the Supreme Court, was announced in March 1857, two days after Buchanan's inauguration. The justices addressed three questions. Could a black

Dred Scott as painted in 1857, the year the Supreme Court ruled that he and his family must remain in slavery.

person be a citizen and therefore sue in federal court? Did residence in a free state make Scott free? Did Congress possess the power to prohibit slavery in a territory? All nine justices issued individual opinions. But essentially, the Court divided 6-3 (with Justice Robert C. Grier of Pennsylvania, at Buchanan's behind-the-scenes urging, joining a southern majority). Speaking for the majority, Chief Justice Roger B. Taney declared that only white persons could be citizens of the United States. The nation's founders, Taney insisted, believed that blacks "had no rights which the white man was bound to respect." Descended from different ancestors and lacking a history of freedom, blacks, he continued, could never be part of the nation's "political family."

Congress's powerlessness to restrict slavery

The case could have ended there, since Scott had no right to sue, but inspired by the idea of resolving the slavery issue, Taney pressed on. Scott, he declared, remained a slave. Illinois law had no effect on him after his return to Missouri. As for his residence in Wisconsin, Congress possessed no power under the Constitution to bar slavery from a territory. The Missouri Compromise, recently repealed by the Kansas-Nebraska Act, had been unconstitutional, and so was any measure interfering with southerners' right to bring slaves into the western territories. The decision in effect declared unconstitutional the Republican platform of restricting slavery's expansion. It also seemed to undermine Douglas's doctrine of popular sovereignty. For if Congress lacked the power to prohibit slavery in a territory, how could a territorial legislature created by Congress do so? The Court, a Georgia newspaper exulted, "covers every question regarding slavery and settles it in favor of the South."

The Decision's Aftermath

The Scott family

Perhaps the person least directly affected by the Dred Scott decision was the plaintiff himself, for a new master immediately emancipated Scott and his family. Scott died in 1858, having enjoyed his freedom for less than two years. Harriet Scott lived until 1876, long enough to see Taney's ruling invalidated by the laws and constitutional amendments of Reconstruction. Their youngest daughter, Lizzie, survived to the age of 99. She died in 1954, having experienced the long era of segregation and the birth of the modern civil rights movement. The impact on the party system was more far-reaching. Among the decision's casualties was the reputation of the Court itself, which, in the North, sank to the lowest level in all of American history. Rather than abandoning their opposition to the expansion of slavery, Republicans now viewed the Court as controlled by the Slave Power.

The Lecompton battle

Slavery, announced President Buchanan, henceforth existed in all the territories, "by virtue of the Constitution." In 1858, his administration attempted to admit Kansas as a slave state under the Lecompton Constitution, which had been drafted by a pro-southern convention and never submitted to a popular vote. Outraged by this violation of popular sovereignty, Douglas formed an unlikely alliance with congressional Republicans to block the attempt. Kansas remained a territory; it would join the Union as a free state on the eve of the Civil War. The Lecompton battle convinced southern Democrats that they could not trust their party's most popular northern leader.

Lincoln and Slavery

The depth of Americans' divisions over slavery were brought into sharp focus in 1858 in one of the most storied election campaigns in the nation's history. Seeking reelection to the Senate as both a champion of popular sovereignty and the man who had prevented the administration from forcing slavery on the people of Kansas, Douglas faced an unexpectedly strong challenge from Abraham Lincoln, then little known outside of Illinois. Born into a modest farm family in Kentucky in 1809, Lincoln had moved as a youth to frontier Indiana and then Illinois. Although he began running for public office at the age of twenty-one, until the mid-1850s his career hardly seemed destined for greatness. He had served four terms as a Whig in the state legislature and one in Congress from 1847 to 1849.

Lincoln reentered politics in 1854 as a result of the Kansas-Nebraska Act. He once said that he "hated slavery as much as any abolitionist." Unlike abolitionists, however, Lincoln was willing to compromise with the South to preserve the Union. "I hate to see the poor creatures hunted down," he once wrote of fugitive slaves, "but I bite my lip and keep silent." But on one question he was inflexible—stopping the expansion of slavery.

Lincoln developed a critique of slavery and its expansion that gave voice to the central values of the emerging Republican Party and the millions of northerners whose loyalty it commanded. His speeches combined the moral fervor of the abolitionists with the respect for order and the Constitution of more conservative northerners. "I hate it," he said in 1854 of the prospect of slavery's expansion, "because of the monstrous injustice of slavery itself. I hate it because it deprives our republican example of its just influence in the world—enables the enemies of free institutions, with plausibility, to taunt us as hypocrites—causes the real friends of freedom to doubt our sincerity." If slavery were allowed to expand, he warned, the "love of liberty" would be extinguished and with it America's special mission to be a symbol of democracy for the entire world.

In a sense, Lincoln's own life personified the free labor ideology and the opportunities northern society offered to laboring men. During the 1850s, property-owning farmers, artisans, and shopkeepers far outnumbered wage earners in Illinois. Lincoln was fascinated and disturbed by the writings of proslavery ideologues like George Fitzhugh (discussed in Chapter 11), and he rose to the defense of northern society. "I want every man to have the chance," said Lincoln, "and I believe a black man is entitled to it, in which he *can* better his condition." Blacks might not be the equal of whites in all respects, but in their "natural right" to the fruits of their labor, they were "my equal and the equal of all others."

The Lincoln-Douglas Campaign

The campaign against Douglas, the North's preeminent political leader, created Lincoln's national reputation. Accepting his party's nomination for the Senate in June 1858, Lincoln etched sharply the differences between them. "A house divided against itself," he announced, "cannot stand. I believe this government cannot endure, permanently half *slave* and half

Abraham Lincoln

Abraham Lincoln's nickname "The Rail-splitter" recalled his humble origins. An unknown artist created this larger-than-life portrait. The White House is visible in the distance. The painting is said to have been displayed during campaign rallies in 1860.

Left: Abraham Lincoln in 1858, the year of the Lincoln-Douglas debates. *Right*: Stephen A. Douglas in a daguerreotype from around 1853.

free." Lincoln's point was not that civil war was imminent, but that Americans must choose between favoring and opposing slavery. There could be no middle ground. Douglas's policy of popular sovereignty, he insisted, reflected a moral indifference that could only result in the institution's spread throughout the entire country.

The **Lincoln-Douglas debates**, held in seven Illinois towns and attended by tens of thousands of listeners, remain classics of American political oratory. Clashing definitions of freedom lay at their heart. To Lincoln, freedom meant opposition to slavery. The nation needed to rekindle the spirit of the founding fathers, who, he claimed, had tried to place slavery on the path to "ultimate extinction." Douglas argued that the essence of freedom lay in local self-government and individual self-determination. A large and diverse nation could only survive by respecting the right of each locality to determine its own institutions. In response to a question posed by Lincoln during the Freeport debate, Douglas insisted that popular sovereignty was not incompatible with the Dred Scott decision. Although territorial legislatures could no longer exclude slavery directly, he argued, if the people wished to keep slaveholders out, all they needed to do was refrain from giving the institution legal protection.

In a critique not only of the antislavery movement but also of the entire reform impulse deriving from religious revivalism, Douglas insisted that politicians had no right to impose their own moral standards on society as a whole. "I deny the right of Congress," he declared, "to force a good thing upon a people who are unwilling to receive it." If a community wished to own slaves, it had a right to do so. Of course, when Douglas spoke of the "people," he meant whites alone. He spent much of his time in the debates attempting to portray Lincoln as a dangerous radical whose positions threatened to degrade white Americans by reducing them to equality with blacks. The United States government, Douglas proclaimed, had been created "by white men for the benefit of white men and their posterity for ever."

Lincoln shared many of the racial prejudices of his day. He opposed giving Illinois blacks the right to vote or serve on juries and spoke frequently of colonizing blacks overseas as the best solution to the problems of slavery and race. Yet, unlike Douglas, Lincoln did not use appeals to racism to garner votes. And he refused to exclude blacks from the human family. No less than whites, they were entitled to the inalienable rights of the Declaration of Independence, which applied to "all men, in all lands, everywhere," not merely to Europeans and their descendants.

> *Illinois divided*

The Illinois election returns revealed a state sharply divided, like the nation itself. Southern Illinois, settled from the South, voted strongly Democratic, while the rapidly growing northern part of the state was firmly in the Republican column. Until the adoption of the Seventeenth Amendment in the early twentieth century, each state's legislature chose its U.S. senators. In 1858, Republican candidates for the legislature won more votes statewide than Democrats. But because the apportionment of seats, based on the census of 1850, did not reflect the growth of northern Illinois since then, the Democrats emerged with a narrow margin in the legislature. Douglas was reelected. His victory was all the more remarkable because elsewhere in the North Republicans swept to victory in 1858. Resentment over the administration's Kansas policy split the Democratic Party, sometimes producing two Democratic candidates (pro-Douglas and pro-Buchanan) running against a single Republican. Coupled with the impact of the economic recession that began in 1857, this helped to produce Republican victories even in Indiana and Pennsylvania, which Democrats had carried two years earlier.

> *Douglas's win*

John Brown at Harpers Ferry

An armed assault by the abolitionist John Brown on the federal arsenal at **Harpers Ferry, Virginia**, further heightened sectional tensions. Brown had a long career of involvement in antislavery activities. In the 1830s and 1840s, he had befriended fugitive slaves and, although chronically in debt, helped to finance antislavery publications. Like other abolitionists, Brown was a deeply religious man. But his God was not the forgiving Jesus of the revivals, who encouraged men to save themselves through conversion, but the vengeful Father of the Old Testament. During the civil war in Kansas, Brown traveled to the territory. In May 1856, after the attack on Lawrence, he and a few followers murdered five proslavery settlers at Pottawatomie Creek. For the next two years, he traveled through the North and Canada, raising funds and enlisting followers for a war against slavery.

On October 16, 1859, with twenty-one men, five of them black, Brown seized Harpers Ferry. Militarily, the plan made little sense. Brown's band was soon surrounded and killed or captured by a detachment of federal soldiers headed by Colonel Robert E. Lee. Placed on trial for treason to the state of Virginia, Brown conducted himself with dignity and courage, winning admiration from millions of northerners who disapproved of his violent deeds. When Virginia's governor, Henry A. Wise, spurned pleas for clemency and ordered Brown executed, he turned Brown into a martyr to much of the North. Henry David Thoreau pronounced him "a crucified hero." Since Brown's death, radicals of both the left and right have revered Brown as a man willing to take action against an institution he considered immoral. Black leaders have long hailed him as a rare white person willing to sacrifice himself for the cause of racial justice.

John Brown, in an 1856 photograph.

To the South, the failure of Brown's assault seemed less significant than the adulation he seemed to arouse from much of the northern public. His raid and

VOICES OF FREEDOM

From THE LINCOLN-DOUGLAS DEBATES (1858)

The most famous political campaign in American history, the 1858 race for the U.S. Senate between Senator Stephen A. Douglas (a former Illinois judge) and Abraham Lincoln was highlighted by seven debates in which they discussed the politics of slavery and contrasting understandings of freedom.

DOUGLAS: Mr. Lincoln says that this government cannot endure permanently in the same condition in which it was made by its framers—divided into free and slave states. He says that it has existed for about seventy years thus divided, and yet he tells you that it cannot endure permanently on the same principles and in the same relative conditions in which our fathers made it.... One of the reserved rights of the states, was the right to regulate the relations between master and servant, on the slavery question.

Now, my friends, if we will only act conscientiously upon this great principle of popular sovereignty which guarantees to each state and territory the right to do as it pleases on all things local and domestic instead of Congress interfering, we will continue to be at peace one with another.

LINCOLN: Judge Douglas says, "Why can't this Union endure permanently, half slave and half free?" "Why can't we let it stand as our fathers placed it?" That is the exact difficulty between

us.... I say when this government was first established it was the policy of its founders to prohibit the spread of slavery into the new territories of the United States, where it had not existed. But Judge Douglas and his friends have broken up that policy and placed it upon a new basis by which it is to become national and perpetual. All I have asked or desired anywhere is that it should be placed back again upon the basis that the founders of our government originally placed it—restricting it from the new territories....

Judge Douglas assumes that we have no interest in them—that we have no right to interfere.... Do we not wish for an outlet for our surplus population, if I may so express myself clear? Do we not feel an interest in getting to that outlet with such institutions as we would like to have prevail there? Now irrespective of the moral aspect of this question as to whether there is a right or wrong in enslaving a negro, I am still in favor of our new territories being in such a condition that white men may find a home. I am in favor of this not merely for our own people, but as an outlet for *free white people everywhere*, the world over—in which Hans and Baptiste and Patrick, and all other men from all the world, may find new homes and better their conditions in life.

DOUGLAS: For one, I am opposed to negro citizenship in any and every form. I believe this government was made on the white basis. I believe it was made by white men, for the benefit of white men and their posterity forever. . . . I do not believe that the Almighty made the negro capable of self-government. I say to you, my fellow-citizens, that in my opinion the signers of the Declaration of Independence had no reference to the negro whatever when they declared all men to be created equal. They desired to express by that phrase, white men, men of European birth and European descent . . . when they spoke of the equality of men.

LINCOLN: I have no purpose to introduce political and social equality between the white and the black races. There is a physical difference between the two, which in my judgment will probably forever forbid their living together upon the footing of perfect equality, and inasmuch as it becomes a necessity that there must be a difference, I, as well as Judge Douglas, am in favor of the race to which I belong, having the superior position. . . . But I hold that notwithstanding all this, there is no reason in the world why the negro is not entitled to all the natural rights enumerated in the Declaration of Independence, the right to life, liberty, and the pursuit of happiness. I hold that he is as much entitled to these as the white man. I agree with Judge Douglas he is not my equal in many respects—certainly not in color, perhaps not in moral or intellectual endowment. But in the right to eat the bread, without leave of anybody else, which his own hand earns, *he is my equal and the equal of Judge Douglas, and the equal of every living man.*

DOUGLAS: He tells you that I will not argue the question whether slavery is right or wrong. I tell you why I will not do it. . . . I hold that the people of the slaveholding states are civilized men as well as ourselves, that they bear consciences as well as we, and that they are accountable to God and their posterity and not to us. It is for them to decide therefore the moral and religious right of the slavery question for themselves within their own limits. . . . He says that he looks forward to a time when slavery shall be abolished everywhere. I look forward to a time when each state shall be allowed to do as it pleases.

LINCOLN: I suppose that the real difference between Judge Douglas and his friends, and the Republicans, is that the Judge is not in favor of making any difference between slavery and liberty . . . and consequently every sentiment he utters discards the idea that there is any wrong in slavery. . . . That is the real issue. That is the issue that will continue in this country when these poor tongues of Judge Douglas and myself shall be silent. It is the eternal struggle between these two principles—right and wrong—throughout the world.

QUESTIONS

1. *How do Lincoln and Douglas differ on what rights black Americans are entitled to enjoy?*

2. *Why does Lincoln believe the nation cannot exist forever half slave and half free, whereas Douglas believes it can?*

3. *How does each of the speakers balance the right of each state to manage its own affairs against the right of every person to be free?*

An 1835 painting of the federal arsenal at Harpers Ferry, Virginia (now West Virginia). John Brown's raid on Harpers Ferry in October 1859 helped to bring on the Civil War.

execution further widened the breach between the sections. Brown's last letter was a brief, prophetic statement: "I, John Brown, am quite certain that the crimes of this guilty land will never be purged away but with blood."

The Rise of Southern Nationalism

With the Republicans continuing to gain strength in the North, Democrats might have been expected to put a premium on party unity as the election of 1860 approached. By this time, however, a sizable group of southerners viewed their region's prospects as more favorable outside the Union than within it. Throughout the 1850s, influential writers and political leaders kept up a drumbeat of complaints about the South's problems. The sky-high price of slaves made it impossible for many planters' sons and upwardly mobile small farmers to become planters in their own right. Many white southerners felt that the opportunity was eroding for economic independence through ownership of land and slaves—liberty as they understood it. The North, secessionists charged, reaped the benefits of the cotton trade, while southerners fell deeper and deeper into debt. To remain in the Union meant to accept "bondage" to the North. But an independent South could become the foundation of a slave empire ringing the Caribbean and embracing Cuba, other West Indian islands, Mexico, and parts of Central America.

A slave empire

More and more southerners were speaking openly of southward expansion. In 1854, Pierre Soulé of Louisiana, the American ambassador to Spain, had persuaded the ministers to Britain and France to join him in signing the Ostend Manifesto, which called on the United States to purchase or seize Cuba, where slavery was still legal, from Spain. Meanwhile, the military adventurer William Walker led a series of "filibustering" expeditions (the term derived from the Spanish word for pirate, *filibustero*) in Central America.

Born in Tennessee, Walker had headed to California to join the gold rush. Failing to strike it rich, he somehow decided to try to become the leader of a Latin American country. Walker moved to establish himself as ruler of Nicaragua in Central America, and to open that country to slavery. Nicaragua at the time was engaged in a civil war, and one faction invited Walker to assist it by bringing 300 armed men. In 1855, Walker captured the city of Granada and in the following year proclaimed himself president. The administration of Franklin Pierce recognized Walker's government, but neighboring countries sent in troops, who forced Walker to flee. His activities represented clear violations of American neutrality laws. But Walker won acclaim in the South, and when federal authorities placed him on trial in New Orleans in 1858, the jury acquitted him.

William Walker

By the late 1850s, southern leaders were bending every effort to strengthen the bonds of slavery. "Slavery is our king," declared a South Carolina politician in 1860. "Slavery is our truth, slavery is our divine right." New state laws further restricted access to freedom. One in Louisiana stated simply: "After the passage of this act, no slave shall be emancipated in this state." Some southerners called for the reopening of the African slave trade, hoping that an influx of new slaves would lower the price, thereby increasing the number of whites with a vested interest in the peculiar institution. By early 1860, seven states of the Deep South had gone on record demanding that the Democratic platform pledge to protect slavery in all the territories that had not yet been admitted to the Union as states. Virtually no northern politician could accept this position. For southern leaders to insist on it would guarantee the destruction of the Democratic Party as a national institution. But southern nationalists, known as "fire-eaters," hoped to split the party and the country and form an independent southern Confederacy.

Strengthening slavery

The "fire-eaters"

The Democratic Split

When the Democratic convention met in April 1860, Douglas's supporters commanded a majority but not the two-thirds required for a presidential nomination. Because of his fight against Kansas's Lecompton Constitution and his refusal to support congressional laws imposing slavery on all the territories, Douglas had become unacceptable to political leaders of the Deep South. They were still determined to bring Kansas into the Union as a slave state. When the convention adopted a platform reaffirming the doctrine of popular sovereignty, delegates from the seven slave states of the Lower South walked out and the gathering recessed in confusion. Six weeks later, it reconvened, replaced the bolters with Douglas supporters, and nominated him for president. In response, southern Democrats placed their own ticket in the field, headed by John C. Breckinridge of Kentucky. Breckinridge insisted that slavery must be protected in the western territories.

The Democratic Party, the last great bond of national unity, had been shattered. National conventions had traditionally been places where party managers, mindful of the need for unity in the fall campaign, reconciled their differences. But in 1860, neither northern nor southern Democrats were interested in conciliation. Southern Democrats no longer trusted their northern counterparts. Douglas's backers, for

Democratic Party shattered

their part, would not accept a platform that doomed their party to certain defeat in the North.

The Nomination of Lincoln

Meanwhile, Republicans gathered in Chicago and chose Lincoln as their standard-bearer. Although he entered the convention with fewer delegates than William H. Seward, Lincoln did not suffer from Seward's political liabilities. Former Know-Nothings, a majority of whom had by now joined Republican ranks, bitterly resented Seward's efforts as governor of New York to channel state funds to Catholic schools. Seward had a not entirely deserved reputation for radicalism as a result of his "higher law" and "irrepressible conflict" speeches, discussed earlier.

Lincoln's appeal

Lincoln's devotion to the Union appealed to moderate Republicans, and his emphasis on the moral dimension of the sectional controversy made him acceptable to Republicans from abolitionist backgrounds. Having never associated with the Know-Nothings, he could appeal to immigrant voters, and nativists preferred him to the hated Seward. Most important, coming from Illinois, Lincoln was better positioned to carry the pivotal "doubtful states" essential for Republican victory. On the third ballot, he was nominated. The party platform denied the validity of the Dred Scott decision, reaffirmed Republicans' opposition to slavery's expansion, and added economic planks designed to appeal to a broad array of northern voters—free homesteads in the West, a protective tariff, and government aid in building a transcontinental railroad.

The Election of 1860

In effect, two presidential campaigns took place in 1860. In the North, Lincoln and Douglas were the combatants. In the South, the Republicans had no presence and three candidates contested the election—Douglas, Breckinridge, and John Bell of Tennessee, the candidate of the hastily organized Constitutional Union Party. A haven for Unionist former Whigs, this new party adopted a platform consisting of a single pledge—to preserve "the Constitution as it is [that is, with slavery] and the Union as it was [without sectional discord]."

The most striking thing about the election returns was their sectional character. Lincoln carried all of the North except New Jersey, receiving 1.8 million popular votes (54 percent of the regional total and 40 percent of the national) and 180 electoral votes (a clear majority). Breckinridge captured most of the slave states, although Bell carried three Upper South states and about 40 percent of the southern vote as a whole. Douglas placed first only in Missouri, but his 1.3 million popular votes were second in number only to Lincoln's. Douglas was the only candidate with significant support in all parts of the country, a vindication, in a sense, of his long effort to transcend sectional divisions. But his failure to carry either section suggested that a traditional political career based on devotion to the Union was no longer possible.

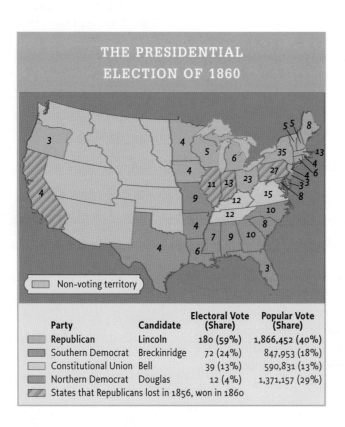

THE PRESIDENTIAL ELECTION OF 1860

Non-voting territory

Party	Candidate	Electoral Vote (Share)	Popular Vote (Share)
Republican	Lincoln	180 (59%)	1,866,452 (40%)
Southern Democrat	Breckinridge	72 (24%)	847,953 (18%)
Constitutional Union	Bell	39 (13%)	590,831 (13%)
Northern Democrat	Douglas	12 (4%)	1,371,157 (29%)
States that Republicans lost in 1856, won in 1860			

Without a single vote in ten southern states, Lincoln was elected the nation's sixteenth president. He failed to secure a majority of the national popular vote. But because of the North's superiority in population, Lincoln would still have carried the electoral college and thus been elected president even if the votes of his three opponents had all been cast for a single candidate.

THE IMPENDING CRISIS

The Secession Movement

In the eyes of many white southerners, Lincoln's victory placed their future at the mercy of a party avowedly hostile to their region's values and interests. Those advocating secession did not believe Lincoln's administration would take immediate steps against slavery in the states. But if, as seemed quite possible, the election of 1860 marked a fundamental shift in power, the beginning of a long period of Republican rule, who could say what the North's antislavery sentiment would demand in five years, or ten? Slaveowners, moreover, feared Republican efforts to extend their party into the South by appealing to non-slaveholders. Rather than accept permanent minority status in a nation governed by their opponents, Deep South political leaders boldly struck for their region's independence. At stake, they believed, was not a single election, but an entire way of life.

In the months that followed Lincoln's election, seven states stretching from South Carolina to Texas seceded from the Union. These were the states of the Cotton Kingdom, where slaves represented a larger part of the total population than in the Upper South. First to secede was South Carolina, the state with the highest percentage of slaves in its population and a long history of political radicalism. On December 20, 1860, the legislature unanimously voted to leave the Union. Its *Declaration of the Immediate Causes of Secession* placed the issue of slavery squarely at the center of the crisis. The first and longest complaint against the free states was interference with the return of fugitive slaves. The document indicated that not only northern actions but also northern public opinion regarding slavery compelled the state to leave the Union. The North had "assumed the right of deciding upon the propriety of our domestic institutions." Lincoln was a man "whose opinions and purposes are hostile to slavery." Experience had proved "that slaveholding states cannot be safe in subjection to nonslaveholding states." Secessionists equated their movement with the struggle for American independence. Proslavery ideologue George Fitzhugh, however, later claimed that southern secession was even more significant than the "commonplace affair" of 1776, since the South rebelled not merely against a particular government but against the erroneous modern idea of freedom based on "human equality" and "natural liberty."

A colorful Republican campaign banner from the 1860 campaign emphasizes the party's opposition to the expansion of slavery and promise of free homesteads for settlers in the West.

South Carolina

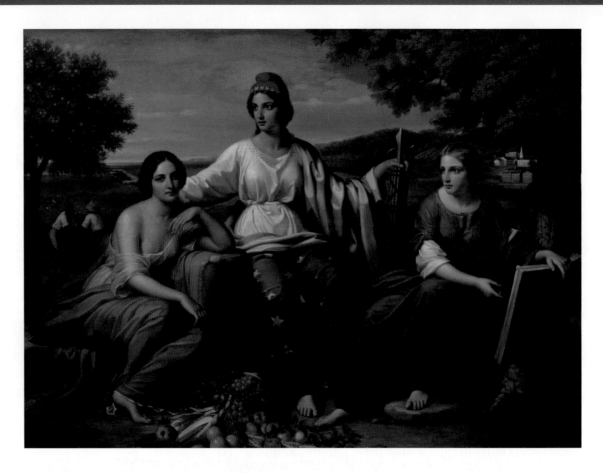

An Allegory of the North and the South, painted in 1858 by the Connecticut-born artist Luther Terry, offers a symbolic portrait of the United States on the eve of the Civil War. At the center is a female figure representing the nation and wearing a cap of liberty, with a horn of plenty at her feet. The figure of the South, on the left, is seated on a bale of cotton, with slaves visible in the fields behind her. The North, on the right, holds a book, *Useful Arts and Sciences*, and sits before a New England town with a church and textile mill. The sectional harmony portrayed here would soon be replaced by bloody warfare.

> *Lincoln's opposition to the Crittenden plan*

The Secession Crisis

As the Union unraveled, President Buchanan seemed paralyzed. He denied that a state could secede, but he also insisted that the federal government had no right to use force against it. Other political leaders struggled to find a formula to resolve the crisis. Senator John J. Crittenden of Kentucky, a slave state on the border between North and South, offered the most widely supported compromise plan of the secession winter. Embodied in a series of unamendable constitutional amendments, Crittenden's proposal would have guaranteed the future of slavery in the states where it existed, and extended the Missouri Compromise line to the Pacific Ocean, dividing between slavery and free soil all territories "now held, or hereafter acquired." The seceding states rejected the compromise as too little, too late. But many in the Upper South and North saw it as a way to settle sectional differences and prevent civil war.

Crittenden's plan, however, foundered on the opposition of Abraham Lincoln. Willing to conciliate the South on issues like the return of fugitive slaves, Lincoln took an unyielding stand against the expansion of slavery. Here, he informed one Republican leader, he intended to "hold firm, as with a chain of steel." A fundamental principle of democracy, Lincoln believed, was at stake. "We have just carried an election," he wrote, "on principles fairly stated to the people. Now we are told in advance that the government shall be broken up unless we surrender to those we have beaten, before we take the offices. . . . If we surrender, it is the end of us and the end of the government." Lincoln, moreover, feared that Crittenden's reference to land "hereafter acquired" offered the South a thinly veiled invitation to demand the acquisition of Cuba, Mexico, and other territory suited to slavery.

Before Lincoln assumed office on March 4, 1861, the seven seceding states formed the Confederate States of America, adopted a constitution, and chose as their president Jefferson Davis of Mississippi. With a few alterations—the president served a single six-year term; cabinet members, as in Britain, could sit in Congress— the Confederate constitution was modeled closely on that of the United States. It departed from the federal Constitution, however, in explicitly guaranteeing slave property both in the states and in any territories the new nation acquired. The "cornerstone" of the Confederacy, announced Davis's vice president, Alexander H. Stephens of Georgia, was "the great truth that the negro is not equal to the white man, that slavery, subordination to the superior race, is his natural and normal condition."

The Confederate States of America

And the War Came

Even after rejecting the Crittenden Compromise, Lincoln did not believe war inevitable. When he became president, eight slave states of the Upper South remained in the Union. Here, slaves and slaveholders made up a considerably lower proportion of the population than in the Deep South, and large parts of the white population did not believe Lincoln's election justified dissolving the Union. Even within the Confederacy, whites had divided over secession, with considerable numbers of non-slaveholding farmers in opposition. In time, Lincoln believed, secession might collapse from within.

In his inaugural address, Lincoln tried to be conciliatory. He rejected the right of secession but denied any intention of interfering with slavery in the states. He said nothing of retaking the forts, arsenals, and customs houses the Confederacy

Lincoln's response to secession

An 1860 engraving of a mass meeting in Savannah, Georgia, shortly after Lincoln's elction as president, which called for the state to secede from the Union. The banner on the obelisk at the center reads, "Our Motto State's Rights, Equality of the States, Don't Tread on Me"—the last a slogan from the American Revolution.

A Richmond, Virginia, cartoonist in April 1861 depicts Lincoln as a cat seeking to catch the southern states as mice fleeing the Union, which lies dead on the left.

Fort Sumter

had seized, although he did promise to "hold" remaining federal property in the seceding states. But Lincoln also issued a veiled warning: "In your hands, my dissatisfied fellow countrymen, and not in mine, is the momentous issue of civil war."

In his first month as president, Lincoln walked a tightrope. He avoided any action that might drive more states from the Union, encouraged southern Unionists to assert themselves within the Confederacy, and sought to quiet a growing clamor in the North for forceful action against secession. Knowing that the risk of war existed, Lincoln strove to ensure that if hostilities did break out, the South, not the Union, would fire the first shot. And that is precisely what happened on April 12, 1861, at **Fort Sumter**, an enclave of Union control in the harbor of Charleston, South Carolina.

A few days earlier, Lincoln had notified South Carolina's governor that he intended to replenish the garrison's dwindling food supplies. Viewing Fort Sumter's presence as an affront to southern nationhood, and perhaps hoping to force the wavering Upper South to join the Confederacy, Jefferson Davis ordered batteries to fire on the fort. On April 14, its commander surrendered. The following day, Lincoln proclaimed that an insurrection existed in the South and called for 75,000 troops to suppress it. Civil war had begun. Within weeks, Virginia, North Carolina, Tennessee, and Arkansas joined the Confederacy. "Both sides deprecated war," Lincoln later said, "but one of them would *make* war rather than let the nation survive; and the other would *accept* war rather than let it perish. And the war came."

In 1842, Henry Wadsworth Longfellow published *Poems on Slavery*, a collection that included a work entitled simply "The Warning." In it, Longfellow compared the American slave to the mighty biblical figure of Samson, who after being blinded and chained, managed to destroy the temple of his tormentors:

Inauguration of Mr. Lincoln, a photograph taken on March 4, 1861. The unfinished dome of the Capitol building symbolizes the precarious state of the Union at the time Lincoln assumed office.

> There is a poor, blind Samson in this land,
> Shorn of his strength, and bound in bonds of steel,
> Who may, in some grim revel, raise his hand,
> And shake the pillars of this Commonweal,
> Till the vast Temple of our liberties
> A shapeless mass of wreck and rubbish lies.

In 1861, Longfellow's warning came to pass. The Union created by the founders lay in ruins. The struggle to rebuild it would bring about a new birth of American freedom.

SUGGESTED READING

BOOKS

- Anbinder, Tyler. *Nativism and Slavery: The Northern Know-Nothings and the Politics of the 1850s* (1992). A detailed study of the relationship between nativism and antislavery politics in the North.

- Cronon, William. *Nature's Metropolis: Chicago and the Great West* (1992). An influential account of the rise of Chicago and the city's relationship to its agricultural hinterland.

- Current, Richard N. *Lincoln and the First Shot* (1963). Examines the decisions and strategy of both Lincoln and Jefferson Davis that produced the firing on Fort Sumter that began the Civil War.

- Dean, Adam W. *An Agrarian Republic: Farming, Antislavery Politics, and Nature Parks in the Civil War Era* (2015). Challenges the idea of the coming of the Civil War as a clash between an agricultural South and an industrialized North by stressing the agrarian origins of political antislavery.

- DeLay, Brian. *War of a Thousand Deserts: Indian Raids and the U.S.-Mexican War* (2008). A history of the Mexican war that emphasizes its impact on Native Americans.

- Earle, Jonathan H. *Jacksonian Antislavery and the Politics of Free Soil, 1824–1854* (2004). Emphasizes the role of northern Jacksonians in antislavery politics.

- Foner, Eric. *Free Soil, Free Labor, Free Men: The Ideology of the Republican Party before the Civil War* (1970). A discussion of the basic ideas that united Republicans in the 1850s, especially their "free labor ideology."

- Haas, Lisbeth. *Conquests and Historical Identities in California, 1769–1936* (1995). Contains a detailed description of how California's acquisition by the United States affected the state's diverse population groups.

- Levine, Bruce. *Half Slave and Half Free: The Roots of the Civil War* (1992). A survey of the coming of the Civil War, stressing irreconcilable differences between North and South.

- Montejano, David. *Anglos and Mexicans in the Making of Texas* (1987). A history of cultural relations among the varied populations of Texas.

- Potter, David M. *The Impending Crisis, 1848–1861* (1976). Still the standard account of the nation's history in the years before the Civil War.

- Sinha, Manisha. *The Counterrevolution of Slavery: Politics and Ideology in Antebellum South Carolina* (2002). A detailed study of how a vigorous defense of slavery developed in South Carolina, which justified the decision for secession.

- Stampp, Kenneth. *And the War Came: The North and the Secession Crisis, 1860–61* (1950). An examination of northern actions and attitudes during the secession crisis.

- Stephanson, Anders. *Manifest Destiny: American Expansionism and the Empire of Right* (1995). Considers how the idea of an American mission to spread freedom and democracy has affected American foreign policy throughout the country's history.

WEBSITES

- Getting the Message Out! National Campaign Materials, 1840–1860: http://lincoln.lib.niu.edu/message/

- Gold Rush!: www.museumca.org/goldrush/

- The Mexican-American War and the Media, 1845–1858: www.history.vt.edu/MxAmWar/INDEX.HTM

- The Oregon Trail: http://oregontrail101.com

- Record of Fugitives: https://exhibitions.cul.columbia.edu/exhibits/show/fugitives/record_fugitives

- Uncle Tom's Cabin and American Culture: http://jefferson.village.virginia.edu/utc/

CHAPTER REVIEW AND ONLINE RESOURCES

REVIEW QUESTIONS

1. Explain the justifications for the doctrine of manifest destiny, including material and idealistic motivations.

2. Why did many Americans criticize the Mexican War? How did they see expansion as a threat to American liberties?

3. How did the concept of "race" develop by the mid-nineteenth century, and how did it enter into the manifest destiny debate?

4. How did western expansion affect the sectional tensions between the North and South?

5. How did the market revolution contribute to the rise of the Republican Party? How did those economic and political factors serve to unite groups in the Northeast and in the Northwest, and why was that unity significant?

6. What was the "Slave Power," and why did many northerners feel threatened by it?

7. Based on the Lincoln-Douglas debates, how did the two differ on the expansion of slavery, equal rights, and the role of the national government? Use examples of their words to illustrate your points.

8. Why did Stephen Douglas, among others, believe that "popular sovereignty" could resolve sectional divisions of the 1850s? Why did the idea not work out?

9. Explain how sectional voting patterns in the 1860 presidential election allowed southern "fire-eaters" to justify secession.

10. What do the California gold rush and the opening of Japan reveal about the United States' involvement in a global economic system?

KEY TERMS

Tejanos (p. 461)

Antonio López de Santa Anna (p. 461)

the Texas Revolt (p. 462)

Mexican War (p. 465)

Gadsden Purchase (p. 466)

gold rush (p. 469)

Commodore Matthew Perry (p. 472)

Wilmot Proviso (p. 473)

Free Soil Party (p. 473)

Compromise of 1850 (p. 476)

Fugitive Slave Act (p. 476)

popular sovereignty (p. 478)

Kansas-Nebraska Act (p. 479)

Know-Nothing Party (p. 482)

the Slave Power (p. 483)

"Bleeding Kansas" (p. 484)

Dred Scott v. Sandford (p. 485)

Lincoln-Douglas debates (p. 488)

Harpers Ferry, Virginia (p. 489)

Fort Sumter (p. 498)

Go to 🐇 INQUIZITIVE

To see what you know—and learn what you've missed—with personalized feedback along the way.

Visit the *Give Me Liberty!* **Student Site** for primary source documents and images, interactive maps, author videos featuring Eric Foner, and more.

CHAPTER 14

A NEW BIRTH OF FREEDOM: THE CIVIL WAR

★

1861-1865

Like hundreds of thousands of other Americans, Marcus M. Spiegel volunteered in 1861 to fight in the Civil War. Born into a Jewish family in Germany in 1829, Spiegel took part in the failed German revolution of 1848. In the following year he emigrated to Ohio, where he married the daughter of a local farmer. When the Civil War broke out, the nation's 150,000 Jews represented less than 1 percent of the total population. But Spiegel shared wholeheartedly in American patriotism. He went to war, he wrote to his brother-in-law, to defend "the flag that was ever ready to protect you and me and every one who sought its protection from oppression."

Spiegel rose to the rank of colonel in the 120th Ohio Infantry and saw action in Virginia, Mississippi, and Louisiana. He corresponded frequently with his wife, Caroline. "I have seen and learned much," he wrote in 1863. "I have seen men dying of disease and mangled by the weapons of death; I have witnessed hostile armies arrayed against each other, the charge of infantry, [and] cavalry hunting men down like beasts." But he never wavered in his commitment to the "glorious cause" of preserving the Union and its heritage of freedom.

What one Pennsylvania recruit called "the magic word *Freedom*" shaped how many Union soldiers understood the conflict. The war's purpose, wrote Samuel McIlvaine, a sergeant from Indiana, was to preserve the American nation as "the beacon light of liberty and freedom to the human race." But as the war progressed, prewar understandings of liberty gave way to something new. Millions of northerners who had not been abolitionists became convinced that preserving the Union as an embodiment of liberty required the destruction of slavery.

Marcus Spiegel's changing views mirrored the transformation of a struggle to save the Union into a war to end slavery. Spiegel was an ardent Democrat. He shared the era's racist attitudes and thought Lincoln's Emancipation Proclamation a serious mistake. Yet as the Union army penetrated the heart of the Deep South, Spiegel became increasingly opposed to slavery. "Since I am here," he wrote to his wife from Louisiana in January 1864, "I have learned and seen . . . the horrors of slavery. You know it takes me long to say anything that sounds antidemocratic [opposed to Democratic Party policies], but . . . never hereafter will I either speak or vote in favor of slavery."

Marcus Spiegel was killed in a minor engagement in Louisiana in May 1864, one of hundreds of thousands of Americans to perish in the Civil War.

THE FIRST MODERN WAR

The American Civil War is often called the first modern war. Never before had mass armies confronted each other on the battlefield with the deadly weapons created by the industrial revolution. The resulting casualties dwarfed anything in the American experience. Beginning as a battle of army versus army, the war became a conflict of society against society, in which the distinction between military and civilian targets often disappeared. In a war of this kind, the effectiveness of political

FOCUS QUESTIONS

Why is the Civil War considered the first modern war? *–p. 503*

How did a war to preserve the Union become a war to end slavery? *–p. 511*

How did the Civil War transform the national economy and create a stronger nation-state? *–p. 519*

How did the war effort and leadership problems affect the society and economy of the Confederacy? *–p. 532*

What were the military and political turning points of the war? *–p. 538*

What were the most important wartime "rehearsals for Reconstruction"? *–p. 541*

Union General George B. McClellan drilling his troops during the winter of 1861–1862, a painting by an unknown artist.

leadership, the ability to mobilize economic resources, and a society's willingness to keep up the fight despite setbacks are as crucial to the outcome as success or failure on individual battlefields.

The Two Combatants

Almost any comparison between Union and Confederacy seemed to favor the Union. The population of the North and the loyal border slave states numbered 22 million in 1860, while only 9 million persons lived in the Confederacy, 3.5 million of them slaves. In manufacturing, railroad mileage, and financial resources, the Union far outstripped its opponent. On the other hand, the Union confronted by far the greater task. To restore the shattered nation, it had to invade and conquer an area larger than western Europe. Confederate soldiers were highly motivated fighters defending their homes and families. Like Washington's forces during the American Revolution, southern armies could lose most of the battles and still win the war if their opponent tired of the struggle. "No people," Confederate general P. G. T. Beauregard later claimed, "ever warred for independence with more relative advantages than the Confederacy."

On both sides, the outbreak of war stirred powerful feelings of patriotism. Recruits rushed to enlist, expecting a short, glorious war. Later, as enthusiasm waned, both sides resorted to a draft. The Confederacy in the spring of 1862 passed the first draft law in American history, and the North soon followed. By 1865, more than 2 million men had served in the Union army and 900,000 in the Confederate army. Each was a cross section of its society: the North's was composed largely of farm boys, shopkeepers, artisans, and urban workers, while the South's consisted mostly of non-slaveholding small farmers, with slaveowners dominating the officer corps.

Few recruits had any military experience. Ideas about war were highly romantic, based on novels, magazine articles, and lithographs of soldiers covering themselves with glory. One private wrote home in 1862 that his notion of combat had come from the pictures of battles he had seen: "they would all be in a line, all standing in a nice level field fighting, a number of ladies taking care of the wounded, etc. But it isn't so." Nor were the recruits ready for military regimentation. "It comes rather hard at first to be deprived of liberty," wrote an Illinois soldier. Initially, the constant round of drilling, ditch digging, and other chores was only occasionally interrupted by fierce bursts of fighting on the battlefield. According to one estimate, during the first two years of the war the main Union force, the Army of the Potomac, spent only thirty days in actual combat.

The Technology of War

Neither the soldiers nor their officers were prepared for the way technology had transformed warfare. The Civil War was the first major conflict in which the railroad transported troops and supplies and the first to see railroad junctions such as Atlanta and Petersburg become major military objectives. The famous sea battle between the Union vessel *Monitor* and the Confederate *Merrimac* in 1862 was the first demonstration of the superiority of ironclads over wooden ships, revolutionizing naval warfare. The war saw the use of the telegraph for military

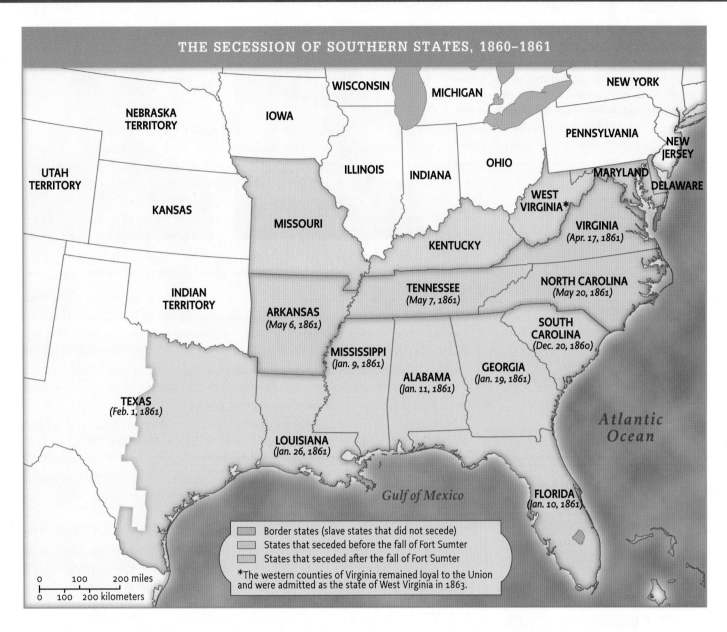

THE SECESSION OF SOUTHERN STATES, 1860–1861

Border states (slave states that did not secede)
States that seceded before the fall of Fort Sumter
States that seceded after the fall of Fort Sumter

*The western counties of Virginia remained loyal to the Union and were admitted as the state of West Virginia in 1863.

communication, the introduction of observation balloons to view enemy lines, and even primitive hand grenades and submarines.

Perhaps most important, a revolution in arms manufacturing had replaced the traditional musket, accurate at only a short range, with the more modern rifle, deadly at 600 yards or more because of its grooved (or "rifled") barrel. This development changed the nature of combat, emphasizing the importance of heavy fortifications and elaborate trenches and giving those on the defensive—usually southern armies—a significant advantage over attacking forces. "My men," said Confederate general Thomas "Stonewall" Jackson, "sometimes fail to drive the enemy from his position, but to hold one, never." The war of rifle and trench produced the appalling casualty statistics of Civil War battles. The most recent estimate of those who perished in the war—around 750,000 men—represents the equivalent, in terms of today's population, of more than 7 million. These figures

By the time secession ran its course, eleven slave states had left the Union.

War of rifle and trench

Sergeant James W. Travis, Thirty-eighth Illinois Infantry, Union army, and Private Edwin Francis Jemison, Second Louisiana Regiment, Confederate army, two of the nearly 3 million Americans who fought in the Civil War. Before going off to war, many soldiers sat for photographs like these, reproduced on small cards called *cartes de visite*, which they distributed to friends and loved ones. Jemison was killed in the Battle of Malvern Hill in July 1862.

In nearly every resource for warfare, the Union enjoyed a distinct advantage. But this did not make Union victory inevitable; as during the War of Independence, the stronger side sometimes loses.

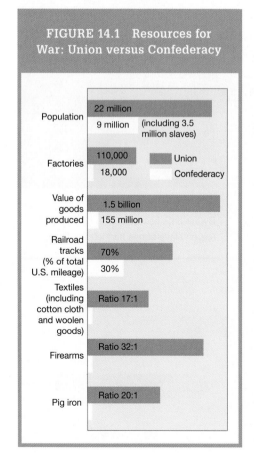

FIGURE 14.1   Resources for War: Union versus Confederacy

do not include the thousands of civilians who became victims of battles or who perished in disease-ridden camps for runaway slaves or in conflicts between Unionist and Confederate families that raged in parts of the South. The death toll in the Civil War exceeds the total number of Americans who died in all the nation's other wars, from the Revolution to the wars in Iraq and Afghanistan.

Nor was either side ready for other aspects of modern warfare. Medical care remained primitive. "I believe the doctors kill more than they cure," wrote an Alabama private in 1862. Diseases like measles, dysentery, malaria, and typhus swept through army camps, killing more men than did combat. The Civil War was the first war in which large numbers of Americans were captured by the enemy and held in dire conditions in military prisons. Some 50,000 men died in these prisons, victims of starvation and disease, including 13,000 Union soldiers at Andersonville, Georgia.

Everywhere in the world, war was becoming more destructive. The scale of Civil War bloodshed was unique in American history, but not in the nineteenth-century world. The Taiping Rebellion in China (1850–1864) resulted in 23 million deaths. The War of the Triple Alliance in South America (1864–1870), which pitted Argentina, Brazil, and Uruguay against Paraguay, caused the death of half of Paraguay's prewar population of around 525,000.

The Public and the War

Another modern feature of the Civil War was that both sides were assisted by a vast propaganda effort to mobilize public opinion. In the Union, an outpouring of lithographs, souvenirs, sheet music, and pamphlets issued by patriotic organizations and the War Department reaffirmed northern values, tarred the Democratic Party with the brush of treason, and accused the South of numerous crimes against Union soldiers and loyal civilians. Comparable items appeared in the Confederacy.

At the same time, the war's brutal realities were brought home with unprecedented immediacy to the public at large. War correspondents accompanied the

War Spirit at Home, an 1866 painting by the New Jersey artist Lilly M. Spencer, depicts a family reading the news of the Union capture of Vicksburg in 1863. The household is now composed of women and children; the husband may be off in the army. While the children play as soldiers, the cross in the folds of the newspaper suggests a less celebratory reflection on the conflict. Newspapers brought news of the war into American homes.

armies, and newspapers reported the results of battles on the following day and quickly published long lists of casualties. The infant art of photography carried images of war into millions of American living rooms. Beginning in 1862, when photographers entered the battlefield to take shocking pictures of the dead at Antietam, the camera, in the words of one journalist, "brought the bodies and laid them in our door-yards." Mathew Brady, who organized a corps of photographers to cover the war, found the conflict a passport to fame and wealth. For photography itself, it was a turning point in its growth as an art and a business enterprise.

Reporting on the war

Mobilizing Resources

The outbreak of the war found both sides unprepared. In 1861, there was no national railroad gauge (the distance separating the two rails), so trains built for one line could not run on another. There were no national banking system, no tax system capable of raising the enormous funds needed to finance the war, and not even accurate maps of the southern states. Soon after the firing on Fort Sumter, Lincoln proclaimed a naval blockade of the South. But the navy, charged with patrolling the 3,500-mile coastline, consisted of only ninety vessels, fewer than half of them steam-powered. Not until late in the war did the blockade become effective.

Logistical problems

Then there was the problem of purchasing and distributing the food, weapons, and other supplies required by the soldiers. The Union army eventually became the best-fed and best-supplied military force in history. By the war's third year, on the other hand, southern armies were suffering from acute shortages of food, uniforms, and shoes. Yet the chief of the Confederacy's Ordnance Bureau, Josiah Gorgas

An eight-inch cannon, one of the weapons forged in the industrial revolution and deployed in the Civil War.

(a transplanted northerner), proved brilliantly resourceful in arming southern troops. Under his direction, the Confederate government imported weapons from abroad and established arsenals of its own to turn out rifles, artillery, and ammunition.

Military Strategies

Each side tried to find ways to maximize its advantages. Essentially, the Confederacy adopted a defensive strategy, with occasional thrusts into the North. General Robert E. Lee, the leading southern commander, was a brilliant battlefield tactician who felt confident of his ability to fend off attacks by larger Union forces. He hoped that a series of defeats would weaken the North's resolve and lead it eventually to abandon the conflict and recognize southern independence.

Lincoln's early generals found it impossible to bring the Union's advantages in manpower and technology to bear on the battlefield. In April 1861, the regular army numbered little more than 15,000 men, most of whom were stationed west of the Mississippi River. Its officers had been trained to lead small, professional forces into battle, not the crowds of untrained men who assembled in 1861. The North also suffered from narrowness of military vision. Its generals initially concentrated on occupying southern territory and attempting to capture Richmond, the Confederate capital. They attacked sporadically and withdrew after a battle, thus sacrificing the North's manpower superiority and allowing the South to concentrate its smaller forces when an engagement impended.

Well before his generals, Lincoln realized that simply capturing and occupying territory would not win the war, and that defeating the South's armies, not capturing its capital, had to be the North's battlefield objective. And when he came to adopt the policy of emancipation, Lincoln acknowledged that to win the war, the Union must make the institution that lay at the economic and social foundation of southern life a military target.

The War Begins

In the East, most of the war's fighting took place in a narrow corridor between Washington and Richmond—a distance of only 100 miles—as a succession of Union generals led the Army of the Potomac (as the main northern force in the East was called) toward the Confederate capital, only to be turned back by southern forces. The first significant engagement, the **first Battle of Bull Run**, took place in northern Virginia on July 21, 1861. It ended with the chaotic retreat of the Union soldiers, along with the sightseers and politicians who had come to watch the battle. Almost 800 men died at Bull Run, a toll eclipsed many times in the years to come, but more Americans than had been killed in any previous battle in the nation's history. The encounter disabused both sides of the idea that the war would be a brief lark.

A surgeon's kit used in the Civil War, containing amputation instruments, knives, and tourniquets. With medical knowledge and practices primitive at best, far more men died from wounds, infections, and disease than in battle.

In the wake of Bull Run, George B. McClellan, an army engineer who had recently won a minor engagement with Confederate troops in western Virginia, assumed command of the Union's Army of the Potomac. A brilliant organizer, McClellan succeeded in welding his men into a superb fighting force. He seemed reluctant, however, to commit them to battle, since he tended to overestimate the size of enemy forces. And as a Democrat, he hoped that compromise might end the war without large-scale loss of life or a weakening of slavery. Months of military inactivity followed.

George B. McClellan

The War in the East, 1862

Not until the spring of 1862, after a growing clamor for action by Republican newspapers, members of Congress, and an increasingly impatient Lincoln, did McClellan lead his army of more than 100,000 men into Virginia. Here they confronted the smaller Army of Northern Virginia under the command of the Confederate general Joseph E. Johnston, and after he was wounded, Robert E. Lee. A brilliant battlefield tactician, Lee had been offered a command in the Union army but chose to fight for the Confederacy because of his devotion to Virginia. In the Seven Days' Campaign, a series of engagements in June 1862 on the peninsula south of Richmond, Lee blunted McClellan's attacks and forced him to withdraw to the vicinity of Washington, D.C. In August 1862, Lee again emerged victorious at the **second Battle of Bull Run** against Union forces under the command of General John Pope.

The Seven Days' Campaign

Successful on the defensive, Lee now launched an invasion of the North. He hoped to bring the border slave states into the Confederacy, persuade Britain and France to recognize southern independence, influence the North's fall elections, and perhaps capture Washington, D.C. At the **Battle of Antietam**, in Maryland, McClellan and the Army of the Potomac repelled Lee's advance. In a single day of fighting, nearly 4,000 men were killed and 18,000 wounded (2,000 of whom later died of their injuries). The dead, one survivor recalled, lay three deep in the field, mowed down "like grass before the scythe." More Americans died on September 17, 1862, when the Battle

Departure of the 7th Regiment, a lithograph from 1861 illustrating the departure of a unit of the New York State militia for service in the Civil War. A contemporary writer captured the exuberant spirit of the early days of the war: "New York was certainly raving mad with excitement. The ladies laughed, smiled, sighed, sobbed, and wept. The men cheered and shouted as never men cheered and shouted before."

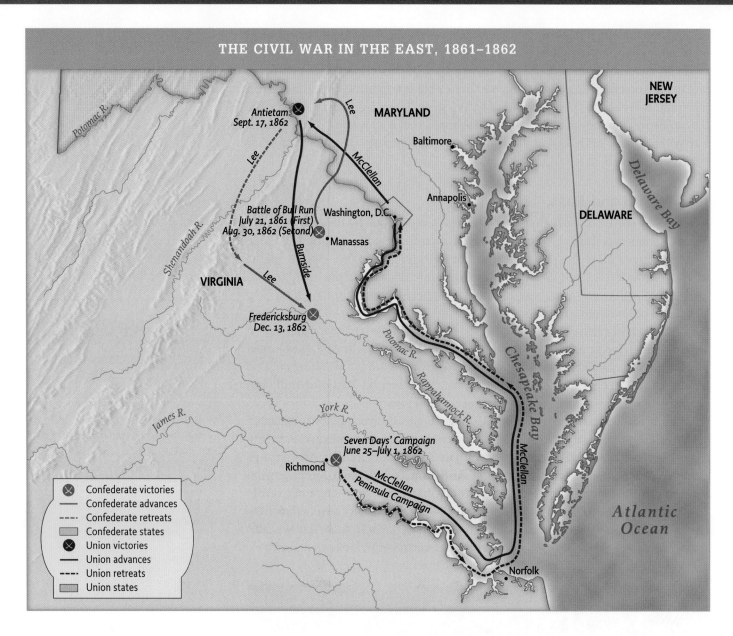

During the first two years of the war, most of the fighting took place in Virginia and Maryland.

Fredericksburg

of Antietam was fought, than on any other day in the nation's history, including Pearl Harbor and D-Day in World War II and the terrorist attacks of September 11, 2001.

Since Lee was forced to retreat, the North could claim Antietam as a victory. It was to be the Union's last success in the East for some time. In December 1862, the Union suffered one of its most disastrous defeats of the war when General Ambrose E. Burnside, who had replaced McClellan as the head of the Army of the Potomac, assaulted Lee's army, which was entrenched on heights near Fredericksburg, Virginia. "It was not a fight," wrote one Union soldier to his mother, "it was a massacre."

The War in the West

While the Union accomplished little in the East in the first two years of the war, events in the West followed a different course. Here, the architect of early success was Ulysses S. Grant. A West Point graduate who had resigned from the army in

The Battle of Antietam, a painting of a Union advance by Captain James Hope of the Second Vermont Volunteers. More than 4,000 men died on September 17, 1862, when the Battle of Antietam was fought.

1854 in part because of allegations of excessive drinking, Grant had been notably unsuccessful in civilian life. When the war broke out, he was working as a clerk in his brother's leather store in Galena, Illinois. But after being commissioned as a colonel in an Illinois regiment, Grant quickly displayed the daring, the logical mind, and the grasp of strategy he would demonstrate throughout the war.

In February 1862, Grant won the Union's first significant victory when he captured Forts Henry and Donelson in Tennessee. In April, naval forces under Admiral David G. Farragut steamed into New Orleans, giving the Union control of the South's largest city and the rich sugar plantation parishes to its south and west. At the same time, Grant withstood a surprise Confederate attack at Shiloh, Tennessee. But Union momentum in the West then stalled.

THE COMING OF EMANCIPATION

Slavery and the War

War, it has been said, is the midwife of revolution. And the Civil War produced far-reaching changes in American life. The most dramatic of these was the destruction of slavery, the central institution of southern society. Between 1831, when the British abolished slavery in their empire, and 1888, when emancipation came to Brazil, some 6 million slaves gained their freedom in the Western Hemisphere. Of these, nearly 4 million, two-thirds of the total, lived in the southern United States. In numbers, scale, and the economic power of the institution of slavery, American emancipation dwarfed that of any other country (although far

Emancipation in the Western Hemisphere

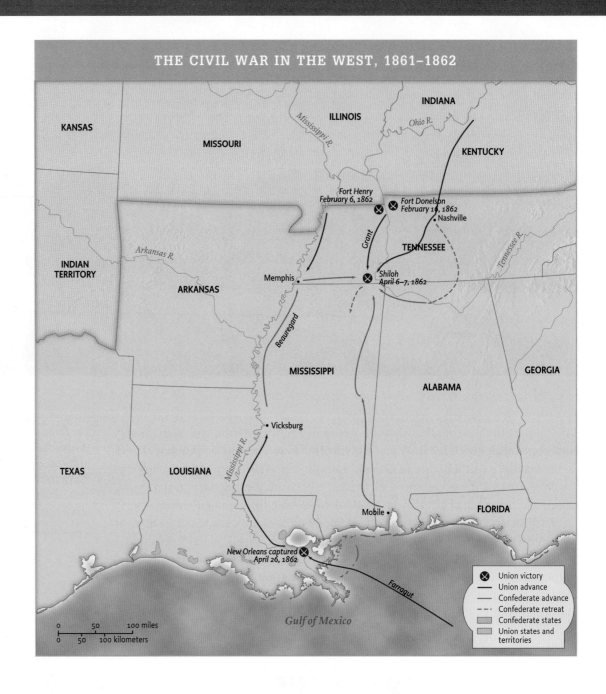

THE CIVIL WAR IN THE WEST, 1861–1862

Most of the Union's victories in the first two years of the war occurred in the West, especially at Shiloh and New Orleans.

more people were liberated in 1861 when Czar Alexander II abolished serfdom in the Russian empire).

At the outset of the war, Lincoln invoked time-honored northern values to mobilize public support. In a message to Congress, he identified the Union cause with the fate of democracy for the "whole family of man." He identified the differences between North and South in terms of the familiar free labor ideology: "This is essentially a people's struggle. On the side of the Union, it is a struggle for maintaining in the world, that form and substance of government, whose leading object is to elevate the condition of men . . . to afford all, an unfettered start, and a fair chance, in the race of life."

But while appealing to free labor values, Lincoln initially insisted that slavery was irrelevant to the conflict. In the war's first year, his paramount concerns were to keep the border slave states—Delaware, Maryland, Kentucky, and Missouri—in the Union and to build the broadest base of support in the North for the war effort. Action against slavery, he feared, would drive the border, with its white population of 2.6 million and nearly 500,000 slaves, into the Confederacy and alienate conservative northerners.

Early Union policy on slavery

The Unraveling of Slavery

Thus, in the early days of the war, a nearly unanimous Congress adopted a resolution proposed by Senator John J. Crittenden of Kentucky, which affirmed that the Union had no intention of interfering with slavery. Northern military commanders even returned fugitive slaves to their owners, a policy that raised an outcry in antislavery circles. Yet as the Confederacy set slaves to work as military laborers and blacks began to escape to Union lines, the policy of ignoring slavery unraveled. By the end of 1861, the military had adopted the plan, begun in Virginia by General Benjamin F. Butler, of treating escaped blacks as contraband of war—that is, property of military value subject to confiscation. Butler's order added a word to the war's vocabulary. Escaping slaves became known as "**the contrabands**." They were housed by the army in "contraband camps" and educated in new "contraband schools."

The Crittenden Resolution

Meanwhile, slaves took actions that helped propel a reluctant white America down the road to emancipation. Well before Lincoln made emancipation a war aim, blacks, in the North and the South, were calling the conflict the "freedom war." In 1861 and 1862, as the federal army occupied Confederate territory, slaves by the thousands headed for Union lines. Unlike fugitives before the war, these runaways included large numbers of women and children, as entire families abandoned the plantations. Not a few passed along military intelligence and detailed knowledge of the South's terrain. "The most valuable and reliable information of the enemy's movements in our vicinity that we have been able to get," noted the Union general Daniel E. Sickles, "derived from Negroes who came into our lines." In southern Louisiana, the arrival of the Union army in 1862 led slaves to sack plantation houses and refuse to work unless wages were paid. Slavery there, wrote a northern reporter, "is forever destroyed and worthless, no matter what Mr. Lincoln or anyone else may say on the subject."

A Civil War photograph depicts African-American men, women, and children who have escaped to Union lines in a mule-drawn covered wagon. The actions of fugitives like these helped propel the nation down the road to emancipation.

Steps toward Emancipation

At first, blacks' determination to seize the opportunity presented by the war proved a burden to the army and an embarrassment to the administration. But the failure of traditional strategies to produce victory strengthened the hand of antislavery northerners. Since slavery stood at the foundation of the southern economy, they insisted, emancipation was necessary to weaken the South's ability to sustain the war.

The most uncompromising opponents of slavery before the war, abolitionists and **Radical Republicans**, quickly concluded that the institution must become a target of the Union war effort. "It is plain," declared Thaddeus Stevens, a Radical Republican congressman from Pennsylvania, "that nothing approaching the present policy will subdue the rebels." Outside of Congress, few pressed the case for emancipation more eloquently than Frederick Douglass. From the outset, he insisted that it was futile to "separate the freedom of the slave from the victory of the government." "Fire must be met with water," Douglass declared, "darkness with light, and war for the destruction of liberty must be met with war for the destruction of slavery."

Steps toward emancipation

These appeals won increasing support in a Congress frustrated by lack of military success. In March 1862, Congress prohibited the army from returning fugitive slaves. Then came abolition in the District of Columbia (with monetary compensation for slaveholders) and the territories, followed in July by the Second Confiscation Act, which liberated slaves of disloyal owners in Union-occupied territory, as well as slaves who escaped to Union lines.

The Second Confiscation Act

Throughout these months, Lincoln struggled to retain control of the emancipation issue. In August 1861, John C. Frémont, commanding Union forces in Missouri, a state racked by a bitter guerrilla war between pro-northern and pro-southern bands, decreed the freedom of its slaves. Fearful of the order's impact on the border states, Lincoln swiftly rescinded it. In November, the president proposed that the border states embark on a program of gradual emancipation with the federal government paying owners for their loss of property. He also revived the idea of colonization. In August 1862, Lincoln met at the White House with a delegation of black leaders and urged them to promote emigration from the United States. "You and we are different races," he declared. "It is better for us both to be separated." As late as December 1862, the president signed an agreement with a shady entrepreneur to settle former slaves on an island off the coast of Haiti.

Abe Lincoln's Last Card, an engraving from the British magazine *Punch*, October 18, 1862, portrays the Preliminary Emancipation Proclamation as the last move of a desperate gambler

Lincoln's Decision

During the summer of 1862, Lincoln concluded that emancipation had become a political and military necessity. Many factors contributed to his decision—lack of military success, hope that emancipated slaves might help meet the army's growing manpower needs, changing northern public opinion, and the calculation that making slavery a target of the war effort would counteract sentiment in Britain for recognition of the Confederacy. But on the

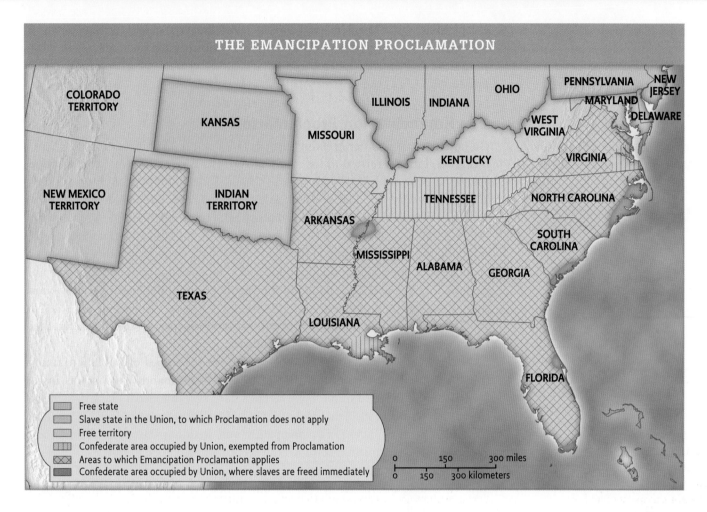

THE EMANCIPATION PROCLAMATION

Legend:
- Free state
- Slave state in the Union, to which Proclamation does not apply
- Free territory
- Confederate area occupied by Union, exempted from Proclamation
- Areas to which Emancipation Proclamation applies
- Confederate area occupied by Union, where slaves are freed immediately

With the exception of a few areas, the Emancipation Proclamation applied only to slaves in parts of the Confederacy not under Union control on January 1, 1863. Lincoln did not "free the slaves" with a stroke of his pen, but the Proclamation did change the nature of the Civil War.

advice of Secretary of State William H. Seward, Lincoln delayed his announcement until after a Union victory, lest it seem an act of desperation. On September 22, 1862, five days after McClellan's army forced Lee to retreat at Antietam, Lincoln issued the Preliminary Emancipation Proclamation. It warned that unless the South laid down its arms by the end of 1862, he would decree abolition.

The Preliminary Emancipation Proclamation

The initial northern reaction was not encouraging. In the fall elections of 1862, Democrats made opposition to emancipation the centerpiece of their campaign, warning that the North would be "Africanized"—inundated by freed slaves who would compete for jobs and seek to marry white women. The Republicans suffered sharp reverses. They lost control of the legislatures of Indiana and Illinois and the governorship of New York, and saw their majorities dangerously reduced in other states. In his annual message to Congress, early in December, Lincoln tried to calm northerners' racial fears, reviving the ideas of gradual emancipation and colonization. He concluded, however, on a higher note: "Fellow citizens, we cannot

Political backlash

escape history. . . . The fiery trial through which we pass, will light us down, in honor or dishonor, to the latest generation. . . . In giving freedom to the slave, we assure freedom to the free—honorable alike in what we give, and what we preserve."

The Emancipation Proclamation

On January 1, 1863, after greeting visitors at the annual White House New Year's reception, Lincoln retired to his study to sign the **Emancipation Proclamation**. The document did not liberate all the slaves—indeed, on the day it was issued, it applied to very few. Because its legality derived from the president's authority as military commander-in-chief to combat the South's rebellion, the Proclamation exempted areas firmly under Union control (where the war, in effect, had already ended). Thus, it did not apply to the loyal border slave states that had never seceded or to areas of the Confederacy occupied by Union soldiers, such as Tennessee and parts of Virginia and Louisiana. But the vast majority of the South's slaves—more than 3 million men, women, and children—it declared "henceforward shall be free." Since most of these slaves were still behind Confederate lines, however, their liberation would have to await Union victories.

Despite its limitations, the Proclamation set off scenes of jubilation among free blacks and abolitionists in the North and "contrabands" and slaves in the South. "Sound the loud timbrel o'er Egypt's dark sea," intoned a black preacher at a celebration in Boston. "Jehovah hath triumphed, his people are free." By making the Union army an agent of emancipation and wedding the goals of Union and abolition, the Proclamation sounded the eventual death knell of slavery.

Not only did the Emancipation Proclamation alter the nature of the Civil War and the course of American history, but it also represented a turning point in

Freed Negroes Celebrating President Lincoln's Decree of Emancipation, a fanciful engraving from the French periodical *Le Monde Illustré*, March 21, 1863.

Lincoln's own thinking. It contained no reference to compensation to slaveholders or to colonization of the freed people. For the first time, it committed the government to enlisting black soldiers in the Union army. Lincoln now became in his own mind the Great Emancipator—that is, he assumed the role that history had thrust upon him, and he tried to live up to it. He would later refuse suggestions that he rescind or modify the Proclamation in the interest of peace. Were he to do so, he told one visitor, "I should be damned in time and eternity."

The Civil War, begun to preserve the prewar Union, now portended a far-reaching transformation in southern life and a redefinition of American freedom. Decoupling emancipation from colonization meant that the freed slaves would become part of American life. A new system of labor, politics, and race relations would have to replace the shattered institution of slavery. "Up to now," wrote the socialist thinker Karl Marx, observing events from London, "we have witnessed only the first act of the Civil War—the constitutional waging of war. The second act, the revolutionary waging of war, is at hand." The evolution of Lincoln's emancipation policy displayed the hallmarks of his wartime leadership—his capacity for growth and his ability to develop broad public support for his administration.

The regimental banner and motto of a unit of African-American soldiers embodies the hope that service in the Union army will lead to citizenship in the postwar world.

Enlisting Black Troops

Of the Proclamation's provisions, few were more radical in their implications than the enrollment of blacks into military service. Since sailor had been one of the few occupations open to free blacks before the war, Secretary of the Navy Gideon Welles had already allowed African-Americans to serve on Union warships. But as during the American Revolution, when George Washington initially excluded blacks from the Continental army, blacks in the Civil War had to fight for the right to fight on land. Early in the war, Harry Jarvis, a Virginia slave, escaped to Fortress Monroe and offered to enlist in the Union army. General Benjamin F. Butler, Jarvis later recalled, "said *it wasn't a black man's war.* I told him it *would* be a black man's war before they got through."

At the outset, the Union army refused to accept northern black volunteers. The administration feared that whites would not be willing to fight alongside blacks, and that enlisting black soldiers would alienate the border slave states that remained in the Union. By the end of 1861, however, the army was employing escaped slaves as cooks, laundresses, and laborers. Preliminary steps to enlist combat troops were taken in a few parts of the South in 1862. White abolitionist Thomas Wentworth Higginson was sent to the South Carolina Sea Islands, which the Union navy had seized early in the war, to enroll slaves in the First South Carolina Volunteers. But only after the Emancipation Proclamation did the recruitment of black soldiers begin in earnest.

Concerns about volunteers

By the end of the war, more than 180,000 black men had served in the Union army, and 24,000 in the navy. One-third died in battle, or of wounds or disease. Fifteen black soldiers and eight sailors received the Medal of Honor, the highest

COME AND JOIN US BROTHERS.

PUBLISHED BY THE SUPERVISORY COMMITTEE FOR RECRUITING COLORED REGIMENTS
1210 CHESTNUT ST. PHILADELPHIA.

This widely reprinted recruiting poster urged African-American men to join the Union army after Congress and the president changed the policy of allowing only whites to serve.

A photograph of a black washerwoman for the Union army wearing a small American flag reflects how the war and emancipation led African-Americans to identify strongly with the nation.

award for military valor. Some black units won considerable notoriety, among them the Fifty-fourth Massachusetts Volunteers, a company of free blacks from throughout the North commanded by Robert Gould Shaw, a young reformer from a prominent Boston family. The bravery of the Fifty-fourth in the July 1863 attack on Fort Wagner, South Carolina, where nearly half the unit, including Shaw, perished, helped to dispel widespread doubts about blacks' ability to withstand the pressures of the Civil War battlefield. (The exploits of Shaw and the Fifty-fourth Massachusetts were popularized in the 1989 film *Glory*.)

Most black soldiers were emancipated slaves who joined the army in the South. After Union forces in 1863 seized control of the rich plantation lands of the Mississippi Valley, General Lorenzo Thomas raised fifty regiments of black soldiers—some 76,000 men in all. Another large group hailed from the border states exempted from the Emancipation Proclamation, where enlistment was, for most of the war, the only route to freedom. Here black military service undermined slavery, for Congress expanded the Emancipation Proclamation to liberate the families of black soldiers.

The Black Soldier

For black soldiers themselves, military service proved to be a liberating experience. "No negro who has ever been a soldier," wrote a northern official in 1865, "can again be imposed upon; they have learned what it is to be free and they will infuse their feelings into others." Service in the army established men as community leaders and opened a door to political advancement. Out of the army came many of the leaders of the Reconstruction era. At least 130 former soldiers served in political office after the Civil War. In time, the memory of black military service would fade from white America's collective memory. Of the hundreds of Civil War monuments that still dot the northern landscape, fewer than a dozen contain an image of a black soldier. But well into the twentieth century, it remained a point of pride in black families throughout the United States that their fathers and grandfathers had fought for freedom.

The Union navy treated black sailors pretty much the same as white sailors. Conditions on ships made racial segregation impossible. Black and white sailors lived and dined together in the same quarters. They received equal pay and had the same promotion opportunities. Within the army, however, black soldiers received treatment that was anything but equal to their white counterparts. Organized into segregated units under sometimes abusive white officers, they initially received lower pay (ten dollars per month, compared to sixteen dollars for white soldiers).

They were disproportionately assigned to labor rather than combat, and they could not rise to the rank of commissioned officer until the very end of the war. If captured by Confederate forces, they faced the prospect of sale into slavery or immediate execution. In a notorious incident in 1864, 200 of 262 black soldiers died when southern troops under the command of Nathan B. Forrest overran Fort Pillow in Tennessee. Some of those who perished had been killed after surrendering.

Nonetheless, black soldiers played a crucial role not only in winning the Civil War but also in defining the war's consequences. "Once let a black man get upon his person the brass letters U.S.," wrote Frederick Douglass in urging blacks to enlist, "and there is no power on earth which can deny that he has earned the right to citizenship in the United States." As Douglass predicted, thanks in part to black military service many Republicans in the last two years of the war came to believe that emancipation must bring with it equal protection of the laws regardless of race. One of the first acts of the federal government to recognize this principle was the granting of retroactive equal pay to black soldiers early in 1865. Racism was hardly eliminated from national life. But, declared George William Curtis, the editor of *Harper's Weekly*, the war and emancipation had transformed a government "for white men" into one "for mankind."

The service of black soldiers affected Lincoln's own outlook. He insisted that they must be treated the same as whites when captured and suspended prisoner-of-war exchanges when the Confederacy refused to include black troops. In 1864, Lincoln, who before the war had never supported suffrage for African-Americans, urged the governor of Union-occupied Louisiana to work for the partial enfranchisement of blacks, singling out soldiers as especially deserving. At some future time, he observed, they might again be called upon to "keep the *jewel of Liberty* in the family of freedom."

This is the only known photograph of a black Union soldier with his family.

A songbook compiled and illustrated by a Union soldier includes "John Brown's Body," sung to the melody of a Methodist hymn.

THE SECOND AMERICAN REVOLUTION

"Old things are passing away," wrote a black resident of California in 1862, "and eventually old prejudices must follow. The revolution has begun, and time alone must decide where it is to end." The changing status of black Americans was only one dramatic example of what some historians call the **Second American Revolution**—the transformation of American government and society brought about by the Civil War.

Liberty and Union

Never was freedom's contested nature more evident than during the Civil War. "We all declare for liberty," Lincoln observed in 1864, "but in using the same *word*

The illustration accompanying "The American Flag," a piece of patriotic Civil War sheet music, exemplifies how the war united the ideals of liberty and nationhood.

Lincoln and the Female Slave, by the free black artist David B. Bowser. Working in Philadelphia, Bowser painted flags for a number of black Civil War regiments. Lincoln confers freedom on a kneeling slave, an image that downplays blacks' role in their own emancipation.

we do not all mean the same *thing*." To the North, he continued, freedom meant for "each man" to enjoy "the product of his labor." To southern whites, it conveyed mastership—the power to do "as they please with other men, and the product of other men's labor." The Union's triumph consolidated the northern understanding of freedom as the national norm.

The attack on Fort Sumter crystallized in northern minds the direct conflict between freedom and slavery that abolitionists had insisted upon for decades. The war, as Frederick Douglass recognized as early as 1862, merged "the cause of the slaves and the cause of the country." "Liberty and Union," he continued, "have become identical." As during the American Revolution, religious and secular understandings of freedom joined in a celebration of national destiny. "As He died to make men holy, let us die to make men free," proclaimed the popular song "Battle Hymn of the Republic," written by Julia Ward Howe and published in 1862.

Lincoln's Vision

But it was Lincoln himself who linked the conflict with the deepest beliefs of northern society. It is sometimes said that the American Civil War was part of a broader nineteenth-century process of nation building. Throughout the world, powerful, centralized nation-states developed in old countries, and new nations emerged where none had previously existed. The Civil War took place as modern states were consolidating their power and reducing local autonomy. The Meiji Restoration in Japan saw the emperor reclaim power from local lords, or shoguns. As in the United States, economic development quickly followed national unification. Japan soon emerged as a major economic power.

Lincoln has been called the American equivalent of Giuseppe Mazzini or Otto von Bismarck, who during this same era created nation-states in Italy and Germany from disunited collections of principalities. But Lincoln's nation was different from those being constructed in Europe. They were based on the idea of unifying a particular people with a common ethnic, cultural, and linguistic heritage. To Lincoln, the American nation embodied, instead, a set of universal ideas, centered on political democracy and human liberty. The United States represented to the world the principle that government should rest on popular consent and that all men should be free. These ideals, Lincoln declared, allowed immigrants from abroad, who could not "trace their connection by blood" to the nation's birth, nonetheless to become fully American.

Lincoln summarized his conception of the war's meaning in November 1863 in brief remarks at the dedication of a military cemetery at the site of the war's greatest battle. The Gettysburg Address is considered his finest speech (see the Appendix for the full text). In less than three minutes, he identified the nation's mission with the principle that "all men are created equal," spoke of the war as bringing about a "new birth of freedom," and defined the essence of democratic government. The sacrifices of Union soldiers, he declared, would ensure that "government of the people, by the people, for the people, shall not perish from the earth."

The mobilization of the Union's resources for modern war brought into being a new American nation-state with greatly expanded powers and responsibilities. The United States remained a federal republic with sovereignty divided between the state and national governments. But the war forged a new national

The Eagle's Nest, an 1861 antisecession cartoon promising "annihilation to traitors." The eggs representing seceding states have become rotten and are hatching monsters.

self-consciousness, reflected in the increasing use of the word "nation"—a unified political entity—in place of the older "Union" of separate states. In his inaugural address in 1861, Lincoln used the word "Union" twenty times, while making no mention of the "nation." By 1863, "Union" does not appear at all in the 269-word Gettysburg Address, while Lincoln referred five times to the "nation."

A new political identity

The War and American Religion

The upsurge of patriotism, and of national power, was reflected in many aspects of American life. Even as the war produced unprecedented casualties, the northern Protestant clergy strove to provide it with a religious justification and to reassure their congregations that the dead had not died in vain. The religious press now devoted more space to military and political developments than to spiritual matters. In numerous wartime sermons, Christianity and patriotism were joined in a civic religion that saw the war as God's mechanism for ridding the United States of slavery and enabling it to become what it had never really been—a land of freedom. Lincoln, one of the few American presidents who never joined a church, shrewdly marshaled religious symbolism to generate public support, declaring days of Thanksgiving after northern victories and encouraging northern clergymen to support Republican candidates for office. Of course, the southern clergy was equally convinced that the Confederate cause represented God's will. In 1863, Methodist bishop George Pierce, in an address to the Confederate Congress, declared that the struggle for southern independence enjoyed "the seal of the divine blessing."

Mass grief, religion, and patriotism

The Sisters of Charity, an order of nuns, photographed with doctors and soldiers at a hospital in Philadelphia in 1863. Many of the wounded from the Battle of Gettysburg were sent here for treatment. The Catholic contribution to the Union war effort mitigated the nativist bias so prominent in the 1850s.

Satulee Hospital — West Phila.

Coping with mass death

A girl in mourning dress holds a framed photograph of her father, a cavalryman.

Religious beliefs enabled Americans to cope with the unprecedented mass death the war involved. Of course, equating death with eternal life is a central tenet of Christianity. But the war led to what one historian calls a "transformation of heaven," as Americans imagined future celestial family reunions that seemed more and more like gatherings in middle-class living rooms. Some Americans could not wait until their own deaths to see the departed. Spiritualism—belief in the ability to communicate with the dead—grew in popularity. Mary Todd Lincoln held seances in the White House to experience again the presence of her young son Willie, who succumbed to disease in 1862.

Coping with death also required unprecedented governmental action, from notifying next of kin to accounting for the dead and missing. Both the Union and Confederacy established elaborate systems for gathering statistics and maintaining records of dead and wounded soldiers, an effort supplemented by private philanthropic organizations. After the war ended, the federal government embarked on a program to locate and re-bury hundreds of thousands of Union soldiers in national military cemeteries. Between 1865 and 1871, the government reinterred more than 300,000 Union (but not Confederate) soldiers—including black soldiers, who were buried in segregated sections of military cemeteries.

Liberty in Wartime

This intense new nationalism made criticism of the war effort—or of the policies of the Lincoln administration—seem to Republicans equivalent to treason. Although there had been sporadic persecution of opponents of the Mexican War, the Civil War presented, for the first time since the Revolution, the issue of the limits of wartime dissent. During the conflict, declared the Republican *New York Times*, "the safety of the nation is the supreme law." Arbitrary arrests numbered in the thousands. They included opposition newspaper editors, Democratic politicians, individuals who discouraged enlistment in the army, and ordinary civilians like the Chicago man briefly imprisoned for calling the president a "damned fool." With the Constitution unclear as to who possessed the power to suspend the writ of habeas corpus (thus allowing prisoners to be held without charge), Lincoln claimed the right under the presidential war powers and twice suspended the writ throughout the entire Union for those accused of "disloyal activities."

Arbitrary arrests and the suspension of habeas corpus

The courts generally gave the administration a free hand. They refused to intervene when a military court convicted Clement L. Vallandigham, a leading Ohio Democrat known for his blistering antiwar speeches, of treason. On Lincoln's order, Vallandigham was banished to the Confederacy. In 1861, Chief Justice Roger B. Taney ordered the president to release John Merryman, a civilian who had been arrested by military authorities in Maryland, but the president ignored him. Not until 1866, after the fighting had ended, did the Supreme Court, in the case ***Ex parte Milligan***, declare it unconstitutional to bring accused persons before military tribunals where civil courts were operating. The Constitution, declared Justice David Davis, is not suspended in wartime—it remains "a law for rulers and people, equally in time of war and peace."

The Constitution in wartime

Lincoln was not a despot. Most of those arrested were quickly released, the Democratic press continued to flourish, and contested elections were held throughout the war. But the policies of the Lincoln administration offered proof—to be repeated during later wars—of the fragility of civil liberties in the face of assertive patriotism and wartime demands for national unity.

Fragility of civil liberties in wartime

The North's Transformation

Even as he invoked traditional values, Lincoln presided over far-reaching changes in northern life. The effort to mobilize the resources of the Union greatly enhanced the power not only of the federal government but also of a rising class of capitalist entrepreneurs. Unlike the South, which suffered economic devastation, the North experienced the war as a time of prosperity.

Northern prosperity

Nourished by wartime inflation and government contracts, the profits of industry boomed. New England mills worked day and night to supply the army with blankets and uniforms, and Pennsylvania coal mines and ironworks rapidly expanded their production. Mechanization proceeded apace in many industries, especially those like boot and shoe production and meatpacking that supplied the army's ever-increasing needs. Agriculture also flourished, for even as farm boys by the hundreds of thousands joined the army, the frontier of cultivation pushed westward, with machinery and immigrants replacing lost labor. Wisconsin furnished 90,000 men to the Union army, yet its population, grain production, and farm income continued to grow.

Government and the Economy

As in contemporary Germany and Japan, the new American nation-state that emerged during the Civil War was committed to rapid economic development.

Sheet music for two of the best-known patriotic songs written during the Civil War.

Congress adopted policies that promoted economic growth and permanently altered the nation's financial system. With the South now unrepresented, the lawmakers adopted policies long advocated by many northerners. To spur agricultural development, the **Homestead Act** offered 160 acres of free public land to settlers in the West. It took effect on January 1, 1863, the same day as the Emancipation Proclamation, and like the Proclamation, tried to implement a vision of freedom. By the 1930s, more than 400,000 families had acquired farms under its provisions. In addition, the Morrill Land Grant College Act, named for Justin S. Morrill of Vermont, who introduced the measure, assisted the states in establishing "agricultural and mechanic colleges."

Congress also made huge grants of money and land for internal improvements, including up to 100 million acres to the Union Pacific and Central Pacific, two companies chartered in 1862 and charged with building a railroad from the Missouri River to the Pacific coast. (These were the first corporate charters issued by the federal government since the Second Bank of the United States in 1816.)

When first proposed by Asa Whitney in 1846, the idea of a **transcontinental railroad** had been considered by Congress "too gigantic" and "entirely impracticable." And, indeed, the project was monumental. The Central Pacific progressed only twenty miles a year for the first three years of construction because the Sierra Nevada range was almost impassable. It required some 20,000 men to lay the tracks across prairies and mountains, a substantial number of them immigrant Chinese contract laborers, called "coolies" by many Americans. Hundreds of Chinese workers died blasting tunnels and building bridges through this treacherous terrain. When it was completed in 1869, the transcontinental railroad, which ran from Omaha, Nebraska, to San Francisco, reduced the time of a cross-country journey from four or five months to six days. It expanded the national market, facilitated the spread of settlement and investment in the West, and heralded the doom of the Plains Indians.

The West and the War

Most accounts of the Civil War say little or nothing about the West. Yet the conflict engulfed Missouri, Kansas, and Indian Territory, and spread into the Southwest borderlands. The war divided western communities as residents flocked to both armies.

Since the beginning of the republic, the question of slavery had been tied up with the status of new western lands. Jefferson Davis had long been interested in the expansion of slavery into the Southwest. In pursuit of this goal, in October 1861, Confederate units from Texas launched an invasion of New Mexico (which Texans had long claimed as part of their state). They hoped to conquer the region as a gateway to acquisition of southern California and northern Mexico, a continuation of a southern version of manifest destiny, evidenced before the war in filibustering expeditions in the Caribbean. But the Confederates were defeated at Glorieta Pass in March 1862 by a small Union army contingent reinforced by volunteers from Colorado and California. With their retreat to Texas died the dream of a slave empire in the Far West.

The invasion of New Mexico

The war had a profound impact on western Indians. One of Lincoln's first orders as president was to withdraw federal troops from the West so that they could protect Washington, D.C. Recognizing that this would make it impossible for the army to keep white interlopers from intruding on Indian land, as treaties required it to do, Indian leaders begged Lincoln to reverse this decision, but to no avail. Inevitably, conflict flared in the West between Native Americans and white settlers, with disastrous results. During the Civil War, the Sioux killed hundreds of white farmers in Minnesota before being subdued by the army at Fort Ridgely. After a military court sentenced more than 300 Indians to death, Lincoln commuted the sentences of all but 38. But their hanging in December 1862 remains the largest official execution in American history.

In November 1864, Colorado militiamen attacked a group of around 700 Cheyennes and Arapahos camped along Sand Creek in Colorado. Led by Colonel John Chivington, an abolitionist and a former Methodist minister, the soldiers were bent on punishing Indians responsible for raids on nearby settlements. They failed to locate the hostile Indians, but chose to assault the peaceful encampment with rifles and artillery, killing more than 150 men, women, and children. The incident sparked intensified warfare on the southern plains, as Cheyennes and Arapahos retaliated with attacks of their own. It also helped to inspire a movement for the reform of Indian policies to emphasize peaceful assimilation over military conquest. Congress investigated the massacre and condemned Chivington's actions. It even promised reparations to the survivors.

The Union army also launched a series of campaigns in the Southwest against tribes like the Kiowas and Comanches, whose violent raids on ranches and settlements had been an essential, although disruptive, part of the borderlands economy, organized around trading and exchanging captives (usually women), livestock, and horses. They had taken tens of thousands of horses and cattle each year, to use as a kind of currency in trade with other Indians and Anglos.

A lithograph depicts the hanging of thirty-eight Sioux Dakotas at Mankato, Minnesota, in December 1862, the largest mass execution in American history.

A Union soldier stands guard over a group of Indians during the Navajo's Long Walk, in which the army removed them from their New Mexico homeland to a reservation hundreds of miles away.

VOICES OF FREEDOM

From FREDERICK DOUGLASS, MEN OF COLOR TO ARMS (1863)

The Emancipation Proclamation opened the door to the large-scale recruitment of black men into the Union army. In March 1863, in a speech in Rochester, New York, Frederick Douglass called on northern blacks to volunteer for the Fifty-fourth Massachusetts Volunteers, a company of blacks from throughout the free states commanded by Robert Gould Shaw, a young reformer from a prominent Boston family.

———————————

When first the rebel cannon shattered the walls of Sumter and drove away its starving garrison, I predicted that the war then and there inaugurated would not be fought out entirely by white men. Every month's experience during these dreary years has confirmed that opinion. A war undertaken and brazenly carried on for the perpetual enslavement of colored men, calls logically and loudly for colored men to help suppress it. . . . With every reverse to the national arms, with every exulting shout of victory raised by the slaveholding rebels, I have implored the imperiled nation to unchain against her foes, her powerful black hand. Slowly and reluctantly that appeal is beginning to be heeded. Stop not now to complain that it was not heeded sooner. . . . When the war is over, the country is saved, peace is established, and the black man's rights are secured, as they will

be, history with an impartial hand will dispose of that and sundry other questions. Action! Action! not criticism is the plain duty of this hour. . . . Liberty won by white men would lose half its luster. . . .

I have not thought lightly of the words I am now addressing you. The counsel I give comes of close observation of the great struggle now in progress, and of the deep conviction that this is your hour and mine. In good earnest then, and after the best deliberation, I now for the first time during this war feel at liberty to call and counsel you to arms. By every consideration which binds you to your enslaved fellow-countrymen, and the peace and welfare of your country; by every aspiration which you cherish for the freedom and equality of yourselves and your children; by all the ties of blood and identity which make us one with the brave black men now fighting our battles in Louisiana and in South Carolina, I urge you to fly to arms, and smite with death the power that would bury the government and your liberty in the same hopeless grave. . . . The chance is now given you to end in a day the bondage of centuries, and to rise in one bound from social degradation to the plane of common equality with all other varieties of men. . . . This is our golden opportunity.

From ABRAHAM LINCOLN, ADDRESS AT SANITARY FAIR, BALTIMORE (APRIL 18, 1864)

Abraham Lincoln's speech at a Sanitary Fair (a grand bazaar that raised money for the care of Union soldiers) offers a dramatic illustration of the contested meaning of freedom during the Civil War.

The world has never had a good definition of the word liberty, and the American people, just now, are much in want of one. We all declare for liberty; but in using the same *word* we do not all mean the same *thing*. With some the word liberty may mean for each man to do as he pleases with himself, and the product of his labor; while with others the same word may mean for some men to do as they please with other men, and the product of other men's labor. Here are two, not only different, but incompatible things, called by the same name—liberty. And it follows that each of the things is, by the respective parties, called by two different and incompatible names—liberty and tyranny.

The shepherd drives the wolf from the sheep's throat, for which the sheep thanks the shepherd as a *liberator*, while the wolf denounces him for the same act as the destroyer of liberty, especially as the sheep was a black one. Plainly the sheep and the wolf are not agreed upon a definition of the word liberty; and precisely the same difference prevails today among us human creatures, even in the North, and all professing to love liberty. Hence we behold the process by which thousands are daily passing from under the yoke of bondage, hailed by some as the advance of liberty, and bewailed by others as the destruction of all liberty. Recently, as it seems, the people of Maryland have been doing something to define liberty [abolishing slavery in the state]; and thanks to them that, in what they have done, the wolf's dictionary, has been repudiated.

QUESTIONS

1. *What benefits does Douglass think blacks will derive from service in the Union army?*

2. *What does Lincoln identify as the essential difference between northern and southern definitions of freedom?*

3. *While both men desire the end of slavery, are there subtle differences in how they seem to understand freedom?*

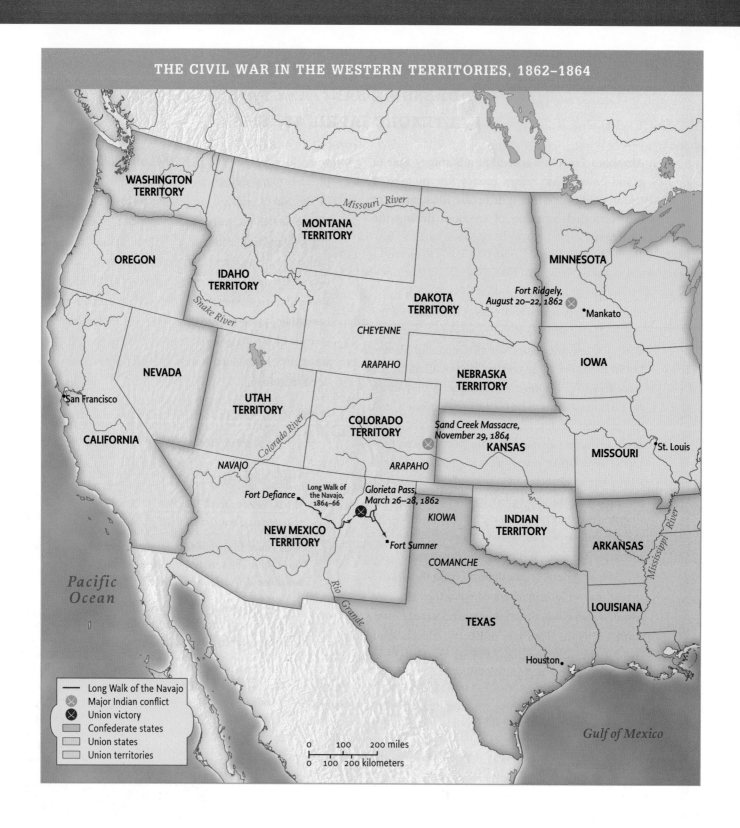

THE CIVIL WAR IN THE WESTERN TERRITORIES, 1862–1864

WASHINGTON TERRITORY

OREGON

IDAHO TERRITORY

MONTANA TERRITORY

Missouri River

DAKOTA TERRITORY

MINNESOTA

Fort Ridgely, August 20–22, 1862

Mankato

Snake River

CHEYENNE

NEVADA

ARAPAHO

NEBRASKA TERRITORY

IOWA

San Francisco

UTAH TERRITORY

Colorado River

COLORADO TERRITORY

Sand Creek Massacre, November 29, 1864

CALIFORNIA

NAVAJO

ARAPAHO

KANSAS

MISSOURI

St. Louis

Fort Defiance

Long Walk of the Navajo, 1864–66

Glorieta Pass, March 26–28, 1862

KIOWA

INDIAN TERRITORY

ARKANSAS

NEW MEXICO TERRITORY

Fort Sumner

COMANCHE

Pacific Ocean

Rio Grande

Mississippi River

LOUISIANA

TEXAS

Houston

Legend:
— Long Walk of the Navajo
⊗ Major Indian conflict
⊗ Union victory
▢ Confederate states
▢ Union states
▢ Union territories

0   100   200 miles
0   100   200 kilometers

Gulf of Mexico

The army also made war on the Navajo, who were more victims than perpetrators of these raids. Indian raiding parties had stolen more than 50,000 sheep from their settlements in 1860 alone. Union forces destroyed their orchards and sheep and forced 8,000 people to move to a reservation set aside by the government. The **Navajo's Long Walk** became as central to their historical experience as the Trail of Tears to the Cherokee (see Chapter 10). Unlike the eastern Indians, however, the Navajo were eventually allowed to return to a portion of their lands. The wars against Native Americans, a small part of the violence that engulfed the nation during the Civil War, would continue for more than two decades after the sectional conflict ended.

War with the Navajo

Ironically, the Confederacy, although defending slavery, treated Native Americans more fairly than the Union. The Confederate Constitution provided for Indian tribes to elect representatives to Congress, and the Davis administration removed state jurisdiction over Indian reservations, allowing them complete self-government. Some tribes that owned slaves, like the Cherokee, sided with the Confederacy. After 1865, they were forced to cede much of their land to the federal government and to accept former slaves into the Cherokee nation and give them land (the only slaveowners required to do so). Their status remains a point of controversy to this day. The Cherokee constitution was recently amended to exclude descendants of slaves from citizenship, leading to lawsuits that have yet to be resolved.

The Confederacy's treatment of Indians

A New Financial System

The need to pay for the war produced dramatic changes in financial policy. To raise money, the government increased the tariff to unprecedented heights (thus promoting the further growth of northern industry), imposed new taxes on the production and consumption of goods, and enacted the nation's first income tax. It also borrowed more than $2 billion by selling interest-bearing bonds, thus creating an immense national debt. And it printed more than $400 million worth of paper money, called "greenbacks," declared to be legal tender—that is, money that must be accepted for nearly all public and private payments and debts. To rationalize banking, Congress established a system of nationally chartered banks, which were required to purchase government bonds and were given the right to issue bank notes as currency. A heavy tax drove money issued by state banks out of existence. Thus, the United States, whose money supply before the war was a chaotic mixture of paper notes issued by state and local banks, now had essentially two kinds of national paper currency—greenbacks printed directly by the federal government, and notes issued by the new national banks.

Along with profitable contracts to supply goods for the military effort, wartime economic policies greatly benefited northern manufacturers, railroad men, and financiers. Numerous Americans who would take the lead in reshaping the nation's postwar economy created or consolidated their fortunes during the Civil War, among them iron and steel entrepreneur Andrew Carnegie, oil magnate John D. Rockefeller, financiers Jay Gould and J. P. Morgan, and Philip D. Armour, who earned millions supplying beef to the Union army. These and other "captains of industry" managed to escape military service, sometimes by purchasing exemptions or hiring substitutes, as allowed by the draft law.

Filling Cartridges at the U.S. Arsenal of Watertown, Massachusetts, an engraving from *Harper's Weekly*, September 21, 1861. Both men and women were drawn to work in the booming war-related industries of the North.

A female nurse photographed between two wounded Union soldiers in a Nashville military hospital in 1862. Many northern women served the army as nurses during the war.

Taken together, the Union's economic policies vastly increased the power and size of the federal government. The federal budget for 1865 exceeded $1 billion—nearly twenty times that of 1860. With its new army of clerks, tax collectors, and other officials, the government became the nation's largest employer. And while much of this expansion proved temporary, the government would never return to its weak and fragmented condition of the prewar period.

Women and the War

For many northern women, the conflict opened new doors of opportunity. Women took advantage of the wartime labor shortage to move into jobs in factories and into certain largely male professions, particularly nursing. The expansion of the activities of the national government opened new jobs for women as clerks in government offices. Many of these wartime gains were short-lived, but in white-collar government jobs, retail sales, and nursing, women found a permanent place in the workforce.

Some northern women took a direct part in military campaigns. Clara Barton, a clerk in the Patent Office in Washington, D.C., when the war began, traveled with the Army of Virginia, helping to organize supply lines and nursing wounded soldiers. Barton worked alone rather than as a part of the Department of Female Nurses, and she never received compensation from the government.

Hundreds of thousands of northern women took part in organizations that gathered money and medical supplies for soldiers and sent books, clothing, and food to freedmen. The United States Sanitary Commission emerged as a centralized national relief agency to coordinate donations on the northern home front. Although control at the national level remained in male hands, patriotic women did most of the grassroots work. Women played the leading role in organizing **Sanitary Fairs**—grand bazaars that displayed military banners, uniforms, and

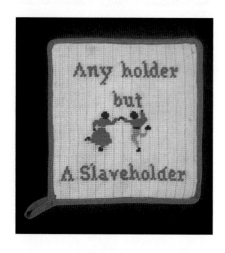

Whimsical potholders expressing hope for a better life for emancipated slaves were sold at the Chicago Sanitary Fair of 1865, to raise money for soldiers' aid.

other relics of the war and sold goods to raise money for soldiers' aid. New York City's three-week fair of 1864 attracted a crowd of 30,000 and raised more than $1 million.

Many men understood women's war work as an extension of their "natural" capacity for self-sacrifice. But the very act of volunteering to work in local soldiers' aid societies brought many northern women into the public sphere and offered them a taste of independence. The suffrage movement suspended operations during the war to devote itself to the Union and emancipation. But women's continuing lack of the vote seemed all the more humiliating as their involvement in war work increased.

From the ranks of this wartime mobilization came many of the leaders of the postwar movement for women's rights. Mary Livermore, the wife of a Chicago minister, for example, toured military hospitals to assess their needs, cared for injured and dying soldiers, and organized two Sanitary Fairs. She emerged from the war with a deep resentment of women's legal and political subordination and organized her state's first woman suffrage convention. Women, she had concluded, must "think and act for themselves." After the war, Clara Barton not only became an advocate of woman suffrage but, as president of the American National Red Cross, lobbied for the United States to endorse the First Geneva Convention of 1864, which mandated the humane treatment of battlefield casualties. Largely as a result of Barton's efforts, the Senate ratified the convention in 1882. (Subsequent Geneva Conventions in the twentieth century would deal with the treatment of prisoners of war and civilians during wartime.)

Camp of Thirty-first Pennsylvania Infantry, Near Washington, D.C., an 1862 photograph by the Mathew Brady studio. Many women worked for the army as laundresses. Some accompanied their husbands and even brought their children.

The Divided North

Despite Lincoln's political skills, the war and his administration's policies divided northern society. Republicans labeled those opposed to the war Copperheads, after a poisonous snake that strikes without warning. Mounting casualties and rapid societal changes divided the North. Disaffection was strongest among the large southern-born population of states like Ohio, Indiana, and Illinois and working-class Catholic immigrants in eastern cities.

As the war progressed, it heightened existing social tensions and created new ones. The growing power of the federal government challenged traditional notions of local autonomy. The Union's draft law, which allowed individuals to provide a substitute or buy their way out of the army, caused widespread indignation. Workers resented manufacturers and financiers who reaped large profits while their own real incomes dwindled because of inflation. The war witnessed the rebirth of the northern labor movement, which organized numerous strikes for higher wages. The prospect of a sweeping change in the status of blacks called forth a racist reaction in many parts of the North. Throughout the war, the

Social tensions in the North

The Riots in New York: The Mob Lynching a Negro in Clarkson Street, an engraving from the British magazine *Illustrated London News*, August 8, 1863, reveals how the New York City draft riots escalated from an attempt to obstruct the draft into an assault on the city's black population.

Democratic Party subjected Lincoln's policies to withering criticism, although it remained divided between "War Democrats," who supported the military effort while criticizing emancipation and the draft, and those who favored immediate peace.

On occasion, dissent degenerated into outright violence. In July 1863, the introduction of the draft provoked four days of rioting in New York City. The mob, composed largely of Irish immigrants, assaulted symbols of the new order being created by the war—draft offices, the mansions of wealthy Republicans, industrial establishments, and the city's black population, many of whom fled to New Jersey or took refuge in Central Park. Only the arrival of Union troops quelled the uprising, but not before more than 100 persons had died.

The New York City draft riots

THE CONFEDERATE NATION

Leadership and Government

Jefferson Davis

The man charged with the task of rallying public support for the Confederacy proved unequal to the task. Born in 1808 in Kentucky, within eight months and 100 miles of Lincoln's birth, Jefferson Davis moved to Mississippi as a youth, attended West Point, and acquired a large plantation. Aloof, stubborn, and humorless, he lacked Lincoln's common touch and political flexibility. Although known before the war as the "Cicero of the Senate" for his eloquent speeches, Davis, unlike Lincoln, proved unable to communicate the war's meaning effectively to ordinary men and women. Moreover, the Confederacy's lack of a party system proved to be a political liability. Like the founders of the American republic, southern leaders saw parties as threats to national unity. As a result, Davis lacked a counterpart

The centrality of slavery to the Confederacy is illustrated by the paper money issued by state governments and private banks, which frequently juxtaposed scenes of slaves at work with other revered images. The ten-dollar note of the Eastern Bank of Alabama depicts slaves working in the field and at a port, along with an idealized portrait of southern white womanhood. Alabama's five-dollar bill includes an overseer directing slaves in the field, and a symbol of liberty.

to the well-organized Republican Party, which helped to mobilize support for the Lincoln administration.

Under Davis, the Confederate nation became far more centralized than the Old South had been. The government raised armies from scratch, took control of southern railroads, and built manufacturing plants. But it failed to find an effective way of utilizing the South's major economic resource, cotton. In the early part of the war, the administration tried to suppress cotton production, urging planters to grow food instead and banning cotton exports. This, it was hoped, would promote economic self-sufficiency and force Great Britain, whose textile mills could not operate without southern cotton, to intervene on the side of the Confederacy.

Centralizing the South

"**King Cotton diplomacy**" turned out to be ineffective. Large crops in 1859 and 1860 had created a huge stockpile in English warehouses. By the time distress hit the manufacturing districts in 1862, the government of Prime Minister Palmerston had decided not to intervene, partly because Britain needed northern wheat almost as much as southern cotton. But the Confederate policy had far-reaching global consequences. Recognizing their overdependence on southern cotton, other nations moved to expand production. Britain promoted cultivation of the crop in Egypt and India, and Russia did the same in parts of Central Asia. As a result, the resumption of American cotton production after the war led directly to a worldwide crisis of overproduction that drove down the price of cotton, impoverishing farmers around the world.

The international dimension

A drawing by Langdon Cheves III, the teenage grandson of a prominent South Carolina political leader, depicts a Confederate killing a Yankee officer.

Commodity shortages

Nor did Davis deal effectively with obstructionist governors like Joseph E. Brown of Georgia, who denounced the Confederate draft as "a dangerous usurpation" of states' rights and individual liberty. All in all, Davis was so inferior to Lincoln as a wartime leader that one historian has suggested that had the North and South exchanged presidents, the South would have won the war.

The Inner Civil War

As the war progressed, social change and internal turmoil engulfed much of the Confederacy. At the outset, most white southerners rallied to the Confederate cause. No less fervently than northern troops, southern soldiers spoke of their cause in the language of freedom. "We are fighting for our liberty," wrote one volunteer, without any sense of contradiction, "against tyrants of the North . . . who are determined to destroy slavery." But public disaffection eventually became an even more serious problem for the Confederacy than for the Union.

One grievance was the draft. Like the Union, the Confederacy allowed individuals to provide a substitute. Because of the accelerating disintegration of slavery, it also exempted one white male for every twenty slaves on a plantation (thus releasing many overseers and planters' sons from service). The "twenty-negro" provision convinced many yeomen that the struggle for southern independence had become "a rich man's war and a poor man's fight."

Economic Problems

Economic deprivation also sparked disaffection. As the blockade tightened, areas of the Confederacy came under Union occupation, and production by slaves declined, shortages arose of essential commodities such as salt, corn, and meat. The war left countless farms, plantations, businesses, and railroads in ruins. The economic crisis, which stood in glaring contrast to the North's boom, was an unavoidable result of the war. But Confederate policies exaggerated its effects. War requires sacrifice, and civilian support for war depends, in part, on the belief that sacrifice is being fairly shared. Many non-slaveholders, however, became convinced that they were bearing an unfair share of the war's burdens.

Like the Union, the Confederacy borrowed heavily to finance the war. Unlike federal lawmakers, however, the planter-dominated Confederate Congress proved unwilling to levy heavy taxes that planters would have to pay. It relied on paper money, of which it issued $1.5 billion, far more than the North's greenbacks. Congress also authorized military officers to seize farm goods to supply the army, paying with increasingly worthless Confederate money. Small farmers deeply resented this practice, known as "impressment." "The Rebel army treated us a heap worse than [Union general William T.] Sherman did," a Georgia farmer later recalled. "I had hogs, and a mule, and a horse, and they took them all." Numerous yeoman families, many of whom had gone to war to preserve their economic independence, sank into poverty and debt. Food riots broke out in many places, including Richmond, Virginia, and Mobile, Alabama, where in 1863 large crowds of women plundered army food supplies.

Confederate financing of the war

In 1862, Joshua B. Moore, a slaveholder in northern Alabama, commented on how slavery threatened the Confederate war effort: "Men who have no interest in it," he wrote, "are not going to fight through a long war to save it—never. They will tire of it and quit." As the war progressed, desertion became what one officer called a "crying evil" for the southern armies. By the war's end, more than 100,000 men had deserted, almost entirely from among "the poorest class of nonslaveholders whose labor is indispensable to the daily support of their families." Men, another official noted, "cannot be expected to fight for the government that permits their wives and children to starve."

Desertion

Southern Unionists

Continued loyalty to the Union was a dangerous stance in the Confederate South. Georgia in 1861 passed a law making it punishable by death (hardly the action of a government committed to individual liberty and the rights of minorities). Nonetheless, by 1864, organized peace movements had appeared in several southern states, and secret societies such as the Heroes of America were actively promoting disaffection. Confederate military tribunals imprisoned hundreds of Unionists. Others were violently driven from their homes, and a few were executed by the

An engraving in the *New York Illustrated News* depicts the bread riot that took place in Mobile, Alabama, in the fall of 1863.

army or civilian authorities. But southerners loyal to the Union made a significant contribution to northern victory. By the end of the war, an estimated 50,000 white southerners had fought in the Union armies.

Elizabeth Van Lew

One of the most celebrated Union heroes of the war was Elizabeth Van Lew of Richmond, who had persuaded her mother to free the family's slaves when her father died in 1843. During the war she frequently visited Libby Prison in the Confederate capital, bringing supplies to Union prisoners of war and helping some of them to escape. With the aid of Mary Elizabeth Bowser, a former slave of the Van Lew family who worked as a servant in the southern White House, Van Lew passed information about Confederate plans to Union forces.

Women and the Confederacy

Experiences of white women in the South

Even more than in the North, the war placed unprecedented burdens on southern white women. Left alone on farms and plantations, they were often forced to manage business affairs and discipline slaves, previously the responsibility of men. As in the North, women mobilized to support soldiers in the field and stepped out of their traditional "sphere" to run commercial establishments and work in arms factories. In Richmond, "government girls" staffed many of the clerkships in the new Confederate bureaucracy. Rose Greenhow, the widow of a former American diplomat, headed an espionage ring in Washington, D.C., that passed valuable information about Union troop movements to the Confederacy early in the war. Even after her arrest and jailing, she managed to smuggle out intelligence until she was exiled to Richmond in 1862. Jefferson Davis rewarded Greenhow with $2,500 for her services.

Painted in 1864 by the Virginia artist William D. Washington, *The Burial of Latané* depicts a common wartime scene. The deceased is Confederate cavalry officer William Latané. The work illustrates how women, children, and slaves predominated on the southern homefront. Having finished digging the grave, the slave on the left has a faraway look in his eyes; perhaps he is listening for the sound of the approaching Union army. The painting was displayed in Richmond accompanied by a bucket into which viewers were urged to deposit contributions to the southern cause.

THE CIVIL WAR, 1863

All Confederate women struggled to cope as their loved ones were drawn off into the army. The war led to the political mobilization, for the first time, of non-slaveholding white women. Lacking the aid of slave labor, they found that the absence of their husbands from their previously self-sufficient farms made it impossible to feed their families. They flooded Confederate authorities with petitions seeking assistance, not as charity but as a right. Politicians could not ignore the pleas of soldiers' wives, and state governments began to distribute supplies to needy families.

Southern women's self-sacrificing devotion to the cause became legendary. But as the war went on and the death toll mounted, increasing numbers of women came to believe that the goal of independence was not worth the cost. The growing disaffection of southern white women, conveyed in letters to loved ones at the front, contributed to the decline in civilian morale and encouraged desertion from the army.

In July 1863, the Union won major victories at Gettysburg and Vicksburg.

Black Soldiers for the Confederacy

The growing shortage of white manpower eventually led Confederate authorities to a decision no one could have foreseen when the war began: they authorized the arming of slaves to fight for the South. As early as September 1863, a Mississippi newspaper had argued for freeing and enlisting able-bodied black men. "Let them," it wrote, "be declared free, placed in the ranks, and told to fight for their homes and country." But many slaveholders fiercely resisted this idea, and initially, the Confederate Senate rejected it. Not until March 1865, after Robert E. Lee had endorsed the plan, did the Confederate Congress authorize the arming of slaves. To be sure, enlisting blacks in the Confederate army did not necessarily mean the end of slavery. Both the British and Americans had used slave soldiers in the War of Independence, but slavery survived, as it undoubtedly would have had the Confederacy managed to win the Civil War.

The war ended before substantial recruitment of black Confederate soldiers— the only ones who reached the front were two companies impressed into service in Richmond a few days before the city's surrender. But the Confederate army did employ numerous blacks, nearly all of them slaves, as laborers. This later led to some confusion over whether blacks actually fought for the Confederacy—apart from a handful who "passed" for white, none in fact did. But the South's decision to raise black troops illustrates how the war undermined not only slavery but also the proslavery ideology. "The day you make soldiers of them is the beginning of the end of the revolution," declared Howell Cobb, a Georgia planter and politician. "If slaves make good soldiers, our whole theory of slavery is wrong."

TURNING POINTS

Gettysburg and Vicksburg

Despite the accelerating demise of slavery and the decline of morale in the South, the war's outcome remained very much in doubt for much of its third and fourth years. In April 1863, "Fighting Joe" Hooker, who had succeeded Ambrose E. Burnside as the Union commander in the East, brought the Army of the Potomac into central Virginia to confront Lee. Outnumbered two to one, Lee repelled Hooker's attack at Chancellorsville, although he lost his ablest lieutenant, "Stonewall" Jackson, mistakenly killed by fire from his own soldiers.

Lee now gambled on another invasion of the North, although his strategic objective remains unclear. Perhaps he believed a defeat on its own territory would destroy the morale of the northern army and public. In any event, the two armies, with Union soldiers now under the command of General George G. Meade, met at Gettysburg, Pennsylvania, on the first three days of July 1863. With 165,000 troops involved, the **Battle of Gettysburg** remains the largest battle ever fought on the North American continent. Lee found himself in the unusual position of confronting entrenched Union forces. After two days of failing to dislodge them, he decided to attack the center of the Union line. On July 3, Con-

Generals Robert E. Lee and Ulysses S. Grant, leaders of the opposing armies in the East, 1864–1865.

federate forces, led by Major General George E. Pickett's crack division, marched across an open field toward Union forces. Withering artillery and rifle fire met the charge, and most of Pickett's soldiers never reached Union lines. Of the 14,000 men who made the advance—the flower of Lee's army—fewer than half returned. Later remembered as "the high tide of the Confederacy," Pickett's Charge was also Lee's greatest blunder. His army retreated to Virginia, never again to set foot on northern soil.

Pickett's charge

On the same day that Lee began his retreat from Gettysburg, the Union achieved a significant victory in the West. Late in 1862, Grant had moved into Mississippi toward the city of Vicksburg. From its heights, defended by miles of trenches and earthworks, the Confederacy commanded the central Mississippi River. When direct attacks failed, as did an attempt to divert the river by digging a canal, Grant launched a siege. On July 4, 1863, Vicksburg surrendered, and with it John C. Pemberton's army of 30,000 men, a loss the Confederacy could ill afford. The entire Mississippi Valley now lay in Union hands. The simultaneous defeats at Gettysburg and the **Battle of Vicksburg** dealt a heavy blow to southern morale. "Today absolute ruin seems our portion," one official wrote in his diary. "The Confederacy totters to its destruction."

1864

Nearly two years, however, would pass before the war ended. Brought east to take command of Union forces, Grant in 1864 began a war of attrition against Lee's army in Virginia. That is, he was willing to accept high numbers of casualties, knowing that the North could replace its manpower losses while the South could not. Grant understood that to bring the North's manpower advantage into play, he must attack continuously "all along the line," thereby preventing the enemy from concentrating its forces or retreating to safety after an engagement.

A war of attrition

In May 1864, the 115,000-man Army of the Potomac crossed the Rapidan River to do battle with Lee's forces in Virginia. A month of the war's bloodiest fighting

Confederate dead at Spotsylvania, Virginia, the site of a bloody battle in 1864.

A sketch by William Waud, an artist who covered the war for *Harper's Weekly*, depicts Pennsylvania soldiers voting in their army camp in the 1864 election.

A political cartoon from 1864 suggests the difficulty faced by the Democratic candidate, George B. McClellan, in reconciling the party's war and peace wings.

YOU TRIED TO RIDE THEM TWO HOSSES ON THE PENINSULA FOR TWO YEARS MAC BUT IT WOULDN'T WORK

LITTLE MAC (confidentially)—*Curse them busilly Horses—I can't manage the Act no how. One throw me in Virginia, and the other is bound the wrong way.*

PEACE.

WAR

LITTLE MAC, IN HIS GREAT TWO HORSE ACT, IN THE PRESIDENTIAL CANVASS OF 1864.

followed. Grant and Lee first encountered each other in the Wilderness, a wild, shrub-covered region where, one participant recalled, "it was as though Christian men had turned to fiends, and hell itself had usurped the place of earth." Grant's army suffered 18,000 casualties, while Lee's far smaller forces incurred 7,500. Previous Union generals had broken off engagements after losses of this magnitude. But Grant continued to press forward, attacking again at Spotsylvania and then at Cold Harbor. At the end of six weeks of fighting, Grant's casualties stood at 60,000—almost the size of Lee's entire army—while Lee had lost 30,000 men. The sustained fighting in Virginia was a turning point in modern warfare. With daily combat and a fearsome casualty toll, it had far more in common with the trench warfare of World War I (discussed in Chapter 19) than the almost gentlemanly fighting with which the Civil War began.

Grant had become the only Union general to maintain the initiative against Lee, but at a cost that led critics to label him a "butcher of men." Victory still eluded him. Grant attempted to capture Petersburg, which controlled the railway link to Richmond, but Lee got to Petersburg first, and Grant settled in for a prolonged siege. Meanwhile, General William T. Sherman, who had moved his forces into Georgia from Tennessee, encountered dogged resistance from Confederate troops. Not until September 1864 did he finally enter Atlanta, seizing Georgia's main railroad center.

As casualty rolls mounted in the spring and summer of 1864, northern morale sank to its lowest point of the war. Lincoln for a time believed he would be unable to win reelection. In May, hoping to force Lincoln to step aside, Radical Republicans nominated John C. Frémont on a platform calling for a constitutional amendment to abolish slavery, federal protection of the freedmen's rights, and confiscation of the land of leading Confederates. The Democratic candidate for president, General George B. McClellan, was hampered from the outset of the campaign by a platform calling for an immediate cease-fire and peace conference—a plan that even war-weary northerners viewed as equivalent to surrender. In the end, Frémont withdrew, and buoyed by Sherman's capture of Atlanta, Lincoln won a sweeping victory. He captured every state but Kentucky, Delaware, and New Jersey. The result ensured that the war would continue until the Confederacy's defeat.

REHEARSALS FOR RECONSTRUCTION AND THE END OF THE WAR

As the war drew toward a close and more and more parts of the Confederacy came under Union control, federal authorities found themselves presiding over the transition from slavery to freedom. In South Carolina, Louisiana, and other parts of the South, debates took place over issues—access to land, control of labor, and the new structure of political power—that would reverberate in the postwar world.

The Sea Islands Experiment

The most famous "rehearsal for Reconstruction" took place on the Sea Islands just off the coast of South Carolina. The war was only a few months old when, in November 1861, the Union navy occupied the islands. Nearly the entire white population fled, leaving behind some 10,000 slaves. The navy was soon followed by other northerners—army officers, Treasury agents, prospective investors in cotton land, and a group known as Gideon's Band, which included black and white reformers and teachers committed to uplifting the freed slaves. Each of these groups, in addition to the islands' black population, had its own view of how the transition to freedom should be organized. And journalists reported every development on the islands to an eager reading public in the North.

Gideon's Band

Convinced that education was the key to making self-reliant, productive citizens of the former slaves, northern-born teachers like Charlotte Forten, a member of one of Philadelphia's most prominent black families, and Laura M. Towne, a white native of Pittsburgh, devoted themselves to teaching the freed blacks. Towne, who in 1862 helped to establish Penn school on St. Helena Island,

Forten and Towne

Diagram of plots selected by former slaves on Port Royal Island, South Carolina, January 25, 1864. Taking advantage of a sale of abandoned property, eighteen blacks (seventeen men and one woman) selected plots on a Sea Island plantation for purchase.

A school for freed people established in 1862 on St. Helena Island, South Carolina, by an aid association in Pennsylvania.

remained there as a teacher until her death in 1901. Like many of the Gideonites, Towne and Forten assumed that blacks needed outside guidance to appreciate freedom. But they sympathized with the former slaves' aspirations, central to which was the desire for land.

Other northerners, however, believed that the transition from slave to free labor meant not giving blacks land but enabling them to work for wages in more humane conditions than under slavery. When the federal government put land on the islands up for sale, most was acquired not by former slaves but by northern investors bent upon demonstrating the superiority of free wage labor and turning a tidy profit at the same time. By 1865, the **Sea Islands experiment** was widely held to be a success. Black families were working for wages, acquiring education, and enjoying better shelter and clothing and a more varied diet than under slavery. But the experiment also bequeathed to postwar Reconstruction the contentious issue of whether landownership should accompany black freedom.

Wartime Reconstruction in the West

A very different rehearsal for Reconstruction, involving a far larger area and population than the Sea Islands, took place in Louisiana and the Mississippi Valley. After the capture of Vicksburg, the Union army established regulations for plantation labor. Military authorities insisted that the emancipated slaves must sign labor contracts with plantation owners who took an oath of loyalty. But, unlike before the war, the laborers would be paid wages and provided with education, physical punishment was prohibited, and their families were safe from disruption by sale.

Regulations for plantation labor

Neither side was satisfied with the new labor system. Blacks resented having to resume working for whites and being forced to sign labor contracts. Planters complained that their workers were insubordinate. Without the whip, they insisted, discipline could not be enforced. But only occasionally did army officers seek to implement a different vision of freedom. At Davis Bend, Mississippi, site of the cotton plantations of Jefferson Davis and his brother Joseph, General Grant decided to establish a "negro paradise." Here, rather than being forced to labor for white owners, the emancipated slaves saw the land divided among themselves. In addition, a system of government was established that allowed the former slaves to elect their own judges and sheriffs.

The Politics of Wartime Reconstruction

As the Civil War progressed, the future political status of African-Americans emerged as a key dividing line in public debates. Events in Union-occupied Louisiana brought the issue to national attention. Hoping to establish a functioning civilian government in the state, Lincoln in 1863 announced his **Ten-Percent Plan of Reconstruction**. He essentially offered an amnesty and full restoration

Lincoln's Ten-Percent Plan

of rights, including property except for slaves, to nearly all white southerners who took an oath affirming loyalty to the Union and support for emancipation. When 10 percent of the voters of 1860 had taken the oath, they could elect a new state government, which would be required to abolish slavery. Lincoln's plan offered no role to blacks in shaping the post-slavery order. His leniency toward southern whites seems to have been based on the assumption that many former slaveholders would come forward to accept his terms, thus weakening the Confederacy, shortening the war, and gaining white support for the ending of slavery.

Another group now stepped onto the stage of politics—the free blacks of New Orleans, who saw the Union occupation as a golden opportunity to press for equality before the law and a role in government for themselves. Their complaints at being excluded under Lincoln's Reconstruction plan won a sympathetic hearing from Radical Republicans in Congress. By the summer of 1864, dissatisfaction with events in Louisiana helped to inspire the **Wade-Davis Bill**, named for two leading Republican members of Congress. This bill required a majority (not one-tenth) of white male southerners to pledge support for the Union before Reconstruction could begin in any state, and it guaranteed blacks equality before the law, although not the right to vote. The bill passed Congress only to die when Lincoln refused to sign it and Congress adjourned. As the war drew to a close, it was clear that while slavery was dead, no agreement existed as to what social and political system should take its place.

Wade-Davis Bill

Victory at Last

After Lincoln's reelection, the war hastened to its conclusion. In November 1864, Sherman and his army of 60,000 set out from Atlanta on their March to the Sea. Cutting a sixty-mile-wide swath through the heart of Georgia, they destroyed railroads, buildings, and all the food and supplies they could not use. His aim, Sherman wrote, was "to whip the rebels, to humble their pride, to follow them to their innermost recesses, and make them fear and dread us." Here was modern war in all its destructiveness, even though few civilians were physically harmed. In January 1865, after capturing Savannah, Sherman moved into South Carolina, bringing even greater destruction. Anarchy reigned on the plantations as slaves drove off remaining overseers, destroyed planters' homes, plundered smokehouses and storerooms, and claimed the land for themselves.

Sherman's March to the Sea

General William T. Sherman photographed in 1864.

On January 31, 1865, Congress approved the **Thirteenth Amendment**, which abolished slavery throughout the entire Union—and in so doing, introduced the word "slavery" into the Constitution for the first time. In March, in his second inaugural address, Lincoln called for reconciliation: "with malice toward none, with charity for all, . . . let us . . . bind up the nation's wounds." Yet he also leveled a harsh judgment on the nation's past. Unlike the northern and southern clergy, who were sure of what God intended, Lincoln suggested that man does not know God's will—a remarkably modest statement on the eve of Union victory. Perhaps, Lincoln suggested, God had brought on the war to punish the entire nation, not just the South, for the sin of slavery. And if God willed that the war continue until all the wealth created by 250 years of slave labor had been destroyed, and "every drop

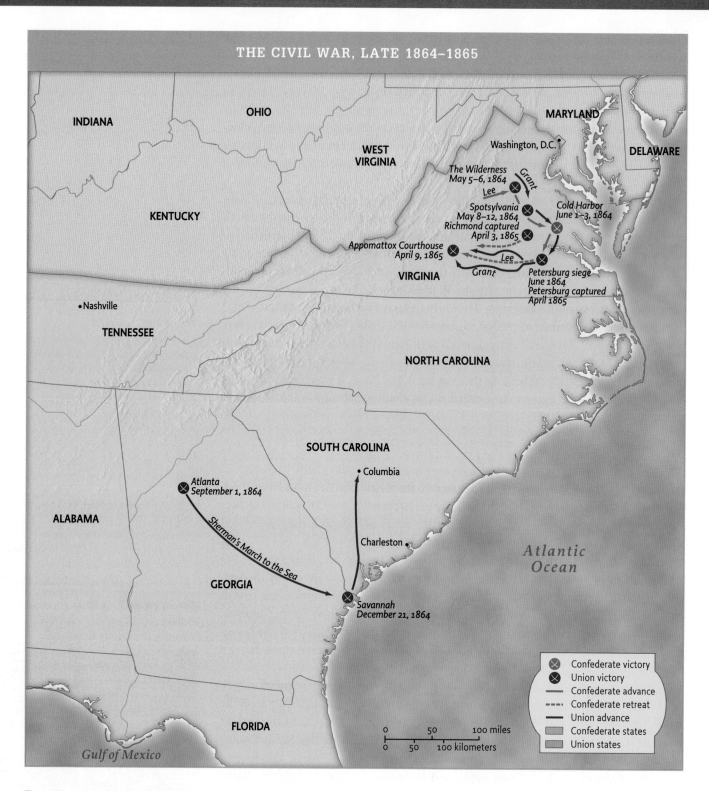

THE CIVIL WAR, LATE 1864–1865

INDIANA

OHIO

WEST VIRGINIA

MARYLAND

Washington, D.C.

DELAWARE

KENTUCKY

The Wilderness
May 5–6, 1864

Grant

Lee

Spotsylvania
May 8–12, 1864

Cold Harbor
June 1–3, 1864

Richmond captured
April 3, 1865

Appomattox Courthouse
April 9, 1865

Lee

VIRGINIA

Grant

Petersburg siege
June 1864
Petersburg captured
April 1865

•Nashville

TENNESSEE

NORTH CAROLINA

SOUTH CAROLINA

•Columbia

Atlanta
September 1, 1864

ALABAMA

Sherman's March to the Sea

Charleston •

Atlantic Ocean

GEORGIA

Savannah
December 21, 1864

FLORIDA

Gulf of Mexico

0	50	100 miles
0	50	100 kilometers

Confederate victory
Union victory
Confederate advance
Confederate retreat
Union advance
Confederate states
Union states

The military defeat of the Confederacy came in the East, with Sherman's March to the Sea, Grant's occupation of Richmond, and the surrender of Robert E. Lee's army.

of blood drawn with the lash shall be paid by another drawn with the sword," this too would be an act of justice (see the Appendix for the full text).

April 1865 brought some of the most momentous events in American history. On April 2, Grant finally broke through Lee's lines at Petersburg, forcing the Army of Northern Virginia to abandon the city and leaving Richmond defenseless. The following day, Union soldiers occupied the southern capital. At the head of one black army unit marched its chaplain, Garland H. White, a former fugitive from slavery. Called upon by a large crowd to make a speech, White, as he later recalled, proclaimed "for the first time in that city freedom to all mankind." Then the "doors of all the slave pens were thrown open and thousands came out shouting and praising God, and Father, or Master Abe."

On April 4, heedless of his own safety, Lincoln walked the streets of Richmond accompanied only by a dozen sailors. At every step he was besieged by former slaves, some of whom fell on their knees before the embarrassed president, who urged them to remain standing. Meanwhile, Lee and his army headed west, only to be encircled by Grant's forces. Realizing that further resistance was useless, Lee surrendered at **Appomattox Courthouse, Virginia**, on April 9. Although some Confederate units remained in the field, the Civil War was over.

Lincoln did not live to savor victory. On April 11, in what proved to be his last speech, he called publicly for the first time for limited black suffrage in the South. Three days later, while attending a performance at Ford's Theatre in Washington, D.C., the president was mortally wounded by John Wilkes Booth, one of the nation's most celebrated actors. Lincoln died the next morning. A train carried the president's body to its final resting place in Illinois on a winding 1,600-mile journey that illustrated how tightly the railroad now bound the northern states. Grieving crowds lined the train route, and solemn processions carried the president's body to lie in state in major cities so that mourners could pay their respects. It was estimated that 300,000 persons passed by the coffin in Philadelphia, 500,000 in New York, and 200,000 in Chicago. On May 4, 1865, Lincoln was laid to rest in Springfield.

> *Occupation at Richmond*

The ruins of a Charleston railroad depot, in an 1865 photograph by George N. Barnard.

The War and the World

In 1877, soon after retiring as president, Ulysses S. Grant embarked with his wife on a two-year tour of the world. At almost every location, he was greeted as a modern-day hero. What did America in the aftermath of the Civil War represent to the world? In England, the son of the duke of Wellington greeted Grant as a military genius, the primary architect of victory in one of the greatest wars in human history, and a fitting successor to Wellington's own father, the general who had vanquished Napoleon. In Newcastle, parading English workers hailed him as the man whose military prowess

A redesign of the American flag proposed in 1863 illustrates the linkage of nationalism and freedom that was solidified by the Civil War. The thirty-five stars forming the word "FREE" include the eleven Confederate states.

had saved the world's leading experiment in democratic government, and as a "Hero of Freedom," whose commander-in-chief, Abraham Lincoln, had vindicated the principles of free labor by emancipating America's slaves. In Berlin, Otto von Bismarck, the chancellor of Germany, welcomed Grant as a nation-builder, who had accomplished on the battlefield something—national unity—that Bismarck was attempting to create for his own people. "You had to save the Union," Bismarck commented, "just as we had to save Germany." Grant corrected him—"Not only to save the Union, but to destroy slavery."

The War in American History

The Civil War laid the foundation for modern America, guaranteeing the Union's permanence, destroying slavery, and shifting power in the nation from the South to the North (and, more specifically, from slaveowning planters to northern capitalists). It dramatically increased the power of the federal government and accelerated the modernization of the northern economy. And it placed on the postwar agenda the challenge of defining and protecting African-American freedom.

Paradoxically, both sides lost something they had gone to war to defend. Slavery was the cornerstone of the Confederacy, but the war led inexorably to slavery's destruction. In the North, the war hastened the transformation of Lincoln's America—the world of free labor, of the small shop and independent farmer—into an industrial giant. Americans, in the words of the abolitionist Wendell Phillips, would "never again . . . see the republic in which we were born."

Winslow Homer's painting *The Veteran in a New Field*, completed in the fall of 1865, offers a reflection on the Civil War and its legacy. The former Union soldier, whose army jacket lies in the right corner, is at work cutting wheat. The scythe brings to mind the grim reaper, a symbol of death, perhaps a reference not only to war casualties but also Lincoln's assassination. But the bountiful field suggests national regeneration.

Late in May 1865, a little over a month after Lincoln's death, some 200,000 veterans paraded through Washington, D.C., for the Grand Review of the Union armies, a final celebration of the nation's triumph. The scene inspired the poet Bret Harte to imagine a very different parade—a "phantom army" of the Union dead:

> The martyred heroes of Malvern Hill,
> Of Gettysburg and Chancellorsville,
> The men whose wasted figures fill
> The patriot graves of the nation . . .
> And marching beside the others,
> Came the dusky martyrs of Pillow's fight.

To Harte, the war's meaning ultimately lay in the sacrifices of individual soldiers. He included in his reverie the black troops, including those massacred at Fort Pillow. Blacks, Harte seemed to be saying, had achieved equality in death. Could the nation give it to them in life?

Here was the problem that confronted the United States as the postwar era known as Reconstruction began. "Verily," as Frederick Douglass declared, "the work does not *end* with the abolition of slavery, but only *begins*."

SUGGESTED READING

BOOKS

- Ayers, Edward L. *In the Presence of Mine Enemies: War in the Heart of America, 1859–1863* (2003). A study of the experiences of Americans in two counties—one in Pennsylvania, one in Virginia—in the early years of the Civil War.

- Foner, Eric. *The Fiery Trial: Abraham Lincoln and American Slavery* (2010). A study of the evolution of Lincoln's ideas and policies relating to slavery over the course of his life.

- Glatthaar, Joseph T. *Forged in Battle: The Civil War Alliance of Black Soldiers and White Officers* (1990). Relates the complex experience of black Civil War soldiers and their officers.

- Kelman, Ari. *A Misplaced Massacre: Struggling Over the Memory of Sand Creek* (2013). Examines the massacre at Sand Creek and the modern controversy over how to commemorate it.

- Lawson, Melinda. *Patriot Fires: Forging a New Nationalism in the Civil War North* (2002). Considers how both public and private groups, in order to mobilize support for the war effort, promoted a new idea of American nationalism.

- McCurry, Stephanie. *Confederate Reckoning: Power and Politics in the Civil War South* (2010). A pioneering study of the political mobilization of poorer white women and slaves in the Confederacy.

- McPherson, James M. *Battle Cry of Freedom: The Civil War Era* (1988). The standard account of the coming of the war, its conduct, and its consequences.

- Mitchell, Reid. *Civil War Soldiers* (1988). A look at the Civil War from the point of view of the experience of ordinary soldiers.

- Neely, Mark E. *The Fate of Liberty: Abraham Lincoln and Civil Liberties* (1991). Explores how the Lincoln administration did and did not meet the challenge of preserving civil liberties while fighting the war.

- Oakes, James. *Freedom National: The Destruction of Slavery in the United States* (2012). A careful account of the complex path to emancipation.

- Rable, George C. *God's Almost Chosen People: A Religious History of the Civil War* (2010). How on both sides religious conviction helped to sustain the war effort.

- Richardson, Heather C. *Greatest Nation of the Earth: Republican Economic Policies during the Civil War* (1997). Considers the far-reaching impact of the economic measures adopted by the Union during the war.

- Rose, Willie Lee. *Rehearsal for Reconstruction: The Port Royal Experiment* (1964). Traces the unfolding of the issues of Reconstruction in the Sea Islands of South Carolina in the midst of the war.

- Rubin, Anne S. *Shattered Nation: The Rise and Fall of the Confederacy, 1861–1868* (2005). An up-to-date account of the Confederate experience.

- Silber, Nina. *Daughters of the Union: Northern Women Fight the Civil War* (2005). Examines the participation of northern women in the war effort and how this did and did not alter their lives.

WEBSITES

- Civil War Photographs: http://memory.loc.gov/ammem /cwphtml/cwphome.html

- Civil War Women: http://library.duke.edu /specialcollections/collections/digitized/civil-war-women/

- A House Divided: America in the Age of Lincoln: www.digitalhistory.uh.edu/exhibits/ahd/index.html

- The Valley of the Shadow: Two Communities in the American Civil War: http://valley.vcdh.virginia.edu

CHAPTER REVIEW AND ONLINE RESOURCES

REVIEW QUESTIONS

1. What made the American Civil War the first modern war?

2. How was the North's victory over the South tied to the different ways the market revolution had developed in the two regions?

3. Describe how President Lincoln's war aims evolved between 1861 and 1863, changing from simply preserving the Union to also ending slavery.

4. How did the actions of slaves themselves, northern military strategy, and the Emancipation Proclamation combine to end slavery?

5. What role did blacks play in winning the Civil War and in defining the war's consequences?

6. How did federal policies undertaken during the Civil War transform the United States into a stronger nation-state—economically, politically, and ideologically?

7. What was the impact of the Civil War on civil liberties?

8. Compare and contrast women's efforts in the North and South to support the war effort and their families.

9. In what ways did the outcome of the Civil War change the United States' status in the world?

KEY TERMS

first Battle of Bull Run (p. 508)

second Battle of Bull Run (p. 509)

Battle of Antietam (p. 509)

"the contrabands" (p. 513)

Radical Republicans (p. 514)

Emancipation Proclamation (p. 516)

Second American Revolution (p. 519)

Ex parte Milligan (p. 523)

Homestead Act (p. 524)

transcontinental railroad (p. 524)

Navajo's Long Walk (p. 529)

Sanitary Fairs (p. 530)

"King Cotton diplomacy" (p. 533)

Battle of Gettysburg (p. 538)

Battle of Vicksburg (p. 539)

Sea Islands experiment (p. 542)

Ten-Percent Plan of Reconstruction (p. 542)

Wade-Davis Bill (p. 543)

Thirteenth Amendment (p. 543)

Appomattox Courthouse, Virginia (p. 545)

Go to 🐰 INQUIZITIVE

To see what you know—and learn what you've missed—with personalized feedback along the way.

Visit the *Give Me Liberty!* **Student Site** for primary source documents and images, interactive maps, author videos featuring Eric Foner, and more.

CHAPTER 15

"WHAT IS FREEDOM?": RECONSTRUCTION

★

1865-1877

On the evening of January 12, 1865, less than a month after Union forces captured Savannah, Georgia, twenty leaders of the city's black community gathered for a discussion with General William T. Sherman and Secretary of War Edwin M. Stanton. Mostly Baptist and Methodist ministers, the group included several men who within a few years would assume prominent positions during the era of Reconstruction that followed the Civil War. Ulysses S. Houston, pastor of the city's Third African Baptist Church, and James Porter, an episcopal religious leader who had operated a secret school for black children before the war, in a few years would win election to the Georgia legislature. James D. Lynch, who had been born free in Baltimore and educated in New Hampshire, went on to serve as secretary of state of Mississippi.

The conversation revealed that the black leaders brought out of slavery a clear definition of freedom. Asked what he understood by slavery, Garrison Frazier, a Baptist minister chosen as the group's spokesman, responded that it meant one person's "receiving by irresistible power the work of another man, and not by his consent." Freedom he defined as "placing us where we could reap the fruit of our own labor, and take care of ourselves." The way to accomplish this was "to have land, and turn it and till it by our own labor." Frazier insisted that blacks possessed "sufficient intelligence" to maintain themselves in freedom and enjoy the equal protection of the laws.

Sherman's meeting with the black leaders foreshadowed some of the radical changes that would take place during the era known as Reconstruction (meaning, literally, the rebuilding of the shattered nation). In the years following the Civil War, former slaves and their white allies, North and South, would seek to redefine the meaning and boundaries of American freedom. Previously an entitlement of whites, freedom would be expanded to include black Americans. The laws and Constitution would be rewritten to guarantee African-Americans, for the first time in the nation's history, recognition as citizens and equality before the law. Black men would be granted the right to vote, ushering in a period of interracial democracy throughout the South. Black schools, churches, and other institutions would flourish, laying the foundation for the modern African-American community. Many of the advances of Reconstruction would prove temporary, swept away during a campaign of violence in the South and the North's retreat from the ideal of equality. But Reconstruction laid the foundation for future struggles to extend freedom to all Americans.

All this, however, lay in the future in January 1865. Four days after the meeting, Sherman responded to the black delegation by issuing Special Field Order 15. This set aside the Sea Islands and a large area along the South Carolina and Georgia coasts for the settlement of black families on forty-acre plots of land. He also offered them broken-down mules that the army could no longer use. In Sherman's order lay the origins of the phrase "forty acres and a mule," that would reverberate across the South in the next few years. By June, some 40,000 freed slaves had been settled on "Sherman land." Among the emancipated slaves, Sherman's order raised hopes that the end of slavery would be accompanied by the economic independence that they, like other Americans, believed essential to genuine freedom.

FOCUS QUESTIONS

What visions of freedom did the former slaves and slaveholders pursue in the postwar South? –p. 552

What were the sources, goals, and competing visions for Reconstruction? –p. 564

What were the social and political effects of Radical Reconstruction in the South? –p. 574

What were the main factors, in both the North and South, for the abandonment of Reconstruction? –p. 579

The Shackle Broken—by the Genius of Freedom. This 1874 lithograph depicts Robert B. Elliott, a black congressman from South Carolina, delivering a celebrated speech supporting the bill that became the Civil Rights Act of 1875.

THE MEANING OF FREEDOM

With the end of the Civil War, declared an Illinois congressman in 1865, the United States was a "new nation," for the first time "wholly free." The destruction of slavery, however, made the definition of freedom the central question on the nation's agenda. "What is freedom?" asked Congressman James A. Garfield in 1865. "Is it the bare privilege of not being chained? If this is all, then freedom is a bitter mockery, a cruel delusion." Did freedom mean simply the absence of slavery, or did it imply other rights for the former slaves, and if so, which ones: equal civil rights, the vote, ownership of property? During Reconstruction, freedom became a terrain of conflict, its substance open to different, often contradictory interpretations. Out of the conflict over the meaning of freedom arose new kinds of relations between black and white southerners, and a new definition of the rights of all Americans.

Blacks and the Meaning of Freedom

African-Americans' understanding of freedom was shaped by their experiences as slaves and their observation of the free society around them. To begin with, freedom meant escaping the numerous injustices of slavery—punishment by the lash, the separation of families, denial of access to education, the sexual exploitation of black women by their owners—and sharing in the rights and opportunities of American citizens. "If I cannot do like a white man," Henry Adams, an emancipated slave in Louisiana, told his former master in 1865, "I am not free."

Blacks relished the opportunity to demonstrate their liberation from the regulations, significant and trivial, associated with slavery. They openly held mass meetings and religious services free of white supervision, and they acquired dogs, guns, and liquor, all barred to them under slavery. No longer required to obtain a pass from their owners to travel, former slaves throughout the South left the plantations in search of better jobs, family members, or simply a taste of personal liberty. Many moved to southern towns and cities, where, it seemed, "freedom was free-er."

Families in Freedom

With slavery dead, institutions that had existed before the war, like the black family, free blacks' churches and schools, and the secret slave church, were strengthened, expanded, and freed from white supervision. The family was central to the postemancipation black community. Former slaves made remarkable efforts to locate loved ones from whom they had been separated under slavery. One northern reporter in 1865 encountered a freedman who had walked more than 600 miles from Georgia to North Carolina, searching for the wife and children from whom he had been sold away before the war. Meanwhile, widows of black soldiers successfully claimed survivors' pensions, forcing the federal government to acknowledge the validity of prewar relationships that slavery had attempted to deny.

But while Reconstruction witnessed the stabilization of family life, freedom subtly altered relationships within the family. Emancipation increased the power of black men and brought to many black families the nineteenth-century notion that men and women should inhabit separate "spheres." Immediately after the Civil War, planters complained that freedwomen had "withdrawn" from field labor and work as house servants. Many black women preferred to devote more time to their families than had been possible under slavery, and men considered it a badge of honor to see their wives remain at home. Eventually, the dire poverty of the black community would compel a far higher proportion of black women than white women to go to work for wages.

Church and School

At the same time, blacks abandoned white-controlled religious institutions to create churches of their own. On the eve of the Civil War, 42,000 black Methodists worshiped in biracial South Carolina churches; by the end of Reconstruction, only 600 remained. The rise of the independent black church, with Methodists and Baptists commanding the largest followings, redrew the religious map of the South. As the major institution independent of white control, the church played a central role in the black community. A place of worship, it also housed schools, social events, and political gatherings. Black ministers came to play a major role in politics. Some 250 held public office during Reconstruction.

Another striking example of the freedpeople's quest for individual and community improvement was their desire for education. Education, declared a Mississippi freedman, was "the next best thing to liberty." The thirst for learning sprang from many sources—a desire to read the Bible, the need to prepare for the economic marketplace, and the opportunity, which arose in 1867, to take part in politics. Blacks of all ages flocked to the schools established by northern missionary societies, the Freedmen's Bureau, and groups of ex-slaves themselves. Northern journalist Sidney Andrews, who toured the South in 1865, was impressed by how much education also took place outside of the classroom: "I had occasion very frequently to notice that porters in stores and laboring men in warehouses, and cart drivers on the streets, had spelling books with them, and were studying them during the time they were not occupied with their work." Reconstruction also witnessed the creation of the nation's first black colleges, including Fisk University in Tennessee, Hampton Institute in Virginia, and Howard University in the nation's capital.

Political Freedom

In a society that had made political participation a core element of freedom, the right to vote inevitably became central to the former slaves' desire for empowerment and equality. As Frederick Douglass put it soon after the South's surrender in 1865, "Slavery is not abolished until the black man has the ballot." In a "monarchial government," Douglass explained, no "special" disgrace applied to those denied the right to vote. But in a democracy, "where universal suffrage is the rule," excluding

Family Record, a lithograph marketed to former slaves after the Civil War, is an idealized portrait of a middle-class black family, with scenes of slavery and freedom.

Mother and Daughter Reading, Mt. Meigs, Alabama, an 1890 photograph by Rudolph Eickemeyer. During Reconstruction and for years thereafter, former slaves exhibited a deep desire for education, and learning took place outside of school as well as within.

Five Generations of a Black Family, an 1862 photograph that suggests the power of family ties among emancipated slaves

any group meant branding them with "the stigma of inferiority." As soon as the Civil War ended, and in some parts of the South even earlier, free blacks and emancipated slaves claimed a place in the public sphere. They came together in conventions, parades, and petition drives to demand the right to vote and, on occasion, to organize their own "freedom ballots."

Anything less than full citizenship, black spokesmen insisted, would betray the nation's democratic promise and the war's meaning. Speakers at black conventions reminded the nation of Crispus Attucks, who fell at the Boston Massacre, and of black soldiers' contribution to the War of 1812 and during "the bloody struggle through which we have just passed." To demonstrate their patriotism, blacks throughout the South organized Fourth of July celebrations. For years after the Civil War, white southerners would "shut themselves within doors" on Independence Day, as a white resident of Charleston recorded in her diary, while former slaves commemorated the holiday themselves.

Land, Labor, and Freedom

Former slaves' ideas of freedom, like those of rural people throughout the world, were directly related to landownership. Only land, wrote Merrimon Howard, a freedman from Mississippi, would enable "the poor class to enjoy the sweet boon of freedom." On the land they would develop independent communities free of white control. Many former slaves insisted that through their unpaid labor, they had acquired a right to the land. "The property which they hold," declared an Alabama black convention, "was nearly all earned by the sweat of *our* brows." In some parts of the South, blacks in 1865 seized property, insisting that it belonged

Landownership

The First African Church, Richmond, as depicted in *Harper's Weekly*, June 27, 1874. The establishment of independent black churches was an enduring accomplishment of Reconstruction.

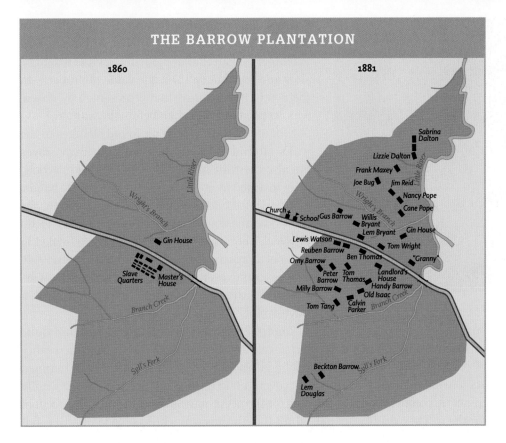

THE BARROW PLANTATION

1860   1881

Two maps of the Barrow plantation illustrate the effects of emancipation on rural life in the South. In 1860, slaves lived in communal quarters near the owner's house. Twenty-one years later, former slaves working as sharecroppers lived scattered across the plantation and had their own church and school.

to them. On one Tennessee plantation, former slaves claimed to be "joint heirs" to the estate and, the owner complained, took up residence "in the rooms of my house."

In its individual elements and much of its language, former slaves' definition of freedom resembled that of white Americans—self-ownership, family stability, religious liberty, political participation, and economic autonomy. But these elements combined to form a vision very much their own. For whites, freedom, no matter how defined, was a given, a birthright to be defended. For African-Americans, it was an open-ended process, a transformation of every aspect of their lives and of the society and culture that had sustained slavery in the first place. Although the freedpeople failed to achieve full freedom as they understood it, their definition did much to shape national debate during the turbulent era of Reconstruction.

> *Freedom's meaning to former slaves*

Masters without Slaves

Most white southerners reacted to military defeat and emancipation with dismay, not only because of the widespread devastation but also because they must now submit to northern demands. "The demoralization is complete," wrote a Georgia girl. "We are whipped, there is no doubt about it." The appalling loss of life, a disaster without parallel in the American experience, affected all classes of southerners. Nearly 260,000 men died for the Confederacy—more than one-fifth of the

> *Confederate deaths*

Winslow Homer's 1876 painting *A Visit from the Old Mistress* depicts an imaginary meeting between a southern white woman and her former slaves. Their stance and gaze suggest the tensions arising from the birth of a new social order. Homer places his subjects on an equal footing, yet maintains a space of separation between them. He exhibited the painting to acclaim at the Paris Universal Exposition in 1878.

Free labor and the good society

South's adult male white population. The wholesale destruction of work animals, farm buildings, and machinery ensured that economic revival would be slow and painful. In 1870, the value of property in the South, not counting that represented by slaves, was 30 percent lower than before the war.

Planter families faced profound changes in the war's aftermath. Many lost not only their slaves but also their life savings, which they had patriotically invested in now-worthless Confederate bonds. Some, whose slaves departed the plantation, for the first time found themselves compelled to do physical labor. General Braxton Bragg returned to his "once prosperous" Alabama home to find "*all, all* was lost, except my debts." Bragg and his wife, a woman "raised in affluence," lived for a time in a slave cabin.

Southern planters sought to implement an understanding of freedom quite different from that of the former slaves. As they struggled to accept the reality of emancipation, most planters defined black freedom in the narrowest manner. As journalist Sidney Andrews discovered late in 1865, "The whites seem wholly unable to comprehend that freedom for the negro means the same thing as freedom for them. They readily enough admit that the government has made him free, but appear to believe that they have the right to exercise the same old control." Southern leaders sought to revive the antebellum definition of freedom as if nothing had changed. Freedom still meant hierarchy and mastery; it was a privilege not a right, a carefully defined legal status rather than an open-ended entitlement. Certainly, it implied neither economic autonomy nor civil and political equality. "A man may be free and yet not independent," Mississippi planter Samuel Agnew observed in his diary in 1865. A Kentucky newspaper summed up the stance of much of the white South: the former slave was "*free*, but free only to labor."

The Free Labor Vision

Along with former slaves and former masters, the victorious Republican North tried to implement its own vision of freedom. Central to its definition was the antebellum principle of free labor, now further strengthened as a definition of the good society by the Union's triumph. In the free labor vision of a reconstructed South, emancipated blacks, enjoying the same opportunities for advancement as northern workers, would labor more productively than they had as slaves. At the same time, northern capital and migrants would energize the economy. The South would eventually come to resemble the "free society" of the North, complete with public schools, small towns, and independent farmers. Unified on the basis of free labor, proclaimed Carl Schurz, a refugee from the failed German revolution of 1848 who rose to become a leader of the Republican Party, America would become "a republic, greater, more populous, freer, more prosperous, and more powerful" than any in history.

With planters seeking to establish a labor system as close to slavery as possible, and former slaves demanding economic autonomy and access to land, a long period of conflict over the organization and control of labor followed on plantations throughout the South. It fell to **the Freedmen's Bureau**, an agency established by Congress in March 1865, to attempt to establish a working free labor system.

The Freedmen's Bureau

Under the direction of O. O. Howard, a graduate of Bowdoin College in Maine and a veteran of the Civil War, the Bureau took on responsibilities that can only be described as daunting. The Bureau was an experiment in government social policy that seems to belong more comfortably to the New Deal of the 1930s or the Great Society of the 1960s (see Chapters 21 and 25, respectively) than to nineteenth-century America. Bureau agents were supposed to establish schools, provide aid to the poor and aged, settle disputes between whites and blacks and among the freedpeople, and secure for former slaves and white Unionists equal treatment before the courts. "It is not . . . in your power to fulfill one-tenth of the expectations of those who framed the Bureau," General William T. Sherman wrote to Howard. "I fear you have Hercules' task."

The Bureau lasted from 1865 to 1870. Even at its peak, there were fewer than 1,000 agents in the entire South. Nonetheless, the Bureau's achievements in some areas, notably education and health care, were striking. While the Bureau did not establish schools itself, it coordinated and helped to finance the activities of

The Great Labor Question from a Southern Point of View, a cartoon by the artist Winslow Homer, published in *Harper's Weekly*, July 29, 1865. Homer satirizes the attitudes of many white southerners. While blacks labor in the fields, an idle planter warns a former slave, "My boy, we've toiled and taken care of you long enough—now you've got to work!"

The Freedmen's Bureau, an engraving from *Harper's Weekly*, July 25, 1868, depicts the Bureau agent as a promoter of racial peace in the violent postwar South.

Winslow Homer's 1876 painting *The Cotton Pickers*, one of a series of studies of rural life in Virginia, portrays two black women as dignified figures, without a trace of the stereotyping so common in the era's representations of former slaves. The expressions on their faces are ambiguous, perhaps conveying disappointment that eleven years after the end of slavery they are still at work in the fields.

northern societies committed to black education. By 1869, nearly 3,000 schools, serving more than 150,000 pupils in the South, reported to the Bureau. Bureau agents also assumed control of hospitals established by the army during the war, and expanded the system into new communities. They provided medical care and drugs to both black and white southerners. In economic relations, however, the Bureau's activities proved far more problematic.

The Failure of Land Reform

The idea of free labor, wrote one Bureau agent, was "the noblest principle on earth." All that was required to harmonize race relations in the South was fair wages, good working conditions, and the opportunity to improve the laborer's situation in life. But blacks wanted land of their own, not jobs on plantations. One provision of the law establishing the Bureau gave it the authority to divide abandoned and confiscated land into forty-acre plots for rental and eventual sale to the former slaves.

A nursemaid and her charge, from a daguerreotype around 1865.

In the summer of 1865, however, President Andrew Johnson, who had succeeded Lincoln, ordered nearly all land in federal hands returned to its former owners. A series of confrontations followed, notably in South Carolina and Georgia, where the army forcibly evicted blacks who had settled on "Sherman land." When O. O. Howard, head of the Freedmen's Bureau, traveled to the Sea Islands to inform blacks of the new policy, he was greeted with disbelief and protest. A committee of former slaves drew up petitions to Howard and President Johnson. "We want Homesteads," they declared, "we were promised Homesteads by the government." Land, the freedmen insisted, was essential to the meaning of freedom. Without it, they declared, "we have not bettered our condition" from the days of slavery—"you will see, this is not the condition of really free men."

Because no land distribution took place, the vast majority of rural freedpeople remained poor and without property during Reconstruction. They had no alternative but to work on white-owned plantations, often for their former owners. Far from

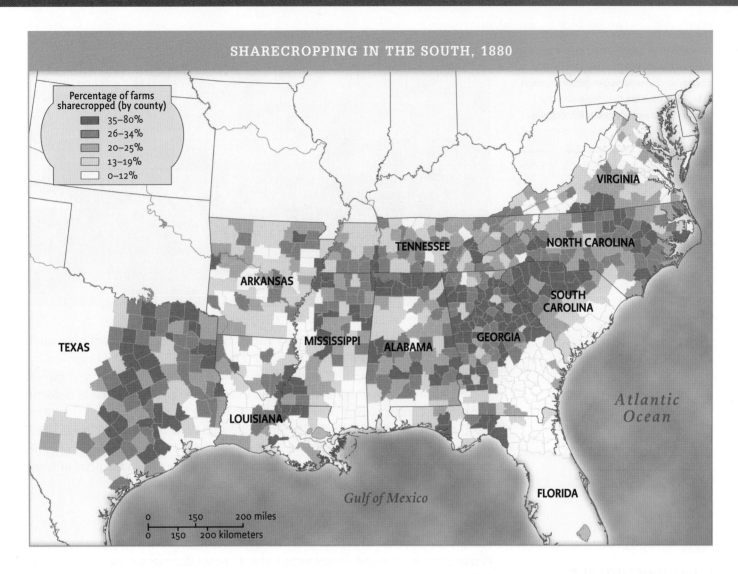

SHARECROPPING IN THE SOUTH, 1880

Percentage of farms
sharecropped (by county)

- 35–80%
- 26–34%
- 20–25%
- 13–19%
- 0–12%

VIRGINIA

TENNESSEE

NORTH CAROLINA

ARKANSAS

SOUTH CAROLINA

TEXAS

MISSISSIPPI   ALABAMA   GEORGIA

LOUISIANA

Atlantic Ocean

Gulf of Mexico

FLORIDA

0 — 150 — 200 miles
0 — 150 — 200 kilometers

being able to rise in the social scale through hard work, black men were largely confined to farm work, unskilled labor, and service jobs, and black women to positions in private homes as cooks and maids. Their wages remained too low to allow for any accumulation. By the turn of the century, a significant number of southern African-Americans had managed to acquire small parcels of land. But the failure of land reform produced a deep sense of betrayal that survived among the former slaves and their descendants long after the end of Reconstruction. "No sir," Mary Gaffney, an elderly ex-slave, recalled in the 1930s, "we were not given a thing but freedom."

By 1880, sharecropping had become the dominant form of agricultural labor in large parts of the South. The system involved both white and black farmers.

Toward a New South

Out of the conflict on the plantations, new systems of labor emerged in the different regions of the South. The task system, under which workers were assigned daily tasks, completion of which ended their responsibilities for that day, survived in the rice kingdom of South Carolina and Georgia. Closely supervised wage labor predominated on the sugar plantations of southern Louisiana. Sharecropping came to dominate the Cotton Belt and much of the Tobacco Belt of Virginia and North Carolina.

Labor systems

The cotton depot at Guthrie, Texas. Bales of cotton have been loaded onto trains for shipment. After the Civil War, more and more white farmers began growing cotton to support their families, permanently altering their formerly self-sufficient way of life.

Sharecropping initially arose as a compromise between blacks' desire for land and planters' demand for labor discipline. The system allowed each black family to rent a part of a plantation, with the crop divided between worker and owner at the end of the year. Sharecropping guaranteed the planters a stable resident labor force. Former slaves preferred it to gang labor because it offered them the prospect of working without day-to-day white supervision. But as the years went on, sharecropping became more and more oppressive. Sharecroppers' economic opportunities were severely limited by a world market in which the price of farm products suffered a prolonged decline.

The rise of sharecropping

The White Farmer

The plight of the small farmer was not confined to blacks in the postwar South. Wartime devastation set in motion a train of events that permanently altered the independent way of life of white yeomen, leading to what they considered a loss of freedom. Before the war, most small farmers had concentrated on raising food for their families and grew little cotton. With much of their property destroyed, many yeomen saw their economic condition worsened by successive crop failures after the war. To obtain supplies from merchants, farmers were forced to take up the growing of cotton and pledge a part of the crop as collateral (property the creditor can seize if a debt is not paid). This system became known as the **crop lien**. Since interest rates were extremely high and the price of cotton fell steadily, many farmers found themselves still in debt after marketing their portion of the crop at year's end. They had no choice but to continue to plant cotton to obtain new loans. By the mid-1870s, white farmers, who cultivated only 10 percent of the South's cotton crop in 1860, were growing 40 percent, and many who had owned their land had fallen into dependency as sharecroppers, who now rented land owned by others.

The crop-lien system

Both black and white farmers found themselves caught in the sharecropping and crop-lien systems. A far higher percentage of black than white farmers in the South rented land rather than owned it. But every census from 1880 to 1940 counted more white than black sharecroppers. The workings of sharecropping and the crop-lien system are illustrated by the case of Matt Brown, a Mississippi farmer who borrowed money each year from a local merchant. He began 1892 with a debt of $226 held over from the previous year. By 1893, although he produced cotton worth $171, Brown's debt had increased to $402, because he had borrowed $33 for food, $29 for clothing, $173 for supplies, and $112 for other items. Brown never succeeded in getting out of debt. He died in 1905; the last entry under his name in the merchant's account book is a coffin.

The burden of debt

The Urban South

Even as the rural South stagnated economically, southern cities experienced remarkable growth after the Civil War. As railroads penetrated the interior, they enabled merchants in market centers like Atlanta to trade directly with the North, bypassing coastal cities that had traditionally monopolized southern commerce. A new urban middle class of merchants, railroad promoters, and bankers reaped the benefits of the spread of cotton production in the postwar South.

Thus, Reconstruction brought about profound changes in the lives of southerners, black and white, rich and poor. In place of the prewar world of master, slave, and self-sufficient yeoman, the postwar South was peopled by new social classes—landowning employers, black and white sharecroppers, cotton-producing white farmers, wage-earning black laborers, and urban entrepreneurs. Each of these groups turned to Reconstruction politics in an attempt to shape to its own advantage the aftermath of emancipation.

Postwar southern society

Aftermath of Slavery

The United States, of course, was not the only society to confront the problem of the transition from slavery to freedom. Indeed, many parallels exist between the debates during Reconstruction and struggles that followed slavery in other parts of the Western Hemisphere over the same issues of land, control of labor, and political power. In every case, former planters (or, in Haiti, where the planter class had been destroyed, the government itself) tried to encourage or require former slaves to go back to work on plantations to grow the same crops as under slavery. Planters elsewhere held the same stereotypical views of black laborers as were voiced by their counterparts in the United States—former slaves were supposedly lazy, were lacking in ambition, and thought that freedom meant an absence of labor.

Emancipation in the Western Hemisphere

For their part, former slaves throughout the hemisphere tried to carve out as much independence as possible, both in their daily lives and in their labor. They attempted to reconstruct family life by withdrawing women and children from field labor (in the West Indies, women turned to marketing their families' crops to earn income). Wherever possible, former slaves acquired land of their own and devoted more time to growing food for their families than to growing crops for the international market. In many places, the plantations either fell to pieces, as in Haiti, or continued operating with a new labor force composed of indentured servants from India and China, as in Jamaica, Trinidad, and British Guiana. Southern planters in the United States brought in a few Chinese laborers in an attempt to replace freedmen, but since the federal government opposed such efforts, the Chinese remained only a tiny proportion of the southern workforce.

VOICES OF FREEDOM

From PETITION OF COMMITTEE IN BEHALF OF THE FREEDMEN TO ANDREW JOHNSON (1865)

In the summer of 1865, President Andrew Johnson ordered land that had been distributed to freed slaves in South Carolina and Georgia returned to its former owners. A committee of freedmen drafted a petition asking for the right to obtain land. Johnson did not, however, change his policy.

We the freedmen of Edisto Island, South Carolina, have learned from you through Major General O. O. Howard . . . with deep sorrow and painful hearts of the possibility of [the] government restoring these lands to the former owners. We are well aware of the many perplexing and trying questions that burden your mind, and therefore pray to god (the preserver of all, and who has through our late and beloved President [Lincoln's] proclamation and the war made us a free people) that he may guide you in making your decisions and give you that wisdom that cometh from above to settle these great and important questions for the best interests of the country and the colored race.

Here is where secession was born and nurtured. Here is where we have toiled nearly all our lives as slaves and treated like dumb driven cattle.

This is our home, we have made these lands what they were, we are the only true and loyal people that were found in possession of these lands. We have been always ready to strike for liberty and humanity, yea to fight if need be to preserve this glorious Union. Shall not we who are freedmen and have always been true to this Union have the same rights as are enjoyed by others? . . . Are not our rights as a free people and good citizens of these United States to be considered before those who were found in rebellion against this good and just government? . . .

[Are] we who have been abused and oppressed for many long years not to be allowed the privilege of purchasing land but be subject to the will of these large land owners? God forbid. Land monopoly is injurious to the advancement of the course of freedom, and if government does not make some provision by which we as freedmen can obtain a homestead, we have not bettered our condition. . . .

We look to you . . . for protection and equal rights with the privilege of purchasing a homestead—a homestead right here in the heart of South Carolina.

From A SHARECROPPING CONTRACT (1866)

Few former slaves were able to acquire land in the post–Civil War South. Most ended up as sharecroppers, working on white-owned land for a share of the crop at the end of the growing season. This contract, typical of thousands of others, originated in Tennessee. The laborers signed with an X, as they were illiterate.

————————————

Thomas J. Ross agrees to employ the Freedmen to plant and raise a crop on his Rosstown Plantation. . . . On the following Rules, Regulations and Remunerations.

The said Ross agrees to furnish the land to cultivate, and a sufficient number of mules & horses and feed them to make and house said crop and all necessary farming utensils to carry on the same and to give unto said Freedmen whose names appear below one half of all the cotton, corn and wheat that is raised on said place for the year 1866 after all the necessary expenses are deducted out that accrues on said crop. Outside of the Freedmen's labor in harvesting, carrying to market and selling the same the said Freedmen . . . covenant and agrees to and with said Thomas J. Ross that for and in consideration of one half of the crop before mentioned that they will plant, cultivate, and raise under the management control and Superintendence of said Ross, in good faith, a cotton, corn and oat crop under his management for the year 1866. And we the said Freedmen agrees to furnish ourselves & families in provisions, clothing, medicine and medical bills and all, and every kind of other expenses that we may incur on said plantation for the year 1866 free of charge to said Ross. Should the said Ross furnish us any of the above supplies or any other kind of expenses, during said year, [we] are to settle and pay him out of the net proceeds of our part of the crop the retail price of the county at time of sale or any price we may agree upon—The said Ross shall keep a regular book account, against each and every one or the head of every family to be adjusted and settled at the end of the year.

We furthermore bind ourselves to and with said Ross that we will do good work and labor ten hours a day on an average, winter and summer. . . . We further agree that we will lose all lost time, or pay at the rate of one dollar per day, rainy days excepted. In sickness and women lying in childbed are to lose the time and account for it to the other hands out of his or her part of the crop. . . .

We furthermore bind ourselves that we will obey the orders of said Ross in all things in carrying out and managing said crop for said year and be docked for disobedience. All is responsible for all farming utensils that is on hand or may be placed in care of said Freedmen for the year 1866 to said Ross and are also responsible to said Ross if we carelessly, maliciously maltreat any of his stock for said year to said Ross for damages to be assessed out of our wages.

Samuel (X) Johnson, Thomas (X) Richard, Tinny (X) Fitch, Jessie (X) Simmons, Sophe (X) Pruden, Henry (X) Pruden, Frances (X) Pruden, Elijah (X) Smith

QUESTIONS

1. *Why do the black petitioners believe that owning land is essential to the enjoyment of freedom?*

2. *In what ways does the contract limit the freedom of the laborers?*

3. *What do these documents suggest about competing definitions of black freedom in the aftermath of slavery?*

But if struggles over land and labor united its postemancipation experience with that of other societies, in one respect the United States was unique. Only in the United States were former slaves, within two years of the end of slavery, granted the right to vote and, thus, given a major share of political power. Few anticipated this development when the Civil War ended. It came about as the result of one of the greatest political crises of American history—the battle between President Andrew Johnson and Congress over Reconstruction. The struggle resulted in profound changes in the nature of citizenship, the structure of constitutional authority, and the meaning of American freedom.

THE MAKING OF RADICAL RECONSTRUCTION

Andrew Johnson

To Lincoln's successor, Andrew Johnson, fell the task of overseeing the restoration of the Union. Born in poverty in North Carolina, as a youth Johnson worked as a tailor's apprentice. After moving to Tennessee, he achieved success through politics. Beginning as an alderman (a town official), he rose to serve in the state legislature, the U.S. Congress, and for two terms as governor of Tennessee. Johnson identified himself as the champion of his state's "honest yeomen" and a foe of large planters, whom he described as a "bloated, corrupted aristocracy." A strong defender of the Union, he became the only senator from a seceding state to remain at his post in Washington, D.C., when the Civil War began in 1861. When northern forces occupied Tennessee, Abraham Lincoln named him military governor. In 1864, Republicans nominated him to run for vice president as a symbol of the party's hope of extending its organization into the South.

In personality and outlook, Johnson proved unsuited for the responsibilities he shouldered after Lincoln's death. A lonely, stubborn man, he was intolerant of criticism and unable to compromise. He lacked Lincoln's political skills and keen sense of public opinion. A fervent believer in states' rights, Johnson insisted that since secession was illegal, the southern states had never actually left the Union or surrendered the right to govern their own affairs. Moreover, while Johnson had supported emancipation once Lincoln made it a goal of the war effort, he held deeply racist views. African-Americans, Johnson believed, had no role to play in Reconstruction.

The Failure of Presidential Reconstruction

A little over a month after Lee's surrender at Appomattox, and with Congress out of session until December, Johnson in May 1865 outlined his plan for reuniting the nation. He issued a series of proclamations that began the period of Presidential Reconstruction (1865–1867). Johnson offered a pardon (which restored political and property rights, except for slaves) to nearly all white southerners who took an oath of allegiance to the Union. He excluded Confederate leaders and wealthy planters whose prewar property had been valued at more than $20,000. This exemption suggested at first that Johnson planned a more punitive Reconstruction than Lincoln had intended. Most of those exempted, however, soon received individual pardons from the president. Johnson also appointed provisional governors and ordered them to call state conventions, elected by whites alone, that would establish loyal governments in the South. Apart from the requirement that they abolish slavery, repudiate secession, and refuse to pay the Confederate debt—all unavoidable consequences of southern defeat—he granted the new governments a free hand in managing local affairs.

Johnson's program

At first, most northerners believed Johnson's policy deserved a chance to succeed. The conduct of the southern governments elected under his program, however, turned most of the Republican North against the president. By and large, white voters returned prominent Confederates and members of the old elite to power. Reports of violence directed against former slaves and northern visitors in the South further alarmed Republicans.

The Black Codes

But what aroused the most opposition to Johnson's Reconstruction policy were the **Black Codes**, laws passed by the new southern governments that attempted to regulate the lives of the former slaves. These laws granted blacks certain rights, such as legalized marriage, ownership of property, and limited access to the courts. But they denied them the rights to testify against whites, to serve on juries or in state militias, or to vote. And in response to planters' demands that the freedpeople be required to work on the plantations, the Black Codes declared that those who failed to sign yearly labor contracts could be arrested and hired out to white landowners. Some states limited the occupations open to blacks and barred them from acquiring land, and others provided that judges could assign black children to work for their former owners without the consent of the parents. "We are not permitted to own the land whereon to build a schoolhouse or a church," complained a black convention in Mississippi. "Where is justice? Where is freedom?"

Regulating the former slaves

Selling a Freedman to Pay His Fine at Monticello, Florida, an engraving from Frank Leslie's Illustrated Newspaper, January 19, 1867. Under the Black Codes enacted by southern legislatures immediately after the Civil War, blacks convicted of "vagrancy"—often because they refused to sign contracts to work on plantations—were fined and, if unable to pay, auctioned off to work for the person who paid the fine.

Thaddeus Stevens, leader of the Radical Republicans in the House of Representatives during Reconstruction.

Clearly, the death of slavery did not automatically mean the birth of freedom. But the Black Codes so completely violated free labor principles that they called forth a vigorous response from the Republican North. Wars—especially civil wars—often generate hostility and bitterness. But few groups of rebels in history have been treated more leniently than the defeated Confederates. A handful of southern leaders were arrested but most were quickly released. Only one was executed—Henry Wirz, the commander of Andersonville prison, where thousands of Union prisoners of war had died. Most of the Union army was swiftly demobilized. What motivated the North's turn against Johnson's policies was not a desire to "punish" the white South, but the inability of the South's political leaders to accept the reality of emancipation. "We must see to it," announced Republican senator William Stewart of Nevada, "that the man made free by the Constitution of the United States is a freeman indeed."

The Radical Republicans

When Congress assembled in December 1865, Johnson announced that with loyal governments functioning in all the southern states, the nation had been reunited. In response, Radical Republicans, who had grown increasingly disenchanted with Johnson during the summer and fall, called for the dissolution of these governments and the establishment of new ones with "rebels" excluded from power and black men guaranteed the right to vote. Radicals tended to represent constituencies in New England and the "burned-over" districts of the rural North that had been home to religious revivalism, abolitionism, and other reform movements. Although they differed on many issues, Radicals shared the conviction that Union victory created a golden opportunity to institutionalize the principle of equal rights for all, regardless of race.

The Radicals fully embraced the expanded powers of the federal government born during the Civil War. Traditions of federalism and states' rights, they insisted, must not obstruct a sweeping national effort to protect the rights of all Americans.

The most prominent Radicals in Congress were Charles Sumner, a senator from Massachusetts, and Thaddeus Stevens, a lawyer and iron manufacturer who represented Pennsylvania in the House of Representatives. Before the Civil War, both had been outspoken foes of slavery and defenders of black rights. Early in the Civil War, both had urged Lincoln to free and arm the slaves, and both in 1865 favored black suffrage in the South. "The same national authority," declared Sumner, "that destroyed slavery must see that this other pretension [racial inequality] is not permitted to survive."

Thaddeus Stevens

Thaddeus Stevens's most cherished aim was to confiscate the land of disloyal planters and divide it among former slaves and northern migrants to the South. "The whole fabric of southern society," he declared, "*must* be changed. Without this, this Government can never be, as it has never been, a true republic." But his plan to make "small independent landholders" of the former slaves proved too radical even for many of his Radical colleagues. Congress, to be sure, had already offered free land to settlers in the West in the Homestead Act of 1862. But this land had been in the possession of the federal government, not private individuals (although originally, of course, it had belonged to Indians). Most congressmen believed too deeply in the sanctity of property rights to be willing to take land from one group of owners and distribute it to others. Stevens's proposal failed to pass.

The Origins of Civil Rights

With the South unrepresented, Republicans enjoyed an overwhelming majority in Congress. But the party was internally divided. Most Republicans were moderates, not Radicals. Moderates believed that Johnson's plan was flawed, but they desired to work with the president to modify it. They feared that neither northern nor southern whites would accept black suffrage. Moderates and Radicals joined in refusing to seat the southerners recently elected to Congress, but moderates broke with the Radicals by leaving the Johnson governments in place.

Early in 1866, Senator Lyman Trumbull of Illinois proposed two bills, reflecting the moderates' belief that Johnson's policy required modification. The first extended the life of the Freedmen's Bureau, which had originally been established for only one year. The second, the **Civil Rights Bill of 1866**, was described by one congressman as "one of the most important bills ever presented to the House for its action." It defined all persons born in the United States as citizens and spelled out rights they were to enjoy without regard to race. Equality before the law was central to the measure—no longer could states enact laws like the Black Codes discriminating between white and black citizens. So were free labor values. According to the law, no state could deprive any citizen of the right to make contracts, bring lawsuits, or enjoy equal protection of one's person and property. These, said Trumbull, were the "fundamental rights belonging to every man as a free man." The bill made no mention of the right to vote for blacks. In constitutional terms, the Civil Rights Bill represented the first attempt to give concrete meaning to the Thirteenth Amendment, which had abolished slavery, to define in law the essence of freedom.

To the surprise of Congress, Johnson vetoed both bills. Both, he said, would centralize power in the national government and deprive the states of the authority to regulate their own affairs. Moreover, he argued, blacks did not deserve the rights of citizenship. By acting to secure their rights, Congress was discriminating

President Andrew Johnson, in an 1868 lithograph by Currier and Ives. Because of Johnson's stubborn opposition to the congressional Reconstruction policy, one disgruntled citizen drew a crown on his head with the words, "I am King."

THE FREEDMAN'S BUREAU!
AN AGENCY TO KEEP THE NEGRO IN IDLENESS AT THE EXPENSE OF THE WHITE MAN.
TWICE VETOED BY THE PRESIDENT, AND MADE A LAW BY CONGRESS.
SUPPORT CONGRESS & YOU SUPPORT THE NEGRO.   SUSTAIN THE PRESIDENT & YOU PROTECT THE WHITE MAN

A Democratic Party broadside from the election of 1866 in Pennsylvania uses racist imagery to argue that government assistance aids lazy former slaves at the expense of hardworking whites.

Black suffrage

Significance of the Fourteenth Amendment

"against the white race." The vetoes made a breach between the president and nearly the entire Republican Party inevitable. Congress failed by a single vote to muster the two-thirds majority necessary to override the veto of the Freedmen's Bureau Bill (although later in 1866, it did extend the Bureau's life to 1870). But in April 1866, the Civil Rights Bill became the first major law in American history to be passed over a presidential veto.

The Fourteenth Amendment

Congress now proceeded to adopt its own plan of Reconstruction. In June, it approved and sent to the states for ratification the **Fourteenth Amendment**, which placed in the Constitution the principle of citizenship for all persons born in the United States, and which empowered the federal government to protect the rights of all Americans. The amendment prohibited the states from abridging the "privileges or immunities" of citizens or denying any person of the "equal protection of the laws." This broad language opened the door for future Congresses and the federal courts to breathe meaning into the guarantee of legal equality.

In a compromise between the radical and moderate positions on black suffrage, the amendment did not grant blacks the right to vote. But it did provide that if a state denied the vote to any group of men, that state's representation in Congress would be reduced. (This provision did not apply when states barred women from voting.) The abolition of slavery threatened to increase southern political power, since now all blacks, not merely three-fifths as in the case of slaves, would be counted in determining a state's representation in Congress. The Fourteenth Amendment offered the leaders of the white South a choice—allow black men to vote and keep their state's full representation in the House of Representatives, or limit the vote to whites and sacrifice part of their political power.

The Fourteenth Amendment produced an intense division between the parties. Not a single Democrat in Congress voted in its favor, and only 4 of 175 Republicans were opposed. Radicals, to be sure, expressed their disappointment that the amendment did not guarantee black suffrage. (It was far from perfect, Stevens told the House, but he intended to vote for it, "because I live among men and not among angels.") Nonetheless, by writing into the Constitution the principle that equality before the law regardless of race is a fundamental right of all American citizens, the amendment made the most important change in that document since the adoption of the Bill of Rights.

The Reconstruction Act

The Fourteenth Amendment became the central issue of the political campaign of 1866. Johnson embarked on a speaking tour of the North, called by journalists the "swing around the circle," to urge voters to elect members of Congress committed to his own Reconstruction program. Denouncing his critics, the president made wild accusations that the Radicals were plotting to assassinate him. His behavior further undermined public support for his policies, as did riots that broke out in Memphis and New Orleans, in which white policemen and citizens killed dozens of blacks.

In the northern congressional elections that fall, Republicans opposed to Johnson's policies won a sweeping victory. Nonetheless, at the president's urging, every southern state but Tennessee refused to ratify the Fourteenth Amendment. The intransigence of Johnson and the bulk of the white South pushed moderate Republicans toward the Radicals. In March 1867, over Johnson's veto, Congress adopted the **Reconstruction Act**, which temporarily divided the South into five military districts and called for the creation of new state governments, with black men given the right to vote. Thus began the period of Radical Reconstruction, which lasted until 1877.

A variety of motives combined to produce Radical Reconstruction—demands by former slaves for the right to vote, the Radicals' commitment to the idea of equality, widespread disgust with Johnson's policies, the desire to fortify the Republican Party in the South, and the determination to keep ex-Confederates from office. But the conflict between President Johnson and Congress did not end with the passage of the Reconstruction Act.

Impeachment and the Election of Grant

In March 1867, Congress adopted the **Tenure of Office Act**, barring the president from removing certain officeholders, including cabinet members, without the consent of the Senate. Johnson considered this an unconstitutional restriction on his authority. In February 1868, he removed Secretary of War Edwin M. Stanton, an ally of the Radicals. The House of Representatives responded by approving articles of **impeachment**—that is, it presented charges against Johnson to the Senate, which had to decide whether to remove him from office.

That spring, for the first time in American history, a president was placed on trial before the Senate for "high crimes and misdemeanors." By this point, virtually all Republicans considered Johnson a failure as president. But some moderates disliked Benjamin F. Wade, a Radical who, as temporary president of the Senate, would become president if Johnson were removed. Others feared that conviction would damage the constitutional separation of powers between Congress and the executive. Johnson's lawyers assured moderate Republicans that, if acquitted, he would stop interfering with Reconstruction policy. The final tally was 35–19 to convict Johnson, one vote short of the two-thirds necessary to remove him. Seven Republicans had joined the Democrats in voting to acquit the president.

A few days after the vote, Republicans nominated Ulysses S. Grant, the Union's most prominent military hero, as their candidate for president. Grant's Democratic opponent was Horatio Seymour, the former governor of New York. Reconstruction became the central issue of the bitterly fought 1868 campaign. Republicans identified their opponents with secession and treason, a tactic known as "waving the bloody shirt." Democrats denounced Reconstruction as unconstitutional and

A Republican campaign poster from 1868 depicts Ulysses S. Grant and his running mate Henry Wilson not as a celebrated general and U.S. senator but as ordinary workingmen, embodiments of the dignity of free labor.

Johnson's acquittal

A Democratic ribbon from the election of 1868, with Horatio Seymour and Francis P. Blair Jr., the party's candidates for president and vice president. The ribbon illustrates the explicit appeals to racism that marked the campaign.

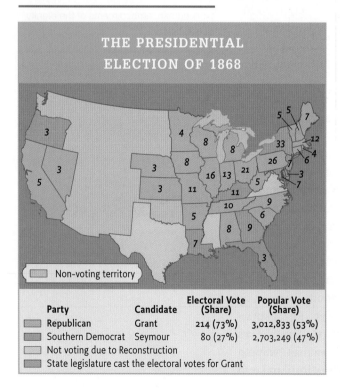

THE PRESIDENTIAL
ELECTION OF 1868

Non-voting territory

Party	Candidate	Electoral Vote (Share)	Popular Vote (Share)
Republican	Grant	214 (73%)	3,012,833 (53%)
Southern Democrat	Seymour	80 (27%)	2,703,249 (47%)
Not voting due to Reconstruction			
State legislature cast the electoral votes for Grant			

condemned black suffrage as a violation of America's political traditions. They appealed openly to racism. Seymour's running mate, Francis P. Blair Jr., charged Republicans with placing the South under the rule of "a semi-barbarous race" who longed to "subject the white women to their unbridled lust."

The Fifteenth Amendment

Grant won the election of 1868, although by a margin—300,000 of 6 million votes cast—that many Republicans found uncomfortably slim. The result led Congress to adopt the era's third and final amendment to the Constitution. In February 1869, it approved the **Fifteenth Amendment**, which prohibited the federal and state governments from denying any citizen the right to vote because of race. Bitterly opposed by the Democratic Party, it was ratified in 1870.

Although the Fifteenth Amendment opened the door to suffrage restrictions not explicitly based on race—literacy tests, property qualifications, and poll taxes—and did not extend the right to vote to women, it marked the culmination of four decades of abolitionist agitation. As late as 1868, even after Congress had enfranchised black men in the South, only eight northern states allowed African-American men to vote. With the Fifteenth Amendment, the American Anti-Slavery Society disbanded, its work, its members believed, now complete. "Nothing in all history," exclaimed veteran abolitionist William Lloyd Garrison, equaled "this wonderful, quiet, sudden transformation of four millions of human beings from . . . the auction-block to the ballot-box."

The "Great Constitutional Revolution"

The laws and amendments of Reconstruction reflected the intersection of two products of the Civil War era—a newly empowered national state and the idea of a national citizenry enjoying equality before the law. What Republican leader Carl Schurz called the "great Constitutional revolution" of Reconstruction transformed the federal system and with it, the language of freedom so central to American political culture.

Before the Civil War, American citizenship had been closely linked to race. The first Congress, in 1790, had limited to whites the right to become a naturalized citizen when immigrating from abroad. No black person, free or slave, the Supreme Court had declared in the *Dred Scott* decision of 1857, could be a citizen of the United States. The laws and amendments of Reconstruction repudiated the idea that citizenship was an entitlement of whites alone. The principle of equality before the law, moreover, did not apply only to the South. The Reconstruction amendments voided many northern laws discriminating on the basis of race. And, as one congressman noted, the amendments expanded the liberty of whites as well as blacks, including "the millions of people of foreign birth who will flock to our shores."

The new amendments also transformed the relationship between the federal government and the states. The Bill of Rights had linked civil liberties to the autonomy of the states.

Uncle Sam's Thanksgiving Dinner, an engraving by Thomas Nast from *Harper's Weekly*, November 20, 1868, shortly after the election of Ulysses S. Grant, graphically illustrates how the boundaries of freedom had expanded during Reconstruction. The guests include, among others, African-Americans, Asian-Americans, and Native Americans, men and women, all enjoying a harmonious feast. The table's centerpiece contains the slogan, "universal suffrage."

Its language—"Congress shall make no law"—reflected the belief that concentrated national power posed the greatest threat to freedom. The authors of the Reconstruction amendments assumed that rights required national power to enforce them. Rather than a threat to liberty, the federal government, in Charles Sumner's words, had become "the custodian of freedom."

The Reconstruction amendments transformed the Constitution from a document primarily concerned with federal-state relations and the rights of property into a vehicle through which members of vulnerable minorities could stake a claim to freedom and seek protection against misconduct by all levels of government. In the twentieth century, many of the Supreme Court's most important decisions expanding the rights of American citizens were based on the Fourteenth Amendment, perhaps most notably the 1954 *Brown* ruling that outlawed school segregation (see Chapter 24).

Boundaries of Freedom

Reconstruction redrew the boundaries of American freedom. Lines of exclusion that limited the privileges of citizenship to white men had long been central to the practice of American democracy. Only in an unparalleled crisis could they have been replaced, even temporarily, by the vision of a republic of equals embracing black Americans as well as white. That the United States was a "white man's government" had been a widespread belief before the Civil War. It is not difficult to understand why Andrew Johnson, in one of his veto messages, claimed that federal protection of blacks' civil rights violated "all our experience as a people."

Race and rights

Another illustration of the new spirit of racial inclusiveness was the Burlingame Treaty, negotiated by Anson Burlingame, an antislavery congressman from Massachusetts before being named American envoy to China. Other treaties with China had been one-sided, securing trading and political advantages for European

The Burlingame Treaty

powers. The Burlingame Treaty reaffirmed China's national sovereignty, and provided reciprocal protection for religious freedom and against discrimination for citizens of each country emigrating or visiting the other. When Burlingame died, Mark Twain wrote a eulogy that praised him for "outgrow[ing] the narrow citizenship of a state [to] become a citizen of the world."

Reconstruction Republicans' belief in universal rights had its limits. In his remarkable "Composite Nation" speech of 1869, Frederick Douglass condemned prejudice against immigrants from China. America's destiny, he declared, was to transcend race by serving as an asylum for people "gathered here from all corners of the globe by a common aspiration for national liberty." A year later, Charles Sumner moved to strike the word "white" from naturalization requirements. Senators from the western states objected. At their insistence, the naturalization law was amended to make Africans eligible to obtain citizenship when migrating from abroad. But Asians remained ineligible. The racial boundaries of nationality had been redrawn, but not eliminated. The juxtaposition of the amended naturalization law and the Fourteenth Amendment created a significant division in the Asian-American community. Well into the twentieth century, Asian immigrants could not become citizens, but their native-born children automatically did.

Amendment of naturalization law

The Rights of Women

"The contest with the South that destroyed slavery," wrote the Philadelphia lawyer Sidney George Fisher in his diary, "has caused an immense increase in the popular passion for liberty and equality." But advocates of women's rights encountered the limits of the Reconstruction commitment to equality. Women activists saw Reconstruction as the moment to claim their own emancipation. No less than blacks, proclaimed Elizabeth Cady Stanton, women had arrived at a "transition period, from slavery to freedom." The rewriting of the Constitution, declared suffrage leader Olympia Brown, offered the opportunity to sever the blessings of freedom from sex as well as race and to "bury the black man and the woman in the citizen."

Women activists

The destruction of slavery led feminists to search for ways to make the promise of free labor real for women. Every issue of the new women's rights journal, *The Agitator*, edited by Mary Livermore, who had led fund-raising efforts for aid to Union soldiers during the war, carried stories complaining of the limited job opportunities and unequal pay for females who entered the labor market. Other feminists debated how to achieve "liberty for married women." Demands for liberalizing divorce laws (which generally required evidence of adultery, desertion, or extreme abuse to terminate a marriage) and for recognizing "woman's control over her own body" (including protection against domestic violence and access to what later generations would call birth control) moved to the center of many feminists' concerns. "Our rotten marriage institution," one Ohio woman wrote, "is the main obstacle in the way of woman's freedom."

Feminists and Radicals

In one place, women's political rights did expand during Reconstruction—not, however, in a bastion of radicalism such as Massachusetts, but in the Wyoming territory. This had less to do with the era's egalitarian impulse than with the desire to attract female emigrants to an area where men outnumbered women five to one. In 1869, Wyoming's diminutive legislature (it consisted of fewer than twenty men) extended the right to vote to women, and the bill was then signed by the governor, a federal appointee. Wyoming entered the Union in 1890, becoming the first state since New Jersey in the late eighteenth century to allow women to vote.

In general, however, talk of woman suffrage and redesigning marriage found few sympathetic male listeners. Even Radical Republicans insisted that Reconstruction was the "Negro's hour" (the hour, that is, of the black male). The Fourteenth Amendment for the first time introduced the word "male" into the Constitution, in its clause penalizing a state for denying any group of men the right to vote. The Fifteenth Amendment outlawed discrimination in voting based on race but not gender. These measures produced a bitter split both between feminists and Radical Republicans, and within feminist circles.

Some leaders, like Stanton and Susan B. Anthony, opposed the Fifteenth Amendment because it did nothing to enfranchise women. They denounced their former abolitionist allies and moved to sever the women's rights movement from its earlier moorings in the antislavery tradition. On occasion, they appealed to racial and ethnic prejudices, arguing that native-born white women deserved the vote more than non-whites and immigrants. "Patrick and Sambo and Hans and Yung Tung, who do not know the difference between a monarchy and a republic," declared Stanton, had no right to be "making laws for [feminist leader] Lucretia Mott." But other abolitionist-feminists, like Abby Kelley and Lucy Stone, insisted that despite their limitations, the Reconstruction amendments represented steps in the direction of truly universal suffrage and should be supported. The result was a split in the movement and the creation in 1869 of two hostile women's rights organizations—the National Woman Suffrage Association, led by Stanton, and the American Woman Suffrage Association, with Lucy Stone as president. They would not reunite until 1890.

Thus, even as it rejected the racial definition of freedom that had emerged in the first half of the nineteenth century, Reconstruction left the gender boundary largely intact. When women tried to use the rewritten legal code and Constitution to claim equal rights, they found the courts unreceptive. Myra Bradwell invoked the idea of free labor in challenging an Illinois statute limiting the practice of law to men, but the Supreme Court in 1873 rebuffed her claim. Free labor principles, the justices declared, did not apply to women, since "the law of the Creator" had assigned them to "the domestic sphere."

Despite their limitations, the Fourteenth and Fifteenth Amendments and the Reconstruction Act of 1867 marked a radical departure in American history.

A Delegation of Advocates of Woman Suffrage Addressing the House Judiciary Committee, an engraving from *Frank Leslie's Illustrated Newspaper*, February 4, 1871. The group includes Elizabeth Cady Stanton, seated just to the right of the speaker, and Susan B. Anthony, at the table on the extreme right.

The gender boundary intact

America's great departure

"We have cut loose from the whole dead past," wrote Timothy Howe, a Republican senator from Wisconsin, "and have cast our anchor out a hundred years" into the future. The Reconstruction Act of 1867 inaugurated America's first real experiment in interracial democracy.

RADICAL RECONSTRUCTION IN THE SOUTH

"The Tocsin of Freedom"

Political action by African-Americans

Among the former slaves, the passage of the Reconstruction Act inspired an outburst of political organization. At mass political meetings—community gatherings attended by men, women, and children—African-Americans staked their claim to equal citizenship. Blacks, declared an Alabama meeting, deserved "exactly the same rights, privileges and immunities as are enjoyed by white men. We ask for nothing more and will be content with nothing less."

These gatherings inspired direct action to remedy long-standing grievances. Hundreds took part in sit-ins that integrated horse-drawn public streetcars in cities across the South. Plantation workers organized strikes for higher wages. Speakers, male and female, fanned out across the South. Frances Ellen Watkins Harper, a black veteran of the abolitionist movement, embarked on a two-year tour, lecturing on "Literacy, Land, and Liberation." James D. Lynch, a member of the group that met with General Sherman in 1865, organized Republican meetings. He became known, in the words of a white contemporary, as "a great orator, fluid and graceful," who "stirred the emotions" of his listeners "as no other man could do."

The Union League

Determined to exercise their new rights as citizens, thousands joined the Union League, an organization closely linked to the Republican Party, and the vast majority of eligible African-Americans registered to vote. James K. Green,

Electioneering at the South, an engraving from *Harper's Weekly*, July 25, 1868, depicts a speaker at a political meeting in the rural South. Women as well as men took part in these grassroots gatherings.

a former slave in Hale County, Alabama, and a League organizer, went on to serve eight years in the Alabama legislature. In the 1880s, Green looked back on his political career. Before the war, he declared, "I was entirely ignorant; I knew nothing more than to obey my master; and there were thousands of us in the same attitude. . . . But the tocsin [warning bell] of freedom sounded and knocked at the door and we walked out like free men and shouldered the responsibilities."

By 1870, all the former Confederate states had been readmitted to the Union, and in a region where the Republican Party had not existed before the war, nearly all were under Republican control. Their new state constitutions, drafted in 1868 and 1869 by the first public bodies in American history with substantial black representation, marked a considerable improvement over those they replaced. The constitutions greatly expanded public responsibilities. They established the region's first state-funded systems of free public education, and they created new penitentiaries, orphan asylums, and homes for the insane. The constitutions guaranteed equality of civil and political rights and abolished practices of the antebellum era such as whipping as a punishment for crime, property qualifications for officeholding, and imprisonment for debt. A few states initially barred former Confederates from voting, but this policy was quickly abandoned by the new state governments.

From the Plantation to the Senate, an 1883 lithograph celebrating African-American progress during Reconstruction. Among the black leaders pictured at the top are Reconstruction congressmen Benjamin S. Turner, Josiah T. Walls, and Joseph H. Rainey; Hiram Revels of Mississippi, the first African-American senator; religious leader Richard Allen; and abolitionists Frederick Douglass and William Wells Brown. At the center emancipated slaves work in the cotton fields, and below children attend school and a black family stands outside its home.

The Black Officeholder

Throughout Reconstruction, black voters provided the bulk of the Republican Party's support. But African-Americans did not control Reconstruction politics, as their opponents frequently charged. The highest offices remained almost entirely in white hands, and only in South Carolina, where blacks made up 60 percent of the population, did they form a majority of the legislature. Nonetheless, the fact that some 2,000 African-Americans occupied public offices during Reconstruction represented a fundamental shift of power in the South and a radical departure in American government.

African-Americans were represented at every level of government. Fourteen were elected to the national House of Representatives. Two blacks served in the U.S. Senate during Reconstruction, both representing Mississippi. Hiram Revels, who had been born free in North Carolina, was educated in Illinois, and served as a chaplain in the wartime Union army, in 1870 became the first black senator in American history. The second, Blanche K. Bruce, a former slave, was elected in 1875. The next African-American elected to the Senate was Edward W. Brooke of Massachusetts, who served 1967–1978.

Pinckney B. S. Pinchback of Louisiana, the Georgia-born son of a white planter and a free black woman, served briefly during the winter of 1872–1873 as America's first black governor. More than a century would pass before L. Douglas Wilder of Virginia, elected in 1989, became the second. Some 700 blacks sat in state legislatures during Reconstruction, and scores held local offices ranging

The First Vote, an engraving from *Harper's Weekly*, November 16, 1867, depicts the first biracial elections in southern history. The voters represent key sources of the black political leadership that emerged during Reconstruction—the artisan carrying his tools, the well-dressed city person (probably free before the war), and the soldier.

from justice of the peace to sheriff, tax assessor, and policeman. The presence of black officeholders and their white allies made a real difference in southern life, ensuring that blacks accused of crimes would be tried before juries of their peers and enforcing fairness in such aspects of local government as road repair, tax assessment, and poor relief.

In South Carolina and Louisiana, homes of the South's wealthiest and best-educated free black communities, most prominent Reconstruction officeholders had never experienced slavery. In addition, a number of black Reconstruction officials, like Pennsylvania-born Jonathan J. Wright, who served on the South Carolina Supreme Court, had come from the North after the Civil War. The majority, however, were former slaves who had established their leadership in the black community by serving in the Union army, working as ministers, teachers, or skilled craftsmen, or engaging in Union League organizing. Among the most celebrated black officeholders was Robert Smalls, who had worked as a slave on the Charleston docks before the Civil War and who won national fame in 1862 by secretly guiding the *Planter*, a Confederate vessel, out of the harbor and delivering it to Union forces. Smalls became a powerful political leader on the South Carolina Sea Islands and was elected to five terms in Congress.

Carpetbaggers and Scalawags

The new southern governments also brought to power new groups of whites. Many Reconstruction officials were northerners who for one reason or another had made their homes in the South after the war. Their opponents dubbed them **carpetbaggers**, implying that they had packed all their belongings in a suitcase and left their homes in order to reap the spoils of office in the South. Some carpetbaggers were undoubtedly corrupt adventurers. The large majority, however, were former Union soldiers who decided to remain in the South when the war ended, before there was

Black and white members of the Mississippi senate, 1874–1875, shortly before the end of Reconstruction in the state. The woman in the bottom row is a postmistress.

any prospect of going into politics. Others were investors in land and railroads who saw in the postwar South an opportunity to combine personal economic advancement with a role in helping to substitute, as one wrote, "the civilization of freedom for that of slavery." Teachers, Freedmen's Bureau officers, and others who came to the region genuinely hoping to assist the former slaves represented another large group of carpetbaggers.

Most white Republicans had been born in the South. Former Confederates reserved their greatest scorn for these **scalawags**, whom they considered traitors to their race and region. Some southern-born Republicans were men of stature and wealth, like James L. Alcorn, the owner of one of Mississippi's largest plantations and the state's first Republican governor.

Most scalawags, however, were non-slaveholding white farmers from the southern upcountry. Many had been wartime Unionists, and they now cooperated with the Republicans in order to prevent "rebels" from returning to power. Others hoped Reconstruction governments would help them recover from wartime economic losses by suspending the collection of debts and enacting laws protecting small property holders from losing their homes to creditors. In states like North Carolina, Tennessee, and Arkansas, Republicans initially commanded a significant minority of the white vote. Even in the Deep South, the small white Republican vote was important, because the population remained almost evenly divided between blacks (almost all of whom voted for the party of Lincoln) and whites (overwhelmingly Democratic).

A portrait of Hiram Revels, the first black U.S. senator, by Theodore Kaufmann, a German-born artist who emigrated to the United States in 1855. Lithograph copies sold widely in the North during Reconstruction. Frederick Douglass, commenting on the dignified image, noted that African-Americans "so often see ourselves described and painted as monkeys, that we think it a great piece of fortune to find an exception to this general rule."

Southern Republicans in Power

In view of the daunting challenges they faced, the remarkable thing is not that Reconstruction governments in many respects failed, but how much they did accomplish. Perhaps their greatest achievement lay in establishing the South's first state-supported public schools. The new educational systems served both black and white children, although generally in schools segregated by race. Only in New Orleans were the public schools integrated during Reconstruction, and only in South Carolina did the state university admit black students (elsewhere, separate colleges were established). By the 1870s, in a region whose prewar leaders had made it illegal for slaves to learn and had done little to provide education for poorer whites, more than half the children, black and white, were attending public schools. The new governments also pioneered civil rights legislation. Their laws made it illegal for railroads, hotels, and other institutions to discriminate on the basis of race. Enforcement varied considerably from locality to locality, but Reconstruction established for the first time at the state level a standard of equal citizenship and a recognition of blacks' right to a share of public services.

State-supported public schools

Republican governments also took steps to strengthen the position of rural laborers and promote the South's economic recovery. They passed laws to ensure that agricultural laborers and sharecroppers had the first claim on harvested crops, rather than merchants to whom the landowner owed money. South Carolina created a state Land Commission, which by 1876 had settled 14,000 black families and a few poor whites on their own farms.

Plans for economic recovery

Emancipation, an 1865 lithograph, is unusual because along with the familiar images of Lincoln and emancipated slaves, it also portrays a poor white family, suggesting that all Americans will benefit from the end of slavery and Reconstruction.

The Quest for Prosperity

Rather than land distribution, however, the Reconstruction governments pinned their hopes for southern economic growth and opportunity for African-Americans and poor whites alike on regional economic development. Railroad construction, they believed, was the key to transforming the South into a society of booming factories, bustling towns, and diversified agriculture. "A free and living republic," declared a Tennessee Republican, would "spring up in the track of the railroad." Every state during Reconstruction helped to finance railroad construction, and through tax reductions and other incentives tried to attract northern manufacturers to invest in the region. The program had mixed results. Economic development in general remained weak. With abundant opportunities existing in the West, few northern investors ventured to the Reconstruction South.

To their supporters, the governments of Radical Reconstruction presented a complex pattern of disappointment and accomplishment. A revitalized southern economy failed to materialize, and most African-Americans remained locked in poverty. On the other hand, biracial democratic government, a thing unknown in American history, for the first time functioned effectively in many parts of the South. Public facilities were rebuilt and expanded, school systems established, and legal codes purged of racism. The conservative elite that had dominated southern government from colonial times to 1867 found itself excluded from political power, while poor whites, newcomers from the North, and former slaves cast ballots, sat on juries, and enacted and administered laws. "We have gone through one of the most remarkable changes in our relations to each other," declared a white South Carolina lawyer in 1871, "that has been known, perhaps, in the history of the world." It is a measure of how far change had progressed that the reaction against Reconstruction proved so extreme.

A group of black students and their teacher in a picture taken by an amateur photographer, probably a Union army veteran, while touring Civil War battlefields.

THE OVERTHROW OF RECONSTRUCTION

Reconstruction's Opponents

The South's traditional leaders—planters, merchants, and Democratic politicians—bitterly opposed the new governments. They denounced them as corrupt, inefficient, and examples of "black supremacy." "Intelligence, virtue, and patriotism" in public life, declared a protest by prominent southern Democrats, had given way to "ignorance, stupidity, and vice." Corruption did exist during Reconstruction, but it was confined to no race, region, or party. The rapid growth of state budgets and the benefits to be gained from public aid led in some states to a scramble for influence that produced bribery, insider dealing, and a get-rich-quick atmosphere. Southern frauds, however, were dwarfed by those practiced in these years by the Whiskey Ring, which involved high officials of the Grant administration, and by New York's Tweed Ring, controlled by the Democrats, whose thefts ran into the tens of millions of dollars. (These are discussed in the next chapter.) The rising taxes needed to pay for schools and other new public facilities and to assist railroad development were another cause of opposition to Reconstruction. Many poor whites who had initially supported the Republican Party turned against it when it became clear that their economic situation was not improving.

Sources of opposition

The most basic reason for opposition to Reconstruction, however, was that most white southerners could not accept the idea of former slaves voting, holding office, and enjoying equality before the law. In order to restore white supremacy in southern public life and to ensure planters a disciplined, reliable labor force, they believed, Reconstruction must be overthrown. Opponents launched a campaign of violence in an effort to end Republican rule. Their actions posed a fundamental challenge both for Reconstruction governments in the South and for policymakers in Washington, D.C.

Campaign of violence

"A Reign of Terror"

The Civil War ended in 1865, but violence remained widespread in large parts of the postwar South. In the early years of Reconstruction, violence was mostly

A cartoon from around 1870 illustrates a key theme of the racist opposition to Reconstruction—that blacks had forced themselves upon whites and gained domination over them. A black schoolteacher inflicts punishment on a white student in an integrated classroom, and a racially mixed jury judges a white defendant.

A Prospective Scene in the City of Oaks, a cartoon in the September 1, 1868, issue of the *Independent Monitor*, a Democratic newspaper published in Tuscaloosa, Alabama. The cartoon sent a warning to the Reverend A. S. Lakin, who had moved from Ohio to become president of the University of Alabama, and Dr. N. B. Cloud, a southern-born Republican serving as Alabama's superintendent of public education. The Ku Klux Klan forced both men from their positions. While most of the Klan's victims were black, the two men pictured here are white.

Colfax

The Enforcement Acts

local and unorganized. Blacks were assaulted and murdered for refusing to give way to whites on city sidewalks, using "insolent" language, challenging end-of-year contract settlements, and attempting to buy land. The violence that greeted the advent of Republican governments after 1867, however, was far more pervasive and more directly motivated by politics. In wide areas of the South, secret societies sprang up with the aim of preventing blacks from voting and destroying the organization of the Republican Party by assassinating local leaders and public officials.

The most notorious such organization was the **Ku Klux Klan**, which in effect served as a military arm of the Democratic Party in the South. From its founding in 1866 in Tennessee, the Klan was a terrorist organization. It quickly spread into nearly every southern state. Led by planters, merchants, and Democratic politicians, men who liked to style themselves the South's "respectable citizens," the Klan committed some of the most brutal criminal acts in American history. In many counties, it launched what one victim called a "reign of terror" against Republican leaders, black and white.

The Klan's victims included white Republicans, among them wartime Unionists and local officeholders, teachers, and party organizers. William Luke, an Irish-born teacher in a black school, was lynched in 1870. But African-Americans—local political leaders, those who managed to acquire land, and others who in one way or another defied the norms of white supremacy—bore the brunt of the violence. In York County, South Carolina, where nearly the entire white male population joined the Klan (and women participated by sewing the robes and hoods Klansmen wore as disguises), the organization committed eleven murders and hundreds of whippings.

On occasion, violence escalated from assaults on individuals to mass terrorism and even local insurrections. In Meridian, Mississippi, in 1871, some thirty blacks were murdered in cold blood, along with a white Republican judge. The bloodiest act of violence during Reconstruction took place in Colfax, Louisiana, in 1873, where armed whites assaulted the town with a small cannon. Hundreds of former slaves were murdered, including fifty members of a black militia unit after they had surrendered.

Unable to suppress the Klan, the new southern governments appealed to Washington for help. In 1870 and 1871, Congress adopted three **Enforcement Acts**, outlawing terrorist societies and allowing the president to use the army against them. These laws continued the expansion of national authority during Reconstruction. They defined crimes that aimed to deprive citizens of their civil and political rights as federal offenses rather than violations of state law. In 1871, President Grant dispatched federal marshals, backed up by troops in some areas, to arrest hundreds of accused Klansmen. Many Klan leaders fled the South. After a series of well-publicized trials, the Klan went out of existence. In 1872, for the first time since before the Civil War, peace reigned in most of the former Confederacy.

The Liberal Republicans

Despite the Grant administration's effective response to Klan terrorism, the North's commitment to Reconstruction waned during the 1870s. Many Radicals, including Thaddeus Stevens, who died in 1868, had passed from the scene. Within the Republican Party, their place was taken by politicians less committed to the ideal of equal rights for blacks. Northerners increasingly felt that the South should be able to solve its own problems without constant interference from Washington. The federal government had freed the slaves, made them citizens, and given them the right to vote. Now, blacks should rely on their own resources, not demand further assistance.

In 1872, an influential group of Republicans, alienated by corruption within the Grant administration and believing that the growth of federal power during and after the war needed to be curtailed, formed their own party. They included Republican founders like Lyman Trumbull and prominent editors and journalists such as E. L. Godkin of *The Nation*. Calling themselves Liberal Republicans, they nominated Horace Greeley, editor of the *New York Tribune*, for president.

The Liberals' alienation from the Grant administration initially had little to do with Reconstruction. They claimed that corrupt politicians had come to power in the North by manipulating the votes of immigrants and workingmen, while men of talent and education like themselves had been pushed aside. Democratic criticisms of Reconstruction, however, found a receptive audience among the Liberals. As in the North, they became convinced, the "best men" of the South had been excluded from power while "ignorant" voters controlled politics, producing corruption and misgovernment. Power in the South should be returned to the region's "natural leaders." During the campaign of 1872, Greeley repeatedly called on Americans to "clasp hands across the bloody chasm" by putting the Civil War and Reconstruction behind them.

A Tennessee member of the Ku Klux Klan, photographed in his hooded disguise around 1870.

The Old Plantation Home, a lithograph from 1872 produced by the prominent firm of Currier and Ives in New York City, illustrates how a nostalgic image of slavery as a time of carefree happiness for African-Americans was being promoted even as Reconstruction took place.

Changes in graphic artist Thomas Nast's depiction of blacks in *Harper's Weekly* mirrored the evolution of Republican sentiment in the North. *And Not This Man?*, August 5, 1865, shows the black soldier as an upstanding citizen deserving of the vote. *Colored Rule in a Reconstructed (?) State*, March 14, 1874, suggests that Reconstruction legislatures had become travesties of democratic government.

A bankbook issued by the Freedman's Savings and Trust Company, a private corporation established by Congress to promote thrift among the former slaves. Black individuals, families, church groups, and civic organizations deposited nearly $2 million in branches scattered across the South. The bank failed in 1874 because of mismanagement, and thousands of depositors lost their savings.

Greeley had spent most of his career, first as a Whig and then as a Republican, denouncing the Democratic Party. But with the Republican split presenting an opportunity to repair their political fortunes, Democratic leaders endorsed Greeley as their candidate. Many rank-and-file Democrats, unable to bring themselves to vote for Greeley, stayed at home on election day. As a result, Greeley suffered a devastating defeat by Grant, whose margin of more than 700,000 popular votes was the largest in a nineteenth-century presidential contest. But Greeley's campaign placed on the northern agenda the one issue on which the Liberal reformers and the Democrats could agree—a new policy toward the South.

The North's Retreat

The Liberal attack on Reconstruction, which continued after 1872, contributed to a resurgence of racism in the North. Journalist James S. Pike, a leading Greeley supporter, in 1874 published *The Prostrate State*, an influential account of a visit to South Carolina. The book depicted a state engulfed by political corruption, drained by governmental extravagance, and under the control of "a mass of black barbarism." The South's problems, Pike insisted, arose from "Negro government." The solution was to restore leading whites to political power. Newspapers that had long supported Reconstruction now began to condemn black participation in southern government. They expressed their views visually as well. Engravings depicting the former slaves as heroic Civil War veterans, upstanding citizens, or victims of violence were increasingly replaced by caricatures presenting them as little more than unbridled animals. Resurgent racism offered a convenient explanation for the alleged "failure" of Reconstruction.

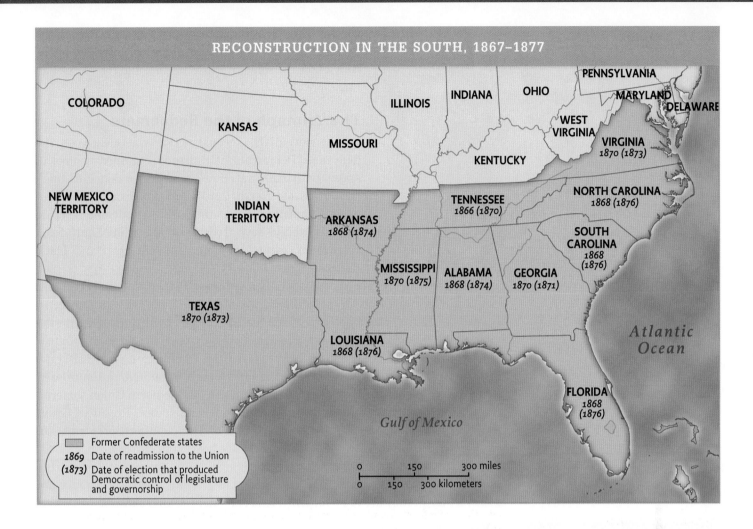

RECONSTRUCTION IN THE SOUTH, 1867–1877

Former Confederate states

1869 Date of readmission to the Union

(1873) Date of election that produced Democratic control of legislature and governorship

Other factors also weakened northern support for Reconstruction. In 1873, the country plunged into a severe economic depression. Distracted by economic problems, Republicans were in no mood to devote further attention to the South. The depression dealt the South a severe blow and further weakened the prospect that Republicans could revitalize the region's economy. Democrats made substantial gains throughout the nation in the elections of 1874. For the first time since the Civil War, their party took control of the House of Representatives. Before the new Congress met, the old one enacted a final piece of Reconstruction legislation, the **Civil Rights Act of 1875**. This outlawed racial discrimination in places of public accommodation like hotels and theaters. But it was clear that the northern public was retreating from Reconstruction.

Politics and the economy

The Supreme Court whittled away at the guarantees of black rights Congress had adopted. In the *Slaughterhouse Cases* (1873), white butchers excluded from a state-sponsored monopoly in Louisiana went to court, claiming that their right to equality before the law guaranteed by the Fourteenth Amendment had been violated. The justices rejected their claim, ruling that the amendment had not altered traditional federalism. Most of the rights of citizens, it declared, remained under state

Court rulings on rights

Of Course He Wants to Vote the Democratic Ticket, a cartoon from *Harper's Weekly*, October 21, 1876, comments on the campaign of terror launched by South Carolina Democrats in an attempt to carry the election of 1876.

THE PRESIDENTIAL ELECTION OF 1876

Non-voting territory

Party	Candidate	Electoral Vote (Share)	Popular Vote (Share)
Republican	Hayes	185 (50%)	4,036,298 (48%)
Democrat	Tilden	184 (50%)	4,300,590 (51%)
Greenback	Cooper	0 (0%)	93,895 (1%)
Disputed (assigned to Hayes by electoral commission)			

control. Three years later, in *United States v. Cruikshank*, the Court gutted the Enforcement Acts by throwing out the convictions of some of those responsible for the Colfax Massacre of 1873.

The Triumph of the Redeemers

By the mid-1870s, Reconstruction was clearly on the defensive. Democrats had already regained control of states with substantial white voting majorities such as Tennessee, North Carolina, and Texas. The victorious Democrats called themselves **Redeemers**, since they claimed to have "redeemed" the white South from corruption, misgovernment, and northern and black control.

In those states where Reconstruction governments survived, violence again erupted. This time, the Grant administration showed no desire to intervene. In contrast to the Klan's activities—conducted at night by disguised men—the violence of 1875 and 1876 took place in broad daylight, as if to underscore Democrats' conviction that they had nothing to fear from Washington. In Mississippi, in 1875, white rifle clubs drilled in public and openly assaulted and murdered Republicans. When Governor Adelbert Ames, a Maine-born Union general, frantically appealed to the federal government for assistance, President Grant responded that the northern public was "tired out" by southern problems. On election day, armed Democrats destroyed ballot boxes and drove former slaves from the polls. The result was a Democratic landslide and the end of Reconstruction in Mississippi. "A revolution has taken place," wrote Ames, "and a race are disfranchised—they are to be returned to . . . an era of second slavery."

Similar events took place in South Carolina in 1876. Democrats nominated for governor former Confederate general Wade Hampton. Hampton promised to respect the rights of all citizens of the state, but his supporters, inspired by Democratic tactics in Mississippi, launched a wave of intimidation. Democrats intended to carry the election, one planter told a black official, "if we have to wade in blood knee-deep."

The Disputed Election and Bargain of 1877

Events in South Carolina directly affected the outcome of the presidential campaign of 1876. To succeed Grant, the Republicans nominated Governor Rutherford B. Hayes of Ohio. Democrats chose as his opponent New York's governor, Samuel J. Tilden. By this time, only South Carolina, Florida, and Louisiana remained under Republican control. The election turned out to be so close that whoever captured these states—which both parties claimed to have carried—would become the next president.

Unable to resolve the impasse on its own, Congress in January 1877 appointed a fifteen-member Electoral Commission, composed of senators, representatives, and Supreme Court justices. Republicans enjoyed an 8–7 majority on the commission, and to no one's surprise, the members decided by that margin that Hayes had carried the disputed southern states and had been elected president. Even as the commission deliberated, however, behind-the-scenes negotiations took place between leaders of the two parties. Hayes's representatives agreed to recognize Democratic control of the entire South and to avoid further intervention in local affairs. They also pledged that Hayes would place a southerner in the cabinet position of postmaster general and that he would work for federal aid to the Texas and Pacific railroad, a transcontinental line projected to follow a southern route. For their part, Democrats promised not to dispute Hayes's right to office and to respect the civil and political rights of blacks.

Thus was concluded the **Bargain of 1877**. Not all of its parts were fulfilled. But Hayes became president, and he did appoint David M. Key of Tennessee as postmaster general. Hayes quickly ordered federal troops to stop guarding the state houses in Louisiana and South Carolina, allowing Democratic claimants to become governor. (Contrary to legend, Hayes did not remove the last soldiers from the South—he simply ordered them to return to their barracks.) But the Texas and Pacific never did get its land grant. Of far more significance, the triumphant southern Democrats failed to live up to their pledge to recognize blacks as equal citizens.

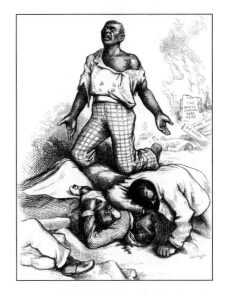

Is This a Republican Form of Government?, a cartoon by Thomas Nast in *Harper's Weekly*, September 2, 1876, illustrates his conviction that the overthrow of Reconstruction meant that the United States was not prepared to live up to its democratic ideals or protect the rights of black citizens threatened by violence.

The End of Reconstruction

As a historical process—the nation's adjustment to the destruction of slavery—Reconstruction continued well after 1877. Blacks continued to vote and, in some states, hold office into the 1890s. But as a distinct era of national history—when Republicans controlled much of the South, blacks exercised significant political power, and the federal government accepted the responsibility for protecting the fundamental rights of all American citizens—Reconstruction had come to an end. Despite its limitations, Reconstruction was a remarkable chapter in the story of American freedom. Nearly a century would pass before the nation again tried to bring equal rights to the descendants of slaves. The civil rights era of the 1950s and 1960s would sometimes be called the Second Reconstruction.

Even while it lasted, however, Reconstruction revealed some of the tensions inherent in nineteenth-century discussions of freedom. The policy of granting black men the vote while denying them the benefits of land ownership strengthened the idea that the free citizen could be a poor, dependent laborer. Reconstruction placed on the national agenda a problem that would dominate political discussion for the next half-century—how, in a modern society, to define the economic essence of freedom.

SUGGESTED READING

BOOKS

- Bottoms, D. Michael. *An Aristocracy of Color: Race and Reconstruction in California and the West*, 1850–1890 (2013). A study of changing race relations, and definitions of race, in the western states.

- Butchart, Ronald E. *Schooling the Freed People: Teaching, Learning, and the Struggle for Black Freedom* (2010). Relates the efforts of black and white teachers to educate the former slaves and some of the conflicts that arose over the purposes of such education.

- Downs, Gregory. *Declarations of Dependence: The Long Reconstruction of Popular Politics in the South, 1861–1908* (2011). Traces the changing ways black and white southerners sought aid and protection from the government during and after the Civil War and Reconstruction.

- Downs, James. *Sick from Freedom: The Deadly Consequences of Emancipation* (2012). How disease shaped the experience of freedom and how the Freedmen's Bureau and other agencies sought to cope with widespread illness among former slaves.

- DuBois, Ellen C. *Feminism and Suffrage: The Emergence of an Independent Women's Movement in America, 1848–1869* (1978). Explores how the split over the exclusion of women from the Fourteenth and Fifteenth Amendments gave rise to a movement for woman suffrage no longer tied to the abolitionist tradition.

- Edwards, Laura. *Gendered Strife and Confusion: The Political Culture of Reconstruction* (1997). Considers how issues relating to gender relations affected the course of southern Reconstruction.

- Fields, Barbara J. *Slavery and Freedom on the Middle Ground: Maryland during the Nineteenth Century* (1985). A study of slavery and emancipation in a key border state.

- Foner, Eric. *Nothing but Freedom: Emancipation and Its Legacy* (1983). Includes a comparison of the emancipation experience in different parts of the Western Hemisphere.

- Foner, Eric. *Reconstruction: America's Unfinished Revolution, 1863–1877* (1988). A comprehensive account of the Reconstruction era.

- Hahn, Steven. *A Nation under Our Feet: Black Political Struggles in the Rural South from Slavery to the Great Migration* (2003). A detailed study of black political activism, stressing nationalist consciousness and emigration movements.

- Hyman, Harold M. *A More Perfect Union: The Impact of the Civil War and Reconstruction on the Constitution* (1973). Analyzes how the laws and constitutional amendments of Reconstruction changed the Constitution and the rights of all Americans.

- Jung, Moon-Ho. *Coolies and Cane: Race, Labor, and Sugar in the Age of Emancipation* (2006). Tells the story of Chinese laborers brought to work in the sugar fields after the end of slavery.

- Litwack, Leon F. *Been in the Storm So Long: The Aftermath of Slavery* (1979). A detailed look at the immediate aftermath of the end of slavery and the variety of black and white responses to emancipation.

- Rable, George C. *But There Was No Peace: The Role of Violence in the Politics of Reconstruction* (1984). The only full-scale study of violence in the Reconstruction South.

- Richardson, Heather C. *West from Appomattox* (2007). An account that fully integrates the West into the history of the Reconstruction era.

- Rodrigue, John C. *Reconstruction in the Cane Fields: From Slavery to Free Labor in Louisiana's Sugar Parishes, 1862–1880* (2001). A study of how an often-neglected part of the South experienced the aftermath of slavery.

- Summers, Mark W. *Railroads, Reconstruction, and the Gospel of Prosperity: Aid under the Radical Republicans, 1865–1877* (1984). A detailed look at southern governments' efforts to promote economic development, and the political corruption that sometimes accompanied it.

WEBSITES

- After Slavery: Race, Labor, and Politics in the Post-Emancipation Carolinas: www.afterslavery.com

- America's Reconstruction: People and Politics after the Civil War: www.digitalhistory.uh.edu/exhibits/reconstruction/index.html

- The Andrew Johnson Impeachment Trial: www.law.umkc.edu/faculty/projects/ftrials/impeach/impeachmt.htm

- Freedmen and Southern Society Project: www.history.umd.edu/Freedmen/

- Freedmen's Bureau Online: http://www.freedmensbureau.com/

CHAPTER REVIEW AND ONLINE RESOURCES

REVIEW QUESTIONS

1. In 1865, former Confederate general Robert Richardson remarked that "the emancipated slaves own nothing, because nothing but freedom has been given to them." Explain whether this would be an accurate assessment of Reconstruction twelve years later.

2. The women's movement split into two separate national organizations in part because the Fifteenth Amendment did not give women the vote. Explain why the two groups split.

3. How did black families, churches, schools, and other institutions contribute to the development of African-American culture and political activism in this period?

4. Why did ownership of land and control of labor become major points of contention between former slaves and whites in the South?

5. By what methods did southern whites seek to limit African-American civil rights and liberties? How did the federal government respond?

6. How did the failure of land reform and continued poverty lead to new forms of servitude for both blacks and whites?

7. What caused the confrontation between President Johnson and Congress over Reconstruction policies?

8. What national issues and attitudes combined to bring an end to Reconstruction by 1877?

9. By 1877, how did the condition of former slaves in the United States compare with that of freedpeople around the globe?

KEY TERMS

the Freedmen's Bureau (p. 557)

sharecropping (p. 560)

crop lien (p. 560)

Black Codes (p. 565)

Civil Rights Bill of 1866 (p. 567)

Fourteenth Amendment (p. 568)

Reconstruction Act (p. 569)

Tenure of Office Act (p. 569)

impeachment (p. 569)

Fifteenth Amendment (p. 570)

carpetbaggers (p. 576)

scalawags (p. 577)

Ku Klux Klan (p. 580)

Enforcement Acts (p. 580)

Civil Rights Act of 1875 (p. 583)

Redeemers (p. 584)

Bargain of 1877 (p. 585)

Go to INQUIZITIVE

To see what you know—and learn what you've missed—with personalized feedback along the way.

Visit the *Give Me Liberty!* **Student Site** for primary source documents and images, interactive maps, author videos featuring Eric Foner, and more.

APPENDIX

THE DECLARATION OF INDEPENDENCE (1776)

When in the course of human events, it becomes necessary for one people to dissolve the political bands which have connected them with another, and to assume among the Powers of the earth, the separate and equal station to which the Laws of Nature and of Nature's God entitle them, a decent respect to the opinions of mankind requires that they should declare the causes which impel them to the separation.

We hold these truths to be self-evident, that all men are created equal, that they are endowed by their Creator with certain unalienable rights, that among these are Life, Liberty, and the pursuit of Happiness. That to secure these rights, Governments are instituted among Men, deriving their just powers from the consent of the governed. That whenever any Form of Government becomes destructive of these ends, it is the Right of the People to alter or to abolish it, and to institute new Government, laying its foundation on such principles and organizing its powers in such form, as to them shall seem most likely to effect their Safety and Happiness. Prudence, indeed, will dictate that Governments long established should not be changed for light and transient causes; and accordingly all experience hath shown, that mankind are more disposed to suffer, while evils are sufferable, than to right themselves by abolishing the forms to which they are accustomed. But when a long train of abuses and usurpations, pursuing invariably the same Object evinces a design to reduce them under absolute Despotism, it is their right, it is their duty, to throw off such Government, and to provide new Guards for their future security.—Such has been the patient sufferance of these Colonies; and such is now the necessity which constrains them to alter their former Systems of Government. The history of the present King of Great Britain is a history of repeated injuries and usurpations, all having in direct object the establishment of an absolute Tyranny over these States. To prove this, let Facts be submitted to a candid world.

He has refused his Assent to Laws, the most wholesome and necessary for the public good.

He has forbidden his Governors to pass Laws of immediate and pressing importance, unless suspended in their operation till his Assent should be obtained; and when so suspended, he has utterly neglected to attend to them.

He has refused to pass other Laws for the accommodation of large districts of people, unless those people would relinquish the right of Representation in the Legislature, a right inestimable to them and formidable to tyrants only.

He has called together legislative bodies at places unusual, uncomfortable, and distant from the depository of their public Records, for the sole purpose of fatiguing them into compliance with his measures.

He has dissolved Representative Houses repeatedly, for opposing with manly firmness his invasions on the rights of the people.

He has refused for a long time, after such dissolutions, to cause others to be elected; whereby the Legislative powers, incapable of Annihilation, have returned to the People at large for their exercise; the State remaining in the mean time exposed to all dangers of invasion from without, and convulsions within.

He has endeavoured to prevent the population of these States; for that purpose obstructing the Laws of Naturalization of Foreigners; refusing to pass others to encourage their migrations hither, and raising the conditions of new Appropriations of Lands.

He has obstructed the Administration of Justice, by refusing his Assent to Laws for establishing Judiciary powers.

He has made Judges dependent on his Will alone, for the tenure of their offices, and the amount and payment of their salaries.

He has erected a multitude of New Offices, and sent hither swarms of Officers to harass our People, and eat out their substance.

He has kept among us, in times of peace, Standing Armies without the Consent of our legislatures.

He has affected to render the Military independent of and superior to the Civil Power.

He has combined with others to subject us to a jurisdiction foreign to our constitution, and unacknowledged by our laws; giving his Assent to their Acts of pretended Legislation:

For quartering large bodies of armed troops among us:

For protecting them, by a mock Trial, from Punishment for any Murders which they should commit on the Inhabitants of these States:

For cutting off our Trade with all parts of the world:

For imposing taxes on us without our Consent:

For depriving us of many cases, of the benefits of Trial by jury:

For transporting us beyond Seas to be tried for pretended offences:

For abolishing the free System of English Laws in a neighbouring Province, establishing therein an Arbitrary government, and enlarging its Boundaries so as to render it at once an example and fit instrument for introducing the same absolute rule into these Colonies:

For taking away our Charters, abolishing our most valuable Laws, and altering fundamentally the Forms of our Governments:

For suspending our own Legislatures, and declaring themselves invested with Power to legislate for us in all cases whatsoever.

He has abdicated Government here, by declaring us out of his Protection and waging War against us.

He has plundered our seas, ravaged our Coasts, burnt our towns, and destroyed the lives of our people.

He is at this time transporting large armies of foreign mercenaries to compleat the works of death, desolation, and tyranny, already begun with circumstances of Cruelty & perfidy scarcely paralleled in the most barbarous ages, and totally unworthy the Head of a civilized nation.

He has constrained our fellow Citizens taken Captive on the high Seas to bear Arms against their Country, to become the executioners of their friends and Brethren, or to fall themselves by their Hands.

He has excited domestic insurrections amongst us, and has endeavoured to bring on the inhabitants of our frontiers, the merciless Indian Savages, whose known rule of warfare, is an undistinguished destruction of all ages, sexes, and conditions.

In every stage of these Oppressions We have Petitioned for Redress in the most humble terms: Our repeated Petitions have been answered only by repeated injury. A Prince, whose character is thus marked by every act which may define a Tyrant, is unfit to be the ruler of a free people.

Nor have We been wanting in attention to our British brethren. We have warned them from time to time of attempts by their legislature to extend an unwarrantable jurisdiction over us. We have reminded them of the circumstances of our emigration and settlement here. We have appealed to their native justice and magnanimity, and we have conjured them by the ties of our common kindred to disavow these usurpations, which, would inevitably interrupt our connections and correspondence. They too must have been deaf to the voice of justice and of consanguinity. We must, therefore, acquiesce in the necessity, which denounces our Separation, and hold them, as we hold the rest of mankind, Enemies in War, in Peace Friends.

WE, THEREFORE, the Representatives of the UNITED STATES OF AMERICA, in General Congress, Assembled, appealing to the Supreme Judge of the world for the rectitude of our intentions, do, in the Name, and by Authority of the good People of these Colonies, solemnly publish and declare, That these United Colonies are, and of Right ought to be FREE AND INDEPENDENT STATES; that they are Absolved from all Allegiance to the British Crown, and that all political connection between them and the State of Great Britain, is and ought to be totally dissolved; and that as Free and Independent States, they have full Power to levy War, conclude Peace, contract Alliances, establish Commerce, and to do all other Acts and Things which Independent States may of right do. And for the support of this Declaration, with a firm reliance on the Protection of Divine Providence, we mutually pledge to each other our Lives, our Fortunes, and our sacred Honor.

The foregoing Declaration was, by order of Congress, engrossed, and signed by the following members:

John Hancock

NEW HAMPSHIRE
Josiah Bartlett
William Whipple
Matthew Thornton

MASSACHUSETTS BAY
Samuel Adams
John Adams
Robert Treat Paine
Elbridge Gerry

RHODE ISLAND
Stephen Hopkins
William Ellery

CONNECTICUT
Roger Sherman
Samuel Huntington
William Williams
Oliver Wolcott

NEW YORK
William Floyd
Philip Livingston
Francis Lewis
Lewis Morris

NEW JERSEY
Richard Stockton
John Witherspoon
Francis Hopkinson
John Hart
Abraham Clark

PENNSYLVANIA
Robert Morris
Benjamin Rush
Benjamin Franklin
John Morton
George Clymer
James Smith
George Taylor
James Wilson
George Ross

DELAWARE
Caesar Rodney
George Read
Thomas M'Kean

MARYLAND
Samuel Chase
William Paca
Thomas Stone
Charles Carroll, of Carrollton

VIRGINIA
George Wythe
Richard Henry Lee
Thomas Jefferson
Benjamin Harrison
Thomas Nelson, Jr.
Francis Lightfoot Lee
Carter Braxton

NORTH CAROLINA
William Hooper
Joseph Hewes
John Penn

SOUTH CAROLINA
Edward Rutledge
Thomas Heyward, Jr.
Thomas Lynch, Jr.
Arthur Middleton

GEORGIA
Button Gwinnett
Lyman Hall
George Walton

Resolved, That copies of the Declaration be sent to the several assemblies, conventions, and committees, or councils of safety, and to the several commanding officers of the continental troops; that it be proclaimed in each of the United States, at the head of the army.

THE CONSTITUTION OF THE UNITED STATES (1787)

We the People of the United States, in order to form a more perfect Union, establish Justice, insure domestic Tranquility, provide for the common defence, promote the general Welfare, and secure the Blessings of Liberty to ourselves and our Posterity, do ordain and establish this Constitution for the United States of America.

ARTICLE. I.

Section. 1. All legislative Powers herein granted shall be vested in a Congress of the United States, which shall consist of a Senate and House of Representatives.

Section. 2. The House of Representatives shall be composed of Members chosen every second Year by the People of the several States, and the Electors in each State shall have the Qualifications requisite for Electors of the most numerous Branch of the State Legislature.

No Person shall be a Representative who shall not have attained to the Age of twenty five Years, and been seven Years a Citizen of the United States, and who shall not, when elected, be an Inhabitant of that State in which he shall be chosen.

Representatives and direct Taxes shall be apportioned among the several States which may be included within this Union, according to their respective Numbers, which shall be determined by adding to the whole Number of free Persons, including those bound to Service for a Term of Years, and excluding Indians not taxed, three fifths of all other Persons. The actual Enumeration shall be made within three Years after the first Meeting of the Congress of the United States, and within every subsequent Term of ten Years, in such Manner as they shall by Law direct. The Number of Representatives shall not exceed one for every thirty Thousand, but each State shall have at Least one Representative; and until such enumeration shall be made, the State of New Hampshire shall be entitled to chuse three, Massachusetts eight, Rhode-Island and Providence Plantations one, Connecticut five, New York six, New Jersey four, Pennsylvania eight, Delaware one, Maryland six, Virginia ten, North Carolina five, South Carolina five, and Georgia three.

When vacancies happen in the Representation from any state, the Executive Authority thereof shall issue Writs of Election to fill such Vacancies.

The House of Representatives shall chuse their Speaker and other Officers; and shall have the sole Power of Impeachment.

Section. 3. The Senate of the United States shall be composed of two Senators from each State, chosen by the legislature thereof, for six Years; and each Senator shall have one Vote.

Immediately after they shall be assembled in Consequence of the first Election, they shall be divided as equally as may be into three Classes. The Seats of the Senators of the first Class shall be vacated at the Expiration of the second Year, of the second Class at the Expiration of the fourth Year, and of the third Class at the Expiration of the sixth Year, so that one third may be chosen every second Year; and if Vacancies happen by Resignation, or otherwise, during the Recess of the Legislature of any State, the Executive thereof may make temporary Appointments until the next Meeting of the Legislature, which shall then fill such Vacancies.

No Person shall be a Senator who shall not have attained to the Age of thirty Years, and been nine Years a Citizen of the United States, and who shall not, when elected, be an Inhabitant of that State for which he shall be chosen.

The Vice President of the United States shall be President of the Senate, but shall have no Vote, unless they be equally divided.

The Senate shall chuse their other Officers, and also a President pro tempore, in the Absence of the Vice President, or when he shall exercise the Office of President of the United States.

The Senate shall have the sole Power to try all Impeachments. When sitting for that Purpose, they shall be on Oath or Affirmation. When the President of the United States is tried, the Chief Justice shall preside: And no Person shall be convicted without the Concurrence of two thirds of the Members present.

Judgment in Cases of Impeachment shall not extend further than to removal from Office, and disqualification to hold and enjoy any Office of honor, Trust or Profit under the United States: but the Party convicted shall nevertheless be liable and subject to Indictment, Trial, Judgment and Punishment, according to Law.

Section. 4. The Times, Places and Manner of holding Elections for Senators and Representatives, shall be prescribed in each State by the Legislature thereof; but the Congress may at any time by Law make or alter such Regulations, except as to the Places of chusing Senators.

The Congress shall assemble at least once in every Year, and such Meeting shall be on the first Monday in December, unless they shall by Law appoint a different Day.

Section. 5. Each House shall be the Judge of the Elections, Returns and Qualifications of its own Members, and a Majority of each shall constitute a Quorum to do Business; but a smaller Number may adjourn from day to day, and may be authorized to compel the Attendance of absent Members, in such Manner, and under such Penalties as each House may provide.

Each House may determine the Rules of its Proceedings, punish its Members for disorderly Behaviour, and, with the Concurrence of two thirds, expel a Member.

Each House shall keep a Journal of its Proceedings, and from time to time publish the same, excepting such Parts as may in their Judgment require Secrecy; and the Yeas and Nays of the Members of either House on any question shall, at the Desire of one fifth of those Present, be entered on the Journal.

Neither House, during the Session of Congress, shall, without the Consent of the other, adjourn for more than three days, not to any other Place than that in which the two Houses shall be sitting.

Section. 6. The Senators and Representatives shall receive a Compensation for their Services, to be ascertained by Law, and paid out of the Treasury of the United States. They shall in all Cases, except Treason, Felony and Breach of the Peace, be privileged from Arrest during their Attendance at the Session of their respective Houses, and in going to and returning from the same; and for any Speech or Debate in either House, they shall not be questioned in any other Place.

No Senator or Representative shall, during the Time for which he was elected, be appointed to any civil Office under the Authority of the United States, which shall have been created, or the Emoluments whereof shall have been encreased during such time; and no Person holding any Office under the United States, shall be a Member of either House during his Continuance in Office.

Section. 7. All Bills for raising Revenue shall originate in the House of Representatives; but the Senate may propose or concur with Amendments as on other Bills.

Every Bill which shall have passed the House of Representatives and the Senate shall, before it become a Law, be presented to the President of the United States; If he approve he shall sign it, but if not he shall return it, with his Objections to that House in which it shall have originated, who shall enter the Objections at large on their Journal, and proceed to reconsider it. If after such Reconsideration two thirds of that House shall agree to pass the Bill, it shall be sent, together with the Objections, to the other House, by which it shall likewise be reconsidered, and if approved by two thirds of that House, it shall become a Law. But in all such Cases the Votes of both Houses shall be determined by Yeas and Nays, and the Names of the Persons voting for and against the Bill shall be entered on the Journal of each House respectively. If any Bill shall not be returned by the President within ten Days (Sundays excepted) after it shall have been presented to him, the Same shall be a Law, in like Manner as if he had signed it, unless the Congress by their Adjournment prevent its Return, in which Case it shall not be a Law.

Every Order, Resolution, or Vote to which the Concurrence of the Senate and House of Representatives may be necessary (except on a question of Adjournment) shall be presented to the President of the United States; and before the Same shall take Effect, shall be approved by him, or being disapproved by him, shall be repassed by two thirds of the Senate and House of Representatives, according to the Rules and Limitations prescribed in the Case of a Bill.

Section. 8. The Congress shall have Power To lay and collect Taxes, Duties, Imposts and Excises, to pay the Debts and provide for the common Defence and general Welfare of the United States; but all Duties, Imposts and Excises shall be uniform throughout the United States;

To borrow Money on the credit of the United States;

To regulate Commerce with foreign Nations, and among the several States, and with the Indian Tribes;

To establish an uniform Rule of Naturalization, and uniform Laws on the subject of Bankruptcies throughout the United States;

To coin Money, regulate the Value thereof, and of foreign Coin, and fix the Standard of Weights and Measures;

To provide for the Punishment of counterfeiting the Securities and current Coin of the United States;

To establish Post Offices and Post Roads;

To promote the Progress of Science and useful Arts, by securing for limited Times to Authors and Inventors the exclusive Right to their respective Writings and Discoveries;

To constitute Tribunals inferior to the supreme Court;

To define and punish Piracies and Felonies committed on the high Seas, and Offences against the Law of Nations;

To declare War, grant Letters of Marque and Reprisal, and make Rules concerning Captures on Land and Water;

To raise and support Armies, but no Appropriation of Money to that Use shall be for a longer Term than two Years;

To provide and maintain a Navy;

To make Rules for the Government and Regulation of the land and naval Forces;

To provide for calling forth the Militia to execute the Laws of the Union, suppress Insurrections and repel Invasions;

To provide for organizing, arming, and disciplining, the Militia, and for governing such Part of them as may be employed in the Service of the United States, reserving to the States respectively, the Appointment of the Officers, and the Authority of training the Militia according to the discipline prescribed by Congress;

To exercise exclusive Legislation in all Cases whatsoever, over such District (not exceeding ten Miles square) as may, by Cession of Particular States, and the Acceptance of Congress, become the Seat of the Government of the United States, and to exercise like Authority over all Places purchased by the Consent of the Legislature of the State in which the Same shall be, for the Erection of Forts, Magazines, Arsenals, dock-Yards, and other needful Buildings;—And

To make all Laws which shall be necessary and proper for carrying into Execution the foregoing Powers, and all other Powers vested by this Constitution in the Government of the United States, or in any Department or Officer thereof.

Section. 9. The Migration or Importation of such Persons as any of the States now existing shall think proper to admit, shall not be prohibited by the Congress prior to the Year one thousand eight hundred and eight, but a Tax or duty may be imposed on such Importation, not exceeding ten dollars for each Person.

The Privilege of the Writ of Habeas Corpus shall not be suspended, unless when in Cases of Rebellion or Invasion the public Safety may require it.

No Bill of Attainder or ex post facto Law shall be passed.

No Capitation, or other direct, Tax shall be laid, unless in Proportion to the Census or Enumeration herein before directed to be taken.

No Tax or Duty shall be laid on Articles exported from any State.

No Preference shall be given by any Regulation of Commerce or Revenue to the Ports of one State over those of another: nor shall Vessels bound to, or from, one State, be obliged to enter, clear, or pay Duties in another.

No Money shall be drawn from the Treasury, but in Consequence of Appropriations made by Law; and a regular Statement and Account of the Receipts and Expenditures of all public Money shall be published from time to time.

No Title of Nobility shall be granted by the United States: And no Person holding any Office of Profit or Trust under them, shall, without the Consent of the Congress, accept of any present, Emolument, Office, or Title, of any kind whatever, from any King, Prince, or foreign State.

Section. 10. No State shall enter into any Treaty, Alliance, or Confederation; grant Letters of Marque and Reprisal; coin Money; emit Bills of Credit; make any Thing but gold and silver Coin a Tender in Payment of Debts; pass any Bill of Attainder, ex post facto Law, or Law impairing the Obligation of Contracts, or grant any Title of Nobility.

No State shall, without the Consent of the Congress, lay any Imposts or Duties on Imports or Exports, except what may be absolutely necessary for executing its inspection Laws: and the net Produce of all Duties and Imposts, laid by any State on Imports or Exports, shall be for the Use of the Treasury of the United States; and all such Laws shall be subject to the Revision and Controul of the Congress.

No State shall, without the Consent of Congress, lay any Duty of Tonnage, keep Troops, or Ships of War in time of Peace, enter into any Agreement or Compact with another State, or with a foreign Power, or engage in War, unless actually invaded, or in such imminent Danger as will not admit of delay.

ARTICLE. II.

Section. 1. The executive Power shall be vested in a President of the United States of America. He shall hold his Office during the term of four Years, and, together with the Vice President, chosen for the same Term, be elected, as follows:

Each State shall appoint, in such Manner as the Legislature thereof may direct, a Number of Electors, equal to the whole Number of Senators and Representatives to which the State may be entitled in the Congress: but no Senator or Representative, or Person holding an Office of Trust or Profit under the United States, shall be appointed an Elector.

The Electors shall meet in their respective States, and vote by Ballot for two Persons, of whom one at least shall not be an Inhabitant of the same State with themselves. And they shall make a List of all the Persons voted for, and of the Number of Votes for each; which List they shall sign and certify, and transmit sealed to the Seat of the Government of the United States, directed to the President of the Senate. The President of the Senate shall, in the Presence of the Senate and House of Representatives, open all the Certificates, and the Votes shall then be counted. The Person having the greatest Number of Votes shall be the President, if such Number be a Majority of the whole Number of Electors appointed; and if there be more than one who have such Majority, and have an equal Number of Votes, then the House of Representatives shall immediately chuse by Ballot one of them for President; and if no Person have a Majority, then from the five highest on the List the said House shall in like Manner chuse the President. But in chusing the President, the Votes shall be taken by States, the Representation from each State having one Vote; A quorum for this Purpose shall consist of a Member or Members from two thirds of the States, and a Majority of all the States shall be necessary to a Choice. In every Case, after the Choice of the President, the Person having the greatest Number of Votes of the Electors shall be the Vice President. But if there should remain two or more who have equal Votes, the Senate shall chuse from them by Ballot the Vice President.

The Congress may determine the Time of chusing the Electors, and the Day on which they shall give their Votes; which Day shall be the same throughout the United States.

No Person except a natural born Citizen, or a Citizen of the United States, at the time of the Adoption of this Constitution, shall be eligible to the Office of President; neither shall any Person be eligible to that Office who shall not have attained to the Age of thirty five Years, and been fourteen Years a Resident within the United States.

In Case of the Removal of the President from Office, or of his Death, Resignation, or Inability to discharge the Powers and Duties of the said Office, the Same shall devolve on the Vice President, and the Congress may by Law provide for the Case of Removal, Death, Resignation or Inability, both of the President and Vice President, declaring what Officer shall then act as President, and such Officer shall act accordingly, until the Disability be removed, or a President shall be elected.

The President shall, at stated Times, receive for his Services, a Compensation, which shall neither be encreased or diminished during the Period for which he shall have been elected, and he shall not receive within that Period any other Emolument from the United States, or any of them.

Before he enters on the Execution of his Office, he shall take the following Oath or Affirmation:—"I do solemnly swear (or affirm) that I will faithfully execute the Office of President of the United States, and will to the best of my Ability, preserve, protect and defend the Constitution of the United States."

Section. 2. The President shall be Commander in Chief of the Army and Navy of the United States, and of the Militia of the several States, when called into the actual Service of the United States; he may require the Opinion, in writing, of the principal Officer in each of the executive Departments, upon any Subject relating to the Duties of their respective Offices, and he shall have Power to grant Reprieves and Pardons for Offences against the United States, except in Cases of Impeachment.

He shall have Power, by and with the Advice and Consent of the Senate, to make Treaties, provided two thirds of the Senators present concur; and he shall nominate, and by and with the Advice and Consent of the Senate, shall appoint Ambassadors, other public Ministers and Consuls, Judges of the supreme Court, and all other Officers of the United States, whose Appointments are not herein otherwise provided for, and which shall be established by Law; but the Congress may by Law vest the Appointment of such inferior Officers, as they think proper, in the President alone, in the Courts of Law, or in the Heads of Departments.

The President shall have Power to fill up all Vacancies that may happen during the Recess of the Senate, by granting Commissions which shall expire at the End of their next Session.

Section. 3. He shall from time to time give to the Congress Information of the State of the Union, and recommend to their Consideration such Measures as he shall judge necessary and expedient; he may, on extraordinary Occasions, convene both Houses, or either of them, and in Case of Disagreement between them, with Respect to the Time of Adjournment, he may adjourn them to such Time as he shall think proper; he shall receive Ambassadors and other public Ministers; he shall take Care that the Laws be faithfully executed, and shall Commission all the Officers of the United States.

Section. 4. The President, Vice President and all civil Officers of the United States, shall be removed from Office on Impeachment for, and Conviction of, Treason, Bribery, or other high Crimes and Misdemeanors.

ARTICLE. III.

Section. 1. The judicial Power of the United States, shall be vested in one supreme Court, and in such inferior Courts as the Congress may from time to time ordain and establish. The Judges, both of the supreme and inferior Courts, shall hold their Offices during good Behavior, and shall, at stated Times, receive for their Services, a Compensation, which shall not be diminished during their Continuance in Office.

Section. 2. The judicial Power shall extend to all Cases, in Law and Equity, arising under this Constitution, the Laws of the United States, and Treaties made, or which shall be made, under their Authority;—to all Cases affecting Ambassadors, other public Ministers and Consuls;—to all Cases of admiralty and maritime Jurisdiction;—the Controversies to which the United States shall be a Party;—to Controversies between two or more States;—between a State and Citizens of another State;—between Citizens of different States;—between Citizens of the same State claiming Lands under Grants of different States, and between a State, or the Citizens thereof, and foreign States, Citizens or Subjects.

In all cases affecting Ambassadors, other public Ministers and Consuls, and those in which a State shall be Party, the supreme Court shall have original Jurisdiction. In all the other Cases before mentioned, the supreme Court shall have appellate Jurisdiction, both as to Law and Fact, with such Exceptions, and under such Regulations as the Congress shall make.

The Trial of all Crimes, except in Cases of Impeachment, shall be by Jury; and such Trial shall be held in the State where the said Crimes shall have been committed; but when not committed within any State, the Trial shall be at such Place or Places as the Congress may by Law have directed.

Section. 3. Treason against the United States, shall consist only in levying War against them, or in adhering to their Enemies, giving them Aid and Comfort. No Person shall be convicted of Treason unless on the Testimony of two Witnesses to the same overt Act, or on Confession in open Court.

The Congress shall have Power to declare the Punishment of Treason, but no Attainder of Treason shall work Corruption of Blood, or Forfeiture except during the Life of the Person attainted.

ARTICLE. IV.

Section. 1. Full Faith and Credit shall be given in each State to the public Acts, Records, and judicial Proceedings of every other State. And the Congress may by general Laws prescribe the Manner in which such Acts, Records and Proceedings shall be proved, and the Effect thereof.

Section. 2. The Citizens of each State shall be entitled to all Privileges and Immunities of Citizens in the several States.

A Person charged in any State with Treason, Felony, or other Crime, who shall flee from Justice, and be found in another State, shall on Demand of the executive Authority of the State from which he fled, be delivered up, to be removed to the State having Jurisdiction of the Crime.

No Person held to Service or Labour in one State, under the Laws thereof, escaping into another, shall, in Consequence of any Law or Regulation therein, be discharged from such Service or Labour, but shall be delivered up on Claim of the Party to whom such Service or Labour may be due.

Section. 3. New States may be admitted by the Congress into this Union; but no new State shall be formed or erected within the Jurisdiction of any other State; nor any State be formed by the Junction of two or more States, or Parts of States, without the consent of the Legislatures of the States concerned as well as of the Congress.

The Congress shall have Power to dispose of and make all needful Rules and Regulations respecting the Territory or other Property belonging to the United States; and nothing in this Constitution shall be so construed as to Prejudice any Claims of the United States, or of any particular States.

Section. 4. The United States shall guarantee to every State in this Union a Republican Form of Government, and shall protect each of them against Invasion; and on Application of the Legislature, or of the Executive (when the Legislature cannot be convened) against domestic Violence.

ARTICLE. V.

The Congress, whenever two thirds of both Houses shall deem it necessary, shall propose Amendments to this Constitution, or, on the Application of the Legislatures of two thirds of the several States, shall call a Convention for proposing Amendments, which, in either Case, shall be valid to all Intents and Purposes, as Part of this Constitution, when ratified by the Legislatures of three fourths of the several States, or by Conventions in three fourths thereof, as the one or the other Mode of Ratification may be proposed by the Congress; Provided that no Amendment which may be made prior to the Year One thousand eight hundred and eight shall in any Manner affect the first and fourth Clauses in the Ninth Section of the first Article; and that no State, without its Consent, shall be deprived of its equal Suffrage in the Senate.

ARTICLE. VI.

All Debts contracted and Engagements entered into, before the Adoption of this Constitution, shall be as valid against the United States under this Constitution, as under the Confederation.

This Constitution, and the Laws of the United States which shall be made in Pursuance thereof; and all Treaties made, or which shall be made, under the Authority of the United States, shall be the supreme Law of the Land; and the Judges in every State shall be bound thereby, any Thing in the Constitution or Laws of any State to the Contrary notwithstanding.

The Senators and Representatives before mentioned, and the Members of the several State Legislatures, and all executive and judicial Officers, both of the United States and of the several States, shall be bound by Oath or Affirmation, to support this Constitution; but no religious Test shall ever be required as a Qualification to any Office or public Trust under the United States.

ARTICLE. VII.

The Ratification of the Conventions of nine States, shall be sufficient for the Establishment of this Constitution between the States so ratifying the Same.

Done in Convention by the Unanimous Consent of the States present the Seventeenth Day of September in the Year of our Lord one thousand seven hundred and Eighty seven and of the Independence of the United States of America the Twelfth. In witness thereof We have hereunto subscribed our Names,

G°. WASHINGTON—Presd*.
and deputy from Virginia

NEW HAMPSHIRE
John Langdon
Nicholas Gilman

MASSACHUSETTS
Nathaniel Gorham
Rufus King

CONNECTICUT
Wm Saml Johnson
Roger Sherman

NEW YORK
Alexander Hamilton

NEW JERSEY
Wil: Livingston
David A. Brearley
Wm Paterson
Jona: Dayton

PENNSYLVANIA
B Franklin
Thomas Mifflin
Robt Morris
Geo. Clymer
Thos FitzSimons
Jared Ingersoll
James Wilson
Gouv Morris

DELAWARE
Geo: Read
Gunning Bedford jun
John Dickinson
Richard Bassett
Jaco: Broom

MARYLAND
James McHenry
Dan of St Thos Jenifer
Danl Carroll

VIRGINIA
John Blair—
James Madison Jr.

NORTH CAROLINA
Wm Blount
Richd Dobbs Spaight
Hu Williamson

SOUTH CAROLINA
J. Rutledge
*Charles Cotesworth
  Pinckney*
Charles Pinckney
Pierce Butler

GEORGIA
William Few
Abr Baldwin

AMENDMENTS TO THE CONSTITUTION

Articles in addition to, and Amendment of the Constitution of the United States of America, proposed by Congress, and ratified by the Legislatures of the several States, pursuant to the fifth Article of the original Constitution.

AMENDMENT I.*

Congress shall make no law respecting an establishment of religion, or prohibiting the free exercise thereof; or abridging the freedom of speech, or of the press; or the right of the people peaceably to assemble, and to petition the Government for a redress of grievances.

AMENDMENT II.

A well regulated Militia, being necessary to the security of a free State, the right of the people to keep and bear Arms, shall not be infringed.

AMENDMENT III.

No Soldier shall, in time of peace be quartered in any house, without the consent of the Owner, nor in time of war, but in a manner to be prescribed by law.

AMENDMENT IV.

The right of the people to be secure in their persons, houses, papers, and effects, against unreasonable searches and seizures, shall not be violated, and no Warrants shall issue, but upon probable cause, supported by Oath or affirmation, and particularly describing the place to be searched, and the persons or things to be seized.

AMENDMENT V.

No person shall be held to answer for a capital, or otherwise infamous crime, unless on a presentment or indictment of a Grand Jury, except in cases arising in the land or naval forces, or in the Militia, when in actual service in time of War or public danger; nor shall any person be subject for the same offence to be twice put in jeopardy of life or limb; nor shall be compelled in any criminal case to be a witness against himself, nor be deprived of life, liberty, or property, without due process of law; nor shall private property be taken for public use, without just compensation.

*The first ten Amendments (the Bill of Rights) were ratified in 1791.

AMENDMENT VI.

In all criminal prosecutions, the accused shall enjoy the right to a speedy and public trial, by an impartial jury of the State and district wherein the crime shall have been committed, which district shall have been previously ascertained by law, and to be informed of the nature and cause of the accusation; to be confronted with the witnesses against him; to have compulsory process for obtaining witnesses in his favor, and to have the Assistance of Counsel for his defence.

AMENDMENT VII.

In Suits at common law, where the value in controversy shall exceed twenty dollars, the right of trial by jury shall be preserved, and no fact tried by a jury, shall be otherwise re-examined in any Court of the United States, than according to the rules of the common law.

AMENDMENT VIII.

Excessive bail shall not be required, nor excessive fines imposed, nor cruel and unusual punishments inflicted.

AMENDMENT IX.

The enumeration in the Constitution, of certain rights, shall not be construed to deny or disparage others retained by the people.

AMENDMENT X.

The powers not delegated to the United States by the Constitution, nor prohibited by it to the States, are reserved to the States respectively, or to the people.

AMENDMENT XI.

The Judicial power of the United States shall not be construed to extend to any suit in law or equity, commenced or prosecuted against one of the United States by Citizens of another State, or by Citizens or Subjects of any Foreign State. [January 8, 1798]

AMENDMENT XII.

The Electors shall meet in their respective states, and vote by ballot for President and Vice-President, one of whom, at least, shall not be an inhabitant of the same state with themselves; they shall name in their ballots the person voted for as President, and in distinct ballots the person voted for as Vice-President, and they shall make distinct lists of all persons voted for as President, and of all persons voted for as Vice President, and of the number of votes for each, which lists they shall sign and certify, and transmit sealed to the seat of the government of the United States, directed to the President of the Senate;—The President of the Senate shall, in the presence of the Senate and House of Representatives, open all the certificates and the votes shall then be counted;—The person having the greatest number of votes for President, shall be the President, if such number be a majority of the whole number of Electors appointed; and if no person have such majority, then from the persons having the highest numbers not exceeding three on the list of those voted for as President, the House of Representatives shall choose immediately, by ballot, the President. But in choosing the President, the votes shall be taken by states, the representation from each state having one vote; a quorum for this purpose shall consist of a member or members from two-thirds of the states, and a majority of all the states shall be necessary to a choice. And if the House of Representatives shall not choose a President whenever the right of choice shall devolve upon them, before the fourth day of March next following, then the Vice-President shall act as President, as in the case of the death or other constitutional disability of the President.— The person having the greatest number of votes as Vice-President, shall be the Vice-President, if such number be a majority of the whole number of Electors appointed, and if no person have a majority, then from the two highest numbers on the list, the Senate shall choose the Vice-President; a quorum for the purpose shall consist of two-thirds of the whole number of Senators, and a majority of the whole number shall be necessary to a choice. But no person constitutionally ineligible to the office of President shall be eligible to that of Vice-President of the United States. [September 25, 1804]

AMENDMENT XIII.

Section 1. Neither slavery nor involuntary servitude, except as a punishment for crime whereof the party shall have been duly convicted, shall exist within the United States, or any place subject to their jurisdiction.

Section 2. Congress shall have power to enforce this article by appropriate legislation. [December 18, 1865]

AMENDMENT XIV.

Section 1. All persons born or naturalized in the United States, and subject to the jurisdiction thereof, are citizens of the United States and of the State wherein they reside. No State shall make or enforce any law which shall abridge the privileges or immunities of citizens of the United States; nor shall any State deprive any person of life, liberty, or property, without due process of law; nor deny to any person within its jurisdiction the equal protection of the laws.

Section 2. Representatives shall be apportioned among the several States according to their respective numbers, counting the whole number of persons in each State, excluding Indians not taxed. But when the right to vote at any election for the choice of electors for President and Vice President of the United States, Representatives in Congress, the Executive and Judicial officers of a State, or the members of the Legislature thereof, is denied to any of the male inhabitants of such State, being twenty-one years of age, and citizens of the United States, or in any way abridged, except for participation in rebellion, or other crime, the basis of representation therein shall be reduced in the proportion which the number of such male citizens shall bear to the whole number of male citizens twenty-one years of age in such State.

Section 3. No person shall be a Senator or Representative in Congress, or elector of President and Vice President, or hold any office, civil or military, under the United States, or under any State, who, having previously taken an oath, as a member of Congress, or as an officer of the United States, or as a member of any State legislature, or as an executive or judicial officer of any State, to support the Constitution of the United States, shall have engaged in insurrection or rebellion against the same, or given aid or comfort to the enemies thereof. But Congress may by a vote of two-thirds of each House, remove such disability.

Section 4. The validity of the public debt of the United States, authorized by law, including debts incurred for payment of pensions and bounties for services in suppressing insurrection or rebellion, shall not be questioned. But neither the United States nor any State shall assume or pay any debt or obligation incurred in aid of insurrection or rebellion against the United States, or any claim for the loss or emancipation of any slave; but all such debts, obligations and claims shall be held illegal and void.

Section 5. The Congress shall have power to enforce, by appropriate legislation, the provisions of this article. [July 28, 1868]

AMENDMENT XV.

Section 1. The right of citizens of the United States to vote shall not be denied or abridged by the United States or by any State on account of race, color, or previous condition of servitude—

Section 2. The Congress shall have power to enforce this article by appropriate legislation. [March 30, 1870]

AMENDMENT XVI.

The Congress shall have power to lay and collect taxes on incomes, from whatever source derived, without apportionment among the several States, and without regard to any census or enumeration. [February 25, 1913]

AMENDMENT XVII.

The Senate of the United States shall be composed of two senators from each State, elected by the people thereof, for six years; and each Senator shall have one vote. The electors in each State shall have the qualifications requisite for electors of the most numerous branch of the State legislatures.

When vacancies happen in the representation of any State in the Senate, the executive authority of such State shall issue writs of election to fill such vacancies: *Provided,* That the legislature of any State may empower the executive thereof to make temporary appointments until the people fill the vacancies by election as the legislature may direct.

This amendment shall not be so construed as to affect the election or term of any senator chosen before it becomes valid as part of the Constitution. [May 31, 1913]

AMENDMENT XVIII.

After one year from the ratification of this article, the manufacture, sale, or transportation of intoxicating liquors within, the importation thereof into, or the exportation thereof from the United States and all territory subject to the jurisdiction thereof for beverage purposes is hereby prohibited.

The Congress and the several States shall have concurrent power to enforce this article by appropriate legislation.

This article shall be inoperative unless it shall have been ratified as an amendment to the Constitution by the legislatures of the several States, as provided in the Constitution, within seven years from the date of the submission thereof to the States by Congress. [January 29, 1919]

AMENDMENT XIX.

The right of citizens of the United States to vote shall not be denied or abridged by the United States or by any State on account of sex.

The Congress shall have power by appropriate legislation to enforce the provisions of this article. [August 26, 1920]

AMENDMENT XX.

Section 1. The terms of the President and Vice-President shall end at noon on the twentieth day of January, and the terms of Senators and Representatives at noon on the third day of January, of the years in which such terms would have ended if this article had not been ratified; and the terms of their successors shall then begin.

Section 2. The Congress shall assemble at least once in every year, and such meeting shall begin at noon on the third day of January, unless they shall by law appoint a different day.

Section 3. If, at the time fixed for the beginning of the term of the President, the President-elect shall have died, the Vice-President-elect shall become President. If a President shall not have been chosen before the time fixed for the beginning of his term, or if the President-elect shall have failed to qualify, then the Vice-President-elect shall act as President until a President shall have qualified; and the Congress may by law provide for the case wherein neither a President-elect nor a Vice-President-elect shall have qualified, declaring who shall then act as President, or the manner in which one who is to act shall be selected, and such person shall act accordingly until a President or Vice-President shall have qualified.

Section 4. The Congress may by law provide for the case of the death of any of the persons from whom the House of Representatives may choose a President whenever the right of choice shall have devolved upon them, and for the case of the death of any of the persons from whom the Senate may choose a Vice-President whenever the right of choice shall have devolved upon them.

Section 5. Sections 1 and 2 shall take effect on the 15th day of October following the ratification of this article.

Section 6. This article shall be inoperative unless it shall have been ratified as an amendment to the Constitution by the legislatures of three-fourths of the several States within seven years from the date of its submission. [February 6, 1933]

AMENDMENT XXI.

Section 1. The eighteenth article of amendment to the Constitution of the United States is hereby repealed.

Section 2. The transportation or importation into any State, Territory or possession of the United States for delivery or use therein of intoxicating liquors, in violation of the laws thereof, is hereby prohibited.

Section 3. This article shall be inoperative unless it shall have been ratified as an amendment to the Constitution by convention in the several States, as provided in the Constitution, within seven years from the date of the submission thereof to the States by the Congress. [December 5, 1933]

AMENDMENT XXII.

Section 1. No person shall be elected to the office of the President more than twice, and no person who has held the office of President, or acted as President, for more than two years of a term to which some other person was elected President shall be elected to the office of the President more than once. But this Article shall not apply to any person holding the office of President when this Article was proposed by the Congress, and shall not prevent any person who may be holding the office of President, or acting as President, during the term within which this Article becomes operative from holding the office of President or acting as President during the remainder of such term.

Section 2. This article shall be inoperative unless it shall have been ratified as an amendment to the Constitution by the legislatures of three-fourths of the several States within seven years from the date of its submission to the States by the Congress. [February 27, 1951]

AMENDMENT XXIII.

Section 1. The District constituting the seat of government of the United States shall appoint in such manner as the Congress may direct:

A number of electors of President and Vice-President equal to the whole number of Senators and Representatives in Congress to which the District would be entitled if it were a State, but in no event more than the least populous State; they shall be in addition to those appointed by the States, but they shall be considered, for the purposes of the election of President and Vice-President, to be electors appointed by a State; and they shall meet in the District and perform such duties as provided by the twelfth article of amendment.

Section 2. The Congress shall have the power to enforce this article by appropriate legislation. [March 29, 1961]

AMENDMENT XXIV.

Section 1. The right of citizens of the United States to vote in any primary or other election for President or Vice President, for electors for President or Vice President, or for Senator or Representative in Congress, shall not be denied or abridged by the United States or any State by reason of failure to pay any poll tax or other tax.

Section 2. The Congress shall have power to enforce this article by appropriate legislation. [January 23, 1964]

AMENDMENT XXV.

Section 1. In case of the removal of the President from office or of his death or resignation, the Vice President shall become President.

Section 2. Whenever there is a vacancy in the office of Vice President, the President shall nominate a Vice President who shall take office upon confirmation by a majority vote of both Houses of Congress.

Section 3. Whenever the President transmits to the President pro tempore of the Senate and the Speaker of the House of Representatives his written declaration that he is unable to discharge the powers and duties of his office, and until he transmits to them a written declaration to the contrary, such powers and duties shall be discharged by the Vice President as Acting President.

Section 4. Whenever the Vice President and a majority of either the principal officers of the executive departments or of such other body as Congress may by law provide, transmit to the President pro tempore of the Senate and the Speaker of the House of Representatives their written declaration that the President is unable to discharge the powers and duties of his office, the Vice President shall immediately assume the powers and duties of the office as Acting President.

Thereafter, when the President transmits to the President pro tempore of the Senate and the Speaker of the House of Representatives his written declaration that no inability exists, he shall resume the powers and duties of his office unless the Vice President and a majority of either the principal officers of the executive departments or of such other body as Congress may by law provide, transmit within four days to the President pro tempore of the Senate and the Speaker of the House of Representatives their written declaration that the President is unable to discharge the powers and duties of his office. Thereupon Congress shall decide the issue, assembling within forty-eight hours for that purpose if not in session. If the Congress, within twenty-one days after receipt of the latter written declaration, or, if Congress is not in session, within twenty-one days after Congress is required to assemble, determines by two-thirds vote of both Houses that the President is unable to discharge the powers and duties of his office, the Vice-President shall continue to discharge the same as Acting President; otherwise, the President shall resume the powers and duties of his office. [February 10, 1967]

AMENDMENT XXVI.

Section 1. The right of citizens of the United States, who are eighteen years of age or older, to vote shall not be denied or abridged by the United States or by any State on account of age.

Section 2. The Congress shall have power to enforce this article by appropriate legislation. [June 30, 1971]

AMENDMENT XXVII.

No law, varying the compensation for the services of the Senators and Representatives shall take effect, until an election of Representatives shall have intervened. [May 8, 1992]

FROM GEORGE WASHINGTON'S FAREWELL ADDRESS (1796)

Friends and Citizens:

The period for a new election of a citizen to administer the executive government of the United States being not far distant, and the time actually arrived when your thoughts must be employed in designating the person who is to be clothed with that important trust, it appears to me proper, especially as it may conduce to a more distinct expression of the public voice, that I should now apprise you of the resolution I have formed, to decline being considered among the number of those out of whom a choice is to be made.

★ ★ ★

In looking forward to the moment which is intended to terminate the career of my public life, my feelings do not permit me to suspend the deep acknowledgment of that debt of gratitude which I owe to my beloved country for the many honors it has conferred upon me; still more for the steadfast confidence with which it has supported me; and for the opportunities I have thence enjoyed of manifesting my inviolable attachment, by services faithful and persevering, though in usefulness unequal to my zeal. If benefits have resulted to our country from these services, let it always be remembered to your praise, and as an instructive example in our annals, that under circumstances in which the passions, agitated in every direction, were liable to mislead, amidst appearances sometimes dubious, vicissitudes of fortune often discouraging, in situations in which not unfrequently want of success has countenanced the spirit of criticism, the constancy of your support was the essential prop of the efforts, and a guarantee of the plans by which they were effected. Profoundly penetrated with this idea, I shall carry it with me to my grave, as a strong incitement to unceasing vows that heaven may continue to you the choicest tokens of its beneficence; that your union and brotherly affection may be perpetual; that the free Constitution, which is the work of your hands, may be sacredly maintained; that its administration in every department may be stamped with wisdom and virtue; that, in fine, the happiness of the people of these States, under the auspices of liberty, may be made complete by so careful a preservation and so prudent a use of this blessing as will acquire to them the glory of recommending it to the applause, the affection, and adoption of every nation which is yet a stranger to it.

Here, perhaps, I ought to stop. But a solicitude for your welfare, which cannot end but with my life, and the apprehension of danger, natural to that solicitude, urge me, on an occasion like the present, to offer to your solemn contemplation, and to recommend to your frequent review, some sentiments which are the result of much reflection, of no inconsiderable observation, and which appear to me all-important to the permanency of your felicity as a people. These will be offered to you with the more freedom, as you can only see in them the disinterested warnings of a parting friend, who can possibly have no personal motive to bias his counsel. Nor can I forget, as an encouragement to it, your indulgent reception of my sentiments on a former and not dissimilar occasion.

Interwoven as is the love of liberty with every ligament of your hearts, no recommendation of mine is necessary to fortify or confirm the attachment.

The unity of government which constitutes you one people is also now dear to you. It is justly so, for it is a main pillar in the edifice of your real independence, the support of your tranquility at home, your peace abroad; of your safety; of your prosperity; of that very liberty which you so highly prize. But as it is easy to foresee that, from different causes and from different quarters, much pains will be taken, many artifices employed to weaken in your minds the conviction of this truth; as this is the point in your political fortress against which the batteries of internal and external enemies will be most constantly and actively (though often covertly and insidiously) directed, it is of infinite moment that you should properly estimate the immense value of your national union to your collective and individual happiness; that you should cherish a cordial, habitual, and immovable attachment to it; accustoming yourselves to think and speak of it as of the palladium of your political safety and prosperity; watching for its preservation with jealous anxiety; discountenancing whatever may suggest even a suspicion that it can in any event be abandoned; and indignantly frowning upon the first dawning of every attempt to alienate any portion of our country from the rest, or to enfeeble the sacred ties which now link together the various parts.

For this you have every inducement of sympathy and interest. Citizens, by birth or choice, of a common country, that country has a right to concentrate your affections. The name of American, which belongs to you in your national capacity, must always exalt the just pride of patriotism more than any appellation derived from local discriminations. With slight shades of difference, you have the same religion, manners, habits, and political principles. You have in a common cause fought and triumphed together; the independence and liberty you possess are the work of joint counsels, and joint efforts of common dangers, sufferings, and successes.

But these considerations, however powerfully they address themselves to your sensibility, are greatly outweighed by those which apply more immediately to your interest. Here every portion of our country finds the most commanding motives for carefully guarding and preserving the union of the whole.

The North, in an unrestrained intercourse with the South, protected by the equal laws of a common government, finds in the productions of the latter great additional resources of maritime and commercial enterprise and precious materials of manufacturing industry. The South, in the same intercourse, benefiting by the agency of the North, sees its agriculture grow and its commerce expand. Turning partly into its own channels the seamen of the North, it finds its particular navigation invigorated; and, while it contributes, in different ways, to nourish and increase the general mass of the national navigation, it looks forward to the protection of a maritime strength, to which itself is unequally adapted. The East, in a like intercourse with the West, already finds, and in the progressive improvement of interior communications by land and water, will more and more find a valuable vent for the commodities which it brings from abroad, or manufactures at home. The West derives from the East supplies requisite to its growth and comfort, and, what is perhaps of still greater consequence, it must of necessity owe the secure enjoyment of indispensable outlets for its own productions to the weight, influence, and the future maritime strength of the Atlantic side of the Union, directed by an indissoluble community of interest as one nation. Any other tenure by which the West can hold this essential advantage, whether derived from its own separate strength, or from an apostate and unnatural connection with any foreign power, must be intrinsically precarious.

While, then, every part of our country thus feels an immediate and particular interest in union, all the parts combined cannot fail to find in the united mass of means and efforts greater strength, greater resource, proportionably greater security from external danger, a less frequent interruption of their peace by foreign nations; and, what is of inestimable value, they must derive from union an

exemption from those broils and wars between themselves, which so frequently afflict neighboring countries not tied together by the same governments, which their own rival ships alone would be sufficient to produce, but which opposite foreign alliances, attachments, and intrigues would stimulate and embitter. Hence, likewise, they will avoid the necessity of those overgrown military establishments which, under any form of government, are inauspicious to liberty, and which are to be regarded as particularly hostile to republican liberty. In this sense it is that your union ought to be considered as a main prop of your liberty, and that the love of the one ought to endear to you the preservation of the other.

These considerations speak a persuasive language to every reflecting and virtuous mind, and exhibit the continuance of the Union as a primary object of patriotic desire. Is there a doubt whether a common government can embrace so large a sphere? Let experience solve it. To listen to mere speculation in such a case were criminal. We are authorized to hope that a proper organization of the whole with the auxiliary agency of governments for the respective subdivisions, will afford a happy issue to the experiment. It is well worth a fair and full experiment. With such powerful and obvious motives to union, affecting all parts of our country, while experience shall not have demonstrated its impracticability, there will always be reason to distrust the patriotism of those who in any quarter may endeavor to weaken its bands.

★ ★ ★

To the efficacy and permanency of your Union, a government for the whole is indispensable. No alliance, however strict, between the parts can be an adequate substitute; they must inevitably experience the infractions and interruptions which all alliances in all times have experienced. Sensible of this momentous truth, you have improved upon your first essay, by the adoption of a constitution of government better calculated than your former for an intimate union, and for the efficacious management of your common concerns. This government, the offspring of our own choice, uninfluenced and unawed, adopted upon full investigation and mature deliberation, completely free in its principles, in the distribution of its powers, uniting security with energy, and containing within itself a provision for its own amendment, has a just claim to your confidence and your support. Respect for its authority, compliance with its laws, acquiescence in its measures, are duties enjoined by the fundamental maxims of true liberty. The basis of our political systems is the right of the people to make and to alter their constitutions of government. But the Constitution which at any time exists, till changed by an explicit and authentic act of the whole people, is sacredly obligatory upon all. The very idea of the power and the right of the people to establish government presupposes the duty of every individual to obey the established government.

★ ★ ★

I have already intimated to you the danger of parties in the State, with particular reference to the founding of them on geographical discriminations. Let me now take a more comprehensive view, and warn you in the most solemn manner against the baneful effects of the spirit of party generally.

This spirit, unfortunately, is inseparable from our nature, having its root in the strongest passions of the human mind. It exists under different shapes in all governments, more or less stifled, controlled, or repressed; but, in those of the popular form, it is seen in its greatest rankness, and is truly their worst enemy.

The alternate domination of one faction over another, sharpened by the spirit of revenge, natural to party dissension, which in different ages and countries has perpetrated the most horrid enormities, is itself a frightful despotism. But this leads at length to a more formal and permanent despotism. The disorders and miseries which result gradually incline the minds of men to seek security and repose in the absolute power of an individual; and sooner or later the chief of some prevailing faction, more able or more fortunate than his competitors, turns this disposition to the purposes of his own elevation, on the ruins of public liberty.

Without looking forward to an extremity of this kind (which nevertheless ought not to be entirely out of sight), the common and continual mischiefs of the spirit of party are sufficient to make it the interest and duty of a wise people to discourage and restrain it.

It serves always to distract the public councils and enfeeble the public administration. It agitates the community with ill-founded jealousies and false alarms, kindles the animosity of one part against another, foments occasionally riot and insurrection. It opens the door to foreign influence and corruption, which finds a facilitated access to the government itself through the channels of party passions. Thus the policy and the will of one country are subjected to the policy and will of another.

There is an opinion that parties in free countries are useful checks upon the administration of the government and serve to keep alive the spirit of liberty. This within certain limits is probably true; and in governments of a monarchical cast, patriotism may look with indulgence, if not with favor, upon the spirit of party. But in those of the popular character, in governments purely elective, it is a spirit not to be encouraged. From their natural tendency, it is certain there will always be enough of that spirit for every salutary purpose. And there being constant danger of excess, the effort ought to be by force of public opinion, to mitigate and assuage it. A fire not to be quenched, it demands a uniform vigilance to prevent its bursting into a flame, lest, instead of warming, it should consume.

It is important, likewise, that the habits of thinking in a free country should inspire caution in those entrusted with its administration, to confine themselves within their respective constitutional spheres, avoiding in the exercise of the powers of one department to encroach upon another. The spirit of encroachment tends to consolidate the powers of all the departments in one, and thus to create, whatever the form of government, a real despotism. A just estimate of that love of power, and proneness to abuse it, which predominates in the human heart, is sufficient to satisfy us of the truth of this position. The necessity of reciprocal checks in the exercise of political power, by dividing and distributing it into different depositaries, and constituting each the guardian of the public weal against invasions by the others, has been evinced by experiments ancient and modern; some of them in our country and under our own eyes. To preserve them must be as necessary as to institute them. If, in the opinion of the people, the distribution or modification of the constitutional powers be in any particular wrong, let it be corrected by an amendment in the way which the Constitution designates. But let there be no change by usurpation; for though this, in one instance, may be the instrument of good, it is the customary weapon by which free governments are destroyed. The precedent must always greatly overbalance in permanent evil any partial or transient benefit, which the use can at any time yield.

★ ★ ★

Observe good faith and justice towards all nations; cultivate peace and harmony with all. Religion and morality enjoin this conduct; and can it be, that good policy does not equally enjoin it? It will be worthy of a free, enlightened, and at no distant period, a great nation, to give to mankind the magnanimous and too novel example of a people always guided by an exalted justice and benevolence. Who can doubt that, in the course of time and things, the fruits of such a plan would richly repay any temporary advantages which might be lost by a steady adherence to it? Can it be that Providence has not connected the permanent felicity of a nation with its virtue? The experiment, at least, is recommended by every sentiment which ennobles human nature. Alas! is it rendered impossible by its vices?

In the execution of such a plan, nothing is more essential than that permanent, inveterate antipathies against particular nations, and passionate attachments for others, should be excluded; and that, in place of them, just and amicable feelings towards all should be cultivated. The nation which indulges towards another a habitual hatred or a habitual fondness is in some degree a slave. It is a slave to its animosity or to its affection, either of which is sufficient to lead it astray from its duty and its interest. Antipathy in one nation against another disposes each more readily to offer insult and injury, to lay hold of slight causes of umbrage, and to be haughty and intractable, when accidental or trifling occasions of dispute occur. Hence, frequent collisions, obstinate, envenomed, and bloody contests. The nation, prompted by ill-will and resentment, sometimes impels to war the government, contrary to the best calculations of policy. The government sometimes participates in the national propensity, and adopts through passion what reason would reject; at other times it makes the animosity of the nation subservient to projects of hostility instigated by pride, ambition, and other sinister and pernicious motives. The peace often, sometimes perhaps the liberty, of nations, has been the victim.

★ ★ ★

The great rule of conduct for us in regard to foreign nations is in extending our commercial relations, to have with them as little political connection as possible. So far as we have already formed engagements, let them be fulfilled with perfect good faith. Here let us stop. Europe has a set of primary interests which to us have none; or a very remote relation. Hence she must be engaged in frequent controversies, the causes of which are essentially foreign to our concerns. Hence, therefore, it must be unwise in us to implicate ourselves by artificial ties in the ordinary vicissitudes of her politics, or the ordinary combinations and collisions of her friendships or enmities.

Our detached and distant situation invites and enables us to pursue a different course. If we remain one people under an efficient government, the period is not far off when we may defy material injury from external annoyance; when we may take such an attitude as will cause the neutrality we may at any time resolve upon to be scrupulously respected; when belligerent nations, under the impossibility of making acquisitions upon us, will not lightly hazard the giving us provocation; when we may choose peace or war, as our interest, guided by justice, shall counsel.

Why forego the advantages of so peculiar a situation? Why quit our own to stand upon foreign ground? Why, by interweaving our destiny with that of any part of Europe, entangle our peace and prosperity in the toils of European ambition, rivalship, interest, humor or caprice?

It is our true policy to steer clear of permanent alliances with any portion of the foreign world; so far, I mean, as we are now at liberty to do it; for let me not be understood as capable of patronizing infidelity to existing engagements. I hold the maxim no less applicable to public than to private affairs, that honesty is always the best policy. I repeat it, therefore, let those engagements be observed in their genuine sense. But, in my opinion, it is unnecessary and would be unwise to extend them.

Taking care always to keep ourselves by suitable establishments on a respectable defensive posture, we may safely trust to temporary alliances for extraordinary emergencies.

Harmony, liberal intercourse with all nations, are recommended by policy, humanity, and interest. But even our commercial policy should hold an equal and impartial hand; neither seeking nor granting exclusive favors or preferences; consulting the natural course of things; diffusing and diversifying by gentle means the streams of commerce, but forcing nothing; establishing (with powers so disposed, in order to give trade a stable course, to define the rights of our merchants, and to enable the government to support them) conventional rules of intercourse, the best that present circumstances and mutual opinion will permit, but temporary, and liable to be from time to time abandoned or varied, as experience and circumstances shall dictate; constantly keeping in view that it is folly in one nation to look for disinterested favors from another; that it must pay with a portion of its independence for whatever it may accept under that character; that, by such acceptance, it may place itself in the condition of having given equivalents for nominal favors, and yet of being reproached with ingratitude for not giving more.

★ ★ ★

Relying on its kindness in this as in other things, and actuated by that fervent love towards it, which is so natural to a man who views in it the native soil of himself and his progenitors for several generations, I anticipate with pleasing expectation that retreat in which I promise myself to realize, without alloy, the sweet enjoyment of partaking, in the midst of my fellow-citizens, the benign influence of good laws under a free government, the ever-favorite object of my heart, and the happy reward, as I trust, of our mutual cares, labors, and dangers.

Geo. Washington

THE SENECA FALLS DECLARATION OF SENTIMENTS AND RESOLUTIONS (1848)

1. DECLARATION OF SENTIMENTS

When, in the course of human events, it becomes necessary for one portion of the family of man to assume among the people of the earth a position different from that which they have hitherto occupied, but one to which the laws of nature and of nature's God entitle them, a decent respect to the opinions of mankind requires that they should declare the causes that impel them to such a course.

We hold these truths to be self-evident: that all men and women are created equal; that they are endowed by their Creator with certain inalienable rights; that among these are life, liberty, and the pursuit of happiness; that to secure these rights governments are instituted, deriving their just powers from the consent of the governed. Whenever any form of government becomes destructive of these ends, it is the right of those who suffer from it to refuse allegiance to it, and to insist upon the institution of a new government, laying its foundation on such principles, and organizing its powers in such form, as to them shall seem most likely to effect their safety and happiness. Prudence, indeed, will dictate that governments long established should not be changed for light and transient causes; and accordingly all experience hath shown that mankind are more disposed to suffer, while evils are sufferable, than to right themselves by abolishing the forms to which they are accustomed. But when a long train of abuses and usurpations, pursuing invariably the same object, evinces a design to reduce them under absolute despotism, it is their duty to throw off such government, and to provide new guards for their future security. Such has been the patient sufferance of the women under this government, and such is now the necessity which constrains them to demand the equal station to which they are entitled. The history of mankind is a history of repeated injuries and usurpations on the part of man toward woman, having in direct object the establishment of an absolute tyranny over her. To prove this, let facts be submitted to a candid world.

He has never permitted her to exercise her inalienable right to the elective franchise.

He has compelled her to submit to laws, in the formation of which she had no voice.

He has withheld from her rights which are given to the most ignorant and degraded men—both natives and foreigners.

Having deprived her of this first right of a citizen, the elective franchise, thereby leaving her without representation in the halls of legislation, he has oppressed her on all sides.

He has made her, if married, in the eye of the law, civilly dead. He has taken from her all right in property, even to the wages she earns.

He has made her, morally, an irresponsible being, as she can commit many crimes with impunity, provided they be done in the presence of her husband.

In the covenant of marriage, she is compelled to promise obedience to her husband, he becoming, to all intents and purposes, her master—the law giving him power to deprive her of her liberty, and to administer chastisement.

He has so framed the laws of divorce, as to what shall be the proper causes, and in case of separation, to whom the guardianship of the children shall be given, as to be wholly regardless of the happiness of women—the law, in all cases, going upon a false supposition of the supremacy of man, and giving all power into his hands.

After depriving her of all rights as a married woman, if single, and the owner of property, he has taxed her to support a government which recognizes her only when her property can be made profitable to it.

He has monopolized nearly all the profitable employments, and from those she is permitted to follow, she receives but a scanty remuneration. He closes against her all the avenues to wealth and distinction which he considers most honorable to himself. As a teacher of theology, medicine, or law, she is not known.

He has denied her the facilities for obtaining a thorough education, all colleges being closed against her.

He allows her in Church, as well as State, but a subordinate position, claiming Apostolic authority for her exclusion from the ministry, and, with some exceptions, from any public participation in the affairs of the Church.

He has created a false public sentiment by giving to the world a different code of morals for men and women, by which moral delinquencies which exclude women from society, are not only tolerated, but deemed of little account in man.

He has usurped the prerogative of Jehovah himself, claiming it as his right to assign for her a sphere of action, when that belongs to her conscience and to her God.

He has endeavored, in every way that he could, to destroy her confidence in her own powers, to lessen her self-respect and to make her willing to lead a dependent and abject life.

Now, in view of this entire disfranchisement of one-half the people of this country, their social and religious degradation—in view of the unjust laws above mentioned, and because women do feel themselves aggrieved, oppressed, and fraudulently deprived of their most sacred rights, we insist that they have immediate admission to all the rights and privileges which belong to them as citizens of the United States.

In entering upon the great work before us, we anticipate no small amount of misconception, misrepresentation, and ridicule; but we shall use every instrumentality within our power to effect our object. We shall employ agents, circulate tracts, petition the State and National legislatures, and endeavor to enlist the pulpit and the press in our behalf. We hope this Convention will be followed by a series of Conventions embracing every part of the country.

2. RESOLUTIONS

WHEREAS, The great precept of nature is conceded to be, that "man shall pursue his own true and substantial happiness." Blackstone in his Commentaries remarks, that this law of Nature being coeval with mankind, and dictated by God himself, is of course superior in obligation to any other. It is binding over all the globe, in all countries and at all times; no human laws are of any validity if contrary to this, and such of them as are valid, derive all their force, and all their validity, and all their authority, mediately and immediately, from this original; therefore,

Resolved, That such laws as conflict, in any way, with the true and substantial happiness of woman, are contrary to the great precept of nature and of no validity, for this is "superior in obligation to any other."

Resolved, That all laws which prevent woman from occupying such a station in society as her conscience shall dictate, or which place her in a position inferior to that of man, are contrary to the great precept of nature, and therefore of no force or authority.

Resolved, That woman is man's equal—was intended to be so by the Creator, and the highest good of the race demands that she should be recognized as such.

Resolved, That the women of this country ought to be enlightened in regard to the laws under which they live, that they may no longer publish their degradation by declaring themselves satisfied with their present position, nor their ignorance, by asserting that they have all the rights they want.

Resolved, That inasmuch as man, while claiming for himself intellectual superiority, does accord to woman moral superiority, it is pre-eminently his duty to encourage her to speak and teach, as she has an opportunity, in all religious assemblies.

Resolved, That the same amount of virtue, delicacy, and refinement of behavior that is required of woman in the social state, should also be required of man, and the same transgressions should be visited with equal severity on both man and woman.

Resolved, That the objection of indelicacy and impropriety, which is so often brought against woman when she addresses a public audience, comes with a very ill-grace from those who encourage, by their attendance, her appearance on the stage, in the concert. Or in feats of the circus.

Resolved, That woman has too long rested satisfied in the circumscribed limits which corrupt customs and a perverted application of the Scriptures have marked out for her, and that it is time she should move in the enlarged sphere which her great Creator has assigned her.

Resolved, That it is the duty of the women of this country to secure to themselves their sacred right to the elective franchise.

Resolved, That the equality of human rights results necessarily from the fact of the identity of the race in capabilities and responsibilities.

Resolved, therefore, That, being invested by the Creator with the same capabilities, and the same consciousness of responsibility for their exercise, it is demonstrably the right and duty of woman, equally with man, to promote every righteous cause by every righteous means; and especially in regard to the great subjects of morals and religion, it is self-evidently her right to participate with her brother in teaching them, both in private and in public, by writing and by speaking, by any instrumentalities proper to be used, and in any assemblies proper to be held; and this being a self-evident truth growing out of the divinely implanted principles of human nature, any custom or authority adverse to it, whether modern or wearing the hoary sanction of antiquity, is to be regarded as a self-evident falsehood, and at war with mankind.

Resolved, That the speedy success of our cause depends upon the zealous and untiring efforts of both men and women, for the overthrow of the monopoly of the pulpit, and for the securing to women an equal participation with men in the various trades, professions, and commerce.

FROM FREDERICK DOUGLASS'S "WHAT, TO THE SLAVE, IS THE FOURTH OF JULY?" SPEECH (1852)

★ ★ ★

This, for the purpose of this celebration, is the Fourth of July. It is the birthday of your National Independence, and of your political freedom. This, to you, is what the Passover was to the emancipated people of God. It carries your minds back to the day, and to the act of your great deliverance; and to the signs and to the wonders associated with that act and that day. This celebration also marks the beginning of another year of your national life; and reminds you that the Republic of America is now seventy-six years old. I am glad, fellow citizens, that your nation is so young. Seventy-six years, though a good old age for a man, is but a mere speck in the life of a nation. Three score years and ten is the allotted time for individual men; but nations number their years by thousands. According to this fact, you are, even now, only in the beginning of your national career, still lingering in the period of childhood. I repeat, I am glad this is so. There is hope in the thought, and hope is much needed, under the dark clouds which lower above the horizon. The eye of the reformer is met with angry flashes, portending disastrous times; but his heart may well beat lighter at the thought that America is young, and that she is still in the impressible stage of her existence. May he not hope that high lessons of wisdom, of justice and of truth, will yet give direction to her destiny? Were the nation older, the patriot's heart might be sadder and the reformer's brow heavier. Its future might be shrouded in gloom and the hope of its prophets go out in sorrow. There is consolation in the thought that America is young. Great streams are not easily turned from channels worn deep in the course of ages. They may sometimes rise in quiet and stately majesty, and inundate the land, refreshing and fertilizing the earth with their mysterious properties. They may also rise in wrath and fury, and bear away on their angry waves the accumulated wealth of years of toil and hardship. They, however, gradually flow back to the same old channel and flow on as serenely as ever. But, while the river may not be turned aside, it may dry up and leave nothing behind but the withered branch and the unsightly rock, to howl in the abyss-sweeping wind, the sad tale of departed glory. As with rivers, so with nations.

Fellow citizens, I shall not presume to dwell at length on the associations that cluster about this day. The simple story of it is, that seventy-six years ago the people of this country were British subjects. The style and title of your "sovereign people" (in which you now glory) was not then born. You were under the British Crown. Your fathers esteemed the English government as the home government, and England as the fatherland. This home government, you know, although a considerable distance from your home, did, in the exercise of its parental prerogatives, impose upon its colonial children such restraints, burdens and limitations as, in its mature judgment, it deemed wise, right and proper.

★ ★ ★

Feeling themselves harshly and unjustly treated by the home government, your fathers, like men of honesty and men of spirit, earnestly sought redress. They petitioned and remonstrated; they did so in a decorous, respectful and loyal manner. Their conduct was wholly unexceptionable. This, however, did not answer the purpose. They saw themselves treated with sovereign indifference, coldness and scorn. Yet they persevered. They were not the men to look back.

★ ★ ★

Citizens, your fathers . . . succeeded; and today you reap the fruits of their success. The freedom gained is yours; and you, therefore, may properly celebrate this anniversary. The Fourth of July is the first great fact in your nation's history—the very ringbolt in the chain of your yet undeveloped destiny.

Pride and patriotism, not less than gratitude, prompt you to celebrate and to hold it in perpetual remembrance. I have said that the Declaration of Independence is the ringbolt to the chain of your nation's destiny; so, indeed, I regard it. The principles contained in that instrument are saving principles. Stand by those principles, be true to them on all occasions, in all places, against all foes, and at whatever cost.

★ ★ ★

[The fathers of this republic] were peace men, but they preferred revolution to peaceful submission to bondage. They were quiet men; but they did not shrink from agitating against oppression. They showed forbearance, but that they knew its limits. They believed in order, but not in the order of tyranny. With them, nothing was "settled" that was not right. With them, justice, liberty and humanity were "final," not slavery and oppression. You may well cherish the memory of such men. They were great in their day and generation. Their solid manhood stands out the more as we contrast it with these degenerate times.

★ ★ ★

Fellow citizens, pardon me, allow me to ask, why am I called upon to speak here today? What have I, or those I represent, to do with your national independence? Are the great principles of political freedom and of natural justice, embodied in that Declaration of Independence, extended to us? and am I, therefore, called upon to bring our humble offering to the national altar and to confess the benefits and express devout gratitude for the blessings resulting from your independence to us?

★ ★ ★

But such is not the state of the case. I say it with a sad sense of the disparity between us. I am not included within the pale of this glorious anniversary! Your high independence only reveals the immeasurable distance between us. The blessings in which you, this day, rejoice, are not enjoyed in common. The rich inheritance of justice, liberty, prosperity and independence, bequeathed by your fathers, is shared by you, not by me. The sunlight that brought light and healing to you, has brought stripes and death to me. This Fourth of July is *yours*, not *mine*. *You* may rejoice, *I* must mourn.

★ ★ ★

Fellow citizens, above your national, tumultuous joy I hear the mournful wail of millions! whose chains, heavy and grievous yesterday, are today rendered more intolerable by the jubilee shouts that reach them. If I do forget, if I do not faithfully remember those bleeding children of sorrow this day, "may my right hand forget her cunning, and may my tongue cleave to the roof of my mouth!" To forget them, to pass lightly over their wrongs and to chime in with the popular theme would be treason most scandalous and shocking and would make me a reproach before God and the world. My subject, then, fellow citizens, is American slavery. I shall see this day and its popular characteristics from the slave's point of view. Standing there identified with the American bondman, making his wrongs mine, I do not hesitate to declare, with all my soul, that the character and conduct of this nation never looked

blacker to me than on this Fourth of July. Whether we turn to the declarations of the past or to the professions of the present, the conduct of the nation seems equally hideous and revolting. America is false to the past, false to the present, and solemnly binds herself to be false to the future.

★ ★ ★

For the present, it is enough to affirm the equal manhood of the Negro race. It is not astonishing that, while we are plowing, planting and reaping, using all kinds of mechanical tools, erecting houses, constructing bridges, building ships, working in metals of brass, iron, copper, silver and gold; that, while we are reading, writing and ciphering, acting as clerks, merchants and secretaries, having among us lawyers, doctors, ministers, poets, authors, editors, orators and teachers; that, while we are engaged in all manner of enterprises common to other men, digging gold in California, capturing the whale in the Pacific, feeding sheep and cattle on the hillside, living, moving, acting, thinking, planning, living in families as husbands, wives and children, and, above all, confessing and worshiping the Christian's God and looking hopefully for life and immortality beyond the grave, we are called upon to prove that we are men!

Would you have me argue that man is entitled to liberty? that he is the rightful owner of his own body? You have already declared it. Must I argue the wrongfulness of slavery? Is that a question for republicans? Is it to be settled by the rules of logic and argumentation, as a matter beset with great difficulty, involving a doubtful application of the principle of justice, hard to be understood? How should I look today, in the presence of Americans, dividing and subdividing a discourse, to show that men have a natural right to freedom, speaking of it relatively and positively, negatively and affirmatively? To do so would be to make myself ridiculous and to offer an insult to your understanding. There is not a man beneath the canopy of heaven that does not know that slavery is wrong *for him*.

★ ★ ★

What, to the American slave, is your Fourth of July? I answer: a day that reveals to him, more than all other days in the year, the gross injustice and cruelty to which he is the constant victim. To him, your celebration is a sham; your boasted liberty an unholy license; your national greatness swelling vanity; your sounds of rejoicing are empty and heartless; your denunciation of tyrants brass-fronted impudence; your shouts of liberty and equality hollow mockery; your prayers and hymns, your sermons and thanksgivings, with all your religious parade and solemnity, are to Him mere bombast, fraud, deception, impiety and hypocrisy—a thin veil to cover up crimes which would disgrace a nation of savages. There is not a nation on the earth guilty of practices more shocking and bloody than are the people of the United States at this very hour.

Go where you may, search where you will, roam through all the monarchies and despotisms of the Old World, travel through South America, search out every abuse, and when you have found the last, lay your facts by the side of the everyday practices of this nation, and you will say with me, that, for revolting barbarity and shameless hypocrisy, America reigns without a rival.

★ ★ ★

Americans! your republican politics, not less than your republican religion, are flagrantly inconsistent. You boast of your love of liberty, your superior civilization and your pure Christianity, while the whole political power of the nation (as embodied in the two great political parties) is solemnly pledged to support and perpetuate the enslavement of three millions of your countrymen. You hurl your anathemas at the crowned-headed tyrants of Russia and Austria and pride yourselves on your democratic institutions, while you yourselves consent to be the mere *tools* and *bodyguards* of the tyrants of Virginia and Carolina. You invite to your shores fugitives of oppression from abroad, honor them with banquets, greet them with ovations, cheer them, toast them, salute them, protect them, and pour out your money to them like water; but the fugitives from your own land you advertise, hunt, arrest, shoot and kill. You glory in your refinement and your universal education; yet you maintain a system as barbarous and dreadful as ever stained the character of a nation—a system begun in avarice, supported in pride, and perpetuated in cruelty. You shed tears over fallen Hungary, and make the sad story of her wrongs the theme of your poets, statesmen and orators, till your gallant sons are ready to fly to arms to vindicate her cause against the oppressor;* but, in regard to the ten thousand wrongs of the American slave, you would enforce the strictest silence and would hail him as an enemy of the nation who dares to make those wrongs the subject of public discourse! You are all on fire at the mention of liberty for France or for Ireland, but are as cold as an iceberg at the thought of liberty for the enslaved of America. You discourse eloquently on the dignity of labor; yet, you sustain a system which, in its very essence, casts a stigma upon labor. You can bare your bosom to the storm of British artillery to throw off a three-penny tax on tea, and yet wring the last hard-earned farthing from the grasp of the black laborers of your country. You profess to believe "that of one blood God made all nations of men to dwell on the face of all the earth"† and hath commanded all men, everywhere, to love one another; yet you notoriously hate (and glory in your hatred) all men whose skins are not colored like your own. You declare before the world, and are understood by the world to declare, that you "*hold these truths to be self-evident, that all men are created equal; and are endowed by their Creator with certain unalienable rights; and that among these are, life, liberty and the pursuit of happiness*"; and yet, you hold securely, in a bondage which, according to your own Thomas Jefferson, "*is worse than ages of that which your fathers rose in rebellion to oppose," a seventh part* of the inhabitants of your country.

Fellow citizens, I will not enlarge further on your national inconsistencies. The existence of slavery in this country brands your republicanism as a sham, your humanity as a base pretense, and your Christianity as a lie. It destroys your moral power abroad; it corrupts your politicians at home. It saps the foundation of religion; it makes your name a hissing and a byword to a mocking earth. It is the antagonistic force in your government, the only thing that seriously disturbs and endangers your union. It fetters your progress; it is the enemy of improvement; the deadly foe of education; it fosters pride; it breeds insolence; it promotes vice; it shelters crime; it is a curse to the earth that supports it; and yet you cling to it as if it were the sheet anchor of all your hopes.

★ ★ ★

Allow me to say, in conclusion, notwithstanding the dark picture I have this day presented, of the state of the nation, I do not despair of this country. There are forces in operation which must inevitably work the downfall of slavery.

★ ★ ★

---

*The fledgling Hungarian republic was invaded by Austria and Russia in 1849.
†Acts 17:26.

THE GETTYSBURG ADDRESS (1863)

Four score and seven years ago our fathers brought forth on this continent, a new nation, conceived in Liberty, and dedicated to the proposition that all men are created equal.

Now we are engaged in a great civil war, testing whether that nation, or any nation so conceived and so dedicated, can long endure. We are met on a great battle field of that war. We have come to dedicate a portion of that field, as a final resting place for those who here gave their lives that that nation might live. It is altogether fitting and proper that we should do this.

But, in a larger sense, we can not dedicate—we can not consecrate—we can not hallow—this ground. The brave men, living and dead, who struggled here, have consecrated it, far above our poor power to add or detract. The world will little note, nor long remember what we say here, but it can never forget what they did here. It is for us the living, rather, to be dedicated here to the unfinished work which they who fought here have thus far so nobly advanced. It is rather for us to be here dedicated to the great task remaining before us—that from these honored dead we take increased devotion to that cause for which they gave the last full measure of devotion—that we here highly resolve that these dead shall not have died in vain—that this nation, under God, shall have a new birth of freedom—and that government of the people, by the people, for the people, shall not perish from the earth.

Abraham Lincoln
November 19, 1863

ABRAHAM LINCOLN'S SECOND INAUGURAL ADDRESS (1865)

Fellow Countrymen:

At this second appearing to take the oath of the presidential office, there is less occasion for an extended address than there was at the first. Then a statement, somewhat in detail, of a course to be pursued, seemed fitting and proper. Now, at the expiration of four years, during which public declarations have been constantly called forth on every point and phase of the great contest which still absorbs the attention, and engrosses the energies of the nation, little that is new could be presented. The progress of our arms, upon which all else chiefly depends, is as well known to the public as to myself; and it is, I trust, reasonably satisfactory and encouraging to all. With high hope for the future, no prediction in regard to it is ventured.

On the occasion corresponding to this four years ago, all thoughts were anxiously directed to an impending civil war. All dreaded it—all sought to avert it. While the inaugural address was being delivered from this place, devoted altogether to *saving* the Union without war, insurgent agents were in the city seeking to *destroy* it without war—seeking to dissolve the Union, and divide effects, by negotiation. Both parties deprecated war; but one of them would *make* war rather than let the nation survive; and the other would *accept* war rather than let it perish. And the war came.

One eighth of the whole population were colored slaves, not distributed generally over the Union, but localized in the southern part of it. These slaves constituted a peculiar and powerful interest. All knew that this interest was, somehow, the cause of the war. To strengthen, perpetuate, and extend this interest was the object for which the insurgents would rend the Union, even by war; while the government claimed no right to do more than to restrict the territorial enlargement of it. Neither party expected for the war, the magnitude, or the duration, which it has already attained. Neither anticipated that the *cause* of the conflict might cease with, or even before, the conflict itself should cease. Each looked for an easier triumph, and a result less fundamental and astounding. Both read the same Bible, and pray to the same God; and each invokes His aid against the other. It may seem strange that any men should dare to ask a just God's assistance in wringing their bread from the sweat of other men's faces; but let us judge not that we be not judged. The prayers of both could not be answered; that of neither has been answered fully. The Almighty has His own purposes. "Woe unto the world because of offences! for it must needs be that offences come; but woe to that man by whom the offence cometh." If we shall suppose that American slavery is one of those offences which, in the providence of God, must needs come, but which, having continued through His appointed time, He now wills to remove, and that He gives to both North and South, this terrible war, as the woe due to those by whom the offence came, shall we discern therein any departure from those divine attributes which the believers in a living God always ascribe to Him? Fondly do we hope, fervently do we pray—that this mighty scourge of war may speedily pass away. Yet, if God wills that it continue until all the wealth piled by the bondsman's two hundred and fifty years of unrequited toil shall be sunk, and until every drop of blood drawn with the lash shall be paid by another drawn with the sword, as was said three thousand years ago, so still it must be said "the judgments of the Lord are true and righteous altogether."

With malice toward none; with charity for all; with firmness in the right as God gives us to see the right, let us strive on to finish the work we are in; to bind up the nation's wounds; to care for him who shall have borne the battle and for his widow and his orphan, to do all which may achieve and cherish a just and a lasting peace, among ourselves and with all nations.

THE POPULIST PLATFORM OF 1892

Assembled upon the 116th anniversary of the Declaration of Independence, the People's Party of America, in their first national convention, invoking upon their action the blessing of Almighty God, puts forth in the name and on behalf of the people of this country, the following preamble and declaration of principles:

PREAMBLE

The conditions which surround us best justify our cooperation; we meet in the midst of a nation brought to the verge of moral, political, and material ruin. Corruption dominates the ballot-box, the Legislatures, the Congress, and touches even the ermine of the bench. The people are demoralized; most of the States have been compelled to isolate the voters at the polling places to prevent universal intimidation and bribery. The newspapers are largely subsidized or muzzled, public opinion silenced, business prostrated, homes covered with mortgages, labor impoverished, and the land concentrating in the hands of the capitalists. The urban workmen are denied the right to organize for self-protection, imported pauperized labor beats down their wages, a hireling standing army, unrecognized by our laws, is established to shoot them down, and they are rapidly degenerating into European conditions. The fruits of the toil of millions are boldly stolen to build up the fortunes for a few, unprecedented in the history of mankind; and the possessors of these, in turn, despise the Republic and endanger liberty. From the same prolific womb of governmental injustice we breed the two great classes—tramps and millionaires.

The national power to create money is appropriated to enrich bondholders; a vast public debt, payable in legal tender currency, has been funded into gold-bearing bonds, thereby adding millions to the burdens of the people. Silver, which has been accepted as coin since the dawn of history, has been demonetized to add to the purchasing power of gold by decreasing the value of all forms of property as well as human labor, and the supply of currency is purposely abridged to fatten usurers, bankrupt enterprise, and enslave industry. A vast conspiracy against mankind has been organized on two continents, and it is rapidly taking possession of the world. If not met and overthrown at once it forebodes terrible social convulsions, the destruction of civilization, or the establishment of an absolute despotism.

We have witnessed for more than a quarter of a century the struggles of the two great political parties for power and plunder, while grievous wrongs have been inflicted upon the suffering people. We charge that the controlling influences dominating both these parties have permitted the existing dreadful conditions to develop without serious effort to prevent or restrain them. Neither do they now promise us any substantial reform. They have agreed together to ignore in the coming campaign every issue but one. They propose to drown the outcries of a plundered people with the uproar of a sham battle over the tariff, so that capitalists, corporations, national banks, rings, trusts, watered stock, the demonetization of silver, and the oppressions of the usurers may all be lost sight of. They propose to sacrifice our homes, lives, and children on the altar of mammon; to destroy the multitude in order to secure corruption funds from the millionaires.

Assembled on the anniversary of the birthday of the nation, and filled with the spirit of the grand general and chief who established our independence, we seek to restore the government of the Republic to the hands of "the plain people," with which class it originated. We assert our purpose to be identical with the purposes of the National Constitution, "to form a more perfect union and establish justice, insure domestic tranquility, provide for the common defense, promote the general welfare, and secure the blessings of liberty for ourselves and our posterity." We declare that this Republic can only endure as a free government while built upon the love of the whole people for each other and for the nation; that it cannot be pinned together by bayonets; that the civil war is over, and that every passion and resentment which grew out of it must die with it; and that we must be in fact, as we are in name, one united brotherhood of free men.

Our country finds itself confronted by conditions for which there is no precedent in the history of the world; our annual agricultural productions amount to billions of dollars in value, which must, within a few weeks or months, be exchanged for billions of dollars of commodities consumed in their production; the existing currency supply is wholly inadequate to make this exchange; the results are falling prices, the formation of combines and rings, the impoverishment of the producing class. We pledge ourselves, if given power, we will labor to correct these evils by wise and reasonable legislation, in accordance with the terms of our platform. We believe that the power of government—in other words, of the people—should be expanded (as in the case of the postal service) as rapidly and as far as the good sense of an intelligent people and the teaching of experience shall justify, to the end that oppression, injustice, and poverty shall eventually cease in the land.

While our sympathies as a party of reform are naturally upon the side of every proposition which will tend to make men intelligent, virtuous, and temperate, we nevertheless regard these questions—important as they are—as secondary to the great issues now pressing for solution, and upon which not only our individual prosperity but the very existence of free institutions depend; and we ask all men to first help us to determine whether we are to have a republic to administer before we differ as to the conditions upon which it is to be administered, believing that the forces of reform this day organized will never cease to move forward until every wrong is remedied, and equal rights and equal privileges securely established for all the men and women of this country.

PLATFORM

We declare, therefore—

First.—That the union of the labor forces of the United States this day consummated shall be permanent and perpetual; may its spirit enter into all hearts for the salvation of the Republic and the uplifting of mankind!

Second.—Wealth belongs to him who creates it, and every dollar taken from industry without an equivalent is robbery. "If any will not work, neither shall he eat." The interests of rural and civic labor are the same; their enemies are identical.

Third.—We believe that the time has come when the railroad corporations will either own the people or the people must own the railroads; and, should the government enter upon the work of owning and managing all railroads, we should favor an amendment to the Constitution by which all persons engaged in the government service shall be placed under a civil-service regulation of the most rigid character, so as to prevent the increase of the power of the national administration by the use of such additional government employees.

FINANCE.—We demand a national currency, safe, sound, and flexible, issued by the general government only, a full legal tender for all debts, public and private, and that without the use of banking corporations, a just, equitable, and efficient means of distribution direct to the people, at a tax not to exceed two per cent per annum, to be provided as set forth in the sub-treasury plan of the Farmers' Alliance, or a better system; also by payments in discharge of its obligations for public improvements.

1. We demand free and unlimited coinage of silver and gold at the present legal ratio of 16 to 1.

2. We demand that the amount of circulating medium be speedily increased to not less than $50 per capita.

3. We demand a graduated income tax.

4. We believe that the money of the country should be kept as much as possible in the hands of the people, and hence we demand that all State and national revenues shall be limited to the necessary expenses of the government, economically and honestly administered.

5. We demand that postal savings banks be established by the government for the safe deposit of the earnings of the people and to facilitate exchange.

TRANSPORTATION.—Transportation being a means of exchange and a public necessity, the government should own and operate the railroads in the interest of the people. The telegraph and telephone, like the post-office system, being a necessity for the transmission of news, should be owned and operated by the government in the interest of the people.

LAND.—The land, including all the natural sources of wealth, is the heritage of the people, and should not be monopolized for speculative purposes, and alien ownership of land should be prohibited. All land now held by railroads and other corporations in excess of their actual needs, and all lands now owned by aliens should be reclaimed by the government and held for actual settlers only.

EXPRESSION OF SENTIMENTS

Your committee on Platform and Resolutions beg leave unanimously to report the following:

Whereas, Other questions have been presented for our consideration, we hereby submit the following, not as a part of the Platform of the People's Party, but as resolutions expressive of the sentiment of this Convention:

1. *Resolved*, That we demand a free ballot and a fair count in all elections, and pledge ourselves to secure it to every legal voter without federal intervention, through the adoption by the States of the unperverted Australian or secret ballot system.

2. *Resolved*, That the revenue derived from a graduated income tax should be applied to the reduction of the burden of taxation now levied upon the domestic industries of this country.

3. *Resolved*, That we pledge our support to fair and liberal pensions to ex-Union soldiers and sailors.

4. *Resolved*, That we condemn the fallacy of protecting American labor under the present system, which opens our ports to the pauper and criminal classes of the world, and crowds out our wage-earners; and we denounce the present ineffective laws against contract labor, and demand the further restriction of undesirable emigration.

5. *Resolved*, that we cordially sympathize with the efforts of organized workingmen to shorten the hours of labor, and demand a rigid enforcement of the existing eight-hour law on Government work, and ask that a penalty clause be added to the said law.

6. *Resolved*, That we regard the maintenance of a large standing army of mercenaries, known as the Pinkerton system, as a menace to our liberties, and we demand its abolition; and we condemn the recent invasion of the Territory of Wyoming by the hired assassins of plutocracy, assisted by federal officers.

7. *Resolved*, That we commend to the favorable consideration of the people and the reform press the legislative system known as the initiative and referendum.

8. *Resolved*, That we favor a constitutional provision limiting the office of President and Vice-President to one term, and providing for the election of Senators of the United States by a direct vote of the people.

9. *Resolved*, That we oppose any subsidy or national aid to any private corporation for any purpose.

10. *Resolved*, That this convention sympathizes with the Knights of Labor and their righteous contest with the tyrannical combine of clothing manufacturers of Rochester, and declare it to be the duty of all who hate tyranny and oppression to refuse to purchase the goods made by the said manufacturers, or to patronize any merchants who sell such goods.

FRANKLIN D. ROOSEVELT'S FIRST INAUGURAL ADDRESS (1933)

I am certain that my fellow Americans expect that on my induction into the Presidency I will address them with a candor and a decision which the present situation of our Nation impels. This is preeminently the time to speak the truth, the whole truth, frankly and boldly. Nor need we shrink from honestly facing conditions in our country today. This great Nation will endure as it has endured, will revive and will prosper. So, first of all, let me assert my firm belief that the only thing we have to fear is fear itself—nameless, unreasoning, unjustified terror which paralyzes needed efforts to convert retreat into advance. In every dark hour of our national life a leadership of frankness and vigor has met with that understanding and support of the people themselves which is essential to victory. I am convinced that you will again give that support to leadership in these critical days.

In such a spirit on my part and on yours we face our common difficulties. They concern, thank God, only material things. Values have shrunken to fantastic levels; taxes have risen; our ability to pay has fallen; government of all kinds is faced by serious curtailment of income; the means of exchange are frozen in the currents of trade; the withered leaves of industrial enterprise lie on every side; farmers find no markets for their produce; the savings of many years in thousands of families are gone.

More important, a host of unemployed citizens face the grim problem of existence, and an equally great number toil with little return. Only a foolish optimist can deny the dark realities of the moment.

Yet our distress comes from no failure of substance. We are stricken by no plague of locusts. Compared with the perils which our forefathers conquered because they believed and were not afraid, we have still much to be thankful for. Nature still offers her bounty and human efforts have multiplied it. Plenty is at our doorstep, but a generous use of it languishes in the very sight of the supply. Primarily this is because the rulers of the exchange of mankind's goods have failed, through their own stubbornness and their own incompetence, have admitted their failure, and abdicated. Practices of the unscrupulous money changers stand indicted in the court of public opinion, rejected by the hearts and minds of men.

True they have tried, but their efforts have been cast in the pattern of an outworn tradition. Faced by failure of credit they have proposed only the lending of more money. Stripped of the lure of profit by which to induce our people to follow their false leadership, they have resorted to exhortations, pleading tearfully for restored confidence. They know only the rules of a generation of self-seekers. They have no vision, and when there is no vision the people perish.

The money changers have fled from their high seats in the temple of our civilization. We may now restore that temple to the ancient truths. The measure of the restoration lies in the extent to which we apply social values more noble than mere monetary profit.

Happiness lies not in the mere possession of money; it lies in the joy of achievement, in the thrill of creative effort. The joy and moral stimulation of work no longer must be forgotten in the mad chase of evanescent profits. These dark days will be worth all they cost us if they teach us that our true destiny is not to be ministered unto but to minister to ourselves and to our fellow men.

Recognition of the falsity of material wealth as the standard of success goes hand in hand with the abandonment of the false belief that public office and high political position are to be valued only by the standards of pride of place and personal profit; and there must be an end to a conduct in banking and in business which too often has given to a sacred trust the likeness of callous and selfish wrongdoing. Small wonder that confidence languishes, for it thrives only on honesty, on honor, on the sacredness of obligations, on faithful protection, on unselfish performance; without them it cannot live.

Restoration calls, however, not for changes in ethics alone. This Nation asks for action, and action now.

Our greatest primary task is to put people to work. This is no unsolvable problem if we face it wisely and courageously. It can be accomplished in part by direct recruiting by the Government itself, treating the task as we would treat the emergency of a war, but at the same time, through this employment, accomplishing greatly needed projects to stimulate and reorganize the use of our natural resources.

Hand in hand with this we must frankly recognize the overbalance of population in our industrial centers and, by engaging on a national scale in a redistribution, endeavor to provide a better use of the land for those best fitted for the land. The task can be helped by definite efforts to raise the values of agricultural products and with this the power to purchase the output of our cities. It can be helped by preventing realistically the tragedy of the growing loss through foreclosure of our small homes and our farms. It can be helped by insistence that the Federal, State, and local governments act forthwith on the demand that their cost be drastically reduced. It can be helped by the unifying of relief activities which today are often scattered, uneconomical, and unequal. It can be helped by national planning for and supervision of all forms of transportation and of communications and other utilities which have a definitely public character. There are many ways in which it can be helped, but it can never be helped merely by talking about it. We must act and act quickly.

Finally, in our progress toward a resumption of work we require two safeguards against a return of the evils of the old order; there must be a strict supervision of all banking and credits and investments; there must be an end to speculation with other people's money, and there must be provision for an adequate but sound currency.

There are the lines of attack. I shall presently urge upon a new Congress, in special session, detailed measures for their fulfillment, and I shall seek the immediate assistance of the several States.

Through this program of action we address ourselves to putting our own national house in order and making income balance outgo. Our international trade relations, though vastly important, are in point of time and necessity secondary to the establishment of a sound national economy. I favor as a practical policy the putting of first things first. I shall spare no effort to restore world trade by international economic readjustment, but the emergency at home cannot wait on that accomplishment.

The basic thought that guides these specific means of national recovery is not narrowly nationalistic. It is the insistence, as a first consideration, upon the interdependence of the various elements in all parts of the United States—a recognition of the old and permanently important manifestation of the American spirit of the pioneer. It is the way to recovery. It is the immediate way. It is the strongest assurance that the recovery will endure.

In the field of world policy I would dedicate this Nation to the policy of the good neighbor—the neighbor who resolutely respects himself and, because he does so, respects the rights of others—the neighbor who respects his obligations and respects the sanctity of his agreements in and with a world of neighbors.

If I read the temper of our people correctly, we now realize as we have never realized before our interdependence on each other; that we cannot merely take but we must give as well; that if we are to go forward, we must move as a trained and loyal army willing to sacrifice for the good of a common discipline, because without such discipline no progress is made, no leadership becomes effective. We are, I know, ready and willing to submit our lives and property to such discipline, because it makes possible a leadership which aims at a larger good. This I propose to offer, pledging that the larger purposes will bind upon us all as a sacred obligation with a unity of duty hitherto evoked only in time of armed strife.

With this pledge taken, I assume unhesitatingly the leadership of this great army of our people dedicated to a disciplined attack upon our common problems.

Action in this image and to this end is feasible under the form of government which we have inherited from our ancestors. Our Constitution is so simple and practical that it is possible always to meet extraordinary needs by changes in emphasis and arrangement without loss of essential form. That is why our constitutional system has proved itself the most superbly enduring political mechanism the modern world has produced. It has met every stress of vast expansion of territory, of foreign wars, of bitter internal strife, of world relations.

It is to be hoped that the normal balance of executive and legislative authority may be wholly adequate to meet the unprecedented task before us. But it may be that an unprecedented demand and need for undelayed action may call for temporary departure from that normal balance of public procedure.

I am prepared under my constitutional duty to recommend the measures that a stricken nation in the midst of a stricken world may require. These measures, or such other measures as the Congress may build out of its experience and wisdom, I shall seek, within my constitutional authority, to bring to speedy adoption.

But in the event that the Congress shall fail to take one of these two courses, and in the event that the national emergency is still critical, I shall not evade the clear course of duty that will then confront me. I shall ask the Congress for the one remaining instrument to meet the crisis—broad Executive power to wage a war against the emergency, as great as the power that would be given to me if we were in fact invaded by a foreign foe.

For the trust reposed in me I will return the courage and the devotion that befit the time. I can do no less.

We face the arduous days that lie before us in the warm courage of national unity; with the clear consciousness of seeking old and precious moral values; with the clean satisfaction that comes from the stern performance of duty by old and young alike. We aim at the assurance of a rounded and permanent national life.

We do not distrust the future of essential democracy. The people of the United States have not failed. In their need they have registered a mandate that they want direct, vigorous action. They have asked for discipline and direction under leadership. They have made me the present instrument of their wishes. In the spirit of the gift I take it.

In this dedication of a Nation we humbly ask the blessing of God. May He protect each and every one of us. May He guide me in the days to come.

FROM THE PROGRAM FOR THE MARCH ON WASHINGTON FOR JOBS AND FREEDOM (1963)

WHAT WE DEMAND*

1. Comprehensive and effective *civil rights legislation* from the present Congress—without compromise or filibuster—to guarantee all Americans

> access to all public accommodations
> decent housing
> adequate and integrated education
> the right to vote

2. Withholding of Federal funds from all programs in which discrimination exists.

3. *Desegregation of all school districts in 1963.*

4. Enforcement of the *Fourteenth Amendment*—reducing Congressional representation of states where citizens are disfranchised.

5. A new *Executive Order* banning discrimination in all housing supported by federal funds.

6. Authority for the Attorney General to institute *injunctive suits* when any constitutional right is violated.

7. A massive federal program to train and place all unemployed workers—Negro and white—on meaningful and dignified jobs at decent wages.

8. A national *minimum wage* act that will give all Americans a decent standard of living. (Government surveys show that anything less than $2.00 an hour fails to do this.)

9. A broadened *Fair Labor Standards Act* to include all areas of employment which are presently excluded.

10. A federal *Fair Employment Practices Act* barring discrimination by federal, state, and municipal governments, and by employers, contractors, employment agencies, and trade unions.

*Support of the March does not necessarily indicate endorsement of every demand listed. Some organizations have not had an opportunity to take an official position on all of the demands advocated here.

RONALD REAGAN'S FIRST INAUGURAL ADDRESS (1981)

WEST FRONT OF THE U.S. CAPITOL, JANUARY 20, 1981

Senator Hatfield, Mr. Chief Justice, Mr. President, Vice President Bush, Vice President Mondale, Senator Baker, Speaker O'Neill, Reverend Moomaw, and my fellow citizens:

To a few of us here today this is a solemn and most momentous occasion, and yet in the history of our nation it is a commonplace occurrence. The orderly transfer of authority as called for in the Constitution routinely takes place, as it has for almost two centuries, and few of us stop to think how unique we really are. In the eyes of many in the world, this every-four-year ceremony we accept as normal is nothing less than a miracle.

Mr. President, I want our fellow citizens to know how much you did to carry on this tradition. By your gracious cooperation in the transition process, you have shown a watching world that we are a united people pledged to maintaining a political system which guarantees individual liberty to a greater degree than any other, and I thank you and your people for all your help in maintaining the continuity which is the bulwark of our republic. The business of our nation goes forward. These United States are confronted with an economic affliction of great proportions. We suffer from the longest and one of the worst sustained inflations in our national history. It distorts our economic decisions, penalizes thrift, and crushes the struggling young and the fixed-income elderly alike. It threatens to shatter the lives of millions of our people.

Idle industries have cast workers into unemployment, human misery, and personal indignity. Those who do work are denied a fair return for their labor by a tax system which penalizes successful achievement and keeps us from maintaining full productivity. But great as our tax burden is, it has not kept pace with public spending. For decades we have piled deficit upon deficit, mortgaging our future and our children's future for the temporary convenience of the present. To continue this long trend is to guarantee tremendous social, cultural, political, and economic upheavals.

You and I, as individuals, can, by borrowing, live beyond our means, but for only a limited period of time. Why, then, should we think that collectively, as a nation, we're not bound by that same limitation? We must act today in order to preserve tomorrow. And let there be no misunderstanding: We are going to begin to act, beginning today. The economic ills we suffer have come upon us over several decades. They will not go away in days, weeks, or months, but they will go away. They will go away because we as Americans have the capacity now, as we've had in the past, to do whatever needs to be done to preserve this last and greatest bastion of freedom.

In this present crisis, government is not the solution to our problem; government is the problem. From time to time we've been tempted to believe that society has become too complex to be managed by self-rule, that government by an elite group is superior to government for, by, and of the people. Well, if no one among us is capable of governing himself, then who among us has the capacity to govern someone else? All of us together, in and out of government, must bear the burden. The solutions we seek must be equitable, with no one group singled out to pay a higher price.

We hear much of special interest groups. Well, our concern must be for a special interest group that has been too long neglected. It knows no sectional boundaries or ethnic and racial divisions, and it crosses political party lines. It is made up of men and women who raise our food, patrol our streets, man our mines and factories, teach our children, keep our homes, and heal us when we're sick—professionals, industrialists, shopkeepers, clerks, cabbies, and truck drivers. They are, in short, "we the people," this breed called Americans.

Well, this administration's objective will be a healthy, vigorous, growing economy that provides equal opportunities for all Americans, with no barriers born of bigotry or discrimination. Putting America back to work means putting all Americans back to work. Ending inflation means freeing all Americans from the terror of runaway living costs. All must share in the productive work of this "new beginning," and all must share in the bounty of a revived economy. With the idealism and fair play which are the core of our system and our strength, we can have a strong and prosperous America, at peace with itself and the world.

So, as we begin, let us take inventory. We are a nation that has a government—not the other way around. And this makes us special among the nations of the Earth. Our government has no power except that granted it by the people. It is time to check and reverse the growth of government, which shows signs of having grown beyond the consent of the governed.

It is my intention to curb the size and influence of the federal establishment and to demand recognition of the distinction between the powers granted to the federal government and those reserved to the states or to the people. All of us need to be reminded that the federal government did not create the states; the states created the federal government.

Now, so there will be no misunderstanding, it's not my intention to do away with government. It is rather to make it work—work with us, not over us; to stand by our side, not ride on our back. Government can and must provide opportunity, not smother it; foster productivity, not stifle it.

If we look to the answer as to why for so many years we achieved so much, prospered as no other people on earth, it was because here in this land we unleashed the energy and individual genius of man to a greater extent than has ever been done before. Freedom and the dignity of the individual have been more available and assured here than in any other place on earth. The price for this freedom at times has been high, but we have never been unwilling to pay the price.

It is no coincidence that our present troubles parallel and are proportionate to the intervention and intrusion in our lives that result from unnecessary and excessive growth of government. It is time for us to realize that we're too great a nation to limit ourselves to small dreams. We're not, as some would have us believe, doomed to an inevitable decline. I do not believe in a fate that will fall on us no matter what we do. I do believe in a fate that will fall on us if we do nothing. So, with all the creative energy at our command, let us begin an era of national renewal. Let us renew our determination, our courage, and our strength. And let us renew our faith and our hope.

We have every right to dream heroic dreams. Those who say that we're in a time when there are no heroes, they just don't know where to look. You can see heroes every day going in and out of factory gates. Others, a handful in number, produce enough food to feed all of us and then the world beyond. You meet heroes across a counter, and they're on both sides of that counter. There are entrepreneurs with faith in themselves and faith in an idea who create new jobs, new wealth and opportunity. They're individuals and families whose taxes support the government and whose voluntary gifts support church, charity, culture, art, and education. Their patriotism is quiet, but deep. Their values sustain our national life.

Now, I have used the words "they" and "their" in speaking of these heroes. I could say "you" and "your," because I'm addressing the heroes of whom I speak—you, the citizens of this blessed land. Your dreams, your hopes, your goals are going to be the dreams, the hopes, and the goals of this administration, so help me God.

We shall reflect the compassion that is so much a part of your makeup. How can we love our country and not love our countrymen; and loving them, reach out a hand when they fall, heal them when they're sick, and provide opportunity to make them self-sufficient so they will be equal in fact and not just in theory?

Can we solve the problems confronting us? Well, the answer is an unequivocal and emphatic "yes." To paraphrase Winston Churchill, I did not take the oath I've just taken with the intention of presiding over the dissolution of the world's strongest economy.

In the days ahead I will propose removing the roadblocks that have slowed our economy and reduced productivity. Steps will be taken aimed at restoring the balance between the various levels of government. Progress may be slow, measured in inches and feet, not miles, but we will progress. It is time to reawaken this industrial giant, to get government back within its means, and to lighten our punitive tax burden. And these will be our first priorities, and on these principles there will be no compromise.

On the eve of our struggle for independence a man who might have been one of the greatest among the Founding Fathers, Dr. Joseph Warren, president of the Massachusetts Congress, said to his fellow Americans, "Our country is in danger, but not to be despaired of . . . . On you depend the fortunes of America. You are to decide the important questions upon which rests the happiness and the liberty of millions yet unborn. Act worthy of yourselves." Well, I believe we, the Americans of today, are ready to act worthy of ourselves, ready to do what must be done to ensure happiness and liberty for ourselves, our children, and our children's children. And as we renew ourselves here in our own land, we will be seen as having greater strength throughout the world. We will again be the exemplar of freedom and a beacon of hope for those who do not now have freedom.

To those neighbors and allies who share our freedom, we will strengthen our historic ties and assure them of our support and firm commitment. We will match loyalty with loyalty. We will strive for mutually beneficial relations. We will not use our friendship to impose on their sovereignty, for our own sovereignty is not for sale. As for the enemies of freedom, those who are potential adversaries, they will be reminded that peace is the highest aspiration of the American people. We will negotiate for it, sacrifice for it; we will not surrender for it, now or ever.

Our forbearance should never be misunderstood. Our reluctance for conflict should not be misjudged as a failure of will. When action is required to preserve our national security, we will act. We will maintain sufficient strength to prevail if need be, knowing that if we do so we have the best chance of never having to use that strength. Above all, we must realize that no arsenal or no weapon in the arsenals of the world is so formidable as the will and moral courage of free men and women. It is a weapon our adversaries in today's world do not have. It is a weapon that we as Americans do have. Let that be understood by those who practice terrorism and prey upon their neighbors. I'm told that tens of thousands of prayer meetings are being held on this day, and for that I'm deeply grateful. We are a nation under God, and I believe God intended for us to be free. It would be fitting and good, I think, if on each Inaugural Day in future years it should be declared a day of prayer.

This is the first time in our history that this ceremony has been held, as you've been told, on the West Front of the Capitol. Standing here, one faces a magnificent vista, opening up on the city's special beauty and history. At the end of this open mall are those shrines to the giants on whose shoulders we stand.

Directly in front of me, the monument to a monumental man, George Washington, father of our country. A man of humility who came to greatness reluctantly. He led Americans out of revolutionary victory into infant nationhood. Off to one side, the stately memorial to Thomas Jefferson. The Declaration of Independence flames with his eloquence. And then, beyond the Reflecting Pool, the dignified columns of the Lincoln Memorial. Whoever would understand in his heart the meaning of America will find it in the life of Abraham Lincoln.

Beyond those monuments to heroism is the Potomac River, and on the far shore the sloping hills of Arlington National Cemetery, with its row upon row of simple white markers bearing crosses and Stars of David. They add up to only a tiny fraction of the price that has been paid for our freedom. Each one of those markers is a monument to the kind of hero I spoke of earlier. Their lives ended in places called Belleau Wood, the Argonne, Omaha Beach, Salerno, and halfway around the world on Guadalcanal, Tarawa, Pork Chop Hill, the Chosin Reservoir, and in a hundred rice paddies and jungles of a place called Vietnam.

Under one such marker lies a young man, Martin Treptow, who left his job in a small town barbershop in 1917 to go to France with the famed Rainbow Division. There, on the western front, he was killed trying to carry a message between battalions under heavy artillery fire.

We're told that on his body was found a diary. On the flyleaf under the heading "My Pledge," he had written these words: "America must win this war. Therefore I will work, I will save, I will sacrifice, I will endure, I will fight cheerfully and do my utmost, as if the issue of the whole struggle depended on me alone."

The crisis we are facing today does not require of us the kind of sacrifice that Martin Treptow and so many thousands of others were called upon to make. It does require, however, our best effort and our willingness to believe in ourselves and to believe in our capacity to perform great deeds, to believe that together with God's help we can and will resolve the problems which now confront us.

And after all, why shouldn't we believe that? We are Americans.

God bless you, and thank you.

BARACK OBAMA'S FIRST INAUGURAL ADDRESS (2009)

My fellow citizens: I stand here today humbled by the task before us, grateful for the trust you've bestowed, mindful of the sacrifices borne by our ancestors.

I thank President Bush for his service to our nation—(*applause*)—as well as the generosity and cooperation he has shown throughout this transition.

Forty-four Americans have now taken the presidential oath. The words have been spoken during rising tides of prosperity and the still waters of peace. Yet, every so often, the oath is taken amidst gathering clouds and raging storms. At these moments, America has carried on not simply because of the skill or vision of those in high office, but because we, the people, have remained faithful to the ideals of our forebears and true to our founding documents.

So it has been: so it must be with this generation of Americans.

That we are in the midst of crisis is now well understood. Our nation is at war against a far-reaching network of violence and hatred. Our economy is badly weakened, a consequence of greed and irresponsibility on the part of some, but also our collective failure to make hard choices and prepare the nation for a new age. Homes have been lost, jobs shed, businesses shuttered. Our health care is too costly, our schools fail too many—and each day brings further evidence that the ways we use energy strengthen our adversaries and threaten our planet.

These are the indicators of crisis, subject to data and statistics. Less measurable, but no less profound, is a sapping of confidence across our land; a nagging fear that America's decline is inevitable, that the next generation must lower its sights.

Today I say to you that the challenges we face are real. They are serious and they are many. They will not be met easily or in a short span of time. But know this America: They will be met. (*Applause*)

On this day, we gather because we have chosen hope over fear, unity of purpose over conflict and discord. On this day, we come to proclaim an end to the petty grievances and false promises, the recriminations and worn-out dogmas that for far too long have strangled our politics. We remain a young nation. But in the words of Scripture, the time has come to set aside childish things. The time has come to reaffirm our enduring spirit; to choose our better history; to carry forward that precious gift, that noble idea passed on from generation to generation; the God-given promise that all are equal, all are free, and all deserve a chance to pursue their full measure of happiness. (*Applause*)

In reaffirming the greatness of our nation we understand that greatness is never a given. It must be earned. Our journey has never been one of short-cuts or settling for less. It has not been the path for the faint-hearted, for those that prefer leisure over work, or seek only the pleasures of riches and fame. Rather, it has been the risk-takers, the doers, the makers of things—some celebrated, but more often men and women obscure in their labor—who have carried us up the long rugged path towards prosperity and freedom.

For us, they packed up their few worldly possessions and traveled across oceans in search of a new life. For us, they toiled in sweatshops, and settled the West, endured the lash of the whip, and plowed the hard earth. For us, they fought and died in places like Concord and Gettysburg, Normandy and Khe Sahn.

Time and again these men and women struggled and sacrificed and worked till their hands were raw so that we might live a better life. They saw America as bigger than the sum of our individual ambitions, greater than all the differences of birth or wealth or faction.

This is the journey we continue today. We remain the most prosperous, powerful nation on Earth. Our workers are no less productive than when this crisis began. Our minds are no less inventive, our goods and services no less needed than they were last week, or last month, or last year. Our capacity remains undiminished. But our time of standing pat, of protecting narrow interests and putting off unpleasant decisions—that time has surely passed. Starting today, we must pick ourselves up, dust ourselves off, and begin again the work of remaking America. (*Applause*)

For everywhere we look, there is work to be done. The state of our economy calls for action, bold and swift. And we will act, not only to create new jobs, but to lay a new foundation for growth. We will build the roads and bridges, the electric grids and digital lines that feed our commerce and bind us together. We'll restore science to its rightful place, and wield technology's wonders to raise health care's quality and lower its cost. We will harness the sun and the winds and the soil to fuel our cars and run our factories. And we will transform our schools and colleges and universities to meet the demands of a new age. All this we can do. All this we will do.

Now, there are some who question the scale of our ambitions, who suggest that our system cannot tolerate too many big plans. Their memories are short, for they have forgotten what this country has already done, what free men and women can achieve when imagination is joined to common purpose, and necessity to courage. What the cynics fail to understand is that the ground has shifted beneath them, that the stale political arguments that have consumed us for so long no longer apply.

The question we ask today is not whether our government is too big or too small, but whether it works—whether it helps families find jobs at a decent wage, care they can afford, a retirement that is dignified. Where the answer is yes, we intend to move forward. Where the answer is no, programs will end. And those of us who manage the public's dollars will be held to account, to spend wisely, reform bad habits, and do our business in the light of day, because only then can we restore the vital trust between a people and their government.

Nor is the question before us whether the market is a force for good or ill. Its power to generate wealth and expand freedom is unmatched. But this crisis has reminded us that without a watchful eye, the market can spin out of control. The nation cannot prosper long when it favors only the prosperous. The success of our economy has always depended not just on the size of our gross domestic product, but on the reach of our prosperity, on the ability to extend opportunity to every willing heart—not out of charity, but because it is the surest route to our common good. (*Applause*)

As for our common defense, we reject as false the choice between our safety and our ideals. Our Founding Fathers—(*applause*)—our Founding Fathers, faced with perils that we can scarcely imagine, drafted a charter to assure the rule of law and the rights of man—a charter expanded by the blood of generations. Those ideals still light the world, and we will not give them up for expedience sake. (*Applause*)

And so, to all the other peoples and governments who are watching today, from the grandest capitals to the small village where my father was born, know that America is a friend of each nation, and every man, woman and child who seeks a future of peace and dignity. And we are ready to lead once more. (*Applause*)

Recall that earlier generations faced down fascism and communism not just with missiles and tanks, but

with the sturdy alliances and enduring convictions. They understood that our power alone cannot protect us, nor does it entitle us to do as we please. Instead they knew that our power grows through its prudent use; our security emanates from the justness of our cause, the force of our example, the tempering qualities of humility and restraint.

We are the keepers of this legacy. Guided by these principles once more we can meet those new threats that demand even greater effort, even greater cooperation and understanding between nations. We will begin to responsibly leave Iraq to its people and forge a hard-earned peace in Afghanistan. With old friends and former foes, we'll work tirelessly to lessen the nuclear threat, and roll back the specter of a warming planet.

We will not apologize for our way of life, nor will we waver in its defense. And for those who seek to advance their aims by inducing terror and slaughtering innocents, we say to you now that our spirit is stronger and cannot be broken—you cannot outlast us, and we will defeat you. (*Applause*)

For we know that our patchwork heritage is a strength, not a weakness. We are a nation of Christians and Muslims, Jews and Hindus, and non-believers. We are shaped by every language and culture, drawn from every end of this Earth: and because we have tasted the bitter swill of civil war and segregation, and emerged from that dark chapter stronger and more united, we cannot help but believe that the old hatreds shall someday pass; that the lines of tribe shall soon dissolve; that as the world grows smaller, our common humanity shall reveal itself; and that America must play its role in ushering in a new era of peace.

To the Muslim world, we seek a new way forward, based on mutual interest and mutual respect. To those leaders around the globe who seek to sow conflict, or blame their society's ills on the West, know that your people will judge you on what you can build, not what you destroy. (*Applause*)

To those who cling to power through corruption and deceit and the silencing of dissent, know that you are on the wrong side of history, but that we will extend a hand if you are willing to unclench your fist. (*Applause*)

To the people of poor nations, we pledge to work alongside you to make your farms flourish and let clean waters flow; to nourish starved bodies and feed hungry minds. And to those nations like ours that enjoy relative plenty, we say we can no longer afford indifference to the suffering outside our borders, nor can we consume the world's resources without regard to effect. For the world has changed, and we must change with it.

As we consider the role that unfolds before us, we remember with humble gratitude those brave Americans who at this very hour patrol far-off deserts and distant mountains. They have something to tell us, just as the fallen heroes who lie in Arlington whisper through the ages.

We honor them not only because they are the guardians of our liberty, but because they embody the spirit of service—a willingness to find meaning in something greater than themselves.

And yet at this moment, a moment that will define a generation, it is precisely this spirit that must inhabit us all. For as much as government can do, and must do, it is ultimately the faith and determination of the American people upon which this nation relies. It is the kindness to take in a stranger when the levees break, the selflessness of workers who would rather cut their hours than see a friend lose their job which sees us through our darkest hours. It is the firefighter's courage to storm a stairway filled with smoke, but also a parent's willingness to nurture a child that finally decides our fate.

Our challenges may be new. The instruments with which we meet them may be new. But those values upon which our success depends—honesty and hard work, courage and fair play, tolerance and curiosity, loyalty and patriotism—these things are old. These things are true. They have been the quiet force of progress throughout our history.

What is demanded, then, is a return to these truths. What is required of us now is a new era of responsibility—a recognition on the part of every American that we have duties to ourselves, our nation and the world; duties that we do not grudgingly accept, but rather seize gladly, firm in the knowledge that there is nothing so satisfying to the spirit, so defining of our character than giving our all to a difficult task.

This is the price and the promise of citizenship. This is the source of our confidence—the knowledge that God calls on us to shape an uncertain destiny. This is the meaning of our liberty and our creed, why men and women and children of every race and every faith can join in celebration across this magnificent mall; and why a man whose father less than 60 years ago might not have been served in a local restaurant can now stand before you to take a most sacred oath. (*Applause*)

So let us mark this day with remembrance of who we are and how far we have traveled. In the year of America's birth, in the coldest of months, a small band of patriots huddled by dying campfires on the shores of an icy river. The capital was abandoned. The enemy was advancing. The snow was stained with blood. At the moment when the outcome of our revolution was most in doubt, the father of our nation ordered these words to be read to the people:

"Let it be told to the future world…that in the depth of winter, when nothing but hope and virtue could survive… that the city and the country, alarmed at one common danger, came forth to meet [it]."

America: In the face of our common dangers, in this winter of our hardship, let us remember these timeless words. With hope and virtue, let us brave once more the icy currents, and endure what storms may come. Let it be said by our children's children that when we were tested we refused to let this journey end, that we did not turn back nor did we falter; and with eyes fixed on the horizon and God's grace upon us, we carried forth that great gift of freedom and delivered it safely to future generations.

Thank you. God bless you. And God bless the United States of America. (*Applause*)

PRESIDENTIAL ELECTIONS

Year	Number of States	Candidates	Parties	Popular Vote	% of Popular Vote	Electoral Vote	% Voter Participation
1789	11	**GEORGE WASHINGTON**	NO PARTY			69	
		John Adams	DESIGNATIONS			34	
		Other candidates				35	
1792	15	**GEORGE WASHINGTON**	NO PARTY			132	
		John Adams	DESIGNATIONS			77	
		George Clinton				50	
		Other candidates				5	
1796	16	**JOHN ADAMS**	FEDERALIST			71	
		Thomas Jefferson	Republican			68	
		Thomas Pinckney	Federalist			59	
		Aaron Burr	Republican			30	
		Other candidates				48	
1800	16	**THOMAS JEFFERSON**	REPUBLICAN			73	
		Aaron Burr	Republican			73	
		John Adams	Federalist			65	
		Charles C. Pinckney	Federalist			64	
		John Jay	Federalist			1	
1804	17	**THOMAS JEFFERSON**	REPUBLICAN			162	
		Charles C. Pinckney	Federalist			14	
1808	17	**JAMES MADISON**	REPUBLICAN			122	
		Charles C. Pinckney	Federalist			47	
		George Clinton	Republican			6	
1812	18	**JAMES MADISON**	REPUBLICAN			128	
		DeWitt Clinton	Federalist			89	

Year	Number of States	Candidates	Parties	Popular Vote	% of Popular Vote	Electoral Vote	% Voter Participation
1816	19	**JAMES MONROE**	REPUBLICAN			183	
		Rufus King	Federalist			34	
1820	24	**JAMES MONROE**	REPUBLICAN			231	
		John Quincy Adams	Independent			1	
1824	24	**JOHN QUINCY ADAMS**	NO PARTY	108,740	31.0	84	26.9
		Andrew Jackson	DESIGNATIONS	153,544	43.0	99	
		William H. Crawford		46,618	13.0	41	
		Henry Clay		47,136	13.0	37	
1828	24	**ANDREW JACKSON**	DEMOCRAT	647,286	56.0	178	57.6
		John Quincy Adams	National Republican	508,064	44.0	83	
1832	24	**ANDREW JACKSON**	DEMOCRAT	687,502	54.5	219	55.4
		Henry Clay	National Republican	530,189	37.5	49	
		William Wirt	Anti-Masonic	101,051	8.0	7	
		John Floyd	Democrat			11	
1836	26	**MARTIN VAN BUREN**	DEMOCRAT	765,483	51.0	170	57.8
		William H. Harrison	Whig			73	
		Hugh L. White	Whig	739,795	49.0	26	
		Daniel Webster	Whig			14	
		William P. Mangum	Whig			11	
1840	26	**WILLIAM H. HARRISON**	WHIG	1,274,624	53.0	234	80.2
		Martin Van Buren	Democrat	1,127,781	47.0	60	

Year	Number of States	Candidates	Parties	Popular Vote	% of Popular Vote	Electoral Vote	% Voter Participation
1844	26	**JAMES K. POLK**	DEMOCRAT	1,338,464	50.0	170	78.9
		Henry Clay	Whig	1,300,097	48.0	105	
		James G. Birney	Liberty	62,300	2.0		
1848	30	**ZACHARY TAYLOR**	WHIG	1,360,967	47.5	163	72.7
		Lewis Cass	Democrat	1,222,342	42.5	127	
		Martin Van Buren	Free Soil	291,263	10.0		
1852	31	**FRANKLIN PIERCE**	DEMOCRAT	1,601,117	51.0	254	69.6
		Winfield Scott	Whig	1,385,453	44.0	42	
		John P. Hale	Free Soil	155,825	5.0		
1856	31	**JAMES BUCHANAN**	DEMOCRAT	1,832,955	45.0	174	78.9
		John C. Frémont	Republican	1,339,932	33.0	114	
		Millard Fillmore	American	871,731	22.0	8	
1860	33	**ABRAHAM LINCOLN**	REPUBLICAN	1,865,593	40.0	180	81.2
		Stephen A. Douglas	Northern Democrat	1,382,713	29.0	12	
		John C. Breckinridge	Southern Democrat	848,356	18.0	72	
		John Bell	Constitutional Union	592,906	13.0	39	
1864	36	**ABRAHAM LINCOLN**	REPUBLICAN	2,206,938	55.0	212	73.8
		George B. McClellan	Democrat	1,803,787	45.0	21	
1868	37	**ULYSSES S. GRANT**	REPUBLICAN	3,013,421	53.0	214	78.1
		Horatio Seymour	Democrat	2,706,829	47.0	80	

Year	Number of States	Candidates	Parties	Popular Vote	% of Popular Vote	Electoral Vote	% Voter Participation
1872	37	**ULYSSES S. GRANT**	REPUBLICAN	3,596,745	55.6	286	71.3
		Horace Greeley	Democrat	2,843,446	43.9	66	
1876	38	**RUTHERFORD B. HAYES**	REPUBLICAN	4,036,572	48.0	185	81.8
		Samuel J. Tilden	Democrat	4,284,020	51.0	184	
1880	38	**JAMES A. GARFIELD**	REPUBLICAN	4,453,295	48.4	214	79.4
		Winfield S. Hancock	Democrat	4,414,082	48.3	155	
		James B. Weaver	Greenback-Labor	308,578	3.5		
1884	38	**GROVER CLEVELAND**	DEMOCRAT	4,879,507	48.5	219	77.5
		James G. Blaine	Republican	4,850,293	48.2	182	
		Benjamin F. Butler	Greenback-Labor	175,370	1.8		
		John P. St. John	Prohibition	150,369	1.5		
1888	38	**BENJAMIN HARRISON**	REPUBLICAN	5,447,129	47.9	233	79.3
		Grover Cleveland	Democrat	5,537,857	48.6	168	
		Clinton B. Fisk	Prohibition	249,506	2.2		
		Anson J. Streeter	Union Labor	146,935	1.3		
1892	44	**GROVER CLEVELAND**	DEMOCRAT	5,555,426	46.1	277	74.7
		Benjamin Harrison	Republican	5,182,690	43.0	145	
		James B. Weaver	People's	1,029,846	8.5	22	
		John Bidwell	Prohibition	264,133	2.2		
1896	45	**WILLIAM McKINLEY**	REPUBLICAN	7,102,246	51.0	271	79.3
		William J. Bryan	Democrat	6,492,559	47.0	176	

Year	Number of States	Candidates	Parties	Popular Vote	% of Popular Vote	Electoral Vote	% Voter Participation
1900	45	**WILLIAM McKINLEY**	REPUBLICAN	7,218,491	52.0	292	73.2
		William J. Bryan	Democrat; Populist	6,356,734	46.0	155	
		John C. Wooley	Prohibition	208,914	1.5		
1904	45	**THEODORE ROOSEVELT**	REPUBLICAN	7,628,461	56.4	336	65.2
		Alton B. Parker	Democrat	5,084,223	37.6	140	
		Eugene V. Debs	Socialist	402,283	3.0		
		Silas C. Swallow	Prohibition	258,536	1.9		
1908	46	**WILLIAM H. TAFT**	REPUBLICAN	7,675,320	52.0	321	65.4
		William J. Bryan	Democrat	6,412,294	43.4	162	
		Eugene V. Debs	Socialist	420,793	2.8		
		Eugene W. Chafin	Prohibition	253,840	1.7		
1912	48	**WOODROW WILSON**	DEMOCRAT	6,296,547	41.9	435	58.8
		Theodore Roosevelt	Progressive	4,118,571	27.4	88	
		William H. Taft	Republican	3,486,720	23.2	8	
		Eugene V. Debs	Socialist	900,672	6.0		
		Eugene W. Chafin	Prohibition	206,275	1.4		
1916	48	**WOODROW WILSON**	DEMOCRAT	9,127,695	49.4	277	61.6
		Charles E. Hughes	Republican	8,533,507	46.2	254	
		A. L. Benson	Socialist	585,113	3.2		
		J. Frank Hanly	Prohibition	220,506	1.2		
1920	48	**WARREN G. HARDING**	REPUBLICAN	16,153,115	60.6	404	49.2
		James M. Cox	Democrat	9,133,092	34.3	127	
		Eugene V. Debs	Socialist	915,490	3.4		
		P. P. Christensen	Farmer-Labor	265,229	1.0		
1924	48	**CALVIN COOLIDGE**	REPUBLICAN	15,719,921	54.0	382	48.9
		John W. Davis	Democrat	8,386,704	29.0	136	
		Robert M. La Follette	Progressive	4,832,532	16.5	13	

Year	Number of States	Candidates	Parties	Popular Vote	% of Popular Vote	Electoral Vote	% Voter Participation
1928	48	**HERBERT C. HOOVER**	REPUBLICAN	21,437,277	58.2	444	56.9
		Alfred E. Smith	Democrat	15,007,698	40.9	87	
1932	48	**FRANKLIN D. ROOSEVELT**	DEMOCRAT	22,829,501	57.7	472	56.9
		Herbert C. Hoover	Republican	15,760,684	39.8	59	
		Norman Thomas	Socialist	884,649	2.2		
1936	48	**FRANKLIN D. ROOSEVELT**	DEMOCRAT	27,757,333	60.8	523	61.0
		Alfred M. Landon	Republican	16,684,231	36.6	8	
		William Lemke	Union	892,267	2.0		
1940	48	**FRANKLIN D. ROOSEVELT**	DEMOCRAT	27,313,041	54.9	449	62.5
		Wendell L. Willkie	Republican	22,348,480	44.9	82	
1944	48	**FRANKLIN D. ROOSEVELT**	DEMOCRAT	25,612,610	53.5	432	55.9
		Thomas E. Dewey	Republican	22,017,617	46.0	99	
1948	48	**HARRY S. TRUMAN**	DEMOCRAT	24,179,345	49.7	303	53.0
		Thomas E. Dewey	Republican	21,991,291	45.3	189	
		J. Strom Thurmond	States' Rights	1,176,125	2.4	39	
		Henry A. Wallace	Progressive	1,157,326	2.4		
1952	48	**DWIGHT D. EISENHOWER**	REPUBLICAN	33,936,234	55.1	442	63.3
		Adlai E. Stevenson	Democrat	27,314,992	44.4	89	

Year	Number of States	Candidates	Parties	Popular Vote	% of Popular Vote	Electoral Vote	% Voter Participation
1956	48	**DWIGHT D. EISENHOWER**	REPUBLICAN	35,590,472	57.6	457	60.6
		Adlai E. Stevenson	Democrat	26,022,752	42.1	73	
1960	50	**JOHN F. KENNEDY**	DEMOCRAT	34,226,731	49.7	303	62.8
		Richard M. Nixon	Republican	34,108,157	49.6	219	
1964	50	**LYNDON B. JOHNSON**	DEMOCRAT	43,129,566	61.0	486	61.9
		Barry M. Goldwater	Republican	27,178,188	38.4	52	
1968	50	**RICHARD M. NIXON**	REPUBLICAN	31,785,480	43.2	301	60.9
		Hubert H. Humphrey	Democrat	31,275,166	42.6	191	
		George C. Wallace	American Independent	9,906,473	12.9	46	
1972	50	**RICHARD M. NIXON**	REPUBLICAN	47,169,911	60.7	520	55.2
		George S. McGovern	Democrat	29,170,383	37.5	17	
		John G. Schmitz	American	1,099,482	1.4		
1976	50	**JIMMY CARTER**	DEMOCRAT	40,830,763	50.0	297	53.5
		Gerald R. Ford	Republican	39,147,793	48.0	240	
1980	50	**RONALD REAGAN**	REPUBLICAN	43,904,153	50.9	489	52.6
		Jimmy Carter	Democrat	35,483,883	41.1	49	
		John B. Anderson	Independent	5,720,060	6.6		
		Ed Clark	Libertarian	921,299	1.1		

Year	Number of States	Candidates	Parties	Popular Vote	% of Popular Vote	Electoral Vote	% Voter Participation
1984	50	**RONALD REAGAN**	REPUBLICAN	54,455,075	58.8	525	53.1
		Walter F. Mondale	Democrat	37,577,185	40.5	13	
1988	50	**GEORGE H. BUSH**	REPUBLICAN	48,886,097	53.4	426	50.1
		Michael Dukakis	Democrat	41,809,074	45.6	111	
1992	50	**BILL CLINTON**	DEMOCRAT	44,909,326	42.9	370	55.0
		George H. Bush	Republican	39,103,882	37.4	168	
		H. Ross Perot	Independent	19,741,657	18.9		
1996	50	**BILL CLINTON**	DEMOCRAT	47,402,357	49.2	379	49.0
		Bob Dole	Republican	39,198,755	40.7	159	
		H. Ross Perot	Reform Party	8,085,402	8.4		
2000	50	**GEORGE W. BUSH**	REPUBLICAN	50,455,156	47.9	271	50.4
		Albert Gore	Democrat	50,992,335	48.4	266	
		Ralph Nader	Green Party	2,882,738	2.7		
2004	50	**GEORGE W. BUSH**	REPUBLICAN	62,040,610	50.7	286	56.2
		John F. Kerry	Democrat	59,028,111	48.3	251	
2008	50	**BARACK H. OBAMA**	DEMOCRAT	66,882,230	52.9	365	56.8
		John S. McCain	Republican	58,343,671	45.7	173	
2012	50	**BARACK H. OBAMA**	DEMOCRAT	62,611,250	57.1	332	53.6
		W. Mitt Romney	Republican	59,134,475	47.2	206	

Candidates receiving less than 1 percent of the popular vote have been omitted. Thus, the percentage of popular vote given for any election year may not total 100 percent.

Before the passage of the Twelfth Amendment in 1804, the electoral college voted for two presidential candidates; the runner-up became vice president.

ADMISSION OF STATES

Order of Admission	State	Date of Admission	Order of Admission	State	Date of Admission
1	Delaware	December 7, 1787	26	Michigan	January 26, 1837
2	Pennsylvania	December 12, 1787	27	Florida	March 3, 1845
3	New Jersey	December 18, 1787	28	Texas	December 29, 1845
4	Georgia	January 2, 1788	29	Iowa	December 28, 1846
5	Connecticut	January 9, 1788	30	Wisconsin	May 29, 1848
6	Massachusetts	February 7, 1788	31	California	September 9, 1850
7	Maryland	April 28, 1788	32	Minnesota	May 11, 1858
8	South Carolina	May 23, 1788	33	Oregon	February 14, 1859
9	New Hampshire	June 21, 1788	34	Kansas	January 29, 1861
10	Virginia	June 25, 1788	35	West Virginia	June 30, 1863
11	New York	July 26, 1788	36	Nevada	October 31, 1864
12	North Carolina	November 21, 1789	37	Nebraska	March 1, 1867
13	Rhode Island	May 29, 1790	38	Colorado	August 1, 1876
14	Vermont	March 4, 1791	39	North Dakota	November 2, 1889
15	Kentucky	June 1, 1792	40	South Dakota	November 2, 1889
16	Tennessee	June 1, 1796	41	Montana	November 8, 1889
17	Ohio	March 1, 1803	42	Washington	November 11, 1889
18	Louisiana	April 30, 1812	43	Idaho	July 3, 1890
19	Indiana	December 11, 1816	44	Wyoming	July 10, 1890
20	Mississippi	December 10, 1817	45	Utah	January 4, 1896
21	Illinois	December 3, 1818	46	Oklahoma	November 16, 1907
22	Alabama	December 14, 1819	47	New Mexico	January 6, 1912
23	Maine	March 15, 1820	48	Arizona	February 14, 1912
24	Missouri	August 10, 1821	49	Alaska	January 3, 1959
25	Arkansas	June 15, 1836	50	Hawaii	August 21, 1959

POPULATION OF THE UNITED STATES

Year	Number of States	Population	% Increase	Population per Square Mile
1790	13	3,929,214		4.5
1800	16	5,308,483	35.1	6.1
1810	17	7,239,881	36.4	4.3
1820	23	9,638,453	33.1	5.5
1830	24	12,866,020	33.5	7.4
1840	26	17,069,453	32.7	9.8
1850	31	23,191,876	35.9	7.9
1860	33	31,443,321	35.6	10.6
1870	37	39,818,449	26.6	13.4
1880	38	50,155,783	26.0	16.9
1890	44	62,947,714	25.5	21.1
1900	45	75,994,575	20.7	25.6
1910	46	91,972,266	21.0	31.0
1920	48	105,710,620	14.9	35.6
1930	48	122,775,046	16.1	41.2
1940	48	131,669,275	7.2	44.2
1950	48	150,697,361	14.5	50.7
1960	50	179,323,175	19.0	50.6
1970	50	203,235,298	13.3	57.5
1980	50	226,504,825	11.4	64.0
1985	50	237,839,000	5.0	67.2
1990	50	250,122,000	5.2	70.6
1995	50	263,411,707	5.3	74.4
2000	50	281,421,906	6.8	77.0
2005	50	296,410,404	5.3	81.7
2010	50	308,745,538	4.2	87.4
2015	50	321,418,820	4.1	91.0

LABOR FORCE—SELECTED CHARACTERISTICS EXPRESSED AS A PERCENTAGE OF THE LABOR FORCE, 1800–2010

Year	Agriculture	Manufacturing	Domestic service	Clerical, sales, and service	Professions	Slave	Nonwhite	Foreign-born	Female
1800	74.4	—	2.4	—	—	30.2	32.6	—	21.4
1860	55.8	13.8	5.4	4.8[1]	3.0[1]	21.7	23.6	24.5[1]	19.6
1910	30.7	20.8	5.5	14.1	4.7	—	13.4	22.0	20.8
1950	12.0	26.4	2.5	27.3	8.9	—	10.0	8.7	27.9
2000	2.4	14.7	0.6	38.0[2]	15.6	—	16.5	10.3[2]	46.6
2010	1.6	10.1	1.6	40.2	22.2	—	18.7	15.8	46.7

[1]Values for 1870 are presented here because the available data for 1860 exclude slaves.
[2]1990.
Note: "Clerical, sales, and service" excludes domestic service.

IMMIGRATION, BY ORIGIN (in thousands)

Period	Europe	Americas	Asia
1820–30	106	12	—
1831–40	496	33	—
1841–50	1,597	62	—
1851–60	2,453	75	42
1861–70	2,065	167	65
1871–80	2,272	404	70
1881–90	4,735	427	70
1891–1900	3,555	39	75
1901–10	8,065	362	324
1911–20	4,322	1,144	247
1921–30	2,463	1,517	112
1931–40	348	160	16
1941–50	621	355	32
1951–60	1,326	997	150
1961–70	1,123	1,716	590
1971–80	800	1,983	1,588
1981–90	762	3,616	2,738
1991–2000	1,360	4,487	2,796
2001–10	1,318	4,478	3,621

UNEMPLOYMENT RATE, 1890–2015

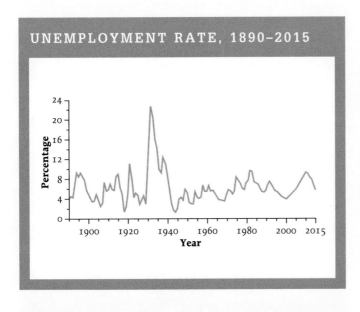

UNION MEMBERSHIP AS A PERCENTAGE OF NONAGRICULTURAL EMPLOYMENT, 1880–2015

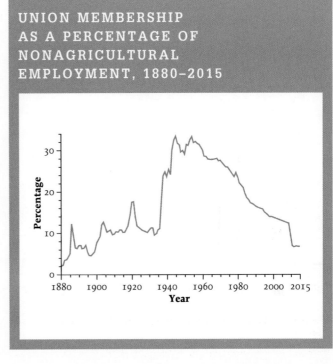

VOTER PARTICIPATION IN PRESIDENTIAL ELECTIONS, 1824–2012

BIRTHRATE, 1820–2015

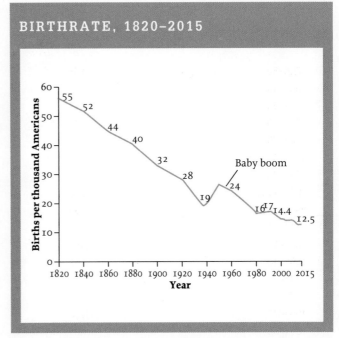

GLOSSARY

abolition Social movement of the pre–Civil War era that advocated the immediate emancipation of the slaves and their incorporation into American society as equal citizens.

Act Concerning Religion (or Maryland Toleration Act) 1649 law that granted free exercise of religion to all Christian denominations in colonial Maryland.

Adkins v. Children's Hospital 1923 Supreme Court case that reversed *Muller v. Oregon*, the 1908 case that permitted states to set maximum hours to protect working women. Justices ruled in *Adkins* that women no longer deserved special treatment because they could vote.

affirmative action Policy efforts to promote greater employment opportunities for minorities.

Agricultural Adjustment Act New Deal legislation passed in 1933 that established the Agricultural Adjustment Administration (AAA) to improve agricultural prices by limiting market supplies; declared unconstitutional in *United States v. Butler* (1936).

Albany Plan of Union A failed 1754 proposal by the seven northern colonies in anticipation of the French and Indian War, urging the unification of the colonies under one crown-appointed president.

Alien and Sedition Acts Four measures passed in 1798 during the undeclared war with France that limited the freedoms of speech and press and restricted the liberty of noncitizens.

American Anti-Slavery Society Founded in 1833, the organization that sought an immediate end to slavery and the establishment of equality for black Americans. It split in 1840 after disputes about the role of women within the organization and other issues.

American Civil Liberties Union Organization founded during World War I to protest the suppression of freedom of expression in wartime; played a major role in court cases that achieved judicial recognition of Americans' civil liberties.

American Colonization Society Organized in 1816 to encourage colonization of free blacks to Africa; West African nation of Liberia founded in 1822 to serve as a homeland for them.

American exceptionalism The belief that the United States has a special mission to serve as a refuge from tyranny, a symbol of freedom, and a model for the rest of the world.

American Federation of Labor A federation of trade unions founded in 1881, composed mostly of skilled, white, native-born workers; its long-term president was Samuel Gompers.

American Indian Movement (AIM) Movement founded in 1963 by Native Americans who were fed up with the poor conditions on Indian reservations and the federal government's unwillingness to help. In 1973, AIM led 200 Sioux in the occupation of Wounded Knee. After a ten-week standoff with the federal authorities, the government agreed to reexamine Indian treaty rights and the occupation ended.

"American standard of living" The Progressive-era idea that American workers were entitled to a wage high enough to allow them full participation in the nation's mass consumption economy.

American System Program of internal improvements and protective tariffs promoted by Speaker of the House Henry Clay in his presidential campaign of 1824; his proposals formed the core of Whig ideology in the 1830s and 1840s.

American system of manufactures A system of production that relied on the mass production of interchangeable parts that could be rapidly assembled into standardized finished products. First perfected in Connecticut by clockmaker Eli Terry and by small-arms producer Eli Whitney in the 1840s and 50s.

Americans with Disabilities Act 1990 law that prohibited the discrimination against persons with disabilities in both hiring and promotion. It also mandated accessible entrances for public buildings.

the *Amistad* Ship that transported slaves from one port in Cuba to another, seized by the slaves in 1839. They made their way northward to the United States, where the status of the slaves became the subject of a celebrated court case; eventually most were able to return to Africa.

Anglican Church The established state church of England, formed by Henry VII after the pope refused to annul his marriage to Catherine of Aragon.

annuity system System of yearly payments to Native American tribes by which the federal government justified and institutionalized its interference in Indian tribal affairs.

Antietam, Battle of One of the bloodiest battles of the Civil War, fought to a standoff on September 17, 1862, in western Maryland.

Anti-Federalists Opponents of the Constitution who saw it as a limitation on individual and states' rights; their demands led to the addition of a Bill of Rights to the document.

Anti-Imperialist League Coalition of anti-imperialist groups united in 1899 to protest American territorial expansion, especially in the Philippine Islands; its membership included prominent politicians, industrialists, labor leaders, and social reformers.

Appomattox Courthouse, Virginia Site of the surrender of Confederate general Robert E. Lee to Union general Ulysses S. Grant on April 9, 1865, marking the end of the Civil War.

Army-McCarthy hearings Televised U.S. Senate hearings in 1954 on Senator Joseph McCarthy's charges of disloyalty in the army; his tactics contributed to his censure by the Senate.

Arnold, Benedict A traitorous American commander who planned to sell out the American garrison at West Point to the British. His plot was discovered before it could be executed and he joined the British army.

Articles of Confederation First frame of government for the United States; in effect from 1781 to 1788, it provided for a weak central authority and was soon replaced by the Constitution.

Atlanta Compromise Speech to the Cotton States and International Exposition in 1895 by educator Booker T. Washington, the leading black spokesman of the day; black

scholar W. E. B. Du Bois gave the speech its derisive name and criticized Washington for encouraging blacks to accommodate segregation and disenfranchisement.

Atlantic Charter Agreement issued August 12, 1941, following meetings in Newfoundland between President Franklin D. Roosevelt and British Prime Minister Winston Churchill, that signaled the Allies' cooperation and stated their war aims.

Atlantic slave trade The systematic importation of African slaves from their native continent across the Atlantic Ocean to the New World, largely fueled by rising demand for sugar, rice, coffee, and tobacco.

Attucks, Crispus During the Boston Massacre, the individual who was supposedly at the head of the crowd of hecklers and who baited the British troops. He was killed when the British troops fired on the crowd.

Axis powers In World War II, the nations of Germany, Italy, and Japan.

Aztec Mesoamerican people who were conquered by the Spanish under Hernan Cortes, 1519–1528.

baby boom Markedly higher birthrate in the years following World War II; led to the biggest demographic "bubble" in American history.

backcountry In colonial America, the area stretching from central Pennsylvania southward through the Shenandoah Valley of Virginia and into upland North and South Carolina.

Bacon's Rebellion Unsuccessful 1676 revolt led by planter Nathaniel Bacon against Virginia governor William Berkeley's administration because of governmental corruption and because Berkeley had failed to protect settlers from Indian raids and did not allow them to occupy Indian lands.

Balkan crisis A series of ethnic and political crises that arose following the dissolution of Yugoslavia in the 1990s. Many atrocities were committed during the conflict, and NATO, the United Nations, and the United States intervened several times.

Bank of the United States Proposed by the first secretary of the treasury, Alexander Hamilton, the bank that opened in 1791 and operated until 1811 to issue a uniform currency, make business loans, and collect tax monies. The Second Bank of the United States was chartered in 1816 but President Andrew Jackson vetoed the recharter bill in 1832.

Bank War Political struggle in the early 1830s between President Jackson and financier Nicholas Biddle over the renewing of the Second Bank's charter.

Barbary Wars The first wars fought by the United States, and the nation's first encounter with the Islamic world. The wars were fought from 1801 to 1805 against plundering pirates off the Mediterranean coast of Africa after President Thomas Jefferson's refusal to pay them tribute to protect American ships.

Bargain of 1877 Deal made by a Republican and Democratic special congressional commission to resolve the disputed presidential election of 1876; Republican Rutherford B. Hayes, who had lost the popular vote, was declared the winner in exchange for the withdrawal of federal troops from involvement in politics in the South, marking the end of Reconstruction.

Bay of Pigs Invasion U.S. mission in which the CIA, hoping to inspire a revolt against Fidel Castro, sent 1,500 Cuban exiles to invade their homeland on April 17, 1961; the mission was a spectacular failure.

the Beats A term coined by Jack Kerouac for a small group of poets and writers who railed against 1950s mainstream culture.

Bill for Establishing Religious Freedom A Virginia law, drafted by Thomas Jefferson in 1777 and enacted in 1786, that guarantees freedom of, and from, religion.

Bill of Rights First ten amendments to the U.S. Constitution, adopted in 1791 to guarantee individual rights against infringement by the federal government.

birth control movement An offshoot of the early twentieth-century feminist movement that saw access to birth control and "voluntary motherhood" as essential to women's freedom. The birth-control movement was led by Margaret Sanger.

Black Codes Laws passed from 1865 to 1866 in southern states to restrict the rights of former slaves; to nullify the codes, Congress passed the Civil Rights Act of 1866 and the Fourteenth Amendment.

Black Legend Idea that the Spanish New World empire was more oppressive toward the Indians than other European empires; was used as a justification for English imperial expansion.

Black Lives Matter Civil rights movement sparked by a series of incidents of police brutality and lethal force against people of color.

Black Power Post-1966 rallying cry of a more militant civil rights movement.

"Bleeding Kansas" Violence between pro- and antislavery settlers in the Kansas Territory, 1856.

bonanza farms Large farms that covered thousands of acres and employed hundreds of wage laborers in the West in the late nineteenth century.

borderland A place between or near recognized borders where no group of people has complete political control or cultural dominance.

Boston Massacre Clash between British soldiers and a Boston mob, March 5, 1770, in which five colonists were killed.

Boston Tea Party The incident on December 16, 1773, in which the Sons of Liberty, dressed as Indians, dumped hundreds of chests of tea into Boston Harbor to protest the Tea Act of 1773. Under the Tea Act, the British exported to the colonies millions of pounds of cheap—but still taxed—tea, thereby undercutting the price of smuggled tea and forcing payment of the tea duty.

***bracero* program** System agreed to by Mexican and American governments in 1942 under which tens of thousands of Mexicans entered the United States to work temporarily in agricultural jobs in the Southwest; lasted until 1964 and inhibited labor organization among farm workers since *braceros* could be deported at any time.

Brant, Joseph The Mohawk leader who led the Iroquois against the Americans in the Revolutionary War.

Bretton Woods conference International meeting held in the town of Bretton Woods, New Hampshire, in 1944 in which participants agreed that the American dollar would replace the British pound as the most important international currency. The conference also created the World Bank and International Monetary Fund to promote rebuilding after

World War II and to ensure that countries did not devalue their currencies.

Brook Farm Transcendentalist commune in West Roxbury, Massachusetts, populated from 1841 to 1847 principally by writers (Nathaniel Hawthorne, for one) and other intellectuals.

Brown v. Board of Education 1954 U.S. Supreme Court decision that struck down racial segregation in public education and declared "separate but equal" unconstitutional.

Bull Run, first Battle of The first land engagement of the Civil War which took place on July 21, 1861, at Manassas Junction, Virginia, and at which Union troops quickly retreated.

Bull Run, second Battle of Civil War engagement that took place one year after the first Battle of Bull Run, on August 29–30, during which Confederates captured the federal supply depot at Manassas Junction, Virginia, and forced Union troops back to Washington.

Bunker Hill, Battle of First major battle of the Revolutionary War; it actually took place at nearby Breed's Hill, Massachusetts, on June 17, 1775.

the Bush Doctrine President George W. Bush's foreign policy principle wherein the United States would launch a war on terrorism.

Bush v. Gore U.S. Supreme Court case that determined the winner of the disputed 2000 presidential election.

busing The means of transporting students via buses to achieve school integration in the 1970s.

Camp David Accords Peace agreement between the leaders of Israel and Egypt, brokered by President Jimmy Carter in 1978.

captivity narratives Accounts written by colonists after their time in Indian captivity, often stressing the captive's religious convictions.

caravel A fifteenth-century European ship capable of long-distance travel.

carpetbaggers Derisive term for northern emigrants who participated in the Republican governments of the Reconstruction South.

checks and balances A systematic balance to prevent any one branch of the national government from dominating the other two.

Chinese Exclusion Act 1882 law that halted Chinese immigration to the United States.

Church of Jesus Christ of Latter-Day Saints Religious sect founded in 1830 by Joseph Smith; it was a product of the intense revivalism of the "burned-over district" of New York. Smith's successor Brigham Young led 15,000 followers to Utah in 1847 to escape persecution.

Civil Rights Act (1964) Law that outlawed discrimination in public accommodations and employment.

Civil Rights Act of 1875 The last piece of Reconstruction legislation, which outlawed racial discrimination in places of public accommodation such as hotels and theaters. Many parts of it were ruled unconstitutional by the Supreme Court in 1883.

Civil Rights Bill of 1866 Along with the Fourteenth Amendment, legislation that guaranteed the rights of citizenship to former slaves.

Civil Service Act of 1883 Law that established the Civil Service Commission and marked the end of the spoils system.

Civilian Conservation Corps (CCC) 1933 New Deal public work relief program that provided outdoor manual work for unemployed men, rebuilding infrastructure and implementing conservation programs. The program cut the unemployment rate, particularly among young men.

Cold War Term for tensions, 1945–1989, between the Soviet Union and the United States, the two major world powers after World War II.

collective bargaining The process of negotiations between an employer and a group of employees to regulate working conditions.

Columbian Exchange The transatlantic flow of goods and people that began with Columbus's voyages in 1492.

Committee of Correspondence Group organized by Samuel Adams in retaliation for the *Gaspée* incident to address American grievances, assert American rights, and form a network of rebellion.

common school Tax-supported state schools of the early nineteenth century open to all children.

Common Sense A pamphlet anonymously written by Thomas Paine in January 1776 that attacked the English principles of hereditary rule and monarchical government.

Commonwealth v. Hunt Landmark 1842 ruling of the Massachusetts Supreme Court establishing the legality of labor unions.

communitarianism Social reform movement of the nineteenth century driven by the belief that by establishing small communities based on common ownership of property, a less competitive and individualistic society could be developed.

Compromise of 1850 Complex compromise devised by Senator Henry Clay that admitted California as a free state, included a stronger fugitive slave law, and delayed determination of the slave status of the New Mexico and Utah territories.

Congress of Industrial Organizations Umbrella organization of semiskilled industrial unions, formed in 1935 as the Committee for Industrial Organization and renamed in 1938.

conquistadores Spanish term for "conquerors," applied to Spanish and Portuguese soldiers who conquered lands held by indigenous peoples in central and southern America as well as the current states of Texas, New Mexico, Arizona, and California.

conservation movement A progressive reform movement focused on the preservation and sustainable management of the nation's natural resources.

Constitutional Convention Meeting in Philadelphia, May 25–September 17, 1787, of representatives from twelve colonies—excepting Rhode Island—to revise the existing Articles of Confederation; the convention soon resolved to produce an entirely new constitution.

containment General U.S. strategy in the Cold War that called for containing Soviet expansion; originally devised by U.S. diplomat George F. Kennan.

Continental army Army authorized by the Continental Congress in 1775 to fight the British; commanded by General George Washington.

Continental Congress First meeting of representatives of the colonies, held in Philadelphia in 1774 to formulate actions against British policies; in the Second Continental Congress (1775–1789), the colonial representatives conducted the war and adopted the Declaration of Independence and the Articles of Confederation.

"the contrabands" Slaves who sought refuge in Union military camps or who lived in areas of the Confederacy under Union control.

Contract with America A list of conservatives' promises in response to the supposed liberalism of the Clinton administration, that was drafted by Speaker of the House Newt Gingrich and other congressional Republicans as the GOP platform for the 1994 midterm elections. It was more a campaign tactic than a practical program; few of its proposed items ever became law.

cotton gin Invented by Eli Whitney in 1793, the machine that separated cotton seed from cotton fiber, speeding cotton processing and making profitable the cultivation of the more hardy, but difficult to clean, short-staple cotton; led directly to the dramatic nineteenth-century expansion of slavery in the South.

"Cotton Is King" Phrase from Senator James Henry Hammond's speech extolling the virtues of cotton, and, implicitly, the slave system of production that led to its bounty for the South. "King Cotton" became a shorthand for Southern political and economic power.

Cotton Kingdom Cotton-producing region, relying predominantly on slave labor, that spanned from North Carolina west to Louisiana and reached as far north as southern Illinois.

counterculture "Hippie" youth culture of the 1960s, which rejected the values of the dominant culture in favor of illicit drugs, communes, free sex, and rock music.

Court packing President Franklin D. Roosevelt's failed 1937 attempt to increase the number of U.S. Supreme Court justices from nine to fifteen in order to save his Second New Deal programs from constitutional challenges.

Covenant Chain Alliance formed in the 1670s between the English and the Iroquois nations.

coverture Principle in English and American law that a married woman lost her legal identity, which became "covered" by that of her husband, who therefore controlled her person and the family's economic resources.

Coxey's Army A march on Washington organized by Jacob Coxey, an Ohio member of the People's Party. Coxey believed in abandoning the gold standard and printing enough legal tender to reinvigorate the economy. The marchers demanded that Congress create jobs and pay workers in paper currency not backed by gold.

creoles Persons born in the New World of European ancestry.

crop lien Credit extended by merchants to tenants based on their future crops; under this system, high interest rates and the uncertainties of farming often led to inescapable debts.

Cuban missile crisis Tense confrontation caused when the United States discovered Soviet offensive missile sites in Cuba in October 1962; the U.S.-Soviet confrontation was the Cold War's closest brush with nuclear war.

cult of domesticity The nineteenth-century ideology of "virtue" and "modesty" as the qualities that were essential to proper womanhood.

Culture Wars Battles over moral values that occurred throughout the 1990s. The Culture Wars touched many areas of American life—from popular culture to academia. Flashpoints included the future of the nuclear family and the teaching of evolution.

Dartmouth College v. Woodward 1819 U.S. Supreme Court case in which the Court upheld the original charter of the college against New Hampshire's attempt to alter the board of trustees; set the precedent of support of contracts against state interference.

Dawes Act Law passed in 1887 meant to encourage adoption of white norms among Indians; broke up tribal holdings into small farms for Indian families, with the remainder sold to white purchasers.

D-Day June 6, 1944, when an Allied amphibious assault landed on the Normandy coast and established a foothold in Europe, leading to the liberation of France from German occupation.

Declaration of Independence Document adopted on July 4, 1776, that made the break with Britain official; drafted by a committee of the Second Continental Congress, including principal writer Thomas Jefferson.

decolonization The process by which African and Asian colonies of European empires became independent in the years following World War II.

Defense of Marriage Act 1996 law that barred gay couples from receiving federal benefits. Ruled unconstitutional in 2013.

deindustrialization Term describing decline of manufacturing in old industrial areas in the late twentieth century as companies shifted production to low-wage centers in the South and West or in other countries.

Deism Enlightenment thought applied to religion; emphasized reason, morality, and natural law.

Democracy in America Two works, published in 1835 and 1840, by the French thinker Alexis de Tocqueville on the subject of American democracy. Tocqueville stressed the cultural nature of American democracy, and the importance and prevalence of equality in American life.

Democratic-Republican societies Organizations created in the mid-1790s by opponents of the policies of the Washington administration and supporters of the French Revolution.

Denmark Vesey's conspiracy An 1822 failed slave uprising in Charleston, South Carolina, purported to have been led by Denmark Vesey, a free black man.

deregulation Reagan-Clinton era legislation that removed regulations on many industries, including finance and air travel.

détente Period of improving relations between the United States and Communist nations, particularly China and the Soviet Union, during the Nixon administration.

disenfranchisement To deprive of the right to vote; in the United States, exclusionary policies were used to deny groups, especially African-Americans and women, their voting rights.

Dissenters Protestants who belonged to denominations outside of the established Anglican Church.

division of powers The division of political power between the state and federal governments under the U.S. Constitution (also known as federalism).

Dix, Dorothea An important figure in increasing the public's awareness of the plight of the mentally ill. After a two-year investigation of the treatment of the mentally ill in Massachusetts, she presented her findings and won the support of leading reformers. She eventually convinced twenty states to reform their treatment of the mentally ill.

Dixiecrats Deep South delegates who walked out of the 1948 Democratic National Convention in protest of the party's support for civil rights legislation and later formed the States' Rights Democratic (Dixiecrat) Party, which nominated Strom Thurmond of South Carolina for president.

Dollar Diplomacy A foreign policy initiative under President William Howard Taft that promoted the spread of American influence through loans and economic investments from American banks.

Dominion of New England Consolidation into a single colony of the New England colonies—and later New York and New Jersey—by royal governor Edmund Andros in 1686; dominion reverted to individual colonial governments three years later.

"Don't ask, don't tell" President Clinton's compromise measure that allowed gay people to serve in the military incognito, as officers could no longer seek them out for dismissal but they could not openly express their identity. "Don't ask, don't tell" was ended under the Obama administration, when gay military service was allowed.

the Dorr War A movement in Rhode Island against property qualifications for voting. The movement formed an extralegal constitutional convention for the state and elected Thomas Dorr as a governor, but was quashed by federal troops dispatched by President John Tyler.

double-V Led by *The Pittsburgh Courier*, the movement that pressed for victory over fascism abroad and over racism at home. It argued that since African-Americans were risking their lives abroad, they should receive full civil rights at home.

dower rights In colonial America, the right of a widowed woman to inherit one-third of her deceased husband's property.

Dred Scott v. Sandford 1857 U.S. Supreme Court decision in which Chief Justice Roger B. Taney ruled that Congress could not prohibit slavery in the territories, on the grounds that such a prohibition would violate the Fifth Amendment rights of slaveholders, and that no black person could be a citizen of the United States.

Dust Bowl Great Plains counties where millions of tons of topsoil were blown away from parched farmland in the 1930s; massive migration of farm families followed.

Eighteenth Amendment Prohibition amendment passed in 1919 that made illegal the manufacture, sale, or transportation of alcoholic beverages; repealed in 1933.

Ellis Island Reception center in New York Harbor through which most European immigrants to America were processed from 1892 to 1954.

Emancipation Proclamation Declaration issued by President Abraham Lincoln; the preliminary proclamation on September 22, 1862, freed the slaves in areas under Confederate control as of January 1, 1863, the date of the final proclamation, which also authorized the enrollment of black soldiers into the Union army.

Embargo Act Attempt in 1807 to exert economic pressure by prohibiting all exports from the United States, instead of waging war in reaction to continued British impressment of American sailors; smugglers easily circumvented the embargo, and it was repealed two years later.

Emergency Banking Act Passed in 1933, the First New Deal measure that provided for reopening the banks under strict conditions and took the United States off the gold standard.

empire of liberty The idea, expressed by Jefferson, that the United States would not rule its new territories as colonies, but rather would eventually admit them as full member states.

enclosure movement A legal process that divided large farm fields in England that were previously collectively owned by groups of peasants into smaller, individually owned plots. The enclosure movement took place over several centuries, and resulted in eviction for many peasants.

Enforcement Acts Three laws passed in 1870 and 1871 that tried to eliminate the Ku Klux Klan by outlawing it and other such terrorist societies; the laws allowed the president to deploy the army for that purpose.

English Bill of Rights A series of laws enacted in 1689 that inscribed the rights of Englishmen into law and enumerated parliamentary powers such as taxation.

English liberty The idea that English people were entitled to certain liberties, including trial by jury, habeas corpus, and the right to face one's accuser in court. These rights meant that even the English king was subject to the rule of law.

English Toleration Act A 1690 act of Parliament that allowed all English Protestants to worship freely.

Enlightenment Revolution in thought in the eighteenth century that emphasized reason and science over the authority of traditional religion.

Equal Rights Amendment Amendment to guarantee equal rights for women, introduced in 1923 but not passed by Congress until 1972; it failed to be ratified by the states.

Era of Good Feelings Contemporary characterization of the administration of popular Republican president James Monroe, 1817–1825.

Erie Canal Most important and profitable of the canals of the 1820s and 1830s; stretched from Buffalo to Albany, New York, connecting the Great Lakes to the East Coast and making New York City the nation's largest port.

Espionage Act 1917 law that prohibited spying and interfering with the draft as well as making "false statements" that hurt the war effort.

ethnic cleansing The systematic removal of an ethnic group from a territory through violence or intimidation in order to create a homogeneous society; the term was popularized by the Yugoslav policy brutally targeting Albanian Muslims in Kosovo.

Ex parte Milligan 1866 Supreme Court case that declared it unconstitutional to bring accused persons before military tribunals where civil courts were operating.

Exposition and Protest Document written in 1828 by Vice President John C. Calhoun of South Carolina to protest the so-called Tariff of Abominations, which seemed to favor northern industry; introduced the concept of state interposition and became the basis for South Carolina's Nullification Doctrine of 1833.

Fair Deal Domestic reform proposals of the Truman administration; included civil rights legislation, national health insurance, and repeal of the Taft-Hartley Act, but only extensions of some New Deal programs were enacted.

family values Set of beliefs usually associated with conservatism that stressed the superiority of nuclear family, heterosexual marriage, and traditional gender roles.

family wage Idea that male workers should earn a wage sufficient to enable them to support their entire family without their wives' having to work outside the home.

Federal Housing Administration (FHA) A government agency created during the New Deal to guarantee mortgages, allowing lenders to offer long-term (usually thirty-year) loans with low down payments (usually 10 percent of the asking price). The FHA seldom underwrote loans in racially mixed or minority neighborhoods.

Federal Trade Commission (FTC) Independent agency created by the Wilson administration that replaced the Bureau of Corporations as an even more powerful tool to combat unfair trade practices and monopolies.

federalism A system of government in which power is divided between the central government and the states.

The Federalist Collection of eighty-five essays that appeared in the New York press in 1787–1788 in support of the Constitution; written by Alexander Hamilton, James Madison, and John Jay and published under the pseudonym "Publius."

Federalists and Republicans The two increasingly coherent political parties that appeared in Congress by the mid-1790s. The Federalists, led by George Washington, John Adams, and Alexander Hamilton, favored a strong central government. The Republicans, first identified during the early nineteenth century, supported a strict interpretation of the Constitution, which they believed would safeguard individual freedoms and states' rights from the threats posed by a strong central government.

The Feminine Mystique The book widely credited with sparking second-wave feminism in the United States. Author Betty Friedan focused on college-educated women, arguing that they would find fulfillment by engaging in paid labor outside the home.

feminism Term that entered the lexicon in the early twentieth century to describe the movement for full equality for women, in political, social, and personal life.

Fifteenth Amendment Constitutional amendment ratified in 1870, which prohibited states from discriminating in voting privileges on the basis of race.

flappers Young women of the 1920s whose rebellion against prewar standards of femininity included wearing shorter dresses, bobbing their hair, dancing to jazz music, driving cars, smoking cigarettes, and indulging in illegal drinking and gambling.

Force Act 1833 legislation, sparked by the nullification crisis in South Carolina, that authorized the president's use of the army to compel states to comply with federal law.

Fordism Early twentieth-century term describing the economic system pioneered by Ford Motor Company based on high wages and mass consumption.

Fort McHenry Fort in Baltimore Harbor unsuccessfully bombarded by the British in September 1814; Francis Scott Key, a witness to the battle, was moved to write the words to "The Star-Spangled Banner."

Fort Sumter First battle of the Civil War, in which the federal fort in Charleston (South Carolina) Harbor was captured by the Confederates on April 14, 1861, after two days of shelling.

Four Freedoms Freedom of speech, freedom of worship, freedom from want, and freedom from fear, as described by President Franklin D. Roosevelt during his January 6, 1941, State of the Union Address.

Fourteen Points President Woodrow Wilson's 1918 plan for peace after World War I; at the Versailles peace conference, however, he failed to incorporate all of the points into the treaty.

Fourteenth Amendment 1868 constitutional amendment that guaranteed rights of citizenship to former slaves, in words similar to those of the Civil Rights Act of 1866.

franchise The right to vote.

free blacks African-American persons not held in slavery; immediately before the Civil War, there were nearly a half million in the United States, split almost evenly between North and South.

Free Soil Party Political organization formed in 1848 to oppose slavery in the territory acquired in the Mexican War; nominated Martin Van Buren for president in 1848. By 1854 most of the party's members had joined the Republican Party.

free trade The belief that economic development arises from the exchange of goods between different countries without governmental interference.

the Freedmen's Bureau Reconstruction agency established in 1865 to protect the legal rights of former slaves and to assist with their education, jobs, health care, and landowning.

freedom petitions Arguments for liberty presented to New England's courts and legislatures in the early 1770s by enslaved African-Americans.

Freedom Rides Bus journeys challenging racial segregation in the South in 1961.

French and Indian War The last—and most important—of four colonial wars fought between England and France for control of North America east of the Mississippi River.

Fugitive Slave Act 1850 law that gave the federal government authority in cases involving runaway slaves; aroused considerable opposition in the North.

fugitive slaves Slaves who escaped from their owners.

fundamentalism Anti-modernist Protestant movement started in the early twentieth century that proclaimed the literal truth of the Bible; the name came from *The Fundamentals*, published by conservative leaders.

Gabriel's Rebellion An 1800 uprising planned by Virginian slaves to gain their freedom. The plot was led by a blacksmith named Gabriel, but was discovered and quashed.

Gadsden Purchase Thirty thousand square miles in present-day Arizona and New Mexico bought by Congress from Mexico in 1853 primarily for the Southern Pacific Railroad's transcontinental route.

gag rule Rule adopted by House of Representatives in 1836 prohibiting consideration of abolitionist petitions;

opposition, led by former president John Quincy Adams, succeeded in having it repealed in 1844.

Garvey, Marcus The leading spokesman for Negro Nationalism, which exalted blackness, black cultural expression, and black exclusiveness. He called upon African-Americans to liberate themselves from the surrounding white culture and create their own businesses, cultural centers, and newspapers. He was also the founder of the Universal Negro Improvement Association.

Geneva Accords A 1954 document that had promised elections to unify Vietnam and established the Seventeenth Parallel demarcation line which divided North and South Vietnam.

"gentlemen of property and standing" Well-to-do merchants who often had commercial ties to the South and resisted abolitionism, occasionally inciting violence against its adherents.

Gettysburg, Battle of Battle fought in southern Pennsylvania, July 1–3, 1863; the Confederate defeat and the simultaneous loss at Vicksburg marked the military turning point of the Civil War.

Ghost Dance A spiritual and political movement among Native Americans whose followers performed a ceremonial "ghost dance" intended to connect the living with the dead and make the Indians bulletproof in battles intended to restore their homelands.

GI Bill of Rights The 1944 legislation that provided money for education and other benefits to military personnel returning from World War II.

Gibbons v. Ogden 1824 U.S. Supreme Court decision reinforcing the "commerce clause" (the federal government's right to regulate interstate commerce) of the Constitution; Chief Justice John Marshall ruled against the State of New York's granting of steamboat monopolies.

the Gilded Age The popular but derogatory name for the period from the end of the Civil War to the turn of the century, after the title of the 1873 novel by Mark Twain and Charles Dudley Warner.

globalization Term that became prominent in the 1990s to describe the rapid acceleration of international flows of commerce, financial resources, labor, and cultural products.

Glorious Revolution A coup in 1688 engineered by a small group of aristocrats that led to William of Orange taking the British throne in place of James II.

gold rush The massive migration of Americans into California territory in the late 1840s and 1850s in pursuit of gold, which was discovered there in 1848.

gold standard Policy at various points in American history by which the value of a dollar is set at a fixed price in terms of gold (in the post–World War II era, for example, $35 per ounce of gold).

Good Neighbor Policy Policy proclaimed by President Franklin D. Roosevelt in his first inaugural address in 1933 that sought improved diplomatic relations between the United States and its Latin American neighbors.

gradual emancipation A series of acts passed in state legislatures throughout the North in the years following the Revolution that freed slaves after they reached a certain age, following lengthy "apprenticeships."

grandfather clause Loophole created by southern disenfranchising legislatures of the 1890s for illiterate white males whose grandfathers had been eligible to vote before the Civil War.

Great Awakening Fervent religious revival movement in the 1720s through the 1740s that was spread throughout the colonies by ministers like New England Congregationalist Jonathan Edwards and English revivalist George Whitefield.

Great Depression Worst economic depression in American history; it was spurred by the stock market crash of 1929 and lasted until World War II.

Great League of Peace An alliance of the Iroquois tribes, originally formed sometime between 1450 and 1600, that used their combined strength to pressure Europeans to work with them in the fur trade and to wage war across what is today eastern North America.

Great Migration Large-scale migration of southern blacks during and after World War I to the North, where jobs had become available during the labor shortage of the war years.

Great Migration (1630s) The migration of approximately 21,000 English Puritans to the Massachusetts Bay Colony.

Great Railroad Strike A series of demonstrations, some violent, held nationwide in support of striking railroad workers in Martinsburg, West Virginia, who refused to work due to wage cuts.

Great Recession A period of major economic stagnation across the United States and western Europe, characterized by rising unemployment and inflation and a 37 percent decline in the stock market between March and December 1974.

Great Society Term coined by President Lyndon B. Johnson in his 1965 State of the Union address, in which he proposed legislation to address problems of voting rights, poverty, diseases, education, immigration, and the environment.

Griswold v. Connecticut Supreme Court decision that, in overturning Connecticut law prohibiting the use of contraceptives, established a constitutional right to privacy.

Guantánamo Bay A detention center at the American naval base at Guantánamo Bay, Cuba, where beginning in 2002 suspected terrorists and war prisoners were held indefinitely and tried by extrajudicial military tribunals. During his 2008 presidential campaign, Senator Barack Obama pledged to close the prison, but as of 2015 it remained open.

Gulf of Tonkin resolution Legislation passed by Congress in 1964 in reaction to supposedly unprovoked attacks on American warships off the coast of North Vietnam; it gave the president unlimited authority to defend U.S. forces and members of SEATO.

Gulf oil spill Environmental disaster that occurred in 2010 after an explosion on the *Deepwater Horizon* oil rig. Hundreds of millions of gallons of oil were spilled into the Gulf of Mexico, resulting in one of the largest environmental calamities in human history.

Gulf War Military action in 1991 in which an international coalition led by the United States drove Iraq from Kuwait, which it had occupied the previous year.

hacienda Large-scale farm in the Spanish New World empire worked by Indian laborers.

Haitian Revolution A slave uprising that led to the establishment of Haiti as an independent country in 1804.

Half-Way Covenant A 1662 religious compromise that allowed baptism and partial church membership to colonial New Englanders whose parents were not among the Puritan elect.

Harlem Renaissance African-American literary and artistic movement of the 1920s centered in New York City's Harlem neighborhood; writers Langston Hughes, Jean Toomer, Zora Neale Hurston, and Countee Cullen were among those active in the movement.

Harpers Ferry, Virginia Site of abolitionist John Brown's failed raid on the federal arsenal, October 16–17, 1859; Brown became a martyr to his cause after his capture and execution.

Hart-Celler Act 1965 law that eliminated the national origins quota system for immigration established by laws in 1921 and 1924; led to radical change in the origins of immigrants to the United States, with Asians and Latin Americans outnumbering Europeans.

Hartford Convention Meeting of New England Federalists on December 15, 1814, to protest the War of 1812; proposed seven constitutional amendments (limiting embargoes and changing requirements for officeholding, declaration of war, and admission of new states), but the war ended before Congress could respond.

Haymarket Affair Violence during an anarchist protest at Haymarket Square in Chicago on May 4, 1886; the deaths of eight, including seven policemen, led to the trial of eight anarchist leaders for conspiracy to commit murder.

Haynes, Lemuel A black member of the Massachusetts militia and celebrated minister who urged that Americans extend their conception of freedom to enslaved Africans during the Revolutionary Era.

headright system A land-grant policy that promised fifty acres to any colonist who could afford passage to Virginia, as well as fifty more for any accompanying servants. The headright policy was eventually expanded to include any colonists—and was also adopted in other colonies.

Helsinki Accords 1975 agreement between the USSR and the United States that recognized the post–World War II boundaries of Europe and guaranteed the basic liberties of each nation's citizens.

Hessians German soldiers, most from Hesse-Cassel principality (hence, the name), paid to fight for the British in the Revolutionary War.

Hollywood Ten A group called before the House Un-American Activities Committee who refused to speak about their political leanings or "name names"—that is, identify communists in Hollywood. Some were imprisoned as a result.

Holocaust Systematic racist attempt by the Nazis to exterminate the Jews of Europe, resulting in the murder of over 6 million Jews and more than a million other "undesirables."

Homestead Act 1862 law that authorized Congress to grant 160 acres of public land to a western settler, who had to live on the land for five years to establish title.

horizontal expansion The process by which a corporation acquires or merges with its competitors.

House of Burgesses The first elected assembly in colonial America, established in 1619 in Virginia. Only wealthy landowners could vote in its elections.

House Un-American Activities Committee (HUAC) Committee formed in 1938 to investigate subversives in the government and holders of radical ideas more generally; best-known investigations were of Hollywood notables and of former State Department official Alger Hiss, who was accused in 1948 of espionage and Communist Party membership. Abolished in 1975.

Hundred Days Extraordinarily productive first three months of President Franklin D. Roosevelt's administration in which a special session of Congress enacted fifteen of his New Deal proposals.

Hurricane Katrina 2005 hurricane that devastated much of the Gulf Coast, especially New Orleans. The Bush administration's response was widely criticized as inadequate.

illegal alien A new category established by the Immigration Act of 1924 that referred to immigrants crossing U.S. borders in excess of the new immigration quotas.

Immigration Restriction League A political organization founded in 1894 that called for reducing immigration to the United States by requiring a literacy test for immigrants.

impeachment Bringing charges against a public official; for example, the House of Representatives can impeach a president for "treason, bribery, or other high crimes and misdemeanors" by majority vote, and after the trial the Senate can remove the president by a vote of two-thirds. Two presidents, Andrew Johnson and Bill Clinton, have been impeached and tried before the Senate; neither was convicted.

impressment The British navy's practice of using press-gangs to kidnap men in British and colonial ports who were then forced to serve in the British navy.

"In God We Trust" Phrase placed on all new U.S. currency as of 1954.

indentured servants Settlers who signed on for a temporary period of servitude to a master in exchange for passage to the New World; Virginia and Pennsylvania were largely peopled in the seventeenth and eighteenth centuries by English and German indentured servants.

Indian New Deal Phrase that refers to the reforms implemented for Native Americans during the New Deal era. John Collier, the commissioner of the Bureau of Indian Affairs (BIA), increased the access Native Americans had to relief programs and employed more Native Americans at the BIA. He worked to pass the Indian Reorganization Act. However, the version of the act passed by Congress was a much diluted version of Collier's original proposal and did not greatly improve the lives of Native Americans.

Indian Removal Act 1830 law signed by President Andrew Jackson that permitted the negotiation of treaties to obtain the Indians' lands in exchange for their relocation to what would become Oklahoma.

individualism Term that entered the language in the 1820s to describe the increasing emphasis on the pursuit of personal advancement and private fulfillment free of outside interference.

Industrial Workers of the World Radical union organized in Chicago in 1905 and nicknamed the Wobblies; its opposition to World War I led to its destruction by the federal government under the Espionage Act.

inflation An economic condition in which prices rise continuously.

Insular Cases Series of cases between 1901 and 1904 in which the Supreme Court ruled that constitutional protection of individual rights did not fully apply to residents of "insular" territories acquired by the United States in the Spanish-American War, such as Puerto Rico and the Philippines.

Interstate Commerce Commission Organization established by Congress, in reaction to the U.S. Supreme Court's ruling in *Wabash Railroad v. Illinois* (1886), in order to curb abuses in the railroad industry by regulating rates.

interstate highway system National network of interstate superhighways; its construction began in the late 1950s for the purpose of commerce and defense. The interstate highways would enable the rapid movement of military convoys and the evacuation of cities after a nuclear attack.

Intolerable Acts Four parliamentary measures in reaction to the Boston Tea Party that forced payment for the tea, disallowed colonial trials of British soldiers, forced their quartering in private homes, and reduced the number of elected officials in Massachusetts.

Iran-Contra Affair Scandal of the second Reagan administration involving sales of arms to Iran in partial exchange for release of hostages in Lebanon and use of the arms money to aid the Contras in Nicaragua, which had been expressly forbidden by Congress.

Iraq War Military campaign in 2003 in which the United States, unable to gain approval by the United Nations, unilaterally occupied Iraq and removed dictator Saddam Hussein from power.

iron curtain Term coined by Winston Churchill to describe the Cold War divide between western Europe and the Soviet Union's eastern European satellites.

ISIS An insurgency that emerged from the sectarian civil wars that destabilized Syria and post–Saddam Hussein Iraq. Beginning in 2014, ISIS forces attacked towns and cities in Iraq, Syria, and Lybia, systematically murdering members of ethnic and religious minorities.

isolationism The desire to avoid foreign entanglements that dominated the U.S. Congress in the 1930s; beginning in 1935, lawmakers passed a series of Neutrality Acts that banned travel on belligerents' ships and the sale of arms to countries at war.

Japanese-American internment Policy adopted by the Roosevelt administration in 1942 under which 110,000 persons of Japanese descent, most of them American citizens, were removed from the West Coast and forced to spend most of World War II in internment camps; it was the largest violation of American civil liberties in the twentieth century.

Jay's Treaty Treaty with Britain negotiated in 1794 by Chief Justice John Jay; Britain agreed to vacate forts in the Northwest Territories, and festering disagreements (border with Canada, prewar debts, shipping claims) would be settled by commission.

Kansas Exodus A migration in 1879 and 1880 by some 40,000–60,000 blacks to Kansas to escape the oppressive environment of the New South.

Kansas-Nebraska Act 1854 law sponsored by Illinois senator Stephen A. Douglas to allow settlers in newly organized territories north of the Missouri border to decide the slavery issue for themselves; fury over the resulting repeal of the Missouri Compromise of 1820 led to violence in Kansas and to the formation of the Republican Party.

"King Cotton diplomacy" An attempt during the Civil War by the South to encourage British intervention by banning cotton exports.

King Philip's War A multiyear conflict that began in 1675 with an Indian uprising against white colonists. Its end result was broadened freedoms for white New Englanders and the dispossession of the region's Indians.

Knights of Labor Founded in 1869, the first national union; lasted, under the leadership of Terence V. Powderly, only into the 1890s; supplanted by the American Federation of Labor.

Know-Nothing Party Nativist, anti-Catholic third party organized in 1854 in reaction to large-scale German and Irish immigration; the party's only presidential candidate was Millard Fillmore in 1856.

Korean War Conflict touched off in 1950 when Communist North Korea invaded South Korea; fighting, largely by U.S. forces, continued until 1953.

Korematsu v. United States 1944 Supreme Court case that found Executive Order 9066 to be constitutional. Fred Korematsu, an American-born citizen of Japanese descent, defied the military order that banned all persons of Japanese ancestry from designated western coastal areas. The Court upheld Korematsu's arrest and internment.

Ku Klux Klan Group organized in Pulaski, Tennessee, in 1866 to terrorize former slaves who voted and held political offices during Reconstruction; a revived organization in the 1910s and 1920s that stressed white, Anglo-Saxon, fundamentalist Protestant supremacy; revived a third time to fight the civil rights movement of the 1950s and 1960s in the South.

Kyoto Protocol A 1997 international agreement that sought to combat global warming. To great controversy, the Bush administration announced in 2001 that it would not abide by the Kyoto Protocol.

Las Casas, Bartolomé de A Catholic missionary who renounced the Spanish practice of coercively converting Indians and advocated their better treatment. In 1552, he wrote *A Brief Relation of the Destruction of the Indies*, which described the Spanish's cruel treatment of the Indians.

League of Nations Organization of nations to mediate disputes and avoid war established after World War I as part of the Treaty of Versailles; President Woodrow Wilson's "Fourteen Points" speech to Congress in 1918 proposed the formation of the league, which the United States never joined.

League of United Latin American Citizens Often called LULAC, an organization that challenged restrictive housing, employment discrimination, and other inequalities faced by Latino Americans.

Lend-Lease Act 1941 law that permitted the United States to lend or lease arms and other supplies to the Allies, signifying increasing likelihood of American involvement in World War II.

Letters from an American Farmer 1782 book by Hector St. John de Crèvecoeur that popularized the notion that the United States was a "melting pot" while excluding people of color from the process of assimilation.

Levittown Low-cost, mass-produced developments of suburban tract housing built by William Levitt after World War II on Long Island and elsewhere.

Lewis and Clark expedition Led by Meriwether Lewis and William Clark, a mission to the Pacific coast commissioned for the purposes of scientific and geographical exploration.

Lexington and Concord, Battles of The first shots fired in the Revolutionary War, on April 19, 1775, near Boston; approximately 100 minutemen and 250 British soldiers were killed.

liberal internationalism Woodrow Wilson's foreign policy theory, which rested on the idea that economic and political freedom went hand in hand, and encouraged American intervention abroad in order to secure these freedoms globally.

liberalism Originally, political philosophy that emphasized the protection of liberty by limiting the power of government to interfere with the natural rights of citizens; in the twentieth century, belief in an activist government promoting greater social and economic equality.

liberty of contract A judicial concept of the late nineteenth and early twentieth centuries whereby the courts overturned laws regulating labor conditions as violations of the economic freedom of both employers and employees.

Liberty Party Abolitionist political party that nominated James G. Birney for president in 1840 and 1844; merged with the Free Soil Party in 1848.

Lincoln-Douglas debates Series of senatorial campaign debates in 1858 focusing on the issue of slavery in the territories; held in Illinois between Republican Abraham Lincoln, who made a national reputation for himself, and incumbent Democratic senator Stephen A. Douglas, who managed to hold on to his seat.

the Little Bighorn, Battle of Most famous battle of the Great Sioux War; took place in 1876 in the Montana Territory; combined Sioux and Cheyenne warriors massacred a vastly outnumbered U.S. Cavalry commanded by Lieutenant Colonel George Armstrong Custer.

Long Telegram A telegram by American diplomat George Kennan in 1946 outlining his views of the Soviet Union that eventually inspired the policy of containment.

Lord Dunmore's proclamation A proclamation issued in 1775 by the earl of Dunmore, the British governor of Virginia, that offered freedom to any slave who fought for the king against the rebelling colonists.

Lords of Trade An English regulatory board established to oversee colonial affairs in 1675.

the Lost Cause A romanticized view of slavery, the Old South, and the Confederacy that arose in the decades following the Civil War.

Louisiana Purchase President Thomas Jefferson's 1803 purchase from France of the important port of New Orleans and 828,000 square miles west of the Mississippi River to the Rocky Mountains; it more than doubled the territory of the United States at a cost of only $15 million.

Loyalists Colonists who remained loyal to Great Britain during the War of Independence.

Lusitania British passenger liner sunk by a German U-boat, May 7, 1915, creating a diplomatic crisis and public outrage at the loss of 128 Americans (roughly 10 percent of the total aboard); Germany agreed to pay reparations, and the United States waited two more years to enter World War I.

lynching Practice, particularly widespread in the South between 1890 and 1940, in which persons (usually black) accused of a crime were murdered by mobs before standing trial. Lynchings often took place before large crowds, with law enforcement authorities not intervening.

Manhattan Project Secret American program during World War II to develop an atomic bomb; J. Robert Oppenheimer led the team of physicists at Los Alamos, New Mexico.

manifest destiny Phrase first used in 1845 to urge annexation of Texas; used thereafter to encourage American settlement of European colonial and Indian lands in the Great Plains and the West and, more generally, as a justification for American empire.

Marbury v. Madison First U.S. Supreme Court decision to declare a federal law—the Judiciary Act of 1801—unconstitutional.

March on Washington Civil rights demonstration on August 28, 1963, where the Reverend Martin Luther King Jr. gave his "I Have a Dream" speech on the steps of the Lincoln Memorial.

Marshall Plan U.S. program for the reconstruction of post–World War II Europe through massive aid to former enemy nations as well as allies; proposed by General George C. Marshall in 1947.

massive retaliation Strategy that used the threat of nuclear warfare as a means of combating the global spread of communism.

maternalist reforms Progressive-era reforms that sought to encourage women's child-bearing and -rearing abilities and to promote their economic independence.

Mayflower Compact Document signed in 1620 aboard the *Mayflower* before the Pilgrims landed at Plymouth; the document committed the group to majority-rule government.

McCarran-Walter Act Immigration legislation passed in 1952 that allowed the government to deport immigrants who had been identified as communists, regardless of whether or not they were citizens.

McCarthyism Post–World War II Red Scare focused on the fear of Communists in U.S. government positions; peaked during the Korean War; most closely associated with Joseph McCarthy, a major instigator of the hysteria.

McCulloch v. Maryland 1819 U.S. Supreme Court decision in which Chief Justice John Marshall, holding that Maryland could not tax the Second Bank of the United States, supported the authority of the federal government versus the states.

McNary-Haugen bill Vetoed by President Calvin Coolidge in 1927 and 1928, the bill to aid farmers that would have artificially raised agricultural prices by selling surpluses overseas for low prices and selling the reduced supply in the United States for higher prices.

mercantilism Policy of Great Britain and other imperial powers of regulating the economies of colonies to benefit the mother country.

mestizos Spanish word for persons of mixed Native American and European ancestry.

Metacom The chief of the Wampanoags, whom the colonists called King Philip. He resented English efforts to convert Indians to Christianity and waged a war against the English colonists, one in which he was killed.

métis Children of marriages between Indian women and French traders and officials.

Mexican War Controversial war with Mexico for control of California and New Mexico, 1846–1848; the Treaty of Guadalupe

Hidalgo fixed the border at the Rio Grande and extended the United States to the Pacific coast, annexing more than a half-million square miles of Mexican territory.

middle ground A borderland between European empires and Indian sovereignty where various native peoples and Europeans lived side by side in relative harmony.

Middle Passage The hellish and often deadly middle leg of the transatlantic "Triangular Trade" in which European ships carried manufactured goods to Africa, then transported enslaved Africans to the Americas and the Caribbean, and finally conveyed American agricultural products back to Europe; from the late sixteenth to the early nineteenth centuries, some 12 million Africans were transported via the Middle Passage, unknown millions more dying en route.

military-industrial complex The concept of "an immense military establishment" combined with a "permanent arms industry," which President Eisenhower warned against in his 1961 Farewell Address.

mill girls Women who worked at textile mills during the Industrial Revolution who enjoyed new freedoms and independence not seen before.

missile gap The claim, raised by John F. Kennedy during his campaign for president in 1960, that the Soviet Union had developed a technological and military advantage during Eisenhower's presidency.

Missouri Compromise Deal proposed by Kentucky senator Henry Clay in 1820 to resolve the slave/free imbalance in Congress that would result from Missouri's admission as a slave state; Maine's admission as a free state offset Missouri, and slavery was prohibited in the remainder of the Louisiana Territory north of the southern border of Missouri.

Monroe Doctrine President James Monroe's declaration to Congress on December 2, 1823, that the American continents would be thenceforth closed to European colonization, and that the United States would not interfere in European affairs.

Montgomery bus boycott Sparked by Rosa Parks's arrest on December 1, 1955, for refusing to surrender her seat to a white passenger, a successful year-long boycott protesting segregation on city buses; led by the Reverend Martin Luther King Jr.

moral imperialism The Wilsonian belief that U.S. foreign policy should be guided by morality, and should teach other peoples about democracy. Wilson used this belief to both repudiate Dollar Diplomacy and justify frequent military interventions in Latin America.

moral suasion The abolitionist strategy that sought to end slavery by persuading both slaveowners and complicit northerners that the institution was evil.

muckraking Writing that exposed corruption and abuses in politics, business, meatpacking, child labor, and more, primarily in the first decade of the twentieth century; included popular books and magazine articles that spurred public interest in reform.

Muller v. Oregon 1908 Supreme Court decision that held that state interest in protecting women could override liberty of contract. Louis D. Brandeis, with help from his sister-in-law Josephine Goldmark of the National Consumers League, filed a brief in *Muller* that used statistics about women's health to argue for their protection.

multiculturalism Term that became prominent in the 1990s to describe a growing emphasis on group racial and ethnic identity and demands that jobs, education, and politics reflect the increasingly diverse nature of American society.

Murray, Judith Sargent A writer and early feminist thinker prominent in the years following the American Revolution.

My Lai massacre Massacre of 347 Vietnamese civilians in the village of My Lai by Lieutenant William Calley and troops under his command. U.S. army officers covered up the massacre for a year until an investigation uncovered the events. Eventually twenty-five army officers were charged with complicity in the massacre and its cover-up, but only Calley was convicted. He served little time for his crimes.

Nat Turner's Rebellion Most important slave uprising in nineteenth-century America, led by a slave preacher who, with his followers, killed about sixty white persons in Southampton County, Virginia, in 1831.

National Association for the Advancement of Colored People Founded in 1910, the civil rights organization that brought lawsuits against discriminatory practices and published *The Crisis*, a journal edited by African-American scholar W. E. B. Du Bois.

National Defense Education Act 1958 law passed in reaction to America's perceived inferiority in the space race; encouraged education in science and modern languages through student loans, university research grants, and aid to public schools.

National Industrial Recovery Act 1933 law passed on the last of the Hundred Days; it created public-works jobs through the Federal Emergency Relief Administration and established a system of self-regulation for industry through the National Recovery Administration, which was ruled unconstitutional in 1935.

National Organization for Women Organization founded in 1966 by writer Betty Friedan and other feminists; it pushed for abortion rights, nondiscrimination in the workplace, and other forms of equality for women.

National Recovery Administration (NRA) Controversial federal agency created in 1933 that brought together business and labor leaders to create "codes of fair competition" and "fair labor" policies, including a national minimum wage.

nativism Anti-immigrant and anti-Catholic feeling especially prominent in the 1830s through the 1850s; the largest group of its proponents was New York's Order of the Star-Spangled Banner, which expanded into the American (Know-Nothing) Party in 1854.

Navajo's Long Walk The forced removal of 8,000 Navajos from their lands by Union forces to a reservation in the 1860s.

Navigation Act Law passed by the English Parliament to control colonial trade and bolster the mercantile system, 1650–1775; enforcement of the act led to growing resentment by colonists.

neoconservatives The leaders of the conservative insurgency of the early 1980s. Their brand of conservatism was personified in Ronald Reagan, who believed in less government, supply-side economics, and "family values."

Neolin A Native American religious prophet who, by preaching pan-Indian unity and rejection of European technology and commerce, helped inspire Pontiac's Rebellion.

Neutrality Acts Series of laws passed between 1935 and 1939 to keep the United States from becoming involved in war by prohibiting American trade and travel to warring nations.

New Deal Franklin D. Roosevelt's campaign promise, in his speech to the Democratic National Convention of 1932, to combat the Great Depression with a "new deal for the American people"; the phrase became a catchword for his ambitious plan of economic programs.

new feminism A new aspect of the women's rights movement that arose in the early part of the twentieth century. New feminism added a focus on individual and sexual freedom to the movement, and introduced the word "feminism" into American life.

New Freedom Democrat Woodrow Wilson's political slogan in the presidential campaign of 1912; Wilson wanted to improve the banking system, lower tariffs, and, by breaking up monopolies, give small businesses freedom to compete.

New Harmony Community founded in Indiana by British industrialist Robert Owen in 1825; the short-lived New Harmony Community of Equality was one of the few nineteenth-century communal experiments not based on religious ideology.

new immigrants Wave of newcomers from southern and eastern Europe, including many Jews, who became a majority among immigrants to America after 1890.

New Jersey Plan New Jersey's delegation to the Constitutional Convention's plan for one legislative body with equal representation for each state.

New Left Radical youth protest movement of the 1960s, named by leader Tom Hayden to distinguish it from the Old (Marxist-Leninist) Left of the 1930s.

New Nationalism Platform of the Progressive Party and slogan of former president Theodore Roosevelt in the presidential campaign of 1912; stressed government activism, including regulation of trusts, conservation, and recall of state court decisions that had nullified progressive programs.

New Negro Term used in the 1920s, in reference to a slow and steady growth of black political influence that occurred in northern cities, where African-Americans were freer to speak and act. This political activity created a spirit of protest that expressed itself culturally in the Harlem Renaissance and politically in "new Negro" nationalism.

New Orleans, Battle of Last battle of the War of 1812, fought on January 8, 1815, weeks after the peace treaty was signed but prior to the news' reaching America; General Andrew Jackson led the victorious American troops.

New South *Atlanta Constitution* editor Henry W. Grady's 1886 term for the prosperous post–Civil War South he envisioned: democratic, industrial, urban, and free of nostalgia for the defeated plantation South.

new world order President George H. W. Bush's term for the post–Cold War world.

Ninety-Five Theses The list of moral grievances against the Catholic Church by Martin Luther, a German priest, in 1517.

"no taxation without representation" The rallying cry of opponents to the 1765 Stamp Act. The slogan decried the colonists' lack of representation in Parliament.

North American Free Trade Agreement (NAFTA) Approved in 1993, the agreement with Canada and Mexico that allowed goods to travel across their borders free of tariffs. Critics of the agreement argued that American workers would lose their jobs to cheaper Mexican labor.

North Atlantic Treaty Organization (NATO) Alliance founded in 1949 by ten western European nations, the United States, and Canada to deter Soviet expansion in Europe.

Northwest Ordinance of 1787 Law that created the Northwest Territory (area north of the Ohio River and west of Pennsylvania), established conditions for self-government and statehood, included a Bill of Rights, and permanently prohibited slavery.

Notes on the State of Virginia Thomas Jefferson's 1785 book that claimed, among other things, that black people were incapable of becoming citizens and living in harmony alongside white people due to the legacy of slavery and what Jefferson believed were the "real distinctions that nature has made" between races.

NSC-68 Top-secret policy paper approved by President Truman in 1950 that outlined a militaristic approach to combating the spread of global communism.

nullification crisis The 1832 attempt by the State of South Carolina to nullify, or invalidate within its borders, the 1832 federal tariff law. President Jackson responded with the Force Act of 1833.

Obergefell v. Hodges 2015 Supreme Court decision that allowed same-sex couples to marry throughout the United States.

Occupy Wall Street A grassroots movement in 2011 against growing economic inequality, declining opportunity, and the depredations of Wall Street banks.

oil embargo Prohibition on trade in oil declared by the Organization of Petroleum Exporting Countries, dominated by Middle Eastern producers, in October 1973 in response to U.S. and western European support for Israel in the 1973 Yom Kippur War. The rise in gas prices and fuel shortages resulted in a global economic recession and profoundly affected the American economy.

Oneida Utopian community founded in 1848; the Perfectionist religious group practiced "complex marriage" under leader John Humphrey Noyes.

Open Door Policy Demand in 1899 by Secretary of State John Hay, in hopes of protecting the Chinese market for U.S. exports, that Chinese trade be open to all nations.

open immigration American immigration laws under which nearly all white people could immigrate to the United States and become naturalized citizens.

Operation Dixie CIO's largely ineffective post–World War II campaign to unionize southern workers.

Ordinance of 1784 A law drafted by Thomas Jefferson that regulated land ownership and defined the terms by which western land would be marketed and settled; it established stages of self-government for the West. First Congress would govern a territory; then the territory would be admitted to the Union as a full state.

Ordinance of 1785 A law that regulated land sales in the Old Northwest. The land surveyed was divided into 640-acre plots and sold at $1 per acre.

Oslo Accords 1993 roadmap for peace between Israel and the newly created Palestinian Authority, negotiated under the Clinton administration.

Panama Canal Zone The small strip of land on either side of the Panama Canal. The Canal Zone was under U.S. control from 1903 to 1979 as a result of Theodore Roosevelt's assistance in engineering a coup in Colombia that established Panama's independence.

Panic of 1819 Financial collapse brought on by sharply falling cotton prices, declining demand for American exports, and reckless western land speculation.

Panic of 1837 Beginning of major economic depression lasting about six years; touched off by a British financial crisis and made worse by falling cotton prices, credit and currency problems, and speculation in land, canals, and railroads.

paternalism A moral position developed during the first half of the nineteenth century which claimed that slaves were deprived of liberty for their own "good." Such a rationalization was adopted by some slaveowners to justify slavery.

the "peculiar institution" A phrase used by whites in the antebellum South to refer to slavery without using the word "slavery."

Pentagon Papers Informal name for the Defense Department's secret history of the Vietnam conflict; leaked to the press by former official Daniel Ellsberg and published in the *New York Times* in 1971.

Pequot War An armed conflict in 1637 that led to the destruction of one of New England's most powerful Indian groups.

perfectionism The idea that social ills once considered incurable could in fact be eliminated, popularized by the religious revivalism of the nineteenth century.

Perry, Commodore Matthew U.S. naval officer who negotiated the Treaty of Kanagawa in 1854. That treaty was the first step in starting a political and commercial relationship between the United States and Japan.

pet banks Local banks that received deposits while the charter of the Bank of the United States was about to expire in 1836. The choice of these banks was influenced by political and personal connections.

Philippine War American military campaign that suppressed the movement for Philippine independence after the Spanish-American War; America's death toll was over 4,000 and the Philippines' was far higher.

Pilgrims Puritan separatists who broke completely with the Church of England and sailed to the New World aboard the *Mayflower*, founding Plymouth Colony on Cape Cod in 1620.

plantation An early word for a colony, a settlement "planted" from abroad among an alien population in Ireland or the New World. Later, a large agricultural enterprise that used unfree labor to produce a crop for the world market.

Platt Amendment 1901 amendment to the Cuban constitution that reserved the United States' right to intervene in Cuban affairs and forced newly independent Cuba to host American naval bases on the island.

Plessy v. Ferguson U.S. Supreme Court decision supporting the legality of Jim Crow laws that permitted or required "separate but equal" facilities for blacks and whites.

Pontiac's Rebellion An Indian attack on British forts and settlements after France ceded to the British its territory east of the Mississippi River, as part of the Treaty of Paris in 1763, without consulting France's Indian allies.

Popular Front A period during the mid-1930s when the Communist Party sought to ally itself with socialists and New Dealers in movements for social change, urging reform of the capitalist system rather than revolution.

popular sovereignty Program that allowed settlers in a disputed territory to decide the slavery issue for themselves; most closely associated with Senator Stephen A. Douglas of Illinois.

Populists Founded in 1892, a group that advocated a variety of reform issues, including free coinage of silver, income tax, postal savings, regulation of railroads, and direct election of U.S. senators.

Porkopolis Nickname of Cincinnati, coined in the mid-nineteenth century, after its numerous slaughter houses.

Port Huron Statement A manifesto by Students for a Democratic Society that criticized institutions ranging from political parties to corporations, unions, and the military-industrial complex, while offering a new vision of social change.

Potsdam conference Last meeting of the major Allied powers; the conference that took place outside Berlin from July 17 to August 2, 1945, at which U.S. president Harry Truman, Soviet dictator Joseph Stalin, and British prime minister Clement Attlee finalized plans begun at Yalta.

Proclamation of 1763 Royal directive issued after the French and Indian War prohibiting settlement, surveys, and land grants west of the Appalachian Mountains; caused considerable resentment among colonists hoping to move west.

Progressive Party Political party created when former president Theodore Roosevelt broke away from the Republican Party to run for president again in 1912; the party supported progressive reforms similar to those of the Democrats but stopped short of seeking to eliminate trusts. Also the name of the party backing Robert La Follette for president in 1924.

Progressivism Broad-based reform movement, 1900–1917, that sought governmental action in solving problems in many areas of American life, including education, public health, the economy, the environment, labor, transportation, and politics.

proslavery argument The series of arguments defending the institution of slavery in the South as a positive good, not a necessary evil. The arguments included the racist belief that black people were inherently inferior to white people, as well as the belief that slavery, in creating a permanent underclass of laborers, made freedom possible for whites. Other elements of the argument included biblical citations.

Public Works Administration A New Deal agency that contracted with private construction companies to build roads, bridges, schools, hospitals, and other public facilities.

Pueblo Revolt Uprising in 1680 in which Pueblo Indians temporarily drove Spanish colonists out of modern-day New Mexico.

Pure Food and Drug Act Passed in 1906, the first law to regulate manufacturing of food and medicines; prohibited dangerous additives and inaccurate labeling.

Puritans English religious group that sought to purify the Church of England; founded the Massachusetts Bay Colony under John Winthrop in 1630.

Radical Republicans Group within the Republican Party in the 1850s and 1860s that advocated strong resistance to the expansion of slavery, opposition to compromise with the South in the secession crisis of 1860–1861, emancipation and arming of black soldiers during the Civil War, and equal civil and political rights for blacks during Reconstruction.

Reagan Revolution The rightward turn of American politics following the 1980 election of Ronald Reagan. The Reagan Revolution made individual "freedom" a rallying cry for the right.

Reaganomics Popular name for President Ronald Reagan's philosophy of "supply side" economics, which combined tax cuts with an unregulated marketplace.

reconquista The "reconquest" of Spain from the Moors completed by King Ferdinand and Queen Isabella in 1492.

Reconstruction Act 1867 law that established temporary military governments in ten Confederate states—excepting Tennessee—and required that the states ratify the Fourteenth Amendment and permit freedmen to vote.

Reconstruction Finance Corporation Federal program established in 1932 under President Herbert Hoover to loan money to banks and other institutions to help them avert bankruptcy.

Red Scare of 1919–1920 Fear among many Americans after World War I of Communists in particular and noncitizens in general, a reaction to the Russian Revolution, mail bombs, strikes, and riots.

Redeemers Post–Civil War Democratic leaders who supposedly saved the South from Yankee domination and preserved the primarily rural economy.

redemptioners Indentured families or persons who received passage to the New World in exchange for a promise to work off their debt in America.

Regulators Groups of backcountry Carolina settlers who protested colonial policies.

repartimiento **system** Spanish labor system under which Indians were legally free and able to earn wages but were also required to perform a fixed amount of labor yearly. Replaced the *encomienda* system.

republic Representative political system in which citizens govern themselves by electing representatives, or legislators, to make key decisions on the citizens' behalf.

republican motherhood The ideology that emerged as a result of American independence where women played an indispensable role by training future citizens.

republicanism Political theory in eighteenth-century England and America that celebrated active participation in public life by economically independent citizens as central to freedom.

reverse discrimination Belief that affirmative action programs discriminate against white people.

Revolution of 1800 First time that an American political party surrendered power to the opposition party; Jefferson, a Republican, had defeated incumbent Adams, a Federalist, for president.

Roanoke colony English expedition of 117 settlers, including Virginia Dare, the first English child born in the New World; the colony disappeared from Roanoke Island in the Outer Banks sometime between 1587 and 1590.

robber barons Also known as "captains of industry"; Gilded-Age industrial figures who inspired both admiration, for their economic leadership and innovation, and hostility and fear, due to their unscrupulous business methods, repressive labor practices, and unprecedented economic control over entire industries.

Roe v. Wade 1973 U.S. Supreme Court decision requiring states to permit first-trimester abortions.

Roosevelt Corollary 1904 Announcement by President Theodore Roosevelt, essentially a corollary to the Monroe Doctrine, that the United States could intervene militarily to prevent interference from European powers in the Western Hemisphere.

Rwandan genocide 1994 Genocide conducted by the Hutu ethnic group upon the Tutsi minority in Rwanda.

Sacco-Vanzetti case A case held during the 1920s in which two Italian-American anarchists were found guilty and executed for a crime in which there was very little evidence linking them to the particular crime.

Salem witch trials A crisis of trials and executions in Salem, Massachusetts, in 1692 that resulted from anxiety over witchcraft.

salutary neglect Informal British policy during the first half of the eighteenth century that allowed the American colonies considerable freedom to pursue their economic and political interests in exchange for colonial obedience.

Sanitary Fairs Fund-raising bazaars led by women on behalf of Civil War soldiers. The fairs offered items such as uniforms and banners, as well as other emblems of war.

Santa Anna, Antonio López de The military leader who, in 1834, seized political power in Mexico and became a dictator. In 1835, Texans rebelled against him, and he led his army to Texas to crush their rebellion. He captured the missionary called the Alamo and killed all of its defenders, which inspired Texans to continue their resistance and Americans to volunteer to fight for Texas. The Texans captured Santa Anna during a surprise attack, and he bought his freedom by signing a treaty recognizing Texas's independence.

Saratoga, Battle of Major defeat of British general John Burgoyne and more than 5,000 British troops at Saratoga, New York, on October 17, 1777.

scalawags Southern white Republicans—some former Unionists—who supported Reconstruction governments.

Schenck v. United States 1919 U.S. Supreme Court decision upholding the wartime Espionage and Sedition Acts; in the opinion he wrote for the case, Justice Oliver Wendell Holmes set the now-familiar "clear and present danger" standard.

scientific management Management campaign to improve worker efficiency using measurements like "time and motion" studies to achieve greater productivity; introduced by Frederick Winslow Taylor in 1911.

Scopes trial 1925 trial of John Scopes, Tennessee teacher accused of violating state law prohibiting teaching of the theory of evolution; it became a nationally celebrated confrontation between religious fundamentalism and civil liberties.

Scottsboro case Case in which nine black youths were convicted of raping two white women; in overturning the verdicts of this case, the Court established precedents in *Powell v. Alabama* (1932) that adequate counsel must be appointed in capital cases, and in *Norris v. Alabama* (1935) that African-Americans cannot be excluded from juries.

Sea Islands experiment The 1861 pre-Reconstruction social experiment that involved converting slave plantations into places where former slaves could work for wages or own land. Former slaves also received education and access to improved shelter and food.

Second American Revolution The transformation of American government and society brought about by the Civil War.

Second Great Awakening Religious revival movement of the early decades of the nineteenth century, in reaction to the growth of secularism and rationalist religion; began the predominance of the Baptist and Methodist Churches.

second Great Migration The movement of black migrants from the rural South to the cities of the North and West, which occurred from 1941 through World War II, that dwarfed the Great Migration of World War I.

Second Middle Passage The massive trade of slaves from the upper South (Virginia and the Chesapeake) to the lower South (the Gulf states) that took place between 1820 and 1860.

Sedition Act 1918 law that made it a crime to make spoken or printed statements that criticized the U.S. government or encouraged interference with the war effort.

Selective Service Act Law passed in 1917 to quickly increase enlistment in the army for the United States' entry into World War I; required men to register with the draft.

"separate but equal" Principle underlying legal racial segregation, upheld in *Plessy v. Ferguson* (1896) and struck down in *Brown v. Board of Education* (1954).

separation of powers Feature of the U.S. Constitution, sometimes called "checks and balances," in which power is divided between executive, legislative, and judicial branches of the national government so that no one can dominate the other two and endanger citizens' liberties.

Serra, Father Junípero Missionary who began and directed the California mission system in the 1770s and 1780s. Serra presided over the conversion of many Indians to Christianity, but also engaged them in forced labor.

settlement house Late-nineteenth-century movement to offer a broad array of social services in urban immigrant neighborhoods; Chicago's Hull House was one of hundreds of settlement houses that operated by the early twentieth century.

Seven Years' War The last—and most important—of four colonial wars fought between England and France for control of North America east of the Mississippi River.

Seventeenth Amendment Progressive reform passed in 1913 that required U.S. senators to be elected directly by voters; previously, senators were chosen by state legislatures.

Shakers Religious sect founded by Mother Ann Lee in England. The United Society of Believers in Christ's Second Appearing settled in Watervliet, New York, in 1774, and subsequently established eighteen additional communes in the Northeast, Indiana, and Kentucky.

Share Our Wealth movement Program offered by Huey Long as an alternative to the New Deal. The program proposed to confiscate large personal fortunes, which would be used to guarantee every poor family a cash grant of $5,000 and every worker an annual income of $2,500. It also promised to provide pensions, reduce working hours, and pay veterans' bonuses and ensured a college education to every qualified student.

sharecropping Type of farm tenancy that developed after the Civil War in which landless workers—often former slaves—farmed land in exchange for farm supplies and a share of the crop.

Shays's Rebellion Attempt by Massachusetts farmer Daniel Shays and 1,200 compatriots, seeking debt relief through issuance of paper currency and lower taxes, to prevent courts from seizing property from indebted farmers.

Sherman Antitrust Act Passed in 1890, first law to restrict monopolistic trusts and business combinations; extended by the Clayton Antitrust Act of 1914.

Silent Spring A 1962 book by biologist Rachel Carson about the destructive impact of the widely used insecticide DDT that launched the modern environmentalist movement.

single tax Concept of taxing only landowners as a remedy for poverty, promulgated by Henry George in *Progress and Poverty* (1879).

sit-down strike Tactic adopted by labor unions in the mid- and late 1930s, whereby striking workers refused to leave factories, making production impossible; proved highly effective in the organizing drive of the Congress of Industrial Organizations.

sit-ins Tactic adopted by young civil rights activists, beginning in 1960, of demanding service at lunch counters or public accommodations and refusing to leave if denied access; marked the beginning of the most militant phase of the civil rights struggle.

Sixteenth Amendment Constitutional amendment passed in 1913 that legalized the federal income tax.

the Slave Power The Republican and abolitionist term for proslavery dominance of southern and national governments.

Smith, John A swashbuckling soldier of fortune with rare powers of leadership and self-promotion who was appointed to the resident council to manage Jamestown.

Smoot-Hawley Tariff 1930 act that raised tariffs to an unprecedented level and worsened the Great Depression by raising prices and discouraging foreign trade.

Snowden, Edward An NSA contractor turned whistleblower, who released classified information relating to the United States' intelligence gathering both at home and abroad.

social contract Agreement hammered out between labor and management in leading industries; called a new "social contract." Unions signed long-term agreements that left decisions regarding capital investment, plant location, and output in management's hands, and they agreed to try to prevent unauthorized "wildcat" strikes.

Social Darwinism Application of Charles Darwin's theory of natural selection to society; used the concept of the "survival of the fittest" to justify class distinctions and to explain poverty.

Social Gospel Ideals preached by liberal Protestant clergymen in the late nineteenth and early twentieth centuries; advocated the application of Christian principles to social problems generated by industrialization.

Social Security Act 1935 law that created the Social Security system with provisions for a retirement pension, unemployment insurance, disability insurance, and public assistance (welfare).

Socialist Party Political party demanding public ownership of major economic enterprises in the United States as well as reforms like recognition of labor unions and women's suffrage; reached peak of influence in 1912 when presidential candidate Eugene V. Debs received over 900,000 votes.

Society of American Indians Organization founded in 1911 that brought together Native American intellectuals of many tribal backgrounds to promote discussion of the plight of Indian peoples.

Society of Friends (Quakers) Religious group in England and America whose members believed all persons possessed the "inner light" or spirit of God; they were early proponents of abolition of slavery and equal rights for women.

soft money and hard money In the 1830s, "soft money" referred to paper currency issued by banks. "Hard money" referred to gold and silver currency—also called specie.

Sons of Liberty Organizations formed by Samuel Adams, John Hancock, and other radicals in response to the Stamp Act.

Sotomayor, Sonia First Supreme Court Justice of Hispanic descent. Justice Sotomayor was appointed by President Barack Obama in 2009.

Southern Christian Leadership Conference (SCLC) Civil rights organization founded in 1957 by the Reverend Martin Luther King Jr. and other civil rights leaders.

Southern Manifesto A document written in 1956 that repudiated the Supreme Court decision in *Brown v. Board of Education* and supported the campaign against racial integration in public places.

spoils system The term meaning the filling of federal government jobs with persons loyal to the party of the president; originated in Andrew Jackson's first term.

Sputnik First artificial satellite to orbit the earth; launched October 4, 1957, by the Soviet Union.

stagflation A combination of stagnant economic growth and high inflation present during the 1970s.

Stamp Act Parliament's 1765 requirement that revenue stamps be affixed to all colonial printed matter, documents, and playing cards; the Stamp Act Congress met to formulate a response, and the act was repealed the following year.

staple crops Important cash crops; for example, cotton or tobacco.

steamboats Paddlewheelers that could travel both up- and down-river in deep or shallow waters; they became commercially viable early in the nineteenth century and soon developed into America's first inland freight and passenger service network.

stock market crash Also known as Black Tuesday, a stock market panic in 1929 that resulted in the loss of more than $10 billion in market value (worth approximately ten times more today). One among many causes of the Great Depression.

Stonewall Inn A gathering place for New York's gay community, the site of the 1969 police raids and resulting riots that launched the modern gay rights movement.

Stono Rebellion A slave uprising in 1739 in South Carolina that led to a severe tightening of the slave code and the temporary imposition of a prohibitive tax on imported slaves.

Strategic Arms Limitation Talks 1972 talks between President Nixon and Secretary Brezhnev that resulted in the Strategic Arms Limitation Treaty (or SALT), which limited the quantity of nuclear warheads each nation could possess, and prohibited the development of missile defense systems.

Student Nonviolent Coordinating Committee (SNCC) Organization founded in 1960 to coordinate civil rights sit-ins and other forms of grassroots protest.

Students for a Democratic Society (SDS) Major organization of the New Left, founded at the University of Michigan in 1960 by Tom Hayden and Al Haber.

suffrage The right to vote.

Sugar Act 1764 decision by Parliament to tax refined sugar and many other colonial products.

Sunbelt The label for an arc that stretched from the Carolinas to California. During the postwar era, much of the urban population growth occurred in this area.

Taft-Hartley Act 1947 law passed over President Harry Truman's veto; the law contained a number of provisions to weaken labor unions, including the banning of closed shops.

tariff of abominations Tariff passed in 1828 by Parliament that taxed imported goods at a very high rate; aroused strong opposition in the South.

Tariff of 1816 First true protective tariff, intended to protect certain American goods against foreign competition.

Tea Party A grassroots Republican movement that emerged in 2009 named for the Boston Tea Party of the 1770s. The Tea Party opposed the Obama administration's sweeping legislative enactments and advocated for a more stringent immigration policy.

Teapot Dome Harding administration scandal in which Secretary of the Interior Albert B. Fall profited from secret leasing to private oil companies of government oil reserves at Teapot Dome, Wyoming, and Elk Hills, California.

Tecumseh and Tenskwatawa Tecumseh—a leader of the Shawnee tribe who tried to unite all Indians into a confederation to resist white encroachment on their lands. His beliefs and leadership made him seem dangerous to the American government. He was killed at the Battle of the Thames. His brother, Tenskwatawa—a religious prophet who called for complete separation from whites, the revival of traditional Indian culture, and resistance to federal policies.

Tejanos Texas settlers of Spanish or Mexican descent.

temperance movement A widespread reform movement, led by militant Christians, focused on reducing the use of alcoholic beverages.

Tennessee Valley Authority Administrative body created in 1933 to control flooding in the Tennessee River valley, provide work for the region's unemployed, and produce inexpensive electric power for the region.

Tenochtitlán The capital city of the Aztec Empire. The city was built on marshy islands on the western side of Lake Tetzcoco, which is the site of present-day Mexico City.

Ten-Percent Plan of Reconstruction President Lincoln's proposal for reconstruction, issued in 1863, in which southern states would rejoin the Union if 10 percent of the 1860 electorate signed loyalty pledges, accepted emancipation, and had received presidential pardons.

Tenure of Office Act 1867 law that required the president to obtain Senate approval to remove any official whose appointment had also required Senate approval; President Andrew Johnson's violation of the law by firing Secretary of War Edwin Stanton led to Johnson's impeachment.

Tet offensive Surprise attack by the Viet Cong and North Vietnamese during the Vietnamese New Year of 1968; turned American public opinion strongly against the war in Vietnam.

the Texas Revolt The 1830s rebellion of residents of the territory of Texas—many of them Americans emigrants—against Mexican control of the region.

Thirteenth Amendment Constitutional amendment adopted in 1865 that irrevocably abolished slavery throughout the United States.

Three Mile Island Nuclear power plant near Harrisburg, Pennsylvania, site of 1979 accident that released radioactive steam into the air; public reaction ended the nuclear power industry's expansion.

three-fifths clause A provision signed into the Constitution in 1787 that three-fifths of the slave population would be counted in determining each state's representation in the House of Representatives and its electoral votes for president.

Title IX Part of the Educational Amendments Act of 1972 that banned gender discrimination in higher education.

totalitarianism The term that describes aggressive, ideologically driven states that seek to subdue all of civil society to their control, thus leaving no room for individual rights or alternative values.

Townshend Acts 1767 parliamentary measures (named for the chancellor of the Exchequer) that taxed tea and other commodities, and established a Board of Customs Commissioners and colonial vice-admiralty courts.

Trail of Tears Cherokees' own term for their forced removal, 1838–1839, from the Southeast to Indian lands (later Oklahoma); of 15,000 forced to march, 4,000 died on the way.

transcendentalists Philosophy of a small group of mid-nineteenth-century New England writers and thinkers, including Ralph Waldo Emerson, Henry David Thoreau, and Margaret Fuller; they stressed personal and intellectual self-reliance.

transcontinental railroad First line across the continent from Omaha, Nebraska, to Sacramento, California, established in 1869 with the linkage of the Union Pacific and Central Pacific railroads at Promontory, Utah.

Treaty of Greenville 1795 treaty under which twelve Indian tribes ceded most of Ohio and Indiana to the federal government, and which also established the "annuity" system.

Treaty of Paris Signed on September 3, 1783, the treaty that ended the Revolutionary War, recognized American independence from Britain, established the border between Canada and the United States, fixed the western border at the Mississippi River, and ceded Florida to Spain.

Truman Doctrine President Harry S. Truman's program announced in 1947 of aid to European countries—particularly Greece and Turkey—threatened by communism.

trusts Companies combined to limit competition.

Tubman, Harriet Abolitionist who was born a slave, escaped to the North, and then returned to the South nineteen times and guided 300 slaves to freedom.

Tulsa riot A race riot in 1921—the worst in American history—that occurred in Tulsa, Oklahoma, after a group of black veterans tried to prevent a lynching. Over 300 African-Americans were killed, and 10,000 lost their homes in fires set by white mobs.

Uncle Tom's Cabin Harriet Beecher Stowe's 1852 antislavery novel that popularized the abolitionist position.

Underground Railroad Operating in the decades before the Civil War, a clandestine system of routes and safehouses through which slaves were led to freedom in the North.

United Nations Organization of nations to maintain world peace, established in 1945 and headquartered in New York.

Uprising of 1622 Unsuccessful uprising of Virginia Native Americans that wiped out one-quarter of the settler population, but ultimately led to the settlers gaining supremacy.

urban renewal A series of policies supported by all levels of government that allowed local governments and housing authorities to demolish so-called blighted areas in urban centers to replace them with more valuable real estate usually reserved for white people.

USA Patriot Act A 2001 mammoth bill that conferred unprecedented powers on law-enforcement agencies charged with preventing domestic terrorism, including the power to wiretap, read private messages, and spy on citizens.

U.S.S. _Maine_ Battleship that exploded in Havana Harbor on February 15, 1898, resulting in 266 deaths; the American public, assuming that the Spanish had mined the ship, clamored for war, and the Spanish-American War was declared two months later.

utopian communities Ideal communities that offered innovative social and economic relationships to those who were interested in achieving salvation.

V-E Day May 8, 1945, the day World War II officially ended in Europe.

Versailles Treaty The treaty signed at the Versailles peace conference after World War I which established President Woodrow Wilson's vision of an international regulating body, redrew parts of Europe and the Middle East, and assigned economically crippling war reparations to Germany, but failed to incorporate all of Wilson's Fourteen Points.

vertical integration Company's avoidance of middlemen by producing its own supplies and providing for distribution of its product.

Vicksburg, Battle of The fall of Vicksburg, Mississippi, to General Ulysses S. Grant's army on July 4, 1863, after two months of siege; a turning point in the war because it gave the Union control of the Mississippi River.

Vietnam Syndrome The belief that the United States should be extremely cautious in deploying its military forces overseas that emerged after the end of the Vietnam War.

Virginia and Kentucky resolutions Legislation passed in 1798 and 1799 by the Virginia and the Kentucky legislatures; written by James Madison and Thomas Jefferson in response to the Alien and Sedition Acts, the resolutions advanced the state-compact theory of the Constitution. Virginia's resolution called on the federal courts to protect free speech. Jefferson's draft for Kentucky stated that a state could nullify federal law, but this was deleted.

Virginia Company A joint-stock enterprise that King James I chartered in 1606. The company was to spread Christianity in the New World as well as find ways to make a profit in it.

Virginia Plan Virginia's delegation to the Constitutional Convention's plan for a strong central government and a two-house legislature apportioned by population.

virtual representation The idea that the American colonies, although they had no actual representative in Parliament, were "virtually" represented by all members of Parliament.

Voting Rights Act Law passed in the wake of Martin Luther King Jr.'s Selma-to-Montgomery March in 1965; it authorized federal protection of the right to vote and permitted federal enforcement of minority voting rights in individual counties, mostly in the South.

Wade-Davis Bill Radical Republicans' 1864 plan for reconstruction that required loyalty oaths, abolition of slavery, repudiation of war debts, and denial of political rights to high-ranking Confederate officials; President Lincoln refused to sign the bill.

Wagner Act (National Labor Relations Act of 1935) Law that established the National Labor Relations Board and facilitated unionization by regulating employment and bargaining practices.

Walking Purchase An infamous 1737 purchase of Indian land in which Pennsylvanian colonists tricked the Lenni Lanape Indians. The Lanape agreed to cede land equivalent to the distance a man could walk in thirty-six hours, but the colonists marked out an area using a team of runners.

war in Afghanistan War fought against the Taliban and Al-Qaeda in Afghanistan following the attacks of September 11, 2001. It remains the longest war in American history.

War Industries Board Board run by financier Bernard Baruch that planned production and allocation of war materiel, supervised purchasing, and fixed prices, 1917–1919.

War of 1812 War fought with Britain, 1812–1814, over issues that included impressment of American sailors, interference with shipping, and collusion with Northwest Territory Indians; settled by the Treaty of Ghent in 1814.

War on Poverty Plan announced by President Lyndon B. Johnson in his 1964 State of the Union address; under the Economic Opportunity Bill signed later that year, Head Start, VISTA, and the Jobs Corps were created, and programs were created for students, farmers, and businesses in efforts to eliminate poverty.

war on terrorism Global crusade to root out anti-American, anti-Western Islamist terrorist cells; launched by President George W. Bush as a response to the 9/11 attacks.

War Powers Act Law passed in 1973, reflecting growing opposition to American involvement in the Vietnam War; required congressional approval before the president sent troops abroad.

Watergate Washington office and apartment complex that lent its name to the 1972–1974 scandal of the Nixon administration; when his knowledge of the break-in at the Watergate and subsequent cover-up were revealed, Nixon resigned the presidency under threat of impeachment.

The Wealth of Nations The 1776 work by economist Adam Smith that argued that the "invisible hand" of the free market directed economic life more effectively and fairly than governmental intervention.

Webster-Hayne debate U.S. Senate debate of January 1830 between Daniel Webster of Massachusetts and Robert Hayne of South Carolina over nullification and states' rights.

welfare state A term that originated in Britain during World War II to refer to a system of income assistance, health coverage, and social services for all citizens.

Whiskey Rebellion Violent protest by western Pennsylvania farmers against the federal excise tax on whiskey, 1794.

Wilmot Proviso Proposal to prohibit slavery in any land acquired in the Mexican War; defeated by southern senators, led by John C. Calhoun of South Carolina, in 1846 and 1847.

Winthrop, John Puritan leader and governor of the Massachusetts Bay Colony who resolved to use the colony as a refuge for persecuted Puritans and as an instrument of building a "wilderness Zion" in America.

woman suffrage Movement to give women the right to vote through a constitutional amendment, spearheaded by Susan B. Anthony and Elizabeth Cady Stanton's National Woman Suffrage Association.

Worcester v. Georgia 1832 Supreme Court case that held that the Indian nations were distinct peoples who could not be dealt with by the states—instead, only the federal government could negotiate with them. President Jackson refused to enforce the ruling.

Works Progress Administration (WPA) Part of the Second New Deal; it provided jobs for millions of the unemployed on construction and arts projects.

Wounded Knee massacre Last incident of the Indian Wars; it took place in 1890 in the Dakota Territory, where the U.S. Cavalry killed over 200 Sioux men, women, and children.

writs of assistance One of the colonies' main complaints against Britain; the writs allowed unlimited search warrants without cause to look for evidence of smuggling.

XYZ affair Affair in which French foreign minister Talleyrand's three anonymous agents demanded payments to stop French plundering of American ships in 1797; refusal to pay the bribe was followed by two years of undeclared sea war with France (1798–1800).

Yalta conference Meeting of Franklin D. Roosevelt, Winston Churchill, and Joseph Stalin at a Crimean resort to discuss the postwar world on February 4–11, 1945; Joseph Stalin claimed large areas in eastern Europe for Soviet domination.

Yamasee uprising Revolt of Yamasee and Creek Indians, aggravated by rising debts and slave traders' raids, against

Carolina settlers. Resulted in the expulsion of many Indians to Florida.

yellow press Sensationalism in newspaper publishing that reached a peak in the circulation war between Joseph Pulitzer's *New York World* and William Randolph Hearst's *New York Journal* in the 1890s; the papers' accounts of events in Havana Harbor in 1898 led directly to the Spanish-American War.

yeoman farmers Small landowners (the majority of white families in the Old South) who farmed their own land and usually did not own slaves.

Yorktown, Battle of Last battle of the Revolutionary War; General Lord Charles Cornwallis along with over 7,000 British troops surrendered at Yorktown, Virginia, on October 17, 1781.

Zimmerman Telegram Telegram from the German foreign secretary to the German minister in Mexico, February 1917, instructing the minister to offer to recover Texas, New Mexico, and Arizona for Mexico if it would fight the United States to divert attention from Germany in the event that the United States joined the war.

zoot suit riots 1943 riots in which sailors on leave attacked Mexican-American youths.

CREDITS

PHOTOS

Title page: Library of Congress; Frontispiece: Granger Collection; **Author photo:** Flynn Larsen; **p. viii:** Nuestra Senora de Copacabana, Lima, Peru / Bridgeman Images; **p. ix:** Museum of Art, Rhode Island School of Design. Gift of Robert Winthrop. Photography by Erik Gould; **p. x:** *Free Women of Color with Their Children and Servants in a Landscape*, 1770–1796 (oil on canvas), Brunias, Agostino (1728–96) / Brooklyn Museum of Art, New York, USA / Gift of Mrs. Carl H. de Silver in memory of her husband, by exchange and gift of George S. Hellman, by exchange / Bridgeman Images; **p. xi:** Image copyright © The Metropolitan Museum of Art. Image source: Art Resource, NY; **p. xii:** Collection of the New-York Historical Society; **p. xiii:** Shelburne Museum, Vermont / Museum purchase, 1957, acquired from Harry Shaw Newman, The Old Print Shop / Bridgeman Images; **p. xiv:** MPI / Getty Images; **p. xv:** National Portrait Gallery, Smithsonian Institution / Art Resource, NY; **p. xvi:** Art Resource; **p. xvii:** Artist / maker unknown, American Fourth Pennsylvania Cavalry American After 1861 Oil on canvas The Collection of Edgar William and Bernice Chrysler Garbisch, 1968, 1968–222–3 Philadelphia Museum of Art; **p. xviii:** Digital Image © 2016 Museum Associates / LACMA. Licensed by Art Resource, NY; **p. xxi:** Granger Collection; **p. xxii:** Jewett, William S. (1812–1873) *The Promised Land - the Grayson family*, 1850. Oil on canvas, 50 3/4 x 64 in. Daniel J. Terra Collection, 1999.79. Terra Foundation for American Art. Photo Credit: Terra Foundation for American Art, Chicago / Art Resource, NY; **p. xxiv:** Library of Congress; **p. xxvi:** National Archives; **p. 1:** Library of Congress. **Chapter 1: p. 2 (top):** Bridgeman Images; **(bottom):** Self-Portrait, by Thomas Smith, 1948.19, Worcester Art Museum, Worcester, Massachusetts; **p. 3 (top):** Unidentified artist, British, 18th century or first quarter 19th century; Quaker Meeting; Oil on canvas; 64.1 × 76.2cm (25 1/4 × 30in.); Museum of Fine Arts, Boston; Bequest of Maxim Karolik; 64.456. Photograph © 2013 Museum of Fine Arts, Boston; **(bottom):** Granger Collection; **p. 4:** Nuestra Senora de Copacabana, Lima, Peru / Bridgeman Images; **p. 8:** Library of Congress; **p. 9:** Bridgeman Images; **p. 10 (top):** Georg Gerster/ Science Source; **(bottom):** Library of Congress; **p. 12:** Bridgeman Images; **p. 13:** Library of Congress; **p. 14:** Bridgeman Images; **p. 15:** Courtesy Lilly Library, Indiana University, Bloomington, IN; **p. 16:** Library of Congress; **p. 17:** Wikimedia Commons, public domain; **p. 20 (top):** Ellen Mack / Getty Images; **(bottom):** Granger Collection; **p. 21:** Granger Collection; **p. 23:** Granger Collection; **p. 24:** akg-images; **p. 25:** Gianni Dagli Orti / The Art Archive at Art Resource, NY; **p. 26 (top):** Denver Art Museum, Collection of Frederick and Jan Mayer; **(bottom):** Bridgeman Images; **p. 27:** Library of Congress; **p. 28 (top):** Museo de la Basilica de Guadalupe, Mexico City; **(bottom):** Rare Books Division, The New York Public Library, Astor, Lenox, and Tilden Foundations. Art Resource, NY;

p. 29: Library of Congress; **p. 30:** Granger Collection; **p. 33:** Library of Congress, Prints & Photographs Division, Edward S. Curtis Collection; **p. 34:** National Museum of American History, Smithsonian Institution, Behring Center; **p. 38:** Bettmann / Corbis; **p. 42:** GLC03582 Novi Belgi Novaeque Angliae (New Netherland and New England) by Nicholas Visscher, 1682 / Courtesy of The Gilder Lehrman Institute of American History; **p. 43:** Museum of the City of New York; **p. 44:** The Colonial Williamsburg Foundation. **Chapter 2: p. 48:** Granger Collection; **p. 51 (top):** GL Archive / Alamy Stock Photo; **(bottom):** Woburn Abbey, Bedfordshire, UK / Bridgeman Images; **p. 52:** The John Carter Brown Library at Brown University; **p. 53:** Wikimedia, public domain; **p. 54:** Granger Collection; **p. 55:** GLC 4110. Document signed: contracts relating to the indenture of James Mahony, 31 March 1773. (The Gilder Lehrman Collection, courtesy of the Gilder Lehrman Institute of American History, New York.); **p. 56:** © The Trustees of the British Museum / Art Resource, NY; **p. 57:** Museum of Art, Rhode Island School of Design. Gift of Robert Winthrop. Photography by Erik Gould; **p. 59 (top):** Corbis; **(bottom):** National Portrait Gallery, Smithsonian Institution / Art Resource, NY; **p. 60:** Granger Collection; **p. 61 (top):** Library of Congress; **(bottom):** George Arents Collection, New York Public Library. Art Resource, NY; **p. 62:** Mary Evans Picture Library / Alamy; **p. 63:** MPI / Getty Images; **p. 64:** Library of Congress; **p. 65:** American Antiquarian Society; **p. 66:** Granger Collection; **p. 67:** Courtesy of the Massachusetts Archives; **p. 68:** Worcester Art Museum, Worcester, Massachusetts, Gift of William A. Savage; **p. 69:** Massachusetts Historical Society; **p. 70:** The New York Public Library / Art Resource, NY; **p. 73:** Annenberg Rare Book and Manuscript Library, Van Pelt-Dietrich Library Center, U Penn; **p. 76:** Library of Congress; **p. 77:** Self-Portrait, by Thomas Smith, 1948.19, Worcester Art Museum, Worcester, Massachusetts; **p. 78:** Mrs. Elizabeth Freake and Baby Mary, unknown artist, 1963.134, Worcester Art Museum, Worcester, Massachusetts; **p. 79:** Historical Picture Archive / Corbis; **p. 81:** Granger Collection; **p. 82 (top):** Private Collection / Bridgeman Images; **(bottom):** British Library Board / Robana / Art Resource, NY; **p. 83:** The Cromwell Museum, Huntingdon. **Chapter 3: p. 86:** Emmet Collection, Miriam and Ira D. Wallach Division of Art, Prints and Photographs, The New York Public Library, Astor, Lenox and Tilden Foundations; **p. 91:** Library of Congress; **p. 92:** Historical Society of Pennsylvania; **p. 93:** Germantown Historical Society, Philadelphia, PA; **p. 94:** Unidentified artist, British, 18th century or first quarter 19th century; Quaker Meeting; Oil on canvas; 64.1 × 76.2cm (25 1/4 × 30in.); Museum of Fine Arts, Boston; Bequest of Maxim Karolik; 64.456. Photograph © 2013 Museum of Fine Arts, Boston; **p. 95:** *Free Women of Color with Their Children and Servants in a Landscape*, 1770-1796 (oil on can-

vas), Brunias, Agostino (1728-96) / Brooklyn Museum of Art, New York, USA / Gift of Mrs. Carll H. de Silver in memory of her husband, by exchange and gift of George S. Hellman, by exchange / Bridgeman Images; **p. 96:** © British Library Board. All Rights Reserved / The Bridgeman Art Library; **p. 97:** Private Collection / Bridgeman Art Library; **p. 98:** Colonial Williamsburg Foundation; **p. 100:** National Maritime Museum, London; **p. 102:** The John Carter Brown Library at Brown University; **p. 103:** Springhill, County Londonderry, Northern Ireland, National Trust Photographic Library / Derrick E. Witty / Bridgeman Art Library; **p. 105:** Rare Books Division, The New York Public Library, Astor, Lenox and Tilden Foundations. Art Resource, NY; **p. 110 (top):** Houghton Library, Harvard University, Typ 632.96.202; **(bottom):** The Historical Society of Pennsylvania; **p. 114:** Eileen Tweedy / The Art Archive at Art Resource, NY; **p. 115:** The Library Company of Philadelphia; **p. 116:** Winterthur Museum; **p. 117:** The Colonial Williamsburg Foundation; **p. 118:** Photograph © 2015 Museum of Fine Arts, Boston; **p. 119:** Geoffrey Clements / Corbis; **p. 120:** Carter's Grove. Aug 1995. Photo by Melissa Wilkins. http://creativecommons.org/licenses/ by-sa/2.0/deed.en; **p. 121:** Art Resource; **p. 122:** Gift of Edgar William and Bernice Chrysler Garbisch, Image © 2006 Board of Trustees, National Gallery of Art, Washington, D.C. **Chapter 4: p. 126:** Granger Collection; **p. 130 (top):** The John Carter Library at Brown University; **(bottom):** Library of Congress; **p. 132:** © Musée d'histoire de Nantes – Château des ducs de Bretagne / Alain Guillard; **p. 133:** Granger Collection; **p. 134:** Granger Collection; **p. 136:** Jamestown-Yorktown Foundation; **p. 137:** Abby Aldrich Rockefeller Folk Art Museum, Colonial Williamsburg Foundation, Williamsburg, VA; **p. 138:** Image copyright © The Metropolitan Museum of Art. Image source: Art Resource, NY; **p. 139:** Schomburg Center for Research in Black Culture, Photographs and Prints Division, The New York Public Library; **p. 141:** Chicago Historical Museum; **p. 142:** Eileen Tweedy / The Art Archive at Art Resource, NY; **p. 143 (top):** Library of Congress, **(bottom):** © National Portrait Gallery, London; **p. 144:** The Library Company of Philadelphia; **p. 146:** This item is reproduced by permission of The Huntington Library, San Marino, California; **p. 148:** Library of Congress; **p. 149:** Portrait of Benjamin Franklin, Mason Chamberlin, Oil on canvas, 1762, Philadelphia Museum of Art: Gift of Mr. and Mrs Wharton Sinkler, 1956; **p. 150 (top):** Wikimedia, public domain; **(bottom):** National Portrait Gallery, London; **p. 151:** The John Carter Brown Library at Brown University; **p. 152:** Zisterzienserstift Zwettl, Bibliothek; Cod. 420, Appendix: Rolle 2; **p. 154:** Library of Congress; **p. 155:** Czech National Library. **Chapter 5: p. 167 (both):** Library of Congress; **p. 168 (top):** Granger Collection; **(bottom):** Chicago Historical Society; **p. 169 (top):** © New Bedford

Whaling Museum; **(bottom):** Private Collection / Bridgeman Images; **p. 170:** Library of Congress; **p. 173:** By permission of the Houghton Library, Harvard University; **p. 174:** Library of Congress; **p. 175 (top):** Corbis; **(bottom):** The Colonial Williamsburg Foundation; **p. 176:** Library of Congress; **p. 180 (top):** Library of Congress; **(bottom):** Michael Nicholson / Corbis; **p. 182:** Library of Congress; **p. 183:** Special Collections Research Center, University of Chicago Library; **p. 184:** Miriam and Ira D. Wallach Division of Art, Prints and Photographs, New York Public Library. Art Resource, NY; **p. 185:** Chicago Historical Society; **p. 186 (top):** National Portrait Gallery, London; **(bottom):** American Philosophical Society; **p. 190:** Library of Congress; **p. 191:** American Antiquarian Society; **p. 192:** Sid Lapidus Collection. Rare Books Division. Department of Rare Books and Special Collections. Princeton University Library; **p. 193:** © The Trustees of the British Museum / Art Resource, NY; **p. 194:** Anne S. K. Brown Military Collection, Brown University; **p. 195:** Morristown National Historic Park, Morristown, New Jersey, USA; **p. 199 (both):** Library of Congress; **p. 200:** Harvard University Portrait Collection, Bequest of Ward Nicholas Boylston to Harvard College, 1828. **Chapter 6: p. 204:** Collection of the New-York Historical Society; **p. 206:** National Gallery of Art, Washington, Gift of Mrs. Robert Homans; **p. 207:** Winterthur Museum; **p. 208:** Gianni Dagli Orti / The Art Archive at Art Resource, NY; **p. 209:** Historical Society of Pennsylvania; **p. 210:** Courtesy of the Beinecke Rare Book and Manuscript Library, Yale University; **p. 211:** Courtesy of the New-York Historical Society; **p. 212:** North Eastern view, Watertown, Ct. 1836 John Warner Barber / The Connecticut Historical Society, Hartford CT; **p. 213:** York County Historical Society, USA / The Bridgeman Art Library; **p. 215:** American Antiquarian Society; **p. 216:** Library of Congress; **p. 217:** Reproduced by permission of the Huntington Library, San Marino, California; **p. 219:** Library of Congress; **p. 223:** Corbis; **p. 224:** Library Company of Philadelphia. Gift of the artist, 1792; **p. 226 (top):** American Antiquarian Society; **(bottom):** Library of Congress; **p. 227:** Library and Archives Canada, Acc. No. 1938-220-1; **p. 228 (top):** National Archives, London; **(bottom):** Collection of The New-York Historical Society; **p. 229:** Bequest of Miss Lucy T. Aldrich, 39.002; Museum of Art, Rhode Island School of Design, Providence; **p. 232 (top):** Library of Congress; **(bottom):** Southern Historical Collection, Wilson Library, The University of North Carolina at Chapel Hill; **p. 233:** The Philadelphia Museum of Art / Art Resource, NY; **p. 235:** Library of Congress. **Chapter 7: p. 238:** Granger Collection; **p. 242:** National Archives; **p. 243:** American Antiquarian Society; **p. 245:** Print Collection, Miriam and Ira D. Wallach Division of Art, Prints, and Photographs, The New York Public Library; Astor, Lenox, and Tilden Foundations. Art Resource, NY; **p. 247 (top):** Library of Congress; **(bottom):** Image copyright © The Metropolitan Museum of Art. Image source: Art Resource, NY; **p. 248:** Wikimedia, public domain; **p. 249:** Library of Congress; **p. 251:** The Library of Virginia; **p. 252:** From the collection of the National Constitution Center, Philadelphia, gift of Robert L. McNeil, Jr.; **p. 253:** MPI / Getty Images; **p. 254:** Library of Congress; **p. 255:** Granger Collection; **p. 256:** Courtesy of the New-York Historical Society; **p. 257:** Collection of the New-York Historical Society / Bridgeman Art Library; **p. 258:** Collection of The New-York Historical Society; **p. 259:** Library of Congress; **p. 263:** Old Paper Studios / Alamy Stock Photo; **p. 265:** Chicago Historical Society; **p. 266:** Greenville County Museum of Art, Museum purchase with funds from The Museum Association's 1990 and 1991 Collectors Groups and the 1989, 1990 and 1991 Museum Antiques Shows, sponsored by Elliott, Davis & Company, CPAs; artist: unknown (circle of E. Savage) title: *The Plan of Civilization*; date: circa 1800; medium: oil on canvas.; **p. 269:** Virginia Historical Society, Richmond / Bridgeman Art Library. **Chapter 8: p. 272:** Chicago Historical Society; **p. 275 (top):** Chicago Historical Society; **(bottom):** Fenimore Art Museum, Cooperstown, New York. Photo by Richard Walker; **p. 276:** Library of Congress; **p. 277 (top):** Rare Book and Special Collections Division, Library of Congress; **(bottom):** Library of Congress; **p. 278 (top):** Courtesy, Winterthur Museum, Bequest of Hery F. DuPont; **(bottom):** Library of Congress; **p. 279:** The New York Public Library / Art Resource, NY; **p. 280 (top):** Chicago Historical Society; **(bottom):** © National Portrait Gallery, London; **p. 281:** Liberty in the Form of the Goddess of Youth, by Mary Green, 1963.86, Worcester Art Museum, Worcester, Massachusetts; **p. 285:** Library of Congress; **p. 286:** Library of Congress; **p. 287:** Division of Political History, National Museum of American History, Smithsonian Institution; **p. 289:** Photos 12 / Alamy; **p. 290:** I.N. Stokes Collection, Miriam and Ira D. Wallach Division of Art, Prints, and Photographs, The New York Public Library; Astor, Lenox, and Tilden Foundations. Art Resource, NY; **p. 292:** Private Collection; **p. 294:** Missouri Historical Society, St. Louis; **p. 295:** GLC07730 *The attack made on Tripoli on the 3d. August 1804 by John Guerrazzi, August 23rd.* 1852 / Courtesy of The Gilder Lehrman Institute of American History; **p. 296:** Courtesy of the New-York Historical Society; **p. 298 (top):** Royal Ontario Museum; **(bottom):** National Portrait Gallery, Smithsonian Institution / Art Resource, NY; **p. 299 (top):** Photo by Mark Sexton. © Peabody Essex Museum, 2003, all rights reserved; **(bottom):** Library Company of Philadelphia; **p. 300:** Collection of the New-York Historical Society / Bridgeman Images; **p. 302:** American Antiquarian Society, Massachusetts / Bridgeman Art Library; **p. 303:** Photography by Erik Arneson © Nicholas S. West. **Chapter 9: p. 306:** Shelburne Museum, Vermont / Museum purchase, 1957, acquired from Harry Shaw Newman, The Old Print Shop / Bridgeman Images; **p. 309:** I.N. Phelps Stokes Collection, Miriam and Ira D. Wallach Division of Art, Prints and Photographs, The New York Public Library, Astor, Lenox and Tilden Foundations. Art Resource, NY; **p. 311 (top):** Chicago Historical Society; **(bottom):** www.Archive.org, public domain; **p. 312:** Collection of the New-York Historical Society / Bridgeman Images; **p. 315:** Edwin Whitefield, Minnesota Historical Society; **p. 318:** Abby Aldrich Rockefeller Folk Art Museum, Colonial Williamsburg Foundation, Williamsburg, VA; **p. 319:** Cincinnati Museum Center / Getty Images; **p. 321:** Courtesy, The Winterthur Library: Joseph Downs Collection of Manuscripts and Printed Ephemera; **p. 323 (top):** Library of Congress; **(bottom):** Granger Collection; **p. 324 (top):** Barfoot, American, Progress of Cotton, Reeding or Drawing In, No. 9, Mabel Brady Garvan Collection, Yale University Art Gallery; **(bottom):** Courtesy of the Manchester (N.H.) Historic Association; **p. 325:** Granger Collection; **p. 326:** Bishop Hill State Historic Site/Illinois Historic Preservation Agency; **p. 327:** Historical Society of Pennsylvania, medium graphics collection, H. Bucholzer; **p. 328:** Granger Collection; **p. 329:** Library of Congress; **p. 330:** George Eastman Museum; **p. 331 (top):** Corbis; **(bottom):** Brooklyn Museum, HIP / Art Resource, NY; **p. 334:** Library of Congress; **p. 335:** Library of Congress; **p. 336:** Church Archives of The Church of Jesus-Christ of Latter-day Saints; **p. 337:** John Neagle, American, 1796-1865; *Pat Lyon at the Forge, 1826-27;* Oil on canvas; 238.12 × 172.72 cm (93 3/4 × 68 in.); Museum of Fine Arts, Boston; Henry H. and Zoe Oliver Sherman Fund; 1975.806. Photograph © 2013 Museum of Fine Arts, Boston; **p. 338:** Library of Congress; **p. 339:** American Antiquarian Society; **p. 340 (both):** Library of Congress; **p. 341:** Library of Congress; **p. 342:** Granger Collection; **p. 343:** Library of Congress. **Chapter 10: p. 346:** Gift of Stephen C. Clark, Fenimore Art Museum, Cooperstown, New York. Photo by Milo Stewart; **p. 349 (top):** Library of Congress; **(bottom):** Courtesy the Rhode Island Historical Society, Dorr Liberation Society, Rhode Island, 1844, engraving, Rhi X3 6692; **p. 350:** Historical Society of Pennsylvania, large graphics collection, John Lewis Krimmel; **p. 351:** Library of Congress; **p. 352:** Granger Collection; **p. 354:** Library of Congress; **p. 358:** Granger Collection; **p. 361:** Huntington Library, San Marino, California; **p. 365:** Bettmann / Corbis; **p. 366:** Library of Congress; **p. 367:** Private Collection / The Bridgeman Art Library; **p. 368:** The Art Archive at Art Resource, NY; **p. 370:** Saint Louis Art Museum, Missouri / Gift of Bank of America / The Bridgeman Art Library; **p. 371:** Library of Congress; **p. 372:** Library of Congress; **p. 373:** Library of Congress; **p. 374:** Library of Congress; **p. 376 (top):** MPI / Getty Images; **(bottom):** Charles Deas, The Trapper and his Family, Photograph © 2013 Museum of Fine Arts, Boston; **p. 377:** Smithsonian American Art Museum, Washington, DC / Art Resource, NY; **p. 378:** Library of Congress; **p. 380:** Library of Congress; **p. 381:** Library of Congress. **Chapter 11: p. 385:** Bettmann / Corbis; **p. 386 (top):** Hulton Archive / Getty Images; **(bottom):** Chicago History Museum; **p. 387 (top):** Collection of Dr. and Mrs. John Livingston and Mrs. Elizabeth Livingston Jaeger, Photo: Hearts and Hands Media Arts. Photography courtesy of Hearts & Hands Media Arts, from the book and film "Hearts and Hands: A Social History of 19th Century Women and their Quilts" (New Day Films); **(bottom):** Fine Arts Museums of San Francisco, Gift of Joseph Martin, Jr., 1994.120.4; **p. 388:** Hirshhorn Museum & Sculpture Garden, Washington D.C. / Bridgeman Art Library; **p. 391:** MPI / Getty Images; **p. 393:** Library of Congress; **p. 394:** Hulton Archive / Getty Images; **p. 395 (top):** Library of Congress; **(bottom):** Missouri History Museum, St. Louis; **p. 396:** Library of Congress; **p. 398:** Library of Congress; **p. 399:** Merseyside Maritime Museum, Liverpool; **p. 400:** Granger Collection; **p. 401 (top):** Chicago Historical Society; **(bottom):** New Hampshire Historical Society; **p. 402:** Courtesy of South Caroliniana Library, University of South

Carolina, Columbia; **p. 407:** Courtesy of the Maryland Historical Society; **p. 409 (top):** Library of Congress; **(bottom):** Library of Congress; **p. 410 (top):** Library of Congress; **(bottom):** North Carolina Museum of Art, Raleigh, Purchased with funds from the State of North Carolina; **p. 411:** Chicago History Museum; **p. 412:** Abby Aldrich Rockefeller Folk Art Museum, Colonial Williamsburg Foundation, Williamsburg, VA; **p. 413:** Library of Congress; **p. 414:** Historic New Orleans Collection 1960.46; **p. 415:** GLC07238 *$2,500 Reward!* Mississippi Co., Missouri broadside advertising runaway slaves, August 23, 1852 / Courtesy of The Gilder Lehrman Institute of American History; **p. 417:** Library Company of Philadelphia; **p. 420:** Library of Congress. **Chapter 12: p. 424:** Collection of Dr. and Mrs. John Livingston and Mrs. Elizabeth Livingston Jaeger, Photo: Hearts and Hands Media Arts. Photography courtesy of Hearts & Hands Media Arts, from the book and film "Hearts and Hands: A Social History of 19th Century Women and their Quilts" (New Day Films); **p. 427:** Library of Congress; **p. 429:** Bibliotheque Nationale, Paris, France / Archives Charmet / The Bridgeman Art Library; **p. 430:** Library of Congress; **p. 431:** Library of Congress; **p. 432:** NYPL Digital; **p. 433:** Collection of New-York Historical Society; **p. 434:** Granger Collection; **p. 435:** Library of Congress; **p. 436 (top):** Library of Congress; **(bottom):** Courtesy of the Massachusetts Historical Society. Banner, William Lloyd Garrison (1805-1879) "Proclaim Liberty Throughout all the Land unto all the inhabitants thereof." MHS image #332; **p. 437:** Bettmann / Corbis; **p. 438:** The Boston Athenaeum, TBMR VEP. An 847. The Anti-Slavery Alphabet, a children's book (1847); **p. 439:** Library of Congress; **p. 440 (top)** Granger Collection; **(bottom):** Susan Torrey Merritt American, 1826-1879 Anti-Slavery Picnic at Weymouth Landing, Massachusetts, c. 1845 Watercolor, gouache, and collage on paper 660 × 914 mm Gift of Elizabeth R. Vaughan, 1950.1846 The Art Institute of Chicago; **p. 441 (both):** Chicago Historical Society; **p. 442:** Library of Congress; **p. 443 (top):** Samuel J. Miller, Frederick Douglass, 1847-52, cased half-plate daguerreotype, plate: 14x10.6 cm, Major Acquisitions Centennial Endowment, The Art Institute of Chicago; **(bottom):** Library of Congress; **p. 444 (top):** Library of Congress; **(bottom):** American Antiquarian Society, Massachusetts / Bridgeman Art Library; **p. 445:** Destruction by Fire of Pennsylvania Hall, on the Night of the 17th May, 1838 by J.C. Wild, printed by J.T. Bowen. The Library Company of Philadelphia; **p. 448:** Library of Congress; **p. 449:** National Portrait Gallery, Smithsonian Institution / Art Resource, NY; **p. 452:** Bettmann / Corbis; **p. 453:** Bettmann / Corbis; **p. 455:** Library of Congress. **Chapter 13: p. 458:** John Perry Newell, Lazell, Perkins & Co. Bridgewater, Mass., ca. 1860. Yale University Art Gallery, Mabel Brady Garvan Collection; **p. 460 (left):** Library of Congress; **(right):** Architect of the Capitol; **p. 461:** Library of Congress; **p. 463:** Courtesy of the State Preservation Board, Austin, Texas, photographer F. Thomson, Post 1990, CHA 1989.68, post conservation; **p. 464:** Bettmann / Corbis; **p. 465:** Anonymous cartoon published in *El Calavera*, May 7, 1847; **p. 466:** Granger Collection; **p. 468:** Alfred Sully Monterey, California Rancho Scene drawing work on paper c. 1849, Watercolor, Oakland Museum of California Kahn Collection A65.43; **p. 469:** Seguin, Juan Nepomuceno; Accession ID: CHA 1989.096; Courtesy State Preservation Board; Original Artist: Wright, Thomas Jefferson / 1798-1846; Photographer: Perry Huston, 7/28/95 post conservation; **p. 470:** Jewett, William S. (1812-1873) *The Promised Land - The Grayson family*, 1850. Oil on canvas, 50 3/4 × 64 in. Daniel J. Terra Collection, 1999.79. Terra Foundation for American Art Photo Credit: Terra Foundation for American Art, Chicago / Art Resource, NY; **p. 471:** Art Resource; **p. 472:** Image copyright © The Metropolitan Museum of Art/ Art Resource, NY; **p. 476** © The Metropolitan Museum of Art / Art Resource, NY; **p. 478:** Fugitive slave law. *Hamlet in chains.* National anti-slavery standard. Vol. 21 (Oct. 17, 1850), page 82, Rare Book & Manuscript Library, Columbia University in the City of New York; **p. 480:** Chicago Historical Society; **p. 482:** Library of Congress; **p. 483:** Library of Congress; **p. 484:** Bettmann / Corbis; **p. 485:** Collection of New-York Historical Society; **p. 487:** Bettmann / Corbis; **p. 488 (left):** Chicago Historical Society; **(right):** George Eastman House / Getty Images; **p. 489:** Collection of The New-York Historical Society; **p. 492:** Courtesy of the Maryland Historical Society; **p. 495:** Abraham Lincoln Presidential Library and Museum; **p. 496:** Greenville County Museum of Art, Greenville, SC; **p. 497:** Library of Congress; **p. 498:** Fotosearch / Getty Images; **p. 499:** Library of Congress. **Chapter 14: p. 502:** Artist/maker unknown, American; Fourth Pennsylvania Cavalry American, After 1861 Oil on canvas, The Collection of Edgar William and Bernice Chrysler Garbisch, 1968; 1968-222-3, Philadelphia Museum of Art; **p. 506 (both):** Library of Congress; **p. 507:** Newark Museum / Art Resource, NY; **p. 508 (top):** Library of Congress; **(bottom):** Chicago Historical Society; **p. 509:** Museum of Fine Arts, Boston / M. and M. Karolik Collection of American Watercolors and / Drawings, 1800-75 / The Bridgeman Art Library; **p. 511:** Edward Owen / Art Resource, NY; **p. 513:** Library of Congress; **p. 514:** Chicago Historical Society; **p. 516:** Chicago History Museum; **p. 517:** Library of Congress; **p. 518 (top):** Chicago History Museum; **(bottom):** Smithsonian Institution, Photographic History Collection, Division of Information Technology; **p. 519 (top):** Library of Congress; **(bottom):** GLC00968 Unknown (Civil War Songbook). November 24, 1862, p.4 / Courtesy of The Gilder Lehrman Institute of American History; **p. 520 (top):** Library of Congress; **(bottom):** David Bustill Bowser (American, 1820-1900) Untitled (Lincoln and the Female Slave) 1863 Oil on canvas, 19 × 14 1987.1.83 Simpson Collection, The Amistad Center for Art & Culture. Photo by John Groo/The Amistad Center for Art & Culture; **p. 521:** Library of Congress; **p. 522 (top):** Courtesy, Daughters of Charity, Province of St. Louise, St. Louis, MO.; **(bottom):** Library of Congress; **p. 524 (both):** Chicago Historical Society; **p. 525 (top):** Granger Collection; **(bottom):** National Archives; **p. 529:** Chicago Historical Society; **p. 530 (top):** U.S. Army Military History Institute; **(bottom):** Chicago Historical Society; **p. 531:** Library of Congress; **p. 532:** Granger Collection; **p. 533:** Louisiana State University Special Collections From the U.S. Civil War Center exhibit Beyond Face Value, courtesy of Jules d'Hemecourt; **p. 533:** Louisiana State University Special Collections From the U.S. Civil War Center exhibit Beyond Face Value, courtesy of Jules d'Hemecourt; **p. 534:** From the Collections of the South Carolina Historical Society; **p. 539:** Library of Congress; **p. 535:** provided courtesy © HarpWeek., LLC; **p. 536:** The Johnson Collection; **p. 538 (both):** Library of Congress; **p. 540 (both):** Library of Congress; **p. 541:** National Archives; **p. 542:** Library of Congress; **p. 543:** National Archives; **p. 545:** Library of Congress; **p. 546 (top):** provided courtesy © HarpWeek LLC; **(bottom):** © The Metropolitan Museum of Art / Art Resource, NY. **Chapter 15: p. 550:** Chicago Historical Society; **p. 553 (top):** Library of Congress; **(bottom):** Photographic History Collection, Division of Information Technology and Communications, National Museum of American History, Smithsonian Institution; **p. 554 (top):** Library of Congress; **(bottom):** Granger Collection; **p. 556:** Smithsonian American Art Museum, Washington, DC / Art Resource, NY; **p. 557 (both):** Library of Congress; **p. 558 (top):** Digital Image © [year] Museum Associates / LACMA. Licensed by Art Resource, NY; **(bottom):** Cook Collection, Valentine Richmond History Center; **p. 560:** Library of Congress; **p. 564:** Kemper Leila Williams Foundation / The Historic New Orleans Collection; **p. 566 (both):** Library of Congress; **p. 567:** Ed Sullivan Collection, Special Collections, University of Hartford; **p. 568:** Library of Congress; **p. 569:** Library of Congress; **p. 570:** Manuscripts, Archives & Rare Books Division, Schomburg Center for Research in Black Culture, The New York Public Library, Astor, Lenox and Tilden Foundations / Art Resource, NY; **p. 571:** Library of Congress; **p. 573:** Library of Congress; **p. 574:** Library of Congress; **p. 575:** Library of Congress; **p. 567 (both):** Library of Congress; **p. 577:** Granger Collection; **p. 578 (top):** Library of Congress; **(bottom):** Clements Library Collection, University of Michigan; **p. 579:** Granger Collection; **p. 580:** Wikimedia, public domain; **p. 581 (top):** Niday Picture Library / Alamy; **(bottom):** © Fine Arts Museums of San Francisco, Gift of Joseph Martin, Jr., 1994.120.4; **p. 582 (both top):** Library of Congress; **(bottom):** National Archives; **p. 584:** Granger Collection; **p. 585:** Library of Congress.

TEXT

Abigail Adams: "Abigail Adams to John Adams, 31 March 1776." Reprinted by permission of the publisher from *The Adams Papers: Adams Family Correspondence, Volume I and II: December 1761-March 1778*, edited by L. H. Butterfield, Cambridge, Mass.: The Belknap Press of Harvard University Press, Copyright © 1963 by the Massachusetts Historical Society. **Bartolomé de las Casas:** "History of the Indies [1528]", excerpt from *History of the Indies*, translated and edited by Andrée Collard (New York: Harper & Row, 1971), pp. 82, 112-115. Copyright © 1971 by Andrée M. Collard, renewed © 1999 by Joyce J. Contrucci. Reprinted by permission of Joyce J. Contrucci. **Democratic-Republican Society of Pennsylvania:** Excerpt from minutes of The Democratic Society of Pennsylvania, December 18, 1794. The Historical Society of Pennsylvania (HSP), Collection # Am. 315/3150. Reprinted with permission. **Johannes Hanner:** Letter by an Immigrant to Pennsylvania, 1769, *Unpublished Documents on Emigration from the Archives of Switzerland*, Albert B. Faust, *Deutsch-Amerikanische Geschichtsblätter*, Vol 18-19, pp. 37-39.

INDEX

Page numbers in *italics* refer to illustrations.